The Economics of Contemporary Latin

The Economics of Contemporary Latin America

Beatriz Armendáriz and Felipe Larraín B.

The MIT Press
Cambridge, Massachusetts
London, England

© 2017 Massachusetts Institute of Technology

All rights reserved. No part of this book may be reproduced in any form by any electronic or mechanical means (including photocopying, recording, or information storage and retrieval) without permission in writing from the publisher.

This book was set in Palatino by Toppan Best-set Premedia Limited. Printed and bound in the United States of America.

Library of Congress Cataloging-in-Publication Data

Names: Armendáriz, Beatriz, author. | Larraín B., Felipe, author.
Title: The economics of contemporary Latin America / Beatriz Armendáriz and Felipe Larraín B.
Description: Cambridge, MA : MIT Press, 2017. | Includes bibliographical references and index.
Identifiers: LCCN 2016029386 | ISBN 9780262533157 (pbk. : alk. paper)
Subjects: LCSH: Latin America--Economic conditions--21st century. | Latin America--Social conditions--21st century. | Latin America--Politics and government--21st century.
Classification: LCC HC125 .A736 2017 | DDC 330.98--dc23 LC record available at https://lccn.loc.gov/2016029386

10 9 8 7 6 5 4 3 2 1

Figure 1.2 reprinted with permission from *Encyclopædia Britannica*, © 2009 by Encyclopædia Britannica, Inc.

To my sister María Luisa
Beatriz Armendáriz

To my parents Vicente and Marta
Felipe Larraín B.

Contents

Preface xiii
List of Acronyms xvii

I Historical Origins of the Contemporary Latin American Economy 1

1 Geography and the Colonial Legacy 3
1.1 Geography 5
1.2 Legal Origins 9
1.3 Factor Endowments 15
1.4 Institutional Legacy 20
1.5 Ethnolinguistic Fragmentation and Culture 28
1.6 Concluding Remarks 29
Summary 32
Review Questions 33
Further Reading 33

2 Export-Led Growth and the Origins of Protectionism 35
2.1 Independence: Economic Consequences 38
2.2 Diversity across Regions under Export-Led Growth 43
2.3 Stellar Performers: Divergent Trends 45
2.4 Two Special Cases: Brazil and Cuba 48
2.5 Nineteenth-Century Export-Led Growth in Contrast with Modern Days 51
2.6 Concluding Remarks 53
Summary 55

Review Questions 56
Further Reading 57

3 Import Substitution Industrialization 59
  3.1 Historical Background 60
  3.2 Import Substitution Industrialization Policies 66
  3.3 ISI Performance Indicators 71
    3.3.1 Fall of Stellar Performers, Rise of Brazil and Mexico 72
    3.3.2 Criticisms 74
    3.3.3 Adjustments to the ISI Strategy 75
  3.4 Toward a New Consensus 79
  3.5 Concluding Remarks 82
  Summary 83
  Review Questions 85
  Further Reading 85

4 Debt Crises and the Lost Decade 87
  4.1 Background 88
  4.2 The 1930s Debt Crisis 89
  4.3 The 1980s Debt Crisis 91
  4.4 Another Wave of Crises 96
    4.4.1 Mexico, Brazil, and Argentina in the 1990s 96
  4.5 Latin America through the Twenty-First-Century Financial Crises 101
  4.6 Concluding Remarks 104
  Summary 105
  Review Questions 106
  Further Reading 107

II The Social and Political Context 109

5 Poverty and Income Inequality 111
  5.1 Poverty and Inequality: Recent Trends and Diversity 113
  5.2 Poverty: Definition and Consequences 117
  5.3 Measurement 119
    5.3.1 Unsatisfied Basic Needs Approach 120
    5.3.2 Cost of Basic Needs Approach 121
  5.4 Main Determinants of Poverty 122
    5.4.1 Education 123
    5.4.2 Unemployment and Informality 124
    5.4.3 Type of Employment 128
    5.4.4 Age 128

                5.4.5   Gender   129
                5.4.6   Inflation   130
                5.4.7   Ethnicity and Racial Discrimination   131
        5.5   Labor Markets and Poverty   131
                5.5.1   Minimum Wage   132
                5.5.2   Firing Costs   132
                5.5.3   Payroll Taxes   133
        5.6   Emergency Job Creation against Poverty   133
        5.7   Income Inequalities: Measurement and Recent Trends   134
                5.7.1   Income Quintiles and the Gini Coefficient   135
                5.7.2   Recent Trends in Inequality   136
        5.8   Conditional Cash Transfers   136
                5.8.1   Mexico's Progresa/Oportunidades/Prospera Program   138
                5.8.2   Brazil's Bolsa Família and Benefício de Prestação Continuada   140
                5.8.3   Chile's Ingreso Ético Familiar (Ethical Family Income)   140
        5.9   Concluding Remarks   141
        Summary   143
        Review Questions   144
        Further Reading   145

6   **The Political Economy of Latin American Development   147**
        6.1   Populism: Historical Background   148
        6.2   Macroeconomic Populism   150
        6.3   Reforms and the Downfall of Macroeconomic Populism   154
                6.3.1   The Impact of Successful Inflation Stabilization and Growth   155
                6.3.2   The Rise of the Middle Class: Social Stability or Unrest?   157
                6.3.3   Left Behind in Resource-Abundant Economies   158
        6.4   The Rebirth of Populism in the Twenty-First Century   159
                6.4.1   Venezuela   160
                6.4.2   Argentina   161
                6.4.3   Bolivia   163
                6.4.4   Ecuador   164
        6.5   Regulatory Capture   165
        6.6   State-Owned Enterprises   167
        6.7   Concluding Remarks   168
        Summary   170
        Review Questions   170
        Further Reading   171

III The Macroeconomics of Latin America in the Twenty-First Century 173

7 Fiscal Policy for Development 175
- 7.1 The Growth of the Public Sector Prior to the Crisis of the 1980s 176
- 7.2 Forceful Public Sector Contraction 180
- 7.3 Redefining the Economic Role of the State 183
- 7.4 Redistributive Effects of Fiscal Policy 184
- 7.5 Institutional Changes in Fiscal Policy 191
- 7.6 Concluding Remarks 195
- Summary 201
- Review Questions 201
- Further Reading 202

8 The Fight against Inflation 203
- 8.1 Main Roots of Inflation 204
- 8.2 Costs of Inflation 208
- 8.3 Orthodox and Heterodox Stabilization Policies 208
- 8.4 Central Bank Autonomy 212
- 8.5 Fiscal Institutions and Fiscal Prudence 215
- 8.6 Inflation and Exchange Rates 216
- 8.7 Twenty-First-Century Capital Inflows 217
- 8.8 Concluding Remarks 219
- Summary 221
- Review Questions 222
- Further Reading 222

9 Pegging, Sliding, and Floating: Managing Exchange Rates 223
- 9.1 Characterization of Different Exchange Rate Regimes 224
- 9.2 Latin America's Rich Experience with Exchange Rate Regimes 227
- 9.3 Toward a Consensus on Floating Exchange Rates 229
- 9.4 Avoiding Twenty-First-Century Currency Crises 235
- 9.5 Concluding Remarks 238
- Summary 239
- Review Questions 240
- Further Reading 241

IV The Underpinnings of Growth and Development in Twenty-First-Century Latin America   243

10 Trade and Financial Liberalization   245
- 10.1 The Unilateral Trade Liberalization Wave   246
- 10.2 Bilateral Trade Agreements and Trade Blocs   252
  - 10.2.1 MERCOSUR   253
  - 10.2.2 The Community of Andean Nations   256
  - 10.2.3 NAFTA and CAFTA   257
- 10.3 The Pacific Alliance and Trans-Pacific Partnership   263
- 10.4 Financial Liberalization   266
  - 10.4.1 Financial Supervision, Liability Dollarization, and Banking Crises   268
  - 10.4.2 Worker Remittances   269
  - 10.4.3 Managing Capital Inflows in the Twenty-First Century   271
- 10.5 Concluding Remarks   272
- Summary   274
- Review Questions   275
- Further Reading   276

11 Labor Markets, Informality, and Labor Protection Systems   277
- 11.1 Background   278
- 11.2 Labor Market Deregulation and Deunionization   283
- 11.3 A Labor Market Turning Point   287
- 11.4 The Informal Sector and Job Quality   296
- 11.5 Age Structure and Women in the Labor Force   302
- 11.6 Concluding Remarks   303
- Summary   306
- Review Questions   307
- Further Reading   307

12 Growth and Development in Latin America   309
- 12.1 Development in Latin America: A Tale of Frustrated Expectations   310
- 12.2 Growth and Development: A Quest for Answers   313
  - 12.2.1 Savings   313
  - 12.2.2 Initial Per Capita Income Level   316
- 12.3 Structural Factors   317
  - 12.3.1 Country Size   318
  - 12.3.2 Geography   320
  - 12.3.3 Natural Resource Abundance   321

12.4 Economic Policies and Institutions   323
      12.4.1   Trade Openness   323
      12.4.2   Terms of Trade   326
      12.4.3   Education   327
      12.4.4   Fiscal Policy   331
      12.4.5   Financial Development   333
      12.4.6   Inflation   336
      12.4.7   Institutions   337
12.5 Productivity and Innovation   339
12.6 Concluding Remarks   342
Summary   347
Review Questions   348
Further Reading   349

Notes   351
References   371
Index   405

Preface

Latin America is a fascinating region, home to some 600 million people—mostly from indigenous, European, and African descent—whose cultures and talents have melted and spanned like a mosaic over an enormous territory richly endowed with natural resources. Latin America's traditions, established in widely diverse geography with abundant mineral endowments, extraordinarily fertile lands, beautiful coastal areas, and marvelous mountains, have captivated the minds of brilliant writers, who have left behind a rich recollection of sacred beliefs dating back to precolonial times. Historical events under Iberian control have mixed with epics, upheavals, racial tensions, transatlantic nineteenth-century invasions, and some of the most romantic episodes in the motherland of magic realism, which has proliferated in the twentieth century and beyond. The region also hosts enormous ecological wealth, the preservation of which is a constant struggle for the well-being of present and future generations worldwide.

However, this book focuses on Latin America's frustrated expectations in the domain of economic development. How can such a richly endowed region with vast natural resources and a talented populace remain so poor compared to its northern neighbors? Why has no country in Latin America reached living standards and solid democratic institutions like those enjoyed by a vast majority of Western European citizens? Why has the average Latin American resident not experienced the same economic development benefits as some of her Asian counterparts, who were far behind the region's income per capita only half a century ago?

This book attempts to shed light on such important questions and explains the impressive yet scattered and short-lived success stories of Latin America, which can set a precedent for policy makers in the region and beyond. Our first tenet is that it is impossible to understand the contemporary economics of Latin America without an in-depth analysis of its colonial past and post-independence periods, especially during the last decades of the nineteenth century until World War I. Then we must catch a glimpse of the Great Depression, World War II, and the debt crisis in the 1980s, all of which left an indelible imprint on the region.

Several episodes of boom and bust in commodity markets worldwide have tarnished the region, which continues to rely heavily on natural resources. In the most recent episode, triggered by high commodity prices, twenty-first-century Latin America experienced a high-growth spell, which came to an end in 2013. Unlike similar commodity-driven cycles in previous centuries, however, the region now is less poor, is less unequal across and within regions, and, importantly, has an enlarged and more vocal middle class. Moreover, several countries in Latin America's infant democracies have set in motion unstoppable antipoverty programs and have established high-quality fiscal and monetary institutions.

Although you will find a snapshot of growth in the last chapter, growth alone does not equal economic development, which is indeed multidimensional and multidisciplinary. This book therefore delivers a considerably extended analysis of contemporary Latin America's economic development and the major challenges ahead through the lens of selective findings.

Our journey begins in part I, which mainly focuses on the historical roots of underdevelopment, from colonial times to the debt crisis in the 1980s. In chapter 1, we explain the modes of production enacted in Latin America by the Iberian powers, because the roots of Latin America's poverty and income inequalities can be found there. Was the colonial legacy exacerbated during the region's belle époque (1870–1914), which witnessed a commodity boom similar to the recent one in the early twenty-first century? We attempt to answer this question in chapter 2, which focuses on the diverse trajectories of Latin America's newly independent republics.

Although cross-country and intraregional diversity is emphasized throughout this book, the entire region transitioned in the previous century from export-led growth to a protectionist paradigm, better known as import substitution industrialization (ISI). We analyze this period in great detail in chapter 3. It is important to understand the ISI period in order to grasp the extent of the end of yet another commodity boom and its consequences for post–World War II protectionist policies in different shapes and forms. These policies bear a large part of the burden for the debt crisis in the 1980s that ensued and for its devastating consequences. Chapter 4 analyzes in great detail two debt crises—namely, those of the 1930s and the 1980s—highlighting their similarities and differences. We then study in detail the question of why contemporary Latin America was so deeply affected by the debt crisis of the 1980s and comparatively less affected by the twenty-first-century subprime and eurozone crises.

Part II sets the stage. We start our discussion of Latin America's twenty-first century in this part, studying a region in which nearly 40 percent of the population is vulnerable or extremely poor and income inequalities are only rivaled by those in Africa. In chapter 5, we deliver a detailed analysis of poverty and income inequalities. We not only provide a general understanding of the issues and controversies of the region but also pin down specificities, bearing in mind that Brazil and Mexico—Latin America's largest economies—are particularly poverty-stricken. Antipoverty campaigns dating back to the late twentieth century are now widespread throughout all of Latin America, which might in turn be a contributing factor that can mitigate the perils of income inequality. Chapter 6 is the end of our stage-setting section; it analyzes in great detail the ongoing problem of populism—which no one denies is rooted in income inequalities, but the underlying economic policies and patriotic rhetoric held by charismatic leaders have proven time and again to leave economies in a worse state than that of pre-populist cycles.

The remainder of the book, parts III and IV, focuses on the paths to move forward, partly because prudent fiscal policy—the main theme of chapter 7—was heralded and implemented by the prescriptions of structural reforms in the last decades of the twentieth century, but perhaps most importantly because of home-grown, countercyclical fiscal policies and fiscal institutions in several countries. No one can deny that excessive fiscal deficits—when monetized—trigger inflation and hyperinflation, but chapter 8 explains how the fight against inflation has been largely won as Latin America's policy makers have implemented orthodox and heterodox policies that help the region spiral down from triple- to single-digit inflation rates. Chapter 9 provides an in-depth analysis of exchange rate regimes in Latin America, emphasizing the contemporary trend toward flexible exchange rate regimes with inflation targeting managed by independent central banks.

Chapter 10 is devoted to recurrent themes in the book—namely, trade and financial liberalization. Latin America had already lived its belle époque while Europe and the United States industrialized at a fast pace, and contemporary Latin America in the twenty-first century lived through a commodity boom as China industrialized rapidly until 2013. Now, Latin America faces new challenges, but this time, several countries in the region are well equipped with better fiscal and monetary institutions to stand up to the challenge of coping with primary commodities' fluctuations. However, a handful of regions do not possess such institutions yet. Moreover, with the exception of Mexico, the trade liberalization trend has not made a significant dent on the primary commodity dependency, which is leading policy makers again to rethink the best ways to diversify production and exports.

Chapter 11 offers a comprehensive and thorough analysis of labor markets in the region, including trends in regulation and unionization, the issues of job quality and informality, and the important subject of women in the labor force. We ask what is left from the twenty-first-century commodity boom in terms of labor productivity in a dual-labor market made up of the formally employed and the informally employed. We focus on the latter group because the vast informal sector remains socially unprotected and cannot access on-the-job training in order to reap a much-needed labor productivity bonus. Chapter 12 ends with an analysis of inclusive growth policies for development in the Latin American region and the main challenges that lie ahead.

We owe a great deal to the many people who have assisted us as we worked on this book. We gratefully acknowledge the support and valuable comments of our colleagues and students. We are particularly grateful to Francisco Ferreira's input in the very early stages of this book and to Juan Bravo, who has been of great help throughout this project. Laura Connell provided invaluable help and comments throughout. Jeff Williamson and Eliana Cardoso provided exceedingly important and very detailed comments on the first five chapters of this book. Rodolfo de la Torre delivered useful and thoughtful remarks on chapter 5. We gratefully acknowledge Tatiana Ribón's assistance on chapter 9. Maria Ignacia Cuevas and Agustin García offered excellent research assistance through the final and most stressful stages of the book. We would also like to thank six anonymous reviewers who offered extremely useful comments. Last but not least, this book would have never existed without the continued support, encouragement, and extraordinary patience of John Covell from the MIT Press. John's successor, Emily Taber, has been marvelous. Not only has she demonstrated a strong commitment to this project, but she has also helped us get timely reviewers' comments and has delivered her own useful and concise advice in order to speed up the publication process.

Last but not least, we thank our spouses, Georges-Antoine and Francisca, respectively, as well as our families for their graceful tolerance during the mental and emotional challenges we have gone through in this endeavor.

Beatriz Armendáriz and Felipe Larraín B.
August 2016

Acronyms

AD	Acción Democratica (Democratic Action)
ASEAN	Association of South East Asian Nations
Banorte	Banco Mercantil del Norte
BF	Bolsa Família
BIS	Bank of International Settlements
BPC	Benefício de Prestação Continuada
BRIC	Brazil, Russia, India, and China
CACM	Central American Common Market
CAFTA	Central American Free Trade Agreement
CAN	Comunidad Andina de las Naciones (Andean Community of Nations)
CARICOM	Comunidad del Caribe (Caribbean Community and Common Market)
CBN	Cost of basic needs
CEPAL	Comisión Económica para América Latina y el Caribe (United Nations Economic Commission for Latin America and the Caribbean)
DF	Distrito Federal (Federal District)
EBRD	European Bank for Reconstruction and Development
ECLAC	Economic Commission for Latin America and the Caribbean
ESFs	Emergency social funds
ESSF	Economic and Social Stabilization Fund
EU	European Union
FARC	Fuerzas Armadas Revolucionarias de Colombia (Revolutionary Armed Forces of Colombia)

FDI	Foreign direct investment	
FOB	Free on board	
FOSIDES	Fondo Sectorial para la Investigación y el Desarrollo Social (Sectoral Fund for Research and Social Development)	
FTA	Free trade agreement	
FTAA	Free Trade Area of the Americas	
GDP	Gross domestic product	
IADB	Inter-American Development Bank	
ICT	Information and communication technology	
IDB	Inter-American Development Bank	
IEF	Ingreso Ético Familiar (Ethical Family Income)	
ILO	International Labour Organization	
IMF	International Monetary Fund	
INEGI	Instituto Nacional de Estadística y Geografía (National Institute of Statistic and Geography)	
ISI	Import substitution industrialization	
JSI	Job Security Index	
LAFTA	Latin American Free Trade Association	
LAIA	Latin American Integration Association	
LANIC	Latin American Information Network	
LDCs	Less developed countries	
MAS	Movimiento al Socialismo (Movement to Socialism)	
MCCA	Mercado Común Centroamericano (Central American Customs Union)	
MCCTP	Mexican Conditional Cash Transfer Program	
MERCOSUR	Mercado Común del Sur (Southern Common Market)	
NAFTA	North American Free Trade Agreement	
NGOs	Nongovernmental organizations	
OECD	Organisation for Economic Co-operation and Development	
OPEC	Organization of the Petroleum Exporting Countries	
PAN	Partido Acción Nacional (National Action Party)	
PDVSA	Petróleos de Venezuela S.A.	
PEMEX	Petróleos Mexicanos	
PETI	Programa de Erradicação do Trabalho Infantil (Program to Eradicate Child Labor)	
Petrobras	Petróleo Brasileiro S.A.	
PPP	Purchasing power parity	
PRF	Pension Reserve Fund	
PRI	Partido Revolucionario Institucional (Institutional Revolutionary Party)	

Acronyms

PROGRESA	Programa de Educación, Salud y Alimentación
R&D	Research and development
RDA	Regression discontinuity analysis
SEDESOL	Secretaría de Desarrollo Social (Ministry of Social Development)
SME	Small and medium enterprises
SOEs	State-owned enterprises
TFP	Total factor productivity
TTP	Trans-Pacific Partnership
UBN	Unsatisfied basic needs
UK	United Kingdom
UNCTAD	United Nations Conference on Trade and Development
UNDP	United Nations Development Program
VAT	Value-added tax
WEO	World Economic Outlook
WHO	World Health Organization
WITS	World Integrated Trade Solution
WTO	World Trade Organization
YPF	Yacimientos Petrolíficos Fiscales (Fiscal Oilfields)

I Historical Origins of the Contemporary Latin American Economy

1   Geography and the Colonial Legacy

It is impossible to understand the diverse twenty-first century Latin American economies and ongoing debates without understanding their history. The salient features we explain in this opening chapter include Latin America's backwardness relative to that of its more prosperous northern neighbors and the high degree of within-region and across-regions income inequalities. We therefore start here by spelling out various hypotheses on economic development rooted in the region's shared historical background.

An unprecedented movement of exploration and colonization pioneered by the Spaniards and Portuguese took place from the fifteenth through the seventeenth centuries. This movement led first to the discovery of the American continent in 1492 and then to its conquest thereafter. In 1494, the kingdoms of Portugal and Spain divided the newly discovered land between themselves via the *Treaty of Tordesillas*.[1] A few centuries later, the dividing line was redrawn throughout South America by the Iberian powers. From this subdivision, two main colonies emerged: Portuguese America—that is, modern-day Brazil—and Spanish America. The latter comprises dozens of countries inclusive of two pre-Columbian empires: the Incan empire in Peru and the Aztec empire in Mexico.

Other European kingdoms attempted to gain control over this vast territory, but success was confined to a few enclaves, such as Belize in Central America, some islands in the Caribbean, the three Guianas, and the Malvinas or Falkland Islands in the south.

Notwithstanding the relative superiority of the Iberian powers in the Americas throughout the fifteenth and sixteenth centuries, England and France, alongside other non-Iberian kingdoms, succeeded in establishing permanent colonies further north later, in the seventeenth century, leaving the immense majority of the southern territories under direct control of Spain and Portugal.[2] But despite the earlier colonization of South America by the Spaniards and Portuguese, the average income per head of Latin Americans has remained strikingly low compared to that of people living in North America.

In the remainder of this chapter, we provide a novel synthesis of the flourishing historical literature on income disparities between north and south and on income inequalities and poverty within Latin America. Drawing from different hypotheses based on geography, legal origins, institutions, and ethnolinguistic fragmentation, we argue that key insights of these postulates can be woven together into a coherent whole to shed light on contemporary Latin America's underdevelopment when compared to its neighbors in the north.

Recent estimates suggest that per capita gross domestic product (GDP) in Latin America is just 20 percent of that in the United States.[3] Persistent per capita GDP inequalities between North and South America over the last century have become the focus of considerable attention by economists, historians, political scientists, and sociologists. Their views have captivated the minds of numerous researchers in economics over the past two decades.

Is greater proximity to the equator and easy access to seacoast an important determinant of north-south income disparities in the Americas? Is the civil law legacy in former Iberian colonies key to our understanding of underdevelopment in the south? Is inherited institutional legacy an impediment to faster economic development in South America? Do the hundred precolonial languages—still spoken in the region—have a negative impact in terms of promoting poverty, income inequality, social unrest and hindering economic prosperity in the south?

Section 1.1 of this chapter spells out the geography hypothesis. Then, section 1.2 evaluates the merits of the common law heritage in North America versus the civil law legacy in South America to provide a potential explanation of underdevelopment in South America. Section 1.3 delivers an overview of the *factor endowments hypothesis*, according to which relative abundance of land propitious to large-scale agriculture (and relative scarcity of labor) has an effect and persistent influence on development patterns. Likewise, areas with large native populations and land conducive to large-scale crop production or mineral wealth are prone to inequality under a master-servant mode of production. Section 1.4 attempts to shed light on economic underdevelopment in Latin America through the lens of the literature on institutional heritage. The bulk of this literature contends that early settlements and the attitudes of colonial masters to the development of the territories under their control had pervasive effects on per capita income. Section 1.5 delivers widespread perceptions from the literature on ethnolinguistic fragmentation and culture to shed light on chronic poverty and political unrest in some parts of Latin America. Finally, section 1.6 summarizes and explains the extent to which each hypothesis can explain current trends and development challenges in contemporary Latin American economies.

1.1 Geography

In a series of thought-provoking articles, it has been argued that slow economic growth during critical historical periods and consequent underdevelopment until today can be attributed to geographic factors—such as close proximity to the equator and/or temperature, and access to seaports.[4] Although the bulk of this literature focuses on Africa, parallels with Latin America are striking. As column 5 in table 1.1 shows, Latin America ranks second after sub-Saharan Africa in terms of the proportion of land located in the tropics.

The reason that inhabitants of lands located in the tropics are at a disadvantage relative to those populations living in temperate zones is threefold. First, unlike the north, agriculture in the tropics is not blessed with predictable water from defrosting and low exposure to the sun. Second, if trade is positively correlated with per capita income, then landlocked countries in the tropics are at a disadvantage, because sea trade remains the cheapest and most effective means of transport. Third, health-wise, the incidence of tropical diseases such as malaria, yellow fever, dengue, and cholera is much higher in the tropics, where public health standards are low compared to those in the north. Hence, labor productivity due to poor health in the tropics is comparatively low.

There is also a suggestion in most literature on this topic that technological diffusion for agriculture- and health-related technology from the north to the tropics is exceedingly difficult and that more context-specific agricultural research is needed to boost agricultural production in the tropics.[5] This research is unlikely to happen, however, because the innovators in industrialized countries find it unprofitable to invest in context-specific agricultural research south of the border. Moreover, for investments in agricultural research to be profitable, scale must be considered. Microclimates and the rapid pace of urbanization are the main constraints for agricultural research and development in Latin America.

Primarily, a vast majority of small agricultural producers is affected, and they remain poor compared to a minority of large estate owners who benefit from the introduction of technological improvements, thus leading to a high degree of inequality between small, subsistence agricultural producers and relatively large-scale producers that market cash crops domestically and abroad.

Table 1.1
Geography-related features of Latin America relative to other regions

(1)	(2)	(3)	(4)	(5)	(6)	(7)	(8)	(9)	(10)	(11)	(12)	(13)
Region	Number of countries	Land area M sq km	Population in millions (2014)	Population density	Proportion land area in the Tropics	Proportion population w/100 km coast	Proportion population w/100 km coast or river	Proportion population landlocked	Distance to core market (km)2	1,000 km coastline/ sq km area	CIF/ FOB ratio 1995	GDP/ capita (2014)
Sub-Saharan Africa	41	24.29	962.33	39.6	0.91	0.19	0.21	0.28	6,237	1.15	1.20	1,796.0
Western Europe	16	2.863	504	176.0	0.00	0.53	0.89	0.04	922	15.74	1.05	3,0338.3
East and South East Asia	12	24.83	2263	91.1	0.30	0.43	0.61	0.00	3,396	11.54	1.10	9,466.1
South Asia	5	5.14	1,692.2	329.2	0.40	0.23	0.41	0.02	5,744	2.45	1.10	1,541.1
East Europe Tran econ	25	24.86	395.26	15.9	0.00	0.09	0.37	0.28	2,439	0.86	1.08	1,0119.3
Latin America	22	20.43	622	30.4	0.73	0.42	0.43	0.03	4,651	2.54	1.11	10,126.0

Source: Bloom et al. 1998, except for columns 4, 5, and 13; World Bank 2014b for columns 4, 5, and 13.

It is important to note two mitigating factors that have affected all primary commodity producers and exporters positively, however. One is the high and sustained growth rate that twenty-first-century Latin America enjoyed as a result of the commodity boom due to increased trade with industrializing China. The commodity boom lifted millions of Latin Americans from poverty. (We will return to globalization often and to trade liberalization in particular in chapter 9.)

The other factor is better public health service provisions and the removal of poverty-related obstacles. To some extent, health-related poverty traps have been removed via anti-poverty campaigns—targeting low-income peasants in priority—such as the conditional cash transfer program pioneered by Mexico as part of the *Progresa/Oportunidades/Prospera* program. We discuss this and similar programs throughout the region in great detail in chapter 5.[6]

Yet another issue often identified with Sachs's geography hypothesis is population density, which is highest in temperate areas in the north that offer more favorable terrain for technological innovations. Economies of scale, the argument goes, are more prone to take hold in larger markets in which emergent middle classes can afford to buy manufactures and capital-intensive products resulting from region-specific research and development (R&D). Technological innovations in the north are more profitable than in sparsely populated areas in the tropics.[7]

However, in an increasingly globalized world, some Latin American countries such as Colombia and Brazil have been hosting agricultural research centers for improving the productivity of primary commodities such as coffee, soybeans, and other products. This has had an undeniably positive impact on total factor productivity and economic growth in the region.

Despite the striking similarities between sub-Saharan Africa and Latin America with regard to low population density, as shown in table 1.1,[8] recent research reveals divergent trends between the two regions: R&D in agriculture is comparatively less costly in Africa, and it also has greater impact on poverty reduction in Africa. However, it does have a positive impact on employment and trade in Latin America.[9]

With regard to distance to core markets, the geography hypothesis postulates that this distance is longer and transport costs are higher in the tropics. This is also shown in table 1.1, in columns 9 and 11, for sub-Saharan Africa and Latin America. High transport costs, particularly in landlocked areas, and long distances from the hinterlands to the seaports may cripple the ability of many regions' policy makers in Latin America to facilitate profitable exploitation of primary commodities, both in agriculture and mining. Limited primary commodity export performance can in turn contribute to the slow pace of economic prosperity.[10] The main challenge here, as argued throughout follow-up chapters, is that of overcoming centuries of underinvestment in infrastructure.

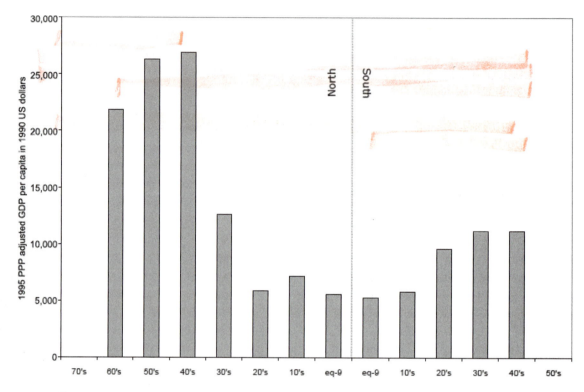

Figure 1.1
Per capita GDP and latitude: North versus South America.
Source: Bloom et al. 1998.

In sum, the geography hypothesis proclaims that low soil fertility, low productivity resulting from relatively high disease burden, limited scope for taking advantage of lucrative trade of primary commodities due to adverse geographic conditions in the tropics, and obstacles to technology transfer from the north are the main reasons Latin America is lagging behind North America. The wide per capita income disparities between North America and South America are therefore due to forces of nature. Figure 1.1 shows different latitude bands along the horizontal axis and GDP per head on the vertical axis, highlighting these disparities.

Notwithstanding the merits of the geography hypothesis, we believe that this is only part of a much broader explanation of Latin American underdevelopment. Investments in infrastructure, health, and education could have mitigated unfavorable geography. Why has the scope and scale of such investments been so limited in middle-income Latin America? We will analyze this important question

1.2 Legal Origins

An influential strand of the literature on north-south income disparities contends that legal origins matter.[11] Common law countries in North America offer better shareholder protection than civil law countries in Latin America. The latter countries imported French civil law when Napoleon conquered the Iberian Peninsula in 1807. Under *civil* or *Napoleonic law* (we use these terms interchangeably), investors are not adequately protected, and ownership concentration—or lack of risk diversification—in the hands of a few economic actors ensues.

Consequent lack of transparency, uncertainty, and the high risk of expropriation have in turn created an adverse investment climate. Moreover, civil law is highly politicized. Since its codification by Napoleon in nineteenth-century France, civil law has often been used as an instrument for the state to enjoy increased powers. This has further deteriorated property rights protection, which is proxied empirically by the risk of expropriation.[12]

In contrast, common law has been shaped by parliamentary democracy, and its main objective is to limit the power of the sovereign and to the benefit of property rights protection for the masses. Better and extended property rights protection for a vast majority of the population is, in turn, conducive to better governance, stabilizing democracy, higher institutional quality, and higher growth rates of per capita income.

From a Latin American perspective, it is difficult to assess the merits of the common versus the civil law hypothesis. Part of the problem is that the dataset on existing empirical work is not confined to Latin America. Cross-country regressions include as many as 152 countries, with only 15 percent of Latin American countries included in the sample. Moreover, existing analyses are limited to the last decades of the twentieth century.

During these last decades, contemporary Latin American economies went through a period of deep economic transformation—with the notable exception of Chile, which, as we will further explain, started its structural transformation earlier. We analyze this important reform period in Latin America during the 1980s and 1990s in greater detail in chapter 4. The structural reform was profound, and most importantly to this section on legal origins, the reform emphasized better protection of private investors' property rights.

Admittedly, most structural reforms need time to take hold. However, we believe that other variables might be playing a prominent role when assessing investment climate in civil law countries. In particular, corruption is a major

Table 1.2
Corruption perceptions index and foreign direct investment across Latin America in 2012

Country	Ranking relative to the rest of the world (1 = best, 176 = worst)	FDI (% of GDP)
Chile	20	11.2
Uruguay	20	5.8
Costa Rica	48	5.8
Brazil	69	3.4
El Salvador	83	2.0
Peru	83	6.0
Panama	83	9.3
Colombia	94	4.2
Argentina	102	2.6
Mexico	105	1.3
Bolivia	105	3.9
Guatemala	113	2.3
Ecuador	118	0.7
Dominican Republic	118	6.5
Paraguay	150	1.4
Venezuela	165	0.6

Source: Authors' own construction from Transparency International (www.transparency.org); World Bank database (www.worldbank.org).

problem in Latin America, and it might be at the root of economic backwardness in the region. Table 1.2 illustrates corruption indices in more than a dozen countries located in Latin America.

According to table 1.2, Chile, Uruguay, Costa Rica, and Brazil are among the least corrupt. These countries also rank high in terms foreign direct investment (FDI) as a share of GDP in recent decades, which accords well with recent empirical studies. These studies show that FDI is negatively correlated with corruption.[13] It is nonetheless important to note that Latin America's recent efforts to reduce corruption have not gone unnoticed.[14] Encouraging findings and stylized facts on improved corruption indices are important, because they seem to encourage not only FDI, but also international community initiatives to, for example, rebuild Haiti and reconstruct Chile after the devastating twenty-first-century natural catastrophes in these two countries.[15]

Corruption alone does not seem to correlate with economic performance, however. Tables 1.2 and 1.3 reveal that, with the exception of Chile, the stellar performers in terms of corruption indices are not necessarily those countries in

Table 1.3
Per capita GDP across Latin America in 2013

Country	GDP per head, PPP adjusted (US dollars)
Chile	19,067
Argentina	18,749
Uruguay	16,723
Panama	16,658
Mexico	15,563
Venezuela	13,605
Costa Rica	12,942
Brazil	12,221
Colombia	11,189
Peru	11,124
Ecuador	10,080
Dominican Republic	9,911
Belize	8,716
El Salvador	7,515
Paraguay	6,823
Bolivia	5,364
Guatemala	5,282
Honduras	4,839
Nicaragua	4,554
Haiti	1,315

Source: IMF 2014c.

which per capita income levels are the highest. This is indeed puzzling and merits further research. On the other hand, attributing underdevelopment—under the narrow definition of per capita GDP—to one single variable, corruption, is unrealistic for we well know that the causes and manifestations of underdevelopment and poverty are multidimensional.

Unsurprisingly, the hypothesis about the superiority of common law countries over civil law counterparts has been stretched beyond corruption indicators. Recent research suggests that there were higher ratios of stock market value to GDP in civil law countries relative to common law countries up until 1929.[16]

This finding is puzzling too. Recall that the entire concept of legal origins relies on the idea that the property rights of shareholders and financiers are better protected under common law. Table 1.4 shows that this is not the case historically, at least prior to the Great Depression of 1929. Follow-up research suggests that

Table 1.4
Stock market capitalization in common and civil law countries before and after the Great Depression of 1929

Country	Legal origin	1913	1929	1938	1950	1960	1970	1980	1990	1999
Australia	English	0.39	0.50	0.91	0.75	0.94	0.76	0.38	0.37	1.13
Canada	English	0.74		1.00	0.57	1.59	1.75	0.46	1.22	1.22
India	English	0.02	0.07	0.07	0.07	0.07	0.06	0.05	0.16	0.46
South Africa	English				0.68	0.91	1.97	1.23	1.33	1.20
United Kingdom	English	1.09	1.38	1.14	0.77	1.06	1.63	0.38	0.81	2.25
United States	English	0.39	0.75	0.56	0.33	0.61	0.66	0.46	0.54	1.52
Avg. common law		0.53	0.68	0.74	0.53	0.86	1.14	0.49	0.74	1.30
Argentina	French	0.17				0.05	0.03	0.11		0.15
Belgium	French	0.99	1.31			0.32	0.23	0.09	0.31	0.82
Brazil	French	0.25						0.05	0.08	0.45
Chile	French	0.17				0.12	0.00	0.34	0.50	1.05
Cuba	French	2.19								
Egypt, Arab Rep.	French	1.09				0.16				0.29
France	French	0.78		0.19	0.08	0.28	0.16			1.17

Table 1.4 (continued)

Country	Legal origin	1913	1929	1938	1950	1960	1970	1980	1990	1999
Italy	French	0.17	0.23	0.26	0.07	0.42	0.14			0.68
Netherlands	French	0.56		0.74	0.25	0.67	0.42			2.03
Russian Federation	French	0.18								0.11
Spain	French							0.17	0.41	0.69
Avg. civil law		0.66	0.77	0.40	0.13	0.29	0.16	0.12	0.28	0.74
Austria	German	0.76					0.09	0.03	0.17	0.17
Germany	German	0.44	0.35	0.18	0.15	0.35	0.16	0.09	0.20	0.67
Japan	German	0.49	1.20	1.81	0.05	0.36	0.23	0.33	1.64	0.95
Switzerland	German	0.58					0.50	0.44	1.93	3.23
Avg German Law		0.57	0.78	1.00	0.1	0.36	0.25	0.22	0.99	1.26
Denmark	Scandinavian	0.36	0.17	0.25	0.10	0.14	0.17	0.09	0.67	0.67
Norway	Scandinavian	0.16	0.22	0.18	0.21	0.26	0.23	0.54	0.23	0.70
Sweden	Scandinavian	0.47	0.41	0.30	0.18	0.24	0.14	0.11	0.39	1.77
Avg. Scandinavian law, similar to civil law in Denmark, Finland, Iceland, Norway, and Sweden		0.33	0.27	0.24	0.16	0.21	0.18	0.25	0.42	1.05

Source: Rajan and Zingales 2003.

property rights' protection laws are not time invariant. In particular, circa 1910 civil law countries' creditors enjoyed better protection relative to common law countries.[17]

We believe that relatively weak property rights' protection in Latin America is indeed a twentieth-century phenomenon, not a nineteenth-century civil law inheritance. In particular, the Great Depression of the 1930s triggered a change of ideology and policy making. Latin America turned increasingly hostile to foreign investment, and government intervention became strong across a wide range of traded and nontraded sectors. We will return to this episode of Latin American history in greater detail in chapter 3.

Two final remarks merit attention. First, table 1.4 includes German and Scandinavian laws, suggesting that the common versus civil law distinction is not as clear-cut as we have been led to believe. From a Latin American standpoint, it is important to note that German and Scandinavian immigration flows prior to 1929 might have influenced institutional quality and/or culture. Even if those European migrants were a minority in comparison with Iberian migrants, Scandinavian migrants might have introduced a particular kind of human capital that gave them a competitive edge relative to the majority of Iberian migrants, and Scandinavian cultures and traditions might have had a positive influence on Latin American development in some regions.[18] This line of thought on the impact of culture in Latin American regions is under-researched. We believe that investigating this idea further is definitely worthwhile, because it gives food for thought about diverse institutional development and contract enforcement in countries such as Chile and Uruguay. Unlike most of their Latin American neighbors, these two countries are now considered high middle-income economies, according to recent studies by the World Bank.[19] Did early migrants' characteristics matter when trying to explain diverse performance across Latin American regions?

Second, when looking at table 1.4 again, yet another important puzzle emerges: How can we explain that Chile, alongside Argentina, Brazil, and Cuba, enjoyed well-developed financial systems by the early twentieth century? The legal origins hypothesis cannot provide a convincing answer. We strongly believe that the law is not static, as a Harvard Business School study suggests.[20] In such Latin American countries, and unlike common law former colonies such as Hong Kong, creditors were well protected in the twentieth century. The reverse is true when one looks at the civil versus common law countries during the second half of the twentieth century: throughout this entire period, Latin America transited from military or semimilitary regimes to nascent democracies. Whether further consolidation of democratic institutions in twenty-first-century Latin America can improve property rights protection indicators remains an open question.

1.3 Factor Endowments

Influential work by economic historians Stanley Engerman and Kenneth Sokoloff suggests that the main reason that the United States and Canada have been more prosperous relative to Latin America is rooted in north-south differences in initial factor endowments.[21]

The authors focus on the idea that soil and climates in the south are more suitable for cultivation of crops that required the use of slaves and Amerindians on a large scale. A typical example is sugar production, which, relative to other crops like wheat, requires tropical soil and climates that can be profitably exploited in large plots of land. In these plots, the production of sugar and other crops required labor—a scarce input of production relative to land in the Americas. Labor shortages in turn triggered large importation of slaves from Africa in relatively more sparsely populated areas, and the use of indentured labor in relatively labor-abundant regions of Spanish America such as Mexico, Peru, and Central America. Large-scale plantation agriculture, in turn, led to high-income inequalities between (1) a small elite of individuals from European descent who owned large plots of land and labor and (2) the vast majority of slaves and native indigenous populations. A similar story applies to countries such as Peru, which was endowed with vast mineral wealth and, relative to other regions, also had a large native population for mineral resource extraction.

In contrast, soil and climatic conditions in the north led to mixed farming, centered on grains and livestock. The potential for taking advantage of scale economies was limited; northern lands took the form of small, family-cultivated plots. In these regions, north of the Chesapeake in the state of Virginia in the United States, a relatively more equal distribution of land and wealth among European colonizers emerged. This, in turn, laid the ground for the emergence and evolution of more democratic political institutions, a relatively larger middle class, larger domestic markets, and the pursuit of more growth-oriented policies relative to those in their southern counterparts, where R&D was not profitable due to the lack of domestic demand rooted in large income inequalities under colonial modes of production (i.e., the vast majority in southern regions did not earn more than subsistence wages).

In contrast to northern regions in the United States, the emergence of a middle class in Latin America is a rather recent phenomenon. It started during the second half of the twentieth century under the so-called import substitution industrialization (ISI) period. We will come back to this in chapter 3. By and large, however, the size of the middle class has increased considerably during the twenty-first century. The emergent middle class has become increasingly vocal, and its concerns now are creating new challenges for Latin America's young democracies, as we will discuss further in chapter 6.

Two additional issues presented by Engerman and Sokoloff's factor endowments hypothesis seem difficult to understand. First, from a Latin American perspective, soil and climatic conditions might be similar and yet growth trajectories very dissimilar between countries—for example, in the case of the Dominican Republic and Haiti. Both are part of the same island of Hispaniola, but the former country has a per capita GDP that is three times higher than that of the latter.[22]

At the other end of the spectrum, when we look at the region's nineteenth-century stellar performers—namely, Argentina, Chile, and Uruguay—the temperate climates that resemble those of North America, we cannot refrain from asking the following question: Why didn't these three relatively similar countries catch up with the living standards of the United States and Canada during the nineteenth and twentieth centuries? We will come back to this question in chapter 3 when we discuss the protracted twentieth-century protectionist period in the region.

The second issue is that in southern US states such as Virginia, Alabama, Georgia, and South Carolina, where large-scale plantation agriculture with extensive use of slaves for the production of cotton and sugar prevailed up until the late nineteenth century, living standards have converged with those of the northern states.[23] These plantation economies' catching-up process began after the start of the American Civil War, in 1861.

Similar plantation-based Latin American regions have just begun to catch up. Rapid growth of agricultural development in Brazil in recent decades, for example, has been impressive. Brazil is now the United States' leading competitor in agricultural products, including soybeans, beef, poultry, and cotton. We will return to this when we analyze the importance of within–Latin America trade integration in chapter 10.

As in Brazil, trade—and, more generally, globalization—has accelerated growth in many other Latin American regions. However, this is a recent phenomenon. Engerman and Sokoloff describe a qualifying distinction among three different groups of countries for most of the eighteenth and nineteenth centuries.

The first category encompasses a group of colonies in which climates and soils were conducive to the production of sugar and other highly valued crops, but the scarcity of labor necessitated large-scale importation of slaves by European colonizers. Chief among this type of plantation colony under Iberian control are countries such as Brazil and Cuba.

A second set of countries includes former Spanish colonies, which are characterized by their relatively large indigenous populations (e.g., Mexico, Guatemala, Bolivia, and Peru). An elite class of Spaniards was granted rights over large plots of land and over indigenous labor under the *encomienda* system. In a nutshell, the *encomienda* was a legal system enforced by the Spanish Crown, under which conquerors were granted land and a large number of natives from whom they could extract tribute in the form of labor and other resources.²⁴ Because indentured laborers under the *encomienda* system could neither be moved nor sold by their masters, economic historians argue that large landowners from Iberian descent found it profitable to operate on a large scale. Note that large-scale agricultural production for the benefit of an elite does not emerge in this case because of soil and climatic characteristics alone; instead, large-scale agriculture results from relative labor abundance under the *encomienda* mode of production. The counterpart in mineral- and labor-abundant areas is the *mita* mode of production, which we analyze later.

A contributing factor to the perpetuation of the *encomienda* system and consequential intergenerational income inequality was the *mayorazgo* institution, directly imported from Spain.²⁵ Ultimately, the outcome in terms of pervasive income inequalities remains the same under both scenarios, but the *mayorazgo* exacerbated inequality specifically, whereas slave agriculture prevailed in countries with soil and climatic conditions prone to plantation agriculture, such as Brazil and Cuba where labor was relatively scarce. By comparison, indentured labor agriculture under the *encomienda* became the predominant mode of production in countries such as Mexico and Peru. Large income inequalities between Europeans from Iberian descent and slaves in the former case and between Europeans from Spanish descent and indigenous populations in the latter were conducive to growth rates of per capita GDP that were considerably lower than those in Canada and the United States since at least the latter countries' industrial revolutions in the nineteenth century. In chapter 5, we analyze in greater detail the relationship between economic growth and income inequality in contemporary Latin American economies.

The third category encompasses a set of southern cone countries—namely, Argentina, Uruguay, and Chile. In these countries, the combination of soil and climatic characteristics and their scarcity of labor—relative to countries such as Mexico and Peru—displays striking similarities to those in northern North America. Engerman and Sokoloff contend that male adult migrants in these regions were able to operate as independent proprietors with limited scope for scale economies, but, unlike North American colonies, income inequalities in the production of grains in Iberian-controlled colonies were deeply rooted in the *encomienda* mode of production, even if in those countries, that is, Argentina, Chile, and Uruguay, there were considerable shortages of indigenous populations in comparison with countries such as Mexico and Peru.

In the particular case of Argentina, inequalities might have been reinforced by the limited scope for scale economies in raising cattle in the *pampas*.²⁶ Massive flows of European migrants in the late nineteenth century together with increased death rates and low fertility among the small indigenous populations gave Argentina, Uruguay, and Chile—often considered to be Latin America's nineteenth-century stellar performers by economic historians—a predominantly European character. We analyze comparative nineteenth-century Latin American countries' performance and diverse trajectories in greater detail in chapter 2.

But why did Argentina, Uruguay, and Chile remain economically backward relative to the United States and Canada? Engerman and Sokoloff suggest that relative to their northern neighbors, European migration flows into Argentina, Chile, and Uruguay arrived comparatively late. Specifically, the flow of migrants produced a relatively low endowment of human capital, because migrants came mostly from Spain, Italy, and Portugal, which were already backward countries in terms of per capita income and human capital relative to those migrants arriving in the United States and Canada at the time. Simply stated, colonizers in the United States and Canada arrived from more advanced northern European regions.

As an aside, and not directly related to Latin American economic development and trajectories, the relative backwardness of the southern United States relative to the north might seem puzzling too. However, we know that the US Civil War and the abolition of slavery during the second half of the nineteenth century played an important role. In particular, the combination of the war and emancipation led to the disappearance of plantation agriculture as a production unit in southeastern United States. Even though large land concentration persisted, small farm, owner-operated units of production dominated the landscape since and boosted domestic demand during the ensuing US industrialization period.

The relative scarcity of physical and human capital in the southern United States, deeply rooted in initial income inequalities, helps to explain why these southern states lagged behind in terms of industrialization. It also explains why it took those southern regions nearly a century to become more urbanized after the 1861 Civil War.

Are there lessons to be learned for Latin America, where land reforms and antipoverty campaigns in rural areas have been in place in recent decades? Chapter 5 addresses antipoverty efforts in the region. As we will discuss later in the book, land reforms and antipoverty campaigns in Latin America are relatively recent when compared to welfare states, in, for example, European countries. Moreover, antipoverty programs and policies across Latin America have a trajectory of their own in different regions. These policies have transformed the landscape of many twenty-first-century Latin American economies. Nonetheless, inclusion of native indigenous and African descent populations remains a challenge. In some regions, twenty-first-century charismatic leaders have appealed to such populations and

Geography and the Colonial Legacy

gained their support via redistributive policies. These policies bear an eerie resemblance to those of populist autocrats, such as Juan and Evita Perón in the twentieth century. We will return to these upsurges of populism in chapter 6.

Engerman and Sokoloff suggest that the former colonies in the United States showed brighter prospects than the plantation-based Iberian colonies for two main reasons. First, southeast United States was unsuitable for sugar production relative to countries such as Cuba. The scale of slave plantation production in comparison was therefore not as large. Consequently, income inequalities were never as extreme as those found in the Iberian colonies. Second, the institutional framework in southeast United States was determined at a federal level and/or via competition between states, and salient and common features shared some similarities with northern, more modern, and more industrialized states.

As a closing remark on the factor endowments hypothesis, notice that the suggested positive correlation between income equality and growth has a demand-side and a supply-side explanation. On the demand side, relative to slaves and indentured laborers under slavery and the *encomienda*, a larger proportion of free whites from European descent would spend a larger share of their income on manufactures, which in turn triggered rapid industrialization in the nineteenth century.

This line of reasoning dates back to Rosenstein and Rodan's 1943 article on industrialization in Eastern Europe.[27] A key assumption in this widely cited article is that rapid industrialization relies on domestic demand. Nascent industrializing economies are assumed to be autarkic as far as trade is concerned. This assumption might have been valid for the case of -nineteenth-century United States, but it was certainly not true during the nineteenth century in Latin America, during which time the entire region could export primary commodities to European regions that were rapidly industrializing; consequent growth led to nascent manufacturing industries in countries such as Argentina. A similar growth spell has been experienced recently as a result of the early twenty-first-century commodity boom triggered by rapid industrialization in China. The real question, then, is why those export-led growth spells in Latin America have failed to trickle down to the vast majority in order to boost domestic demand for manufactures. We will analyze this recent growth spell and its failure to trigger demand-driven industrialization in greater detail in chapter 10 on trade liberalization.

The autarky assumption is also invalid when one looks at other Latin American countries in the twentieth and twenty-first centuries. A case in point is the current wave of export-led growth countries such as Chile, Colombia, Peru, and Mexico. These countries' prospect for rapid industrialization depends heavily on external demand. Labor-abundant China and other Asian economies have already taken the lead, however. Nonetheless, Mexico, along with other Central American countries, has a geographical advantage compared to China; an expanded North American Free Trade Agreement (NAFTA) also has enabled some countries, such as Mexico—Latin America's second-largest economy after Brazil—to diversify their exports away from primary commodities.

Demand for manufactures is not the only factor. On the supply side, a similar argument applies. The profitability of large-scale infrastructure investments in, for example, transport and financial services heavily depends on the number of potential users. In more equal northern regions in the United States, the relative abundance of entrepreneurs in manufacturing activities has made investments in infrastructure profitable.

In contrast, supply-side considerations were not propitious for industrialization to take off in highly unequal Latin America. We should note, however, that the widespread use of slave labor in economies such as those of Brazil and Cuba and in economies in which indigenous populations were used as laborers under the *encomienda* and *mita* modes of production (notably, in Mexico and Peru), combined with relatively low migration inflows, is key to understanding persistent inequality and a scarcity of entrepreneurial-spirited individuals required for rapid industrialization to take off.[28]

1.4 Institutional Legacy

In their groundbreaking work, Acemoglu, Johnson, and Robinson (2001, 2002) argue that although the geography and factor endowment hypotheses pin down interesting stylized facts and correlations, both fail to establish causality. Take the case of population density as an engine of economic growth as an example: Acemoglu, Johnson, and Robinson contend that the geography hypothesis fails to establish whether low population density is caused by adverse climatic characteristics (e.g., migration to tempered regions) or if it is the tropical features that cause low population density due to high mortality rates. In other words, there is an endogeneity problem, which the geography hypothesis is incapable of addressing empirically. This problem makes the geography hypothesis unconvincing at best and misleading at worst.

The empirical work of Acemoglu, Johnson, and Robinson (2001) use settlers' mortality rates as an instrumental variable to demonstrate that institutional colonial legacies in the seventeenth century cause institutions (of private property and extractive) to persist up until these days , and that divergent contemporary economic performances persist via these different institutions to the current day.[29] High per capita GDP corresponds with institutions of private property and low per capita GDP with extractive institutions, that is, institutions where a small group of individuals controls a country's profitable resources and exploits the rest of the population. Acemoglu, Johnson, and Robinson's empirical investigation involves sixty-four seventeenth-century colonies, mostly British, French, Spanish, and Portuguese.

Before we describe the merits of their empirical analysis from a Latin American perspective in greater detail, we examine the graphic representation of what colonial Latin America looked like at the time in figure 1.2.

The Spanish Crown held four viceroyalties—New Spain, New Granada, Peru, and Rio de la Plata—and one *Audiencia* or *Capitania General*—Chile.[30] The main difference between viceroyalties and *Audiencias* is that the latter did not enjoy full judicial powers. An interesting note on the map shown in figure 1.2 is worth mentioning, with regard to the large estate under the viceroyalty of Rio de la Plata, part of which is now Argentina, Bolivia, and Paraguay.

Recall from the introduction that the Spanish crown under the 1494 Treaty of Tordesillas transferred land to the Portuguese.[31] However, the map reflects the Spanish crown wishing to renege on the treaty, which partly explains more recent border conflicts in the southern cone. These conflicts persist until today. We will come back to such conflicts and political upheavals in chapter 2.

Acemoglu, Johnson, and Robinson (2001) suggest that European settlers' mortality rates were public information in various territories that were then already known by their current names. In particular, sailors, bishops, and soldiers knew about mortality rates, which were made public. As a first approximation, they therefore use a sample of seventy-five countries for which settlers' mortality rates are available to show that such rates throughout the seventeenth and up to the nineteenth centuries are negatively correlated with (PPP-adjusted) GDP per capita in 1995. A subsample for the case of Latin America is shown in table 1.5.

Most intriguing in table 1.5 is that, in contrast with the four eighteenth-century Spanish viceroyalties and the Audencia plus the Portuguese viceroyalty during colonial times, the data encompasses nineteen countries in lieu of five or six regions. The data for seventeenth- to nineteenth-century settlers' mortality rates had to be from six regions at most, not nineteen countries. Although we can understand that the sample size had to be increased in order to obtain meaningful econometric results, the researchers' ad hoc subdivision of the five original regions into nineteen "countries" might be misleading. For example, the researchers' original seventeenth-century data sources cannot distinguish settlers' mortality rates in Argentina and neighboring Uruguay—71 and 68.9 percent, respectively—because both countries were part of the same viceroyalty. As a proxy, the researchers use data from Buenos Aires versus Montevideo, the capitals of Argentina and Uruguay, respectively. However, this construct does not include other important cities in Argentina, such as Córdoba, where mortality rates might have been different. More generally, within-region mortality rates in Latin America's

Figure 1.2
Viceroyalties and *Audiencias* in eighteenth-century Latin America.
Source: Carmack, Gasco, and Gossen 2007.

Geography and the Colonial Legacy

Table 1.5
Negative correlation between settlers' mortality rates and per capita GDP

Country	Log of GDP per head	Mortality rates per 1,000
	1995	(1604–1876)
Chile	9.34	68.9
Bahamas	9.29	85.0
Argentina	9.13	68.9
Venezuela	9.07	78.1
Uruguay	9.03	71.0
Mexico	8.94	71.0
Panama	8.84	163.3
Colombia	8.81	71.0
Costa Rica	8.79	78.1
Brazil	8.73	71.0
Ecuador	8.47	71.0
Peru	8.40	71.0
Dominican Republic	8.36	130.0
Guatemala	8.29	71.0
Paraguay	8.21	78.1
Jamaica	8.19	130.0
El Salvador	7.95	78.1
Bolivia	7.93	71.1
Guyana	7.90	32.1
Honduras	7.69	78.1
Nicaragua	7.54	163.3
Haiti	7.15	130.0

Source: Gutiérrez 1986 and Curtin 1989. *Note:* The data reported here is consistent with the data reported at Acemoglu's website: http://economics.mit.edu/faculty/acemoglu/data/ajr2001.

"countries" must have been extremely diverse, which might have led to within-country institutional diversity.

Note that the countries we have listed in table 1.5 are not all Latin American countries, in that the colonizers were neither Spaniards nor Portuguese. We do this deliberately. This is the case for the Bahamas and Jamaica and also for Guyana, first a Dutch colony until 1815, then a British colony until 1966. We could even withdraw Haiti from the list, a French colony until independence in 1805. However, this does not eliminate the numerical discrepancy, for we are still left with five eighteenth-century territories multiplied by a factor of four.

Let us assume for a moment that the countries listed in table 1.5 were not countries but *Audiencias*. This interpretation, however, does not accord well with historical accounts by historians such as, for example, Buckholder and Johnson (2003) for at least two reasons. First, the list provided by Buckholder- and Johnson mostly includes cities, not countries. Second, even if we were to identify a country with a particular city, we are still short of at least three countries/regions. Further research definitely is needed to shed light on divergent institutional trajectories from a Latin American perspective.

Moreover, the geographical proximity of some of the countries listed in table 1.5 in conjunction with their differences in mortality rates is puzzling. Let us start by displaying the geography of contemporary Latin American countries (see figure 1.3).

Tt might seem natural that, due to geographical proximity, Argentina and Chile would have the similar mortality rates shown in table 1.5. However, why nearby Uruguay had higher mortality rates remains a mystery. Moreover, although Chile does feature as an *Audiencia* in the map provided by Carmack, Gasco, and Gossen in 2007 (see figure 1.2), Argentina and Uruguay do not even figure as countries for at least one hundred years during the 1604–1876 period for which mortality rate numbers were reported in table 1.5.

Still more puzzling is the discrepancy between mortality rates in Colombia, Venezuela, and Ecuador and those of Panama, which are more than twice as high. These four countries were part of the viceroyalty of New Granada (see figure 1.2). However, Panama—which along with Nicaragua had the highest mortality rates— ranked above Colombia and Ecuador in terms of per capita GDP in 1995! Meanwhile, Nicaragua, with the same mortality rates as those of Panama, is one of the poorest Latin American countries—slightly above Haiti in terms of per capita GDP in 1995.

As of the time of writing, we have not had access to the dataset interpreted by Acemoglu, Johnson, and Robinson, except for the version provided on Acemoglu's web page. Our point is that basic notion of geographic characteristics influencing mortality rates—and settlements—in Latin American regions needs further scrutiny. However, we understand that dealing with historical data can be exceedingly difficult, and these remarks should not tarnish the main message that the researchers successfully deliver using a much larger dataset including regions outside Latin America.

Specifically, Acemoglu, Johnson, and Robinson have undeniably pioneered empirical research on the colonial period via exploiting exogenous variations to estimate their effect on economic development. Their regressions use various geographical controls, showing that their hypothesis remains robust: early institutional quality persists and determines underdevelopment today.

Geography and the Colonial Legacy

Figure 1.3
Latin American countries today.
Source: Cardoso and Helwege 1992.

Otherwise stated, settlers' mortality rates are used as an instrument for current institutions, and the researchers' results show that institutions, not geography, are the first determinant of prosperity. The authors test for possible direct effects of geographic variables such as latitude and climate. Based on their empirical findings, Acemoglu, Johnson, and Robinson conclude that once institutions are taken into account, geographic variables do not have a significant effect on current economic underdevelopment. That is, geography is not a first-order determinant of economic prosperity today; institutions are.

However, Latin America is exceedingly diverse and requires a larger number of microdata points from context-specific institutions within countries. Even if the sample size was to increase for Latin America, we still share skeptics' views on ending up with a small sample size nonetheless; this eliminates the possibility of controlling for a large number of covariates without losing degrees of freedom.[32]

A more promising venue for understanding Latin America's underdevelopment is found in Acemoglu, Johnson, and Robinson's (2002) reversal of fortunes article, in which the authors suggest that the Aztec and Inca empires that were rich—as proxied by population density and urbanization—in the 1500s became poor; conversely, countries that were poor in the 1500s, such as the United States, became rich. The turning point is detected at the onset of industrialization in the eighteenth century. The reversal took place, according to the authors, because of the poor and persistent institutional quality enacted by the Spanish and Portuguese colonizers. These *extractive* institutions contrast sharply with institutions of *private property* enacted in sparsely populated and underurbanized regions such as the United States and Canada, which are comparatively rich today.

Further evidence of institutional persistence and not geography persistence being at the heart of underdevelopment can be found in the article by Acemoglu and Johnson (2007) in which the authors show that the epidemiological transition in the 1940s affected population but not per capita GDP; hence, not even the disease burden that the geography hypothesis presents as a fundamental cause of poverty seems relevant to our understanding of underdevelopment.[33]

Economic historian John Coatsworth, who focuses on the nineteenth century, presents a competing hypothesis.[34] He argues that in order to shed light on Latin American backwardness, one has to analyze the postindependence period, not the colonial period. We view Coatsworth's contribution as complementary to the institutional hypothesis, as we will further explain in chapter 2.

Acemoglu, Johnson, and Robinson's earlier (2001) idea is a compelling one, we admit. Mortality rates during the colonial period, the researchers argue, affected settlements of European-descended migrants, which in turn affected institutions. These were extractive institutions in the case of Latin America, in that property rights protection was high only for a small elite of families of European descent, whereas the vast majority of the population—slaves and Native Americans, that is, indigenous populations—had nonexistent property rights over their own labor and had exceedingly limited access to land, health, and education. Colonial extractive institutions persisted in most Latin American countries beyond independence (circa 1820s) from Spain and Portugal. Perpetuation of extractive institutions inherited from the Iberian colonizers is thus to be blamed for the per capita income disparities between Latin America and North America, Acemoglu, Johnson, and Robinson would proclaim.

How can one measure institutional quality? Using data from Political Risk Services, Acemoglu, Johnson, and Robinson show that there is a positive correlation between expropriation risk for the 1985–1995 period and the log of per capita GDP in 1995 for a subset of sixty-four countries. Expropriation risk is measured on a scale from 0 to 10, with 0 corresponding to the highest risk and 10 to the lowest risk. The positive correlation between expropriation risk and per capita GDP suggests that countries with low expropriation risk, such as the United States and Canada, enjoy higher income per person relative to those with a higher expropriation risk, such as Mexico, Chile, and Argentina.

In sum, northern European migrants settled in countries where mortality rates were low, such as the United States and Canada. This, in turn, had an impact on institutional quality as proxied by the risk of expropriation. The high quality of institutions (or institutions of private property) then had long-lasting positive effects; high-quality institutions, in turn, had an impact on contemporary per capita GDP. The experience of the United States and Canada contrasts sharply with that of Brazil, Bolivia, and Nicaragua, for example, where comparatively low European migration flows led to extractive institutions, which explains much of the poor performance of such countries in comparison to the performance of their northern neighbors in the late twentieth century.[35]

In recent work, Dell (2010) studies a specific Latin American institution—namely, the *mita*, or forced labor in the region's mines during colonial times. Her main finding is that contemporary levels of human capital—child health, in particular—in areas of Peru and Bolivia that were under the *mita* system is relatively low compared to other regions and, in particular, in comparison to geographically close regions that were under the *encomienda*, in the large plots of land used for plantation agriculture and cattle grazing known as *haciendas*.[36] Dell's finding in turn sheds light on within-region inequalities and persistence of sixteenth-century colonial institutions in the Andes.[37]

1.5 Ethnolinguistic Fragmentation and Culture

Relative to the United States and Canada, Latin America was and continues to be heavily populated by native indigenous populations that speak hundreds of dialects and, in some instances, official languages other than Spanish and Portuguese. In Bolivia and Paraguay, for example, Quechua and Guarani, respectively, are official languages that coexist with Spanish in most official documents. To what extent can ethnolinguistic fragmentation be blamed for social unrest, political instability, and poverty in Latin America?

Again, this question has also been investigated empirically for a larger set of former colonies in other regions.[38] The ethnolinguistic hypothesis suggests that in ethnically heterogeneous societies, groups that come to power expropriate ethnic losers, limiting democratic freedom and ultimately delivering public goods of poor quality, which in turn hinders growth and economic development.

It is difficult to assess whether ethnolinguistic fragmentation is a contributing factor to relatively low per capita income in Latin America, because most empirical cross-section studies include hundreds of countries, African countries prominent among them. Recent work, however, shows that relative to African countries, ethnolinguistic fragmentation in Latin America is statistically insignificant.[39] This seems plausible. Nearly forty African countries have a high degree of ethnical fragmentation, but in Latin America we find only fifteen. Nonetheless, fluency in a local indigenous language is an important asset for populist leaders in twenty-first-century Latin America, and populist leaders' policies do have an impact on economic development and growth trajectories, particularly in the Andean region. We will address this issue in greater detail in chapter 6 on Latin American populism.

As far as culture is concerned, religion is often used as a proxy for a set of values that persist from one generation to another, which can potentially affect economic performance. This line of thought dates back to a distinguished tradition started by Weber (1958), who suggested that relative to Catholicism, the Protestant religion fostered entrepreneurship in the United Kingdom and the United States.[40]

Following this tradition, it has been argued that Protestant populations are more democratic, which in turn provides a fertile land for the creation of high-quality public goods. It has also been suggested that the Protestant religion facilitates the flow of goods, migration, and ideas, all conducive to brighter growth prospects relative to those that other religions would permit.

Empirically, research seems to suggest that the fact that most of Latin America is not Protestant might have limited the scope for property rights protection, freedom, democracy, and economic growth. In these cross-country empirical studies, a cultural dummy variable for the Latin American countries has been introduced for Catholicism. The inclusion of this dummy weakens the results, but it does not eliminate the negative effect that Catholicism has on governance and economic performance.[41] However, such cross-country regressions use data from the late twentieth century when Latin America was experiencing a low growth period compared to the first decade of the twenty-first century. Moreover, stylized facts from the region do not seem to lend support to the hypothesis on Catholicism having a negative impact on growth and prosperity.

In particular, with the exception of Nicaragua and Haiti, all Latin American countries are now ranked as middle-income economies according to latest World Bank estimates. Moreover, Chile, which is mostly Catholic, is now considered a high-income country. Three of the Latin American countries that are also Catholic—namely, Argentina, Mexico, and Brazil—are members of the G-20. Moreover, Brazil, one of the BRIC countries, holds the largest number of Catholics in the world.[42] The apparent contradiction between empirical findings in cross-country studies and the stylized facts from a Latin American perspective merits further empirical investigation.

1.6 Concluding Remarks

In this opening chapter, we reviewed the historical roots of Latin America, from its discovery and colonization through the early nineteenth century. Economists have focused on the colonial period because it is arguably during this period that the source of the economic backwardness of Latin America relative to the United States and Canada can be pinpointed.

We have analyzed five main hypotheses: First, the geography hypothesis contends that climatic conditions in a dozen Latin American countries located near the equator and/or high transport costs to seaports hindered economic development. Landlocked regions, unproductive land, and a high tropical disease burden have limited the scope for growth and trade and lower labor productivity, respectively. Adverse geography has also slowed the pace of technological diffusion and consequent economic prosperity, the geography hypothesis contends.

Second, the legal origins hypothesis proclaims that the forces of nature are not the main cause of underdevelopment. It argues instead that man-made civil law inherited from the Iberian powers is at the root of underdevelopment, relative to Latin American's northern neighbors that "luckily" inherited common law. Under common law, private property rights are better protected, creating a more dynamic investment climate and lower incidence of corruption, the authors of the legal origins' hypothesis proclaim.

Third, the factor endowments hypothesis indicates that propitious soil and climate for large-scale agriculture triggered income inequalities, which turned out to be counterproductive at later stages, particularly during growth spurts in the nineteenth-century industrialization period. During this period, and relative to its northern neighbors, Latin America lagged behind, largely because of high income disparities, which led to low internal demand for manufactures.

Fourth, the institutional hypothesis, undeniably the best empirical investigation of the colonial period, emphasizes the conditions that affected earlier settlements and the attitudes of colonizers to the development of early institutional quality in the territories under their control. For the particular case of Latin America, however, we questioned the mismatch between historical data about settlers' mortality rates pertaining to colonial viceroyalties and colonial regions and recent data on per capita income today in a myriad of independent yet geographically close Latin American countries. We nonetheless acknowledge that the main insights of the institutional hypothesis approach might apply to Latin America. For example, the Aztec Empire in Mexico and Central America was once rich in comparison with the United States, but became comparatively poor—particularly after the industrial revolution. The Andean region under the *mita* system is comparatively poorer than the nearby indentured labor (feudal-style land) regions, also known as *haciendas*.

Fifth, other potential suspects have arguably contributed to Latin America's underdevelopment from colonization until today. These include ethnolinguistic fragmentation and culture as proxied by religion. We argued that these considerations might be contributing factors, but that their validity might be confined to certain regions in which ongoing political unrest might be due to fragmentation. Empirical evidence seems to suggest that ethnolinguistic fragmentation is not relevant in the case of Latin America when compared to the seemingly important role it plays in explaining low income per capita in Africa.

Regarding religion, although cross-country regressions suggest that Catholicism might have had a negative impact, stylized facts do not seem to accord well with such correlations. Further empirical research is needed to shed light on the role of culture -more broadly defined- in Latin America.

Future avenues for solving the puzzle of Latin America's underdevelopment should include the latest research undertaken by behavioral economists. Specifically, we believe that experimental methods used by behavioral scientists can enhance our understanding of chronic distrust and inequalities between Europeans and native populations in the region. These methods have the potential to deliver answers to some of the region's most vexing questions.

Although more avenues for research can contribute to our understanding of underdevelopment in Latin America, we believe that the five hypotheses analyzed in this chapter provide a great deal of food for thought on the big questions of

Latin America's per capita income lagging behind that of its northern neighbors and, perhaps more importantly, across and within regions' income inequalities.

We view the hypotheses discussed in this chapter as complementary. A heavy burden is put on geography and the Iberian colonizers. Geography and seaport accessibility undoubtedly play a role but cannot be easily altered unless the region continues to invest more heavily in infrastructure. Similarly, property rights protection and other variables linked to the risk of expropriation in Latin America are exceedingly difficult to change. Nonetheless, recent research suggests that the rule of law and property rights protection are not time invariant, and recent decades have witnessed progress.

The income inequalities created under the *encomienda* system undeniably took hold in soil and climatic conditions under which large-scale plantation agriculture was possible, but the racial and property concentration issues that are embedded in such institutions are only part of ongoing struggles in some regions. The empirical investigation found in the institutional approach has its merits, but it is exceedingly pessimistic for Latin Americans. The heavy burden of history and the way colonialist modes of production perpetuate themselves is undoubtedly crucial to our understanding of *causality*: poor institutional quality breeds expropriation risk and inequalities, which cause low per capita income and limits the scope for prosperity in the Latin American region. However, we think that the recent globalization trend has made policy makers aware of the need to improve institutional quality, if only because the benefits from FDI in the form of technology transfer, for example, are not within the region's reach without improved institutions that have been specifically enacted in order to protect private property rights.

Finally, we argued that the ethnolinguistic fragmentation hypothesis has a limited impact on Latin America compared to its negative effect on Africa. It might be confined to some regions, affecting a relatively small percent of the approximately six hundred million Latin Americans living in the region in the twenty-first century. The role of culture, on the other hand, might turn out to be relevant in cross-country regressions, but we do not think that it holds true for a small yet very important subset of countries that host the largest number of Latin American households, such as Brazil and Mexico—the region's largest economies.

In sum, the five hypotheses analyzed here paint a grim outlook for Latin Americans. Fighting adverse geographic characteristics is costly at best—and impossible at worst. Shifting from civil to common law is far from easy. Fighting against income inequalities rooted in soil, climate, low migration flows, and poor institutional quality seems like an exceedingly difficult task, as shown by decades of relentless efforts. The pervasiveness of colonial institutions cannot be changed overnight, if at all. Finally, ethnolinguistic fragmentation and religion touch upon sensitive issues close to the hearts of most Latin Americans and are therefore not even discussed in political economy agendas.

Against this backdrop, our next chapter will paint a brighter picture for Latin American economic development by highlighting the marvelous prospects for growth that trade and economic integration can bring to the region. Recent developments will be brought to light by focusing on the region's export performance after independence, especially from the last quarter of the nineteenth century through the onset of World War I in 1914.

Summary

- Adverse geography might be a contributing factor to Latin America's underdevelopment relative to its northern neighbors.
- The legal origins hypothesis suggests that Latin America lags behind its northern neighbors because under the civil law—inherited from the Iberian colonizers—property rights protection is weak compared to common law, which prevails in the United States.
- Latin America is blessed with natural resources, the exploitation of which under *encomienda* and slavery modes of production during the colonial period and beyond might have left an indelible income inequality legacy. Independence from Iberian powers increased the scope for trade with other nations on the one hand, but increased border disputes and thus lowered the scope for intraregional trade and economic growth on the other.
- The institutional approach to underdevelopment suggests that extractive institutions were enacted by Iberian colonizers and that such institutions persist today, which might explain Latin America's low per capita income relative to that of its northern neighbors. Further empirical scrutiny is needed for this hypothesis to hold true from a Latin American perspective.
- Recent research on yet another institutional legacy from colonial times—namely, the *mita*—might shed light on Latin America's within-region income inequalities.
- Ethnical fragmentation does not seem to be an obstacle to economic development in Latin America. However, it might explain diverse trajectories among regions, some of which are—population-wise—more heterogeneous than others.
- Further research is needed in order to understand the role of cultural legacies and their impact on trust, institutions, and economic growth.

Review Questions

1. What are the main similarities between Latin America and Africa from a geographical standpoint?
2. Why is adverse geography a constraint to economic development and how can it be mitigated?
3. Income inequalities are often said to be rooted in the colonial period, when master-servant relationships took the form of *encomienda* and *mita* in some regions and slavery in others. Briefly explain why.
4. Why was *mayorazgo* a cultural tradition that exacerbated income inequalities? Explain.
5. Why are income inequalities an impediment to a rapid pace for economic growth and development? Explain.
6. Can the legacy of extractive institutions explain low per capita income in Latin America relative to the region's northern neighbors?
7. Briefly explain the merits of the institutional approach—when compared to the geography hypothesis—from a Latin American perspective and its main empirical challenges.
8. Is ethnic fragmentation an important determinant of underdevelopment in Latin America? Explain.
9. Is culture playing a role when attempting to shed light on income differentials between Latin America and its northern neighbors? Explain.
10. Latin America is exceedingly diverse, and yet some regions bear an eerie resemblance to one another. Briefly mention similar countries and the reasons that lead you to perceive them as similar.

Further Reading

Sebastian Edwards, Gerardo Esquivel, and Graciela Márquez have edited a comprehensive collection of articles that attempt to explain income differentials between Latin America and its northern neighbors. It delivers a broader picture from colonial times to the late twentieth century. See Edwards, Esquivel, and Márquez 2007. Acemoglu and Robinson 2013 is the most up-to-date and comprehensive analysis on the institutional approach to economic underdevelopment. We see the line of research in this book as an important stepping-stone toward our understanding of Latin America as potentially lacking "contracting institutions," which might be conducive to higher growth rates. Glaeser et al. (2004) have provided an insightful contribution to the empirical controversy over the institutional approach to growth and development.

2   Export-Led Growth and the Origins of Protectionism

In the previous chapter, we focused on Latin America's underdevelopment relative to that of its northern neighbors and the legacy of income inequalities dating back to the colonial period. Although primary commodity exports were the main engine of growth during this period, a small manufacturing/industrial sector emerged. This sector—mostly crafts, textiles, and foodstuffs—was driven by nascent internal demand. The development of emerging manufacturing was hindered, however, because of increased trade with European countries in the aftermath of Latin America's independence from the Iberian powers in the early nineteenth century. The problems caused by trade patterns favoring primary commodity exports became more acute during the late nineteenth century, leaving most Latin American regions trapped as primary commodity exporters. Except for Mexico, the ability of Latin America to pull itself from the commodity export trap is limited still today because of rapid industrialization in Asia. In this chapter, we wish our readers to understand fully this phenomenon and its distinct features across the region. To this end, we spell out the main historical traits during postcolonial Latin America in which the commodity export bias is rooted and explain why income inequalities might have increased further in this time period.[1]

The Napoleonic occupation of the Iberian Peninsula facilitated the movements of independence throughout Latin America from 1810 to the early 1820s. Most of these movements in Spanish America were led by creoles, or *criolus* in Portuguese America. Creoles were individuals from Iberian descent, born in Latin America. They were nonetheless denied access to governing positions. The creoles' independence movement in Brazil was led by Portuguese-born Dom Pedro.[2]

Legendary leaders among the creoles in Spanish America include, among others, Miguel Hidalgo, born in Mexico, a leading figure of his country's independence movement; Simón Bolívar of Venezuela, leader of the independence movement in Great Colombia;[3] José de San Martín of Argentina, who symbolizes the independence movements in both Argentina and Peru; and Bernardo O'Higgins, Chile's most prominent independence leader.

The creoles strongly opposed Iberian taxation. They were outraged by trade restrictions. Their claims for independence echoed the feelings of Amerindians and African American populations who had been working as indentured laborers and slaves. This populace had been denied privileged access to fertile land during three centuries of Iberian colonialism.

In contrast with our previous chapter, in which we discussed Latin America's underdevelopment under Iberian control, in this chapter we follow a distinguished tradition started by economic historians John Coatsworth (1998) and Jeffrey Williamson (1998). Their focus is on nineteenth-century Latin America, which is divided into two periods: First, from around 1820 to 1870, Latin America lagged behind its northern neighbors because of wars and geographic isolation during the nearly five "lost" decades following its independence from the Iberian Peninsula. Second, from 1870 until the outbreak of World War I in 1914, Latin America experienced an unprecedented commodity boom. Specifically, it was not until 1870 that the region was able to take advantage of high industrialization rates in Europe—and, to a lesser extent, in the United States. Coatsworth and Williamson suggest that the growth slowdown during the former period offset the benefits of the latter. Moreover, pervasive effects on income inequalities and protectionism cast doubt on the potential benefits to Latin America during the 1870–1914 period. Therefore, it is during the nineteenth century, and not during the colonial period (as Acemoglu, Johnson, and Robinson 2001 suggest), that Latin America lagged behind its northern neighbors.

The terms of trade bias in favor of primary commodities in 1870 to 1914 exacerbated Latin America's deindustrialization trend. It was during this period that Latin America asserted itself as a leading primary commodity producer and exporter, leaving an indelible imprint on the region as it became increasingly prone to world commodity prices' cyclical fluctuations and an endemic *Dutch disease* problem.[4] It was also during the 1870–1914 period that Latin America's income inequalities seem to have increased further (see Williamson 2009). Moreover, the need to collect revenues via import tariffs, first to finance wars, and then to protect an elite of landowners and nascent manufacturers in the late nineteenth century marked the first and most virulent wave of Latin American protectionism, which extended itself well into the late twentieth century (Coatsworth and Williamson 2002).

On a positive note, from 1870 until the outbreak of World War I in 1914, often referred to as Latin America's belle époque, several countries in the region had access to international capital markets for much-needed long-term investments and were able to use export revenues to construct basic infrastructure.

What are the similarities and differences among the first globalization trend in the nineteenth century (1870–1914) and modern times under the World Trade Organization (WTO), bilateral and regional trade agreements, and industrialization in China? Is Latin America now better positioned to reduce overexploitation of its natural resources? Is the region less prone to experiencing a Dutch disease problem like the one it experienced during its belle époque? Can contemporary Latin America build the necessary infrastructure to diversify export revenues and use these revenues to speed up the pace of industrialization, reduce poverty, and lower income inequalities?

In this chapter, we analyze nineteenth-century Latin America's performance, from the five postindependence lost decades (1820–1870) to the belle époque (1870–1914). Without underestimating the impact of the lost decades of relative isolation, however, our main focus in this chapter is in the striking resemblance between the region's belle époque and the recent commodity boom in the late twentieth century and beyond—within the framework of market-oriented reforms.[5]

There are extraordinarily interesting parallels between the belle époque and the first decade of the twenty-first century: the high demand for Latin America's primary commodities during the nineteenth century was triggered by European countries' industrialization, and industrialization in the United States was a contributing factor; demand for Latin American primary commodities in the twenty-first century has been triggered by high industrialization rates in China. In both instances, the explosion of trade flows acted in support of the development of a booming manufacturing and industrial sector in other regions while leaving most of Latin America underindustrialized and vulnerable to external demand for primary commodity exports.

In section 2.1 in this chapter, we will pin down the main economic advantages and disadvantages of Latin America's independence from Spain and Portugal. In section 2.2, we focus on diversity across Latin American countries in connection with comparative advantages, as proxied by their natural resource endowment differentials and the external demand for such resources. In section 2.3, we analyze the stellar nineteenth-century performers—namely, Argentina, Chile, and Uruguay—in comparison with the rest of the region. In section 2.4, we study two countries with relatively large Afro-Latin American populations—namely, Brazil and Cuba. In section 2.5, we contrast the export-led growth spurt during the late nineteenth century with that of recent decades. Finally, we provide some concluding remarks in section 2.6.

2.1 Independence: Economic Consequences

Key to our understanding of the economic consequences of the Latin American independence movements is the transfer of power in the Iberian Peninsula from the Habsburgs to the Bourbons. This transfer took place long before independence; specifically, it took place at the turn of the eighteenth century. Unlike seventeenth-century Spanish and Portuguese America, in which local authorities in various regions were accountable to the viceroys, the Bourbons in the eighteenth century introduced a decentralized system called *intendencias*, from the French *intendants*.[6]

Under the *intendencia* system, an increasingly large number of regional authorities were no longer accountable to the viceroys. Instead, the *intendencias* were accountable to the Spanish and Portuguese Crowns directly. More importantly, the decentralization reforms—also known as the *Bourbon* and *Pombaline reforms*—allowed for the colonies in Spanish and Portuguese America to trade among themselves. Moreover, the *intendencias* were able to trade with other nations as well, mostly with Britain and the United States.[7] In Portuguese America, trade between Brazil, the Spanish colonies, and Britain was facilitated following the eighteenth-century Bourbon and Pombaline reforms.[8] Table 2.1 provides a qualitative overview of Latin America's trade prior to independence from Spain and Portugal.

Trade of primary commodities within Iberian colonies included wheat, cotton, sugar, cacao, indigo, mercury, and other raw materials. A de facto eighteenth-century custom union was created. This is reminiscent of today's Mercosur, the Andean Community of Nations (CAN), the Caribbean Community and Common Market (CARICOM), and the Central American Customs Union (MCCA).[9]

Trade with non–Latin American regions henceforth was no longer confined to the Iberian Peninsula. Latin America could trade with the United States and, most importantly, with Britain, which was already industrializing at a fast pace.

We should underscore that all European nations at the time were importing vast amounts of bullion—that is, gold and silver. This trend was not necessarily linked to industrialization. Specifically, the high demand for bullion by European countries—as evidenced from table 2.1—reflects the prevailing "mercantilist views" dating back to the sixteenth century.[10]

In brief, the Bourbon and Pombaline reforms that were introduced circa 1739—long before independence—made it possible for transatlantic trade to be more active relative to the earlier colonial period. Nonetheless, and according to

Table 2.1
Latin America's trade at the end of the colonial period

Area	Region	Products	Trade among Latin America's regions	Trade between Latin America's regions and the rest of the world
Mexico	Central	Sugar, textiles	Yes	No
	Oaxaca	Grain	Yes	Yes
	Yucatán	Indigo	Yes	Yes
	North	Cattle, textiles	Yes	No
	North	Silver	No	Yes
Central America and the Caribbean	El Salvador	Indigo	Yes	Yes
	Honduras	Silver	No	Yes
	Costa Rica	Tobacco	Yes	
	Antilles	Sugar	Yes	Yes
Venezuela	Coast	Cacao	Yes	Yes
	Plains	Hides	Yes	Yes
Colombia	Eastern highlands	Gold, silver	No	Yes
	Highlands	Textiles	Yes	No
Ecuador	Highlands	Textiles	Yes	
	Coast	Cacao	Yes	Yes
Peru and Bolivia	Highlands	Silver	No	Yes
	Highlands	Mercury	Yes	No
	North coast	Sugar	Yes	No
	South coast	Cotton	Yes	
Chile	North	Silver	No	Yes
	Central	Wheat	Yes	Yes
Argentina, Paraguay, and Uruguay	North and Central	Artisan products	Yes	Yes
	Cuyo	Wine	Yes	No
	Northeast	Yerba mate, cattle	Yes	No
	Northeast	Sugar	No	Yes
	Río de la Plata	Tallow, hides	Yes	Yes
Brazil	Central	Gold, diamonds	No	Yes
	South	Cattle	Yes	Yes
	Amazonia	Forestry	No	Yes

Coatsworth (1998), throughout the entire preindependence period—circa 1700 to 1820— per capita income growth in Latin America remained stagnant. Williamson suggests that the 1700–1820 period was a low-growth period globally and that Latin America and the United States therefore maintained their relative backwardness vis-à-vis their European colonizers—notably, Britain and France.

However, trade between Latin America and the United States prior to independence was active. It included agricultural commodities such as sugar. International trade of this particular commodity shaped the history of Cuba well into the late twentieth century.

We are often reminded by economic historians that with the notable exception of some southern-cone countries such as Chile, and despite rapid industrialization in Europe, trade flows did not increase immediately after independence. On the contrary, trade remained stagnant during the five postindependence decades because of intraregional conflicts, wars with other nations, and geographic isolation. In particular, trade flows between Europe and Latin America during the (postindependence) 1820–1870 period were tiny in comparison with those between other developing countries in Asia and Europe.

Moreover, despite an extraordinary hike in transatlantic trade flows after the five lost decades—that is, during Latin America's belle époque (1870–1914)—nineteenth-century Latin America's per capita income declined significantly relative to that in North America (see table 2.2). Coatsworth and Williamson therefore contend that it is during the nineteenth century—and not during the colonial period as our preceding chapter suggests—that Latin America fell behind.[11]

Table 2.2
Per capita GDP as a percentage of the US level, 1800 to 1913

Country	1800	1850	1900	1913
Argentina	102		52	55
Brazil	36	39	10	11
Chile	46		38	40
Colombia			18	18
Cuba	112	78		39
Mexico	50	37	35	35
Peru	41		20	20
Venezuela			10	10
Mean	66	51	27	28

Source: Coatsworth 1998.

It is important to further investigate the reasons for export-led underperformance from 1820 to 1870, if only because contemporary Latin America's growth rates crucially depend on fast industrialization in China. What went wrong during export-led postindependence Latin America when the region was exporting primary commodities to Europe and—to a lesser extent—the United States? What lessons can be drawn for the region, which was until recently heavily exporting primary commodities to China? We attempt to answer these questions ahead.

Arguably, and relative to other regions that remained controlled by colonizers well into the twentieth century, there were three main advantages of Latin America's newly independent nations in the nineteenth century. First, independence allowed all regions to access credit in the international capital markets. These loans were used to finance basic infrastructure, such as railways to connect seaports with the hinterlands, for example. Second, following independence, Latin American nations were completely free to trade with European nations other than Spain and Portugal, with the United States, and, most notably, with rapidly industrializing European powers. Third, and perhaps most importantly, Latin America's terms of trade—that is, the region's export commodity prices relative to import prices of manufactures—increased sharply during its belle époque. The hike was stronger than that for any other commodity region exporter.[12]

These advantages have to be weighed against three main drawbacks, however. First, tariffs were enacted across most Latin American regions, leading to a drastic decline in intraregional trade—a huge step back from preindependence Bourbon and Pombaline reforms—and the downfall of bilateral trade agreements *within* Latin America. This situation may have led to "trade diversion".[13] Second, as we underscored previously, Latin America experienced postindependence conflicts and political upheavals within different regions (e.g., the War of the Pacific among Chile, Bolivia, and Peru from 1879 to 1883) and with other nations (e.g., the war between Mexico and the United States from 1846 to 1848). Table 2.3 lists the wars and conflicts that the newly independent Latin American nations engaged in. These wars led to large fiscal deficits and sovereign defaults, which hindered the ability of the region to further invest in infrastructure. Moreover, the region had to enact high tariffs in order to finance war and frontier disputes. This venue for financing budget deficits was perceived as less controversial relative to direct taxation on land owners and nascent manufacturers. Third, favorable commodity export trends did not allow for nascent industry to develop, partly because continuous technological improvements elsewhere, domestic manufacturers could not benefit from technological improvements via imitation because of high tariffs. Low-quality of competing domestic manufactures were unprofitable in most countries. The case of Mexico—Latin America's second largest economy—and its

Table 2.3
Wars and conflicts in nineteenth-century Latin America

War/conflict	Dates	Countries involved
Brazilian—Argentinean War	1825–1828	Argentina and Brasil
Colombian—Peruvian War	1828–1829	Colombia and Peru
Falkland War	1833	Argentina and Great Britain.
Peru—Bolivian Confederation—Argentinean War	1837–1839	Peru, Bolivia and Argentina
Peru—Bolivian Confederation—Chilean War	1837–1839	Peru, Bolivia and Chile
French Blocade of Rio de la Plata	1838	Argentina and France
Pastry war	1838	France and Mexico
Peruvian—Bolivian War	1840	Peru and Bolivia.
Mexican—American War	1846	United States and Mexico
Peruvian—Ecuadorian War	1859	Peru and Ecuador
French intervention in Mexico	1861–1867	Mexico and France
Guatemala—Salvadoran War	1863	Guatemala and El Salvador
Ecuadorian—Colombian Conflict	1863	Ecuador and Colombia
Hispano-Sudamérica War	1864–1866	Peru, Chile, Spain, Bolivia and Ecuador
Triple Aliance War	1865–1870	Brasil, Uruguay, Argentina and Argentina, Brazil, Paraguay and Uruguay
Cuban—Spanish War	1868–1878	Cuba and Spain
Guatemala—Salvadoran War II	1876	Guatemala and El Salvador
War of the Pacific	1879–1883	Chile, Peru and Bolivia.
Guatemala—Salvadoran War III	1885	Guatemala and El Salvador

struggling textile industry in the nineteenth century is a well-documented example.[14]

Favorable terms of trade involved resource allocation toward more lucrative production of primary commodities, which in turn made the region more prone to a Dutch disease problem. Overall, Latin America's growth became more vulnerable to fluctuating world prices of primary commodities from then on.[15]

Unlike Europe in the aftermath of World War II, Latin American warfare-related deficits were unconnected with reconstruction from war and conflict. Specifically, after Latin America's five lost decades, most regions during the late nineteenth century had to invest heavily to build infrastructure from scratch. This, in turn, explains divergent trends and within-country income inequalities. Coastal regions such as those around Rio de Janeiro in Brazil and Buenos Aires in Argentina prospered due to transatlantic export shipping from high-quality ports. At the same time, insufficient infrastructure—railways in particular—left landlocked regions far behind in terms of per capita GDP. Most places along the Pacific coast also remained isolated, leading to low per capita income compared to Atlantic coast regions.[16]

The little infrastructure for trade that the region managed to build dates back to the late nineteenth and early twentieth centuries. It is now very old—particularly the railways, which have been neither maintained nor modernized. Protectionist policies, low inward investments, and the debt crisis of the 1980s amplified the problem. We will analyze these factors in greater detail in chapters 3 and 4.

In sum, the disadvantages of becoming independent from the Iberian Peninsula due to internal strife, poor infrastructure and intraregional protectionism seemed to have offset the gains in terms of potential export revenues with an expanded number of international trade partners. Insufficient access to the interior due to underinvestment in infrastructure in Latin America's largest economies, Brazil and Mexico, was particularly detrimental to the region's average per capita income. The historical persistence of protectionism, which extended itself beyond the region and well into the late twentieth century, was also detrimental as we will see in chapter 3.

Table 2.2 shows the mean income per head as a percentage of the US level, which is estimated to have declined from 66 in 1800 to 28 percent in 1913—one year prior to the outbreak of World War I, when exports to nations overseas collapsed.

If we focus on the last row of table 2.2, displaying the means only, we see a sharp decline from 1800 to 1913 for the entire eight-country sample. Note first that economic retardation stopped, and Latin America moved forward quite rapidly during the last quarter of the nineteenth century until 1913, when the former colonies enjoyed a period of relative political stability. Second, note the sharp decline experienced by Brazil and Mexico throughout the entire period. Finally, it is important to highlight the exceedingly large divergent trends across the newly independent countries, an issue to which we turn next.

2.2 Diversity across Regions under Export-Led Growth

European industrialization led by Britain in the eighteenth and nineteenth centuries had a profound impact on per capita income, not just in Britain and Europe, but also in Japan, the United States, and elsewhere. As Nobel Prize Laureate Robert Lucas (2002, 65) wrote: "For the first time in history, the living standards of the masses of ordinary people had begun to undergo sustained growth."

Key innovations in textiles, cotton, spinning mills, steam power, iron making, petroleum refining, and chemical and electrical industries rapidly diffused across

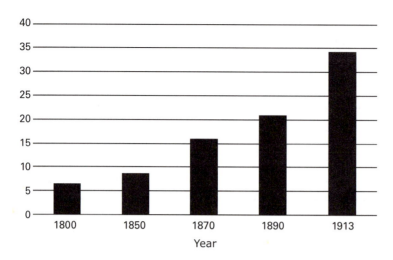

Figure 2.1
Mean exports per capita, 1800–1913 (in current US dollars).
Source: Authors' estimates from Bulmer-Thomas 2003.

Continental Europe, Japan, and the United States. This diffusion had positive externalities on transport, agriculture, mining, and production techniques more generally, fostering greater specialization and efficiency.

Unlike the Latin American colonial period (circa 1500–1820), during which natural resources remained relatively unexploited, European industrialization during the late nineteenth century triggered rapid exploitation and export of natural resources by newly independent nations in the Americas. As figure 2.1 suggests, while Europe was industrializing, Latin American exports increased sevenfold during the region's belle époque. As shown in the third column of table 2.1, however, Latin American exports to the rest of the world—mostly to Europe—were confined to primary commodities such as grain, silver, sugar, and wheat.

In contemporary Latin America, a similar primary commodity export pattern continues. The key difference is that the main importing region is now Asia. This renders contemporary Latin American economies extremely vulnerable to changes in their new trading partners' growth rates—in particular, Chinese growth and, to a lesser extent, the cyclical fluctuations in the United States, Mexico's main trading partner. We will return to this topic in greater detail in chapter 10.

Export growth varied widely across Latin American countries during the region's belle époque. Bulmer-Thomas (2003) attributes such divergent trends to different factor endowments across regions and suggests that European demand for specific commodities was the driving factor. He refers to such a demand-driven phenomenon as *the commodity lottery*: If European industrial demand for a particular primary commodity was not met by developing nations in Africa or Southeast Asia, then Europe turned to Latin America.

The commodity lottery had diverse consequences in the traded and nontraded sectors. Specifically, Bulmer-Thomas distinguishes three groups of export-led countries across the region from circa 1820 to the outbreak of World War I in 1914. The first group shows export-led growth in the traded sectors, with spillovers on nontraded sectors (rural, textile, manufactures, and crafts produced for the domestic market). Three stellar performers fall within this group: Argentina, Chile, and Uruguay. The second group exhibits rapid growth in the traded sector, but slow growth in the nontraded sector. Cuba and Puerto Rico, among other countries, fall into this category. The third group performed poorly in the traded sector, mainly because of sharp and adverse fluctuations in such countries' main export products (e.g., Peru's guano), continued political unrest (e.g., Mexico and Brazil), or both.

Despite the fact that data on this period is poor at best and nonexistent at worse, it is tempting to conjecture that growth in the nonexport sector in the three nineteenth-century stellar performers might have been positively correlated with human capital.[17] As we noted in chapter 1, Argentina, Chile, and Uruguay had a relatively low proportion of low-wage natives and Afro-Latin Americans, which might have given these three countries a leading edge for expanding domestic demand in the nontraded sector because of the relatively high productivity of immigrants of European descent enjoying comparatively higher wages relative to those of indentured laborers and slaves elsewhere in the Latin American region.

2.3 Stellar Performers: Divergent Trends

Argentina's rapid growth of per capita income can be traced back to the last quarter of the nineteenth century.[18] Although Argentinean land has always been propitious for export of meat, hides, and wheat, it was not until the late nineteenth century that Argentina enjoyed a stable political environment, which enabled it to take full advantage of its export potential (see figure 2.2).[19]

Being blessed with natural resources was not enough, however. Argentina's rapid economic development was fueled with inward investments, mostly from Britain and France. Moreover, immigration was a key factor. Large inflows of European immigrants (mainly from Italy and Spain) settled permanently in Argentina. The population grew fivefold in nineteenth-century Argentina compared to the previous century. Recall that making up for capital and labor shortages in land-abundant Latin America was key to economic prosperity—and this still holds true in the region's twenty-first century.

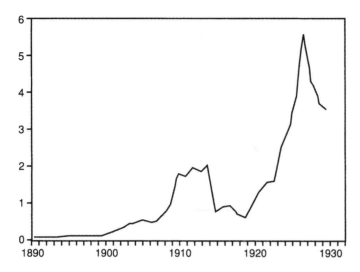

Figure 2.2
Ratio of Argentine to US exports.
Source: Cardoso and Helwege 1992.

The combination of natural resources—which could be more easily transported thanks to FDIs in transport—and population growth from massive immigration allowed Argentina to grow at an exceedingly rapid pace relative to neighboring countries.[20] Argentina's economic growth, as noted earlier, was nevertheless concentrated in the coastal areas, particularly in Buenos Aires. The Argentinean example in turn illustrates most of the within-country income inequalities encountered in contemporary Latin America today, an issue we investigate in greater detail in chapter 5.

Uruguay followed a similar trajectory. Growth rates of per capita agricultural output in Argentina's littoral were of around 2 percent per year between 1825 and 1865. Although data on Uruguay is scarce, based on existing historical estimates it seems reasonable to assume that Uruguay grew at a rate of around 0.8 percent annually during the same first three quarters of the nineteenth century.[21]

This rate is similar to the rate of growth for agricultural produce in Argentina's hinterlands, which, due to lack of adequate infrastructure, could not enjoy privileged access to low coastal transport costs for shipment overseas relative to those areas near Buenos Aires. However, are Uruguay and, in particular, Montevideo not just as strategically well-located as Buenos Aires for facilitating and promoting commerce with the nineteenth-century industrial powers?

The most important reason that Uruguay was comparatively less dynamic than Argentina is often stated to be political strife. Relative to political stability enjoyed by Argentina under the Rosas's dictatorship, Uruguay was a fragile postindependent republic that went through intermittent civil wars and dictatorships.[22] These eventually evolved into two modern political factions: the *Blancos* (Whites) and the *Colorados* (Reds). Political stability did not start to take hold until the early 1900s under the presidency of Battle y Ordóñez.[23]

Nonetheless, geography played its role. Montevideo was by far the best natural harbor in the Atlantic region, from which primary products could be shipped to Europe. Uruguayan commerce and cattle, meat, and hides were exported massively during the last quarter of the nineteenth century. Overall, and despite its high degree of political instability, Uruguay managed to grow relatively fast. It is often ranked second to Argentina in terms of growth of per capita GDP in late nineteenth-century Latin America.[24]

Chile's export-led growth started earlier. Political turmoil was relatively low during the twenty years (1841–1861) when Chile was ruled first by Manuel Bulnes and then by Manuel Montt. Exports during this period were mostly confined to wheat and silver. In 1866, however, Chile was at war. It involved itself in the war between Peru and Spain, which allowed Chile to strengthen its navy and fortify its coast. Later, in 1879, Chile engaged itself in the War of the Pacific with Bolivia and Peru. Coming out victorious, Chile was able to exploit nitrate, a highly profitable export commodity.

However, no product during the nineteenth-century was as intensely competitive as the exceedingly lucrative copper industry. Chilean prominence in copper increased during this period. Chile first challenged and subsequently surpassed Britain as a competitor. It ranked second after the United States as the world-leading producer. Relative to the United States, however, Chile was and continues to be able to produce copper at a much lower cost. Its comparative advantage in the production of copper in turn facilitated the development of infrastructure such as Chile's electricity, gas, street lights, iron structures, and railroad expansion throughout most of the nineteenth century.[25]

In comparison with Argentina and Uruguay, however, most observers rank the Chilean nineteenth-century per capita income level third, mostly because Valparaiso could not rival the strategic location of Buenos Aires and Montevideo for lower-cost transatlantic trade. However, in contemporary Latin America, transpacific trade has become much more important, which in turn gives Chile a comparative geographic advantage vis-à-vis Argentina and Uruguay.

Contrary to the common wisdom about high income inequalities, the ratio of GDP per worker to unskilled wage—a proxy to assess the returns of skilled labor—in Chile was comparable to that of Argentina and Uruguay.[26] Estimates suggest that relative to other Latin American nations—analyzed in section 2.4. Chilean growth, like Argentinean and Uruguayan growth, was not accompanied by a significant deterioration in income inequalities, as Kuznets (1955) inverted-U hypothesis would have predicted.[27]

Large inflows of nineteenth-century immigrants from Europe and the relatively high labor productivity of those migrants also were undeniably contributing factors to Chile's strong nineteenth-century performance.

2.4 Two Special Cases: Brazil and Cuba

Relative to Asia, labor shortages were prevalent throughout all American regions—with the notable exception of Mexico and Peru. In theory, because labor was scarce relative to land, labor's marginal productivity should have been high. Recall from the previous chapter, however, that under the *encomienda* and *mita* modes of production indentured labor was paid at subsistence wages. *Encomienda* and *mita* exacerbated by the *mayorazgo* did not disappear in postindependence Latin America.

Moreover, the Latin American aristocracy owned the fertile land, the mines, and other natural resources, which were key to export-led growth triggered by the primary export boom. Thus, income inequalities must have increased during the region's belle époque as the governments of the newly independent republics protected the elite's interests.[28] This should hold true for Brazil and Cuba, the two plantation economies par excellence, to which we now turn.

After the American Civil War of 1861 to 1865, Brazil and Cuba were the only two countries in which Afro Latin American slavery was permitted well into the nineteenth century. Antislavery laws were not adopted until 1884 and 1888 in Cuba and Brazil, respectively—that is, some forty years after the United States had taken an antislavery stand. Despite the prevalence of indentured labor in other regions, income inequalities in Brazil and Cuba were higher compared to the three stellar performers, and they were also higher relative to indentured labor economies such as Mexico and Peru.

Brazil and Cuba grew fast in an export-led-growth fashion nonetheless, but internal demand remained unsurprisingly low. Exceedingly high income inequalities, relative to those of neighboring countries, shaped the two countries' fate. Against their common backdrop, the economic performance of Brazil and Cuba differed widely throughout the entire nineteenth-century export-led-growth period, however.

We will look first at Brazil. Brazil's independence from Portugal, like that of its neighbors in Spanish America, dates back to the early 1800s. Brazil's main export products to Europe thereafter were coffee produced in the south, cocoa from southern Bahia, and rubber from the Amazon.

Primary commodity Brazilian exports after independence went through periods of boom and bust. Brazil contributed with over 70 percent of world's coffee production in the mid-nineteenth century. However, the international coffee price was highly volatile. For example, it increased sharply during the 1850s, but then experienced a drastic decline in the 1860s as US imports of coffee fell because of the American Civil War.[29] These sharp fluctuations of primary commodity export prices should be factored in when analyzing Brazil's ISI policies, which were implemented in the twentieth century; we will study this period in greater detail in chapter 3.

Price fluctuations alone cannot explain the sharp decline of Brazil's per capita GDP relative to that of the United States, however—from 36 percent in 1800 to 11 percent in 1914 (see table 2.2). Comparatively low FDI in infrastructure played a key role. Railway construction in Brazil, for example, in per capita terms, was nearly half of that in Cuba. Moreover, railways in Brazil tended to bias export-led growth in the coffee-growing south. Immigration flows from Europe were also larger in the south. The north was and remains underdeveloped when compared to the south and also more unequal, because land tended to be concentrated in fewer hands in agricultural production under slavery. Stagnation and income inequalities in the northeast persisted well into the twenty-first century and, in turn, retarded overall per capita growth rates in the entire country.[30]

Let's now turn to Cuba. Infrastructure superiority was not the only factor; strategic location and, perhaps more importantly, historical precedence each played a role. Cuba's per capita exports during the nineteenth century were five times higher than those of Brazil's, because by the turn of the nineteenth century Cuba already had the highest export per capita level—not just relative to that of Brazil, but also relative to all of Latin America. Although it remained a Spanish colony until 1868, Cuba—a traditional sugar plantation economy—enjoyed special trade privileges with the United States; such privileges date back to the seventeenth century.

Recall from table 2.2 that Cuba's per capita GDP compared to that in the United States was high relative to other Latin American regions—Brazil included. The drastic decline of per capita GDP during the nineteenth century in both Cuba and Brazil was similar, however: around 65 percent in Brazil and 69 percent in Cuba.

Because Cuba had a historical trade advantage relative to Brazil, and also relative to other Spanish colonies, its sharp decline throughout the entire nineteenth century enabled the three stellar performers to catch up. Cuba therefore ranked fourth after Argentina, Chile, and Uruguay in terms of per capita GDP during the export-led-growth period—not because of its nineteenth-century export performance, but because it started at a higher per capita GDP level.

More importantly, Cuba's decline throughout the nineteenth century is best explained by labor shortages in sugar production. As Galván (2004) points out, labor shortages in Cuba started long before the abolition of slavery in 1886. Recall that, unlike other Latin American countries, Cuba remained a Spanish colony until 1894. During most of the nineteenth century, Spain was under tremendous pressure to abolish slavery in its largest Caribbean sugar plantation colony, that is, Cuba. Such external pressure, from the Britain and the United States in particular, lowered slave importation on the one hand and triggered recurrent political unrest on the other. Ultimately, external and domestic pressures led to the abolition of slavery, which in turn precipitated the decline of Cuba's supremacy in the production and export of sugar.

Figure 2.3 shows the contrasting details between per capita GDP in the two Latin American plantation economies and the relative positions of these two economies to other Latin American countries.

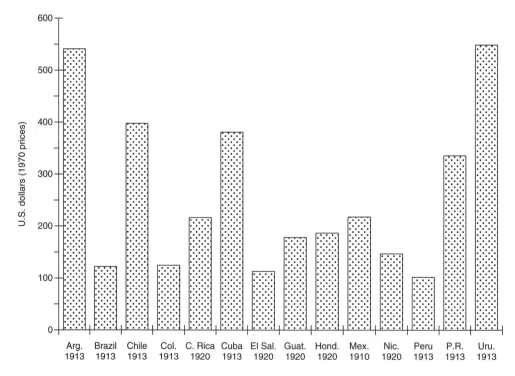

Figure 2.3
Per capita GDP toward the end of the export-led-growth period.
Source: Bulmer-Thomas 2003.

2.5 Nineteenth-Century Export-Led Growth in Contrast with Modern Days

The weight of late nineteenth-century history left a long-lasting imprint. With the exception of Chile—an early starter—trade liberalization in contemporary Latin America was restarted in the late 1980s and early 1990s after a prolonged period of protectionism. Except for Mexico after the 1994 North American Free Trade Agreement (NAFTA), export-led growth continues to rely on primary commodities, for three reasons. First, as we noted at the start of this chapter, Latin America asserted its role in the world economy as a primary commodity exporter during its first globalization wave in the late nineteenth century. Second, the prolonged period of protectionism (1940–1980) under ISI policies—analyzed in great detail in the next chapter—prevented Latin America from industrializing at a fast pace in most regions in the twentieth century. Third, by the time Latin America restarted liberalizing trade in the second half of the 1980s, labor-abundant Asian economies had already established themselves as leading exporters of manufactures—the first stage of industrialization—which placed contemporary Latin America at a historical disadvantage.

With the benefit of hindsight, the nineteenth-century contrast between the stellar performers in the southern cone and the plantation economies is revealing. Deindustrialization during the nineteenth century, followed by protracted protectionism in the twentieth century, combined with endemic labor shortages to place contemporary Latin America economies at a considerable disadvantage during recent attempts by a vast majority of southern cone countries to switch from primary commodity to manufacturing exporters.

Table 2.4 shows the leading traditional Latin American exports up until the early twenty-first century. In the 1996–2013 period, such exports included mining and energy, agriculture, raw materials, food, beverages, oils, and seeds. Over time, most of the economies shown in table 2.4 have intensified their commodity export specialization. These commodities accounted for an average of 56 percent of total Latin American and Caribbean exports in 2010.[31] Mexico stands out as a special case, however. It benefits from its proximity to the United States under NAFTA provisions, which have facilitated Mexican specialization in the export of assembly industries, including vehicles. The increasing trend in export of primary commodities is more evident for exhaustible resources, notably from Venezuela, Bolivia, Chile, Ecuador, Peru, and Colombia (see figure 2.4).

Note that relative to the nineteenth-century export-led growth, the recent trend in Latin America has changed its composition but not its nature as most of the region remains a primary commodity exporting region. The shift of trade patterns to potentially more productivity-enhancing manufactures and services is likely to prove difficult. On the demand-side of the spectrum, however, it is important to

Table 2.4
Latin American exports by country of origin, 1995 to 2013 (percent of total exports)

	Agricultural products		Mining		Fuels	
	1995	2013	1995	2013	1995	2013
Argentina	54.1	50.8	1.6	3.0	10.3	4.3
Bolivia	29.8	16.5	33.7	21.3	13.9	55.8
Brazil	33.7	37.5	10.3	16.9	0.9	7.4
Chile	37.0	27.2	46.8	57.8	0.2	1.0
Colombia	36.5	11.4	N/A	1.1	N/A	66.8
Costa Rica	53.2	36.1	0.8	1.4	0.6	0.0
Ecuador	55.5	34.7	N/A	0.9	N/A	56.8
El Salvador	34.8	22.7	1.7	1.4	0.0	2.3
Guatemala	67.4	48.0	0.5	5.7	2.0	4.6
Honduras	33.5	30.7	0.2	1.5	0.0	1.8
Mexico	9.0	6.6	2.9	3.0	10.3	12.8
Nicaragua	77.9	38.4	N/A	0.7	N/A	0.4
Panama	69.0	6.9	1.0	0.6	2.9	0.0
Paraguay	36.5	66.8	0.1	0.8	0.1	23.9
Peru	31.0	16.9	41.3	38.4	4.9	12.8
Uruguay	59.1	74.9	0.7	0.3	1.0	0.5
Venezuela	3.0	0.1	3.9	0.4	78.9	97.7

Source: World Trade Organization Statistics Database (2015): https://www.wto.org/english/res_e/statis_e/merch_trade_stat_e.htm. *Note:* N/A = not applicable.

emphasize again that it is no longer Europe and the United States are exacerbating the commodity export bias. It is instead high rates of industrialization in Asia and the Pacific, especially in China.

It is often argued that increased trade between Latin America and China has dampened the effects of the 2007 to 2008 financial crisis. Fast-growing Asia is now the second-largest partner of Latin American countries, after the United States and before Europe. In some southern cone countries—such as Chile—Asia is by far the main trading partner. We will return to analyzing the weight of China in Latin America and the implications of the Chinese slowdown growth in recent years in chapter 9.

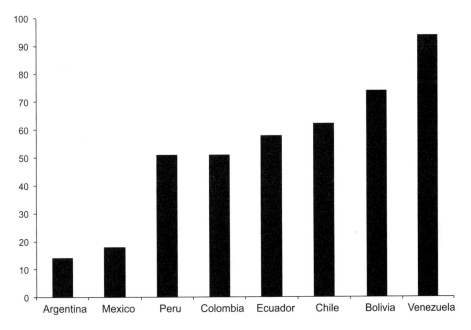

Figure 2.4
Ratio of fuel and mining exports as percentage of total exports (2005–2012 averages).
Source: World Trade Organization International Trade Statistics (2013): https://www.wto.org/english/res_e/statis_e/its2013_e/its2013_e.pdf.

2.6 Concluding Remarks

In this chapter, we discussed the nineteenth-century export-led growth period. Following numerous border disputes and extraregional wars during approximately half a century after the early 1800s' independence movements, exports of primary commodities grew considerably.

Export revenues failed to be channeled toward manufacturing to allow for rapid industrialization to take off. Chenery, Robinson, and Syrquin (1986) document the positive relation between export growth and growth in domestic demand in some parts of Asia, notably in South Korea. This relationship was nonexistent in Latin America. Upsurges of manufacturing growth—in textiles, in particular—such as in Mexico slowed down during the nineteenth century, and nascent industrial development stopped in many regions.

Latin America's belle époque (1870–1914) opened the scope for export diversification and industrial development in some countries, such as Argentina. Industrial development via export growth, however, was interrupted at the outbreak of World War I.

During the nineteenth century, newly independent republics enacted high import tariffs, first, to finance internal wars and foreign invasions, and then to protect powerful elites (landowners and nascent manufacturers). Financing government expenditures via tariffs set a historical precedent. Nineteenth-century protectionism lasted well into the late twentieth century. Contemporary Latin America is still finding it difficult to break with the past. Imposing direct and progressive taxation remains a struggle, because it faces strong opposition from ruling elites. In parallel, governments in the region have resorted to indirect taxation—value added taxes (VAT).

We analyzed the performance in Argentina, Chile, and Uruguay in the nineteenth century prior to 1914. Per capita growth was higher in these three countries relative to the rest of Latin America. Trade openness has continued to promote growth at the turn of the twenty-first century in most southern cone countries.

However, unlike the previous export-led-growth episode during Latin America's belle époque, the current one has been shaped by fast-growing Asian economies, which are now Latin America's second-largest trading partners. In some cases, such as for Chile, Asia is now the number one trading partner.

The growing weight of Asia in trade has hindered manufacturing export growth in Latin America on the one hand and propelled primary commodity export growth on the other. The latter effect has in turn contributed to Latin America not being too affected by the twenty-first century downturns in the United States and Europe.

In addition to the trajectories of Argentina, Chile, and Uruguay, we also examined the nineteenth-century plantation economies: Brazil and Cuba. In comparison, both Brazil and Cuba exported less, grew less rapidly, and had larger income disparities. High income inequalities in turn led to political unrest, which might have obstructed export growth and its potential on per capita GDP and domestic demand, particularly in Cuba.

Overall, per capita GDP relative to that of the United States declined throughout the entire nineteenth century. Although this decline is often attributed to political strife, insufficient infrastructure investment to access the interior in hostile (yet fertile) lands also played a role—the most vivid examples being those of Brazil and Mexico, contemporary Latin America's two largest economies.

Export-led growth in the late nineteenth century continued to be concentrated in primary commodities well into Latin America's twenty-first century—except for the assembly lines and other manufactures and industrial products in Mexico under NAFTA.

The prospect of shifting from producers of primary commodities to producers of higher-value-added goods and services seems grim. Under the umbrella of the

WTO and bilateral and regional trade agreements, the tendency to concentrate production on countries' own comparative advantages has intensified the rewards for low-skilled labor used in primary commodities' exploitation, as the Stolper and Samuelson theorem predicts.[32] Specifically, contemporary Latin America has a difficult task ahead when attempting to compete with labor-abundant and comparatively high-skill labor countries such as China and India.

Another lesson from this chapter is that postindependence Latin American republics missed the opportunity to jump on the industrialization bandwagon in the nineteenth century. As the terms of trade increasingly favored primary commodity exports during that first globalization wave, sharp income inequalities dating back to the colonial period remained because fertile land and mines continued to be under the control of a small elite.

Actually, and according to Williamson (2015), income inequalities increased during Latin America's belle époque. Although handsome revenues from exports accruing to a small elite were on the rise, low-productivity-labor wages remained stagnant under postindependence modes of production, migration and protectionist policies which in turn hindered internal demand.

Have the perils of excessive specialization in primary commodity production disappeared? Our next chapter sheds light on twentieth-century Latin America, in which Brazil's and Mexico's origins with regard to contemporary export trends and domestic demand—away from excessive primary commodity export specialization—can be found.

Summary
- Latin American independence from Iberian powers as of the early 1800s opened the scope for trade with rapidly industrializing European nations and with the United States.
- Postindependence border disputes and conflict with foreign non-Iberian countries prevented most Latin American nations from benefiting from trade until about 1870.
- From 1870 until the outbreak of World War I in 1914, Latin America enjoyed a primary commodity export boom, which accelerated growth but exacerbated Dutch disease, while early manufacturing production either disappeared or remained dormant.
- The three stellar performers during Latin America's belle époque (1870–1914) were Argentina, Chile, and Uruguay. In these three countries trade with industrializing Europe was more active and nascent industrial activity remained active, probably because income inequalities were less pronounced relative to other regions with a higher proportion of indigenous and Afro-Latin American

populations, the purchasing power of which was low due to persistent indentured labor and slavery.
- In comparison, the two plantation economies par excellence—namely, nineteenth-century Brazil and Cuba—declined. In the case of Brazil, poor infrastructure linking the hinterland with seaports for exports is often blamed for poor performance during this period. In both economies, however, the prevalence of pervasive income inequalities and conflict well into the late nineteenth century was a contributing factor.
- The belle époque shaped the future of Latin America as a primary commodity exporter, a development trajectory that has accelerated due to rapidly industrializing China. The "trap" of production and export promotion of primary commodities as an engine of growth represents a major challenge, because contemporary Latin American economies are slowly developing an internal market for domestic production of nascent industrial products.

Review Questions
1. What were the advantages and disadvantages of Latin American countries' independence from the Iberian Peninsula?
2. Why did per capita GDP in the nineteenth-century Latin American stellar performers surpass that of plantation economies?
3. What were the main advantages and disadvantages of Latin America's belle époque?
4. What is the commodity lottery and in what way might it explain growth upsurges in some countries and not in others?
5. In what way can within-country income inequalities be explained by geography considerations?
6. Why might excessive income inequalities have been detrimental to growth from a Latin American perspective during the nineteenth century?
7. Is trade integration within Latin American countries a potential solution to the primary commodity export trap dating back to the nineteenth-century belle époque?
8. Which Latin American countries are more likely to grow out of the primary commodity export bias and why?
9. It is often said that Latin America is resource abundant and will therefore remain underdeveloped. Do you agree?
10. Can trade integration between the entire American continent and Asia be beneficial for Latin America? Briefly explain your answer.

Further Reading

For a comprehensive analysis of the economic consequences of Latin America's independence from Iberian powers, see Prados de la Escosura 2005a, 2005b. For an insightful study of nineteenth-century Latin America focusing on the region's income inequalities, see Bértola et al. 2008. For an interesting analysis of Cuba's past and future prospects—prior to recent initiatives under Barack Obama's and Raúl Castro's administrations—see Domínguez 2006. Parallels between Africa and Latin America from a "resource curse" standpoint are staggering. For relevant analysis of Africa's natural resource extraction, see Collier 2010b.

3 Import Substitution Industrialization

One might argue that the primary commodity export bias discussed in the previous chapter could foster industrial development if the revenues from exports could be successfully converted into man-made capital such as factories and machinery and human capital investments—that is, investments in health and education. Several developed countries have done exactly that—oil-rich Norway is a notable example. In contemporary Latin America, however, the primary commodity export bias has gained traction again as China has industrialized rapidly and at an unprecedented rate and scale.

Why did Latin America remain caught up during the twentieth century in a dormant export sector that did not promote rapid industrialization as it did in other parts of the world—notably in Asia and, in particular, in the four so-called Asian Tigers of South Korea, Taiwan, Hong Kong, and Singapore? In order to answer this important question, we again need to look at the main historical traits first.

The nineteenth-century export-led-growth trend analyzed in the previous chapter stopped at the onset of World War I in 1914. At that point in time, trade flows with Europe and with the United States, Latin America's main trading partners at the time, were severely crippled. After the war, a new economic paradigm gained ground: protectionism.

The protectionist ideology contended that the international trading system was inherently biased against primary commodity–exporting countries and that industrialization in the developing world was a prerequisite for preventing further widening of per capita income disparities between the relatively affluent industrialized north and the developing countries in the south. This ideology was persuasive, particularly after the Great Depression from 1929 to 1933.

Twentieth-century Latin American protectionism manifested itself in various forms. Relative to the nineteenth century, invasive state intervention through both regulation and direct management and control of state-owned enterprises (SOEs) was strong. Inward orientation was geared toward lending support to the development of local manufactures and industry via import substitution industrialization (ISI) policies.[1] Large twentieth-century macroeconomic imbalances were a by-product of such protectionist policies. In particular, ISI policies contributed to Latin America's large fiscal deficits, high inflation, and sovereign debt defaults, particularly during the last quarter of the twentieth century.

This chapter sheds light on key questions of utmost relevance to our understanding of contemporary Latin American economies in the twenty-first century. What are the perils of protectionist policies? Is economic performance in large economies such as those of Brazil and Mexico today linked to twentieth-century ISI policies? What lessons can be drawn from exchange rate policies in Brazil, Colombia, Chile, and Mexico? Are such historical precedents important to better understand ongoing central bank inflation-targeting policies in some countries? To what extent is the twentieth-century "Brazilian miracle" explaining economic performance in contemporary Latin America's largest economy? Has the reversion to export-led-growth policies combined with protectionism been conducive to manufacturing and industrial sector promotion in the twenty-first century?

In section 3.1 in this chapter, we present the historical background that gave rise to the protectionist ideology and explain how this ideology operated in practice. In section 3.2, we describe the ISI policies in brushstrokes. In section 3.3, we question the Latin American protectionist era and explain the adjustments made to the ISI policies in some countries. Successful adjustments and, more importantly, a change in the world macroeconomic environment in the 1980s ploughed the Latin American soil with the seeds of a new paradigm, which we present in section 3.4. We deliver a summary in section 3.5 and conclude by examining contemporary challenges under the new paradigm: stabilization, trade liberalization, privatization, and the consequent need for regulation and avoidance of cronyism. Meeting these challenges is crucial for consolidating and enlarging the middle class legacy in postprotectionist twenty-first-century Latin America.

3.1 Historical Background

As we discussed in chapter 2, Latin America during the late nineteenth century was an export-led region. Primary commodity exports were the engine of

Import Substitution Industrialization

economic growth. Trade flows stopped, first during World War I, then during the 1929 to 1933 Great Depression, and then stopped again during World War II. The Great Depression had an alarming impact on Latin America's export-oriented strategy. Demand for Latin American primary commodities collapsed and their prices plummeted. Between 1929 and 1933, Latin American countries' terms of trade fell by as much 45 percent in some regions.[2] Capital inflows were sharply reduced. The combination of these events drove most Latin American countries into a severe recession; Chile, Peru, and Mexico were the most affected (see figure 3.1).[3] Real interest rates rose sharply with price deflation. Both private and public sector finances deteriorated. Fiscal revenues fell, and debt burdens grew.

The collapse of Latin American trade flows was exacerbated by a fall in world demand for primary commodities, which resulted from protectionist policies in industrialized countries. The protectionist wave started in the United States at the onset of the Great Depression. In 1930, for example, the United States enacted the Smoot-Hawley Tariff Act.[4] Unlike protectionism for industrial promotion in Latin

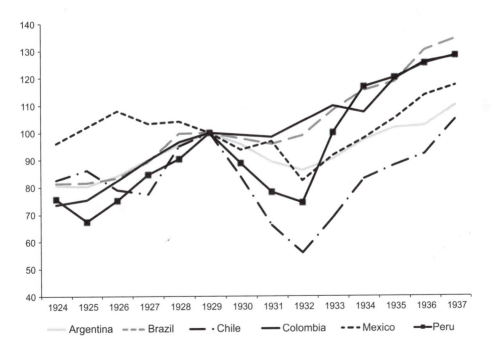

Figure 3.1
Index of total production in selected countries, 1924–1937 (1929 = 100).
Source: Braun et al. 2000.

America, protectionist policies in the United States served a dual purpose: they were aimed at protecting the North American agricultural sector on the one hand and cushioning the economy from rampant unemployment on the other.[5]

Because retaliatory responses were swift, tariffs in the United States worsened the worldwide recession. The retaliation wave swept the world, with an escalation of trade barriers such as quotas, import prohibitions, licensing systems, and ingenious protectionist devices. In 1931, for example, the United Kingdom enacted the Abnormal Importation Act, and other countries followed suit as the recession spread and deepened.[6]

At the turn of the twentieth century and in response to post–World War I reconstruction efforts in Europe, the United States had become the world's largest net creditor.[7] Latin America also contracted loans with the United States in the 1920s. Debtor countries needed to export in order to repay their foreign-currency-denominated debts. As table 3.1 shows, however, the volume and value of Latin American exports during the Great Depression were historically low. Consequently, widespread sovereign defaults on debt owed to private investors both in the United States and Europe ensued.[8] We will return to the Latin American sovereign default record in greater detail in chapter 4.

The international monetary system did not help. On the contrary, the gold standard—a global system of fixed exchange rates—was a contributing factor. Specifically, most observers have argued that the fixed exchange rate regime deepened the Great Depression and transmitted output contraction to other countries at a fast pace.[9] Generating foreign currency in order to repay sovereign debts was virtually impossible in the midst of a worldwide recession and industrialized

Table 3.1
Selected Latin American central government debt to export ratios, 1929–1935

	1929	1931	1933	1935
Argentina	49	73	113	81
Brazil	153	163	215	127
Chile	102	327	842	573
Colombia	58	101	123	67
Costa Rica	96	130	174	158
El Salvador	106	153	183	157
Guatemala	65	97	162	123
Nicaragua	30	42	53	46
Uruguay	147	185	212	148

Source: Eichengreen and Portes 1989 and the League of Nations Annual Statistical Yearbooks 1929, 1931, 1933 and 1935 (http://digital.library.northwestern.edu/league/stat.html).

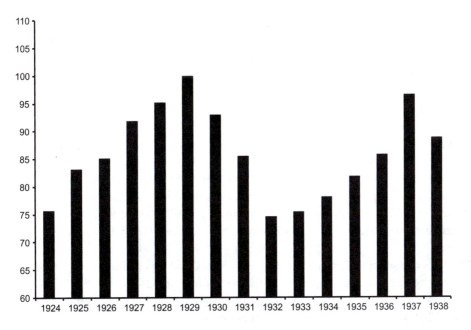

Figure 3.2
World trade, 1924–1938 (1929 = 100).
Source: League of Nations 1939.

countries' protectionist policies. As shown in figure 3.2, world trade decreased drastically. Sovereign debt defaults became the rule rather than the exception. In the aftermath of widespread defaults, debt renegotiations with a multiplicity of foreign bondholders lasted for decades. Latin America could not return to the international capital markets prior to the 1970s—that is, nearly ten years after repayment of the 1930s Great Depression "restructured" debt had been completed.

Trade deficits during the 1930s Great Depression led to current account crises. Most Latin American countries had a fixed-exchange rate system under the gold standard. Predictably, the system became unsustainable because of shortages of foreign currency reserves and gold. Argentina and Uruguay were first to abandon the gold standard in 1929. The ipso facto devaluation of their domestic currencies failed to boost exports, however. Similar failed attempts were attempted by Brazil and Paraguay, and then by Bolivia and Venezuela.

Following the devaluation of the British pound in September 1931, a wave of domestic currency depreciations became unstoppable as several countries that had their currencies pegged to the British pound quit the fixed exchange rate mechanism. Moreover, the depreciation of the British pound vis-à-vis gold and the recurrent depreciations added pressure to the already deteriorated balance of payments accounts in Latin American countries. Several countries resorted to the use of exchange controls to avoid capital flight. Following the protectionist trend in the industrialized economies, Latin America also imposed capital controls. Most nations in the region attempted to prevent capital from flowing out to heavily protected industrialized countries.

It was not until 1933 that the United States abandoned the gold standard. Following the devaluation of the dollar, Central American countries benefited. These countries had pegged their currencies to the dollar, and the depreciation of their currencies had a positive impact on their current accounts; unlike their South American counterparts, Central American depreciations coincided with economic recovery in the United States. At the same time, the 1933 depreciation of the dollar marked a second wave of depreciations in all of post–Great Depression Latin America.[10]

The US recession officially ended in March 1933. At this point in time, a recovery spurt began to spread throughout the rest of the world. In 1934, the US began to relax some trade barriers, and other industrialized countries did the same. As figure 3.2 shows, world trade expanded again. Renewed trade flows in turn promoted export-led economic recovery.

In support of trade barrier dismantling, the devaluation waves in post–Great Depression Latin America were an important exchange rate policy tool to reboost export-led output expansion. Devaluations laid the groundwork for rapid growth of Latin American exports and nascent industrialization. As shown in figure 3.3, sharp real devaluations took place in several regions. Interestingly, such devaluations did not create inflation due to the substantial excess capacity caused by the Great Depression. In other words, the so-called exchange rate pass-through was low.[11]

Some countries recovered faster than others. According to Eichengreen and Sachs (1985) and Eichengreen and Irwin (2010), countries that broke away from the gold standard first and allowed their currencies to depreciate experienced relatively mild recessions and early recoveries because they were able to relax monetary policy. In contrast, countries that kept their currencies fixed against gold were more likely to restrict foreign trade. Lacking the instrument of an independent monetary policy authority, those countries used trade barriers to shift demand toward domestic production in the hope of putting a stop to output contraction and rising unemployment. However, these countries experienced prolonged recessions.

Once the world economic recovery was underway, many Latin American countries maintained high levels of protection. Others reduced their import barriers in the second part of the 1930s. Initially, protectionism was not widespread. For

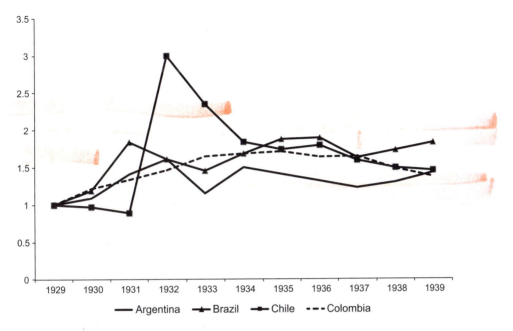

Figure 3.3
Real exchange rates in selected countries, 1929–1939 (1929 = 1).
Source: Based on data from Corbo 1992.

example, countries such as Argentina, Brazil, and Chile forcefully reinstated trade liberalization policies during the interwar years, but such an opening trade interlude was interrupted at the onset of World War II in 1939.

World War II nevertheless had a positive impact on Latin America, because the region was an important supplier of raw materials. However, export potential was stalled due to difficulties with shipping. This kind of trade obstacle reinforced the view of the region as extremely vulnerable to macroeconomic events originating elsewhere, and it also became exceedingly difficult to import intermediary inputs of production for the development of Latin America's nascent manufacturing sectors.[12]

While the impact of World War II on Latin America is difficult to quantify, most observers agree that it was positive. Because of the war, there was a sharp reduction in nonmilitary production in industrialized countries. Relative to primary commodities, the price of manufactures, in which industrialized countries had a comparative advantage, increased. This had two effects: First, it raised the profitability of manufacturing and industrial sectors. This import-substituting sector stimulus was further fueled via domestic currency devaluations. Second, the nascent Latin American industry needed capital-intensive inputs to grow, and a significant portion of domestic resources turned to the production of capital-intensive goods, which could no longer be imported. The two effects reinforced each other, triggering the development of infant industries.

Despite manufacturing and industrial sector stimuli from World War II, Latin America resorted to trade barriers. The United States once more contributed to the recreation of a protectionist environment. It demanded Latin American support for the allies and urged all regions to adopt restrictive measures and legislation against the enemies. It was therefore under US auspices that Latin American governments expanded their role in trade and capital flow restrictions. State intervention in trade in the early 1940s was politically acceptable because of the war, but it set an indelible precedent for follow-up protectionist policies.

3.2 Import Substitution Industrialization Policies

At the end of World War II, Latin American governments and academics engaged themselves in a heated debate over the region's development strategy, forming two ideologically divided camps. The first group was led by exporters, traders of imported goods, representatives of the US chamber of commerce, and many economists. This group advocated a return to free trade and financial openness. However, the effects of the Great Depression and World War II generated a pall of pessimism that hung over this group. According to Edwards (2009), after the end of World War II exporters had lost influence, whereas the state had gained clout.

The second group was optimistic about the state's capacity to promote economic development. This group favored continued and expanded protectionist policies. The World War II experience had demonstrated that Latin America could live in relative autarky. This group proclaimed that isolation could potentially reinforce self-sufficiency and promote manufactures and industrial sector development.

The balance was ultimately tipped in favor of the second group. Intellectual support from the newly created Economic Commission for Latin America and the Caribbean (ECLAC) and, in particular, the pioneering ideas of Raul Prebisch and Hans Singer in the 1950s played a key role.[13] According to Love (2005), Latin American structuralism in its initial form was largely the creation of Raul Prebisch, who introduced the notion of an industrial, hegemonic *center* and an agrarian, dependent *periphery* as a framework for understanding the international division of labor.

The Prebisch-Singer protectionist paradigm was based on two key propositions. First, it predicted a secular and inevitable decline in the price of primary commodities relative to the price of manufactures. Developing countries had specialized in the production of the former and industrialized countries in the latter. Consequently, developing nations would be at a considerable disadvantage over time. These countries would be forced to trade their products in international markets under increasingly unfavorable conditions. Moreover, under the assumption that technical progress is the main determinant of economic growth—and according to Prebisch and Singer technical progress was concentrated in the manufacturing sector—developing countries lagged behind industrialized nations in terms of labor productivity. Trade patterns were therefore creating a growing gap between poor and rich countries.

In theory, however, if technical progress and R&D in the production of primary commodities is lower relative to that in manufactures, the supply of manufactures relative to that of primary commodities should increase. This will lead to a decline in the relative price of manufactures. According to Prebisch and Singer, this theoretical prediction was flawed in practice.[14] Protectionist ideologists held the view that developing-country governments needed to industrialize via ISI policies, explained in greater detail further ahead.

The second proposition was that industrialization required temporary protection of the manufacturing sector. This proposition is based on the well-known infant industry argument from standard international trade textbooks.[15] The argument is that nascent industries in less developed countries (LDCs) are unable to compete successfully against similar ones in developed countries, because infant industries operate on a small scale due to a historical disadvantage. The price that equals or surpasses average costs is therefore significantly higher in developing countries, and in order to cover average costs, an increase in scale is important. Hence, temporary protection is required until infant industries in LDCs attain an efficient scale of production.

In addition, Prebisch emphasized the importance of two issues: structural unemployment, because of the inability of traditional export industries to grow and therefore to absorb excess rural population; and external disequilibrium, because of higher propensities to import industrial goods than to export traditional agricultural and mineral goods. The school of thought that focused on structures, bottlenecks, and imbalances was labeled *structuralism*.[16]

The Prebisch-Singer paradigm was exceedingly influential among economists and policy makers. It soon became the dominant view in Latin America during the 1950s, giving birth to the ISI strategy. Prebisch recommended deliberate state-induced industrialization to substitute products previously imported by domestic ones, with moderate and selective protection. In his view, trade barriers should be high enough to adequately protect industry, but not so high as to put pressure on firms to become more efficient as they developed and gained strength. Selectivity was needed. Protection was meant to target industries generating the greatest

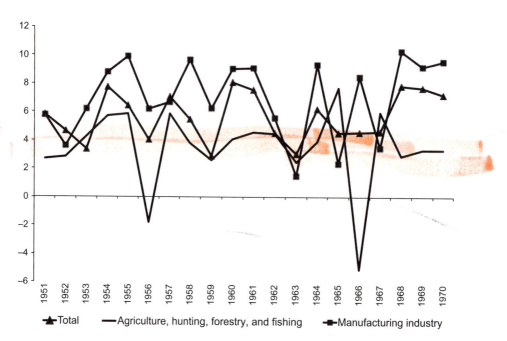

Figure 3.4
GDP growth in Latin America (1970 constant prices), 1951–1970.
Source: Authors' own construction from ECLAC database 2014 (www.cepal.org/en/publications/37647-anuario-estadistico-america-latina-caribe-2014-statistical-yearbook-latin-america).

impact on growth, along the lines of the so-called backward and forward linkages.[17]

In addition to the use of tariffs and other trade restrictions, exchange rate policy was used to provide cheap imported inputs for use by domestic manufacturers. The state was called upon to strengthen infrastructure and to facilitate and subsidize credit to industry via state-owned development banks. State intervention was also needed in key sectors such as the steel industry to directly control and manage large-scale production.

The manufacturing sector in Latin America began to grow fast under protectionist policies, as can be seen in figure 3.4. Total GDP from 1951 to 1960 grew at an average annual rate of 5.6 percent, but manufacturing industrial produce grew at an average of 7.2 percent.

With the benefit of hindsight, however, we know that manufacturing and industrial sector performance did not meet expectations for several reasons. Seven arguments are often invoked. First, protection was excessive and lasted for too long (1940–1985). In many Latin American countries, tariffs averaged over 100 percent in the 1950s and 1960s.[18] Instead of being temporary, as Prebisch and his colleagues had prescribed, protectionism persisted and increased through time. The reason was that the nascent industrial sector required increasingly higher trade barriers and government subsidies in order to face tougher competition from already industrialized countries. Because of historical precedence, industrialized countries continued to make quality improvements to existing products and introduced an entirely new range of products. Increased protection at this juncture, however, discouraged productivity improvements and efficiency in Latin America's nascent industrial sectors and delayed and/or stalled industrialization later on—at the onset of the second globalization trend in the 1990s.

Second, protection was not selective. It was massive and indiscriminate. In practice, it was difficult to pick the winners. Owners and managers in all industries would argue that they had growth potential and that their industries could stimulate the rate of technical progress. Competition for protection led to the emergence of a powerful lobby conducive to rent-seeking behavior.[19] The principal objective of the industrialist lobby was to achieve greater and prolonged protection to avoid foreign competition at all costs. X-inefficiencies were prevalent and widespread throughout a wide range of industrial products.[20] Most observers of contemporary upsurges in crony capitalism in Latin America trace strong links between industrialists and government officials back to protectionist ISI policies during almost the entire second half of the twentieth century.

Third, rising subsidies for manufactures generated large fiscal deficits in many Latin American countries. Such deficits were monetized in many instances, which created strong inflationary pressures. However, inflation spirals were not created by persistent fiscal deficits alone. Increased trade barriers played a role. These barriers raised domestic prices of intermediate inputs of production. Local consumers of domestically produced manufactures therefore also had to pay much higher prices for lower quality products relative to the prices they would have paid under free trade. At such prices, demand for domestically produced manufactures was low.

Fourth, high trade barriers were accompanied by overvalued real exchange rates. The main objective of keeping exchange rates overvalued was twofold: to facilitate imports of capital goods and intermediate inputs via keeping import prices of these goods low on the one hand and to control inflation generated by the antiexport bias on the other. The agricultural sector—and, to a lesser extent, the mining sector—were particularly discriminated against. Protectionist policies in these two sectors were harshly felt. In both sectors, intermediate inputs of production were purchased at higher-than-market prices. Moreover, because exchange rates were kept overvalued, agricultural and mining producers could not sell at competitive prices and did not benefit at all from protection and/or government subsidies. The perverse effects of protectionist policies as proxied by the loss of

Table 3.2
Changes in the structure of the economy in selected countries between 1950 and 1970, percent of GDP (current prices)

Agriculture, hunting, forestry, and fishing	1950	1970
Argentina	14.1	12.2
Brazil	25.1	12.3
Chile	13.2	6.8
Colombia	36.4	25.1
Mexico	20.2	11.3
Manufacturing industry	1950	1970
Argentina	27.5	30.1
Brazil	19.3	29.3
Chile	21.5	25.5
Colombia	17.8	20.7
Mexico	21.4	23.7

Source: Authors' own construction from ECLAC database 2014 (www.cepal.org).

competitiveness in the agricultural and mining sectors also led to a significant change in the economic structure of Latin American countries, as table 3.2 suggests.

Fifth, the Latin American trade balance deteriorated significantly for two reasons: (1) because exports were strongly discouraged and (2) because replacing previously imported consumer goods produced domestically (such as refrigerators, washing machines, and automobiles) increased imports of intermediate inputs of production in order for the nascent industrialization process to take hold.

Sixth, capital inflows were particularly low under protectionist policies. These policies were not designed to attract FDI, and in some instances governments were openly hostile to FDI inflows for ideological reasons.[21] Domestic savings were endemic. Therefore, a "savings gap" could not be filled, leading to underinvestment in nascent industries.[22]

Finally, protectionist policies had a detrimental effect on employment. The subsidized importation of capital goods through overvalued exchange rates or below-market interest rates that helped to finance industrial investments generated price distortions, which promoted the use of more capital-intensive techniques of production. With an increased industrial share and with higher levels of production for capital-intensive manufactures, the industrial sector absorbed a relatively small part of the growing labor force. On the other hand, rural-urban migration flows, largely due to penalized agricultural production, were large.

A lagging agricultural sector still prevails today throughout most contemporary Latin American economies, and rural-urban migrants have joined the ranks of the informally employed or underemployed laborers, in line with the 1970 Harris-Todaro two-sector model predictions. Most observers agree that a high incidence of informal sector activity and urban poverty in Latin America in the twenty-first century dates back to the protectionist period.

However, some of our readers may think that our views on state-led growth performance in Latin America might not do entire justice to ISI policies and their potential achievements in the region, because we are comparing the achievements of state-led intervention in Latin America with those of policies in the four Asian Tigers. These countries grew at an average growth rate of 7 percent per annum between 1960 and 1990.

To some observers, however, ISI policies in Latin America were successful when compared to economic indicators worldwide. In particular, Bértola and Ocampo (2013) argue that annual growth rates of about 5.5 percent during the 1945–1980 period in Latin America were high relative to the world average because ISI policies in various forms and shapes did succeed at creating a solid industrial base and increased labor productivity, particularly in heavily populated countries such as Brazil and Mexico, which offer greater opportunity for scale economies to take hold.

3.3 ISI Performance Indicators

Initially, the protectionist tools described thus far—the ISI policies—induced higher economic growth in Latin America. Eventually, however, the easy phase of import substitution came to an end once the "obvious" substitutions had taken place.[23] At this point, the industrial sector could not continue growing without increased government intervention. But increased government support, particularly via vast amounts of subsidies, became fiscally unsustainable. Output growth slowed sharply in the 1960s.

Protection had brought deteriorating balance of payments accounts, high inflation, rising unemployment rates, and a stagnant agricultural sector. As a result, the ISI policies started to fall into disrepute. They did not generate the expected performance for catching up. Per capita GDP average annual growth between 1951 and 1960 was 2.3 percent in Latin America and 2.8 percent in the world as a whole. In comparison, the Asian Tigers had also opted for protection but exposed their nascent industry to international competition, and they were growing much faster—and unlike their Latin American counterparts, such countries were catching up (see figure 3.5).

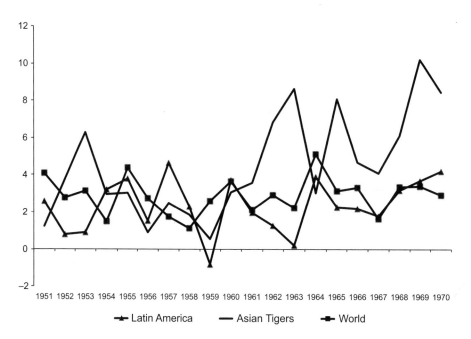

Figure 3.5
Per capita GDP growth in Latin America, the Asian Tigers, and the world, 1951–1970.
Source: Authors' own construction from Maddison Historical Statistics Database 2009 (http://www.ggdc.net/maddison/maddison-project/data.htm).

3.3.1 Fall of Stellar Performers, Rise of Brazil and Mexico

Nonetheless, the controversy over the performance of Latin America during the ISI period is ongoing. According to some observers,[24] Latin America prospered under protectionist policies. In particular, during the 1950s Latin America's economy grew faster than Western economies, and during the entire thirty-year period from 1950 to 1970 the region experienced its own *trente gloriouses*.[25] Latin America's GDP tripled, while population doubled, heavy-machine industrial production began in some regions, and production of basic consumption goods spread out.[26]

However, the arguably positive impact of protectionism was uneven. The nineteenth-century stellar performers reviewed in the previous chapter, Argentina, Uruguay, and Chile, were adversely affected, whereas Latin America's largest economies, Brazil and Mexico, experienced an unprecedented growth spurt (Brazil) and a steady per capita income growth (Mexico). The fall of the stellar performers and the rise of the two largest contemporary Latin American economies is shown in table 3.3.

Table 3.3
Percentage of per capita GDP growth under ISI policies: Brazil and Mexico versus nineteenth-century stellar performers

Country	1941–1949	1950–1959	1960–1969	1970–1979
Brazil	1.6	3.6	2.8	6.1
Mexico	3.7	3.1	3.5	3.2
Argentina	2.3	0.8	2.8	1.3
Chile	1.5	1.3	1.9	0.6
Uruguay	2.5	1.0	0.3	2.5

Source: ECLAC data, from Corbo 1991.

The most popular interpretation of the uneven benefits of protectionist policies relies on market size: domestic demand for manufactures and industry is comparatively high in heavily populated regions. Although this might explain the strong growth performance in Brazil and Mexico under ISI policies, a more nuanced explanation is needed, especially when income inequalities are factored in.

In the case of Brazil, export promotion policies launched in 1965 constitute an undeniable component of the Brazilian miracle (1968–1974). Average per capita GDP growth more than doubled in the 1970s relative to the 1960s. We return to these policies in greater detail further ahead (see section 3.3.3). Such policies were not implemented in neighboring Argentina, Chile, and Uruguay. Although no one really knows what these countries' performance would have been had similar export-oriented policies been implemented during the period in question, recent studies suggest that even small countries such as South Korea can rely on domestic demand for industrialization to take off at early stages.[27]

In the case of Mexico, the 1910 revolution precipitated the downfall of agricultural sector productivity via a sequence of agrarian reforms, which led to a widespread communal form of production called *ejido*. The landed aristocracy abandoned large-scale agriculture and joined an industrial class in the north, which was further enlarged by entrepreneurial-spirited migrants who were escaping the Spanish dictatorship in the 1930s. The manufacturing sector subsequently grew at a robust 7 percent per annum.[28]

Relative to Brazil, Mexico is highly centralized. Nationalization of heavy industry such as petrol under the Cárdenas administration in 1938 gave rise to powerful unions headquartered in Mexico City, or *Ciudad de Mexico*, Mexico's capital. The unions demanded higher wages and infrastructure. Unsurprisingly, utilities such as water, gas, and electricity and construction of infrastructure (public hospitals, schools, and universities included) were sectors in which growth was most vigorous in and around Mexico City. The construction sector grew at an average rate of 11.1 percent per annum from 1940 to 1970.[29]

3.3.2 Criticisms

The ISI strategy was criticized by two different camps. The liberal, promarket group focused first on fiscal deficits.[30] This group argued that fiscal deficits under protectionism were at the root of inflationary pressures. Growing government support for industry, this group proclaimed, could not continue for the sake of protecting a mediocre industry.

The traditional antiprotection critics joined this group. It was argued that high trade barriers and subsidies for industry under ISI generated an inefficient allocation of resources, because countries did not specialize in the production of those commodities for which they had a comparative advantage. Moreover, protectionism caused significant distortions to the economies under it because of *effective protection*—that is, the extent to which the value added of a product is protected, considering the impact of trade barriers on the final product and its imported inputs.[31] In most regions, the effective rates of protection exceeded *nominal protection*, which measures the extent to which protection allows domestic producers to increase their prices above international world prices. Excessive rates of effective protection over nominal protection lowered incentives for domestic producers of manufactures to increase efficiency, reduce costs, and close the gap between domestic and international prices. Durable consumer goods were usually the most favored, with higher effective rates of protection than capital goods and intermediate inputs. Agricultural products, on the other hand, had negative effective rates of protection. Protectionist policies were therefore distorting incentives quite strongly.

Pro-market economists also criticized the massive and indiscriminate way in which protectionist policies had been implemented. These policies did not consider each industry's growth potential. Indiscriminate protection led to meager growth across all industries, lowering the scope for scale economies. This was particularly true in the Latin American regions in which the size of the market was small, such as in the nineteenth-century stellar performers, Argentina, Uruguay, and Chile.

More generally, and according to Baer (1972), in certain industries such as automobiles, numerous governments in LDCs allowed entry of many firms, which hindered the ability of each firm to reap scale economies. This led to inefficient industries operating at a high cost.

Promarket economists also argued that the implementation of ISI resulted from an exceedingly pessimistic view of how the market functions and a very optimistic view of the ability of LDC governments to promote economic development.

Market failures were ever present in the discussion, but government failures were not.[32] Promarket advocates therefore were in favor of redesigning the development strategy by relying on the virtues of the market in which nascent industries would be exposed to foreign competition.

Criticism of the ISI strategy came from yet another group, the new-Marxist group (or dependency theorists). New-Marxists clamored for more state intervention.[33] According to this group, ISI exacerbated dependency or reliance of the *periphery* on the *center*, where the former comprised the vast majority of LDCs and the latter a minority of industrialized countries. In particular, and as we noted in section 3.2, ISI policies increased the need for imported intermediate inputs, which increased LDCs' dependency on the center—or on the "imperialist" countries.

New-Marxists also criticized the failure of ISI to generate employment as the industrial sector was unable to absorb the growing number of laborers migrating from the countryside to the city. Rural-urban migration in turn favored multinational corporations, which benefited from cheap (migrant) labor. The informally employed were perceived as a by-product of insufficient (and deliberate) investments in labor-enhancing technologies by multinationals.

In addition to informal employment, the most important collateral damage of ISI policies, new-Marxists argued, was the worsening of income disparities. Because industrialization was capital intensive and industry was increasing its share in the economy, industrialization led to a greater concentration of income in only a few hands. This exacerbated the problem of income inequality, which in the case of Latin America was rooted in the region's colonial period.

Moreover, because of the skewed distribution of income, demand patterns of final production were determined by a few powerful groups, a minority of individuals with comparatively high purchasing power. The new-Marxist group therefore prescribed redistributive policies to address growing inequality and to increase domestic demand.

As of the time of writing, redistributive policies have been vigorously revisited in the context of high income inequalities in contemporary Latin America under free trade. Thomas Piketty has revived the debate.[34] His dataset includes three Latin American countries: Colombia, Argentina, and Uruguay. We will return to the income inequality issue recurrently throughout this book, particularly in chapter 5.

3.3.3 Adjustments to the ISI Strategy

ISI promoters were receptive to criticisms. In particular, the growing balance of payment problems resulting from endemic scarcity of foreign exchange on the one hand and the small size of the domestic market on the other led policy makers to launch trade-integration initiatives, with the Latin American Free Trade

Association (LAFTA) created in 1961. However, this initiative was ineffective, mostly because of powerful lobbies. Nascent industrialists had been benefiting from heavy protection and fiercely resisted change.

In 1969, a subset of LAFTA members established the Andean Pact, a custom union among Argentina, Bolivia, Chile, Colombia, Ecuador, Peru, and Venezuela. This agreement dismantled trade barriers among member countries and allocated manufacturing activities to each member in an ad hoc manner. The main objective of the Andean Pact was to avoid duplication and exploit economies of scale regionally. The common external tariff for nonmembers was too high, however, and the main protectionist distortions continued to hurt the region's economies.

Efforts to expand market size were accompanied by attempts to relax capital inflows. Because the savings rate in Latin American economies was and continues to be low relative to that in Asia, foreign savings were required to meet the shortage of funds for investment. Instead of opting to provide incentives for FDI to fill the savings gap, governments were able to increase sovereign indebtedness via multilateral institutions, and, years on, via foreign commercial banks. This strategy reflected unresolved debt negotiations with foreign bondholders, which dated back to the 1930s sovereign defaults, and private sector fears of expropriation. We will come back to twentieth-century sovereign defaults and expropriations in chapters 4 and 6, respectively.

Brazil By the mid-1960s, the balance of payment crises had already become recurrent and difficult to address. It was then that the first attempts to break with traditional ISI policies started to emerge. Under the ministry of Roberto Campos in 1965, Brazil launched a program of economic reforms focused on export promotion. One policy measure set up a *crawling peg* exchange rate system, which could potentially control inflation and avoid excessive overvaluations.[35] Most export taxes were eliminated, and a series of tax incentives, cheap credits, and subsidies for export activities were enacted. In addition, stabilization efforts were made to control inflation amid attempts to develop local financial markets.

The Campos policies enabled manufacturing exports to expand strongly, replacing coffee as the main Brazilian export product. Thus, as of the mid-1960s, export-led strategies revitalized the nascent Brazilian industry. From 1966 to 1970, the Brazilian manufacturing sector grew at an average rate of 10.2 percent per annum.

Brazilian pioneering policies not only reduced the antiexport bias embedded in the ISI strategy but also sowed the first seeds of the 1965–1979 Brazilian miracle, during which the economy grew at an average rate of 7.5 percent, with a "golden age" concentrated around the 1968–1973 period. During this period, per capita GDP averaged an unprecedented 10.1 percent per annum, which is very high indeed relative to that in neighboring countries (see table 3.3).

The Brazilian reforms did not completely dismantle the ISI apparatus, however. Instead, the reforms took place in parallel to ISI policies. During the 1970s, for example, Brazil embarked on a new ISI venture via the promotion of primary commodity industrial inputs of production—for example, steel and petrochemicals—in order to contribute to the expansion of infrastructure and exports. However, such a policy mix led to intermediate imports of production growing at a considerably faster pace than that of exports. Current account deficits therefore ensued.

The Brazilian current account deficits were financed through massive foreign borrowing. The expectation was that the combination of ISI policies and export promotion would eventually transform current account deficits into surpluses, which would allow the Brazilian government to service its foreign currency–denominated debt. This never happened, as we will discuss in chapter 4, and Brazil, along with a dozen other Latin American countries, succumbed to yet another debt crisis in 1982.[36]

Colombia Brazil was not the only country that made attempts to mend the ISI strategy. Colombia suffered a balance of payment crisis in 1966. The crisis was linked to foreign exchange shortages due to plummeting international prices of coffee, Colombia's main export product at the time. In 1967, the Colombian government launched a series of policies to stimulate exports without abandoning ISI, in expectation that the industries supported by this strategy would become profitable. The excessive dependence on coffee made policy makers realize the need to diversify Colombia's export base, which led to the creation of ProExpo, a government institution responsible for promoting nontraditional exports. Other mechanisms to stimulate exports were also adopted, such as tax credit certificates (which refunded a percentage of FOB value to exporting companies), simplified requirements for temporary imports, and subsidized credit to exporters. In addition, the average tariff level was reduced and the previous licensing regime for the export of many products dismantled.[37]

Colombia also shifted from a complicated system of multiple exchange rates—which was the rule rather than the exception under ISI policies in Latin America—to a unified system, which eliminated a great deal of confusion and distortions. Like Brazil, Colombia adopted a crawling peg system, which attempted to limit the scope for exchange rate overvaluations.

The reforms introduced by the Colombian government paid off. Export profitability increased, especially in the manufacturing industry, which grew at an average of 7.8 percent per year between 1967 and 1974. Per capita GDP growth rates averaged 6.1 percent during that same period. From 1975 onward, however, the focus shifted to stabilization as inflation rates increased following the oil shock of 1973 on the one hand and the sharp acceleration of aggregate demand following the coffee boom resulting from the coffee frost in Brazil on the other. Ultimately, austerity measures had to be set up. In particular, Colombia had to cut public spending and tighten monetary policy. These policies put an end to the period of high growth under Colombia's modified ISI model. Against this backdrop, and unlike Brazil and other Latin American countries, Colombia did not experience a debt crisis in the 1980s. Whether the reforms to its own ISI model played a role remains an open question. We will return to the 1980s debt crisis in chapter 4.

Chile In Chile, after the failed attempt to stabilize inflation during the Alessandri government (1958–1964), the Frei administration (1964–1970) adopted a crawling peg exchange rate system as well. The system targeted nominal exchange rate adjustments to correct for domestic and international inflation rate differentials. The Chilean crawling peg allowed a reduction in residual uncertainty faced by exporters. Moreover, a "drawback system" was introduced and import tariffs were reduced thanks to high revenues from copper, Chile's main export product.[38] These two policies somewhat mitigated the ISI antiexport bias.

Mexico Starting in 1971, Mexico followed in the steps of Brazil, Colombia, and Chile. In particular, the Mexican government under the Echeverria administration (1970–1976) implemented export-oriented reforms. These reforms included a reduction of trade barriers (especially for industrial inputs), the dispersion of tariffs, and the enactment of direct export subsidies and subsidized credit to export-oriented industries. Manufacturing exports were stimulated for some years, but inflation rates increased, and the need for price stabilization forced the government to suspend its export promotion program in the mid-1970s.

In contemporary Latin America, Brazil, Mexico, Chile, and Colombia reintroduced crawling peg exchange rates to combat inflation in the 1980s and 1990s. These four countries also pioneered inflation-targeting central banks, which in the twenty-first century have become a model for effectively containing inflationary spirals while keeping floating exchange rates in order to avoid currency crises. We will return to inflation targeting and exchange rates in chapters 6, 7, and 8.

The 1970s In the early 1970s, Latin America suffered from high inflation rates and growing balance of payments problems. Disenchantment with the ISI model increased. It also emerged—with the benefit of hindsight—that after two decades of ISI policies, Latin American countries had not caught up with the standards of living of the industrialized world. On the contrary, and as we have already mentioned, the income gap had increased: average per capita GDP growth between

1961 and 1970 was 2.5 percent per annum in Latin America; in comparison, it had reached 3 percent worldwide.

Moreover, as we also highlighted earlier, other emerging market economies performed considerably better than Latin America even when post–World War II growth prospects in such economies were less bright. As shown in figure 3.5, the Asian Tigers took off steadily during the 1960s. Their per capita GDPs increased at an average rate of 6.4 percent per annum, a growth rate nearly three times higher than the average for the entire Latin American region during that same period.

The 1970s was also a period of diverse trajectories within the region. Although the role of the state in economic activity increased in several Latin American countries, state intervention decreased in others. The military regimes that came to power in Chile and Uruguay in 1973 and in Argentina in 1976 gave a final blow to the ISI strategy in these countries. The new governments began a series of reforms set up to reduce inflation, liberalize trade, and decrease state intervention in production processes. Chile moved more radically toward a free market approach, Uruguay did so to a lesser degree, and Argentina made timid and uncoordinated efforts.

With such reforms in place, one might be led to believe that the three nineteenth-century stellar performers would have returned to a pre-1914 economic prosperity period. Despite their efforts to dismantle excessive protection via reduced import barriers, however, export taxes, real exchange rate appreciations, and high inflation continued. These countries used the exchange rate as a stabilization tool, which proved incompatible with the simultaneous introduction of other policies (expansionary fiscal policies in particular), leading to sharp real exchange rate appreciation, deterioration of export performance, and consequential current account deficits. The failed stabilization efforts in these three economies left them exceedingly vulnerable to the debt crisis of the 1980s, which we will analyze in greater detail in chapter 4.

3.4 Toward a New Consensus

Some analysts have argued that the policies of state-led industrialization contributed to the robust growth of Latin America from 1940 to 1970.[39] This is partially correct, especially during the "easy phase" of ISI. However, the evidence is clear on the demise of the ISI model that came about at the onset of the Latin American debt crisis in 1982. As will be explained in greater detail in chapter 4, East Asia performed considerably better than Latin America. East Asia was relatively unaffected by the world financial crisis of the 1980s, which started in the early 1980s under the Reagan and Thatcher administrations in the United States and the

United Kingdom, respectively. Asian countries, despite pursuing somewhat interventionist policies, did not default on their foreign obligations. Thus, the eyes of most scholars turned to East Asia. Many attempted to investigate the differences between the two regions. What factors contributed to the seemingly superior performance of the East Asian Tigers? With the benefit of hindsight, there is now a broad consensus on the differences between the two regions.

First, East Asia had a significantly lower degree of protectionism. Although almost all the East Asian nations went through a first phase of import substitution, by the early 1960s most economies in this region rejected the ISI strategy as a vehicle for economic development and prosperity. Some trade barriers were maintained, but they were much lower and more selective than those of their Latin American counterparts.

Second, East Asia followed an export promotion strategy. As these countries focused on providing incentives to exports, overvalued exchange rates largely were avoided. At the same time, East Asian countries consistently granted credit subsidies and tax incentives to exporters and provided adequate infrastructure financed by FDI and domestic savings. Against this backdrop and unlike Latin America, East Asia avoided recurrent balance of payments crises.

Third, a stable macroeconomic environment in East Asia was the norm rather than the exception. In Latin America, it was common to see large fiscal deficits, high inflation, and balance of payments crises. In East Asia, economic development was based on fiscal prudence and low and stable inflation rates.

Fourth, East Asia imposed fewer controls and regulations. It aimed at facilitating administrative procedures and maintaining a low level of bureaucracy for exporters of manufactures and for producers in general. In addition, labor markets were far more flexible in Asia. Strong labor unions and wage rigidity inhibited job creation in Latin America. Moreover, wage rigidity in highly unionized urban areas created a growing informal sector, exacerbated by massive rural-urban migration as a result of a heavily penalized agricultural sector. Such an informal sector continues to contribute to massive pockets of poverty today, an exceedingly delicate issue of utmost importance that we will explain in greater detail in chapter 5.

Finally, the role of multilateral institutions such as the IMF and the World Bank was another ingredient for consolidation of the new consensus against the ISI strategy. As noted by Edwards (1995), such institutions influenced economic views in Latin America through empirical research, sector analysis, policy dialogue, and conditional lending. Most studies advocated trade liberalization along with outward-oriented policies to promote economic development. These studies were particularly relevant to draw lessons for Eastern European economies after the fall of the Berlin Wall in 1989.

Evidence from international organizations is conclusive. It reveals that a greater degree of openness is associated positively with higher rates of economic growth.⁴⁰ The influence of multilateral institutions went beyond research and dialogue, however; loans granted by the Bretton Woods institutions (particularly the IMF loans) to Latin American countries established strict conditionality on trade liberalization, stabilization, and privatization—the three pillars of the market-oriented reforms that shaped the region's fate in the twenty-first century.

Chile was a case of an early reformer. By the mid-1970s, long before the market-oriented reforms had swept the entire Latin American region, the Chilean government under the military dictatorship of Augusto Pinochet began to unfold an aggressive trade liberalization agenda. When democracy returned in 1990, the Aylwin government counted fervent opponents of the military regime among its ranks. The markets were nervous; it was feared that the new, center-left government would reverse the reforms initiated under the Pinochet regime. However, this did not happen.

The new democratic government legitimized the free market model and, in particular, trade liberalization. At the same time, it maintained and strengthened market-friendly reforms.⁴¹ Such continuity of the market-oriented reforms, which Chile started much before its neighbors did, led to the so-called Chilean golden age of growth between 1986 and 1997, when the economy grew at an average of 7.6 percent per year. Chile, despite its ISI background, rose close to the ranks of East Asian high performers.

ECLAC members themselves recognized the need for reform to the development model in the rest of the region. Some senior members of ECLAC began advocating a shift in economic policy agendas. As Bianchi, Devlin, and Ramos (1987) noted: "The debt problem requires a structural transformation of the economy in at least two ways. First, the growth strategy needs to be outward-oriented. Second, it must be based on a domestic effort to raise savings and productivity." We will analyze the debt problem and the strategies that Bianchi and his colleagues alluded to in chapter 4.

Finally, recent trends in commodity prices seem to revert the downward trend started in the 1980s (see figure 3.6). If sustained, this could lead to a new paradigm, which can potentially prove the Prebisch-Singer predictions wrong. Note that the reversal started in the twenty-first century, as China's weight in the world economy increased significantly. China's slowdown since 2012 has had a significant effect in lowering commodity prices from their peaks—though most are still considerably higher than at the start of the so-called commodity supercycle circa 2004. The extraordinary eruption of China in the world economy has been accompanied by a heartening and major reduction of poverty rates worldwide. We will discuss

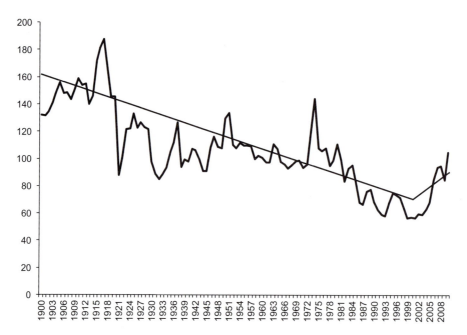

Figure 3.6
Commodity price index deflated by manufacturing value index, the trade-weighted price index of five main industrialized countries' (France, Germany, Japan, the United States, and the United Kingdom) exports of manufactures to developing countries, 1990–2008.
Source: Grilli and Yang 1988; see also http://www.stephan-pfaffenzeller.com/cpi.html.

poverty and income inequality in contemporary Latin America in greater detail in chapter 5.

3.5 Concluding Remarks

In this chapter, we have emphasized the meager performance of Latin America under a protectionist paradigm. The Great Depression of the 1930s set the stage for government intervention in trade and exchange rate protectionist policies known as ISI policies. A brief interlude of trade openness stopped after World War II, when Latin America thought that it potentially could live in autarky.

Against this background, exposing itself to a fluctuating international environment under export-led growth and reverting to the primary commodity export-led growth strategy of the nineteenth century was perceived as risky at best and detrimental to industrialization at worst. ISI policies seemed like a better venue for achieving self-sufficiency in the production of manufactures and industrial goods and for diversifying production and trade patterns, which had a persistent bias in favor of relatively low-productivity primary commodities.

Protectionism under ISI left indelible legacies. First, the structure of the Latin American economy changed radically, from primary commodity production with landed aristocracy as the main beneficiaries of export promotion to an emerging class of industrialists lobbying for continued protection. Nascent industry was inefficient, mostly because it was never fully exposed to international competition. Early reforms to the ISI model in Brazil, Chile, Colombia, and Mexico merit attention for future research, particularly in the area of exchange rate regimes and inflation-targeting central banks. We will return to this topic recurrently in chapters 6, 7, 8, and 9.

Contemporary Latin America remains underindustrialized relative to Asia. This gives food for thought on the perils of excessive protection. Although the role of the state has been redefined, persistent intervention can be invasive in some countries—such as Venezuela and Argentina, two countries that we will analyze in greater detail in chapter 6.

Redefining the role of the state in Latin America within the new globalized world requires some thought on three fundamental issues: First, the protectionist era created a tiny yet powerful blue-collar middle class, both in the private sector and in SOEs. Triggered by high levels of investment in recent decades, its size has grown and it remains powerful. Reforms to SOEs, mostly natural monopolies, can be challenging, because powerful unions oppose private sector participation and exposure to international competition. Second, the protectionist policies did not address persistent income inequalities that date back to the colonial period and were later exacerbated during the region's belle époque. Although the acuteness of poverty has been mitigated by high growth and antipoverty campaigns in recent decades, lowering income disparities and reducing poverty remains one of the region's most important challenges in the twenty-first century. Third, investment in infrastructure was neglected during the protectionist period. This was partly due to low savings rates, low levels of FDI, and the sovereign defaults dating back to the Great Depression. Persistent underinvestment in infrastructure—roads, railways, health, and education—further delays industrialization and economic growth. Long-term investments in infrastructure—inclusive of investments in health and education—do not seem to be prioritized by most governments in the region's nascent democracies. This shortsighted strategy in Latin America can hinder long-term growth and might well be at the root of ongoing political unrest.

Summary
- In contrast with the open-trade policies it followed in the nineteenth century, twentieth-century Latin America has been predominantly a protectionist region.

- The Great Depression in the 1930s had a devastating impact: trade flows decreased, growth slowed down considerably, and unemployment increased. During this period, Latin America experienced one of its worst balance of payments crises ever, which eventually led to the abandonment of the fixed exchange rate system under the gold standard.
- The Great Depression also led to Latin American regions' default on their foreign obligations vis-à-vis bondholders. These obligations were eventually restructured, and it was not until the late 1960s that Latin America finally repaid its sharply reduced foreign obligations. Overall, the early 1930s marked a forty-year period of isolation from private capital inflows.
- The Great Depression was followed by World War II, which further exposed Latin America's vulnerability to cyclical output and demand for primary commodities swings that originated in the United States and Europe.
- Recognizing the perils of excessive reliance on primary commodities, the Latin American governments after World War II launched a set of protectionist policies in order to trigger industrialization via ISI tools, underscoring state intervention in nearly all spheres of production activities. Such antiexport tools penalized agriculture and generated X-inefficiencies in nascent manufacturing and industrial production.
- The countries negatively affected by protectionist ideology and policy included the nineteenth-century stellar performers, Argentina, Uruguay, and Chile. These three countries were superseded by Brazil and Mexico—the region's largest economies—in terms of per capita GDP.
- Mexico's landed aristocracy disappeared starting in the early twentieth century as a result of the 1910 Mexican Revolution, and a new industrialist class emerged in the north. Brazil introduced a series of reforms aimed at boosting exports in the 1960s. These reforms to the ISI model partly explain the 1965 to 1979 Brazilian miracle, during which the economy of Brazil grew at an average rate of about 7 percent per annum.
- A crawling peg exchange rate system was implemented to mitigate the antiexport bias in some countries. The system partially succeeded: it avoided large currency overvaluations and balance of payment crises.
- Relative to Asia, Latin America performed poorly during the ISI period. One main reason was the scope and extent of state intervention. Unlike Latin America, state intervention was biased in favor of exports and allowed for domestic firms to be exposed to foreign competition.
- The ISI model was severely shaken in the 1980s when all Latin American countries could not honor their foreign currency–denominated debts contracted with foreign commercial banks in the 1970s.

Review Questions

1. How did World War I affect Latin American economies?
2. Explain the defining features of Latin America during the Great Depression and after, up to the early 1970s. What was the rationale for implementing protectionist policies after World War II?
3. What were the main propositions of the Prebisch—Singer protectionist paradigm?
4. Briefly explain five salient features of ISI policies in Latin America.
5. What were the main perils of ISI policies in practice?
6. What are the main ideological criticisms against the ISI protectionist paradigm?
7. Why did large economies such as Mexico and Brazil perform well compared to smaller ones, and why was within-region trade integration not helpful for smaller economies?
8. Comment on the merits of the following statement: "A reformed ISI model explains the Brazilian miracle."
9. In what way did the coffee frost in Brazil affect the economy of Colombia, and what type of exchange rate policy was implemented in order to avoid a balance of payment crisis?
10. Why did Latin America under ISI underperform relative to Asia?
11. Recurrent balance of payments crises were the rule rather than the exception under ISI. Explain why.
12. Explain the advantages and disadvantages of privatizing SOEs in the aftermath of the ISI period in the 1980s and beyond.

Further Reading

For a comprehensive and in-depth analysis of ISI in Latin America before and after World War II, the main consequences, and the collapse of the ISI model of economic development in Latin America, see Baer 1972. See also Harberger 1970. With the benefit of hindsight, Braga (2010) delivers an excellent review of Baer's contribution. He pins down academic debate on import substitution, sheds further light on the Brazilian experience, and spells out the post-ISI policies focusing on the reasons why trade liberalization did not deliver the expected stellar results in terms of economic growth.

4 Debt Crises and the Lost Decade

In the previous chapter, we argued that the meager performance of Latin America's exports during the Great Depression changed the region's development strategy. Twentieth-century Latin America reverted to protectionism via the implementation of ISI policies.

Back in the 1930s, and as a result of the Great Depression, Latin America found itself unable to repay its foreign currency–denominated debts. Most nations—with the notable exception of Argentina—defaulted during the interwar period. This is not surprising; Argentina was by far the region's most advanced economy in the early twentieth century. Its growth prospects were just as bright as those of the now-industrialized countries and are often compared with those of Australia and Canada.[1]

In all other countries, nineteenth-century defaults were cyclical, intermittent, and followed by rapid settlements. In contrast, sovereign defaults triggered by the Great Depression were prolonged and imposed severe penalties in terms of Latin America's exclusion from international borrowing for decades.[2]

After the Great Depression, Latin America was not able to return to the international capital markets for four consecutive decades. During the 1970s, Latin America could borrow again quite heavily—but these sovereign loans were defaulted upon in the 1980s.

Interesting work by Reinhart and Rogoff (2009) suggests that the two twentieth-century defaults—those of the Great Depression and those of the 1980s—bear an eerie resemblance. In both instances, macroeconomic policies and disturbing episodes in the main financial centers of industrialized nations were contributing factors of utmost importance. The sovereign defaults of the 1930s were largely due to the Great Depression, started in the United States; those in the 1980s were due to the sudden change in the world macroeconomic environment, sharp interest rate increases, and falling export revenues resulting from industrialized countries' recessions.

In this chapter we emphasize that, compared to the twentieth-century defaults, Latin America was much less affected by the recent twenty-first century financial crises, which also started in industrialized nations. The main question we will ask is this: How vulnerable is contemporary Latin America to a sudden change in the world macroeconomy? In particular, what will be the long-term effects on Latin America of the recent slowdown in China?

In section 4.1 of this chapter, we briefly review the financial crises episodes that preceded the Great Depression defaults. Section 4.2 explains the 1930s debt crisis in great detail in order to shed light on the protracted period of isolation, which was followed by a wild period of international overborrowing in the 1970s. In section 4.3, we analyze the 1980s debt crisis and its consequences. Section 4.4 delivers an overview of crisis episodes in the 1990s and their distinguishing characteristics, focusing on contagion in an increasingly globalized world, and section 4.5 focuses on the twenty-first-century world financial crises in industrialized countries. Unlike previous episodes, the latest crises had a negligible impact on contemporary Latin American economies. We provide a summary and conclusions in section 4.6.

4.1 Background

Nineteenth-century independence from the Iberian Peninsula enabled Latin American nations to contract loans in London—the main financial center at the time.[3] The Monroe Doctrine of 1824 was a contributing factor. It implicitly guaranteed that the United States would fend off a counterattack by transatlantic nations on Latin American countries. This reassured inward foreign investors, which was important at that particular point in time. It is therefore no coincidence that the first nineteenth-century foreign loans contracted by Mexico, for example, date back to that same Monroe Doctrine year—that is, 1824.

Typically, nineteenth-century loans contracted after 1824 were long-term bonds sold in London and had a thirty-year maturity period. The Latin American bonds were contracted at an approximate 6.5 percentage point risk premium. In comparison, the return on relatively safe British consols was 3 percent per annum, whereas the return on Latin American bonds was approximately 9.5 percent.[4]

Debt renegotiations were not new. Most Latin American countries defaulted on their nineteenth-century bonds because of political instability and internal wars in the region. Defaults were renegotiated on a case-by-case basis. Foreign creditors at times accepted losing up to 50 percent or more on the face value of their loans. Remaining sovereign debt was repaid at a considerably lower interest rate. For example, after debt reduction, the remaining Mexican debt—which had been on default throughout the entire 1827–1851 period—was repaid at 3 percent per annum instead of at the 9.5 percent that the original loan contract specified.

Once the Latin American countries had repaid their restructured debts, they were able to return to the international capital markets. In particular, most of the region's nations borrowed heavily during the region's belle époque (1870–1914). Unlike previous loans, which were used to finance internal wars, belle époque loans were mostly utilized for investment in infrastructure. Railway construction to connect hinterlands with seaports was often prioritized. These investments were short-lived, however, due to the outbreak of World War I in 1914. Major trade disruptions prompted a vast majority of Latin American countries to default on their foreign obligations.

Latin America subsequently could borrow in the 1920s in the United States. Simultaneously, all the belle époque loans were partially renegotiated. Unlike previous bilateral renegotiations between Latin American countries and their European creditors, renegotiation and debt restructurings during the 1920s were led by the US Department of State, which had established a consortium of Latin American creditors. However, restructured foreign obligations were defaulted upon at the onset of the Great Depression in 1929. Nonetheless, and despite the consortium of creditors, some Latin American countries successfully negotiated sharp debt reductions.

4.2 The 1930s Debt Crisis

Figure 4.1 illustrates the tremendous impact that the 1929–1933 Great Depression had on Latin America.[5] Despite previous debt restructurings in the early 1920s, which involved debt reductions of up to 70 percent with the remaining debt to be repaid at considerably lower interest rates, foreign debt to export ratios grew drastically, from 1.4 in 1926 to 4.5 in 1932.

Under the auspices of the US Department of State, the Bondholders Protective Council Corporation was created in 1934. The main mandate of the corporation was to renegotiate all outstanding Latin American debt on behalf of the region's foreign creditors/bondholders. The corporation first attempted to sign short-term agreements as a stepping-stone to long-term settlements. However, only Costa Rica and Brazil signed those agreements between 1936 and 1939. The outbreak of

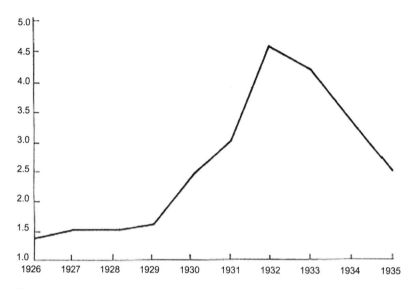

Figure 4.1
Latin America's debt to export ratios, 1926–1935 (US$).
Source: Authors' calculations from Foreign Bondholders Protective Council 1936.

World War II in 1939 made it impossible for the council and other Latin American countries to sign similar settlements.

Export surpluses during World War II enabled Latin American nations to renegotiate permanent repayments on restructured debt with the council. The council was, in principle, opposed to further reductions on the face value of the outstanding Latin American debt. But the council could only recommend not prevent bondholders from accepting offers from sovereign country borrowers involving debt reductions. Successful renegotiations took place from 1940 to 1954. By 1957, only 11 percent of the total outstanding Latin American foreign debt remained in default.

Most Latin American nations had a great deal of bargaining power thanks to their multiplicity of foreign creditors/bondholders acting in an uncoordinated fashion, and the council could only recommend, not act on bondholders' behalf. For example, Chile, Colombia, and Mexico—extended take-it-or-leave-it offers to their creditors. These offers involved considerable face value reductions, and the council, with its strong opposition to such reductions, recommended all Chilean, Colombian, and Mexican creditors not to take those offers. However, foreign bondholders acting independently turned a blind eye to the council's recommendations.

The first country to extend a take-it-or-leave-it offer was Chile in 1935. The offer involved sharp debt reductions on already restructured debt.[6] By 1946, 91 percent of Chilean bondholders had sold their obligations at reduced market prices. The remaining 9 percent never did.

Colombia was next, in 1941.[7] This offer was also fiercely opposed by the council. Only three years later, 90 percent of Colombian bondholders nonetheless had accepted the offer, and by 1945, 100 percent of Colombian foreign creditors had sold their debts at 50 percent of face value.

In 1942, Mexico extended an 80 percent reduced face value offer to all its foreign bondholders.[8] Again, despite the council's strong opposition, 89 percent of Mexico's creditors sold their debts to the Mexican government within the next sixteen years.

By the early 1960s, nearly all Latin American restructured debt had been repaid. Yet it was not until a decade later that Latin America could borrow again in the international financial markets. Thus, contracting long-term debt from private foreign creditors was not possible for Latin American countries for several decades, from the 1930s to the 1970s. Much-needed investments in infrastructure projects were delayed or stalled as a result. This was indeed one of the most severe legacies of the Great Depression debt crisis on Latin America.

After World War II, the World Bank and other multilateral institutions extended long-term loans for infrastructure, but the volume of such loans was comparatively small as the World Bank had other priorities—such as reconstruction of war-torn European nations. Contemporary Latin American economies still struggle today to modernize and expand infrastructure in several areas, such as highways, ports, airports, and railways.

4.3 The 1980s Debt Crisis

Historically, the onset of the debt crisis dates back to August 1982, when Mexico declared a moratorium on the servicing of its external obligations.[9] Relative to previous crises, the nature of these sovereign obligations had changed, however. Specifically, the owners of most Latin American debt were mostly a dozen commercial banks in the industrialized world. The Mexican announcement therefore threatened the world financial system and marked the beginning of a decade of crisis for Latin America. The causes of this decade-long crisis are now well understood. These causes fall into three categories: first, the oil shocks of the 1970s; second, the sudden changes in the world macroeconomy in the early 1980s; and third, inappropriate policies in the borrowing countries that had taken a protectionist stand under ISI.

The connection between the oil shocks and debt accumulation of the 1970s in the market for loans has supply and demand explanations. On the supply side, the oil price hikes in 1973 and 1979 created current account surpluses in oil-producing countries. These surpluses were labeled *petrodollars* and were made available for financial intermediation by the industrialized countries' commercial banks. On the demand side, the Latin American countries were eager to borrow at low interest rates. In addition, non-oil exporters borrowed for consumption-smoothing reasons, because these countries had been adversely affected by the hike in oil prices.

As had been previously the case back in the 1930s, the abrupt changes in the international macroeconomic environment in the early 1980s precipitated a crisis. In the early 1980s, Latin America experienced a sudden increase in interest rates due to tight monetary policies in the United States on the one hand and a rapid fall in export revenues due to the world's 1980s recession on the other.

As table 4.1 shows, the interbank interest rate (Libor) in real terms increased by approximately 28 percentage points from 1979 to 1982. The rate of change of export unit prices first increased by approximately 21 percentage points in 1980 and 1981, and then fell by nearly 24 percentage points from 21.2 in 1980 to -2.8 in 1981, and by a further 11 percentage points in 1982.

Table 4.1
Interest rates and export price changes, 1972–1986

Year	Nominal LIBOR	Rate of change in export unit prices	Real LIBOR
1972	5.4	9.2	-3.5
1973	9.3	33	-17.8
1974	11.2	57.5	-29.4
1975	7.6	-5.7	14.1
1976	6.1	8.1	-1.9
1977	6.4	10.6	-3.8
1978	8.3	-3.7	12.5
1979	12	21	-7.4
1980	14.2	21.2	-5.8
1981	16.5	-2.8	19.9
1982	13.3	-11.2	27.6
1983	9.8	-6.5	17.4
1984	11.2	2.6	8.4
1985	8.6	0.6	8.0
1986	6.7	-12.7	22.2

Source: Larraín and Sachs 1993.

Table 4.2
Latin American countries' vulnerability estimates in 1980

Country	Debt at floating rates	Interest (payments/exports)
Argentina	58.3	15.1
Brazil	64.3	28.3
Colombia	39.2	16.3
Chile	58.2	28.2
Mexico	73.0	19.0
Peru	28.0	19.8
Venezuela	81.4	10.4
All Latin America	64.5	28.0

Source: Larraín and Sachs 1993.

The two effects combined—that is, higher interest rates and lower export revenues—had a drastic impact on the cost of servicing foreign currency-denominated debts. How could Latin America possibly cope with higher cost of servicing its foreign debt in the advent of adverse changes in the world macroeconomy?

Some Latin American countries were more vulnerable than others. As indicated in table 4.2, relative to the average for the region, Mexico and Venezuela—the regions' two main oil exporters at the time—had a higher percentage of their foreign debts contracted at "floating" or variable interest rates. The interest payments to exports ratios were highest in Brazil and Chile, however, because these two countries had high debt to exports ratios at the start of the crisis. Unsurprisingly, these two countries also defaulted on their external obligations in the early 1980s.

The only Latin American country in the sample that did not default was Colombia. Yet all Latin American countries (Colombia included) suffered just as much in terms of GDP growth, because they had no access to international borrowing and had to engage in costly structural reforms. We discuss these reforms ahead.

The recessionary effects of the 1980s debt crisis were particularly severe in 1983, when GDP growth was negative. There was a moderate recovery from 1984 to 1987, followed by a decline during the last years of what came to be known as twentieth-century Latin America's "lost decade," or, simply, the lost decade.

In 1990, Latin America's per capita GDP relative to that of high-income economies was 9 percent lower than that in 1980 and 23 percent lower relative to the world's average. The scope for Latin America to catch up with the standards of living in industrialized nations was severely shattered throughout the region's lost decade.

Table 4.3
Capital flows, 1974–1990

Year	Net capital inflows	Net payments of profits and interest	Net transfer of resources
1974	11.4	5	6.4
1975	14.3	5.6	8.7
1976	17.9	6.8	11.1
1977	17.2	8.2	9.0
1978	26.2	10.2	16.0
1979	29.1	13.6	15.5
1980	32	18.9	13.1
1981	39.8	28.5	11.3
1982	20.1	38.8	-18.7
1983	2.9	34.5	-31.6
1984	10.4	37.3	-26.9
1985	3	35.3	-32.3
1986	9.9	32.7	-22.8
1987	15.1	31.4	-16.3
1988	5.5	34.3	-28.8
1989	10.1	37.4	-27.3
1990	17.9	36.8	-18.9
Total 1974–1981	187.9	96.8	91.1
Total 1982–1990	94.9	318.5	-223.6

Source: Larraín and Sachs 1993.

Another way of measuring the extent of the crisis in the 1980s is via measures of capital inflows into traditionally low-saving Latin American regions. As indicated in table 4.3, net capital inflows during Latin America's lost decade were half those of the previous decade in the 1970s. Net payments of profits and interest tripled, and the net resource transfer between Latin America and the rest of the world was negative.

How does Latin America compare to Asia? In the previous chapter, we discussed the perils of Latin America's ISI policies, but the failure of protectionism became blatant as the entire world witnessed that the sudden interest rate hike and world recession in the 1980s had a mild impact on Asia's economies compared to the impact it had on Latin America's economies. The main differences between the two regions centered on the pro-export policies in Asia and Asian exposure of domestic firms to foreign competition.

Table 4.4
Openness in Latin America and East Asia

	Trade regime*	Exports of goods and services (as % of GDP)
Latin America		
Argentina	1	15
Peru	1	22
Colombia	2	15
Costa Rica	2	32
Mexico	2	16
Brazil	3	14
Chile	3	29
Uruguay	3	25
Average	2.1	21
East Asia		
Indonesia	2	23
Philippines	2	22
Korea	4	36
Malaysia	3	55
Thailand	3	27
Hong Kong	4	106
Singapore	4	129
Average	3.1	56.9

Source: World Bank 1987.

Table 4.4 shows the degree of openness in Latin American economies relative to selected Asian countries as proxied by trade regimes. According to the World Bank classification, the Asian trade regime was, on average, one point higher on a 1 to 4 scale during the 1973–1985 period. Throughout this same period, exports as a percentage of GDP were more than twice as high in Asia.

The 1980s debt crisis came to an end in the early 1990s, when most countries in Latin America embraced market-oriented reforms and signed permanent agreements involving debt restructuring with a consortium of commercial banks. This time, it was not the Bondholders' Protective Council but the International Monetary Fund (IMF) that acted as a coordinating agency. Debt restructurings involved *debt rescheduling*, or postponed repayments at a reduced face value under the so-called Brady Plan—a debt-forgiveness program.[10]

In parallel, a large number of countries bought back their debts at reduced market prices via various schemes, ranging from direct buybacks to debt-for-equity swaps.[11] Direct buybacks at reduced market prices were not new, as noted in the previous section on Chile, Colombia, and Mexico's bond purchases following the 1930s Great Depression debt crisis.

4.4 Another Wave of Crises

On a positive note, one of the main legacies of the lost decade in Latin America during the 1980s was a series of structural reforms. These reforms swept the region with a wave of globalization, characterized by growing trade flows, increased capital flows, technology transfer, and private sector crowding in via mass privatization and deregulation.

Trade liberalization and privatization were only two components of the three pillars of market-oriented reforms in the 1980s and 1990s; the third was stabilization. Once Latin American countries had returned to foreign borrowing in the early 1990s, the region simultaneously attempted to consolidate price stabilization via maintaining fixed or semifixed exchange rate regimes.

4.4.1 Mexico, Brazil, and Argentina in the 1990s

As the region experienced high inflation rates, most governments experimented with various stabilization policies. In this section, our chronological analysis is confined to three Latin American countries' experiences: Mexico, Brazil, and Argentina—the region's three major economies. One common feature was that these three countries implemented exchange rate–based stabilization policies.[12]

Mexico After a period of massive privatization of large, small, and medium state-owned enterprises (SOEs) and deregulation, Mexico's trade liberalization policies included an ambitious plan to become a trade partner of the North American Free Trade Agreement (NAFTA) with the United States and Canada. Simultaneously, Mexico managed to finalize debt-restructuring agreements with its foreign creditors in 1989.

As of 1991, foreign inflows had increased steadily. They took the form of FDI and portfolio flows. A substantial amount of such flows consisted of foreign currency–denominated debts to finance private firms' expansion. As table 4.5 shows, portfolio investment liabilities increased steadily from 1989 to 1993.

Capital inflows, in general, found their way into the newly privatized banking sector, which lacked adequate *prudential regulation*. The main objective of prudential regulation is to ensure that government agencies protect the stability of the financial system and depositors via limiting risk taking and/or setting limits on

Table 4.5
Mexico's balance of payments, 1988–1995 (in billions of US dollars)

	1988	1989	1990	1991	1992	1993	1994	1995
Current account	-2,4	-5,8	-7,5	-14,9	-24,4	-23,4	-29,4	-0,7
Merchandise exports	30,7	35,2	40,7	42,7	46,2	51,9	60,9	79,5
Merchandise imports	-28,1	-34,8	-41,6	-50	-62,1	-65,4	-79,3	-72,5
Trade Balance	2,6	0,4	-0,9	-7,3	-15,9	-13,5	-18,5	7,1
Services (net)	-0,2	-0,7	-2,2	-2,1	-2,7	-2,5	-2,6	0,9
Income (net)	-7.1	-8.1	-8.3	-8.3	-9.2	-11.0	-12.4	-12.6
Net transfers	2.3	2.5	4.0	2.7	3.4	3.6	4.0	4.0
Financial account	-4.5	1.1	8.4	25.1	27.0	33.8	15.8	-11.8
Direct investment (net)	2.0	2.8	2.5	4.7	4.4	4.4	11.0	7.9
Portfolio investment (net)	0.1	-0.7	-4.0	12.1	19.2	28.3	7.6	-10.8
Other investment (net)	-6.7	-2.0	9.9	8.3	3.5	1.1	-2.8	-7.9
Errors and omissions	-3.2	4.5	1.2	-2.3	-0.9	-3.1	-4.0	-2.9
Overall balance (change in reserves)	-10.1	-0.2	2.2	8.0	1.7	7.2	-17.7	-15.3

Source: International Monetary Fund Financial Statistics 1996.

debt/equity ratios. In a vast number of Latin American countries at the time—including Mexico—prudential regulation was impaired by weak accounting standards, poor quality of financial information, and severe shortages of qualified professionals who could assess risk.

Massive capital inflows intermediated by weakly supervised nascent private financial institutions was risky, particularly because the Mexican government had pegged the peso to the dollar in 1988. Shortly after, the peso was allowed to fluctuate within a band, as a part of a "pact" involving the government, the private sector, and the unions. The main objective of the pact was to keep inflation under control.[13]

NAFTA prospects increased capital inflows further, putting pressure on the exchange rate. Inflows were sterilized, however. Nonetheless, the exchange rate remained overvalued, and inflation skyrocketed. As shown in table 4.6, the *exchange rate*—defined as the domestic currency price of foreign goods to domestic goods—was undervalued in 1988 but became overvalued from 1991 to 1994.

Table 4.6
Real exchange rate of the Mexican peso, 1988–1995

	Relative to the United States			Relative to the world	
	CPI based	WPI based	Nominal wage based	CPI based	ULC based
1988	106.3	101.9	126.9	102.3	121.2
1989	107.5	106.6	113.1	102.3	104.8
1990	100.0	100.0	100.0	100.0	100.0
1991	88.4	86.5	83.3	90.3	91.9
1992	80.2	78.0	73.8	83.0	84.8
1993	75.0	72.5	69.5	79.3	83.8
1994	78.6	75.1	73.5	88.0	90.4
1995	134.1	131.5	167.4	-	-

Source: Pill 2002.

The overvalued exchange rate and a series of domestic events (including political unrest in the southern state of Chiapas and the assassination of the PRI Presidential candidate, Luis Donaldo Colosio) triggered a run on Mexico's foreign currency reserves. Consequently, the Mexican peso experienced a sharp devaluation in 1994. Simultaneously, the recently privatized banks became insolvent; most had to be liquidated, and many (except for Banorte) were taken over by foreign banks.

Brazil Brazil also enacted a series of market-friendly reforms. Under the presidency of Fernando Henrique Cardoso in 1994, Brazil tried to tame inflation via a crawling peg exchange rate system. The central bank relaunched the *real*—a currency that had previously circulated. The semifixed exchange rate system, together with the new real and high interest rates, attracted large inflows of FDI. Foreign reserves also increased (see figure 4.2).

Stabilization efforts were successful. Inflation came down from approximately 5,000 percent in 1994 to 1.7 percent in 1998. However, the current account deficit remained persistently high, and foreign reserves dropped considerably from 1996 to 1998 to sustain an overvalued new real. Eventually, investors lost confidence—despite IMF efforts to lend much-needed foreign currency to Brazil to sustain the value of the new real. In 1999, Brazil suffered a major depreciation of its currency as the central bank experienced a run on its foreign reserves, and the new real depreciated by approximately 66 percent against the dollar.[14]

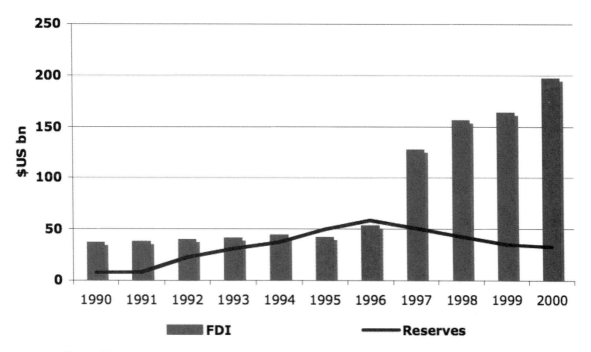

Figure 4.2
Brazil's FDI and foreign reserves, 1990–2000.
Source: Economist intelligence unit in Evangelist and Sathe 2006 (www-personal.umich.edu/~kathrynd/ Brazil.w06.pdf).

Argentina Argentina also engaged in a series of market-friendly economic reforms. In 1991, under the presidency of Carlos Menem, the Argentinean government established a currency board, which consisted of a fixed exchange rate system. Under this system, the Argentinean peso was pegged to the US dollar one-to-one. As in the Mexican and Brazilian experiences, the principal objective of the Argentinean currenc.y board was to lower inflation and keep it under control. The system was successful in that it brought down inflation from about 3,000 percent in 1989 to 3.4 percent in 1994. Moreover, many observers praised the currency board for having resisted contagion from the 1994 Mexican *Tequila* crisis (as the above-mentioned 1994 crisis came to be known), the 1997 East Asian crisis, the 1998 Russian crisis, and the 1999 Brazilian crisis.[15] However, GDP started to contract in 1999 alongside sharp declines in investment and exports (see table 4.7). The current account deficit experienced a tremendous deterioration.

The Argentine convertibility system eventually collapsed in 2001. Although the reasons are still a subject of some debate, no one can deny that output and export

Table 4.7
GDP and various components

	1994	1995	1996	1997	1998	1999	2000	2001
GDP	5.8	-2.8	5.5	8.1	3.9	-3.4	-0.8	-4.5
Private consumption	6.1	-4.4	5.5	9.0	3.5	-2.0	-0.7	-5.8
Public consumption	0.4	0.8	2.2	3.2	3.4	2.6	0.6	-2.1
Investment	13.7	-13.1	8.9	17.7	6.5	-12.6	-6.8	-15.9
Exports	15.3	22.5	7.6	12.2	10.6	-1.3	2.7	2.9
Imports	21.1	-9.8	17.5	26.9	8.4	-11.3	-0.2	-14.0
Export prices	2.9	5.7	6.5	-3.5	-10.4	-11.2	10.2	-3.5

Source: Hausmann and Velasco 2002.

growth prospects as of 1999 created an environment in which investors feared that the Argentine debt, which had been denominated in convertible pesos and therefore dollars, could not be serviced, because export growth was meager and the Argentinean central bank lacked the foreign reserves that were needed to sustain full convertibility under its completely fixed exchange rate regime where the Argentinean peso was overvalued.

Foreign and domestic debts denominated in convertible Argentinean pesos could not be honored in dollars. The central bank experienced a run on its foreign reserves. After unsuccessful attempts to prevent capital outflows of foreign currency, full convertibility completely collapsed in 2001, and the Argentinean peso depreciated by approximately 80 percent. The legacy of the crisis was drastic in terms of GDP growth, inflation, rampant unemployment, and political instability.

When compared to the 1980s debt crisis, the crises in Mexico, Brazil, and Argentina shared four common characteristics. First, the three were generated internally via fixed or semifixed exchange rate policies aimed at lowering and controlling inflation. Second, governments were unable to control spiraling fiscal and current account deficits. Third, two of the three crises were relatively short-lived in comparison to those of the Great Depression and the one in the 1980s. Economic recovery took about two years to revert to precrisis GDP levels. Full recovery to precrisis levels in Argentina, however, took over six years. Last but not least, contagion became evident. In an increasingly globalized world economy as of the 1990s, emerging market economies became more vulnerable to crises in similar low- and middle-income nations.[16]

4.5 Latin America through the Twenty-First-Century Financial Crises

The twenty-first century witnessed two main crises: the dot-com crisis in the early 2000s and the subprime crisis from 2007 to 2008. The causes of these two crises are well-known and are beyond the scope of this chapter. Suffice to say that these boom-bust episodes were, unlike the 1990s crises analyzed in the previous subsection, generated in the industrialized world—notably, in the United States.

The dot-com crisis was triggered by a spectacular appetite for investment in Internet-based start-ups. When the dot-com bubble burst in 2001, investors turned to mortgage-backed securities. When housing prices collapsed, the world's financial system was severely shaken by a second crisis.[17]

Both crises could arguably be blamed on the low-interest, low–inflation rate environment that had prevailed in the 1900s and beyond (see figure 4.3). The declining trend in interest rates has been attributed to a significant extent to increased savings in emerging market economies, particularly in China. This country's high savings were, in turn, a consequence of high and sustained Chinese economic growth. Another reason was the steady decline in investment in industrialized countries due to recessionary trends in these countries.[18]

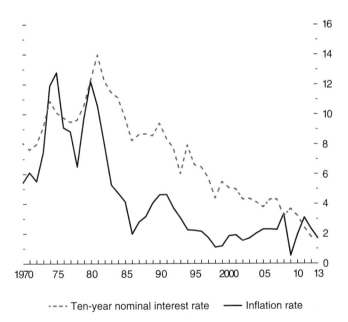

Figure 4.3
World average interest rate and inflation rate, 1970–2013.
Source: IMF World Economic and Financial Surveys, World Economic Outlook 2014 (www.imf.org).

Against this backdrop, Latin America's economic performance has improved considerably since 2004, albeit by less than the world's average. From 1961 to 2008, the world mean average growth rate was 3.2 percent per year, whereas Latin America has expanded by 2.7 percent. If Latin America were to catch up, it would have needed to review far greater per annum GDP growth than that of its industrialized countries' counterparts. Instead, it was about 0.5 percentage point lower.

Relative to rapidly industrializing Asia, the comparison is considerably worse. Latin America's per capita income in the early 1960s was almost double that of Asia. By 2006, per capita income levels in Latin America countries were one-third of those of their Asian counterparts.[19] Relative to Asia, Latin America's poor performance is largely attributed to the region's exceedingly low productivity growth. As shown in figure 4.4, productivity has remained stagnant since the lost decade of the 1980s.

If Latin America could increase current productivity, the living standards of millions of Latin Americans could be lifted. Moreover, widespread increases in labor productivity have the potential of reducing endemic regional income inequalities. The main question is this: How can contemporary Latin American

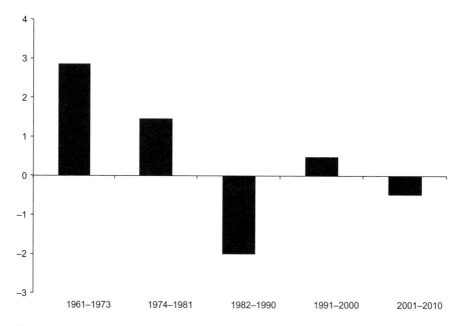

Figure 4.4
Total factor productivity, average annual % change, 1961–2010.
Source: Authors' own construction from ECLAC 2007 and The Conference Board 2015.

governments promote productivity-enhancing policies? We will return to this question in chapter 12.

Despite the less-than stellar performance of Latin America in the twenty-first century, steady growth in Asia (and particularly the high rate of growth in China) explains why Latin America has been relatively unaffected by the twenty-first century financial crises. In fact, we view these crises as a window of opportunity for a brighter Latin American performance outlook in the years to come.

The Chinese growth push and Chinese weight on world demand have increased Latin America's terms of trade and primary commodity prices to unprecedented levels (see figure 4.5). Unsurprisingly, this extraordinary growth of Latin American primary commodity exports has had a positive impact on the region's current accounts, which moved from an average deficit of 4.1 percent of GDP in 1998 to a surplus of approximately 2 percent of GDP in 2006.

However, in 2013 Latin America exhibited a current account deficit nearing 3 percent of GDP, which can be attributed to the region's fall in gross domestic savings. Specifically, the current account surpluses have contributed to foreign reserve accumulation, which has more than doubled—from US$160 billion in 1998 to over US$800 billion in 2012.

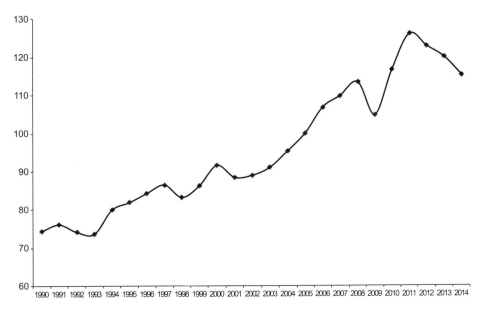

Figure 4.5
Latin America's terms of trade, 1990–2014.
Source: ECLAC 2015.

Another byproduct of the Chinese growth spurt has been reflected in Latin America's public finances, via both taxation and financial surpluses from SOEs. Moreover, external debt burdens have decreased considerably from 4.1 percent of GDP in 2002 to 24.6 percent in 2006, and inflation rates have decreased sharply from hundreds and thousands percentage points in the early 1990s to an average of 7 percent per annum in 2013. These indicators are undoubtedly playing a role in the sharply mitigated impact of the recessions caused by the US dot-com and subprime crises and, more recently, the euro crisis.

Nonetheless, China's recent deceleration is a major test for Latin America. It has already been felt in significant declines in commodity prices, growth rates, and fiscal balances, and Latin America's slowdown can make some countries insolvent. In the case of Venezuela, for example, China's investments and loans are estimated to be about US$70 billion. As of the time of writing, we doubt that Venezuela and other highly indebted countries where China is heavily exposed will be able to service those debts.

4.6 Concluding Remarks

In this chapter, we reviewed the twentieth-century recessions in the industrialized world through the lens of two crises. We argued that, unlike the twentieth-century recessions, which triggered two consecutive debt crises with devastating consequences for Latin American economies, the twenty-first-century recessions in industrialized nations did not provoke a third crisis. Our explanation is rooted in Asia's unprecedented growth rates in general and China's growth in particular.

Growth in Asia has allowed for contemporary Latin American economies to grow at a faster pace in comparison with the continued low rates, which continued to be felt in the United States and Europe. As a result, catching-up with industrialized countries' standards of living started to become a reality prior to the recent Chinese slowdown.

Latin American economies are still vulnerable to external events. The impact of a significant slowdown in China's growth rates has been devastating, mostly because Latin America has not yet capitalized on the export-boom opportunity it enjoyed from 2004 until 2013 to diversify production and exports away from primary commodities. On the contrary, growing demand for primary commodities has exacerbated Latin American reliance on natural resource exploitation. Productivity growth is still stagnant.

Nonetheless, the legacy of market-based reforms in the aftermath of the second debt crisis in the 1980s opened the scope for more productive private and public sectors. Can governments in the region accelerate productivity growth? This major challenge will be discussed in chapter 12.

In the twenty-first century, the revenues of the most recent commodity boom have trickled down. A strong middle class has emerged, and Latin American governments have been able to finance antipoverty campaigns, which have mitigated to some extent the historical legacy and persistence of income inequalities. We turn to this subject in the next chapter.

Summary
- The sovereign defaults of all Latin American governments during the Great Depression left an indelible legacy as the region could no longer contract long-term debt in the international capital markets.
- Foreign bondholders of Latin American debt were diffused, which enabled some Latin American countries to extend advantageous take-it-or-leave-it offers involving sharp debt reduction on the face value of their debts.
- The Great Depression defaults were settled by the end of the 1960s. In the early 1970s, Latin American countries could borrow again in the international financial markets.
- Latin American borrowing during the 1970s was facilitated by the supply of petrodollars resulting from the oil shocks in 1973 and 1979. Petrodollars became available for financial intermediation. Latin America and other regions borrowed heavily from industrialized countries' commercial banks.
- In the early 1980s, interest rates increased as a result of tight monetary policies in the United States and the United Kingdom and of world recession that lowered the demand for primary commodities. The combination of these two events made it impossible for Latin America to service its foreign currency–denominated debt. Widespread defaults ensued.
- After a long period of renegotiation, debt restructuring involving debt reduction and increased maturity for Latin American debt made it possible for most Latin American countries to focus on market-oriented reforms, thereby breaking with the legacy of protectionist ISI policies.
- The traumatic lost decade of unprecedented low growth in Latin America during the 1980s forced most governments to rethink their development strategy. Three main market-oriented reforms were implemented: price stabilization, privatization, and trade liberalization.
- Price stabilizations in Latin America's three major economies—Mexico, Brazil, and Argentina—were exchange-based stabilization in different shapes and forms. Although such stabilizations were successful at bringing inflation down in the short run, endemic overvaluations—partly because of contagion resulting from crises originating in other emerging market regions—led to foreign exchange crises.

- The 1990s balance of payments crises were short-lived relative to the crisis in the 1980s, with the exception of Argentina at the end of the decade.
- After the major debt crises of the 1930s and 1980s, Latin America could have experienced a third crisis in the aftermath of the subprime crisis from 2007 to 2008, but this did not happen. Economic growth rates and employment decreased mildly in comparison with the previous two crises. The main reason was that unlike the twentieth-century crisis, when Latin America was exposed to crises generated in the United States and Europe, during the twenty-first century Latin America became increasingly reliant on China, both as Latin America's main export destination and as a source of portfolio and FDI inflows.
- Recent trends suggest that slowdown of growth in China is affecting Latin American economies. However, the extent and scope of a potential crisis should be limited as a result of the long period of structural reforms and modernization in the region.

Review Questions
1. Briefly explain the similarities and differences between the two main debt crises in Latin America during the twentieth century.
2. What were the main causes of the debt crisis in the 1980s?
3. An unprecedented high inflation rate was one of the main legacies of the crisis in the 1980s. Briefly explain how Latin America's three major economies attempted to resolve this problem.
4. Was price stabilization the only market-oriented reform that Latin American governments implemented in order improve efficiency? Explain your answer.
5. Why were the Latin American financial crises in the 1990s short-lived?
6. The two main crises in the twentieth century were generated in major financial centers outside Latin America, with devastating consequences. Yet the 2007 to 2008 subprime crisis generated in the United States left Latin America relatively unaffected compared to the previous twentieth-century crisis episodes. Explain why.
7. Is twenty-first-century Latin America less vulnerable to commodity price fluctuations in the international markets than it used to be in the twentieth century?
8. Evaluate the merits of the following statement: "Market-friendly reforms started in the late twentieth century have made the region increasingly resilient to financial crises originating elsewhere."
9. Would you expect slow growth in China to have the same effect across the entire Latin American countries? Briefly explain.

10. Detail the main similarities between Latin America's belle époque and the recent commodity boom in the twenty-first century, and briefly explain the merits of the following statement: "Rapid industrialization in other regions can deter industrialization and export diversification in Latin America."

Further Reading

For a detailed and insightful analysis comparing the debt crisis in the 1930s and that in the 1980s, see Barry Eichengreen and Richard Portes 1989b. In a thought-provoking article, William Easterly, Norman Loayza, and Peter Montiel (1997) argue that growth in post–1980s debt crisis Latin America has been disappointing, and they explain why. For a recent and concise overview of Latin America's capital flows since the subprime crisis, see Meier 2015.

II   The Social and Political Context

5   Poverty and Income Inequality

Up to 48.4 percent of Latin Americans were living in poverty in 1990. In 2012, poverty had fallen to 28.2 percent—that is, by 20 percentage points.[1] This extraordinary achievement cannot be dissociated from late twentieth-century structural reforms and the ensuing high and sustained twenty-first-century growth rates in increasingly outward-oriented Latin American economies.

However, despite such an impressive achievement, there still lies a continent marred by pockets of poverty. Approximately 160 million people in contemporary Latin America—nearly one-quarter of the region's inhabitants—still live in poverty.

Poverty eradication is an ethical imperative above all else. It is feasible but exceedingly demanding. Poverty eradication objectives—prioritized in most policy agendas—will bring a growth bonus: as individuals and households pull themselves from poverty, they become part of a growing middle class delivering higher labor productivity, which increases purchasing power and domestic demand for goods and services. Unsurprisingly, entering such a virtuous circle is—and should be—one of the highest aims for all policy makers, from left to right in the political spectrum of the Latin American region.

Who is poor in Latin America? Is poverty endemic to lack of education and opportunities? Is poverty identified with the informally employed and self-employed, with the young, with women heads of households? Is poverty more widespread and acute among indigenous populations and African Americans? Where do we start, and how?

We address these questions in this chapter because identifying the poor and understanding why poverty persists are key ingredients for policy decisions. The challenge is enormous. In parallel with sustaining high rates of economic growth, policy makers must carry out social policies in response to a growing demand for greater access to basic services by the middle class, as recent upsurges in social unrest demonstrate.

We cannot simply wait for the benefits from growth to trickle down. Although growth in the twenty-first century in the region's largest economies is an undeniable force, social policies can potentially reinforce growth-led poverty reduction. In this chapter, we will therefore assess whether antipoverty campaigns such as the *Progresa/Oportunidades/Prospera* program, and the *Benefício de Prestação Continuada* (BPC) and *Bolsa Família* (BBF) in Mexico and Brazil, respectively, have been effective. More recently, the *Ingreso Ético Familiar* (IEF) in Chile has started to gain public attention. Shedding light on these programs requires an in-depth understanding of diverse, inclusive growth trajectories and limitations.

Growth may also be at the root of the region's twenty-first-century declining trend in income inequalities. Despite such an encouraging trend, Latin America's income disparities are indeed pervasive, leading to sluggish social mobility and slow productivity growth. The vast majority continue to lack access to skill acquisition via high-quality secondary and higher education and/or on-the-job training.[2] At the same time, a vibrant and growing middle class is clamoring for increased access to social services in Latin America's young democracies. How have the region's policy makers responded to the dual challenge of fighting poverty and the growing demands of the middle class?

In section 5.1 of this chapter, we present the recent poverty and income inequality trends in Latin America in comparison with the rest of the world. Section 5.2 reviews current definitions of poverty and the received wisdom on why and how poverty should be eradicated. In section 5.3, we discuss two methods for estimating the extent of poverty in the region and their advantages and drawbacks. In section 5.4, we analyze the main determinants of poverty from a Latin American perspective; our focus there is on education, employment, age, gender, and ethnicity. Section 5.5 discusses poverty in connection with labor market policies. Section 5.6 presents emergency job-creation programs for poverty eradication. In section 5.7, we deliver an overview of general concepts of income inequality and measurement. In section 5.8, we discuss the conditional cash transfer programs in Mexico and Brazil—Latin America's largest economies, and also where nearly 50 percent of the region's poor live. Also discussed in this section is the more recent IEF program in Chile, which, in comparison with its counterparts in Mexico and Brazil, targets the entire household, not just children and the elderly. In section 5.9, we deliver a summary and some concluding remarks.

5.1 Poverty and Inequality: Recent Trends and Diversity

According to the World Bank (2013) estimates, poverty rates have declined in all developing country regions (see figure 5.1). In particular, the number of people living on less than 1.25 dollars a day has decreased sharply from 1990 to 2010. Relative to Africa and Asia, the declining trend is less pronounced, however. Still, by this metric, poverty is less acute in Latin America than in Africa. In terms of numbers, East Asia alone hosts nearly 1.5 billion poor, a number that is almost twice as high as the entire Latin American population.[3] Nonetheless, Latin America's poverty seems to be declining at a slower pace compared to other regions.

More recent estimates by ECLAC (2012), as mentioned in the introduction, are more encouraging. These estimates suggest that the declining trend for Latin America is more pronounced than the one that figure 5.1 suggests.

Despite the impressive fall in poverty rates accompanied by comparatively high growth rates during the past decade in the entire developing world, poverty in Latin America is pervasive indeed. As mentioned, Brazil and Mexico host over 50 percent of Latin America's poor. Mexico alone, according to recent estimates by SEDESOL, hosts 53 million poor, which is equivalent to about 40 percent of the entire Mexican population.[4]

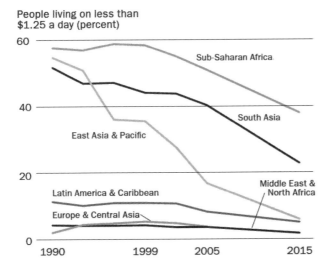

Figure 5.1
Declining poverty trends worldwide, 1990–2015.
Source: World Bank 2014b, forecasts from 2010 to 2015.

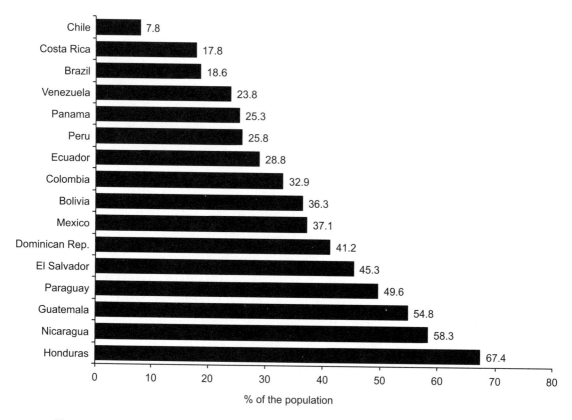

Figure 5.2
Poverty across Latin America in 2012.
Source: Authors' own construction from ECLAC database 2014 (www.cepal.org) and Ministry of Social Development of Chile 2015 (www.ministeriodesarrollosocial.gob.cl).

Overall, and according to recent World Bank estimates, only two Latin American countries—Nicaragua and Haiti—are classified as poor. The rest are classified as middle-income countries. As a percentage of their population, however, considerably smaller Central American countries—with the notable exception of Costa Rica—are worse off. Figure 5.2 shows widespread poverty, and it also shows enormous cross-regional differences. In Chile, for example, 7.8 percent of the population is considered to be poor. In sharp contrast, Honduras marks a staggering 67.4 percent.

With regard to income inequalities, recent data suggests a declining trend—which might be attributed to catch-up growth following the lost decade and structural reforms at the turn of the century. Cornia (2010) and Ocampo and Vallejo (2012) note that the reduction in inequality in Latin America since 2002 is

Poverty and Income Inequality

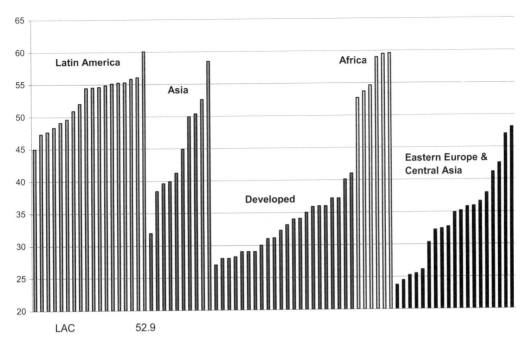

Figure 5.3
Income inequalities in Latin America compared to other regions (2010). *Note:* Each bar represents the Gini coefficient for the distribution of household per capita income in a given country (last available observation in the 1995–2005 period).
Source: Gasparini, Cruces and Tornarolli 2009.

partly due to higher economic growth and a subsequent increase in employment opportunities. We will come back to this point further ahead in sections 5.7 and 5.8. Nonetheless, and just as in the case of poverty, inequalities persist. As figure 5.3 illustrates, Latin America continues to rival Africa in terms of high income disparities, as proxied by the Gini coefficient.[5]

Figure 5.4 also shows a great deal of cross-country diversity. Depending on the region, the top 20 percent high-income households in Latin America have incomes that are from 7 to 25 times higher than their lower-income counterparts. Honduras is the most unequal country according to these estimates. Refer back to figure 5.3 to see that Honduras is also host to the largest proportion of poor households as a percentage of its population.

The case of Honduras is revealing. It suggests that poverty and income inequalities in Latin America take place concurrently. As we will argue in chapter 12, this might well be the case for the entire region: higher growth accompanied by more aggressive social policies may be required for eradicating poverty, and greater

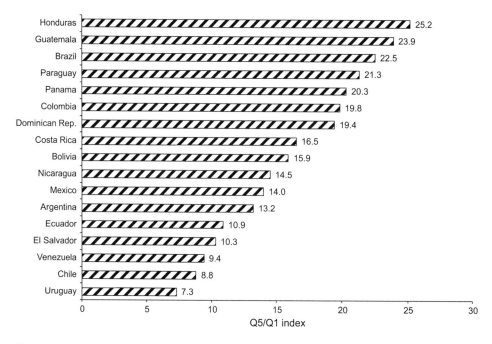

Figure 5.4
Inequalities across Latin American countries, income ratios of fifth quintile (Q5) to first quintile (Q1; 2012 or latest year available).
Source: Authors' own construction from ECLAC database 2014 (www.cepal.org) and Ministry of Social Development in Chile 2015 (www.ministeriodesarrollosocial.gob.cl).

access to social services by the middle class is needed urgently to avoid social unrest and potential upsurges of populism.

Without underestimating efforts to proxy inequality via Gini coefficients and the quintile indices, respectively (see figures 5.3 and 5.4), we believe that lower income inequalities in Latin America are best captured by proxies of the middle class, which now accounts for up to 30 percent of the region's population. The rising trend is shown in figure 5.5.

This upward trend is significantly associated with better governance, deeper credit markets, and more spending on health and education. From a political economy standpoint, Ferreira et al. (2012) find that the thicker middle class in Latin America has enough "voice" or political clout to exert pressure for policy makers to carry out investments in health and education, to improve the quality of governance, to increase democratic participation, and to lower corruption.

Note that according to figure 5.5, the proportion of poor as defined by these metrics (less than four US dollars per day) equals the proportion of the middle class (between ten and fifty US dollars per day). Together, the poor and the middle

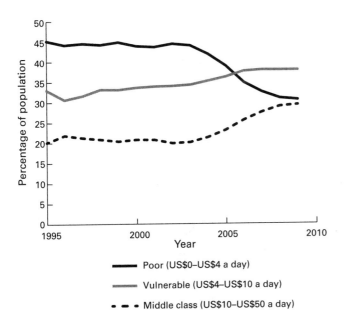

Figure 5.5
Declining poverty and the rise of the middle class.
Source: Ferreira et al. 2012.

class add up to approximately 60 percent of Latin America's population, with the remainder (roughly 40 percent) classified as *vulnerable*. Hence, countries with a large middle class, such as Chile in South America and Costa Rica in Central America, face the dual challenge of meeting the demands of a vocal middle class on the one hand and those of the poor and vulnerable who now aspire to become part of the middle class as social mobility in contemporary Latin America increases on the other.[6] A similar problem is faced by governments in most other regions. The policy responses have been different, however.

Middle-class political pressures recently have been receiving considerable national and international media attention. This might be a reflection of the high effort and the resources that Latin American governments have been putting into their fight to eradicate poverty and vulnerability in the 60 percent of the Latin American population to which we now turn.

5.2 Poverty: Definition and Consequences

There is widespread consensus that the eradication of poverty is the principal objective of economic development. However, there is little agreement on how *poverty* should be defined.

What is poverty? There is not a single and universal explanation of what it is, because poverty is multidimensional and context-specific. This certainly applies to Latin America, which is indeed exceedingly diverse.

Ongoing debates often lead to extremely vague definitions. The World Bank special report on poverty is often taken as a reference point: "Poor people live without fundamental freedoms of action and choice that the better off take for granted. They often lack adequate food and shelter, education and health, deprivations that keep them from leading the kind of life that everyone values. They also face extreme vulnerability to ill health, economic dislocation, and natural disasters" (World Bank 2001). We find this and other definitions, including those by ECLAC specifically on Latin America's poverty, much too broad.[7]

As noted previously, poverty is a multidimensional phenomenon. Also, evolving views of and debates about poverty, hold up the basic tenet of ethics. Simply stated, denying individuals and households the ability to satisfy their basic needs is inhuman—particularly in Latin America, where a vast majority does not have the same standards of living and opportunities that a minority enjoys.

However, there is something else that we think is unique about the region's poverty. This something else is *democracy*. Historically, and unlike other developing regions that remained under the control of colonial powers well into the twentieth century, Latin America gained its independence in the early nineteenth century. The region's policy makers have been dealing with ongoing tensions since. Such tensions have manifested themselves in different forms and shapes—from the Mexican revolution with the rural poor clamoring for rights to fertile land in the northern cone to the urban poor protesting against low wages in Argentina's meatpacking plants in the southern cone in the late nineteenth century. These movements often led to military and/or authoritarian regimes. Military regimes are no longer threatening the poor's rights to enjoy a better standard of living, however. Populism is a major threat instead, as we will explain in chapter 6.

Contemporary Latin American poverty in the region's infant democracies is closely associated with the rural sector and exacerbated by high rural-urban migration creating pockets of urban and semiurban poverty. From a political economy standpoint, high rates of economic growth have made it easier for policy makers to do justice to the rural poor. This accords well with democratically elected politicians' objectives, which are geared toward meeting the demands of the vast majority of the population—or the desires of the median voter.[8]

Purely economic arguments for poverty eradication are pretty straightforward. The following argument is a good example: the poor are talented individuals. Enhancing their access to health and education adds to the existing pool of a productive workforce, which is in turn a much-needed growth-enhancing bonus in many emerging market economies, not just those in Latin America. Moreover, growth-enhancing productivity progress in the region cannot take place without continued structural reforms that require the support of the middle class, an issue to which we return in section 5.7.

A well-known channel through which poverty reduction can positively affect economic growth is clearly explained by Perry et al. (2006). The authors follow a distinguished tradition on credit constraints generally attributed to Banerjee and Newman (1994) in their groundbreaking contribution. Perry et al. contend that social mobility and economic growth crucially depend on access to credit by the vast majority of talented poor. By removing credit constraints faced by the poor, investment is expected to increase, not just in physical capital, but also in health and education, with consequent productivity gains. Credit constraints are common in Latin America. Arguably, microfinance is a mitigating solution.[9]

To close this section, it is important to note the strong link between political economy and purely economic arguments for poverty eradication and reduction of income disparities: high levels of poverty and income disparities in Latin America have often led to political instability, with consequential growth downturns, as predicted by Alesina and Perotti (1996). In practice, persistent poverty and inequality has prompted many Latin American governments to adopt unsustainable populist policies, with devastating long-term consequences from economic and social standpoints. We will wait until the next chapter to address this in greater detail. At this point we must present some basic methodological issues first.

5.3 Measurement

As we have argued from the very start, the extent and acuteness of poverty depends on how it is defined and, perhaps more importantly, how it is measured.

Measuring poverty is extremely relevant for evaluating economic progress. Government, academic institutions, and local and international organizations devote a significant amount of resources to measuring poverty and its evolution through time. From an international development aid standpoint, such measures and cross-section comparisons are based on surveys, which help to prioritize development aid. Local governments, on the other hand, particularly in middle-income Latin America, are often guided by context-specific poverty measures for policy, inclusive of social programs and antipoverty campaigns.

In the following subsections, we present two approaches to measuring poverty in practice: direct and indirect.[10] The *direct approach* attempts to assess the status of the poor and relevant characteristics, depending on how close individuals are to a prespecified set of "standards" that are determined by regional poverty experts. For example, a household with more than two members living in just one room falls short of meeting a standard called *crowding*.

In contrast, the *indirect approach* classifies as poor those who do not have enough income to meet their basic needs, where income is linked, for example, to individuals' ability to consume a basket of goods with enough nutrients depending on age. The latter approach uses the well-known concept of poverty lines, which are predetermined income thresholds below which individuals are considered to be poor.

In Latin America, both poverty measures have been used. The direct method is known as the *unsatisfied basic needs* (UBN) method, and the indirect method is better known as the *cost of basic needs* (CBN) method. Both the UNB and the CBN methods have been guiding Latin America's antipoverty policies for decades now.

5.3.1 Unsatisfied Basic Needs Approach

Let us begin with the UBN method. This used to be the most widespread method for estimating the extent and acuteness of poverty in Latin America up until the 1980s, but it lost ground during the 1990s because it relies too heavily on subjective metrics, which complicates the debate on the ultimate goal of meeting some kind of consensus for policy on such a complex issue. For example, the previously mentioned crowding standard is one that has to be compared with another—say, the average literacy rate within a household, labeled *literacy*. Should literacy be prioritized over crowding, and, if so, why? This is far from obvious in Latin America. For example, an influential Peruvian economist, Hernando de Soto, would argue that crowding is most important.[11] However, this is far from being noncontroversial.[12]

Despite the often disorganized debates on poverty metrics that the UBN method leads to, it nevertheless continues to be regarded as a complementary measure of overall poverty in the region's twenty-first century, because some useful insights still apply, particularly with regard to identifying who the *ultrapoor* are.[13]

The UBN method is based on a definition of poverty associated with "need." The underlying premise is that what matters the most for welfare is whether a set of basic human needs or standards are being effectively satisfied. In practice, the method requires first a definition of basic needs, and, second, setting the threshold for attaining those needs. Filling the need is equivalent to meeting the standard or the threshold beyond which an individual is no longer considered poor.

Using surveys, statisticians gather indicators of need, as dictated by a preestablished set of thresholds or standards via measures of, for example, crowding, literacy, access to water and sanitation, health services, electricity, and shelter. Unsurprisingly, this method delivers confusing indicators of poverty; the numbers obtained are plagued with technical difficulties. It is inherently strenuous in practice to work with numerous indicators.

It is also difficult to decide for or against including key indicators. For example, the UBN method does not include indicators of crucial importance, such as individuals' income volatility (an important proxy of vulnerability), which applies to a vast majority of self-employed individuals in urban areas and seasonally employed household heads in rural areas.[14]

With regard to variables of interest that are included in the UBN method, an observed characteristic, need by need, is compared with a preestablished *normative* threshold. Accordingly, an individual is considered to be poor depending on his or her shortfalls from such a threshold. One shortfall classifies an individual or household as *poor* and more than one as *extremely poor*.

The main advantage of the UBN method is that it enables the mapping of poverty with parameters of interest. This helps policy makers to rank facets of poverty, detect poverty geographically, and draw social program plans accordingly. The method therefore guides local governments in their attempts at prioritizing targets and estimating consequential budgets to attain those targets.

5.3.2 Cost of Basic Needs Approach

The CBN method is the most widespread technique for assessing the extent of poverty in contemporary Latin America. Relative to the UBN, the CBN is an indirect method, because it does not focus on actual consumption and status. Instead, it uses a bundle of goods considered to be essential, and it estimates its cost in order to obtain a region-specific income threshold called a poverty line.

The bundle of goods is chosen by poverty experts and is based on regional consumption patterns. Specifically, the poverty line is constructed in two stages: First, a food component is estimated. This is anchored by nutritional requirements for meeting minimum health standards. Once the bundle of food has been established, its cost is estimated based on prevailing market prices. This allows statisticians to determine the minimum income needed to purchase that nutritious bundle. Second, a non-food-component bundle is estimated. This estimation requires specification of income thresholds to acquire nonfood goods and services in health, education, clothing, utilities, and transport, among others. To establish this rather complex nonfood income threshold, statisticians take a shortcut. They generally multiply the cost of the food income component by a factor of (around) two. Occasionally, statisticians specify the nonfood bundle explicitly and estimate its cost in a similar way to how they proxy the cost of the food component.

Once the costs of the food and nonfood components have been estimated, the income required to acquire a minimum threshold of combined commodities delivers a poverty line, and the poor are those individuals whose incomes fall below that threshold.

According to most recent estimates by the World Bank for Latin America, the income threshold has been set at four US dollars per day.[15] Individuals living below this threshold are considered extremely poor. Those within the four to ten dollars per day range are considered vulnerable in that they risk falling back below the four dollars per day threshold, with an estimated probability of 10 percent. Within the ten to fifty US dollars per day range, individuals are classified as middle-class individuals.

The greatest advantage of this CBN method is its simplicity. It facilitates understanding and follow-up debates. Arguably, it also helps assess the success of social policies through time. The limitations of this method are numerous, however.

A full discussion of the drawbacks of the CBN method is beyond the scope of this book.[16] Some merit special attention, however. First, poverty lines vary across regions and over time, making comparisons difficult and extremely imprecise. Second, the method incorporates value judgments. A typical case in point is that of the choice of food items that meet nutritional standards and their quantities and prices. Third, the nonfood bundle is an issue. What this bundle should contain and how it should be priced is subject to constant debates. Disagreements are not easily reconciled across different multilateral and national statistic agencies. Lastly, the poverty lines derived from the CBN method often do not factor in cross-regional differentials with regard to public procurement of social goods.[17]

5.4 Main Determinants of Poverty

No one can deny that poverty is linked to income. Indeed, there is a vast amount of empirical evidence showing a negative and significant correlation between income growth and poverty; that is, more growth leads to lower poverty, as indicated in table 5.1.

Recent economic analysis suggests that there are fundamental and proximate causes of poverty.[18] *Fundamental causes* affect systematically the income dimension of poverty indirectly. Indirect causes include culture, ethnic composition, rule of law, geography, and climate. In contrast, the *proximate causes* of poverty are those that affect income directly, such as low levels of human and physical capital, technology, efficiency, and, more generally, productivity and labor force participation.

We find this distinction useful in the particular case of Latin America. Not much can be done to fight against fundamental causes of poverty, such as adverse climate or geography. (We have already discussed such fundamental causes in chapter 1.) However, a lot can be done to fight against the proximate causes of poverty, which in turn explains our priority list in this section.

Table 5.1
Empirical research on the relation between economic growth and poverty in different countries and regions

Reference	Effect
Balisacan, Chakravorty and Ravago 2015	Negative or none
Lee et al. 2014	Negative or none
Tovar Jalles 2011	Negative
Perry et al. 2006	Negative
Gupta and Mitra 2004	Negative
Dollar and Kraay 2004	Negative
Bourguignon 2003	Negative
Minujin, Vandemoortele, and Delamonica 2002	Negative or none
Lustig, Arias, and Rigolini 2002	Negative
Heltberg 2002	Negative
Kakwani and Krongkaew 2000	Negative
de Janvry and Sadoulet 2000	Negative or none
Goudie and Ladd 1999	Negative or none
McKay 1997	Negative
Ravallion 1995	Negative
Larrañaga 1994	Negative
Ahluwalia, Carter, and Chenery 1979	Negative

In the following subsections, we will touch upon the roots of poverty from a Latin American perspective. These include mostly the proximate causes of poverty, bearing in mind that Latin America is a middle-income, highly urbanized region ruled by democratically elected governments that need to use a set of growth-enhancing tools to meet the demands of the poor and vulnerable.

5.4.1 Education

There are a few studies that establish the causal effect of education on wages. One of them is the 2002 paper by Esther Duflo on Indonesia, which shows that an additional 0.12 years of education can lead to as much as 1.5 percentage increase in wages (Duflo 2002). A similar study does not exist for Latin America, however.

Nevertheless, serious (albeit less rigorous) research on the region points in the same direction. Specifically, most analyses demonstrate that education is positively correlated with earnings. As income increases, the probability of being poor decreases. This association turns out to be statistically significant in most studies.[19]

Of particular importance to contemporary Latin American economies are the economic returns for higher education—that is, the *educational premium*—which are exceedingly high when compared to those of primary education. Wodon et al. (2001), for example, find that a household head with higher educational attainment delivers an income which is about 97 percent higher than that of household heads with primary education only. Moreover, Perry et al. (2006) suggest that educational shortfalls in poor households deliver an educational poverty trap, in that children with parents whose education endowment is low face a lower probability of attaining higher education and are most likely bound to earn low wages.

Nonetheless, other studies specific to Latin America—such as Manacorda, Sánchez-Páramo, and Schady 2010[20]—suggest that the returns of secondary education, compared to primary education, have fallen as the supply has risen sharply. Evidence also suggests an increase in the educational premium for tertiary education compared to secondary education. According to the authors, this is because the number of people who entered tertiary education grew at a lower rate than those gaining secondary education in every country except Mexico.

In a recent study on the Dominican Republic, Jensen (2010) shows (1) that the returns to secondary education are often underestimated by primary school students and (2) that once students' perceptions with regard to the true returns of education beyond eighth grade are updated upward—via informing eighth graders about the true returns—higher educational attainment is achieved, provided students can afford more years of education. This is an important finding; it calls for government intervention, not only with regard to raising students' awareness about the high returns of additional years of education, but also in making high-quality secondary school affordable.

As noted earlier, with the exceptions of Nicaragua and Haiti, most Latin American countries are classified as middle-income economies. Policy makers therefore should be able to launch initiatives that either increase the costs of not attending secondary education for students from poor backgrounds—via banning child and teenage labor, for example—or provide progressive subsidization as students enroll and progress on the educational ladder.[21] However, where labor laws banning child and teenage labor exist, such laws are poorly enforced if at all.[22]

5.4.2 Unemployment and Informality

Education thus far overemphasizes an income dimension, but it has been shown that education is also linked to formal employment. Unsurprisingly, unemployed (and informally employed) individuals face a higher risk of being poor, as noted in studies by Attanasio and Székely (1999) and Wodon et al. (2001), for example. These studies suggest that job security is of paramount importance to poverty-relief efforts.

Poverty and Income Inequality

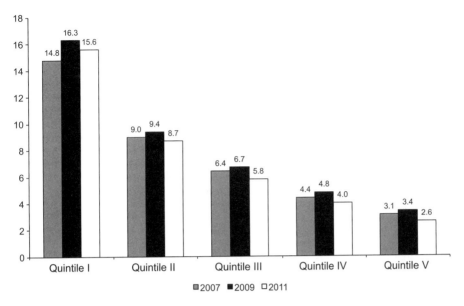

Figure 5.6
Unemployment rates by income quintiles in Latin America; percentage of individuals aged 15 and above, 2007, 2009, and 2011.
Source: ECLAC 2012.

Figure 5.6 shows that poverty is indeed strongly linked to unemployment, which is particularly worrisome in the Latin American region, where there are no welfare safety nets comparable to those of European nations. (Extended family networks are a mitigating factor, however.) Relative to 2007, the 2009 estimates for the region suggest that the unemployment rate increased from 6.9 percent to 7.5 percent (ILO 2013). Nonetheless, as the figure shows, the increase was considerably larger among the poorest quintiles, from 14.8 percent to 16.3 percent, compared to a meager increase from 3.1 percent to 3.4 percent among the richest quintile. In 2011, the unemployment rate in the region fell to 6.5 percent. In contrast, among the poorest quintile the unemployment rate was estimated to be about 15.6 percent—that is, six times higher than the unemployment rate of the richest quintile.

Note that these numbers reflect a slight slowdown in growth as a result of the global financial crisis from 2007 to 2009. Although slow growth seems to be positively and significantly correlated with unemployment and poverty, labor policies in Latin America are also important. Employment regulations dating back to the protectionist 1940–1980 period are still inhibiting employment creation today. We will return to the regulatory environment in chapter 11.

By and large, labor force participation in Latin America is not confined to formal employment. Specifically, a large number of individuals are informally employed. Table 5.2 delivers a snapshot of the extent of informality, which, like poverty and inequality, varies a great deal across countries.

The relation between informality and poverty has been analyzed extensively for many years now. Existing studies deliver similar conclusions. Pribble, Huber, and Stephens (2007), for example, find that the size of the informal sector is positively and significantly correlated with poverty. These findings corroborate the results of Wodon et al. (2001), which show that working in the formal sector is positively and significantly associated with higher income cohorts. Unsurprisingly, formally employed workers also have considerably less income volatility and can therefore smooth consumption over time more easily compared to those who are informally employed. These individuals and households are, broadly speaking, much more vulnerable.

Given that there are clear disadvantages to being informally employed, why do workers choose not to join the formal sector in the first place? Several explanations apply to the Latin American labor market. First, formal sector employment requires skilled labor, which brings us back to educational shortages and the need for policy makers to prioritize enhanced access to postsecondary education and/or via training programs.[23] Second, unskilled labor is often paid relatively high and rigid minimum wages when compared to other regions in, for example, Asia. Firms therefore choose to contract labor offshore and/or pay low wages to imported labor from neighboring regions, i.e., Nicaraguan labor in Costa Rica. Third, there is inadequate social security. According to recent estimates by the Inter-American Development Bank (IDB), up to 43 percent of the salaried work force is not covered by national pension systems, which may in turn discourage workers from joining the formal sector. Fourth, the costs of setting up formal businesses are too high in comparison to those faced by informal enterprises. Excessive bureaucracy and taxes are contributing factors.

The preceeding explanations suggest that there are indeed advantages to informality. First, unskilled labor often finds that setting up an informal business is less costly; petty traders and SMEs are a case in point. These laborers and businesses abound in most cities and semiurban areas in Latin America. Second, relative to men, women have fewer formal skills and bear a disproportionately high share of the household chores. Women in Latin America therefore often find it attractive to engage themselves in informal sector activities while staying at home, because informality is convenient and accords well with social norms.[24]

Social norms are difficult to change, but government failures with regard to limited access to higher education and skill acquisition, taxation, social security, pensions, and day care center provision are largely responsible for informality.

Table 5.2
Formal vs. informal employment in Latin America (2005 or latest figure available)

	Sector	
	Informal	Formal
Latin America		
Total	32.7	67.3
Men	34.6	65.4
Women	30.3	69.7
Argentina		
Total	29.5	70.5
Men	33.4	66.6
Women	23.9	76.1
Brazil		
Total	24.2	75.8
Men	27.6	72.4
Women	20.1	79.9
Colombia		
Total	50.4	49.6
Men	51.0	49.0
Women	49.6	50.4
Ecuador		
Total	34.6	65.4
Men	36.0	64.0
Women	32.8	67.2
Mexico		
Total	34.2	65.8
Men	35.5	64.5
Women	32.4	67.6
Peru		
Total	49.2	50.8
Men	44.7	55.3
Women	54.4	45.6
Venezuela		
Total	35.7	64.3
Men	37.1	62.9
Women	33.7	66.3

Source: ILO 2011.

Table 5.3
Average income of the economically active population employed, as per position held in 2012 or latest year available (shown as multiple of the respective per capita poverty lines)

	Employer	Employed	Self-employed
Argentina	30.1	11.3	16.6
Bolivia	6.8	4.2	3.8
Brazil	18.0	5.4	5.5
Chile	32.8	7.2	9.7
Colombia	8.7	5.1	2.8
Ecuador	13.4	4.3	3.2
Guatemala	17.0	2.8	3.7
Mexico	6.4	2.9	2.1
Peru	8.3	4.3	2.6
Venezuela	11.5	2.7	4.7

Source: ECLAC 2013.

5.4.3 Type of Employment

Informal sector workers lacking skills are often self-employed. Table 5.3 shows that the incomes of the self-employed are considerably lower than those of individuals who are either formally employed or are employers. The table also shows considerable cross-country variation. In all instances, the self-employed earn comparatively less. Their meager earnings often classify them as poor, according to the CBN method. Table 5.3 lends support to the Wodon et al. (2001) findings. In particular, being self-employed—in comparison to having a blue-collar employment status—is associated with lower income.

Self-employment and informal sector employment are related. Both types of laborers are comparatively more prone to experiencing poverty compared to the formally employed, most likely because of their lack of physical and human capital. Self-employment is in many cases synonymous with low-productivity labor, which hinders growth. We will return to this topic in chapter 12.

5.4.4 Age

The population in Latin America is still young compared to other emerging market regions, particularly those in Eastern Europe. Young individuals are more likely to be poor because of lack of skills, experience, and/or being part of the informally employed sector. Figure 5.7 shows that unemployment rates in Latin America are considerably higher for younger people relative to elder cohorts. This holds true for both men and women.

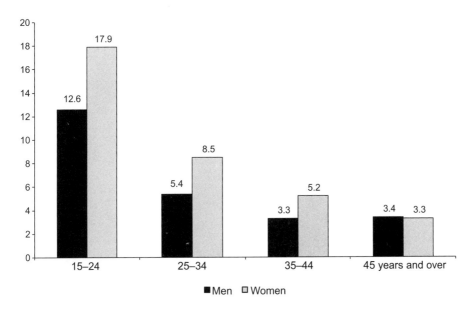

Figure 5.7
Urban unemployment rates (as a percentage of total unemployment) for individuals aged 15 and above in 2012.
Source: ECLAC 2013.

The stylized facts reported for 2012 suggest that the situation has not changed since the early twenty-first century. In particular, Wodon et al. (2001) found that young household heads are more likely to be poor.

5.4.5 Gender

Not surprisingly, Latin America mirrors a well-defined problem worldwide. Relative to men, women are generally poorer and more vulnerable. This is somewhat understandable in middle-income economies, which are predominately rural or semirural and in which physical force is comparatively more important than in urban-sector activities.

Contemporary Latin America is predominantly urban or semiurban, and prevailing poverty from a gender perspective is often attributed to gender discrimination. Table 5.4 delivers an alarming picture of the extent of gender discrimination in the region. Women not only earn less than men at equal levels of educational attainment, but also earn lower incomes for the same types of jobs.

This phenomenon has severe implications for households headed by women, who are indeed more likely to be poor. Empirical studies lend support to the stylized facts reported in table 5.4. Such studies show that woman-headed

Table 5.4
Gender wage ratio in percentages, by year of education completed, in 2012 or latest year available*

	0–5	6–9	10–12	13 and over
Argentina	80.2	74.9	81.5	84.8
Brazil	73.7	68.8	69.6	67.0
Chile	80.4	80.5	76.5	69.0
Colombia	81.4	76.9	77.7	79.2
Mexico	69.6	71.9	83.1	78.1
Peru	70.6	72.7	72.2	78.0
Venezuela	89.1	84.1	84.2	90.0

Source: ECLAC 2013.
*Refers to the ratio of the average pay rate of urban women wage earners to the pay rate of men with similar characteristics in terms of schooling and job held.

households in the labor force have an income that is about 10 percent lower than that of households headed by male counterparts.[25]

Relative to men, unemployment rates are also higher for women (see figure 5.7). This is particularly true for young women. As shown in table 5.2, relative to men, women are overrepresented in the informal sector. Gender considerations should therefore be factored in when designing policies to eradicate poverty in Latin America—and to some extent, they are. In particular, ongoing antipoverty campaigns prioritize women in at least two dimensions. Conditional cash transfers, in general, are handed to women heads of households.[26] Some of these transfers include microfinancing—enhanced access to financial services—in which women are prioritized. Eight out of ten beneficiaries of microfinance programs are women.[27] We will return to these important programs and assess their effectiveness in section 5.8.

5.4.6 Inflation

Urban poverty is exacerbated by inflation, often caused by extremely high budget deficits and exchange rate misalignments. Unlike the minority of wealthy Latin Americans, the poor are less able to hedge against inflation. Experience has shown that in periods of high inflation, the poor have lost purchasing power and become more vulnerable. According to Cardoso (1992), accelerating inflation reduced real wages and increased poverty in Latin America between 1977 and 1989. Inflation is now back in twenty-first-century Latin America—for example, in Venezuela and Argentina. In Venezuela, inflation rates reached around 60 percent in 2014 and have been on an upward trend since. Inflationary spirals of this type are a consequence of twenty-first-century populist policies, an important issue that we discuss in detail in chapter 6.

Efforts to control inflation in most regions involve exchange rate policies. The twenty-first century has witnessed overvalued exchange rates in many regions, and such rates hurt the export sector and have a negative impact on employment and growth, an issue we discuss in greater detail recurrently throughout the remainder of this book.

5.4.7 Ethnicity and Racial Discrimination

Even though ethnicity touches upon fundamental causes of poverty and we have already discussed the issue in chapter 1, we think it is particularly relevant to extreme rural poverty in contemporary Latin America.

According to recent World Bank estimates for 2012, about 13 percent of Latin Americans are indigenous. Most of this indigenous population is concentrated in Mexico, Peru, Guatemala, and Ecuador. Nearly 50 percent of the population in Brazil—Latin America's largest economy—are *mestizos*, or Afro-Latin Americans. These populations often live in rural areas where the incidence of poverty is exceedingly high due to, among other factors, drastic changes in weather conditions in poorly constructed dwellings and lack of access to basic health services, drinking water, sanitation, and adequate school facilities.

High urbanization rates and rural-urban migration might be mitigating the extent and acuteness of ethnicity-related poverty. However, urban areas are also flooded with a multiplicity of ethnic groups, with *mestizos* and Afro-Latin Americans living in the suburbs of many cities filled with pockets of poverty. In such areas, sanitation, health services, and schooling standards are exceedingly low or nonexistent. Unsurprisingly, empirical estimates suggest that racially discriminated ethnic groups are more prone to experiencing poverty.[28]

Local governments and nongovernmental organizations (NGOs) have been fighting to improve living standards and to enhance basic human rights in dozens of Latin American countries. Ongoing struggles often involve a cultural divide dating back to the seventeenth-century master-servant colonialist period. Negligence of indigenous rights by local governments has often led to fatal social conflicts and ethnic strife. The 1994 Zapatista uprising in Chiapas, one of the poorest states in southern Mexico, is a well-known example of negligence and ensuing armed conflict.[29]

5.5 Labor Markets and Poverty

In Latin America, labor market legislation has often been used as a weapon against urban poverty. The design and consequences of legislative amendments have delivered mixed results. In this section, we discuss salient features of such legislation.

5.5.1 Minimum Wage

Most contemporary Latin American economies have adjusted minimum wages—or *wage floors*—upward, with the principal objective of protecting blue-collar incomes from falling below income-based poverty thresholds. These policies have been either ineffective or unenforceable in practice, however. The reason is simple: minimum wage policies may protect the income of those workers who are already formally employed, but not those of the majority whose incomes are derived from informal sector employment or self-employment. As we discussed in the previous section, the informally employed and the self-employed obtain lower incomes than their formally employed counterparts.

Standard arguments against minimum wages in industrialized countries, on the other hand, are based on basic economics textbooks that suggest a positive association between high minimum wages and unemployment. These arguments apply differently in many Latin American countries, where minimum wage laws are not enforceable.

In instances in which minimum wages are enforced, Kristensen and Cunningham (2006) demonstrate that wage floors should be low relative to mean wages, because when floors are low, the informally employed and unemployed (women, young, unskilled, etc.) can more easily access formal sector jobs. This finding accords well with our earlier argument that formally employed individuals are less prone to experiencing poverty.

5.5.2 Firing Costs

Severance payments—compensation awarded to dismissed workers—are relatively high in Latin America due to lack of unemployment insurance. That is, high dismissal compensation in the region somehow replaces insurance protection for workers who find themselves out of the formal sector employment pool.

According to a report issued by the World Bank (2008), firing costs in Latin America amount to approximately 53.9 weeks of salaries per dismissed worker. This figure is twice as high as that in OECD countries, where dismissal costs per worker are equivalent to 25.8 weeks.

Most observers conclude that high firing costs discourage firms from offering formal sector jobs, which is in turn counterproductive, because of the high incidence of poverty among the unemployed, informally employed, and self-employed—in line with our argument in the preceding sections.

We believe that a potential solution might be found if governments in Latin America were to introduce adequate unemployment insurance. To be able to afford unemployment insurance, however, appropriate fiscal policies must be set up first. We discuss fiscal policies in great detail in chapter 7.

5.5.3 Payroll Taxes

Many social protection programs in Latin America, such as old-age pensions and health and unemployment subsidies, are funded via payroll contributions. These are mandatory benefits.

However, social security contributions are perceived poorly in the entire region. In particular, such contributions are often viewed as a tax, which underestimates the benefits. The long-term benefits from social security contributions largely overcome the costs. Nonetheless, short-sighted policy makers in the region often avoid social security contributions because they have a tendency to overemphasize the tax component.

There are several capitalization systems based on individual retirement accounts in Latin America. The pioneering example of the Chilean capitalization system was later followed by Colombia, Mexico, Peru, and Uruguay, among others. This social security scheme demonstrates that employed individuals can more easily perceive their contribution as a benefit to themselves, not as a tax.

Moreover, payroll contributions in many countries are often used to reduce social security deficits. This is indeed a tax, which can in turn reduce the demand for formal sector jobs. The tax—when viewed from the standpoint of how tax revenues are used—can potentially increase the pool of self-employed and informally employed individuals, which is in turn positively (and significantly) correlated with poverty.

Latin America's populations are aging. Social security reforms are therefore of paramount importance in their own right. However, instead of social security contributions, most governments are delivering direct cash transfers to families with elderly members. These policies might aid poverty-reduction efforts, but they do not address the root of the problem—that is, the need to increase access to formal employment and social security contributions for all types of employment.

5.6 Emergency Job Creation against Poverty

A widespread action to fight poverty in Latin America has been the creation of emergency employment programs. These programs provide subsistence to the unemployed poor, particularly during economic downturns. However, these programs generally provide low-productivity jobs and carry the risk of increasing dependency (they are always easier to grow than to scale down). In short, emergency employment is short-term and transitory government aid to the poor, with no lasting effect on their ability to generate income. In this section, we discuss two emergency employment programs that Latin American policy makers have used to combat poverty.

The two programs discussed ahead rely on subsidies. The first one boils down to creating emergency jobs in order to mitigate the perils of unemployment and poverty. Such jobs are short-term and are typically taken up by unskilled workers and involve activities that do not deliver on-the-job training and skill acquisition. Typically, short-term employment in construction of public sector infrastructure, such as roads, is offered by central, regional, and local governments.

We view such programs as a short-term response to a much more fundamental problem. Moreover, the time spent in low-productivity public sector work by unskilled workers can reduce search time by workers who could potentially secure a long-term job in the formal sector, in which they might at least acquire on-the-job training.

In contrast, the second program consists of implementing emergency social funds (ESFs) for job creation in poverty-stricken areas. These programs can have an impact on poverty reduction. ESFs have been created in Bolivia, Nicaragua, Peru, and Honduras, among other Latin American countries. Typically, ESFs are long-term subsidized credit lines extended by multilateral aid agencies for public work creation. The defining feature of ESFs is that the decision about the type of public work to be carried out is made by members of the local community who will benefit directly, not by the federal government in a centralized manner.

ESFs create jobs. Unlike centralized emergency jobs, ESFs subsidize social programs simultaneously in, for example, health, education, and sanitation. Enhanced access to such services is crucial for fighting poverty. However, rigorous impact evaluations of ESFs are needed to shed light on the true effectiveness of these programs.

5.7 Income Inequalities: Measurement and Recent Trends

Before addressing standard textbook technicalities pertaining to income inequalities, it is important to clarify that poverty and income disparities are two different issues, yet interconnected via various channels ranging from access to basic health and education to credit and saving facilities.

In addition, keep two issues in mind. First, unlike the case of poverty, the existing literature on measurement of inequality from a Latin American perspective deals with "soft spots," which touches upon the ultrarich minority of around 1 percent, compared to the over 30 percent of the region's population considered to be poor. Second, this comparison largely underestimates the middle class, which, according to reliable World Bank estimates, exceeds 50 percent in the five most populous regions—namely, Brazil, Mexico, Peru, Argentina, and Colombia—combined. We cannot possibly deal with these two issues in a single chapter. Instead, we will come back to each of these important points recurrently throughout the remainder of the book.

We now turn to the two most standard measures of income inequality worldwide: income quintiles and the Gini coefficient.

5.7.1 Income Quintiles and the Gini Coefficient

The most widely used measures of income inequalities are the Q5/Q1 index and the Gini coefficient. The Q5/Q1 index measures the income ratio of the richest quintile (Q5) to the poorest quintile (Q1):

$$\frac{Q5}{Q1} \; Index = \frac{Income \; Q5}{Income \; Q1}$$

From a technical standpoint, this measure has the obvious advantage of being simple. However, the ratio might be constant over time, which hides what might be happening with the other quintiles—namely, Q2, Q3, and Q4 in ascending income order. This is particularly problematic for the case of contemporary Latin America, which, as already mentioned, has witnessed the upsurge of an important and vigorous middle class in Q2, Q3, and Q4.

In contrast, the Gini coefficient estimates inequality by incorporating the entire population into calculations, not just Q5 and Q1. To fully understand this measure of inequality, we follow a standard procedure via graphic representation of the Lorenz curve, which captures the concept of cumulative distribution of income at a particular point in time. Figure 5.8 shows the cumulative share of the entire

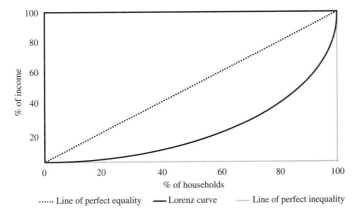

Figure 5.8
The Lorenz curve.
Source: Authors' own construction from Lorenz 1905.

population. (The words population and households are used interchangeably.) The horizontal axis plots income from low to high income (from left to right), and the vertical axis plots the cumulative share of income earned (from bottom to top).

The Gini coefficient is obtained via estimating the ratio of the area below the perfect equality line—and above the continuum of points showing the observed share of total income earned by households—to the total triangle under the perfect equality line. This continuum of points is the U-shaped Lorenz curve. Clearly, as the shape of the U curve becomes more pronounced, income inequalities increase, and so does the Gini coefficient.

In construction, the range of the Gini coefficient is between 0 and 1, or between 0 and 100 when expressed in percentages. The higher the coefficient, the more unequal the distribution of income.

To illustrate the computation of the Gini coefficient, we provide the following example. Suppose that each household head has the same proportion of total income or GDP. In this hypothetical scenario, the Lorenz curve would coincide with the 45-degree line of perfect equality. The Gini coefficient would be 0, because all income is shared equally—by hypothetically identical households in this case. Now, imagine the opposite scenario, in which all national income accrues to one household. This scenario corresponds to a Gini coefficient equaling 1. The mirror image of the L-shaped line shows the perfect inequality case. The Gini coefficient lies between these two extreme scenarios.

5.7.2 Recent Trends in Inequality

Recent estimates of inequality for Latin America are proxied by the Gini coefficient. As shown in figure 5.3, the average Gini coefficient for the region is approximately 0.50, which marks Latin America as one of the most unequal regions in the world.

However, a recent World Bank publication in 2013 demonstrates that, relative to an average Gini coefficient of about 0.54 in the late 1990s, the average Gini coefficient in 2011 fell to approximately 0.48. Figure 5.9 shows the Latin American countries in the income inequality World Bank researchers' dataset. Except for Honduras, where income inequalities increased, income inequalities decreased in the remaining sixteen Latin American countries in the sample. Nicaragua shows the largest decline in income disparities in the first decade of the twenty-first century and Guatemala the smallest. Somewhere in between these two extremes are Brazil and Mexico, to which we now turn.

5.8 Conditional Cash Transfers

To many observers, the twenty-first-century decline in income inequalities in Latin America is due to the fall in average annual Gini coefficients—by 1.17 and 1.03

Poverty and Income Inequality

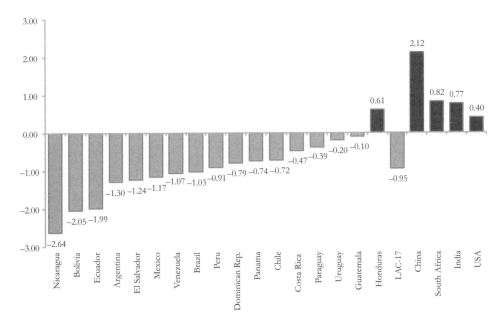

Figure 5.9
Declining income inequality in Latin America by country, 2000–2011 (annual percentage change in the Gini coefficient).
Source: Lustig, Lopez-Calva, and Ortiz-Juarez 2013.

percentage points in Mexico and Brazil, respectively, the region's largest economies. Note that we stick to the Gini approach, rather than using the recent approach of measuring inequalities adopted by Piketty (2014), partly because Piketty's dataset does not include Mexico and Brazil yet.[30]

The reasons for the recent decline in income inequality in Mexico and Brazil are threefold. First, relative to the 1980–1999 period, economic growth in these two economies combined has been multiplied by a factor of three. Second, higher growth in these two regions—where more than half of the Latin American population lives—has been accompanied by a growing middle class. Third, the wage gap between the skilled and unskilled workers (the skill premium) has narrowed down.[31]

Note that two important economies with significantly above-average performance relative to the entire Latin American region—namely, Chile and Peru—also boast important declines in income inequality over the last decade.

Without underestimating the positive effect on income inequalities triggered by economic growth, a growing middle class, and the narrowing of the skilled-unskilled wage gap, in this section we discuss the extent to which conditional and unconditional cash transfers have had an impact on poverty reduction and the decline in income inequalities.

5.8.1 Mexico's Progresa/Oportunidades/Prospera Program

The conditional cash transfer *Progresa/Oportunidades/Prospera* program in Mexico is the pioneering antipoverty campaign project in Latin America and other regions worldwide.[32] It was launched under the name *Progresa* during the Zedillo administration from 1994 to 2000.[33] When the seventy-year-old *Partido Revolucionario Institutional* (PRI) was overthrown in 2000, the program was adopted by the Fox administration from the *Partido Acción Nacional* (PAN). The new administration then rebaptized the program under the name *Oportunidades*, even though the plan was not fundamentally altered. More recently, under Enrique Peña Nieto's administration, from the ranks of the PRI, the project has been relabeled *Prospera*.

Referring to the program as *Progresa/Oportunidades/Prospera* is primarily a semantic choice; only minor changes have taken place to the flagship conditional cash program. Moreover, the project is consensual in that the main center and center-right political parties, PRI and PAN, agree that the program is an effective poverty-reduction tool. Henceforth, we will refer to this particular poverty-alleviation construct as the Mexican Conditional Cash Transfer Program (MCCTP) as *Progresa*—even though, as we have already spelled out, its name has subsequently changed to *Oportunidades* and, more recently, to *Prospera*.

Poverty-stricken households are determined to be Progresa eligible when living in marginalized rural or semirural areas and when they fall below poverty thresholds, as per survey guidance. Recent estimates suggest that approximately 5.8 million households have benefited from the Progresa program, which, as the acronym MCCTP suggests, delivers cash to Mexican women that is earmarked for acquisition of food consumption and nutritional supplements for young children and lactating mothers, *on condition* that children in those eligible households receive preventive health care and attend school.

Eligible households were initially detected in 506 villages. In order to rigorously assess impact, a team of researchers leading the Progresa program randomly chose 320 villages in which eligible households were treated (or given Progresa grants) as of April 1998. In the remaining 186 towns, eligible households were treated as of November 1999.

Taking advantage of the eighteen-month gap between the treatment villages where cash for preventive health care was delivered in April 1998 and the control villages where cash for preventive health care was delivered in November 1999, Gertler and Boyce (2001) were able to assess the impact of the intensity of the treatment on health outcomes such as children's cognitive ability, weight, and height, among others. Higher cumulative transfers delivered comparatively better health outcomes.

With regard to education, Attanasio, Meghir, and Santiago (2012) demonstrate that MCCTP has had a positive impact on primary and post-primary school enrollment and that the program could potentially have an impact on secondary school attainment.

As of the time of writing, it might be too early—or maybe it will never be technically possible—to measure the aggregate impact that the Progresa program has had on human capital, productivity, and wages. Arguably, millions of disadvantaged Mexican households have experienced a lower burden when attempting to simultaneously generate more income and invest in future generations' human capital. Also, as the recent literature on behavioral economics suggests, when the income burden of bringing children up the human capital ladder is lowered, household heads can better focus on their own income-generating potential.[34]

Moreover, anecdotal evidence suggests that an increasingly large number of MCCTP beneficiaries could now "graduate," as such households have joined the ranks of the middle class and therefore are now ineligible. One of the authors of this book is engaged in research efforts by FOSIDES—a Mexican think tank for social development—which is assessing thresholds carefully to classify a growing number of ineligible households.[35]

Finally, MCCTP is biased in favor of women. First, the monetary transfers are handed out to women heads of households. Second, transfers increase with years of school attained; these transfers are higher for girls than for boys. Again, it might be too early to call for the Latin American case, but most econometric studies conducted elsewhere systematically show that increased years of education of women heads of households is a statistically significant variable, delivering a positive effect on household income and investments in human capital. Moreover, some studies show that female earnings are positively and significantly associated with lower income inequality.[36] Third and last, as of 2000 the Progresa program has included subsidies for microfinance programs, the vast majority of which target women. Recent evaluations of flagship microfinance programs in Mexico have demonstrated that microcredit has a positive impact on investment and other outcomes of interest, such as trust and human capital. Positive social effects could be larger if interest rates on microloans were lowered, however.[37]

The overall effect of an expanded version of Progresa program on income inequalities has been estimated. According to Lustig, Lopez-Calva, and Ortiz-Juarez (2011), when comparing the Gini coefficient before and after the program, as much as an 18 percent fall in income inequalities in Mexico can be attributed to Progresa.

5.8.2 Brazil's Bolsa Família and Benefício de Prestação Continuada

The Brazilian conditional cash transfer program, Bolsa Família (BF), is one the largest in the world. The program was launched in 2004 and has grown rapidly since. By 2008, BF covered approximately eleven million Brazilian households. Unlike its Mexican predecessor, BF takes the form of cash transfers, which are higher for lower-income families with a large number of dependent children and elderly members. In other words, unlike Progresa, BF does not target health and education directly, but does target investments in human capital indirectly via a sub-set of BF called the Bolsa-Escola Program (BEP). Under this program, families receive cash transfers per child, thereby lowering the cost of investments in children's human capital accumulation.[38]

In 2007, the Brazilian government decided to specifically target children via lowering the opportunity cost of attending school. In particular, it launched the *Programa de Erradicação do Trabalho Infantil* (PETI), which is a program aimed at stopping child labor that later became part of the BF program. Specifically, the main objective of the PETI program is to stop child labor via direct cash transfers to families with children aged 7 to 15.

Additional transfers to low-income families with children subsequently have been added (including school supplies, gas, and food transfers). The combined effect of the BF program on income inequalities is difficult to assess. Recent estimates, however, suggest that indirect cash transfers to children's investments in health and education via BF has had a minor positive impact on the recent decline in Brazilian income inequalities.[39]

With regard to the elderly, the Brazilian government launched its antipoverty campaign in 1996, *Benefício de Prestação Continuada* (BPC). The program targets low-income households with family members aged 65 and above. According to Ferreira et al (2011) this program has proven to be ineffective at reducing poverty, mostly because food prices have increased considerably during the first decade of the twenty-first century. Lustig, Lopez-Calva, and Ortiz-Juarez (2011), on the other hand, suggest that the combined effect of the BF and BPC explain over 20 percent of the decline in income inequalities in Brazil.

5.8.3 Chile's Ingreso Ético Familiar (Ethical Family Income)

In order to fight poverty, one of the most powerful weapons triggered by the Chilean government in 2011 was IEF. This program consists of both conditional and unconditional cash transfers to the poorest quintiles of the population. IEF operates through a system of comprehensive and continuous support and personalized work with families and vulnerable people in order to facilitate enhanced access to income generation and opportunities for disadvantaged households. It also aims to empower poor families and include working members socially in the pool of the formal sector labor force.

Families in IEF enter into an "axis program." The principal objective of this program is to first prepare a poverty diagnostic and then design an intervention plan, which is followed up to evaluate final outcomes of interest. Following acceptance by qualifying recipients, interventions include psychosocial programs, which target skill acquisition, social inclusion, guidance for insertion into the workforce, and training for undertaking income-generation activities.

In conjunction with these activities, the IEF program grants bonuses and conditional transfers for households living in extreme poverty and an employment subsidy for women. IEF organizes the cash transfers under three pillars: dignity, duties, and achievements. The *dignity* pillar includes unconditional transfers that aim to provide immediate relief to families in extreme poverty. The amount delivered depends on the characteristics of the families. The *duties* pillar comprises conditional transfers. Conditionality implies that children under 6 years of age have compulsory health checkups and that children between six and eighteen years of age have at least 85 percent monthly school-related income attendance. Transfers under the pillars of dignity and duties have a maximum duration of twenty-four months.

Finally, the *achievement* pillar is directed to the most vulnerable 30 percent of the population and, more importantly, provides incentives by giving bonuses to households in which women between the ages of twenty-five and fifty-nine successfully find employment and other bonuses to the best-performing 30 percent of students from fifth grade onward.

In comparison to the Mexican and Brazilian antipoverty programs, a salient feature of IEF is that it aims at providing incentives for families to pull themselves out of poverty on their own—and remain out. The design of the conditional component of IEF transfers combined with psychosocial and employment support are key to avoiding permanent government aid dependency.

Although rigorous academic appraisals of this program have not yet been taken on board by poverty researchers, the program is promising. The idea is appealing indeed: by delivering *incentives* to improve living conditions of *all* family members—adults and children included, not just children and the elderly as in the Mexican and Brazilian conditional cash transfer predecessors—IEF targets households with incentives to all household members as if the economic unit was the household itself and aims to lower dependency ratios within it.

5.9 Concluding Remarks

A large number of Latin Americans live in poverty. Recent declining trends are undeniably linked to higher rates of economic growth in the twenty-first century relative to the periods of crisis, stagflation, reform, and modest recovery in the

1980s and 1990s. Growth acceleration in the twenty-first century has been unequal, however, and poverty reduction therefore reflects uneven growth.

In this chapter, we explained that most definitions of poverty are vague and confusing. Growing concerns by aid agencies and policy makers in Latin America have nonetheless delivered two widespread poverty measures in the region. These measures result from two different methods: UBN and CBN. Despite their numerous shortcomings, such estimates have systematically delivered strikingly high poverty rates. Rough approximations reveal that over 50 percent of households considered to be poor are concentrated in the region's largest economies—namely, Brazil and Mexico.

The bulk of Latin America's poor live in urban and semiurban areas. The poor in such areas include the unemployed or informally employed, the young, women, Afro-Latin Americans, and ethnic groups. Detecting who in Latin America is more likely to be poor has important policy implications with regard to formal employment promotion, policies against gender and racial/ethnic discrimination, and, perhaps more importantly, human capital accumulation. A growing pool of skilled labor should yield a much-needed growth bonus in the region and alleviate the economic costs of the elderly and the fiscal deficit caused by complementary pension and social security reforms.

Poverty and income inequalities are two concurrent phenomena in Latin America. Persistent income inequalities in the region are only rivaled by Africa. Nonetheless, recent data as illustrated by the Gini coefficient—which we have explained in great detail—suggest that a declining trend is under way. Disentangling what portion (if any) of the decline in income inequalities is due to growth and what portion is due to redistributive social projects such as the *Progresa/Oportunidades/Prospera* program in Mexico may turn out to be a challenging question for future research.

What we believe to be unique about contemporary Latin America's income inequalities is on the political economy side of the spectrum. The region had an early start with regard to conflict and political unrest, which are an outgrowth of poverty and income inequalities. More recently, the region's infant democracies have witnessed elected policy makers challenged to meet the dual objectives of reducing poverty and meeting the demands of a growing middle class. The two are not necessarily aligned. Poverty, as manifested via ethnicity and racial discrimination in particular, is context specific, and the challenge here is to provide effective decentralization of well-targeted and well-designed antipoverty campaigns, in which the regions' record is most impressive.

In a broader context, social policies should continue, not just for the sake of escaping poverty, but also for consolidating the vibrant middle class. Redesigning social policies therefore requires careful analysis of the demands for social services by such middle-income cohorts. Unlike the twentieth century, when conflict and political strife might have been triggered by poverty and income inequalities, ongoing social pressures now reappear as a middle-income phenomenon. Social unrest in contemporary Latin America economies has manifested itself in macroeconomic populism, an issue to which we turn in the next chapter.

Summary
- The two most widely used metrics of poverty in Latin America are the UBN and CBN measures. Both have advantages and disadvantages, and they should be perceived as mere proxies and complementary.
- Regardless of the measure used, existing evidence suggests that high growth rates in the early twenty-first-century Latin American economies have been accompanied by lower poverty rates.
- Nonetheless, as much as 30 percent or more of the entire Latin American population is estimated to live in extreme poverty, with the vast majority concentrated in Brazil and Mexico—the region's largest economies.
- Antipoverty campaigns in most regions have contributed to poverty-reduction efforts.
- Recognizing that poverty is most prevalent among the unemployed, informally employed, young, and women heads of households, antipoverty programs have been designed accordingly.
- Although poverty is multidimensional, unemployed and underemployed workers have been detected as main targets, and ESFs for job creation may help to mitigate the problem.
- Chronic and acute poverty in Latin America is identified with Afro-Latin Americans and ethnic groups in rural/semirural areas and with women. These groups suffer from extremely low income levels, from lack of access to health and education, and from social discrimination.
- Persistent gender discrimination against women is linked to poverty. It is prevalent in urban areas, where formally employed women earn less than their male counterparts at equal educational levels.
- The region's young democracies have been underestimating the demands for social services by the growing middle class, which is now an additional source of political conflict and social unrest.
- Income-wise, Latin America is one of the most unequal regions in the world, according to the most widely used proxies of income inequalities—namely, the quintile index and the Gini coefficient.
- Recent evidence suggests that income inequalities have declined in most regions, except in El Salvador.

- In most countries, the income inequality problem has been directly fought via social programs, the principal objective of which is to elevate the status of the poor to the ranks of the middle class.
- Social programs, most notably conditional cash transfer programs, target the health and education of future generations. The elderly have also been targeted in order to reduce the dependency ratio, which can increase a household's income for income generation.
- Most social programs target women. Mexico and Brazil have pioneered such antipoverty social programs with proven results. Relative to Brazil's and Mexico's programs, Chile's social program is more comprehensive and more promising; it emphasizes incentives for the poorest households' members to pull themselves out from poverty permanently.
- The decline in poverty and income inequalities in most regions of contemporary Latin America appears to be linked to both high rates of economic growth on the one hand and social programs on the other. However, estimating the benefits from economic growth and social programs in the region's young democracies remains a challenging task for future research.
- All contemporary Latin American governments face the dual challenge of continuing to finance poverty-relief efforts and consolidating the growing middle class, which is clamoring for enhanced access to social services.

Review Questions
1. Briefly explain the advantages and disadvantages of the two most widely used measures of poverty in Latin America.
2. What are the main characteristics of Latin America's poor?
3. Mention three Latin American countries that are considered to be the poorest and three countries that are considered to be less poor. Briefly explain why.
4. Poverty has declined in twenty-first century Latin America. Briefly explain why and whether democracy has played a role.
5. What are the fundamental and proximate causes of poverty and how can they be fought?
6. Why are women systematically poorer than men, and what policy responses are most adequate to fight against gender discrimination? Deliver concrete examples for the case of Latin America.
7. Do you expect the slowdown in China to reduce the scope for fighting poverty and income inequalities in Latin America? Explain your answer.

Poverty and Income Inequality

8. Briefly spell out the distinguishing features of the Mexican, Brazilian, and Chilean antipoverty campaigns. Which appears to be the most effective and why?
9. One important feature of Brazil's antipoverty campaign is that it targets the elderly. Why has this feature of the Brazilian program proven to be effective?
10. Would you favor replacing direct cash transfers to the elderly with comprehensive pension reform? Explain your answer.
11. Which of the following segments of the Latin American population is more likely to suffer from slowdown growth in China: the poor or the middle class? Explain your answer.

Further Reading

Amartya Sen (1976) authored one of the most often referenced works on poverty lines. From Sen's seminal contribution onward, there has been a large number of less axiomatic articles. For a comprehensive explanation of poverty line measures, see Martin Ravallion 1998. From a policy standpoint, a comprehensive document created by World Bank researchers in 2013 is most relevant to this chapter (see World Bank 2013b). Francisco Ferreira et al. (2012) deliver a clear and concise exposition on the rise of Latin America's middle class and offer venues for future empirical research.

6 The Political Economy of Latin American Development

One of the most pervasive themes in previous chapters has been the relation between institutions and growth-enhancing policies. In sharp contrast to our opening chapter, which focused on income inequalities and long-term growth trajectories dating back to Latin America's colonial period—when the region was predominantly rural—this chapter is closest in spirit to chapter 3 on state intervention under ISI. Specifically, this chapter analyzes the underlying political economy of populist upsurges in predominantly urban areas in which macroeconomic populism has taken hold. The phenomenon is not new. Populism in Latin America dates back to the 1920s.[1] More recently, political economy issues that emphasize the ethnical divide between Latin America's Europeans and *mestizos* and between indigenous and nonindigenous populations have been added to the new wave of populist topics in contemporary Latin America.

Populism is difficult to define. In Latin America, however, the meaning of populism is slightly less difficult to determine. From an economist's standpoint, and paraphrasing Dornbusch and Edwards's groundbreaking work, largely inspired by twentieth-century Latin America, *macroeconomic populism* is an approach to economics that emphasizes growth and income distribution and deemphasizes the risk of inflation and deficit finance, external constraints, and the reaction of economic agents to aggressive nonmarket policies.[2]

Contrary to what chapter 4, with its focus on structural reforms of the 1980s and 1990s, may seem to indicate, macroeconomic populism is not just a ghost from the past. Populism in different forms and shapes is a twenty-first-century Latin American reality. It has reappeared in a handful of countries, regions, and subregions, despite the fact that income inequalities have declined. Indeed, as we document in chapter 5, income inequalities have also decreased in just about every country. Along with poverty and income inequality reduction, an emergent middle class is becoming increasingly important. Yet in countries like Argentina, Bolivia, Ecuador, and Venezuela populist rhetoric and policies are back.

Oil-rich Venezuela is a dramatic example,[3] but even in other countries, regions, and subregions, populist leaders resist market-oriented reforms under the veil of anti-imperialist ideology. What are the roots of such populist revivals? Does the absence of populist rhetoric hide all-powerful entrenched interest groups, which are threaten the development of nascent democracies in the region?

In contemporary Latin American countries such as Mexico, at least three new challenges have emerged. First, private monopolies' and oligopolies' ability to protect entrenched benefits is enormous. Second, public sector workers and unions often resist market-oriented reforms in order to defend insiders at the expense of the truly excluded, to the detriment of foreign investment inflows and consequential productivity enhancements. Third, decentralization has led to local capture by interest groups at the state and municipality levels. Decentralized expenditures for public works and social programs are common examples. How can policy makers effectively fight against institutional capture and all other prevalent forms of corruption?

Section 6.1 in this chapter presents a brief overview of populism dating back to the 1920s. In section 6.2, we deliver concrete examples of macroeconomic populism during the lost decade of the 1980s and beyond. Then, we discuss the decline of macroeconomic populism triggered by the structural reforms of the 1990s in section 6.3. In section 6.4, we analyze the persistence and rebirth of populist policies in extraordinarily diverse regions across Latin America. Twenty-first-century populist movements in Argentina, Bolivia, Ecuador, and Venezuela are covered here. In section 6.5, we develop the theme of regulatory capture of private sector monopolies following privatizations. Section 6.6 discusses SOEs and the most recent nationalization wave in some regions. In section 6.7, we present a summary and some concluding remarks.

6.1 Populism: Historical Background

Conniff (2012, 4) gathers a truly exceptional historical account of populism in Latin America from a political scientist's perspective. He defines *populism* as "an expansive style of election campaigning by colorful and engaging politicians who could draw masses of new voters into their movements and hold their loyalty indefinitely, even after their deaths."[4]

Populism first appeared in Argentina, which by the end of the nineteenth century was the most advanced economy in Latin America. Argentina then featured among the world's top five countries in terms of per capita income. Its growth prospects were rivaled only by those of Australia, which according to most recent statistics ranks fifth among the richest countries on earth.[5] In comparison, Argentina these days ranks sixtieth.[6]

Populism was probably a contributing force in Argentina's precipitous descent during the twentieth century. The country's first populist leader, Hipólito Yrigoyen, was democratically elected in 1916. The constitution did not allow for Yrigoyen to be reelected in 1922, but he nonetheless managed to successfully appoint a successor.[7] His policies identified him with a working-class rural elite at the site of one of the southern-cone Latin America's first upsurges of industrialization: Argentina's meatpacking plant.

The region's most vigorous labor movements since have gathered support from the middle class, first under Juan and Evita Perón's administration at the start of ISI in Latin America in the 1940s. Perón's indelible policies (and tactics) have been replicated by Néstor Kirchner and his wife, former president of Argentina Cristina Fernández de Kirchner—who succeeded her husband as president of Argentina in 2007, was reelected in 2011, and somewhat reluctantly stepped down in 2015 ending thirteen years of Kirchnerism. (In section 6.4 we explain Argentinean populism under the Kirchners in greater detail).

Patriotic rhetoric during most of the twentieth century is a prevailing feature of populism, and not just in Argentina. Since the 1938 nationalization of the oil industry in Mexico under the Lázaro Cárdenas administration, the entire Latin American region has been plagued with anti-foreign-investment leaders.[8] Unsurprisingly, recent energy reforms involving foreign investment into the oil industry and other sectors considered "strategic" for Mexico's economic development have confronted fierce opposition from successors of the ISI ideology—former members of the center-right PRI.[9]

Following the *Acción Democrática* (AD) party—under the leadership of left-wing President Rómulo Betancourt in the 1940s—and its legacy, democratically elected and/or military leaders in Venezuela have often pledged nonintervention from business representatives in national policy making, particularly with regard to FDI.[10]

Under Carlos Andrés Pérez's administration, the 1976 *Great Venezuela Plan* called for an official nationalization of Petróleos de Venezuela S.A. (PDVSA) and production diversification under ISI policies. President Hugo Chávez strengthened state intervention in PDVSA and other industries starting in 1999 and explicitly dictated that a portion of Venezuela's oil industry revenues should be allocated to social programs. Like Argentina under Peronist policies and Mexico under

Echeverría-style PRI policies,[11] Hugo Chávez appointed a successor: Venezuela's current president, Nicolás Maduro.

Chávez's ongoing policies via President Maduro have driven the economy of the seventh largest oil exporter in the world into complete chaos. Venezuela's GDP dropped 4 percent in 2014, and experienced a further decline in excess of 7 percent in 2015, according to recent IMF official statistics. At the same time, the country suffered from exceedingly high inflation rates of over 40 percent in 2013, 62 percent in 2014, and approximately 40 percent in 2015.[12]

Despite the fact that former President Luis Inácio Lula da Silva from Brazil is not characterized by political scientists as a twenty-first-century populist, Lula—as he came to be known—had close business ties to the Chávez administration, which date back to 2003.[13] These included a loan to Venezuela for the construction of a US$14 billion refinery in northeastern Brazil to process oil production from PDVSA and Petrobras (Petróleo Brasileiro S.A.)—Brazil's state-run oil company. However, Brazil's president until 2016—Dilma Rouseff, Lula's former chief of staff—had managed to distance herself from Venezuela's current leader via, for example, calling off the northeast refinery project.

To address populist ideology and practice in every Latin American country is beyond the scope of this chapter. Suffice to say—for the sake of exposition—that the Chávez populist legacy in twenty-first-century Latin America has become a benchmark for populist practices in other regions.

According to Drake 2012, Chile is one of the few Latin American countries where populism—as defined earlier by political scientists—never took hold. Economists tend to disagree, however. Larraín and Meller (1990), for example, conclude that the Allende government was a socialist-populist experiment that left an indelible imprint.

In the future, Drake (2012, 67) warns, with regard to Chile in the twenty-first century, "keeping populism at bay will likely depend on the ability of the parties to recapture their traditional strength, to re-incorporate the masses into political participation, and to re-dress the grievances of the working-class." Drake's predictions are likely to hold true for all of contemporary Latin America's infant democracies.

6.2 Macroeconomic Populism

Simply stated, the Dornbusch—Edwards's definition of macroeconomic populism relates to expansionary policies, which are set in motion by politicians running large budget deficits and prioritizing redistribution over economic growth, quickly leading to stagflation.[14]

Latin America during the twentieth century has suffered from several stagflation spells, and Dornbusch and Edwards's analysis, dating back to the 1990s, delivers important insights with regard to the link between populism and stagflation during the second half of the twentieth century. Specifically, drawing from the historical experiences of Chile under Salvador Allende in the 1970s and Peru under Alan García in the 1980s, the authors pin down a set of populist policies and potential consequences.

In the case of Chile in the 1970s, although the ultimate objectives of the Allende administration were to reignite economic growth, redistribute the benefits from enhanced growth across the poorest quintiles of the Chilean population, and decrease inflation, Allende's policies included nationalization, budget deficit–financed expansionary policies, and price controls (Larraín and Meller 1990).

These policies—also called *structuralist policies* after ECLAC's Prebisch, Furtado, and Singer's ideological influence on ISI tools, as explained in chapter 3—were based on five key assumptions: first, that the economy had excess capacity; second, that excess capacity was linked to unequal distribution of income and consumption; third, that the manufacturing sector was mostly producing luxurious goods under exceedingly high capital/labor ratios; fourth, that inflation was a structural—not a monetary phenomenon—in that it was triggered by low production of basic manufactures, in turn due to wage rigidities and monopolistic pricing; and fifth, that exports could become more diversified regardless of exchange rate fluctuations.

Under these assumptions and with a clear goal of prioritizing redistribution over economic growth, the Allende regime in the aftermath of its election in 1970 undertook aggressive agrarian reforms via expropriation of large estates and masterminded the nationalization of the copper mines, the ownership of which at the time was shared with US investors. Nationalization plans were also drawn to include the banking and manufacturing sectors. Along with massive nationalization projects, salaries in SOEs were increased, favoring low-wage employees. These wages were used as a benchmark for unionized workers in the private sector to claim an increase in their own salaries.

Increased government expenditures were not confined to public sector employee salaries. Expenditures also grew as a result of government outlays used in construction, agriculture, and social security. Most expenditure was paid for via loans from the central bank—that is, via expansionary monetary policies.

Allende's redistributive package involved expansionary fiscal and monetary policies, which were complemented with generalized and tightly enforced price controls. Consequently, after the first year of reforms, growth was reignited, real wages and consumption increased, unemployment decreased, and income distribution—as proxied by the share of GDP accruing to labor—improved.

A year later, however, the Chilean economy stagflated; it went into a recession in 1972 and fell into complete economic collapse in 1973.[15] Then, inflation rates exploded. Next, workers' discontent in private sector firms and a major downfall in productivity growth in SOEs decreased the scope to expand production of intermediate and final goods. After that, real wages decreased to lower-than-pre-reform levels as inflation reached unprecedented three-digit rates. Next, an underground economy developed. Goods and services sold in the black market avoided taxation, further exacerbating the budget deficit. Finally, a key component of stabilization packages at the time implied an overvaluation of the real exchange rate, which in turn lowered foreign reserves on the one hand and penalized exports on the other. This jumbled situation resulted in Allende's *Unidad Popular* coalition being ousted via a violent military coup d'état in September 1973. Allende's incomplete presidential term was followed by a seventeen-year military dictatorship under General Augusto Pinochet.

President Alan García in Peru enacted somewhat similar redistributive policies. García's policies unfolded in the mid-1980s—that is, in the midst of the worst period of Latin America's lost decade, during which Peruvians suffered a dramatic loss of GDP annual growth of up to 4.2 percent on average from 1980 to 1985. Inflation was approximately 250 percent per annum.[16] His policies were labeled *heterodox* because they deviated from IMF policy prescriptions emphasizing budget deficit reductions and nominal price rigidities to prioritize lowering inflation.

Garcia's heterodox package was constructed on four key assumptions: First, imposing nominal wage restrictions is unnecessary, because labor loses purchasing power, hence lowering much needed domestic demand to foster production and GDP growth. Second, further deficit reductions were also unnecessary, as these contribute to lower domestic demand in an economy in which there is excess capacity. Third, devaluations were not needed to close the trade deficit, because devaluations increase the costs of intermediate inputs of production and therefore lower production. A similar argument applies to interest rates that, unlike wages, were restricted in order to lower production costs. Fourth, expansionary monetary policies are necessary to foster liquidity and, thus, demand for money and output.[17]

The Allende and García macroeconomic policies were strikingly similar. In both instances, and under the assumption of excess capacity, internal demand was expected to increase as a result of expansionary fiscal and monetary policies. In both cases, a boost to internal demand was expected to take place following the ISI tradition, which prioritized the internal market at the expense of export promotion.

One key difference is that under the 1985 García administration no immediate nationalization plans were spelt out. Another is that, in an attempt to tame chronic hyperinflation, restore confidence in the national currency, and avoid dollarization, the *sol* (Peru's currency until 1985) was replaced by the *inti*, with one inti equaling one thousand soles. In 1991, the inti was again replaced by the *nuevo sol* (the new sol) under the Presidency of Alberto Fujimori—García's successor—with one new sol equaling one million intis. Another difference is that, having inherited an enormous external debt, the García administration limited external debt service to 10 percent of Peru's exports, with the principal objective of attaining a growth target of around 6 percent per annum—that is, a growth rate nearly four times as high as the one observed in 1985. This growth-enhancing objective was expected to be attained within one year.

Drastically limiting external debt services was perceived as key to the potential success of the García project, because the consequential foreign exchange savings would allow for relaxation of the balance of payments deficit constraints on the one hand, and because imposing further real wage cuts was politically unfeasible on the other. Without external debt limitations, devaluations and an ipso facto inflation hike were imminent, and these inflationary pressures could not be controlled via imposing nominal wage rigidities at that particular point in time; specifically, capping nominal wages was politically unfeasible.

By and large, the immediate effect of the García heterodox policies was a successful one. The inflation rate decreased sharply. Both employment and real wages increased, and the growth rate moved from approximately 2.5 percent in 1985 to 9.5 percent in 1986.[18]

However, in an attempt to control capital flight, García announced a plan aimed at nationalizing the banking sector, which further increased speculation on the government's grand plans to nationalize other sectors. Large capital outflows ensued, leading to a drastic decline in foreign reserves as private investor feared expropriation. This in turn precipitated a large devaluation of the inti and triggered inflation. In addition, price controls were imposed on basic goods and services, which continued production-required subsidies. However, subsidies increased the budget deficit and consequently exacerbated inflationary pressures. Moreover, inflation—due to the devaluations and large public deficits—was also out of control because of the *Olivera-Tanzi effect*; that is, in periods of high inflation the real value of tax collection declines, further exacerbating the deficit and consequential inflation.[19] Inflation ran at around 7,000 percent in 1989.

At such exceedingly high inflation rates, all the first-year gains were lost. Most importantly, real wages fell and unemployment increased, leading to political unrest and the upsurge of a violent Peruvian movement known as the *Shining Path* (*El Sendero Luminoso*). In 1990, García was succeeded by an authoritarian regime led by Alberto Fujimori, and, following charges of corruption and human rights' violations, García sought and found exile in Colombia in 1992.

In addition to Dornbusch and Edwards 1989, from which the preceding discussion borrows, an interesting paper by Sachs (1989) includes an analysis of macroeconomic populism under Juan and Evita Perón in Argentina in the 1950s and under José Sarney in the 1980s in Brazil.[20]

6.3 Reforms and the Downfall of Macroeconomic Populism

No one can deny that the underlying problem that has triggered recurrent populist cycles in Latin America's twentieth century is income inequality. Income inequality creates tensions that contribute to the emergence of populist policies, particularly during slow growth and recessionary spells.

Growth-enhancing reforms against the globalization backdrop in the 1990s are key to our understanding of contemporary Latin American economies. In a nutshell, as we discussed in chapter 4, the structural, market-oriented reforms of the 1980s and 1990s had three key components: stabilization, privatization, and trade liberalization.

On the stabilization front, it was widely acknowledged that fiscal deficits were at the heart of inflation, although contagious effects from crises elsewhere were later recognized as an important contributing factor when attempting to explain failed stabilizations in the 1990s. We return to these issues in chapter 8.

In this section, we first discuss the impact of successful price stabilization and then argue that without the entire package of structural reforms—inclusive of key price-stabilization tools—the downfall of macroeconomic populism in most countries cannot be understood. As growth accelerated in the twenty-first century, poverty rates fell sharply, and, albeit slowly, income inequalities—which are at the heart of macroeconomic populism—have decreased in most countries (see chapter 5).

Although the emergent middle class might prompt new populist waves in the twenty-first century, this trend might be counteracted in Latin America's resource-abundant economies, where democratic institutions are fragile. In fact, natural resource wealth may have adversely affected Latin America's governance—perpetuation of authoritarian regimes in government, rampant corruption by civil servants that go unpunished, among other pervasive manifestations—that are generally referred to as the resource curse. We will come back to the resource curse in subsection 6.3.3.

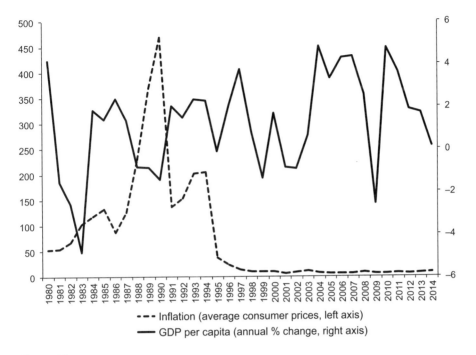

Figure 6.1
Inflation and GDP growth in Latin America, 1980–2014.
Source: IMF 2015.

6.3.1 The Impact of Successful Inflation Stabilization and Growth

Figure 6.1 shows the extraordinary impact of stabilization policies in Latin America at the turn of the century. Success with regard to taming inflation and reigniting growth was so impressive that emerging market economies in Eastern Europe, following the fall of the Berlin Wall in 1990, often requested advice from Latin American policy makers.

Average inflation yearly rates—as proxied by the consumer price index for 1986 to 1996—were nearly 200 percent in Latin America. In sharp contrast, inflation rates fell during the 1997–2006 period to an annual average of 8 percent! This extraordinary achievement resulted from a combination of monetary and fiscal policies in support of stabilization in most countries.

The extent to which lowering inflation supports poverty-reduction efforts was discussed in chapter 5. Simply put, as Latin America becomes increasingly urbanized and thus monetized, the purchasing power of a vast majority of poor households erodes as inflation rises. Hence, while fighting inflation is important in its own right (e.g., productivity increases as menu costs decrease when inflation is

Table 6.1
Labor discontent before and after reforms in Latin America

	Before economic reform	Transition period	Consolidated reform
Bolivia	5.44	3.08	0.78
Chile	27.83	N/A	0.575
Colombia	N/D	0.643	0.599
Costa Rica	0.582	0.644	0.725
Ecuador	1.08	0.88	0.190
El Salvador	0.819	0.445	0.627
Guatemala	0.395	0.221	0.247
Jamaica	2.12	2.52	3.03
Mexico	0.889	0.825	0.105
Peru	3.34	1.43	0.105

Source: Kurtz 2004.

anticipated),[21] it is particularly important in Latin America for political economy considerations as well: the minimum living standards that the vast majority of the urban poor can ask for from policy makers is that the value of their entitlements to basic food and nonfood items be preserved. Unsurprisingly to us, but not to many observers, urban conflict and discontent with policy makers leading reform efforts decreased as inflation vanished.

As table 6.1 shows, reforms were accompanied by exceedingly low levels of open discontent in urban areas, as proxied by labor strikes. This is an interesting finding, given the wide scope of the reforms—inclusive of layoffs, increases in the price of public utilities and social services, and other painful adjustments. Our conjecture is that, had average Latin Americans been asked in early 1990s surveys what they perceived as the most serious problems affecting their lives, the answer would have probably been: inflation![22]

Most Latin Americans live in extended family networks, which serve as a safety net to cope with idiosyncratic shocks. However, inflation is an aggregate shock to poor households' purchasing power—particularly for the poorest quintiles, which, unlike the top quintiles, cannot easily hedge against inflation.

Still more surprising in table 6.1 is that, except for Costa Rica and Jamaica, where the incidence of strikes increased slightly, the structural reform period (circa 1982–2000) coincided with the transistion from military or authoritarian regimes to democracy. The table therefore does not reflect repression of labor movements. More empirical research is needed to fully understand the link between inflation and conflict in Latin America, however.

As for how inflation was eradicated from the region, each country implemented its own price-stabilization policies. To review each case is beyond the scope of this book. However, we return to salient features in greater detail in chapter 8. Nonetheless, two cases merit special attention at this point: Chile and Mexico.

Chile started much earlier than any other country in the region; Mexico started in 1982.[23] Chile implemented orthodox reforms, Mexico heterodox.[24] In both instances, inflation disappeared when compared to prereform periods. Although the causal effect of stabilization on social unrest is difficult to estimate empirically, because stabilization policies were part of a package of market-oriented reforms that ultimately succeeded in terms of higher and sustained economic growth rates starting in 2004, evidence on poverty and inequality reduction arguably played a role.

6.3.2 The Rise of the Middle Class: Social Stability or Unrest?

In most Latin American countries, not just in Chile and Mexico, the share of the population that joined the ranks of the middle class has increased considerably since the turn of the century.

Birdsall (2012) argues that, as figure 6.2 suggests, the rise of the middle class in twenty-first-century Latin America has played an important role in the contain-

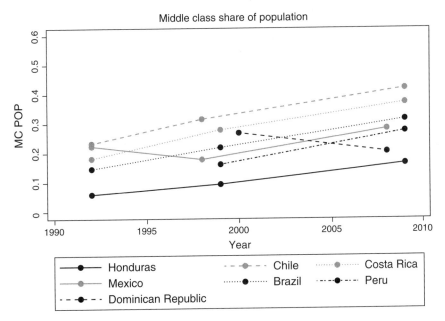

Figure 6.2
The rise of the middle class in selected Latin American countries, 1992–2009, as a percentage of each country's population.
Source: Birdsall 2012.

ment of political instability. Her estimates on the size of the middle class as a proportion of the Latin American population come from the Socioeconomic Database for Latin America and the Caribbean and the World Bank surveys showing that relative to the 1990s and with few exceptions, the middle class in Latin America has almost doubled over the past decade in the region's twenty-first century.

The growing importance of the middle class also reflects growing numbers of educated individuals that are more reliant on stable and effective governments and the rule of law. This growing segment of the population is expected to be more supportive of growth-enhancing reforms. Moreover, recent work suggests that a parallel upward trend in the use of social media can potentially create more participation in public debates and strengthened democracy in contemporary Latin American economies. [25]

On the other hand, even in countries such as Mexico, where the middle class has increased steadily since the mid-1990s, some reforms raised concerns for these groups. For example, subsidies for urban areas (e.g., the *tortilla* and basic services subsidies) declined. Simultaneously, the *Progresa/Oportunidades/Prospera* antipoverty campaign program—launched in the mid-1990s—favored primary and secondary education at the expense of tertiary education, and this also had adverse effects on the middle class, the interests of which were threatened.

Some observers noted that with resource reallocation favoring the poor, the middle class felt vulnerable and saw a more limited scope for social mobility, which in turn helps explain the downfall of the seventy-year-old PRI regime and the rise of PAN in the year 2000.[26]

Chile also experienced a more vocal middle-class discontent in 2011 alongside parallel efforts to reduce poverty via job creation, higher wages, and its antipoverty program, including the *Ingreso Ético Familiar* (IEF). Protesters were mainly middle-class students requesting free education—also perceived by the median voter in Chile as the most important social mobility venue.[27]

6.3.3 Left Behind in Resource-Abundant Economies

Most Latin American countries are predominantly primary commodity export producers. Collier (2010a, 2010b) has studied the political economy features of resource-abundant countries. His analysis of resource abundant economies is pessimistic with regard to stabilizing democracy and consolidating good governance for social stability.

Collier suggests that an excessive reliance on primary commodity exports can lead to rebel predation—or rebels' theft of natural resources to finance confrontation and loot-seeking by rural guerrilla groups that initially hold a political agenda using drug production and trafficking, thus triggering violence and political unrest. A typical example of such a pervasive phenomenon might be the case of the Revolutionary Armed Forces of Colombia (FARC). Moreover, in resource-abundant countries governments might be less accountable, which threatens fragile democratic institutions and can lead to public mistrust and social upheaval. We have already referred earlier to this as a resource curse phenomenon.

Have initial endowments and exploitation of natural resources contributed to the new wave of populism in some Latin American regions? In our view, natural resource windfalls have facilitated the emergence of a new populist wave, especially in countries with weak economic and political institutions. Specifically, growth was not reignited during the 1990s in many Latin American countries, and the approximately ten-year period of reforms left a hostile and grim land, allowing populist leaders to put all the blame for poverty and inequality on corrupt politicians, oligarchs, and multinational corporations that had stakes in natural resources such as oil and mines.

Thus, the market-oriented reforms themselves were questioned by several academics.[28] Nonetheless, most Latin American leaders resisted pressure and did not join the ranks of discontent. John Williamson, who coined the Washington Consensus reforms, namely, stabilization, privatization, and trade liberalization, has spelled out the mixed sentiments in the hearts of Latin Americans until 2003. (We analyze the Washington Consensus reforms in greater detail in chapter 7.) Williamson (2006) argues that on one side of the spectrum, Latin America in the twenty-first century was endowed with (superior) market-friendly institutions, which were Latin America's best bet to pull disadvantaged households from poverty. On the other side of the spectrum, however, Williamson witnessed how public opinion in many countries remained hostile to the market-oriented reforms of the 1980s and 1990s and that such hostility was turning populist, with consequential—and well-known—adverse effects on the middle class and the poor.

6.4 The Rebirth of Populism in the Twenty-First Century

Failed populist attempts to cope with a long period of recurrent stagflation spells led to a very peculiar form of Latin American populism in the twenty-first century. With price stabilization under control, charismatic leaders no longer targeted a majority of Latin American citizens, who had endured inflation and hyperinflation, particularly during the prolonged lost decade of the 1980s. Instead, such leaders seemed to have gathered support from highly heterogeneous segments of the population that were still experiencing the perils of low growth and scarce employment opportunities during the 1998–2004 period—that is, prior to the pronounced commodity boom.

In this section, we review the rebirth of populism in Latin America in chronological order. We first analyze the experience of the 1999 Bolivarian Revolution under Hugo Chávez. We then revisit the case of Argentina, where Néstor and Cristina Kirchner have influenced the economic and political landscape since 2003. We next analyze the case of Bolivia since Evo Morales took office in 2006. Finally, we discuss the case of Ecuador, where Rafael Correa's policies have been most influential since 2007.

Although each country has specificities of its own, it is worth noting that in all instances the countries in question are primary commodity producers and exporters and that their antiglobalization rhetoric is biased against the United States.

6.4.1 Venezuela

The economy of Venezuela is heavily dependent on oil. Venezuela ranks twelfth in world oil production, after Kuwait and before Nigeria, and is the ninth-largest petroleum exporter. Petroleum sales account for over 90 percent of the country's exports. Venezuela has therefore been and continues to be exceedingly dependent on world oil prices.

Along with the vast majority of Latin American countries, Venezuela endured hardships in the lost decade of the 1980s and beyond. By the late 1980s, Venezuela engaged itself in a series of structural reforms, which, just as in most cases in Latin America, did not deliver immediate benefits in terms of growth and produced only meager gains with regard to in income inequality and poverty, if at all.

A temporary increase in GDP growth from 1991 to 1992 came about as a result of US military intervention in Iraq. This intervention in August 1990—also known as Operation Desert Storm—had an impact on oil prices, which doubled from approximately seventeen dollars a barrel to about thirty-six dollars a barrel. As a result, Venezuela's GDP growth in 1991 and 1992 increased to around 8 percent—well above the region's average at the time.

In 1993, however, an internal political crisis erupted, triggered by the liberalization of petroleum prices domestically, which severely affected the cost of living for the average Venezuelan citizen in general and the cost of public transport in particular. Such a hike in the domestic price of oil caused widespread political unrest, leading to *El Caracazo*, after Venezuela's capital, Caracas, where the protests took place. Following charges of embezzlement, then-president Carlos Andrés Pérez was forced to resign.

Venezuela went through one of its worst political crises from 1993 to 1998. In parallel with interim presidents and an election victory by President Caldera, whose legitimacy was questioned due to small electorate turnout and a patchy national congress composed of dozens of political parties, Hugo Chávez's leftist movement known as the *Bolivarian Revolution* gained traction. Chávez won the national election in 1998 against a Yale-educated economist, Enrique Salas Römer. Hugo Chávez remained in office from 1999 until he died in 2013, and he was succeeded by Nicolás Maduro—Venezuela's current president. (Political uncertainty over the fate of the Maduro administration has grown, however; his party lost a huge majority of its seats to the center-right opposition in the 2015 parliamentary elections, widely perceived as the end of Venezuela's era of *Chavismo*).

The Chávez regime was characterized by nationalizations, expropriations, and massive spending on social programs financed by windfall oil revenues. Throughout most of Chávez's mandate, anti-American rhetoric became increasingly confrontational. Fueled by strong links with Cuba, the Venezuelan Bolivarian Revolution turned into a paternalistic government, which went far beyond state intervention during the ISI period. On a positive note, some social indicators improved substantially.[29]

However, average inflation remained well above 20 percent, which is high relative to the average for the Latin American region. A fixed exchange policy regime to contain inflation led to an overvalued *bolivar*—Venezuela's currency. Capital controls and restrictions on imports have led to massive capital flight and severe shortages of basic products such as milk, flour, and medicines. Perhaps more importantly, the sharp decline in oil prices in recent years has made Chávez's economic model unsustainable.

The negative trend is likely to continue. Venezuela's inflation rate, as we mentioned, is the highest in the world. Deep recession has taken hold. As of the time of writing, social unrest that began in February 2014 has escalated. The current chaotic situation may ultimately lead to major political changes even before the next presidential election in 2018, at which point history is likely to mark Venezuela's Chávez/Maduro government as a failed populist regime.

6.4.2 Argentina

Argentina's market-friendly reforms following the debt crisis in the 1980s gained worldwide recognition. Breaking with at least decade-long inflation and failed stabilization attempts, Argentina adopted a currency board in 1991. Such a legal amendment lowered inflationary expectations, bringing inflation down from a yearly average of approximately 3,000 percent in 1989 to 3.4 percent in 1994. At the same time, growth rates increased to an annual rate of around 6.5 percent from 1991 to 1998.

The currency board survived several contagion crises, not only from Latin America but also from other emerging market economies.[30] However, by the end of the millennium, criticism against the currency board was mounting; Argentina's peso was clearly overvalued, export revenues—mostly from primary commodities—began to decrease, and growth rates slowed down. By the end of 2001, the currency board collapsed, leading to a huge depreciation of the Argentinean peso and a complete collapse of a decade-long fixed exchange rate system.

Widespread riots and political upheaval led to President Fernando de la Rúa's resignation in 2001. An interim government followed his presidency until the presidential election of 2003, when the center-left presidential candidate Néstor Kirchner, a Peronist, won the general election. He gained popularity via nationalistic rhetoric favoring state intervention via increased spending in welfare and subsidies, and anti-imperialist trade liberalization, particularly with regard to the Free Trade Area of the Americas (FTAA), an initiative largely perceived as originating in the United States. He instead favored trade with Brazil and other members of Mercosur. Increased ties with Brazil under then-president Luiz Ignácio Lula da Silva went beyond trade and joined investment projects.

Ideology played an important role. Both Lula and Kirchner were ideologically close to the anti-imperialist stance of Venezuela under Chávez. However, Argentina's ties with Chávez went further than those of Lula. Indeed, Venezuela was the only country that bought Argentinean bonds in an effort to help Kirchner cope with the perils of the 2001 financial crisis. Venezuela and Argentina signed bilateral agreements regarding agricultural products, oil exploitation, and technology. Moreover, both countries advocated state intervention in most spheres of production and, in particular, with regard to the financial system.

Initially, Néstor Kirchner's policies seemed to pay off. Robust and sustained recovery started in 2003, with growth rates averaging over 8 percent until the end of his mandate in 2007. Arguably, economic recovery resulted from unprecedented foreign debt renegotiations involving a 65 percent write-off, a sharp devaluation, and a boom in international soybean prices, which triggered an export expansion and an increase in domestic consumption. Inflation rates during the 2003 to 2007 Kirchner administration averaged approximately 10 percent per annum, however, higher than the average for the region.

His wife—Cristina Fernández de Kirchner, who won the presidential election in 2007—succeeded Néstor Kirchner. The two Kirchners shared the same protectionist, state interventionist, and anti-imperialist stance. Despite high growth and prosperity, Fernández de Kirchner inherited an unstable political situation. Inflation and protests from agricultural producers facing export taxes of up to 30 percent dominated Argentina's economic and political landscape at the time.

The situation has worsened since because of government attempts to increase export taxes on agricultural production (soybeans and sunflower oil in particular) in order to finance "social expenditures." Discontent among foreign investors also increased as a result of oil expropriation of foreign stakes in Argentina's *Yacimientos Petrolíficos Fiscales* (YPF). Inflation has continued to increase to nearly 30 percent. After a decade of robust and sustained growth as a result of the commodity boom from 2000 to 2013, the estimated growth rate for 2015 by the IMF was -0.3%. In the recent presidential election, Mauricio Macri, from the ranks of the center-right, won, ending a decade of *Kirchnerismo*. Reverting the populist trend and chaotic economic situation left by the Kirchner predecessors remains a gigantic challenge, and whether the Macri administration will succeed remains an open question.

6.4.3 Bolivia

Inhabited by a large majority of indigenous people from Quechua descent, Bolivia is the only country in twenty-first-century Latin America in which racial issues have taken center stage both domestically and internationally. Bolivia's current leader, Evo Morales, is often referred to as the first indigenous president of Bolivia. Regionally, he has often been compared with Mexico's Benito Juárez, also from indigenous lineage, who dominated the country's political landscape for nearly twenty years during the mid-nineteenth century.

Internationally, Morales has been praised for his fight to defend the rights of rural indigenous populations, often perceived as oppressed and discriminated against by a minority ruling elite of European descent.[31] After winning numerous battles in favor of rural populations in general, and coca growers in particular, Morales fought fiercely against market-friendly urbanites. He led the socialist movement party, *Movimiento al Socialismo* (MAS), he won the presidential election in 2005, and his party secured an overwhelming majority in the Bolivian Congress.

With a clear and strong mandate and an anti-imperialist rhetoric—similar to that of predecessors in Venezuela under Chávez and Argentina under the Kirchners—Morales's first months in office in 2006 gained a great deal of international publicity as he advocated increased state intervention in Bolivia's extraction of natural gas and in mining, electricity, and railways. He first threatened to nationalize and expropriate industries operating "illegally," thereby giving his government a great deal of negotiating clout vis-à-vis Bolivia's international investors.

In practice, the only industry that was truly nationalized was the lucrative gas industry. This enabled the Morales administration to strengthen its government public finances and to devote a nonnegligible portion of state revenues to social investments in infrastructure such as roads, running water, and electricity in remote indigenous communities. Moreover, bilateral gas supply agreements with Brazil and Argentina increased gas exports and attracted private foreign contractors. High rates of growth during the twenty-first-century commodity boom from 2000 to 2013 further strengthened Bolivia's public finances as tax revenues increased.

Relative to Venezuela and Argentina, Bolivia has accumulated a vast amount of foreign reserves. Although this might be due to Morales's desire to assert his anti-imperialist views, particularly via systematically taking a confrontational stance against the United States, foreign reserve accumulation has enabled Bolivia to be fenced off from potential IMF intervention on the one hand and has prevented an inflation upsurge on the other.

In 2014, Morales entered his third term in office. He is the only elected president of Bolivia to have ruled over eight consecutive years. He appeals to the majority of Bolivians from indigenous descent and has managed to weather political upheavals via either retracting his initiatives or via referendums. Whether history will judge Morales as a populist thus far remains an open question.

6.4.4 Ecuador

The economy of Ecuador heavily depends on oil revenues, which account for over half the country's exports. Despite widespread market-friendly reforms in the 1990s, Ecuador suffered from a severe banking crisis in 1999. This was triggered by a number of adverse shocks, including domestic political unrest resulting from fierce internal opposition to the reforms and the 1995 Cenepa War—a boundary dispute with Peru. Moreover, and unlike neighboring countries, Ecuador was incapable of coping with the contagious effects of the Mexican Tequila Crisis in the mid-1990s, partly because it coincided with a sharp decline in the price of oil. Perhaps more importantly, the Central Bank of Ecuador lost credibility, as it did not support the fiscal discipline dictated by the reforms.[32] With output contracting drastically and inflation increasing sharply, a new wave of reforms was introduced.

One of the most important reforms consisted of abandoning the local currency—the sucre—and adopt the US dollar as legal tender in 2000. Dollarization brought inflation down to historical levels and helped to promote growth; the annual increase from 2002 to 2006 was around 5 percent, a high rate of economic growth that Ecuador had not experienced in approximately twenty-five years.[33] Despite such a high growth spell and price stabilization via dollarization, the country continued to experience political instability to the extent that no president has been allowed to complete a four-year term in office since 1996. What seemed to anger the public the most was corruption—an endemic problem indeed.[34]

In 2006, a charismatic left-wing politician, Rafael Correa, emerged from Ecuador's middle class. Among his political assets was his fluency in the indigenous language Quechua, which is widely spoken, particularly among Ecuadoreans from lower quintiles. Unlike Evo Morales, Correa is a highly educated individual, well above average for Latin American standards. He earned a PhD in economics from the University of Illinois at Urbana-Champaign in 2001, but he is considered anti-American and anti-globalization.[35]

Once elected, Correa prioritized economic growth and poverty eradication. He held on to his anti-imperialist manifesto, however, particularly with regard to using oil revenues for social programs. Moreover, Correa defaulted on Ecuador's foreign debt, and a considerable amount of total government expenditures—financed mostly from oil revenues and loans from China—have been devoted to social programs and public investments in infrastructure.

According to recent World Bank estimates, total government expenditures as a percentage of GDP have increased from around 21 percent in 2002 to nearly 41 percent in 2012. Poverty has declined by approximately 12 percentage points, and extreme poverty has decreased by more than 8 percentage points. The number of Ecuadoreans joining the middle class was on the rise in recent estimates, and income disparities have decreased. As proxied by the Gini coefficient, income inequalities decreased from 54 to 48.

President Correa was reelected first in 2010 and then in 2013. Whether his redistributive policies can be sustained crucially depends on external vulnerabilities—most importantly, the price of oil (which has been falling steadily in recent years). Unlike Evo Morales, Rafael Correa is largely perceived as a populist. Ecuador under Correa shares common traits, albeit milder, with Venezuela under Chávez.

6.5 Regulatory Capture

Populism thus far has been linked to the idea of lavish "social spending" in order to gain support from the lower middle class and the lowest income quintiles. However, populism takes a different shape when support from domestic private sector enterprises is needed in order to pursue a political agenda.

Following structural reforms, Latin America in the 1990s witnessed mass privatizations of SOEs. By 1999, Latin America accounted for more than half of the privatizations that took place in the entire developing world.[36] The driving force behind privatizing SOEs is that SOEs are considerably less efficient than privately owned firms.[37] The main reasons for this fact include lack of accountability, leading to a lack of managerial and employee incentives; lack of competition, corruption by government officials; and the use of SOEs to meet political objectives.[38]

Ongoing controversies over privatization cannot be dissociated from welfare considerations, however. For example, in pursuit of profitability, private monopolies have been allowed to increase prices, lower quality, and/or concentrate supply of goods and services in wealthier urban regions at the expense of poorer rural or semirural areas. It has therefore been recognized that following privatization, private monopolies must be effectively regulated.[39]

However, in most instances—as groundbreaking work by Jean-Jacques Laffont and 2014 Nobel Prize winner Jean Tirole (1993) has demonstrated—private monopolies end up manipulating government agencies, which are supposed to control private sector enterprises' actions. This phenomenon is known as *regulatory capture*.

Most observers believe that effective regulation must be designed prior to privatizing SOEs. Effective regulation should aim to clearly define the responsibilities of the main actors involved in the process. Specifically, crafting effective regulation requires coordination and well-defined divisions of labor among national regulators, ministries, and provincial and municipal regulators.

According to the World Bank report on regulation (World Bank 2013a), the experience in Latin America is extremely diverse. Peru, for example, stands out as an example of transparency in the supervision and regulation of its telecommunication system. At the other end of the spectrum, the report shows extreme lack of transparency and predictability along with excessive discretion by the gas regulatory authorities in Argentina. Lack of transparency not only hinders investment and productivity but also affects welfare; the vast majority does not know what "acceptable" gas prices are, because government authorities have been constantly changing policies, negatively affecting energy supplies. In 1999, for example, Argentina's National Electricity Regulatory Authority ordered the country's private electric companies to lower penalties for late payments from 10 to 1.2 percent; the private companies in question openly declared that the government was changing the agreed-upon rules and feared that future changes would further affect them. Changing the rules might in turn hinder private investment in infrastructure.

In the case of Mexico, the constitutional amendments undertaken under the Cárdenas administration back in 1938 (articles 27 and 28 of the Mexican Constitution) pertain to the energy sector. The articles prohibited private sector participation in the oil, gas, and electricity sectors. Underinvestment in these sectors and inefficiencies have adversely affected the Mexican economy for many years, yet it was not until the recent amendments to the constitution under President Peña Nieto's administration that changes to those articles were successfully made, despite sharp divisions within the ranks of legislative power that have left underlying uncertainties as to whether the reform will be reversed.

If well-designed and transparent, effective regulation opens the scope for efficiency gains with minimum welfare losses. However, the regulatory framework in Latin America—inclusive of the banking sector—is still in its infancy. At this particular point in time, the region faces serious challenges with regard to regulatory capture. The lack of an adequate regulatory environment triggers anger and negative feelings against private sector monopolies by the median voter.[40]

Scarcity of expertise, weak accounting and auditing, unclear separation of powers, inefficient lobbying, and corruption prevent current regulatory frameworks from mimicking more developed regulatory frameworks, such as those in the European Union (EU). On a bright note, privatization followed by exposure of local monopolies to foreign competition in the increasingly globalized Latin American economies can mitigate the pervasiveness of regulatory capture.

6.6 State-Owned Enterprises

From an empirical standpoint, it is extremely difficult to compare efficiency in private enterprises and SOEs, because one cannot easily find two exactly comparable private and public firms operating in the same country. However, the theoretical literature on "soft budget constraints" suggests that extensive state ownership exacerbates fiscal deficits.[41]

Regardless of the budget deficits and consequential inflation, some countries in the region have started a new wave of nationalizations under patriotic/protectionist rhetoric, workers' rights, and equity. In 2006, for example, President Evo Morales announced the nationalization of the electric utility *Ibedrola* from Spanish private investors on the grounds of maintaining the service "equitably." Then, in 2012, Morales expropriated the assets of *Red Eléctrica*, also from Spanish private investors, in order "to pay homage to the workers and the Bolivians who have fought for the recovery of natural resources and basic services."[42]

The main problem with such nationalizations is that, in most instances, they tend to protect local elites, ranging from local industrialists to public sector workers and unions. To the eyes of most Latin Americans, nationalizations are a reversal of the ISI period and populist rhetoric, which fell into disrepute in the 1980s. However, to the eyes of international observers, Latin America has a history of nationalizations predating the ISI period, as table 6.2 shows for the case of oil and gas.

Against this background, the recent wave of nationalizations in Venezuela, Ecuador, Bolivia, and Argentina might be affecting foreign investors' expectations, not only in these countries but also in the entire region. Because Latin America is a low-savings region relative to Asia, the return of macroeconomic populism counteracts extraordinary efforts that other governments in the region are making in order to attract FDI to finance much-needed infrastructure and benefit from R&D spillovers.

Table 6.2
Nationalizations of oil and gas in the twentieth and twenty-first centuries

Country	Year(s) of nationalization
Argentina	1922, 1924, 1930, 2004
Bolivia	1937, 1969, 2006
Brazil	1953
Chile	1932, 1950
Colombia	1951
Ecuador	1972, 1974, 2006
Mexico	1938
Peru	1968, 1986
Uruguay	1931
Venezuela	1976, 2001

Source: Berrios, Marak, and Morgenstern 2010.

6.7 Concluding Remarks

This chapter started by reviewing the literature on macroeconomic populism. We have argued that income inequalities and widespread poverty might be at the root of populist upsurges in twentieth-century Latin America. Populist governments assume excess capacity and are characterized by expansionary fiscal and monetary policies, which ultimately lead to high fiscal deficits and inflation, the consequences of which hurt the workers whose interests populist leaders initially claim to defend.

Successful stabilization at the turn of the century brought inflation down in all regions. Key to this major achievement was the enactment of independent central banks—as we will discuss further in chapter 8—which have well-defined mandates. Fiscal prudence has also been a major contributing factor.

The fruits of price stabilization efforts have been supported by external conditions favoring high growth rates during the 2004–2013 commodity boom. As growth has increased, poverty and income inequality indicators have improved. This, along with the disappearance of ISI policies, might in turn explain the downfall of populism in most regions.

However, starting with Chávez in Venezuela, twenty-first-century Latin America has been tainted with populist regimes. A distinguishing feature of such regimes is the use of windfall commodity export revenues from the early twenty-first-century commodity boom for lavish social expenditures. Because the price of primary commodities has declined in recent years, such government expenditures must decrease sharply, at the inevitable cost of exacerbating ongoing social and political upheavals.

Inflation is already spiraling at a fast pace in countries such as Venezuela, which brings us closer to the twentieth-century notion of macroeconomic populism. Argentina, Bolivia, Ecuador, and Venezuela are nearing the end of the populist cycle.

From a political economy standpoint, the congressional elections in 2015 in Venezuela were largely won by the opposition, which may well mark the end of nearly twenty years of *Chavismo*. The end of *Kischnerismo* in 2015 as Mauricio Macri won the presidential election is also revealing. Whether the populist regimes in Ecuador and Bolivia will face a similar fate remains an open question. What we do know, however, is that relative to southern cone nonpopulist neighbors such as Colombia, Chile, and Peru, where fiscal and monetary institutions have been enacted in the twenty-first century, economic indicators in populist regimes are far darker.

Living standards for low-income residents in populist countries normally deteriorate significantly by the end of populist cycles. Redefining the role of the state in such countries and regions requires the long-overdue creation of monetary and fiscal institutions.

The privatization wave has also helped to redefine the role of the state, from larger to wiser, in other regions. Private monopolies still need to be adequately regulated to prevent regulatory capture, however. Despite the lack of solid empirical evidence, case studies in some countries suggest that regulatory frameworks are inefficient compared to those in the EU. A mitigating factor is the exposure of monopolies to international competition and private participation by foreign investors in SOEs.

Currently, the entire region—with the notable exception of Mexico—remains vulnerable to adverse primary commodity shocks. Growth has slowed down considerably in most regions. Keeping expenditures high at current levels to satisfy the needs of an emergent middle class clamoring for better infrastructure and social services will be difficult. Poverty reductions will likely slow down and may come to a complete halt, and governments may be tempted to abandon fiscal prudence for political economy considerations, in which case inflation may again become a problem to be fought against, if only because inflation exacerbates the income inequalities that are at the root of the macroeconomic populist cycles.

Summary
- Latin America has a long history of macroeconomic populism dating back to early twentieth-century Argentina.
- Populist cycles are characterized by key assumptions in the minds of charismatic leaders who have prioritized income redistribution. One of the key assumptions is excess capacity, which has led to overspending, exacerbating fiscal deficits and triggering inflationary spirals.
- Initially, redistributive policies launched by populist leaders have led to enhanced growth and employment along with higher wages and domestic demand for goods and services. After short-lived spells, however, populist regimes have ended up with monetized fiscal deficits, triggering exceedingly high inflation rates. These rates have adversely affected real wages, thereby lowering the living standards of the working class to prepopulist levels and worse.
- In the twentieth century, Latin American populist leaders have been ousted in coup d'états in the midst of economic chaos and social unrest.
- Economic reforms in the 1990s and, in particular, price stabilization policies have delivered a short period of political stability and low incidence of populist upsurges.
- However, chronic income inequalities exacerbated by the long period of reforms and anti-imperialist ideology has triggered a new wave of populism in southern cone countries.
- Venezuela under Hugo Chávez started the new populist wave, the distinguishing feature of which is the use of export revenues from the commodity boom to finance social expenditures.
- Anti-imperialist rhetoric has also taken the form of nationalization of key primary commodity sectors, such as gas and electricity.
- In other countries, natural monopolies, if any, are poorly regulated, leading to regulatory capture. These monopolists have a tendency to increase prices and do not attend to the needs of unprofitable remote areas.
- The lack of ability to enact income taxation effectively leaves the entire Latin American region at the mercy of world commodity price fluctuations. In recent years, slowdown in China has threatened current social expenditures, which might lead to political upheavals and the return of populist rhetoric and policies.

Review Questions
1. Briefly describe the distinguishing features of populist cycles in twentieth-century Latin America. Why did Peru under Alan García experience high growth rates initially, and why was such a growth spell short lived?

2. Why is price stabilization key to standard explanations of the downfall of populist regimes in the late twentieth century?
3. Briefly describe the upsurge of populism in Venezuela under Hugo Chávez. Is it possible to explain its roots and why such a populist regime has been maintained for over fifteen years now?
4. Can the Bolivarian Revolution under Evo Morales's regime be characterized as a populist regime? Briefly explain your answer.
5. In what way has the populist regime in Ecuador under the Correa administration benefited the poor?
6. Briefly explain the merits of the following statement: "A sharp fall in world commodity prices may trigger the downfall of the new wave of populist regimes in Latin America's southern cone."
7. Can slowdown in China trigger a "third wave" of populism in Latin America? Explain your answer.
8. Mexico is the only country in Latin America that has managed to diversify its export revenues. Is this a necessary and sufficient condition for Mexico to avoid future upsurges of populism?
9. Under the structural reforms in the 1980s and 1990s, the role of the state in Latin America has gone from smaller to wiser, yet regulatory capture threatens Latin America's young democracies. Explain.
10. Would you expect the legacy of populism in Venezuela, Argentina, Bolivia, and Ecuador to be the same as that of populist predecessors in the twentieth century?

Further Reading

For a comprehensive review of populist and left-wing regimes in twenty-first-century Latin America with clear exposition from a political scientist's viewpoint, see Seligson 2007. A classic macroeconomic cycle, which might predict the end of the new wave of populism in Latin America, is well-explained in Dornbusch and Edwards 1991. For an insightful analysis of Venezuela under Chávez's populist regime, see Marcano and Barrera 2005.

III The Macroeconomics of Latin America in the Twenty-First Century

7 Fiscal Policy for Development

Fiscal policy has long been at the forefront of economic discussions in Latin America. The role of the state expanded considerably when the region embraced ISI policies. State intervention then was not only confined to import tariffs and other forms of protectionism; the state also reached out to private companies via, for example, preferential tariff rates for intermediate inputs of production, subsidized credit, and direct transfers. SOEs, on the other hand, expanded their reach to several economic sectors, often suffering significant financial losses. SOEs also needed public transfers in order to be kept alive (see chapter 3). Ultimately, by the early 1980s, the size of government in most of Latin America had expanded immensely and this expansion was coupled with growing fiscal deficits. These deficits were generally monetized by subdued central banks. Consequently, inflationary pressures were systematically strong.

Most studies on fiscal policy in Latin America are linked to the symptoms of fiscal deficits. Chief among those is the connection between deficits and inflation. This is understandable in light of the dark and prolonged record of inflation in the region. In this chapter, however, we will attempt to focus instead on their roots—broadly speaking—and policy implications.

We will ask several questions in this chapter, including the following: Why have expansionary fiscal policies taken place for such a long period of time in Latin America? Where did large deficits originate and why? What lessons can be drawn from institutional reforms conducive to fiscal discipline and countercyclical fiscal policies for economic development?

In previous chapters, we argued that despite the existence of a growing middle class, contemporary Latin America remains highly unequal and poverty stricken. The region has consequently experienced persistent populist upsurges, which, as we noted in chapter 6, manifest themselves in shortsighted redistributive responses, leading to large, monetized fiscal deficits followed by high inflation and economic chaos.

In contrast, leading reformers at the end of the twentieth century launched institutional reforms geared toward focusing the role of the state and limiting the scope for large fiscal deficits. Key reforms include but are not limited to tax reforms, fiscal discipline laws, pension reforms, and the creation of sovereign wealth funds.

Section 7.1 in this chapter briefly describes fiscal expansionary policies during the ISI period studied in chapter 3. Section 7.2 analyzes changes in fiscal policies during the lost decade of the 1980s. Section 7.3 examines institutional reforms since the 1980s and 1990s and their effects on fiscal deficits across the Latin American region. Section 7.4 revives the debate on poverty and distribution from a fiscal stance, and section 7.5 lays down the agenda for future fiscal reforms and challenges. Finally, section 7.6 summarizes our conclusions.

7.1 The Growth of the Public Sector Prior to the Crisis of the 1980s

One undisputable feature of the ISI period in Latin America (1940s through 1982) is the invasive role of the state in economic activity. Protectionist policies for the sake of industrialization during this period ranged from high and continued subsidies to inefficient SOEs to high tariffs and export taxes (see chapter 3). We should distinguish between two subperiods, however.[1]

First, under ISI up until the mid-1970s, government expenditures were mostly financed with tax revenues, and therefore government deficits were not particularly high—in the range of 1 to 2 percent of GDP.[2] This is not surprising; since the Great Depression sovereign defaults in the 1930s, Latin America was excluded from international borrowing, except for largely concessional loans from the World Bank, the IDB, and trade credits. At the same time, the region's governments were not able to borrow domestically because of underdeveloped financial markets and the so-called original sin—that is, the inability of domestic governments to issue local currency domestic debt.[3]

Second, major fiscal policy changes started after the 1973 hike in oil prices as oil-producing countries poured windfall petrol revenues into international commercial banks, which in turn extended loans to Latin America and other regions. External funding enabled most Latin American countries to increase expenditures.

Table 7.1
Public sector spending in Latin America, 1970–1982 (consolidated nonfinancial public sector, % of GDP)

	Argentina	Brazil	Chile	Mexico	Peru	Venezuela
1970	38.62	35.92	41.27	22.30	24.50	28.70
1971	37.76	34.44	49.93	20.50	27.10	29.10
1972	37.00	35.19	56.05	23.00	31.20	33.50
1973	40.52	33.96	49.39	25.70	38.60	32.80
1974	47.06	38.81	43.17	27.00	45.10	29.50
1975	46.40	42.74	40.44	31.90	46.10	38.90
1976	43.46	44.17	37.82	32.00	45.80	44.00
1977	43.01	42.04	40.74	30.30	48.40	50.50
1978	48.92	47.56	34.57	31.40	47.60	52.60
1979	45.88	54.45	31.65	33.00	48.40	49.40
1980	49.06	52.66	31.58	35.00	60.10	53.30
1981	53.30	42.70	34.11	41.40	57.40	54.00
1982	49.16	46.06	39.84	46.40	60.20	57.60

Source: Larraín and Selowsky 1991.

According to most studies, these expenditures financed unproductive investments, consumption, and capital flight.[4]

In particular, the decade of the 1970s was characterized by large fiscal expansion. Public expenditure almost doubled in most countries of the region during the 1970–1982 period. As shown in table 7.1, the exception was Chile, which increased public expenditures sharply from 1970 to 1972 but reduced them in subsequent years.

Fiscal expansion was in turn reflected in higher deficits, as there were few increases in fiscal revenues. Thus, unlike developed economies' experiences with fiscal expansion—in which public spending increased gradually over several decades while the tax base was broadened—large fiscal expansion in Latin America took place in just one decade: the 1970s.

Latin America's virtual fiscal explosion was largely based on the external shocks that occurred in this period. Egypt and Syria attacked Israel in October 1973, starting the Yom Kippur War. OPEC proclaimed an embargo on oil exports to penalize the United States and other countries that supported Israel in the conflict, and it later cut production, causing huge oil price increases.

Thus, while most of the world fell into recession, oil-exporting countries accumulated vast foreign exchange windfalls. These were deposited in international commercial banks —and became known as petrodollars. This phenomenon led to a considerable increase in the availability of funds to extend loans to developing countries. Moreover, loans were made available at very low interest rates (even negative real interest rates), and thus developing nations took advantage of the highly liquid environment and increased their foreign indebtedness. International commercial banks seemed to have disregarded the risks of external loans and provided funds incautiously within a highly unregulated banking sector framework. Some major banks went so far as to lend more than 100 percent of their capital to few developing countries.

On the other hand, improvements in the global macroeconomic environment after 1975 contributed to a hike in international primary commodity prices. In turn, export earnings in developing countries grew rapidly, which led foreign investors—mostly foreign commercial banks—to expect that Latin America would honor its contractual obligations, because the region is heavily dependent on primary commodity exports. Further lending ensued.

A similar story can be told about other regions. Overall, borrowing in developing countries increased significantly from 1973 onward. However, the debt structure was not similar across the developing world. Unlike Africa, where most of the foreign currency–denominated loans were granted by governments, international financial institutions, and aid agencies, Latin America's foreign debt was contracted with commercial banks—mostly from the United States and, to a lesser extent, Western Europe.

Internal factors also triggered the surge in public spending. An important portion of Latin America's natural resources was controlled by the state. Ideology played a role in this. Specifically, most governments in the region took a nationalistic stance. They revealed a strong preference for foreign loans over opening their doors to FDI because the latter option meant transferring control over local resources to foreigners. Latin American governments did not trust private domestic investors, either. The received wisdom at the time was that the private sector would concentrate on short-lived investments and abandon the long-term projects that were key to the region's development strategy.

Political economy considerations were also a contributing factor. The availability of cheap external loans allowed many countries to increase public expenditures without needing to raise additional taxes or suffering from high inflation and its consequential costs. However, this option led to large fiscal deficits. Consumers in oil-importing economies, for example, strongly opposed international hikes in oil prices being passed onto domestic prices. Put simply, foreign borrowing was used to satisfy the political needs of incumbent governments and their constituencies instead of relying on criteria based on welfare and economic considerations.

An important cause of expansionary fiscal policies and large fiscal deficits in debtor countries was the implementation of populist policies of the type discussed in chapter 6. Several governments pursued unsustainably expansionary macroeconomic policies in their attempts to build popular support. Pressure for excessive fiscal expenditure tended to to be intense in countries with high income inequalities, a common feature in most of Latin America—and a recurrent theme in this book.

In Latin America, the poor command only a small share of the national income but represent a large percentage of the population. This leads to heavy demands for public spending. At the same time, lack of ability to raise tax revenues and/or enforce tax compliance—particularly income taxes on higher income brackets—exacerbates the problem. In contrast, East Asia is a more equitable region, and therefore pressures for redistributive policies are lower, which results in considerably lower fiscal deficits.

Yet another structural factor of public sector expansion may have been the peculiar way in which governments seemed to form expectations at the time. Instead of assuming rational or adaptive expectations, the public sector seemed to have been governed by a "best expectations" theory: Oil-exporting governments behaved as if the increase in their countries' terms of trade would be permanent, which led them to increase spending. Oil importers, on the other hand, decided against making painful adjustments and financed rising oil import costs via foreign borrowing instead, expecting that the oil shocks were transitory. This asymmetry between oil exporters, who expected the oil shocks to be permanent, and oil importers, who expected the shocks to be transitory, seems to have exacerbated the vicious circle of foreign debt accumulation in most developing countries, particularly those in Latin America and Africa.

A more general issue in the public sector, which was harshly felt during the 1970s, is the principal agent problem.[5] The public sector is not a single entity. Instead, it comprises several agents that do not act in a unified manner. A manager in the public sector does not behave as he or she would in the private sector, because the government cannot—or chooses not to—properly monitor the manager or because public enterprises face soft budget constraints, and also due to the fact that shareholders are diffused. Among private enterprises, management teams respond to shareholders seeking to maximize profits, but managers in public companies and government officials in other state institutions often seek other goals, such as keeping their jobs, helping the government to stay in office, or increasing the size of resources under their control.[6]

7.2 Forceful Public Sector Contraction

Two major changes in the world macroeconomic environment in the early 1980s decisively changed fiscal policies in Latin America. First, the sharp decline in primary commodity exports, and second, the huge increase in world interest rates. These two events are illustrated in figures 7.1 and 7.2, respectively.

The combined effect of the adverse world macroeconomic events prompted Mexico to default on its dollar-denominated obligations in August 1982. All Latin American governments—with the notable exception of Colombia—followed suit. The cascade of sovereign defaults had a major effect on the ability to finance fiscal deficits. In this environment, deficit reduction became unavoidable.

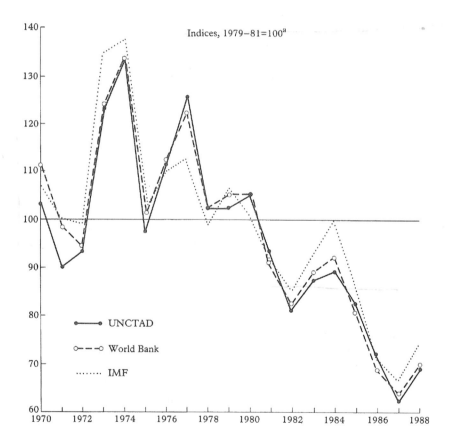

Figure 7.1
The fall in primary commodity prices, 1970–1988.
Source: Maizels 1992.

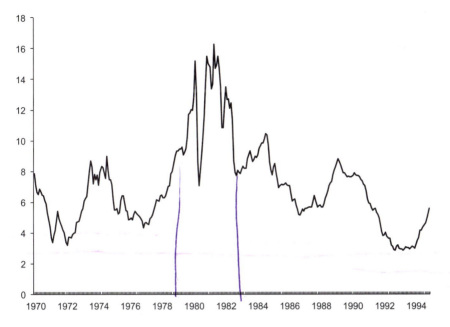

Figure 7.2
The interest rate hike (proxied by the three-month US Treasury bills), 1970–1994.
Source: Authors' own construction from Federal Reserve database (www.federalreserve.gov).

With the outbreak of the crisis, external creditors did not discriminate among countries, and governments of debtor countries faced two problems. The difficulty was not only that real interest rates rose, increasing the burden of the debt unexpectedly, but also that external funding was no longer available. Even Chile, which had followed strict fiscal policies and had reduced the size of its public sector, was equally affected by the credit squeeze. Colombia was less affected by the crisis, both because it had a low debt to GDP ratio in 1982 (26.9 percent) and because it had a low level of financial vulnerability (for 1980–1981, the ratio of debt contracted at floating rates to total debt was only 39.2 percent).[7]

In the absence of external financing, the fiscal adjustment required increased reliance on domestic financing. Most local governments resorted to money creation and the issuing of additional domestic public debt, leading Latin America to experience the highest inflation rates in its entire history. Average inflation for the region reached a peak of 496 percent in 1990.[8] (Chapter 8 studies inflation during this period and beyond.)

Some debtor countries suffered from hyperinflation. The case of Bolivia is illustrative. The government resorted to printing money in order to finance its deficit, which led to a hyperinflation episode from 1984 to 1985. This started a vicious circle, because hyperinflation reduces the real value of tax revenues due to the Olivera-Tanzi effect. That is, high inflation rates erode the tax base, because collected revenues from taxation lag behind tax revenue obligations, and hence fiscal deficits are exacerbated, which fuels inflationary pressures further.[9]

Nonetheless, and as a result of forceful contraction, central government revenues in Bolivia declined to only 1.3 percent of GDP in 1984. Specifically, the fiscal deficit fell in 1983 but rose again in 1984, which increased the need for inflationary financing. It was not until a full-fledged stabilization package was implemented in 1985 that prices stopped rising; fiscal revenues rose quickly as the Olivera-Tanzi effect worked in reverse, and the key price of fuel (a major source of government revenues) increased domestically. This traumatic hyperinflation episode reveals the disastrous consequence that the debt crisis had on public finances.

Again, in this chapter we underscore our view of inflation as a symptom of fiscal problems that manifested themselves in different forms and shapes throughout the entire region. Mismanaged budgets soon became fiscal crises due to a series of events. With the deterioration in the region's terms of trade, the earnings of export-oriented SOEs decreased in many countries, reducing fiscal revenues. On the other hand, tax revenues fell as a result of sharp recessions and inefficient tax collection. Moreover, many private sector firms fell into financial crisis in several countries, and governments had to assume external liabilities and financial losses—partially or totally—raising public sector indebtedness. Countries such as Argentina, Chile, Colombia, Mexico, Peru, Uruguay, and Venezuela experienced extremely costly banking crises in this period, and these crises exacerbated growing fiscal deficits.[10]

Another problem faced by debtor governments was real exchange rate depreciations. Although currency depreciations helped to improve the trade balance and contributed to external adjustment, the foreign debt-servicing burden (interest plus principal amortization) became exceedingly high, which deteriorated the fiscal situation further.

Tax revenues were not growing fast and many times stagnated or dropped after the outbreak of the crisis, due to the weakness of the economies (and often, poor tax administration and enforcement) in most countries. With meager tax revenues, the burden of the fiscal adjustment therefore fell on the expenditure side.

Public expenditure was severely reduced, especially in countries such as Argentina, Bolivia, Chile, and Mexico (see table 7.2), with cuts concentrating on investment, social programs, and associated service networks and public wages, creating strong political and social tensions that produced adverse consequences, especially among the poorer segments of Latin America's populations.

Table 7.2
Public expenditure on education and health (as % of total expenditure)

	Education		Health	
	1972	1988	1972	1988
Argentina	20	6.9	n.a.	2.1
Bolivia	31.3	18.4	6.3	1.9
Chile	14.3	12	8.2	6.3
El Salvador	21.4	17.1	10.9	7.1
Mexico	16.4	7.4	4.5	1.1
Peru	23.6	15.3	5.5	5.8
Uruguay	9.5	7.1	1.6	4.8
Venezuela	18.6	19.6	11.7	10.0

Source: Larraín and Sachs 1993.

7.3 Redefining the Economic Role of the State

Reduction of the debt burden was a necessary, but not a sufficient condition to trigger economic growth in the debtor countries. Along with debt relief, it was necessary to implement deep structural reforms.

The main reforms in debtor countries—which were needed to support the Baker and Brady debt-reduction plans[11]—are summarized in the Washington Consensus, which identified a set of ten reforms supported by Washington-based institutions such as the IMF, the World Bank, and the US Treasury Department, the proper deployment of which Washington [could] muster a reasonable degree of consensus about.[12] The five Washington Consensus goals closer to fiscal policy are as follows:

1. *Fiscal discipline.* Latin American countries had run large and sustained fiscal deficits as a percentage of GDP. Fiscal deficits were indeed perceived as the main source of macroeconomic dislocations in the form of high inflation, balance of payment crises, and capital flight. Therefore, the recommendation was to maintain a budget close to balance, with public expenditures reasonably met via available resources.

2. *Public expenditure redirection.* The main goal of this reform was to reduce indiscriminate subsidization (in products such as gasoline or bread, or agricultural credits) while simultaneously directing government expenditures toward growth-enhancement activities in basic infrastructure and provision of social services in health and education.

3. *Tax reform.* It was recognized that reducing fiscal deficits required increased tax revenues. The proposed reform consisted of broadening the tax base, while marginal rates would be moderate. This meant closing loopholes and eliminating evasion so that revenues could increase without sharp increases in tax rates that would be borne by relatively few taxpayers (especially in the case of direct taxation).
4. *Privatization.* This was another pillar of reform. The common perception was that private firms are more efficient than public firms, because managers either have a direct stake on private firms or are accountable to those who do. Inefficiencies would therefore be abolished if firms were privatized.
5. *Deregulation.* The main goal of this reform was to eliminate excessive regulation, which was preventing entry of new firms and therefore hindering competition. Deregulation was not recommended in special cases, such as when safety and environmental damage were concerns.

There has been intense debate about the consequences of the Washington Consensus reforms.[13] The most relevant reforms for this particular chapter, however, were the first three and, to a lesser extent, privatization and deregulation. Unlike the first three, the latter two remain controversial, not so much because privatization was not seen as relief for the budget burden of loss-making SOEs per se, but because of the often obscure way in which privatization was carried out in practice. With regard to deregulation, although no one can deny that Latin American firms were excessively regulated, exposing regulated firms to foreign competition may have been enough to make a difference in most cases. Moreover, exposure to foreign competition makes the entire debate over whether firms should be privatized or not rather obsolete.

These recommendations involved a profound change in the idea of the role of the public sector, leading to the principle that the state should do only those things that the private sector could not do efficiently.

For structural reforms aimed at lowering the fiscal deficit to be successful, it was necessary to implement institutional changes in the public sector. One of the major problems of existing institutions at the time was the governments' ability to borrow without restrictions from their respective central banks. When central bank independence was granted, however, monetary authorities could refuse to extend financing requirements claimed by the government. We expand on this point at length in chapter 8.

7.4 Redistributive Effects of Fiscal Policy

The Washington Consensus explicitly recognized the impact of fiscal policy on income distribution. Considering the disastrous effects of spending adjustments after the debt crisis, it was necessary to redirect public expenditure in a pro-poor and progrowth manner.[14]

Fiscal policy can affect income distribution by transferring resources from higher-income to lower-income households through public social expenditures and via the way these transfers are financed—that is, tax policy. However, as we will discuss later, fiscal policy can also affect income distribution indirectly—that is, via growth-enhancing policies, which benefit the low-income quintiles. Indeed, social public spending has expanded significantly since the early 1990s and its participation in total public expenditure has also risen, as shown in figure 7.3.

There are several points to consider about the role of public spending to redistribute income. For example, cash transfers to poor households are preferable to indirect methods such as generalized price subsidies, because targeted subsidies go directly to those in need and exert a lower pressure on public resources. Nonetheless, targeting has costs and should therefore be carefully designed. From a purely distributive standpoint, the tax burden should have a solid base of direct taxes (mainly on income). However, developing countries—including Latin American emerging market economies—tend to collect a significantly higher

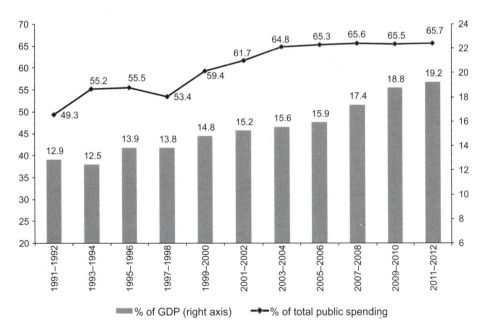

Figure 7.3
Social public spending in Latin America (% of GDP and % of total public spending), from 1991–1992 to 2011–2012.
Source: Authors' own construction from ECLAC database 2014 (www.cepal.org).

Table 7.3
Composition of tax revenue in Latin America, 2013 (% of total tax revenue)

Country	Direct tax revenue	Indirect tax revenue	Other taxes	Social contributions
Argentina	25.3	36.8	2.6	35.3
Brazil	36.7	27.5	0.1	35.6
Chile	37.4	54.0	0.7	7.9
Colombia	50.9	37.4	0.2	11.4
Guatemala	34.2	61.8	0.9	3.0
Mexico	51.7	32.0	1.6	14.7
Nicaragua	27.7	48.3	0.1	23.9
Peru	39.8	43.8	5.5	10.9
Venezuela	29.2	64.2	0.0	6.6

Source: Authors' own construction from ECLAC database 2015 (www.cepal.org).

share of their public revenue from indirect taxes, particularly from general taxes on goods and services, or value-added tax (VAT). Table 7.3 provides a snapshot of the breakdown between direct and indirect taxation in several Latin American countries.

As shown in figure 7.4, when compared with OECD countries, Latin America has a lower tax burden, and funds a much larger portion of its expenditures with indirect taxes. There are several reasons for this, including per capita income differences. It has been widely recognized that the level of tax revenue to GDP increases as countries become richer. It is also a fact that taxes are easier to collect on indirect transactions, with import duties probably being the easiest to collect.

In the Latin American context, low-income taxation is also a consequence of high levels of tax evasion (see table 7.4). Moreover, a large portion of the Latin American population is exempted from personal income taxes, because lower bound exemption levels are high. This holds true even for higher middle-income economies.

In practice, the redistributive impact of fiscal policy in Latin America appears to be mild. Goñi, López, and Servén (2011) analyzed the impact of fiscal policy in six countries of the region and compared it to that in fifteen EU countries. As shown in figure 7.5, the impact of fiscal policy on income redistribution is significantly lower in Latin America compared to the average in Europe, as shown by the mild reduction in Gini coefficients in Latin America compared to significantly larger Gini reductions in Europe after taxes and transfers have taken place.

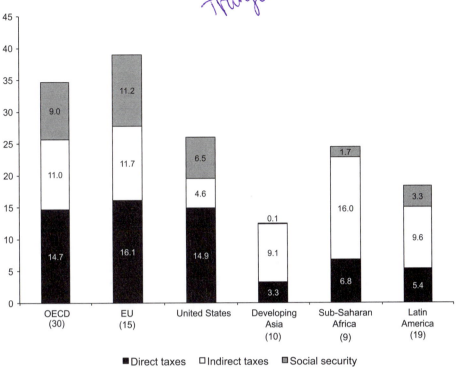

Figure 7.4
International comparison of the structure of the tax burden (% of GDP, 2010 or latest year available).
Source: Jiménez and López 2012, based on data from OECD, IMF, and ECLAC.

Figure 7.5 also shows that in European countries, most of the work to reduce inequality occurs via government cash transfers and only a relatively small portion by taxes. Similar conclusions are obtained by the OECD (2012), which finds that on average 75 percent of the reduction in inequality between gross market income and disposable income (after taxes and transfers) is due to transfers, and only about a quarter to taxes (see figure 7.6).

In line with this information, authors such as Gasparini, Cruces, and Tornarolli (2009) and López-Calva and Lustig (2010) argue that public spending policy in a favorable macroeconomic context—especially pertaining to social spending and specifically the use of conditional cash transfers—should be given credit for the reduction of inequality in Latin America during the twenty-first century, as we discussed in chapter 5.

The IMF (2014b) and other international organizations recommend the use of means-tested cash transfers that restrict eligibility or benefit levels according to

Table 7.4
The evasion of VAT and income taxes

Country	VAT		Income tax			Year
	Estimated evasion rate	Year	Estimated evasion rate			
			Total	Individuals	Corporations	
Argentina	21.2	2006	49.7	--	--	2005
Bolivia (Plurinational State of)	29.0	2004	--	--	--	--
Chile	11.0	2005	47.4	46.0	48.4	2003
Costa Rica	28.7	2002	--	--	--	--
Colombia	23.5	2006	--	--	--	--
Ecuador	21.2	2001	63.8	58.1	65.3	2005
El Salvador	27.8	2006	45.3	36.3	51.0	2005
Guatemala	37.5	2006	63.7	69.9	62.8	2006
Mexico	20.0	2006	41.6	38.0	46.2	2004
Nicaragua	38.1	2006	--	--	--	--
Panama	33.8	2006	--	--	--	--
Peru	37.7		48.5	32.6	52.3	2006
Dominican Republic	31.2	2006	--	--	--	--
Uruguay	26.3	2006	--	--	--	--

Source: Gómez and Jiménez 2012.

income in order to achieve redistributive objectives at a lower cost, as opposed to benefits provided to the entire population. Specifically, the IMF suggests that such transfers be implemented in a manner that avoids adverse effects on the labor market—for example, by gradually phasing out benefits as incomes rise. Where means testing is not feasible, tagging is recommended.[15] However, because "tags" are only imperfectly correlated with need, this method can result in undercoverage of the poor and leakage of benefits to the nonpoor, so that additional cash transfer programs may be needed to protect excluded households. In addition, to be effective tags should not be manipulated easily by individuals or households and should be easily verifiable. On the other hand, according to the World Bank, a conditional cash transfer program should be designed to target poor households that underinvest in children's human capital accumulation.[16]

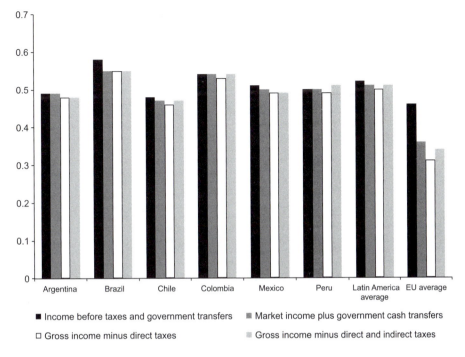

Figure 7.5
Gini coefficients for different income definitions (latest year available).
Source: Goñi, López, and Servén 2011.

However, beyond social spending and taxation, fiscal policy can also affect income distribution through the overall macroeconomic environment. High macroeconomic volatility is most detrimental to low-income households, because these households have limited access to finance and therefore cannot easily smooth consumption over time. The poor are also more prone to experiencing unemployment during downturns. Some are forced to join the ranks of the informally employed, for whom income variations are high. (We defer a detailed discussion of labor markets in Latin America to chapter 11.)

Thus, the higher macroeconomic volatility, the greater income inequality are positively correlated. Indeed, evidence presented by Calderón and Levy Yeyati (2009) shows that output volatility is associated with greater inequality, measured both by the Gini coefficient and by the income share responses across quintiles. Moreover, aggregate volatility has asymmetric, nonlinear effects. Specifically, the authors find that sharp economic *contraction* exerts a more than proportional increase in unemployment, poverty, and inequality, factors that a sharp *expansion* does not completely counteract. These undesired consequences of volatility and

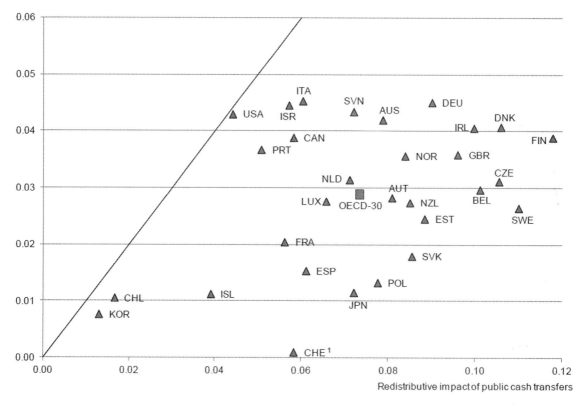

Figure 7.6
Point reduction in the concentration coefficients in the late 2000s. *Note:* The redistributive impact of public cash transfers is measured as the difference between the concentration coefficient of market income and that of income after transfers. The redistributive impact of household taxes is measured as the difference between the concentration coefficient of post-transfer income and that of disposable income (i.e., after tax and transfers). Data for France and Ireland refers to the mid-2000s.
Source: OECD 2012.

Fiscal Policy for Development

negative income shocks vary substantially as a function of country characteristics. Per capita income, public spending levels, or labor protection laws, for example, may mitigate the costs that business cycles and excess volatility have on disadvantaged households.

From an income inequality standpoint, fiscal institutions can play an exceedingly important role in support of generating a stable macroeconomic environment. Fiscal policy must guarantee protection or safety nets for vulnerable households during macroeconomic downturns. Some countries in Latin America have made an effort to meet this challenge via enacting strong fiscal institutions. We turn to this topic next.

7.5 Institutional Changes in Fiscal Policy

Structural reforms applied in most countries of the region after the 1980s crisis helped those countries reap some of the benefits of globalization and growth. Several governments were able to gather the institutional backing to conduct fiscal policy in a responsible, nonpopulist manner. In particular, some Latin American countries have been able to design fiscal policies and institutions in such a way that these policies and institutions have become an asset to the countries' economies, contributing to macroeconomic stability. Thus, in the late 1990s and especially in the 2000s, Latin America was better equipped to confront adverse macroeconomic shocks, as demonstrated by its effectiveness in weathering the 2008 to 2009 subprime crisis (see table 7.5).

Despite significantly improved fundamentals, most Latin American countries remain highly vulnerable. The main reason, as we noted in previous chapters, is that Latin America since the late nineteenth century has been mostly a primary commodity–exporting region. Growth rates fluctuate sharply, mimicking those of world commodity prices, and fiscal revenues change accordingly. Figure 7.7 illustrates the fiscal revenue volatility in middle-income Latin American economies in

Table 7.5
Macroeconomic fundamentals in Latin America in periods previous to crises

	1980–1981	1997–1998	2007–2008
Inflation (average, %)	53.9	11.8	6.7
Current account (% of GDP)	-4	-4.7	-1.1
External debt (% of GDP)	29.4	34.5	21.6
Fiscal balance (% of GDP)	-2.6	-1.8	-0.1

Source: Authors' own construction from IMF database (www.imf.org) and ECLAC database 2014 (www.cepal.org).

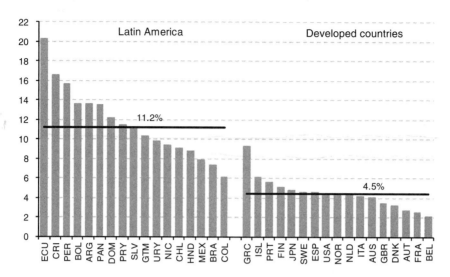

Figure 7.7
Tax revenue volatility without social security, 1980–2008 (standard deviation of revenue income growth in US dollars, 2000).
Source: Jiménez and Kacef 2011.

comparison with that in high-income economies. With the exception of Mexico, such a high degree of vulnerability is due to the fact that fiscal income is dependent on a few exports of primary commodities (mostly metals, oil, and agriculture), as indicated in table 7.6.

In sum, because of high dependence on commodity prices, fiscal revenues are highly volatile. A special problem is that low availability of resources during downturns hits disadvantaged households the most, because social expenditures decrease. Moreover, the procyclicality of fiscal expenditures can easily exacerbate the depth of the recession during downturns.

In countries such as Venezuela, Ecuador, and Bolivia, and even in Chile and Mexico, a significant portion of fiscal revenues are generated from commodities. Figure 7.8 illustrates this phenomenon quite vividly. How should fiscal authorities respond to such a well-documented problem? In our view, the answer partly lies in creating solid fiscal institutions. In this regard, Chile has been a pioneer. In 2000, Chile enacted a *cyclically adjusted* (or *structural*) *balance rule*, which was implemented in 2001. The rule prevails and is enforced by the Ministry of Finance.

The Chilean fiscal rule criterion is rather simple. The rule instructs the government to spend on the basis of its structural (permanent) revenue—as opposed to spending from current revenue. Two independent panels of experts take part for this commitment to be more effective and transparent. One determines potential

Table 7.6
Latin America's high dependence on commodity exports (2009 or latest year available)

	Main commodity exports	Commodity exports as % of total exports
Argentina	Soybeans, oil, wheat, corn	68.0
Bolivia	Natural gas, zinc, tin, silver	92.9
Brazil	Soybeans, corn, sugar, iron ore, crude oil, coffee	60.9
Chile	Copper, fruit, fish, paper and pulp	88.2
Colombia	Oil, coffee, coal, nickel, emeralds	72.8
Costa Rica	Pineapples, coffee, melons	37.6
Ecuador	Bananas, oil, shrimp	90.9
El Salvador	Coffee, sugar	47.0
Guatemala	Coffee, sugar, oil	66.3
Honduras	Coffee, bananas	66.5
Mexico	Oil, silver, copper, tomatoes	24.9
Nicaragua	Coffee, cattle	90.9
Panama	Bananas, shrimp, sugar	90.7
Paraguay	Soybeans, cotton, beef	92.1
Peru	Copper, gold, zinc	87.8
Uruguay	Beef, wheat, corn, dairy	74.8
Venezuela	Oil	92.7

Source: Green and Branford 2013.

GDP growth, the other long-term copper price forecasts. These are the basic inputs for the budget process, because they determine structural fiscal revenue. With this information, the level of spending consistent with a given structural fiscal balance target can be determined. This is an ex-ante, well-known criterion that enjoys both credibility and legitimacy.

In 2006, the structural balance rule was formalized in the Fiscal Responsibility Law. This law requires every incoming Minister of Finance to present a fiscal policy framework consistent with the law within three months after being appointed. The law also allowed for the enactment of two sovereign wealth funds and established the basic institutional framework necessary for their management. The Economic and Social Stabilization Fund (ESSF) is intended to finance fiscal deficits that are due to adverse external shocks. It can also be used to amortize public debt and to contribute to the Pension Reserve Fund (PRF). The PRF was created to fund public guarantees for pension contributions to low-income households.

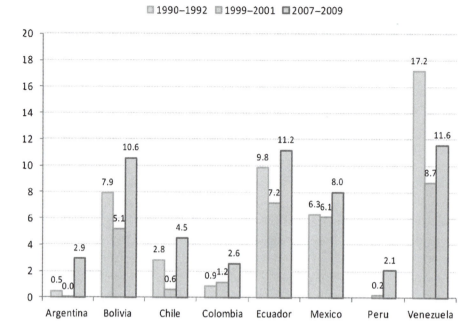

Figure 7.8
Fiscal revenues from commodities (% of GDP).
Source: Jiménez and López 2012.

In 2010, the Ministry of Finance called a commission to analyze and make proposals to improve the fiscal policy framework and the fiscal rule. This commission refined the calculation of the cyclically adjusted fiscal balance rule and proposed the creation of an Advisory Fiscal Council, among other changes. The government adopted many of these proposals, as stated in official documents.[17]

The fiscal council was created by decree in May 2013. Its principal objective is to collaborate on discussion, analysis, and provision of recommendations to the Minister of Finance in matters related to the application of the cyclically adjusted balance rule to the budget. Specific tasks of the council include participating as an observer in the Potential GDP and Copper Price committees, providing an opinion about the estimation of the cyclical adjusted revenue and fiscal balance prepared by the Budget Office, presenting its position and making observations on prospective changes proposed to the fiscal rule by the authority, and delivering advice on fiscal policy issues as per the Minister of Finance's request.

Two other countries in the region have recently established structural fiscal rules: Colombia in 2011 and Peru in 2012 (although Peru suspended the application of the rule for the 2013 budget). In the past, other Latin American countries have set different rules for expenditures and current (as opposed to structural) fiscal balances. Table 7.7 provides a review of fiscal rules in several Latin American countries.

Sometimes, however, the details of setting up a structural fiscal rule are not entirely obvious. In particular, the determination of structural revenue requires the definition of key parameters. In Chile, it is clear that the focus should be on long-term copper prices. In Colombia, it is on oil prices. Other countries—notably, Venezuela and Ecuador—could enact clear and transparent fiscal laws using the price of oil as a benchmark. In Brazil or Costa Rica, for example, the options are less clear.

All countries, however, have the potential of setting up enforceable fiscal rules based on their own specificities. In all cases, fiscal rules should have two principal objectives: (1) to enforce fiscal discipline from a medium- and long-term perspective and (2) to attain macroeconomic stability via expenditure smoothing.

Fiscal institutions in Chile arguably have contributed to macroeconomic stability. This is a significant achievement, considering that fiscal policy has tended to be more procyclical in emerging economies than in advanced ones. In fact, according to Klemm (2014), fiscal policy has been procyclical on average in Latin America, but countercyclical or acyclical in advanced economies. For Argentina and Uruguay, however, the evidence on procyclicality is stronger. Looking at possible changes in recent years, Klemm's paper finds that Brazil, Chile, Colombia, El Salvador, and Mexico have all moved toward a more countercyclical policy. For Chile, Larraín and Parro (2008) have found strong evidence that the introduction of the fiscal rule bears a considerable part of the reduction in GDP growth volatility.

7.6 Concluding Remarks

Latin American public sector deficits experienced a major expansion in the 1970s. The first and second oil shocks during this decade enormously increased the surpluses of oil-exporting countries, which in turn deposited a large part of these surpluses in international commercial banks. These banks used the resources to lend generously to developing countries, particularly to middle-income Latin American nations. Unprecedented access to international capital markets, in turn, enabled most Latin American governments to embark on an unprecedented fiscal expansion without needing to develop a solid tax base. As a result, public deficits increased considerably.

Table 7.7
Fiscal rules in Latin American countries

Country	Type of national rule (year of implementation)	Legal basis	Coverage	Key elements of the rules
Brazil	Expenditure rule (2000)	Statutory	General government or wider	*Expenditure rule, debt rule:* (1) Personnel expenditure is limited to 50 percent of net current revenue for the federal government, and 60 percent for states and municipalities; (2) permanent spending mandates cannot be created without permanent revenue increases or spending cuts; (3) the senate sets debt limits for all levels of government. However, the only limits currently in place are for states and municipalities. There are also limits set by the senate for annual borrowing for states and municipalities. The government sets numerical multiyear targets for the budget balance (for the current year and indicative targets for the next two years), expenditure, and debt.
	Debt rule (2000)	Statutory	General government or wider	
Chile	Budget balance rule (2001)	Statutory	Central government	*Budget balance rule:* Under the structural balance rule, government expenditures are budgeted ex ante in line with structural revenues—that is, revenues that would be achieved if (1) the economy were operating at full potential and (2) the prices of copper and molybdenum were at their long-term levels. Between 2001 and 2007, a constant target for the structural balance (surplus of 1 percent of GDP) was defined; in 2008, a new constant target was specified (surplus of 0.5 percent of GDP). In 2009, while the target was zero structural surplus, a de facto escape clause was used to accommodate countercyclical measures. Further, the 2010 to 2014 administration specified a target path (to converge on 1 percent of GDP structural deficit by 2014).

Table 7.7 (continued)

Country	Type of national rule (year of implementation)	Legal basis	Coverage	Key elements of the rules
Colombia	Expenditure rule (2000)	Statutory	Central government	*Budget balance rule:* The structural balance rule for central government sets a path for fiscal consolidation that lowers the structural deficit for the central government to 2.3 percent of GDP in 2014 and sets a ceiling for a deficit of 1 percent, effective in 2022. The rule also allows for fiscal expansion when the expected output growth rate is at least 2 percentage points. lower than the long-term growth rate and creates a sovereign wealth fund (SWF) to save windfall revenue from natural resources. Annual targets are framed by a medium-term fiscal framework. *Expenditure rule:* On current expenditure growth in central government.
	Budget balance rule (2011)	Statutory	Central government	
Costa Rica	Budget balance rule (2001)	Statutory	Central government	*Budget balance rule:* Costa Rica presently has a type of "golden rule," according to which borrowing can be used only to finance investment spending. This rule is included in Article 6 of the Finance Management Law. The use of cash accounting in practice may lead to the application of a modified golden rule in which the financing of gross (rather than net) investment by borrowing is permitted.
Ecuador	Expenditure rule (2010)	Statutory	General government or wider	*Expenditure rule:* The rule states that permanent expenditure cannot be higher than permanent revenue, though both are unclearly defined. Under xceptional circumstances, nonpermanent revenue may be used to pay for permanent spending if the government deems necessary. This rule is used on a statutory basis and not enforced or monitored outside the government. It was adopted in 2010 and applied to the 2011 and 2012 budgets. The 2002 Fiscal Responsibility, Stabilization, and Transparency Law set fiscal deficit limits; the annual growth of primary central government expenditure must not exceed 3.5 percent in real terms (excluding capital spending), the fiscal deficit as a % of GDP (excluding oil export revenue) must decrease by 0.2 percent each year, and public debt must not exceed 40 percent of GDP. The Fiscal Rule Law and preceding rules were superseded by a new 2010 fiscal rule law (FRL).

Table 7.7 (continued)

Country	Type of national rule (year of implementation)	Legal basis	Coverage	Key elements of the rules
Mexico	Budget balance rule (2006)	Statutory	Central government	*Budget balance rule (since 2006):* Balances the budget on a cash basis established by law. It applies to the federal public sector, which includes the central government, social security, and key public enterprises (e.g., the oil company PEMEX and the electricity company CFE). It includes a reference price for oil that is set by a formula and also a system of four stabilization funds, including an oil stabilization fund. Starting with the 2009 fiscal year, the definition was changed to exclude the investment outlays of the state-owned oil company PEMEX from the balanced-budget rule. This change reflects general reforms aimed at boosting investment in oil projects and the inclusion of all of PEMEX's investment projects as budgetary investment.
Panama	Budget balance rule (2012)	Statutory	General government or wider	*Budget balance rule:* The revised Fiscal Social Responsibility Law (June 2012) and the Savings Fund of Panama Law (2012) introduce the concept of an "adjusted balance" of the nonfinancial public sector (NFPS), for which a statutory limit is set. The adjusted balance of the NFPS is defined as the NFPS balance minus the annual deposits into the newly created Savings Fund of Panama (FAP). Starting in 2015, yearly contributions from the Panama Canal Authority to the budget in excess of 3.5 percent of GDP are to be transferred into the FAP. Should deposits fall short of the 3.5 percent but remain higher than 3 percent of GDP, the government can borrow the difference. From 2012 to 2014, the fiscal rule applies to the nonadjusted balance, because the FAP accumulates funds only from 2015 on. The new budget deficit limits are 2.9 percent of GDP for 2012, 2.8 percent for 2013, 2.7 percent for 2014, 2.0 percent for 2015, 1.5 percent for 2016, 1.0 percent for 2017, and 0.5 percent from 2018 on. New escape clauses have been introduced (state of emergency and economic slowdown). *Debt rule:* Reduce public debt to GDP ratio to below 40 percent by 2017.
	Debt rule (2009)	Statutory	General government or wider	

Table 7.7 (continued)

Country	Type of national rule (year of implementation)	Legal basis	Coverage	Key elements of the rules
Peru	Expenditure rule (2000)	Statutory	Central government	*Budget balance rule:* Deficit ceiling for the nonfinancial public sector. The ceiling was set at 2.0 percent of GDP for 2000 and 2003, 1.5 percent of GDP for 2001 and 2004, and 1.0 percent in 2002 and since 2005.
	Budget balance rule (2000)	Statutory	Central government	

Expenditure rule: Real growth current expenditure ceiling of 2 percent (2000–2002), 3 percent (2003–2008), and 4 percent since 2009. The application of any of the fiscal rules may be suspended for up to three years when (1) real GDP is declining, with the ceiling on the deficit being raised to 2.5 percent of GDP, with a minimum annual reduction of 0.5 percent of GDP until the 1 percent deficit ceiling is reached; and (2) in other emergencies declared by congress at the request of the executive branch. The executive must specify in its request that the ceilings be applied during the period of exception for the deficit and expenditure rules, with the minimum annual reduction of 0.5 percent of GDP on the deficit also applying in this case. In April 2012, the authorities modified the current expenditure limit under the fiscal rule, mainly by excluding infrastructure maintenance from the expenditure cap and current expenditures associated with some social programs and equipment for military and police forces. In addition, the authorities introduced a temporary target for the structural fiscal balance (controlling for commodity prices), requiring an annual adjustment of at least 0.25 percent of GDP to maintain a fiscal path, consistent with reaching zero structural balance over the medium term. However, the structural balance objective was achieved ahead of schedule by the end of 2012 due to the stronger than expected fiscal outcome, and the proposed fiscal adjustment is no longer binding for 2013, because the fiscal accounts have already reached a small structural surplus. Moreover, the 2013 budget approved in December 2012 eliminated the temporary target for the structural fiscal balance introduced in April 2012 and proposed a nondeficit overall fiscal target for 2013.

Source: Authors' own construction from IMF 2013c.

The debt crisis of the 1980s forced countries to adjust. In particular, governments could not continue relying on international credit to finance their deficits. It proved difficult—if not impossible—to raise additional taxes in severely weakened economies, and a large part of the 1980s adjustment took the form of public spending cuts, especially on investment projects, often hurting social programs and thus affecting the poor. However, deficits were not eliminated overnight. In such a complex scenario, several countries had to rely on *seigniorage* (monetary financing), which was a defining force behind the extraordinary inflationary outbursts affecting the region throughout most of the 1980s.

Public finances in Latin America have improved considerably thereon, partly because of relevant market-oriented reforms. By the turn of the millennium, government revenues increased sharply following the upswing of a favorable world commodity boom. In addition, several countries implemented important structural fiscal management reforms. Most notable was the introduction of structural balance rules, starting in Chile, and, more recently, taking place in Colombia and Peru. These rules allow for stronger fiscal discipline and countercyclical fiscal policy.

Latin American countries with federal governments (e.g., Brazil and Argentina), however, face a major challenge regarding fiscal institutions. One well-known problem is that regional governments do not have clear budget constraints. Nonetheless, there are some rules to promote fiscal responsibility in regional governments. The existence of an effectively autonomous central bank is essential, and such a bank needs to have the ability to deny access to credit to regional governments.

It is also important that the central government does not provide collateral for regional or local debts. In principle, governments should only guarantee sovereign debt, though in practice the public sector sometimes needs to rescue local governments and even private debtors.

Finally, it is becoming imperative for all Latin American countries to improve public sector management through the use of information technologies. On the one hand, the state has a role in the diffusion of information technologies across the economy. On the other, the government is an essential user of this information in the procurement process, the management of human resources, the provision of information, and tax administration. In contrast, if and when public purchases and procurement are conducted discretionarily, the scope for corruption becomes wide open. Under well-established and enforceable fiscal rules, information technologies can make an important contribution to most Latin American countries, both in terms of efficiency and transparency.

Fiscal Policy for Development

Summary
- Latin American countries during the 1970s were able to finance large fiscal deficits with foreign commercial bank funding.
- Foreign lending stopped in the early 1980s, and almost all Latin American governments defaulted and resorted to seigniorage in order to finance their deficits.
- Unprecedented inflation rates and an inability to broaden the tax base exacerbated the size of the budget deficits.
- Currency depreciations mitigated the fiscal crisis, but current account surpluses from real depreciations were largely offset by exceedingly high payments of sovereign debt.
- Most governments were forced to decrease expenditures. Particularly affected were expenditure cuts in investments in human capital—health and education.
- Debt restructuring via the Baker and Brady plans alongside a set of Washington Consensus reforms released the pressure on Latin American budget deficits.
- In the 1990s, debt restructurings and reforms started to take hold, and redistributive fiscal policies could further finance cash transfers to disadvantaged sectors of the population despite the region's inability to broaden its tax base via direct taxation.
- The broad scope of the reforms inclusive of stabilization and privatization had a profound impact on the fiscal situation. With stronger macroeconomic fundamentals in the twenty-first century and high rates of economic growth, Latin American countries were able to weather the 2007 to 2008 subprime crisis.
- Most countries in Latin America are primary commodity exporters and thus prone to sharp cyclical fluctuations, which need to be met with countercyclical fiscal policies.
- Countercyclical fiscal policies require strong fiscal institutions, which most countries do not yet have.
- Chile is a pioneer with regard to the adoption of structural fiscal rules. Recent attempts in neighboring countries to mimic the Chilean example seem to be bearing fruit.

Review Questions
1. What are the distinguishing features of Latin America's public deficits in the 1970s?
2. Why did Latin American countries experience a fiscal crisis in the 1980s?
3. What were the main effects of high fiscal deficits during the 1980s, and why were those deficits at the root of a vicious circle?

4. How did Latin American countries manage to resolve their fiscal crises in the early 1990s?
5. Why are fiscal policies redistributive in Latin American countries despite the region's limited scope for direct taxation?
6. Why is direct taxation difficult to implement in most Latin American economies?
7. Why has the fiscal situation in Latin America improved considerably as of 2003 and beyond?
8. What are countercyclical fiscal policies, and why do most Latin American countries need to implement them?
9. What lessons can be drawn from the Chilean experience with regard to the creation of strong fiscal structures for implementing countercyclical fiscal policies?

Further Reading

For a clear presentation of fiscal rules in Latin America, their objectives, and enforceability since the mid-1990s, see Berganza 2012 (written in English, available online at http://www.bde.es/f/webbde/SES/Secciones/Publicaciones/PublicacionesSeriadas/DocumentosOcasionales/12/Fich/do1208e.pdf). In 2015, the IMF published an interesting review on Latin American fiscal policies, emphasizing countercyclical fiscal policies. Crafted by various authors (Celasun et al. 2015), the document bears the title *Fiscal Policy in Latin America: Lessons and Legacies of the Global Financial Crisis* (available online at http://incp.org.co/Site/2015/publicaciones/egerencial/fiscal-policy-in-latin-america.pdf). For best practices in crafting sound fiscal rules in emerging market economies, see Gutiérrez and Revilla 2010.

8   The Fight against Inflation

Inflation—generalized price increases with consequential distortions, efficiency losses, and adverse income redistribution effects—is a pervasive phenomenon. Latin America has an extensive history of inflation. The region endured its most virulent spells over two long decades from 1975 to 1995—but inflation in most regions has declined since. How did policy makers manage to tame inflation by the turn of the century?

Between 1975 and 1990, several countries in Latin America suffered from an *inflation crisis*—that is, inflation running at rates exceeding 20 percent per year— and from *hyperinflation*—that is, inflation rates exceeding 50 percent per month.[1] The precipitous fall of inflation from its 1990 peak, when the region's average inflation exceeded 1,000 percent per year, to 26 percent per annum in 1995 merits attention. Inflation fell further to around an annual rate of 9 percent in 1999, and by the turn of the twenty-first century it continued to decline.

What were the roots of rising inflation spirals in the 1970s, in the 1980s and 1990s? What costs did the region incur? In what way did the world macroeconomic environment help Latin America stand out as a low-inflation region? How did Latin American policy makers manage to tame unprecedented hyperinflation over nearly twenty years of sustained efforts preceding the turn of the twenty-first century? Can inflation be controlled as commodity prices fluctuate? These are some of the questions this chapter will shed light on.

Our understanding of how to tame inflation is crucial—not only because lessons can be drawn from the multiplicity of experiments that are potentially applicable to rampant inflation in some regions such as Venezuela today, but also because inflation remains a real threat for Latin America as a whole.

The entire region is currently exposed to large swings in capital inflows and outflows, which can have significant effects on exchange rates. Most countries are exporters of primary commodities, which have been in high demand from Asia. However, the price of primary commodities is subject to sharp cyclical fluctuations. Indeed, commodity prices have fallen sharply in recent years. Moreover, contagion from emerging markets elsewhere makes the region prone to boom and bust episodes, foreign exchange fluctuations, and balance of payments crises. Taking stock of Latin America's rich experience in price stabilization should help policy makers cope with volatile capital flows, particularly during the current Chinese slowdown and precipitous fall of commodity prices since 2013.

Section 8.1 in this chapter describes the 1975 to 1990 price hikes, to which the roots of contemporary Latin America's inflation can be traced. Section 8.2 explains the negative correlation between growth and inflation and the positive association between income inequality and inflation. Section 8.3 details the rationale behind orthodox and heterodox stabilization policies, their impact, and the role of central banks and fiscal authorities. Sections 8.4 and 8.5 underscore the importance of independent central banks and fiscal prudence, respectively, as the most important tools to keep inflation under control. Section 8.6 analyzes the connection between inflation and exchange rates in brushstrokes, and section 8.7 unveils the reasons behind recent fears of a return to high inflation. Finally, section 8.6 summarizes these points and delivers some concluding comments.

8.1 Main Roots of Inflation

Let us start with some basic macroeconomic identities.[2] We know that total savings, S, are equal to investment, I. But we also know that total savings are national savings (S_N) plus foreign savings, and that foreign savings equal the current account (CA) deficit. Thus, $CA = S_N - I$. However, national savings include government savings $S_G = T - G$, where S_G are government savings, T are tax revenues, and G are government expenditures. Hence, $CA = S_P + S_G - I = S_P - I - (G - T)$, where S_P are private savings and $G - T$ is the public deficit.

Following a sudden fall in commodity prices, a country can reduce its current account deficit via (a) increasing private savings, (b) decreasing private investment, and/or (c) decreasing the public deficit. The close link between the current account and the public deficit is often referred to as the *twin deficit hypothesis*.[3]

Countries often find it politically difficult to reduce their public deficits quickly (*forceful contraction*, to use the terminology from chapter 7) in order

The Fight against Inflation

to improve a deteriorated current account; often times, their only resort is to monetize those deficits via borrowing from their central banks.

More generally, governments can finance their public deficit via issuing local bonds (internal borrowing), via external borrowing, via seigniorage (printing money), or via drawing from its own foreign currency reserves.

As we have been arguing thus far, however, contemporary Latin American economies continue to be vulnerable to external shocks, which are immediately reflected in the current account. Foreign currency reserves fluctuate accordingly. The increase in world commodity prices in the 1970s—oil prices, in particular, tripled in 1973 and rose again in 1979—raised capital inflows. These, along with an external debt explosion resulting from petrodollars enabled Latin American governments to finance large public deficits (see chapters 4 and 7). As shown in figure 8.1, the monetization of high capital inflows to finance large public deficits in turn triggered a rise in inflation rates from single digits in the 1960s to double digits in the 1970s.

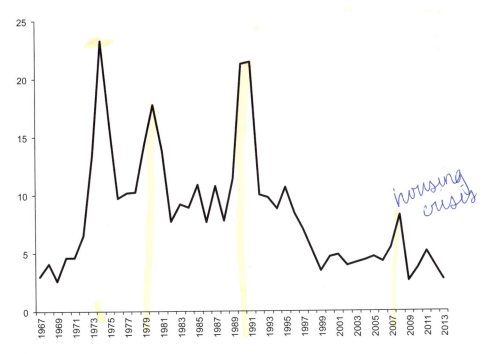

Figure 8.1
Median rate of inflation in Latin America, consumer prices average annual % change, 1967–2013.
Source: World Bank 2014b.

This observation is not new.[4] An important question is how governments should have responded to the inflationary pressures resulting from the oil price increases and consequential inflows of capital in the 1970s. If the fiscal situation was precarious—as it was under ISI policies, reviewed in chapter 3—then the sudden hike in capital inflows and in revenues from the commodity boom should have been met with fiscal prudence in order to avoid an inflation. In other words, the adequate policy response to a sudden hike in capital inflows or in fiscal revenue is to enact *countercyclical fiscal policies*.[5] However, with the notable exception of Chile since 2000, countercyclical fiscal policies in Latin America's infant democracies are unpopular and therefore rare.

Let us now move on to the 1980s, when the region witnessed hyperinflation episodes. The root of the problem is well understood: the sudden stop in capital inflows coincided with a drastic fall in commodity prices. Unable to finance government expenditures with sovereign debt, and with the advent of a sharp fall in foreign exchange reserves as commodity prices decreased, most governments resorted to seigniorage.[6] Note that issuing domestic debt was not feasible because of the "original sin."[7] Seigniorage is at the root of the inflation tax paid by most Latin Americans citizens, who saw the real value of their money holdings sharply eroded. On the other hand, significant public sector contraction was unavoidable (see chapter 7).[8]

Table 8.1 shows that inflation and seigniorage (both as a percentage of government revenues and of GDP) were extraordinarily high in the 1980s relative to subsequent decades. In particular, seigniorage was as high as 129 percent of government revenues in countries such as Bolivia that experienced hyperinflation. As the table shows, this is indeed a gigantic figure relative to that in developed countries such as the United States and Switzerland, where fiscal and monetary institutions are much stronger, that is, where fiscal laws and independent central banks set clear limits to how much the executive can borrow to finance public deficits.

The 1990s witnessed yet another decade of high inflation in some countries, such as Brazil, Latin America's largest economy. Like several other countries (e.g., Mexico and Argentina), Brazil opted for exchange rate–based stabilization, which led to a currency overvaluation and a crisis that started in 1998. Nonetheless, we witnessed a low average inflation in the 1990s relative to the 1980s, partly because the region's largest economies (Argentina, Brazil and Mexico) could finance their deficits through short-term debt as opposed to just money creation.[9]

Sharp swings in volatile capital flows alongside erroneous fiscal and monetary responses are not the only root cause of the traumatic last quarter inflationary period in the last century. Exchange rate policies also played an important role. We will return to such policies in chapter 9. For now, note that most countries—with some exceptions, such as Chile and Colombia—failed in their attempts to

Table 8.1
Seigniorage in selected countries

Country	Inflation			As % of other tax revenue			As % of GDP		
	1980s	1990s	2000s	1980s	1990s	2000s	1980s	1990s	2000s
Bolivia	1382,84	10,52	5,06	129,09	5,17	8,41	5,46	1,19	2,59
Peru	481,28	807,88	2,60	43,72	11,69	3,57	4,73	1,40	0,59
Brazil	328,10	854,78	6,90	113,00	17,84	2,47	2,8	2,30	0,55
Paraguay	20,33	16,49	8,26	23,87	8,94	8,71	2,15	1,35	1,45
South Africa	14,67	9,90	6,13	3,03	2,04	2,07	0,71	0,50	0,55
Philippines	14,17	9,64	5,24	9,60	7,01	7,39	1,29	1,24	1,17
Guatemala	12,30	14,97	7,03	13,14	14,24	11,66	1,16	1,22	1,42
Korea	8,40	5,74	3,12	19,31	20,57	13,07	3,57	3,77	2,87
Canada	6,51	2,20	2,12	10,79	6,72	15,07	1,65	1,14	2,37
United States	5,55	3,01	2,57	1,92	2,42	6,17	0,34	0,44	1,03
Switzerland	3,27	2,34	0,95	0,07	0,64	3,10	0,02	0,19	0,97
Singapore	2,77	1,94	1,49	6,87	5,19	12,46	2,03	1,73	2,67

Source: Larraín and Sachs 2013.

maintain a stable exchange rate regime. Severe devaluations under crawling peg exchange rate systems often went hand in hand with balance of payment crises, triggering massive capital outflows, which further fueled inflationary pressures.

The inability to control high inflation became increasingly complex because of wage and price indexation. In particular, Latin American governments could not credibly commit themselves to monetary tightening and fiscal austerity in an environment in which laborers were clamoring for higher wages, and firms were increasing the price of final products as a result of higher costs of production due to higher wages and higher prices for imported intermediate inputs.

Policy makers' inability to make credible commitments was further exacerbated as a result of *inertial inflation*; that is, economic agents made their own inflation forecasts based on past and current inflation rates. Because these rates were high, future inflation was high as a result, creating a self-fulfilling, vicious circle that was largely beyond policy makers' control.[10]

In periods of high inflation such as those of the 1980s and 1990s, inflation is also difficult to tame because of the Olivera-Tanzi effect.[11] That is, because there is a lag between the moment a tax obligation is born and the moment the tax is paid, higher paid. Higher inflation erodes the real value of tax collection, which amplifies the public deficit and therefore fuels inflation further.

8.2 Costs of Inflation

Standard macroeconomic textbooks distinguish between costs of anticipated inflation versus those of unanticipated inflation.[12] When inflation is anticipated, the economy experiences an efficiency loss due to shoe leather and menu costs.[13] At the same time, and in order to preserve the value of their assets, economic agents invest in relatively safe assets such as real estate, and tend to avoid long-term and potentially more productive investment projects.

Latin Americans have endured these perils of inflation along with capital inflow reversals leading to currency crises, sharp and recurrent devaluations, and macroeconomic instability. The combination of these adverse events creates an environment that is not conducive to productive investments, with consequential negative effects on economic growth and employment.

When inflation is not perfectly anticipated, inaccurate forecasts lead to arbitrary redistribution of income and wealth (e.g., loan contracts based on inaccurate inflation forecasts might lead to borrowers gaining at the expense of lenders). Fixed contracts such as labor and pensions often lead to adverse redistribution against workers and the elderly.

Last but not least, the redistributive impact of inflation often hurts the poor. This is particularly true in Latin America, where a tiny minority of wealthy individuals can more easily hedge themselves against inflation via, for example, savings in hard currency or using sophisticated financial instruments. Conversely, the income of the poor—already eroded by inflation—leaves an exceedingly limited scope for savings, and getting hold of hard currency involves transaction costs that are considerably higher for the poor in comparison with the costs faced by the wealthy.

8.3 Orthodox and Heterodox Stabilization Policies

The debate over how to best tackle inflation crises and hyperinflation episodes (henceforth, stabilization policies) is best understood via shedding light on the divide between monetarists and structuralists.

Dating back to Milton Friedman's (1963) seminal work, *monetarists* contend that excess money creation relative to output growth creates inflation. Their key assumptions are that there is no excess capacity and that the velocity of money is stable. The policy prescription for reducing inflation is therefore to reduce the budget deficit, especially when the deficit is financed via seigniorage, which was indeed the case in the 1980s. (Recall that most Latin American governments at the time could not issue domestic currency–denominated debt.) Budget deficit reduction or orthodox policies for lowering inflation are often identified with IMF policy prescriptions.

In contrast, *structuralists*—notably, Celso Furtado (1967) from ECLAC—contend that although monetized deficits are important, they are not the only cause of inflation. Bottlenecks or shortages of inputs of production play a critical role. Prices, and wages in particular, are sticky downward—creating unemployment. Resulting inflation from wage and price indexation becomes endemic and inertial inflation takes hold.[14] Structuralists advocate wage and price controls as the main tools to combat inflation. Such controls—also known as income policies—are a key ingredient of so-called heterodox policies.

The line between orthodox and heterodox stabilization policies in Latin America is often blurred, mostly because diverse mixtures and trials were used in sequence and often times simultaneously. Ultimately, a broad consensus was reached in the 1990s on prioritizing fiscal, monetary, and exchange rate policies. Although the mixture of these three policies were undeniably at the heart of all successful stabilization programs implemented in the region, external debt restructurings played a key role. In particular, most countries managed to reduce their public deficits via reducing or delaying their foreign currency–denominated interest payments.

As figure 8.2 shows, starting in 1975, the public deficit as a percentage of gross national product (GNP) for the entire Latin America declined until 1983. It then

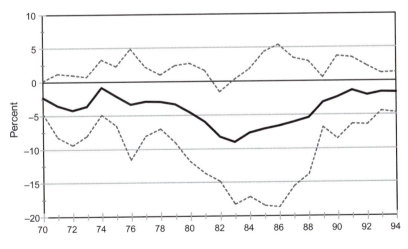

Figure 8.2
Latin American central governments surplus, 1970–1994. *Note:* Dotted lines indicate standard deviations.
Source: Alesina et al. 1999.

started to fall as a result of (a) fiscal austerity or forceful contraction, (b) external debt moratoria, and, (c) successful external debt restructurings. By 1994, the primary surplus had almost reverted to its 1974 average. A great deal of diversity (not shown on the graph) is also well-documented. In some countries (e.g., Mexico, Ecuador, and Chile), the average surplus was positive, whereas in others (e.g., Brazil, Peru, and Venezuela) it remained negative for the entire twenty-year period.[15]

On the monetary side of the spectrum, most reforms were confiscatory. For example, Argentina's Austral Plan and Brazil's Cruzado Plan in the 1980s consisted of swapping old currency for new currency without a change in fundamentals (e.g., lowering budget deficits); with the benefit of hindsight, it is now clear that those policies were not credible.

Uncontrolled inflation in the aftermath of monetary reforms fails to preserve the value of most financial assets and wages. When the value of all assets and liabilities are denominated in domestic currency, inflation erodes their value. A typical example is the case of commercial banks' assets; their value fell as inflation increased, and therefore the risk of widespread bank bankruptcies also increased. Fearing bankruptcy, the deposit base decreased—particularly because depositors were uninsured in most Latin American countries.

This speaks to the fact that, relative to many other countries on the eve of a financial crisis, the Latin American banking sector became extremely fragile. The percentage point change in deposits before the crisis episodes in selected Latin American countries relative to other countries (especially Asian emerging market economies) is revealing, as figure 8.3 shows.

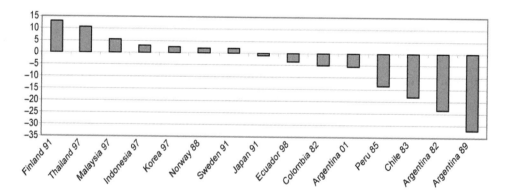

Figure 8.3
Deposits to GDP on the eve of crises (Latin America and several selected countries) (percentage points change).
Source: Rojas-Suarez and Weisbrod 1995 and IMF 2002.

The Fight against Inflation

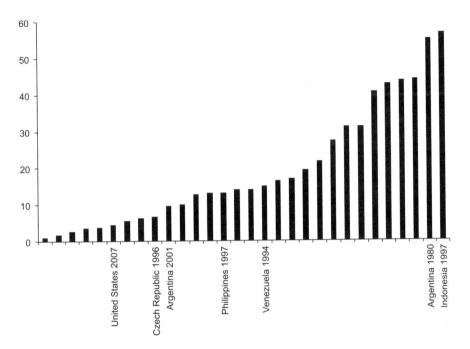

Figure 8.4
Fiscal costs of banking crises as a percentage of GDP in various countries.
Source: Laeven and Valencia 2013.

The fiscal costs of rescuing a bankrupt financial sector have been estimated to be higher for Latin American countries in comparison with other economies. As figure 8.4 shows, Argentina, Chile, Ecuador, Mexico, and Uruguay paid a high cost—in the range of 20 to 55 percent of their GDPs.

Clearly, the various stabilization attempts had an impact on inflation, which in the case of Latin America fell from an average of 496 percent at the peak of the crisis in the late 1980s to nearly 5 percent in 2006, as shown in figure 8.1.

Economic growth, on the other hand, experienced a six-year recovery. As table 8.2 shows, relative to other regions—notably, Asia—Latin America grew strongly until 1997. This growth spurt was followed by a slowdown in the 1998–2003 period, however. To most observers, the slowdown in growth experienced in the region was due to contagion. In particular, Latin America was adversely affected by the Asian and Russian crises from 1997 to 1998. Nevertheless, inflation remained low on average.

Table 8.2
Growth rates in Latin America relative to other regions (annual averages, 1981–2003)

	1981–1990	1991–1997	1998–2003
Latin America	-0.6	2.5	-0.1
Industrial countries	2.5	1.4	1.8
Other developing countries	1.9	2.6	3.3
Asia	4.8	6.5	4.8
Other Asia	2.8	4.1	1.1
Eastern and Central Asia Europe	1.2	0.7	2.6
Middle East	-1.3	1.3	1.8
Sub-Saharan Africa	-0.6	-0.5	0.7

Source: IMF Data (www.imf.org/en/Data).

Relative to the high inflationary period of the 1980s, output volatility in the 1990s decreased albeit slightly for the entire Latin American region. However, as suggested by figure 8.4, large cross-country differences appear once more. Compared to the lost decade, output volatility in Chile, Brazil, and Mexico decreased, while it increased substantially in Venezuela and Argentina.

We now turn to institutional strengthening venues used to prevent inflation.

8.4 Central Bank Autonomy

With the notable exception of Uruguay, countries in Latin America did not have central banks in the nineteenth century.[16] Upon their enactment in the 1920s, central banks' mandate was to finance "key" sectors and to promote growth. The advent of widespread ISI policies in the 1950s de facto enlarged that mandate to include credit to promote economic development—broadly defined—and interest rate controls.

This situation persisted in most countries until the late 1980s, when central bank independence legislation was adopted. Starting in 1989 with the Central Bank of Chile, legislation about central banks' autonomy has been passed in some of the region's major economies, and their mandate has been confined mainly to inflation targeting.

Several authors have reported that there is a negative and statistically significant correlation between the degree of central bank independence and inflation.[17] However, conspicuously absent from table 8.3 is Brazil, where the inflation rate fell precipitously in 1995 but climbed back in 2015 to around 9 percent in the wake

Table 8.3
New central bank laws in Latin America, 1989–2002

Country	Date of new laws	Country	Date of new laws
Chile	1989	Mexico	1993
El Salvador	1991	Bolivia	1995
Argentina	1992 and 2002	Costa Rica	1995
Colombia	1992	Uruguay	1995
Nicaragua	1992 and 1999	Paraguay	1995
Venezuela	1992, 1999, and 2002	Honduras	1996 and 2004
Ecuador	1992 and 1998	Guatemala	2001
Peru	1993	Dominican Republic	2002

Source: Carstens and Jácome 2005.

of significant currency depreciation. Yet Brazil does not have a de jure independent central bank. Specifically, the Brazilian Central Bank president does not have a fixed term length in office and can be dismissed by the executive.[18] Some other countries, like Argentina and Venezuela, do not have a de facto independent central bank.

Table 8.3 and and figure 8.5 suggest that legislative independence—although important—is not a single prerequisite for bringing inflation rates down. Instead, accountability, transparency, inflation targeting, and the fiscal responsibility laws implemented de facto are of paramount importance. These institutional changes have been key to sustaining low inflation rates during the twenty-first century in Latin America, with the exception of Argentina and Venezuela and, more recently, Brazil.

Inflation targeting is a fairly recent phenomenon. The trend formally started in several countries in 2009—that is, after the subprime crisis. Four countries have followed inflation targeting since: Brazil, Colombia, Mexico, and Peru. Chile started earlier, in the year 2000. According to Schmidt-Hebbel (2011), in these five countries the inflation rate has been lower than that of the region's average. More importantly, when compared to other Latin American countries, inflation-targeting countries have greater economic and political central bank independence and better transparency with regard to monetary and accountability indices.

Regarding exchange rate policies, the reforms in the 1990s originally called for central banks to keep semifixed or completely fixed exchange rates, leading to balance of payments crises that reflected vulnerability to external shocks—except in some countries such as Ecuador, which adopted the US dollar as a legal tender.

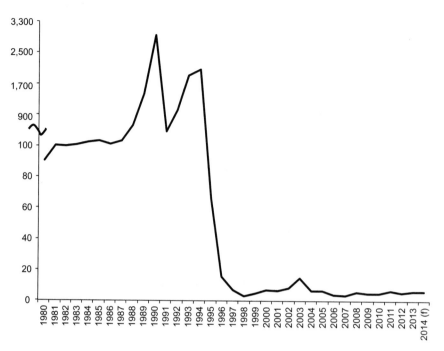

Figure 8.5
Average inflation rate in Brazil, 1980–2014.
Source: IMF 2015.

In the twenty-first century, Latin American central banks have shifted to semiflexible exchange rate regimes anchored by inflation expectations, which has led to lower exposure to contagion from crises originating elsewhere, lower incidence of overvaluations, and lower interest rates. We will return to exchange rate regimes in greater detail in chapter 9.

Following the global financial crisis of 2008, major central banks in the region have been actively undertaking reforms to improve financial regulation and supervision of commercial banks, in accordance with international standards aimed at limiting risk taking and moral hazard. At the same time, restrictions on FDI in the banking sector have been lifted, leading to increased competition. Although national supervisory authorities also regulate foreign banks that operate within their borders, these banks are indirectly accountable to managers in their country of origin, and those managers' actions are strongly supervised by prudential and regulatory institutions elsewhere. The connection between strong fiscal institutions and inflation is the issue to which we now turn.

8.5 Fiscal Institutions and Fiscal Prudence

As analyzed in chapter 7, since the early 1990s, most Latin American countries have embarked on a series of reforms aimed at improving their budget institutions. While delegating budget management and control to finance ministers, laws were enacted to increase transparency, oversight, and accountability. Restrictions on amendments on budget proposals by the executive, constitutional limits on deficit spending, and targets were also part of the reforms to improve fiscal discipline.

Along with this set of reforms, the legislative branches of most Latin American governments were granted greater involvement in approving and potentially modifying budget proposals, greater scrutiny in budget execution, increased ability to monitor performance, and options to ensure accountability.[19]

On the revenue side of the spectrum, a series of tax reforms were introduced. VAT, personal and corporate taxation, excise taxes, and other reforms aimed at broadening the tax base have been a contributing factor in the region's effort to avoid monetization of the deficit and high inflation.

These reforms helped to increase credibility and lower inflationary expectations. However, the extent to which the previously mentioned reforms contributed to deficit reduction in the 1990s remains an open question, because fiscal reforms were introduced in parallel with other corrective measures, such as sovereign debt restructurings and exchange rate policies. Nonetheless, figure 8.6 illustrates the

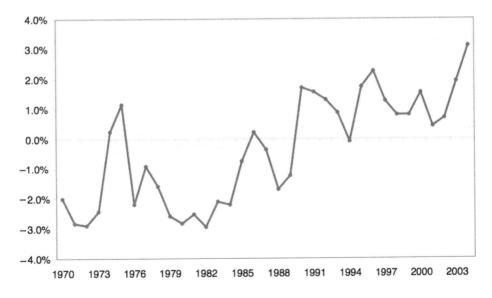

Figure 8.6
Primary budget deficit/surplus in Latin America, 1970–2003.
Source: IMF 2004.

spectacular turnaround of the primary budget from a chronic deficit in the 1970s and 1980s to a surplus as of 1994.

It is important to note that, despite efforts to improve fiscal institutions, the challenges ahead are enormous. First, the divide between de jure and de facto implementation of reforms remains a problem in Latin America's nascent democracies. For example, although the transparency laws are sound, public perceptions on transparency remain poor in some countries. Second, rigidities and ex-ante commitments have a tendency to deliver procyclical budget deficits in a vast majority of countries—with the exceptions of Chile since 2000 and other countries more recently, such as Colombia and Peru. Despite the fact that such rigidities were primarily aimed at preserving key spending categories, they prevent Latin American governments from improving the distribution of fiscal spending. This is particularly detrimental to public finances in countries that remain reliant on primary commodity exports, the prices of which fluctuate enormously.

The recent fall in commodity prices is once more challenging the entire southern-cone region, where domestic currencies have depreciated considerably—except, of course, in countries that have dollarized, such as Ecuador, El Salvador, and Panama. In these countries, tradable sectors are likely to suffer considerably more in comparison with countries under flexible exchange rate regimes.

We now turn to the link between exchange rates and inflation.

8.6 Inflation and Exchange Rates

Latin America is known to have witnessed different exchange rate regimes. On one side of the spectrum, we find fixed exchange rates and dollarization (e.g., Argentina's currency board in the 1990s and Ecuador since 2000). On the extreme opposite side, we find fully flexible exchange rate regimes (e.g., Chile, Colombia, Mexico, Peru, and Uruguay, among others). During the 1990s, however, the choice of exchange rate regime was intrinsically linked to the well-known trade-off between credibility under fixed or semifixed exchange rates and competitiveness under flexible exchange rates.

In this section, we shed light on exchange rate–based stabilization policies by contrasting the case of countries in which inflation at the end of the 1980s was particularly high with that of countries in which inflation rates were moderately high. However, we defer our full-fledged analysis of exchange rate regimes in Latin America during the twenty-first century to chapter 9.

Specifically, stylized facts suggest that in countries in which inflation was exceedingly high in the 1980s, fixed exchange rate regimes enabled such countries to bring inflation down quite quickly. Three of Latin America's large economies illustrate this vividly. According to IMF estimates, Mexico's inflation rate in 1988 had reached 180 percent. Under the so-called *Pacto de Soli[daridad?] intro*duced in that same year, the main pillar of this stabiliz[ation was the] introduction of a semifixed exchange rate regime. The Me[xican peso was allowed] to fluctuate within a narrow band with a sliding ceiling [against the US dollar.] By April 1989—that is, only one year later—inflation had [fallen sharply.]

In Argentina, estimated inflation was approximately 700 [percent in 1991 when] the currency board was introduced.[20] Less than two years l[ater—that is, by] 1994—inflation had fallen to less than 10 percent.

Brazil's inflation rate was as high as 3,000 percent in 19[94. In that same year,] the old currency (the cruzeiro) was exchanged for a new currency (the real). The new currency was linked (not pegged as in the Argentinean case) approximately one-to-one to the US dollar. Only two years later—that is, by 1996—Brazilian inflation had declined to single digits.[21]

In contrast, Colombia had low and stable inflation rates of approximately 10 percent throughout most of the 1990s, and it was not until 1999 that orthodox stabilization brought down inflation to single digits. Similarly, Chile's inflation rate, which stood at about 25 percent in 1990, did not decline to single digits until five years later—that is, by the end of 1994. In both of these countries, as we will discuss in chapter 9, the exchange rate was allowed to float.

These experiences thus suggest that exchange rate stabilization can have a rapid effect on inflation expectations—and, indeed, much of the overall fall in average inflation rates in the 1990s can be attributed to exchange rate stabilizations in Latin America's larger economies. However, substantial gains in credibility via fixed exchange rate commitments compromise competitiveness and the ability of economies to respond to outside shocks (e.g., terms of trade shocks), which were key factors for promoting growth in an increasingly globalized economy—where it was of outmost important to avoid overvalued exchange rates in order to promote exports. We will return to this topic in chapter 9 on exchange rates and then again in chapter 10 on trade and financial liberalization.

Once inflation was under control by the turn of the millennium, Brazil, Chile, Colombia, Guatemala, Mexico, and Uruguay adopted floating exchange rates and embraced inflation targeting.

8.7 Twenty-First-Century Capital Inflows

By the early to mid-1990s, and after a decade of financial isolation, Latin America was again a net recipient of significant capital inflows. In contrast with the inflows of capital that Latin America was a recipient of in the 1970s—basically from commercial bank loans—the new wave of inflows in the 1990s was of a different nature. Capital flowing into the region mainly consisted of short- and long-term

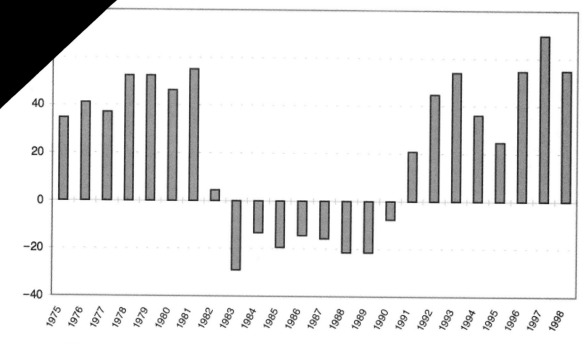

Figure 8.7
Latin American capital inflows, 1975–1998 (in billions of 1990 US dollars)
Source: ECLAC 1999.

portfolio investments and FDI. IMF estimates suggest that net resource transfers reached US$112 billion—that is, more than twice as much as the capital inflows of the 1970s.[22]

The change in the global macroeconomic environment played an important role, but structural reforms and, in particular, tighter budget deficits and low-inflation environments also reignited investors' confidence in Latin America. As figure 8.7 shows, despite the recent record of macroeconomic instability and high inflation in the 1980s, capital inflows started increasing considerably as early as 1991.

In addition, an upward trend in capital inflows continued well into the twenty-first century and beyond the 2007 to 2008 subprime crisis. As we have recurrently highlighted throughout this chapter, however, one of the main features of such inflows is that they are and have always been highly volatile.[23] Despite capital inflow volatility, Latin America weathered the subprime crisis rather well, thanks in part to preceding high growth rates, stronger fundamentals, and, in some instances, twenty-first-century countercyclical fiscal policies.

Let us analyze the impact of capital inflows on inflation. When capital inflows are high, demand for domestic currency increases, and there is a tendency for Latin American currencies to appreciate. The "pass-through" from exchange rate to prices is reflected in disinflationary forces.[24]

On the contrary, capital outflows lead to depreciations and thus to inflationary pressures.[25] This is precisely what Latin America has been experiencing since the onset of the Chinese slowdown in 2013 and the precipitous fall of primary commodity prices that ensued. This tendency can be counteracted via inflation targeting, and indeed several countries in the region have succeeded at counteracting the inflationary pressures of capital inflows via independent inflation-targeting central banks, such as those in Chile, Colombia, Mexico, and Peru.

Although the pass-through from exchange rate to prices has declined, partly because of low inflation and inflation targeting, excess volatility can revert to the high inflation periods depending on (a) the magnitude of the shock, (b) how well equipped inflation-targeting central banks are in terms of foreign reserves, and (c) the ability of fiscal institutions to follow countercyclical policies.

Some countries have pegged their currencies to the dollar in order to avoid overvaluations.[26] One problem in such countries is *imported inflation*. In Mexico, for example, expansionary monetary policies in the United States in particular can generate imported inflation and overvalued exchange rates. Inflation in recent years has been rising as Mexico attempts to counteract current account deficits via depreciations of the peso.

In addition to high volatility under flexible exchange rates, there are some countries such as Venezuela and Argentina in which reforms to contain inflation have been de jure but not de facto; that is, they have been put on words and on paper, but not into action. In these countries, expansionary fiscal policies in support of populist governments are generating high, double-digit inflation rates. As a consequence, capital inflows have stopped and stagflation—that is, slow or negative growth with exceedingly high inflation rates—is back. The trend in Argentina might change, because the newly elected government led by President Macri seems to be coping with the challenge of reverting more than a decade of *Kirchnerist* policies rather well.

8.8 Concluding Remarks

In this chapter, we analyzed the link between current account deficits, budget deficits, and inflation during extraordinarily high episodes of inflation and hyperinflation in Latin America in the late twentieth century. We have also analyzed the effect of stabilization policies in the 1990s. Via reduction in expenditures, new fiscal institutions, central bank independence laws, and, to a lesser extent, an increase in the tax base, the groundwork was laid for stabilization policies to take hold by the turn of the twenty-first century.

In Latin America's largest economies—Brazil and Mexico —inflation in the 1980s was comparatively high, and the introduction of exchange-rate-based stabilization policies had a rapid impact on bringing inflation down from triple- to single-digit rates. In contrast, countries such as Colombia, which started with comparatively low inflation rates in the early 1990s and followed orthodox policies, experienced a longer time frame for bringing inflation down from double to single digits.

Overall, inflation in Latin America fell from an unprecedented 500 percent per annum in the 1980s to approximately 6 percent in the 1990s. However, exchange rate–based stabilizations generated an overvaluation of several countries' currencies, partially contributing to a currency crises in Mexico in 1994, in Brazil in 1998, and in Argentina in 2001, that is, in the region's three major economies.

Low inflation was an undeniable contributing factor to economic growth, which increased during the first half of the 1990s. However, this growth spell was short-lived and highly volatile because, despite structural reforms, Latin America was adversely affected by contagion from crises in other emerging markets—notably in Asia and Russia in 1997 and 1998. These crises had a negative impact on economic growth, but inflation remained low on average compared to the 1980s.

One of the main lessons of this chapter is that taming inflation requires establishing sound de jure and de facto monetary and fiscal institutions. In the case of Venezuela, Argentina, and, to some extent, Brazil, such institutions have not yet been enacted. Consequently, inflation is back. Inflation is hurting other countries in which it is politically unfeasible to lower budget deficits. And indeed, current account deficits are growing due to the Chinese slowdown and the precipitous fall of commodity prices in recent years.

Lowering inflation has a clear effect on reducing consequential taxation for the vast majority of Latin Americans that hold liquid assets denominated in local currencies. The poor, in particular, hold a large proportion of their income in liquid assets, and thus reducing inflation implies comparatively high benefits for less wealthy households—that is, the majority.

The region as a whole might be experiencing a lower exchange rate pass-through because of central bank autonomy and inflation targeting. However, imported inflation from expansionary monetary policies in the main industrial countries may become a problem. The most immediate problem is the fall in commodity prices and capital inflow reversals, which imply that fiscal deficits cannot be financed with windfalls from high commodity prices.

Again, the recent slowdown in China and the fall in commodity prices has brought inflation pressures back to the entire region. The hike in the price of imports followed by recurrent exchange rate depreciations is triggering higher inflation not just in Venezuela and Argentina, but also in other countries in the region, most notably in Brazil. The ability that other countries have to cope with depressed commodity prices and consequential current account deficits very much depends on those countries' past debt to GDP ratios and, in some instances, sovereign wealth funds, such as in Chile. Countries under flexible exchange rate regimes and with solid monetary institutions, such as Chile, Colombia, Mexico, and Peru, may be able to contain inflation. Economies that have dollarized, such as Ecuador, El Salvador, and Panama, might be able to contain inflation completely, but at the expense of a comparatively large output contraction.

Summary
- Inflation rates in the 1970s increased as a result of large capital inflows to which policy makers did not respond via countercyclical fiscal policies.
- Unprecedented high inflation rates were endured by most Latin American economies in the 1980s as a result of highly monetized fiscal deficits despite forceful contraction.
- Orthodox and heterodox stabilization policies contributed to bring inflation rates down in the 1990s,
- Inertial inflation nonetheless remained and was fought against via exchange rate–based stabilization policies in the region's major economies
- Stabilization policies were temporarily successful in the 1990s as volatile capital inflows and crises in other emerging markets triggered balance of payment crises.
- Nonetheless, in some of the region's major economies, independent central banks and sound fiscal rules were enacted; as a result, Latin America is better equipped to fight high inflation spells, because governments have a limited scope to increase budget deficits via seigniorage.
- Inflation elsewhere still remains a threat, and the recent Chinese slowdown may increase the price of traded goods via depreciation with consequential inflation, not just in Venezuela and Argentina, but also in other countries.
- More generally, countries that have not established independent central banks that specifically target inflation and de jure and de facto fiscal rules might be more prone to experiencing high inflation again.
- Countries that are better equipped to control inflation will remain under control via floating exchange rates, inflation-targeting central banks, and strong fiscal institutions.

Review Questions
1. What are the roots of the unprecedented high inflation rates in Latin America during the 1980s?
2. What is the link between current account deficits, public deficits, and inflation in Latin America?
3. What are the costs of high inflation?
4. How did Latin American governments manage to bring inflation down to single-digit rates in the 1990s?
5. What effect do independent central banks and fiscal institutions have on stabilization?
6. What are the advantages and disadvantages of fixed exchange rates for lowering inflation?
7. What are the main effects of a low-inflation environment in Latin America?
8. Why are capital inflows volatile, and what are the consequences of such inflows on inflation?
9. Why are Latin American major economies moving toward floating exchange rates and inflation-targeting central banks?
10. How can inflation-targeting central banks mitigate the effects of inflation when current account deficits are growing?
11. Why is the recent Chinese slowdown and sharp fall in commodity prices threatening a return to high inflation in several Latin American regions?

Further Reading
Latin America's Economy: Diversity Trends and Conflicts by Eliana Cardoso and Ann Helwege (1992) remains a classic for gaining enhanced understanding of orthodox and heterodox stabilization policies during Latin America's lost decade, particularly with regard to Brazil's stabilization policies. For a comprehensive overview of stabilization policies in Latin America in the 1980s and early 1990s, see IMF 1995. For a more recent review on taming inflation and structural reforms in Latin America, see Carstens and Jácome 2005a, 2005b.

9 Pegging, Sliding, and Floating: Managing Exchange Rates

Latin America's experience with exchange rate regimes is long and well-documented. Ever since the region abandoned the fixed exchange rate regime under the Bretton Woods system in the 1950s and 1960s, which established that countries had to maintain their currencies pegged to the US dollar, most countries have oscillated between the two extremes—that is, between hard pegs such as dollarization and currency boards and fully flexible or floating exchange rates. What do these extreme experiments reveal?

In the last chapter, we explained that in periods of high inflation, at least three of the regions' major economies—Mexico, Brazil, and Argentina—reverted to fixed exchange rate regimes in the 1990s as a venue for gaining credibility in order to bring inflation down rapidly and effectively to single-digit levels. The three experiments ended sourly, however. Mexico abandoned its fixed exchange rate mechanism in 1994 after its so-called tequila crisis. Brazil's real plan, which de facto pegged the Brazilian currency to the dollar, was abandoned following the Asian and Russian crises in 1997 and 1998. Finally, Argentina's much-heralded currency board collapsed in 2001.

In this chapter, we first present the different exchange rate regimes that are between the two extremes and briefly assess their context-specific advantages and disadvantages from the vantage point of their effectiveness at cushioning the economy against external shocks and preserving a stable and competitive environment for investment and growth. We then argue that the region is leaning toward implementing floating exchange rate regimes, which require strong fiscal and monetary institutions in order to avoid unmanageable fluctuations that affect inflation and unemployment.

Section 9.1 of this chapter details the defining features of different exchange rate regimes in the 1970s, 1980s, and 1990s. With the benefit of hindsight, section 9.2 assesses those regimes. Section 9.3 then sheds light on floating exchange rate regimes and much-needed institutional support for avoiding sharp and prolonged cyclical fluctuations. Section 9.4 extrapolates from experience to shed light on new mechanisms that can help avoid currency crises in contemporary Latin American economies in the twenty-first century. Finally, section 9.5 summarizes the chapter as a whole and provides some concluding remarks.

9.1 Characterization of Different Exchange Rate Regimes

The IMF classifies different exchange rate regimes by their degree of flexibility.[1] On one end of the spectrum, we find a fully fixed exchange rate regime in which a country uses a foreign currency as its legal tender. Full-fledged dollarization is the most vivid example of such a regime. In Latin America, Ecuador, El Salvador, and Panama fall into this category. Under a completely fixed exchange rate regime like the one that prevails in these three countries, the central banks of the dollarized regions fully surrender monetary authority to the US central bank—that is, the US Federal Reserve (US Fed).

Panama abandoned its own currency, the balboa, shortly after it gained independence from Colombia in 1904. Compared to other cases in Latin America, dollarization in Panama was not preceded by a period of high inflation, nor was it a deliberate attempt to fight inflation. History and geographic strategic location played an important role. Panama's strong links with the United States developed from 1903 to 1914, when the Panama Canal was financed and constructed. This important connection led Panama to adopt the US dollar as its own legal currency for all transactions. The canal was contractually operated by the United States until 1999, and the balboa was completely abandoned for the entire twentieth century and beyond. Nonetheless, balboa coins are still used as a unit of account, but not bills. The use of the dollar as a medium of exchange has produced a great deal of stability in Panama's macroeconomy, in which inflation rates have remained at single-digit levels for over a century—except for the decade of the 1970s, when inflation was particularly high in the United States. Unlike most Latin American countries, however, Panama is a service economy, not a primary commodity exporter. Over three-quarters of its annual GDP derive from operating the canal and from banking, insurance, and tourism. These features have been important contributing factors for macroeconomic stability compared to all other economies in the region.

Unlike Panama, Ecuador is a commodity-exporting country—mostly oil. It failed to stabilize its currency, the sucre, in the last decades of the twentieth century. Failed stabilization attempts led Ecuador to fully dollarize in the year 2000. Specifically, the decision to abandon the sucre was made primarily because its monetary and fiscal institutions are weak, and a succession of governments did not manage to gain credibility. Considerable growth in Ecuador's external debt in the 1970s, sovereign default in the 1980s, and volatile capital flows in the 1990s undermined the country's financial stability. Moreover, sharp fluctuations in the price of oil often drew reserves down, and sharp devaluations ensued. Unstable exchange rates, recurrent balance of payment crises, and inflation were the rule rather than the exception.[2] Since dollarization in 2000, the country's efforts to stabilize have paid off. It regained access to international borrowing and attracted FDI. Ecuadorian growth rates since dollarization have gone from negative to positive. The country has grown at an average rate of 3.5 percent per annum in the twenty-first century. However, Ecuador's heavy reliance on oil and weak fiscal institutions against the current backdrop—slowdown growth in China and lower oil prices—are raising concerns about the sustainability of Ecuador's economic expansion, public spending, and dollarization itself.

Dollarization in El Salvador is somewhat different. In particular, the adoption of the US dollar in El Salvador took place in the context of a relatively stable macroeconomic environment. Between 1993 and 2000, El Salvador pegged its currency, the colón, to the US dollar. Inflation remained low and stable, and the economy was growing. As of 2001, however, the colón was abandoned. The decision was made to strengthen trade links, lower transaction costs with the United States—El Salvador's main trading partner—and reduce domestic interest rates.

Perhaps more importantly, dollarization facilitates the flow of remittances, which are the country's main capital inflow. The adoption of the US dollar as legal tender has thus far served El Salvador rather well. In particular, under a pegged exchange rate and full dollarization, the country has managed to grow at an annual average rate of 2.5 percent. Relative to its Central American neighbors, interest rates are considerably lower.[3] Clearly, El Salvador is not exempt from external shocks in the US economy, however. It experienced a drastic fall in GDP growth after the 2007–2008 subprime crisis, but remittances and exports have resumed in recent years.

A *currency board* is a slightly more flexible regime. The main feature of this regime is its explicit legislative commitment to maintain the value of the domestic currency at a fixed, preestablished level vis-à-vis a foreign currency. A typical example of a currency board is that of Argentina during the 1991–2001 period. We will briefly review the Argentinean currency board and its effect on price stabilization in section 9.2.

Pegged exchange rate systems are fixed exchange rate regimes within narrow fluctuating margins. Under these systems, the monetary authorities (i.e., the central banks) sustain the peg via direct intervention—that is, via buying and selling foreign currency reserves. Argentina and Brazil used pegged exchange rate systems in the mid-1980s in order to lower inflation rates. When pegging is used in this fashion, it is often called a *nominal anchor*. A variant of this regime is a *band*, which specifies a pegged central exchange rate with horizontal bands in reference to lower and upper prespecified bands, typically narrow bands in the 1 to 2 percent range. This system was used by Chile in early stabilization stages circa 1984.

The *crawling peg* system was one of the most widely used exchange rate systems in Latin America during the twentieth century. Under a crawling peg system, the value of the domestic currency vis-à-vis the US dollar—the US was Latin America's main trading partner at the time—is adjusted periodically at a given rate, in small amounts. These adjustments typically take place in response to selective quantitative indicators, such as past inflation or differentials between inflation targets and expected inflation. Colombia launched a crawling peg exchange rate system in the 1960s, and it was maintained throughout most of the debt crisis in the 1980s and beyond. Brazil in the late 1960s—during the so-called Brazilian miracle—was also under a crawling peg system, and during most of the early 1970s, Argentina, Chile, and Uruguay used crawling pegs as price-stabilization devices; by preannouncing gradually declining rates of currency depreciations, the authorities expected domestic inflation convergence on world inflation rates.[4]

Managed floating exchange rate schemes are flexible regimes vis-à-vis a foreign currency (mostly that of the country's main trading partner). In Latin America, it continues to be the US dollar for most countries, although the United States has been losing ground as trading partner to China in recent decades. Under this regime, the monetary authorities intervene discretionarily—that is, without a specific target. Without de facto independent central banks, managed floating systems can be misused for political objectives. The recent experience with managed floating in Argentina is a case in point.

Independent floating is a market-determined exchange rate regime with minimum intervention. Under this system, the monetary authorities intervene in a preventive fashion in order to avoid sharp currency fluctuations, which might be destabilizing. Chile, Colombia, and Mexico are examples of independent floating regimes in recent decades. Central bank interventions are not new, an issue to which we now turn.

9.2 Latin America's Rich Experience with Exchange Rate Regimes

As we have already explained in chapter 4, the oil shocks in the 1970s brought unprecedented inflows of capital into Latin America. In response to these inflows, the monetary authorities in some countries failed to sterilize and kept exchange rates fixed, which led to recurrent balance of payment crises.[5]

A typical case in point is Mexico. A pegged exchange rate regime led to large appreciation of the Mexican peso, and a severe balance of payments ensued. Specifically, the country experienced a sharp and unprecedented depreciation of its currency in 1976. Inflation increased as a result, reaching 20 percent by 1979.

High inflation was also the result of the monetization of large fiscal deficits. Most countries actively promoted exchange rate–based stabilization policies under a crawling peg system called *tablitas*.[6] This system is often identified with southern cone nations—Argentina, Chile, and Uruguay—because Argentina popularized it in the 1980s and neighboring countries followed.

Under the system of *tablitas*, exchange rate devaluations were preannounced with the principal objective of bringing down inflation via gradually declining rates of currency devaluation, which worked directly into prices (through PPP) and also worked by reducing inflationary expectations. Simply stated, the crawling peg under the *tablitas* system used the exchange rate as a nominal anchor. The underlying assumption was that lowering the rates of devaluation would quickly bring down inflation. However, this view had two important shortcomings: First, inflationary inertia was built in, mainly through labor and rental contracts. Second, the increase in private capital inflows since the mid-1970s generally raised the monetary base and aggregate demand. As a result, the exchange rate was systematically overvalued, which in turn led to chronic current account deficits throughout most of the 1970s.

Oil prices increased further in 1979. This shock affected all economies, including the economy of Brazil, which had up until then managed to avoid an appreciation of the cruzeiro, its domestic currency until 1986. Following the 1979 shock, an overvalued cruzeiro provoked a current account deficit, leaving the Brazilian economy exceedingly vulnerable to the external shocks that devastated all Latin American economies in the 1980s.

During the early stages of the sovereign debt crisis in the 1980s, most Latin American countries disregarded the exchange rate as a venue for stabilization. An exception was Chile, which had tried to bring down inflation via crawling pegs and fixed exchange rates already in the 1970s. Then, in 1984 and in the midst of the most virulent crisis, Chile introduced a system of *crawling bands*, which allowed for currency to depreciate within an upper and a lower band. The range was narrow initially, but its main purpose was to generate a capital account surplus via controlled depreciations within the narrow band. By the late 1980s, the range of the crawling band had increased considerably, to such a point that it resembled a floating exchange rate regime. In a nutshell, the Chilean crawling band regime in the 1980s used the exchange rate as a nominal anchor at early stages and then slowly allowed the currency to float freely.

Although the gradual shift from crawling bands to floating exchange rates is often heralded as a success story because it led to significant growth in the 1990s, it is important to note that Chile benefited from international financial institutions' support. Loans were granted to Chile—as the early reformer in the Latin American region since 1984—in order to help this country cope with its exceedingly high debt to GDP ratios. Hence, while faster growth in the 1990s cannot be fully attributed to the gradual move from crawling bands to floating exchange rates, the Chilean gradualist approach set a precedent for other Latin American countries.

In contrast, Mexico's approach to the debt crisis under the so-called Solidarity Pact in 1988 was less straightforward.[7] Mexico first put in place a fixed exchange rate system, which was later changed to a crawling peg, and then to a band scheme. This band had a lower bound, which was fixed, but an upper band that could slide. Because of the fixed floor and discretionary narrow sliding ceiling, the band system was close to a fixed exchange rate regime, which helped to bring inflation down to single-digit levels very quickly. However, an overvalued exchange rate in the mist of political turmoil triggered a sharp depreciation of the currency in 1994. This episode is often referred as the *tequila crisis*. In short, investors' fears and speculation due to political instability—resulting from the assassination of PRI candidate Luis Donaldo Colosio and indigenous uprising in the southern state of Chiapas—provoked a bank run on foreign currency reserves, causing a depreciation of the peso of up to 50 percent. Since 1995, the Mexican peso floats.

A more stringent fixed exchange rate system was implemented in Argentina in 1991. This system is the well-known currency board under which the Argentinean peso was fully pegged one-to-one to the US dollar via a legal provision. The main goal of the currency board was to credibly lower inflationary expectations. The currency board helped Argentina bring inflation down to single-digit levels within a three-year period. The currency board survived potential contagion from the 1994 tequila crisis, but the 1997 to 1998 Asian and Russian currency crises along with a parallel currency crisis in neighboring Brazil marked the beginning of a depression, as proxied by a GDP contraction of around 20 percent in 1998. An overvalued Argentinean peso triggered a depletion of foreign currency reserves and provoked a default on external obligations and a complete collapse of the convertibility system in 2001.

The extreme case of fixed exchange rate regimes at the turn of the millennium was found in dollarization. As we noted previously, Panama, Ecuador, and El Salvador have abandoned their currencies and have de facto adopted the US dollar. Whether dollarization in Ecuador will survive the recent fall in oil prices—Ecuador's most important source of foreign exchange—remains an open question. Academics are watching closely, because lessons can be drawn from Ecuador for the eurozone, where fears still loom about reintroducing old currency in countries such as Greece. Nevertheless, with no international support, it is difficult to imagine a revived sucre (Ecuador's previous currency) without an ipso facto devaluation and skyrocketing inflation.

In sharp contrast with moderate and extreme fixed exchange rate scenarios, during the twenty-first century a consensus has been growing in Latin America in favor of independent floating regimes. These are successful regimes when backed up by strong fiscal and monetary institutions, a topic to which we now turn.

9.3 Toward a Consensus on Floating Exchange Rates

Table 9.1 shows the trend for all Latin American countries. Compared to the 1980s, when up to 84 percent of the region was under a fixed exchange rate regime, this percentage has fallen to 50 in 2004. Intermediate regimes (e.g., semifixed or crawling peg) on the other hand were adopted by a meager 6 percent of the region's total in the 1980s. This percentage increased sharply during the 1990s and has slightly declined since. At the other end of the spectrum, we see an upward trend in number of countries that have adopted a flexible exchange rate system. Specifically, the percentage of countries under flexible exchange rate regimes has more than tripled from 9 percent in the 1980s to 28 percent in 2004.

Figure 9.1 can be viewed through the lens of population. Specifically, nearly 70 percent of the Latin American population—around 400 million—is now under a floating or flexible exchange rate system.

It should be noted, however, that floating exchange rate regimes in Latin America involve inflation-targeting central banks. Mexico started the trend in 1999, which encompassed the use of monetary policy to determine the interest rate. Brazil, Colombia, and Chile followed Mexico's lead. Peru joined the trend of floating inflation-targeting countries in 2002.

As table 9.1 demonstrates, the growing consensus toward floating exchange rates is not exclusive to Latin America. Many developing countries and emerging market economies worldwide that had been under some form of fixed, semifixed, or fully pegged exchange rate systems have slowly moved toward floating exchange rate systems since the mid-1990s. The table also reveals that only 12

Table 9.1
Developing countries: Officially reported exchange rate arrangements as percentage of total, 1976–1998

	1976	1981	1986	1991	1996	1998
Pegged	86	75	67	57	45	41
US dollar	42	32	25	19	15	12
French franc	13	12	11	11	11	9
Other	7	4	4	3	4	8
SDR	12	13	8	5	2	3
Composite	12	14	18	20	14	9
Limited flexibility	3	10	5	4	3	2
Single	3	10	5	4	3	2
Cooperative	-	-	-	-	-	-
More flexible	11	15	28	39	52	57
Set to indicators	6	3	4	4	2	-
Managed floating	4	9	13	16	21	33
Independently Floating	1	4	11	19	29	24
Number of countries	100	113	119	123	123	159

Source: IMF 1997.

percent of developing countries (broadly defined) had their currency pegged in 1998 to the US dollar, relative to 42 percent in 1976.

Globalization is undoubtedly part of the story—particularly increased trade and financial flows. In the case of Latin America, most countries now have an increasingly large number of trading partners, and therefore maintaining a fixed exchange rate system with the US dollar exposes most countries to currency fluctuations between the US dollar and other major currencies, such as the euro and the yen.

Latin America's emerging market economies also are increasingly exposed to sudden reversals of capital inflows, which makes it almost impossible for fixed exchange rate systems to survive. Typical examples of such reversals are the direct effects that the late 1990s Asian and Russian crises had on some of Latin America's major economies, such as Brazil and Argentina.

An even stronger argument for the adoption of floating exchange rates is that most southern-cone Latin American countries are heavily dependent on natural resources and thus remain prone to large commodity price fluctuations. The use

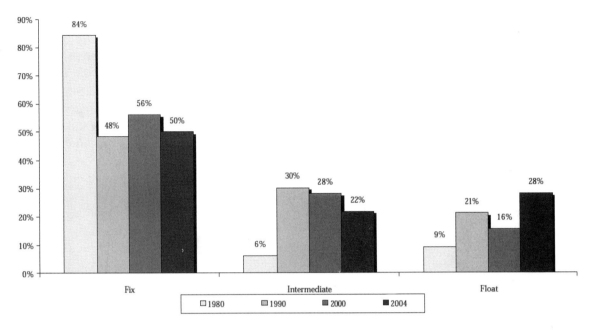

Figure 9.1
Distribution of de facto exchange rate regimes in Latin America, 1980–2004.
Source: Levy Yeyati 2006.

of monetary policy to mitigate shocks therefore is key. Surrendering monetary policy to the US Fed does not make sense.

The theoretical underpinning behind this argument dates back to Mundell 1961, which states that fixing the exchange rate to the US dollar is similar to a *currency union*. Mundell's main argument is that currency unions improve welfare when (1) factors of production—capital and labor—are mobile, (2) countries are subject to correlated shocks, and (3) the structure of the economies of the countries in question is very similar.[8]

In the case of Latin America, workers cannot move freely from one country to another as they do, for example, across the United States. Shocks are uncorrelated, and the structure of Latin American economies is extremely diverse and most definitely uncorrelated. World copper prices, for example, significantly affect Chile—the largest world producer and exporter of copper—and to a lesser extent Peru, but not Argentina, which heavily depends on world prices of soybeans. Colombia heavily depends on oil, coal, and coffee prices. Now, when one looks to Latin America as a whole, commodity price fluctuations severely affecting most southern-cone regions have little impact on the United States' economy, if at all.

Why then did Latin American countries adopt fixed or semifixed exchange rates in the first place? The answer is well-known: the vast majority of countries at the time needed to gain credibility. Specifically, Latin American governments used fixed or semifixed exchange rates as a precommitment device to avoid lax fiscal and monetary policies of the past. In so doing, however, the monetary authorities lost discretionary power to deal with external shocks in general and with capital inflows and outflows in particular. Most notably, with the advent of balance of payment deficits due to, for example, contagion, Latin American countries could not devalue their exchange rates without losing credibility, and this exacerbated the extent of the crises. Not surprisingly, most observers pointed out that all emerging market economies—and Latin American economies in particular, because of their high inflationary record—faced a trade-off between gaining flexibility to more easily accommodate external shocks under floating exchange rates on the one hand and gaining credibility via imposing monetary and fiscal discipline under fixed exchange rate regimes on the other. This trade-off still exists in many of the region's economies, in which de facto independent central banks and sound fiscal rules are missing.

From an empirical standpoint, there is a great deal of evidence to support the view that—except for extreme cases of high inflation and hyperinflation—floating exchange rates offer the opportunity to pull economies out of recession faster than fixed exchange rates, and that floating rates promote growth.[9]

Historical evidence under the fixed exchange rate regimes, on the other hand, is well-documented, most notably under the gold standard.[10] More recently, the debate has been revived with the advent of the eurozone crisis of 2009 and beyond.[11] Relative to the United Kingdom under floating exchange rates, the eurozone countries are worse off—particularly the southern countries, most notably Greece. This highlights an important economic problem with a single currency applying to several countries in a diverse region. In particular, Latin America's degree of economic and institutional integration is tiny in comparison with that of the eurozone countries. The emergence of a regional peso is unthinkable. Moreover, the sour experience of prolonged recessions in eurozone countries over the past decade has completely discouraged other regions, not just Latin America, from adopting a common currency.

Political economy considerations play an important role. It is undeniable that, at least in the case of Latin America, the previously mentioned trade-off between credibility in fiscal and monetary discipline under fixed exchange rates, and competitiveness and efficiency under floating rates exists. This trade-off applies forcefully to countries such as Venezuela and Argentina. Leading economies such as those of Chile, Colombia, Mexico, and Peru have demonstrated that it is possible to leave this trade-off behind so that competitiveness and efficiency can be prioritized.

Larraín and Velasco (2001 and 2002) have highlighted a number of arguments with regard to floating rate skeptics.[12] Their first focus is on wage indexation. Even if a currency depreciation is purely nominal, labor will request higher wages, which will trigger inflation. This will crucially depend on the specificities of the labor market and related political economy considerations. In an environment in which there is a large flow from formal to informal employment, wage differentials between these two labor markets might not be huge, in which case (and somewhat paradoxically) informality plays a mitigating role in lowering the risk of wage indexation. (We will return to labor markets in Latin America in chapter 11.)

Second, initial conditions might be such that the past record of inflation prevents countries from launching a one-off increase in money supply without triggering an unstoppable inflationary spiral. This is not the case for Chile, Colombia, and Mexico, where inflation has been kept under control for over two decades now, but it might be the case in a vast majority of Latin American countries.

Another way of looking at the skeptics' view on floating exchange rates is through the lens of the so-called pass-through—that is, the extent to which depreciation is reflected in price hikes. One might hope that the degree of pass-through is low (as suggested in chapter 8 on inflation). However, the empirical literature on the subject suggests that the degree of pass-through depends on a myriad of factors, such as market structure and the degree of openness. Most importantly, several studies have demonstrated that the degree of pass-through is high only in high-inflation environments.[13] This no longer seems to be the case for the vast majority of Latin American economies in the twenty-first century. In fact, Ghosh (2013) showed a declining pass-through for the region after the turn of the millennium. Whether this will hold true in the new environment with depressed commodity prices remains an open question.

Table 9.2 shows the entire picture for the case of Latin America more clearly, fears of floating aside. Indeed, relative to the 1980s, a large number of Latin American countries have transited from rigid (fixed or semifixed) to floating exchange rate regimes.

Ultimately, the extent to which floating exchange rate regimes trigger a virtuous cycle as theory predicts and empirical evidence seems to support, however, depends on institutions, both fiscal and monetary.[14] As Larraín and Velasco (2001) argue, floating rates by themselves will not suffice. The optimal monetary/exchange rate policy combination includes central bank independence and inflation targeting, along with flexible exchange rates. Indeed, most important economies in the region have been moving in this direction, as table 9.3 further illustrates.

Table 9.2
Exchange rate regimes in Latin America, 1985–2014

	1985	2000	2014
Countries currently using inflation targeting			
Brazil	Intermediate	Floating	Floating
Chile	Intermediate	Floating	Floating
Colombia	Intermediate	Floating	Floating
Guatemala	Pegged	Floating	Intermediate
Mexico	Floating	Floating	Floating
Paraguay	Pegged	Floating	Floating
Peru	Intermediate	Floating	Floating
Countries currently without inflation targeting			
Argentina	Floating	Pegged	Intermediate
Bolivia	Pegged	Intermediate	Intermediate
Costa Rica	Floating	Intermediate	Intermediate
Ecuador	Floating	Pegged	Pegged
El Salvador	Floating	Pegged	Pegged
Honduras	Pegged	Intermediate	Intermediate
Nicaragua	Pegged	Intermediate	Intermediate
Panama	Pegged	Pegged	Pegged
Uruguay	Floating	Intermediate	Floating
Venezuela	Pegged	Intermediate	Pegged

Source: IMF 2008.

Based on data from IMF 2014a, table 9.3 includes seven (not five) Latin American countries under de facto floating exchange rate regimes. These are the five countries mentioned earlier (Brazil, Chile, Colombia, Mexico, and Peru), plus Guatemala and Uruguay. Whether these countries can weather recent events with regard to the Chinese slowdown remains to be seen. Several economies in the region that are under floating rates have already suffered from significant currency appreciation pressures from 2011 to 2012. These pressures were the result of a combination of high commodity prices and quantitative easing in the United States.[15] Economies affected included those of Chile, Colombia, Mexico, and Peru. These pressures have been reversed since; commodity prices have declined, and quantitative easing in the United States officially came to an end in October 2014.

Table 9.3
De facto exchange rate regimes and monetary arrangements in contemporary Latin America

Monetary policy framework	Monetary policy framework	Exchange rate arrangement		
		Floating	No separate legal tender, currency board, or conventional peg	Intermediate regimes/other exchange rate arrangements
	Inflation-targeting	Brazil Chile Colombia Mexico Paraguay Peru		Guatemala
	Monetary aggregate target	Uruguay		
	Exchange rate anchor (US dollar)		Ecuador El Salvador Panama Venezuela	Honduras Nicaragua
	Other			Argentina Bolivia Costa Rica

Source: Authors' own construction, based on IMF 2014a.

9.4 Avoiding Twenty-First-Century Currency Crises

Latin American countries are often singled out as currency crisis countries—and twentieth-century historical evidence shows that this is largely true. In the 1930s, the 1980s, and 1990s—as discussed in chapter 4—most Latin American countries suffered first from sovereign debt crises in the 1930s, in the 1980s, and in the 1990s. What do these three debt crisis episodes have in common?

Large capital inflows is certainly a key element. In the 1930s, Latin American countries defaulted on sovereign debt contracted during the belle époque globalization period and in the 1920s (see chapters 2 and 4). Then, the 1980s were preceded by unprecedented capital inflows during the 1970s petrodollar boom (see chapter 4). Finally, in the 1990s, economic reforms started bearing fruit, triggering private investors' appetite in Latin American markets (see table 9.4).

Table 9.4
Capital inflows in selected Latin American countries

Country	Inflow episode	Cumulative inflows/ GDP at end of episode	Maximum annual inflow
Argentina	1991–1994	9.7	3.8
Brazil	1992–1995	9.4	4.8
Chile	1989–1995	25.8	8.6
Colombia	1992–1995	16.2	6.2
Mexico	1989–1994	27.1	8.5
Peru	1990–1995	30.4	10.8
Venezuela	1992–1993	5.4	3.3

Source: World Bank 1997.

Out of the seven countries shown in table 9.3, four experienced a currency crisis: Mexico, Brazil, Argentina, and Venezuela. Although contagion effects cannot be ruled out, exchange rate policies played an important role. The four countries in question had fixed or semifixed exchange rates.

As in 1982, Mexico was once more the country in which the first signs of crisis appeared. In hindsight, Mexico's 1994 tequila crisis was rooted in the semifixed exchange rate mechanism. Thanks to economic policies applied and a rescue package from international financial institutions and from the US government, Mexico's 1994 crisis was short-lived, and the region benefited from more capital inflows up until the 1997 and 1998 Asian and Russian crises. Investors' fears in emerging markets in general were harshly felt in the entire region. As capital inflows dried up once again, Brazil and then Argentina experienced major currency crises. Chile suffered a recession but did not experience a major crisis. To most observers, that seemed due to Chile's strong fiscal and monetary institutions, and to its adoption of a floating exchange rate system.[16]

Which factors underlie currency crises? Esquivel and Larraín (2000) have empirically analyzed a large group of countries over the period from 1975 to 1996 and have concluded that large current account deficits, significant use of seigniorage, and sharp currency appreciations are at the root of the problem. They also report an important contagion effect; that is, a country's probability of having a currency crisis increases when a regional partner has a crisis.

Other authors have analyzed the role of capital inflows in triggering currency crises. A study at the turn of the millennium analyzed this question empirically for the case of Latin America over a forty-year period.[17] The authors argue that lending booms may be just a natural consequence of economic development and financial deepening but have proven to be dangerous in the long run because of sudden and unexpected reversals. One main finding is that relative to the rest of the world, lending booms in Latin America leave countries considerably more volatile and vulnerable to balance of payment crises. A positive and significant association between lending booms and currency appreciations was also found.

More recently, Furceri, Guichard, and Rusticelli (2012) worked with panel data on developed and emerging economies from 1970 to 2007. The authors show that a large capital inflow episode substantially increases the probability of having a banking or currency crisis in the two following years.

Over the last decade, however, the region has become less vulnerable. As shown in figure 9.2 both public debt and external debt fell significantly since 2003. Ortíz (2014), in particular, argues that Latin America has witnessed a sharp reduction in debt vulnerability as proxied by the average spread of the Emerging Markets Bond Index Plus (EMBI+). Specifically, as figure 9.3 shows, the average spread of the EMBI+ was more than 800 basis points from 1998 to 2003. In contrast, the average spread of the EMBI+ from 2003 to 2011 was around 380 basis points—that is, less than half. He notes that in the current situation, in which growth in

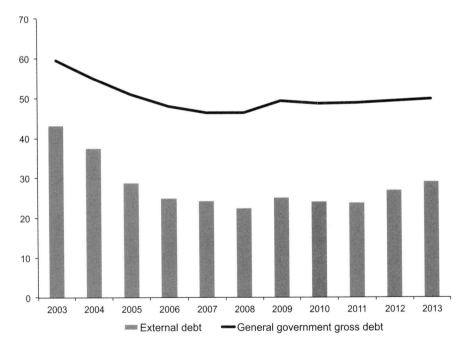

Figure 9.2
Public debt and external debt in Latin America (% of GDP).
Source: IMF 2014b.

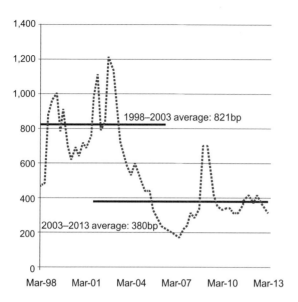

Figure 9.3
Latin American EMBI+ (basis points).
Source: Ortíz 2014.

China has decreased and commodity prices have fallen, Latin America can prevent a crisis if it follows countercyclical fiscal policies and keeps flexible exchange rates with well-anchored inflation expectations—which can potentially be attained via inflation-targeting central banks.

In its most recent World Economic Outlook, the IMF (2015) forecast a slowdown in Latin America's growth rate from 1.3 in 2014 to 0.5 in 2015, mostly because of the Chinese slowdown. It is argued that Latin America can dampen the adverse effect of the slowdown in China and the sharp fall in commodity prices via exchange rate devaluations. Whether such devaluations can take place without triggering inflation remains an open question. We believe it is possible in those countries which have already enacted strong fiscal an monetary institutions.

9.5 Concluding Remarks

This chapter has underscored the paramount importance of exchange rates in support of stabilization efforts during the 1980s and 1990s. In countries in which inflation was exceedingly high, fixed exchange rates—in different forms and shapes—helped some of Latin America's major economies gain credibility and lower inflation rates to single-digit levels quite quickly.

Mexico, Brazil, and Argentina experienced major currency crises. These crises taught the region's leading economies that in an increasingly globalized world, contagion and capital flow volatility requires exchange rate flexibility.

Moreover, with the exception of Mexico, most countries' main exports are primary commodities; for example, commodities account for as much as 76 percent of Argentina's exports, with a substantial concentration in agricultural products. Metal and agricultural products account for nearly 50 percent of Brazil's export products. Approximately 60 percent of Chile's exports are metals, and slightly more than that for Peru. Colombia mainly exports oil and coal. Almost 100 percent of Venezuela's exports are also oil.

Because world prices of primary commodities experience drastic changes, a floating exchange rate regime is appropriate. However, and contrary to theoretical predictions, skeptics view floating rates as dangerous, particularly in countries that are still gaining credibility and in some others that have lost credibility.

The trade-off thus appears to be between credibility under fixed exchange rates, and competitiveness and the ability to adjust to shocks under floating exchange rates. We have argued that this trade-off is not present in some economies in which fiscal and monetary institutions are strong; unfortunately, this is not the case for the entire region.

Although the 2003–2011 period has demonstrated that most of the region's major economies have managed to make important progress, the future is uncertain, especially with the growth slowdown in China, the vertiginous fall in commodity prices. Nonetheless, Latin America has learned from previous crises and thus managed to weather the Great Recession of 2008 to 2009 and its aftermath in much better way than it has in past crisis episodes generated in industrialized nations. Many countries have moved to floating rates, independent central banks, inflation targeting, and better fiscal institutions. This gives hopes that the region can fare better after the onset of the end of the commodity boom in 2014.

Summary
- Since the 1945 Bretton Woods agreement, most Latin-American countries have oscillated between two extreme exchange rate regimes: hard peg and floating regimes.
- The IMF classifies exchange rates regimes according to degree of flexibility. This classification includes fully fixed exchange rate regimes, currency board agreements, pegged exchange rates, crawling pegs, managed floating exchange rates, and independent floating exchange rates.
- Unprecedented capital inflows to Latin America during the oil shocks in the 1970s set the stage for high inflation rate scenarios throughout the region, especially in Argentina, Chile, and Uruguay.

- Fixed exchange rates helped some of Latin America's major economies to gain credibility and to lower high inflation rates from triple to single digits rather quickly in the 1990s.
- Experiences such as the tequila crisis in Mexico, its contagion effect in other Latin American countries, the failure of the currency board in Argentina, and capital inflow volatility in a globalized world have led to a consensus in favor of flexibility in exchange rates in emerging market economies.
- Evidence of the need for a floating exchange rate mechanism is Latin American dependence on primary commodity exports, their consequential high inflows and outflows of capital, and the region's overall exposure to commodity price volatility.
- There is a trade-off between gaining credibility via fixed exchange rate regimes and becoming more competitive and efficient under floating exchange rate systems. However, this trade-off no longer seems to hold true in the case of Brazil, Chile, Colombia, Mexico, and Peru, Latin America's leading economies.
- Skeptics nonetheless view floating rates as dangerous. Wage indexation, high risk of inflationary spiral due to increased money supply, and a high pass-through are some of the reasons supporting such views.
- Latin America has suffered from several currency crises, explained mainly by large capital inflows. However, after the 2003–2011 period, the region has shown to be less vulnerable and has made important institutional progress from the turn of the millennium until 2016.
- More challenges lie ahead. A potential crisis due to the Chinese slowdown in growth is proving to be harmful for Latin America; the entire region must take advantage of its rich experience with exchange rates and engage itself in cautious depreciations in order to dampen the effects of the current slowdown.

Review Questions
1. According to the IMF, what are the different exchange rate regimes?
2. What was the role of exchange rates in stabilizing inflation and boosting economic growth during the 1980s and 1990s?
3. What was the system of *tablitas*? Why was it adopted and later abandoned?
4. What was the main objective of the currency board in Argentina during the 1990s, and why did the currency board collapse?
5. Why are most Latin American economies moving toward a floating exchange rate regime?
6. What are the arguments from skeptics about the dangers of adopting managed floating exchange rates?
7. Explain why volatile capital inflows are at the root of major debt crises in Latin American countries.

8. Why might the trade-off between credibility and competitiveness not apply to the entire Latin American region?

Further Reading

For an excellent historical account of exchange rate regimes in Latin America since the 1960s, see Frenkel and Rapetti 2010. For a comprehensive account of the trend toward floating exchange rate regimes in emerging market economies in general, and in Latin America in particular, see Levy Yeyati 2006. Latin America's vulnerabilities, particularly with regard to growth and development trends in Asia, are discussed in Lederman, Olarreaga, and Perry 2009.

IV The Underpinnings of Growth and Development in Twenty-First-Century Latin America

10   Trade and Financial Liberalization

Dismantling the system of tariff and nontariff barriers that had been erected in the twentieth century to protect domestic industry and to encourage manufacturing and industrial development was a key component of the reforms that most Latin American countries sought to implement after the debt crisis. By reducing the wedges between market and shadow prices, it was hoped that trade liberalization would encourage a more efficient allocation of resources and hence support higher incomes and faster growth.[1] As resources shifted to sectors in which countries had or could rapidly develop a competitive advantage, exports would also grow, relaxing balance of payments constraints and permitting access to imports with higher levels of embodied technology. In addition to opening international trade, the market-oriented reforms that started in the mid-1980s also called for liberalizing financial markets. More than in the case of trade, *financial liberalization* meant different things in different contexts—and sometimes even for different people in the same context. In some cases, like Mexico's, it meant the privatization of the banking sector. In others, it meant the relaxation of exchange rate controls for financial transactions and/or the lifting of barriers to FDI. One general expectation was that reforms should lead to a deeper financial system, with higher credit to GDP ratios. By allowing broader access to capital, it was hoped that this reform too would contribute to faster growth.

This chapter examines the rationale for each of these policy interventions, analyzes how implementation might or might have not upheld the theory behind it, and assesses the consequences for guiding trade and financial liberalization policies.

Section 10.1 of this chapter describes the distinguishing features of Latin America's trade liberalization wave. Section 10.2 assesses the potential positive and negative effects of bilateral trade negotiations and regional trade integration. Section 10.3 highlights the prominence of Asian trade partners, particularly China, and also discusses the extent to which the Pacific Alliance of Latin American countries can serve as a platform for a more ambitious trans-Atlantic alliance. Section 10.4 discusses financial liberalization in the 1990s and the difficulties encountered when trying to balance export-oriented growth with price stabilization, as well as financial flows over the last decade and their origins and trends. Finally, section 10.5 provides a summary and concluding remarks.

10.1 The Unilateral Trade Liberalization Wave

Underscoring the virtuosity of free international trade is not new. Ever since Adam Smith's eighteenth-century writings, economists have entertained the idea that free trade can lead to welfare-improving resource allocation in all countries.

The Ricardian model of trade and the follow-up Hecksher-Ohlin theorem predict trade patterns under laissez-faire. According to the theory, countries will gain from trade by specializing and exporting goods that use their relatively abundant factors of production. Conversely, countries will gain by importing goods that use their relatively scarce factors of production.[2]

Against this background, the Prebisch-Singer hypothesis in the late 1940s proclaimed that North-South trade would lead to unequal trade; developed countries would have a tendency to specialize in the production and export of manufactures, whereas developing countries would remain stuck in the production of low-productivity primary commodities. As we discussed in chapter 3, the Prebisch-Singer hypothesis (closely associated with ECLAC) became the most influential and powerful protectionist ideology behind ISI policies, which were dismantled the 1980s and 1990s. Although developing nascent industry was still recognized as important for economic development, industry was no longer a priority. Reigniting growth was, and countries could no longer afford to subsidize inefficient manufactures and industry in the hope that these sectors might one day become competitive in world markets.

The most important reason at the time for policy makers to seriously question protectionist policies was comparative performance. East Asian export-oriented economies had grown at an average rate of 7.2 percent per annum from 1965 to 1980. During this same period, Latin America grew at an average rate of 6 percent per annum. However, growth rates of around 7 percent were sustained in Asia from 1980 to 1990. In sharp contrast, growth rates fell drastically to a yearly average of 1.6 percent in Latin America in the same decade.[3]

The contrasting performance between the two regions during Latin America's lost decade from 1980 to 1990 was attributed to the outward-oriented strategies in East Asia. Specifically, prior to the lost decade, East Asia's exports had grown at an annual average rate of 10 percent from 1965 to 1980. During this same period, Latin America's average export growth had been around negative 1 percent per year.

In light of the superior performance of East Asia, most Latin American countries no longer debated whether protectionism was better or worse than outward orientation, but rather how to liberalize trade so as to improve market access and boost exports. Indeed, even ECLAC—the very institution in which the Prebisch-Singer protectionist ideology was born—ended up recognizing that the appropriate development course was to follow an open-trade strategy. While this was true for many poor countries and emerging market economies in the 1990s, Latin America's trade liberalization wave had its own specificities to consider.

One option for Latin America was to join (and work through) the multilateral free trade institution known as the World Trade Organization (WTO)—the successor of the General Agreement on Trade and Tariffs (GATT), which had existed since 1948. Indeed, countries such as Brazil, Mexico, Chile, Colombia, Cuba, Peru, and Uruguay had already become members. Some, like Brazil and Cuba, had been founding members since 1948. However, the overall perception in the mid to late 1980s—when Latin American countries were experiencing the urgent need to generate foreign exchange via export promotion—was that negotiations under the umbrella of the WTO were cumbersome, long-lasting, and likely to produce minimal or no results.

The Uruguay Round multilateral negotiations under the WTO spanned from 1986 to 1994, reaching modest achievements in terms of enhanced access to Latin American export products such as textiles, clothing, and agricultural produce. In the vast majority of cases, the agreements reached were nonbinding. Follow-up multilateral negotiations under the umbrella of the WTO delivered equally modest results. The Doha Round (started in 2001 and still not concluded) also proved to be an inadequate trade venue for negotiations with a multiplicity of heterogeneous and geographically distant neighbors. Nonetheless, the Doha negotiations provided a useful platform for trade dispute resolutions internationally, which was particularly useful for countries that had already lifted trade barriers via bilateral agreements, including some in Latin America.

By the mid-1980s, however, and in the midst of a major financial crisis, it seemed easier for Latin American countries to unilaterally lower trade and nontrade restrictions in order to eliminate the antiexport bias imposed by ISI policies, particularly with regard to imports of intermediate inputs of production.[4]

Political economy considerations played a role in trade liberalization, however. Policymakers that advocated unilateral free trade found it politically difficult to embrace it without some reciprocity. Nonetheless, despite fierce opposition from interest groups and parts of public opinion, most Latin American countries significantly lowered their tariff rates unilaterally.

As figure 10.1 shows, tariff reductions in virtually all Latin American countries were quite substantial. During a first trade liberalization wave alone (1985–1992), tariffs were reduced by an average of approximately 35 percentage points. Further reductions of around 3 percentage points on average were observed during a second wave (1992–2003).[5]

Although the effects of tariff reductions on economic growth are empirically difficult to disentangle from other reforms that took place simultaneously, most observers point out that Chile—an early trade liberalizer—achieved substantially higher than average growth rates in the 1990s because of market-oriented policies

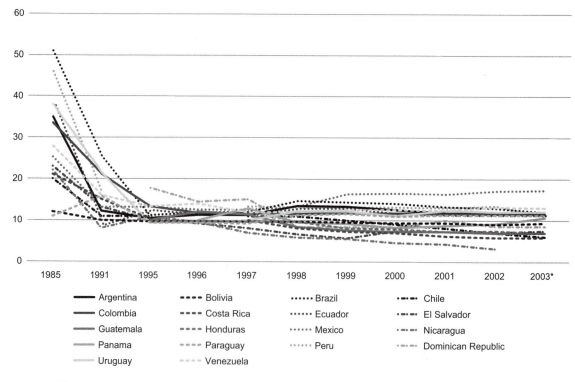

Figure 10.1
Average tariff rates in Latin America, 1985–2003.
Source: Ventura-Dias 2010.

in general and trade liberalization in particular. Indeed, Chile was an early starter. Trade liberalization began during the country´s military dictatorship in 1976. With the advent of the debt crisis in the early 1980s, free trade reforms were temporarily reversed. However, tariffs were later reduced by 22 percentage points from 1985 to 1992 and then by a further 5 percentage points at the turn of the millennium.

Trade liberalization relates not exclusively to the dismantling of tariffs but also, and perhaps more importantly, to nontariff barriers (e.g., import licenses, quotas, administrative and autocratic delays, and more). According to UNCTAD (1994) estimates, by the mid-1980s Chile's nontariff barriers were already the lowest in the region. When compared to neighboring Argentina, for example, nontariff protection as a percentage of all tariff protection estimates in Chile was approximately 16 percent on average, whereas nontariff protection estimates were around 44 percent in Argentina. By 1993, average nontariff protective measures were reduced to 0.4 percent in Chile and to 14.3 percent in Argentina.

Broader estimates of the depth of the trade liberalization reform, considering both tariff and nontariff dismantling, are shown in figure 10.2, where light circles are used for 1986, dark circles for 1999, and black bars for 2009. Within a 0 to 1 scale, with 0 indicating very high trade barriers and 1 indicating complete liberalization, the figure shows that although all countries in the sample reduced tariff and nontariff barriers (in the majority of the countries, the index was higher in 2009 than in 1999 and 1986), the extent and scope of trade reform varies widely. Note that most of the liberalization took place between 1986 and 1999, with little after that. In the cases of Bolivia and Ecuador, there is some reversal in the decade after 1999.

The figure also shows that despite being an early starter, Chile was not alone during the 1985–1999 trade liberalization period. Peru, Guatemala, and Honduras also feature as trade-liberalizing countries. At the other end of the spectrum, we find Brazil and Mexico—Latin America's largest economies—classified as the "worst" performers. This is not surprising. On the one hand, the pace of the reform differed across regions for myriad reasons. On the other, Brazil and Mexico have larger domestic markets and well-known protectionist lobbies with a great deal of political clout. However, the graph hides the key role played by Brazil in trade integration with neighboring countries via MERCOSUR and the importance of Mexico's trade partnership with the United States and Canada via NAFTA. We deliver an in-depth explanation of these trade blocs in section 10.2.

The causal effects of unilateral trade liberalization on economic performance are hard to disentangle, because trade liberalization was part of a wider set of reforms that were adopted differently—both in shape and sequence—across the highly heterogeneous Latin American regions. Nonetheless, World Bank estimates show that exports did grow, possibly as a result of trade liberalization. As

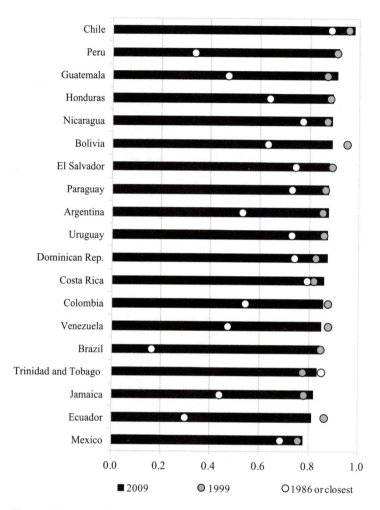

Figure 10.2
Trade reform index for Latin American countries, 1986, 1999, and 2009.
Source: Lora 2012.

mentioned earlier, the annual growth rate of exports in Latin America during the 1965–1980 period was negative. In contrast, exports grew at an average annual rate of 3.6 percent from 1981 to 1989.

Stylized facts, in turn, particularly with regard to the Chilean case, show that trade liberalization can potentially become the main engine of growth. In particular, the unilateral opening of Chile's external sector since 1976 has been praised in numerous studies.[6]

While the rest of Latin America stagnated between 1986 and 1997, Chile—the earlier twentieth-century trade-liberalizing country par excellence—achieved an annual per capita growth rate of approximately 5.7 percent.[7] The extraordinary performance of Chile during the 1986–1997 period is shown in figure 10.3. Relative to Latin America and the world, Chile's average growth rate between 1961 and 1985 was below average. In contrast, during the 1986–1997 period, Chile reached average growth rates that were considerably higher relative to those in Latin

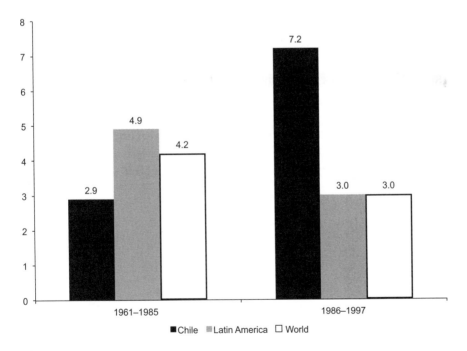

Figure 10.3
Average annual growth rates in Chile relative to other Latin American countries and the world, 1961–1985 and 1986–1997.
Source: Authors' own construction from World Bank (www.worldbank.org) and Central Bank of Chile (www.bcentral.cl) databases.

America and the world. This extraordinary reversal—often referred to as the Chilean miracle, extending throughout the entire 1986–1997 period—is, to an important extent, attributed to trade liberalization.

Moreover, according to Pritchett's (1996) classification of "standards of trade openness," Chile was the only Latin American country to meet all standards. Relative to other countries in the region, Chile stands out as an example of systematically maintaining free trade at the core of all other reforms, including privatization, deregulation, and stabilization. With regard to the latter, and unlike other exchange rate policies in neighboring countries reviewed in chapters 8 and 9, Chile avoided overvalued exchange rates for the sake of export promotion at the expense of rapid price stabilization.[8]

10.2 Bilateral Trade Agreements and Trade Blocs

Somewhat frustrated by their inability to gain wider access to developed countries' markets via multilateral trade agreements under the WTO, unilateral trade liberalization in several Latin American countries rapidly developed alongside bilateral and regional trade-integration blocs.

Theoretical work exists on the potential benefits of negotiating trade agreements bilaterally as opposed to multilaterally.[9] In a nutshell, retaliatory measures for noncompliance under multilateral trade agreements, if any, are more diffused and lengthily to implement. Indeed, this turns out to be true in practice. Multilateral negotiations from a Latin American perspective were perceived as lengthy, and the outcomes of, for example, the Uruguay and Doha negotiation rounds were perceived as difficult to enforce. In a multicountry setting, it is difficult to detect and punish in international courts a country that engages in non-trade-barrier reduction with another country on a bilateral basis, thereby discriminating against others. Reducing such preferential trading—also known as the *most favored nation* principle—is one of the main principles of the WTO. The only exception to this principle, acknowledged by the WTO, is made for a comprehensive free trade agreement between two or more countries.

Negotiating access to markets in other countries bilaterally appeared to be easier and, with the benefit of hindsight, more effective than doing so multilaterally. However, the potential efficiency gains (and losses) from bilateral negotiations are well-known in the international trade literature.[10] In particular, bilateral trade agreements can create and/or divert trade: Trade is *created* when a bilateral agreement allows for more efficient industries to replace existing ones, thereby allowing for member countries to export and import more from other countries, because they are better prepared to face competition internationally. Trade is *diverted* when the resulting lower tariffs agreed upon by member countries discourage imports from more efficient nonmembers, thereby allowing consumers in member countries to face higher prices when compared to a situation in which more efficient producers/exporters are involved. From the standpoint of a single country, trade is potentially beneficial if trade creation outweighs trade diversion.

Such considerations were rarely discussed at the time of preferential trade negotiations. Latin American governments urgently needed to gain access to foreign markets, if only because of political economy considerations. In particular, gaining access to foreign markets was perceived as a mitigating reward from a wide range of painful economic reforms, including adjustments to trade liberalization reforms. Put simply, policymakers thought that bilateral trade agreements in Latin America made sense, because some reciprocity from unilateral tariff and nontariff dismantling reduced the political costs associated with trade globalization.[11]

10.2.1 MERCOSUR

As early as 1985, Brazil and Argentina signed a bilateral trade agreement, which in 1991 became a trade block known as the *Mercado Común del Sur* or MERCOSUR via the 1991 Treaty of Asunción, which involved neighboring Paraguay and Uruguay. More recently, Venezuela joined as a full member of the block in 2012, and Bolivia in 2015. In fact, the treaty has the features of a custom union in that member countries established a common trade policy and tariffs with regard to nonmembers. A small group of permanent MERCOSUR staff professionals is headquartered in Montevideo, Uruguay's capital. MERCOSUR comprises approximately 260 million people, which makes it the fourth most important trading block after the EU, NAFTA, and the Association of South East Asian Nations (ASEAN).

Five salient features of MERCOSUR are worth highlighting here. First, as figure 10.4 shows, when comparing tariff rates before MERCOSUR (prereform) to those in 1995, four years after the 1991 Treaty of Asuncion, tariff reductions were enormous, particularly in the case of Brazil—the largest trading partner within the block. In 1995, tariff rates for MERCOSUR trade partners fell by nearly 46 percentage points. However, it has often been argued that such tariff reductions (in all MERCOSUR countries) were relatively modest when compared to unilateral tariff reductions.[12]

Second, as figure 10.5 shows, there has been a sharp expansion of trade among MERCOSUR members. However, within-export expansion seems to have surpassed within-import expansion, which might be due to Argentina's and Brazil's overvalued exchange rates, because these two countries prioritized price stabilization over trade openness during the 1990s (see chapter 9). Specifically, overvalued

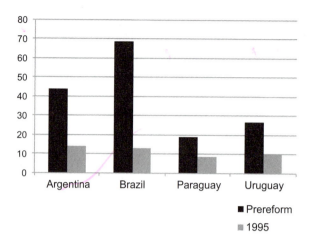

Figure 10.4
Comparative average tariff rates in MERCOSUR countries, 1990 (prereform) and 1995.
Source: IDB 1996.

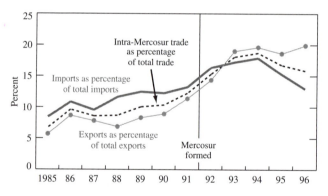

Figure 10.5
Intraregional trade trends among MERCOSUR members, 1985–1996.
Source: Federal Reserve Bank of New York 1999.

exchange rates might have led MERCOSUR members to import more cheaply from nonmember countries.

Third, intraregional exports grew fast between the two main founding members, Brazil and Argentina. Not only because preferential agreements between these two countries began six years prior to the emergence of MERCOSUR's expanded trading block, but also because Brazil and Argentina are considerably larger than other members. Brazil exports mostly petrochemicals, electrical items, and cars. Argentina exports mostly agricultural and natural resource products (soybean-related products, corn, and wheat). Over one-third of Argentina's exports are directed to Brazil, which is now Argentina's second-largest trading partner, after the EU.[13]

Fourth, under MERCOSUR, FDI into the automobile industry has sprung up. Initial concerns by Argentina about Brazil attracting most foreign auto firm investments because of Brazil's lower labor costs were quickly dispelled via a compensated trade clause that prevents Brazil from dominating the automobile market completely. Foreign automobile firms nonetheless took advantage of the two countries' comparative advantage and now gain economies of scale by concentrating production of luxury automobiles in Argentina and standard ones in Brazil.[14]

Fifth, with regard to primary commodities, most notably in agriculture, where MERCOSUR members enjoy comparative advantage, by and large extraregional trade is much more important than intraregional trade, as figure 10.6 shows. This has in turn led MERCOSUR member countries to engage in trade negotiations with the EU and China. One main obstacle in negotiations with the EU has been agriculture—the sector that has been traditionally protected by EU member states. With regard to China, MERCOSUR members are seemingly afraid of destroying

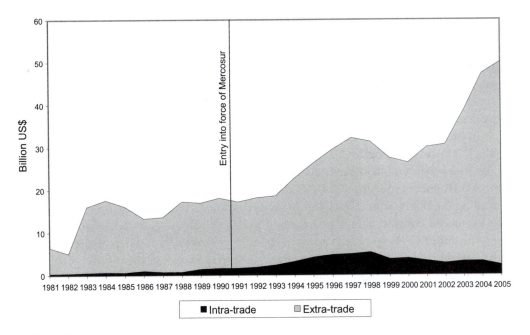

Figure 10.6
Intra- and extraregional MERCOSUR agricultural trade, 1981–2005.
Source: WITS 2015.

nascent industry. Ongoing disputes have not prevented bilateral trade agreements. Most importantly, MERCOSUR does not seem to have prevented member countries from taking advantage of the commodity boom driven by China's increased demand for primary commodities over the past decades.

With regard to trade diversion and trade creation, Yeats (1998) offers a comprehensive study. His empirical investigation includes thirty products that have been traded most actively among MERCOSUR members. He finds a great deal of trade diversion; in particular, MERCOSUR member countries seem to be trading commodities at a higher price than the prevailing one in international markets, particularly in machinery and transport equipment sectors. Because the industries in which trade diversion seems to be occurring are mostly technology driven, including vehicle assembly production, concerns are growing with regard to the potential negative impact of trade diversion on productivity and growth.

10.2.2 The Community of Andean Nations

Despite the fact that efforts toward trade and political integration among Andean Nations dates back to 1969—one of the eldest in the Americas—these efforts were timid until 1992, when the Andean Pact trade block inclusive of Bolivia, Colombia, Ecuador, and Venezuela was created. In comparison with MERCOSUR, the Community of Andean Nations (CAN) is more ambitious in that, at least on paper, member countries adhered to the concept of supranationality, which implies that member countries' joint agreements supersede national legal systems if and when a conflict among them emerges. The institutional structure of CAN is somewhat similar to that of the EU in that it has a de jure presidential council and a court of justice.

In the twenty-first century, CAN is generally viewed as a highly unstable trade block. However, as figure 10.7 shows, studies conducted in the early 2000s suggested a considerable expansion of trade among the four nations.

A distinguishing feature of CAN is the overwhelming importance of two major trading members—namely, Colombia and Venezuela. In particular, Venezuela has experienced considerable economic and political instability, and its trade agreements under CAN were tainted by political tensions within and with Colombia. Unilateral trade reforms have therefore superseded CAN agreements. Nonetheless, earlier studies suggest that CAN played an important role in export expansion, scale economies, and intraindustry trade among partner nations until 1998, when growth slowed down considerably—partly as a result of contagion from financial crises in Russia and Brazil and partly because of Hugo Chávez's coup d'état, which marked the beginning of a populist regime known as the Bolivarian Revolution (see chapter 6).[15]

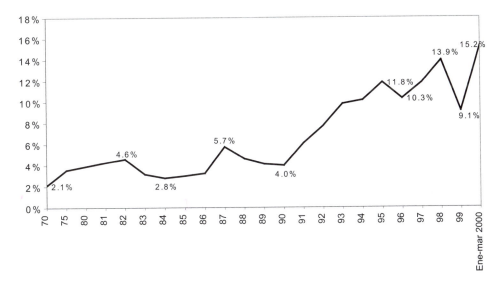

Figure 10.7
Andean community: Intraregional exports as a share of total exports, 1970–2000.
Source: Echavarría and Gamboa 2000.

Colombia—along with other Andean countries outside CAN, such as Peru—has signed free trade agreements with the United States. Both countries have lifted tariffs and nontariff barriers on agricultural imports from the United States within the context of the Andean Preference Act, which was designed to encourage alternatives to coca trade. This has in turn fueled further tensions between Colombia and Venezuela due to ongoing strained relations between Venezuela—under the leadership of Nicolás Maduro, Chavez's successor—and the United States.

Against this backdrop, trade-integration efforts between CAN and MERCOSUR have been pursued since the 2004 Cuzco declaration geared toward a South American Community of Nations. It is fair to say that such efforts have been unsuccessful. Most observers believe that Brazil is pursuing South-South integration to strengthen its bargaining power in multilateral trade negotiations. Venezuela withdrew from CAN in 2006 and has proposed instead a trade union of Bolivarian nations, not allied with the United States.

10.2.3 NAFTA and CAFTA

The well-fought and highly publicized North American Free Trade Agreement was signed in 1994 among three member states: Mexico, the United States, and Canada. However, NAFTA was different from southern cone trade block predecessors in that it promised more interindustry trade. As the Ricardian model of trade predicts, Mexico is relatively labor abundant when compared to Canada and the United States, and thus the least one could expect from NAFTA was high growth rates propelled by labor-intensive manufactures—better known as *maquiladoras*. Indeed, Mexico's labor-intensive *maquila* assembly plants seemed to have had an enormous impact on the number of *maquila*-related plants and employment, particularly in cities located on the border between Mexico and the United States.[16] Arguably, the post-NAFTA *maquila* assembly boom has been a contributing factor of Mexico's export diversification. Exports from the energy sector have decreased, whereas exports of cars and audio and other communication equipment, for example, have increased significantly.

Mexico is now the only Latin American country that has managed to significantly diversify its exports away from commodities. As shown in figure 10.8, the share of manufactures in Mexico's global exports has grown considerably. The trend had been increasing since the early 1980s, but most observers noted an accelerated pace after NAFTA—that is, during the second half of the 1990s. In particular, exports of manufactures grew by approximately 37 percent of total exports from 1980 to 1993. In comparison, the post-NAFTA manufacture exports (1994–2000) share reached 80 percent of Mexican exports.

Moreover, as table 10.1 suggests, Mexico's trade sector—both for imports and exports—is now one of the most diversified when compared to other emerging market economies in Latin America. This in turn has placed Mexico with a con-

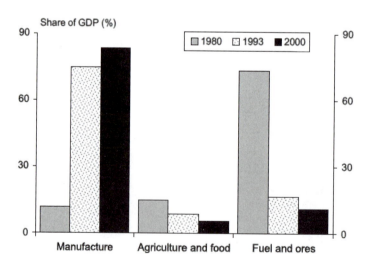

Figure 10.8
Mexico's post-NAFTA export diversification as percentage of exports.
Source: IMF 2004.

Table 10.1
Mexico's export diversification compared to other emerging markets, 1990–2000; share of exports as a percentage of total exports

	Argentina	Brazil	Chile	Indonesia	Korea	Malaysia	Mexico	Peru	Philippines	Thailand	Turkey	Uruguay
Exports												
Manufacturing												
1980–1993	25.9	47.5	9.8	23.0	91.9	39.8	37.1	15.9	33.4	46.5	57.1	37.1
1994–2000	32.9	54.8	15.8	50.4	91.9	77.2	81.2	18.3	75.7	73.2	76.1	39.1
Agriculture and food												
1980–1993	67.0	36.9	32.5	17.1	5.5	34.1	11.9	25.3	29.3	47.9	35.5	62.0
1994–2000	52.3	32.9	36.5	16.1	3.3	13.1	7.2	34.1	9.8	22.5	19.4	59.4
Fuel and ores												
1980–1993	7.1	14.5	56.8	59.8	2.5	25.8	50.9	58.8	11.6	4.4	7.3	0.5
1994–2000	14.2	10.9	45.8	29.2	4.7	8.8	11.5	17.6	4.1	2.6	3.8	1.5
Imports												
Manufacturing												
1980–1993	78.0	47.4	69.9	71.8	57.6	75.4	74.9	68.2	49.3	65.8	57.3	62.9
1994–2000	88.0	73.7	76.9	66.5	63.7	84.8	84.9	72.1	78.4	77.7	72.1	74.9
Agriculture and food												
1980–1993	8.6	11.6	11.4	11.8	15.4	11.5	16.7	23.2	11.7	9.6	8.7	11.8
1994–2000	6.6	11.2	8.6	17.4	9.7	6.7	7.6	16.4	9.7	8.0	9.4	13.7
Fuel and ores												
1980–1993	13.3	40.9	16.8	16.0	26.7	12.6	6.5	7.2	23.0	20.8	33.8	25.3
1994–2000	5.1	15.0	13.5	15.9	26.2	6.5	4.7	11.4	11.7	12.7	16.4	11.7

Source: IMF 2004.

siderable advantage compared to its southern cone neighbors in recent years when world commodity prices have collapsed.

A World Bank study (Lederman, Maloney, and Servén 2003) assessing some other impacts from NAFTA on the Mexican economy concluded that NAFTA helped Mexico get closer to the levels of development in the United States and Canada. The study suggests that NAFTA helped Mexican manufactures to adapt US technological innovations more quickly, which in turn had a positive impact on the number of high-quality jobs. Another finding was that since NAFTA went into effect, overall macroeconomic volatility has declined. Business cycles in Mexico, the United States, and Canada have had higher levels of synchronicity.

However, other studies present a less bright scenario.[17] Anticipating the signing of NAFTA in the early 1990s, FDI increased considerably. These flows stopped, however, in 1994—the year that NAFTA came into effect—due to a sequence of domestic economic and political setbacks. The financial crisis, known as the 1994 *tequila crisis*, together with political unrest due to the assassination of a presidential candidate and the *Zapatista* uprising in the southern state of Chiapas, was particularly damaging (see chapter 9).

Regional integration has facilitated bilateral agreements between trading blocs in the twenty-first century. The 2005 Central American Free Trade Agreement (CAFTA), for example, includes five Central American countries: Costa Rica, El Salvador, Guatemala, Honduras, Nicaragua, and one Caribbean nation—namely, the Dominican Republic. This can be considered a de facto extension of NAFTA.

Ongoing debates over the potential benefits of an extended NAFTA, however, suggest that economic integration has not been clearly accompanied by economic prosperity in the region. On the one hand, *maquila*-style exports by Central American economies have increased. On the other hand, some observers associate extended NAFTA with rising levels of insecurity, drug trafficking, increased crime rates, and rising outflows of illegal migrants, because it has become easier to transport human beings with export commodities to the United States—using Mexico as the natural venue.[18]

Estimates by the US Census Bureau on migration flows are reported in figure 10.9. The bureau's figures suggest that between 2000 and 2010, the amount of Central American–born people living in the United States increased by 51 percent, exceeding all of South America (46 percent), Mexico (28 percent), and the Caribbean (26 percent).

No one doubts that drug trafficking already existed prior to NAFTA. However, after 1994 and under a new regime, Mexico became increasingly decentralized, which in turn led to emerging "local" drug traffickers fighting against each other for an increased market share. Escalating violence followed. The situation

Trade and Financial Liberalization

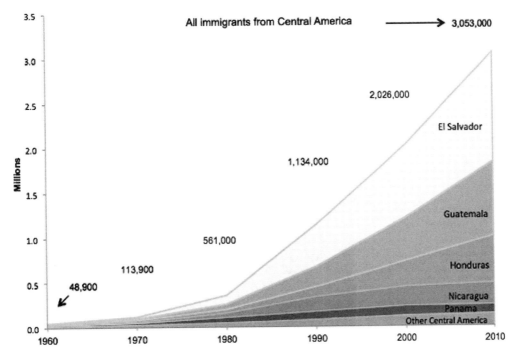

Figure 10.9
Central American migrants, 1960–2010.
Source: US Census Bureau 2011.

worsened when, in 2006, a new regime from the center-right *Partido Acción Nacional* (PAN) fought fiercely against drug traffickers.

Groundbreaking empirical work by Dell (2014) analyzes drug-trafficking and violence escalation in Mexico, which indeed became Latin American's main venue for millions of routes to transport illegal substances produced within Mexico itself and south of the border in Central America.

Dell constructs an econometric model for predicting the millions of new drug-trafficking routes that opened up once PAN gained ground in local electoral victories from 2007 to 2012. Because PAN has fought harshly against drug trafficking, Dell is able to predict the opening of new routes for diverting drug trafficking away from PAN-governed municipalities. She convincingly argues that violence escalates with the opening of new drug routes. Figure 10.10 provides a snapshot of the magnitude of the problem.

Along with regional trade block creation, a large number of bilateral trade agreements have sprung up. In the last two decades, the WTO (2011) reports a

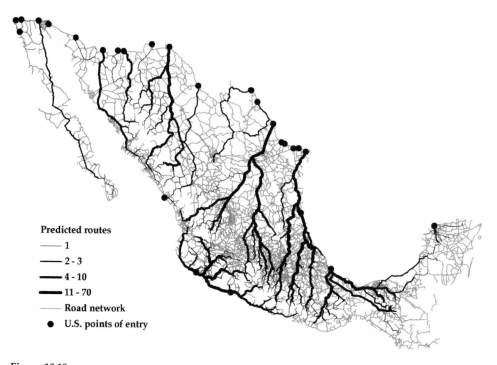

Figure 10.10
Road network and predicted trafficking routes. *Note:* The least cost routes plotted in this figure are predicted using the network model with congestion costs.
Source: Dell 2014.

grand total of sixty-five bilateral agreements between Latin American countries and eleven industrialized countries, plus fifty-four with other developing countries inside and outside the developing region.

It is important to note that this trend is not unique to Latin America. In the twenty-first century, most countries and blocks of countries have engaged in free trade negotiations, which suggests that globalization initiated during the 1980s in Latin America is here to stay. However, a reversal of protectionist policies in some countries, such as Argentina, has also taken place.

Nonetheless, the overwhelming importance of Asia in world trade markets cannot be rivaled by any other developing region. As shown in figure 10.11, although Latin America's (and all other developing and emerging market economies') share in world export markets from 1980 to 2009 has increased slightly, Asia's share has more than tripled.

This trend is revealing. Geographical proximity and increased access to world markets via trade liberalization in general, and via bilateral agreements in

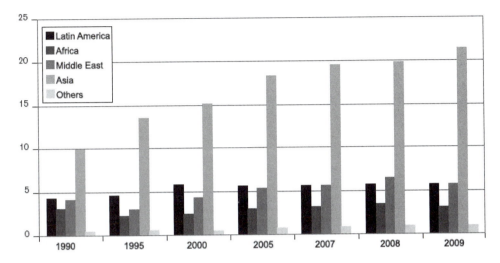

Figure 10.11
Share of developing countries in the value of world exports by region, 1990–2009.
Source: World Trade Organization 2015; see the Millennium Development Goals for trade and development at https://www.wto.org/english/thewto_e/coher_e/mdg_e/development_e.htm.

particular, can explain the modest increase in Latin America's share, but heavily populated Asia continues to have a comparative advantage in manufacturing relative to *all* other regions, not just Latin America. On the other hand, Asia is an early starter and thus enjoys a historical advantage, which prevents other regions from breaking into important value chains for international buyers that have been part of Asia's development strategies for more than three decades now.

From a welfare perspective, this is not necessarily good for Latin America and the world. In particular, even if other regions could produce manufactures more efficiently, Asia—and China in particular—has gained considerable economies of scale via its continued increase in export market penetration at a fast pace. Can Latin America gain from increased trade partnerships with Asia? We turn to this question next.

10.3 The Pacific Alliance and Trans-Pacific Partnership

Trade negotiations involving Latin American blocs and trade blocs in other continents are not new. As of this writing, MERCOSUR member states continue to negotiate a trans-Atlantic free trade agreement with the EU. These negotiations started in the early 2000s. To most observers, however, trans-Atlantic free-trade agreements do not offer much hope for export-led growth. For example, in

Argentina and Brazil (the two most prominent members of MERCOSUR), only a meager 12 percent of total exports are directed toward the EU. The situation might change if growth rates in the EU are reignited, but increasing trade ties with industrializing Asia seem more promising.

An important step in this direction was taken in 2011 when a new trading block known as the Pacific Alliance—comprising Chile, Colombia, Mexico, and Peru—was created. Trade integration among these countries has the potential to foster trade further and to facilitate free movement of capital and citizens across the countries bordering the Pacific.

Most importantly, the Pacific Alliance may become a platform to deepen Latin America's integration with the Pacific. Indeed, negotiations for a Trans-Pacific Trade Partnership (TPP) involving Australia, Brunei, Canada, Chile, Japan, Malaysia, Mexico, New Zealand, Peru, Singapore, the United States, and Vietnam have just crystallized, but these agreements need to be ratified by national legislatures. In this way, free trade might be further propelled, because countries involved in the TPP represent approximately 40 percent of the world's GDP as a whole and one-third of world exports. Meanwhile, however, Chile and Peru have already negotiated bilateral trade agreements with China.

Trade with Asia has become increasingly important for Latin America; Asia is the third-largest destination of Latin American exports, after the United States and the EU. However, although Latin American trade flows with the latter two regions have been decreasing, trade with the former shows an increasing trend. Moreover, for some countries in the region, Asia has already become their main trading partner. The most notable case is that of Chile, which sends about one-quarter of its exports to China alone, and half to Asia. Overall, and as figure 10.12 shows, both imports and exports between Asia and Latin America have increased considerably in the twenty-first century.

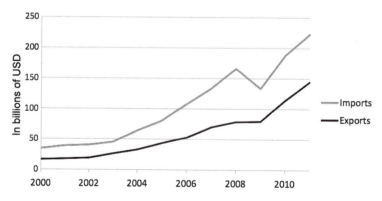

Figure 10.12
Trade between Latin America and Asia, 2000–2010.
Source: Feinberg 2013.

Trade and Financial Liberalization

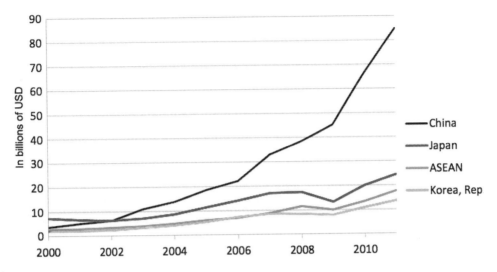

Figure 10.13
Latin American exports to Asia by country and region, 2000–2010.
Source: Feinberg 2013.

Not surprisingly, the main destination of Latin American exports within Asia is rapidly industrializing China—but as figure 10.13 also shows, highly industrialized Japan and Korea as well as other ASEAN countries (Brunei, Cambodia, Indonesia, Laos, Myanmar, the Philippines, Singapore, Thailand, and Vietnam) are rapidly increasing their import share from Latin American economies.

Ongoing US-China tensions do not permit a full-fledged trans-Pacific alliance involving China at this point in time. However, two Latin American countries in the Pacific Alliance—namely, Chile and Peru—have managed to negotiate a free trade agreement first with the United States, and then with China. Both Chile and Peru have the most diversified export destinations. It seems unlikely that other nations within the Pacific Alliance, notably Mexico and Central American countries, will follow in Chile's and Peru's steps.

Mexico has signed forty-five bilateral agreements, but China is not on its list. If anything, tensions are growing in that relationship, because China and Mexico already have industrial export sectors, and Mexico fears this sector will be threatened with the advent of Chinese competition.

We should note that although increased trade with China, and to a lesser extent with India, might improve welfare, Latin America's efforts to develop a stronger manufacturing and industrial sector might be severely hindered. As in Latin America's belle époque (see chapter 2), the pattern of trade is biased further in favor of production of primary commodity exports, which served Latin America well from 2003 to 2013. However, time has come to confront once more the end of a commodity boom and attempt to increase trade with other regions, with continued efforts to diversify existing export sectors.

Despite the sharp price decline in recent years of copper, iron ore, soybeans, oil, and other primary commodities, declines in growth rates in Chile, Colombia, and Peru have not been as drastic as the those observed in Argentina, Brazil and Venezuela. One important reason is that all three commodity-exporting countries, Chile, Colombia, and Peru, managed the commodity boom well in macroeconomic terms, via creating economic institutions that helped, such as structural fiscal rules and sovereign funds, which we discussed in chapter 7. Moreover, credit ratings in these three countries have improved, an issue to which we now turn.

10.4 Financial Liberalization

Alongside trade liberalization, Latin America also made bold steps toward financial openness. In the 1990s, and within a market-friendly reform framework, lifting restrictions on capital mobility was perceived as an essential component of enhanced access to foreign capital and as a magnet for technology diffusion via FDI. To this end, restrictions on capital inflows and outflows were lifted significantly.

The scope of the financial reform was huge. Estimates reported in Edwards (1995) suggest that if we normalize the index for capital mobility at 100, the index increased by approximately 35 points—from 40 in the mid-1980s to 75 in the early 1990s. Comparatively, the index for Asia increased by 20 points during the same period—from roughly 40 in the mid-1980s to 60 in the early 1990s. More recent estimates by Lora (2012) suggest that on a scale of 0 to 1, the average index for all Latin American countries and all structural policy areas increased from 0.39 in 1985 to 0.6 at the end of the 1990s, with the most significant progress in the areas of trade and financial liberalization.

Again, it is difficult to disentangle the effects of financial liberalization on foreign capital inflows. However, prior to the Asian crisis in 1997, the IMF estimates that net capital inflows—that is, after repayment of foreign debt—reached $36.2 billion dollars. For the 1990s, capital inflows were estimated to be 200 percent larger than those in the 1980s. Broadly, capital inflows took the form of short-term loans channeled via Latin American commercial banks, and FDI.[19]

By and large, significant capital inflow fluctuations can be explained by macroeconomic fundamentals (including exchange rate–based stabilization) and contagion. Indeed, in their efforts to lower inflation, countries like Mexico, Brazil, and Argentina maintained overvalued and unsustainable exchange rate regimes. As a result, the three Latin American major economies each suffered a financial crisis, in 1994, 1998, and 2001, respectively.

On the other hand, high growth rates in the world's advanced economies during the 1990s, and in the United States in particular, along with foreign investors' confidence, triggered large flows of capital for financial intermediation in emerging markets in general.

The Asian and Russian financial crises affected investors' expectations. In a financially integrated world economy, cyclical fluctuations and highly volatile capital flows were not only affected by crises within the Latin American region, such as the 1994 tequila crisis, but also by crises originating in emerging markets elsewhere, such as Thailand or Russia.[20]

Large cyclical fluctuations other than FDI inflows—resulting from internally generated crises and contagion—have continued throughout the 2000s, as figure 10.14 shows. It is important to note the trends. The financial accounts—capturing

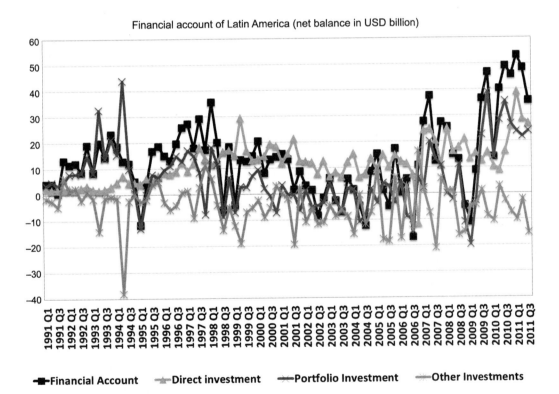

Figure 10.14
Latin American capital flows, 1991–2011.
Source: de Paula, Ferrari-Filho, and Gomes 2014, based on ECLAC and IMF statistics.

all short-term investments under different categories—display an upward trend until the 1994 tequila crisis. After their sudden collapse in 1994, the upward trend gained traction. Following the Brazilian crisis in 1998 and then the 2000–2001 Argentinean crisis, investors seemed to have lost confidence in Latin American markets. This was not surprising, considering that the sequence of crises occurred in the region's three largest economies in less than half a decade.

Not all Latin American countries have suffered from volatile short-term capital inflows. Notwithstanding the difficulties involved in sterilization attempts in the 1990s in countries such as Chile and Colombia, consequential interest rate hikes triggered more short-term capital inflows. In response, both Chile and Colombia introduced a sort of Tobin tax which succeeded—to some extent—in lengthening the maturity of capital inflows, but it did not reduce total inflows.[21]

The debate about financial liberalization remains open. The current position of the IMF is that despite the positive effects of free capital mobility (the ability to attract financial flows for productive investments in countries with low savings, promote risk diversification, and contribute to financial market development, among others), large capital inflows generate undesirable macroeconomic effects in recipient countries—particularly appreciation pressures, affecting the competitiveness of the tradable sector, and increasing financial fragility by generating domestic credit booms or price bubbles. In this regard, the IMF states that controls on capital flows may be useful under certain circumstances, especially at times when transitory capital inflows boom. However, the decision to implement capital controls should factor in the benefits of reducing financial fragility and greater macroeconomic control as well as the implementation costs and the distortions they cause. Multilateral repercussions and the potential reprisals of other countries should also be considered, particularly when capital controls are used by countries with undervalued currencies to prevent domestic currency appreciations.[22]

10.4.1 Financial Supervision, Liability Dollarization, and Banking Crises

An important magnifying problem of the financial crises was the exceedingly weak banking systems in most of the region. In terms of Latin America's largest economies, Brazil privatized its banks in the 1980s, and Mexico nationalized and privatized its banks in the 1980s and 1990s. Alongside privatizations, pedestrian regulatory and supervisory frameworks allowed for local commercial banks to take excessive risks in the 1990s. Consequently, the sudden slowdown of economic activity in the face of sudden reversals of capital inflows—as it happened in 1994 and 1998 in Mexico and Brazil, respectively—gave rise to poor-quality loans and considerable losses in already undercapitalized (and poorly supervised) commercial banks.

Trade and Financial Liberalization 269

Moreover, exchange rate depreciations exposed currency mismatches in balance sheets. In particular, a phenomenon known as *liability dollarization* was present in many countries in the region in which the US dollar and the local currencies were used interchangeably for financial transactions. Commercial banks in countries suffering from liability dollarization extended US dollar–denominated loans to borrowers, both individuals and corporations, whose revenues were obtained in local currency. Such individuals and corporations were not in the tradable sector. A sharp depreciation of the exchange rate implied that these borrowers were not able to service their foreign currency–denominated debts, whereas domestic banks had committed to service dollar-denominated loans. This problem magnified the extent of the wave of crises in the 1990s. More recently, the Argentinean and Uruguayan crises of the early 2000s provide vivid examples of liability dollarization and consequential banking crises.

During the 2007 to 2008 subprime crisis, exchange rates suffered severe depreciations in most Latin American nations, and some countries, such as Mexico, faced a sharp recession, albeit for a limited period of time compared to previous crises in the 1930s and the 1980s. However, no twenty-first-century country in the region—with the exception of Argentina—has experienced a banking crisis that, as argued in this chapter, magnified the perverse effects of sudden capital flow reversals.

The fundamental difference between the rather recent subprime crisis and previous crises lies in improved regulation and supervision standards in most countries along with improved risk-assessment mechanisms in a number of large banks in the region. According to the IMF (2009), financial solvency indicators have improved considerably in Latin America. Despite these improvements, domestic financial systems remain fragile because confidence is not yet restored, which is consistent with the low private saving ratios observed in the region, an issue to which we will return in chapter 12.[23]

10.4.2 Worker Remittances

A mitigating factor that has dampened the potential negative effects that sudden reversals of capital inflows and financial crises can have on the poor has been the steady flow of worker remittances, particularly in Mexico, Central America, and the Caribbean. As figure 10.15 shows, per capita remittances increased steadily in the crisis spells in the 1980s and 1990s, mostly in Mexico, which hosts a large number of poor (see chapter 5). The largest recipients of per capita remittances in Latin America are Mexico and El Salvador.

The upward trend continued in the twenty-first century. Prior to the subprime crisis in 2008, remittances increased at an average yearly rate of 17 percent. The average fell drastically by nearly 7 percentage points in 2009, but increased again

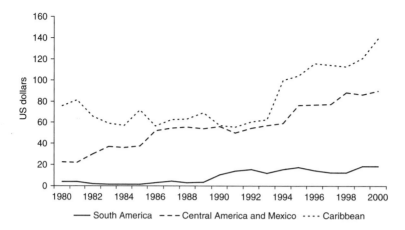

Figure 10.15
Worker remittances per capita in three Latin American regions, 1980–2000.
Source: Fajnzylber and López 2008.

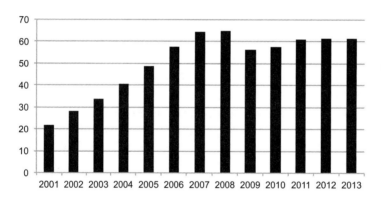

Figure 10.16
Worker remittances to Latin America and the Caribbean, 2001–2013.
Source: Maldonado and Hayem 2014.

as the US economy started to recover. Figure 10.16 captures remittances from other parts of the world as well—most notably those of Spain, from Ecuadorian migrants. However, recent stagnation in the flow of remittances has raised concerns, most notably in Mexico.

In particular, remittances from the United States to Mexico are estimated to be the second-largest source of foreign exchange, after oil and above FDI and tourism receipts.[24] Concerns about a slowdown in the flow of remittances, on the other hand, might stem from recent estimates suggesting that Mexico-US migration has fallen considerably in recent years, which might be due to a myriad of factors affecting both the economy and demographics in Mexico and in the United States. It might also be due to tighter border controls in the United States.[25]

10.4.3 Managing Capital Inflows in the Twenty-First Century

In 2004, a renewed upsurge in capital inflows to Latin America took place as a result of low interest rates in the United States and investors' high expectations for the region due to the commodity boom triggered by China's increasing demand for primary commodities. The subprime crisis of 2007–2008 precipitated a sudden stop, which—as argued earlier—was short-lived. In 2009, inflows restarted, until 2011–2012, when a slowdown was observed—most probably because of renewed concerns about Europe and a deceleration of economic growth rates in China, Latin America's largest foreign investor.

Not surprisingly and as figure 10.17 shows, fluctuating capital flows, which—as mentioned earlier—are by and large short-term flows, differ across countries. In a sample of the seven largest Latin American economies—those of Argentina, Brazil, Chile, Colombia, Mexico, Peru, and Venezuela—the more pronounced cyclical fluctuations seemed to have taken place in Brazil. Short-term flows appeared to have been fairly stable throughout the entire seventeen-year period of the study (1994–2011) in Peru, Colombia, and Chile.

According to an insightful compilation of articles by the Bank for International Settlements (BIS 2008), the relative stability of capital inflows in Peru compared to Latin America as a whole can be attributed to the fact that most inflows have taken the form of either FDI or long-term debt. In the case of Chile—Latin America's trade liberalizer par excellence—the problem of short-term inflows has been a difficult problem to cope with. Ramírez (2011) argued that the extraordinary performance of Chile's export sector attracted capital inflows, resulting in a strong tendency toward foreign exchange overvaluations. The Chilean authorities, however, have taken a pragmatic approach to ensure that the Chilean peso will not become overvalued. Their policies include regulation of exchange rate movements via reserve requirements, quotas, fees, foreign exchange interventions, and relaxing restrictions on capital outflows.[26]

It appears that Brazil's capital account has been subject to larger swings in capital flows than have other countries. Brazil, like all other regions in the southern cone, has until recently enjoyed not only lax external financing conditions but also terms of trade gains because of strong prices for its commodity exports. An important difference relative to other countries that are equally exposed to large fluctuations in commodity prices—most notably, Chile, Colombia, and Peru—lies in the inadequate management of debt to GDP ratios during the good times to

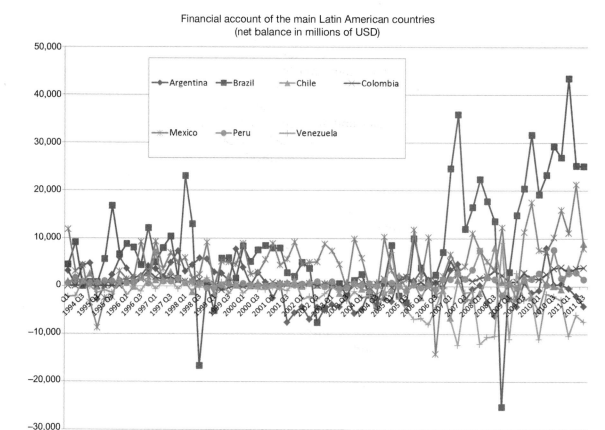

Figure 10.17
Capital flows in seven Latin American countries, 1994–2011.
Source: de Paula, Ferrari-Filho, and Gomes 2014.

avoid boom-bust cycles and exchange rate misalignment along with not-yet-independent central banks.

10.5 Concluding Remarks

A major trade liberalization wave started in Latin America in the late 1980s and early 1990s, with the notable exception of Chile, which had an early start in the mid-1970s. In this chapter, we highlighted the difficulties involved when trying to disentangle the effects of trade and financial liberalization, which took place within a framework of broader market-friendly reforms, including privatization and stabilization.

Efforts to attain price stabilization via using the exchange rate as a nominal anchor in the 1990s counteracted export-led growth in at least the region's three major economies, Argentina, Brazil, and Mexico. Export-led growth was nevertheless propelled via trade integration and bilateral (as opposed to multilateral), cumbersome trade agreements under the umbrella of the WTO. In parallel to participation in the Uruguay and Doha trade negotiations, most Latin American countries found it easier, faster, and more effective to lift tariff and nontariff trade restrictions unilaterally in parallel with trade bloc creation.

The extent to which trade diversion has outweighed trade creation in trading blocs such as MERCOSUR, NAFTA, and CAFTA is not completely clear. It appears that in the case of NAFTA, Mexico has benefited from FDI and technology diffusion. At the same time, NAFTA has facilitated Mexico's export diversification. Relative to other Latin American countries, Mexico is the only country that has managed to move away from primary commodity exports and toward export diversification. In particular, manufactures as a share of total Mexican exports increased considerably. Relative to other emerging market economies, post-NAFTA Mexico is by far the most diversified.

Such benefits have been tainted by political instability, social unrest, and rising drug trafficking and criminality, however, particularly with the advent of an extended NAFTA further south. Fighting drug trafficking and criminality has proved difficult, because the drug network extends itself in search of new venues and routes to cross the US border.

As for the vast majority of Latin American countries, in which growth is strongly linked to commodity prices, only Chile, Colombia, and Peru seem to have managed the commodity boom rather well. This shows that trade can be further enhanced with appropriate fiscal and monetary institutions while trade diversification takes hold.

One trade agreement that offers much promise is the Pacific Alliance involving Chile, Colombia, Peru, and Mexico. Since its foundation in 2012, this alliance has already produced deep integration of trade and financial markets and can serve as a platform for negotiating wider trade agreements.

At the same time, all countries in the region have signed as many as sixty-five bilateral agreements, eleven of which have been signed with highly industrialized countries. Chile and Peru have managed to sign bilateral free trade agreements with both the United States and China in sequence.

The weight of China in twenty-first-century Latin American economies is huge. China is now the third-largest recipient of Latin American exports—after the United States and the EU. China has also played an important role in the provision of capital inflows—particularly in the southern cone, which, unlike Mexico, still remains a primary commodity–exporting region.

Trade openness and financial liberalization in the twenty-first century have prompted a broad set of policies ranging from exchange rate to capital controls in order to achieve the dual objectives of avoiding overvalued exchange rates and creating less short-term capital flows volatility.

A sequence of financial crises in the region's three major economies during the 1990s hindered long-term capital inflows until 2004, when interest rates in the United States reached historically low levels, and the region—particularly southern cone countries—enjoyed a commodity boom from high demand from China for its primary commodities.

The region's reliance on China, particularly for the vast majority of South American countries, has delivered extraordinary benefits. As we argued in chapter 4, despite the fact that Latin America endured two crises originating in the United States in the twentieth century, increased trade and financial liberalization and the growing importance of China allowed the region to limit serious effects from the subprime crisis.

Excessive reliance on China might prove dangerous, however, as indicated by the positive relationship between growth slowdowns in China and those in South American regions—although the fall in growth rates has been less drastic in Chile, Colombia, and Peru, because these three countries have managed the commodity boom rather well via improved economic institutions.

The hope is that enhanced trade ties with other regions and a growth revival in the United States, the EU, and other industrialized regions will allow Latin America to further diversify its exports, benefit from FDI and other long-term capital inflows, and gain from an enhanced diffusion of technology.

Summary
- A distinguishing feature of the trade liberalization wave in Latin America was the unilateral dismantling of tariffs and nontariff barriers.
- Access to foreign markets was gained by potential exporters via signing bilateral trade agreements and creating regional trade blocs.
- The most important trade blocs include MERCOSUR, the Andean Pact, NAFTA, CAFTA, and the recent Pacific Alliance. All these agreements have elements of trade diversion and trade creation, though the more open a trade pact remains to the outside world, the more likely it becomes that the benefits of trade creation will outweigh the losses from trade diversion.
- Existing studies focus on the potential benefits for Mexico from NAFTA. The studies suggest that Mexico's growth performance was less than stellar relative

to the high expectations prior to 1994. Nonetheless, without NAFTA, Mexico would not have been able to diversify its exports and move away from the primary commodity exporter status it held prior to NAFTA. However, it is also possible that drug trafficking and crime rates would not have increased as they did after NAFTA.
- CAFTA is often perceived as an extension of NAFTA to Central America that has not lived up to its potential. One indication of this unfulfilled potential might be the sharp flow of Central American migrants into the United States.
- The country in Latin America with the most empirical evidence for and stylized facts backing the idea of trade openness as the main engine of growth is Chile. Not only was Chile an early trade liberalizer relative to other Latin American countries, but it has also placed trade liberalization at the center of most policies. Policy makers have been systematically mindful about export-oriented policies, especially with regard to policies for avoiding exchange rate overvaluations.
- Financial liberalization delivered sharp cyclical swings of short-term capital inflows, partly as a result of overvaluation of the exchange rate in the region's three major economies and contagion in the 1990s.
- Since 2004 and until recent years, financial liberalization has triggered a steady, upward capital inflow trend, which has been relatively stable in countries like Peru and Chile.
- The performance of Latin American countries—except for Mexico—has generally improved since 2004. The weight of China in the Latin American economies has become increasingly important, not only due to China's status as the third-greatest destination of Latin America's exports after the United States and the EU, but also due to its status as Latin America's main source of capital inflows more recently.
- The extent to which Latin American countries can continue exporting and benefitting from FDI depends not only on further trade integration via trans-Atlantic trade blocs but also on growth in China, the United States, and the EU and on domestic policies, particularly with regard to capital inflows and their impact on exchange rates.

Review Questions

1. Why did Latin American countries decide to unilaterally dismantle tariffs and nontariff barriers?
2. Do the Heckscher-Ohlin predictions accord well with Latin American trade patterns during the 1990s and beyond?
3. What are the potential benefits and costs of regional trade integration blocs?
4. What do most studies suggest with regard to the benefits from NAFTA for Mexico?

5. Why do most observers believe that the Chilean miracle is the result of above-average export growth?
6. Is trade with China beneficial or detrimental to most Latin American economies?
7. What can one expect from trans-Atlantic trade integration versus trans-Pacific trade integration?
8. What are the main concerns about financial liberalization on the basis of capital flows and export performance in the 1990s from a Latin American perspective?
9. Why is sterilization a concern, and what policies can mitigate speculative capital flows?
10. If worker remittances surpass FDI inflows of capital in Mexico, why should the Mexican government worry about trying to attract FDI?

Further Reading

For a well-researched and insightful historical analysis of Latin America's experience with regard to trade liberalization, see Nenci and Pietrobelli 2008. A comprehensive and concise review of trade liberalization in the 1990s is provided by de Ferranti et al. 2003. For an interesting overview of capital flows in Latin America since the 1990s, see Allendorf et al. 2011.

11 Labor Markets, Informality, and Labor Protection Systems

Perhaps the area in which reforms are hardest to implement is the realm of labor markets and worker protection. The potential beneficiaries of deregulation in this market are more numerous but are generally poorer, unorganized, informal sector workers, whereas the potential losers (at least in the short run) often are more highly organized formal sector (or even public sector) workers. How have Latin American governments dealt with labor market laws, unions, and the informal sector throughout the reform period and beyond?

In the particular case of privatization, excess employment in newly privatized firms had to be reduced for the sake of competitiveness and efficiency. The hope was that crowding in private sector enterprises would reabsorb labor and that labor would be protected. However, the transition was economically and politically difficult, particularly in countries lacking safety nets. It was also unrealistic; moving formally employed labor across industries proved exceedingly challenging. In the vast majority of cases, the immediate effect of broad economic reforms under the umbrella of the Washington Consensus was an increase in unemployment and informal employment. Laid-off labor was somewhat compensated via severance payments, handouts of shares in privatized firms, and early retirement schemes.

This chapter links with the political economy considerations underscored in chapter 6 to set up the nature of the problem. It describes employment and unemployment statistics and participation rates (for both men and women) in various countries in the region. It then presents evidence on informality and job quality and assesses the inefficiency and equity costs that arise from having a large pool of informally employed workers while pinning down skill shortages in the informal sector as a contributing factor in persistent income inequalities.

The chapter also reviews the basic features of worker protection, including pension contributions (and subsidies), severance payments, unemployment benefits, and firing rules. The consequent costs of hiring and firing have been estimated for many countries, and we report them here.

Section 11.1 of this chapter analyzes the change in the employment situation as Latin America transitioned from ISI to trade liberalization policies throughout the last two decades of the twentieth century. Section 11.2 analyzes the labor market in Latin America in the 1990s through the lens of political economy considerations, insider-outsider theory, and other hypotheses. This section highlights the most important empirical contributions as the reform took hold in the late twentieth century and beyond. Section 11.3 spells out the stylized facts from the most recent findings of the International Labor Organization (ILO), which deliver an upshot of twenty-first-century Latin America's labor trends prior to and after 2004—the so-called turning point year. This section also discusses the need for labor market reforms in favor of women and the young. Section 11.4 analyzes the informal sector and job quality: roots, costs, and challenges ahead. Section 11.5 touches upon the demographic transition process, the aging structure of the labor force in Latin America, youth skill shortages, and women's labor force participation. Finally, section 6 presents a summary and some concluding remarks.

11.1 Background

Latin America's labor markets during the ISI period—roughly between the late 1940s and mid-1980s—were characterized by large, rural to urban migration flows. These flows generated a highly segmented urban labor market.

Most economists tend to view such a phenomenon through the lens of the Harris-Todaro model (Harris and Todaro 1970). This model sheds light on urban formal sector employment, in which wages are higher than market-clearing wages due to institutional arrangements—most notably as a result of powerful labor unions and minimum wage laws.[1]

The received wisdom is that during the ISI period, the pace of urbanization in Latin America was extremely high, because agricultural producers were systematically penalized in order to promote industrial growth. Relative to Asia, for example, where the number of people living in urban areas increased from 17.4 percent in 1950 to 36.7 percent in 2000, ECLAC (2002) estimates that during that same period, Latin America's urbanization rates increased from 41.4 to 75.3.[2]

As labor moved at a strikingly fast pace from rural to urban areas on the expectation of higher wages, a large number of laborers did not find jobs in the formal sector, either because wages were above-market-clearing wages or because industry was absorbing relatively high skilled labor. Otherwise stated, investors were investing in labor-saving technologies.

Because agriculture offered meager earnings, migrants stayed in urban areas nonetheless, thus creating a pool of informally employed workers. As this pool grew, the Harris-Todaro model predicted that the expected wage for the informally employed would fall and that, in equilibrium, rural to urban migration flows would stop once wages in agriculture equaled the expected wage in urban areas.

The Harris-Todaro model delivers interesting insights for the case of Latin America. In particular, the model predicts a segmented urban sector in which formal sector employees enjoy above-market-clearing wages coexisting with an informal sector. The informal sector comprises self-employed individuals, part-time workers, labor employed in microenterprises that avoid taxation, and unemployed or partially unemployed individuals. Informal sector workers earn comparatively less than formal sector employees and, perhaps most importantly for policy, do not benefit from social protection.

The pool of informally employed individuals has increased in post-ISI Latin America. At the same time, labor unions have lost power. This phenomenon is often attributed to trade liberalization.[3] During the 1990s, the argument goes, a relatively small proportion of high-skilled labor became employed in firms exposed to foreign competition and services, whereas a vast majority of unskilled labor was confined to informal self-employment and partial employment in microenterprises that produced for the domestic market; this exacerbated income inequalities, because skill premiums of the skilled and formally employed laborers grew, while earnings in the informal sector either remained stagnant or escalated at a considerably slower pace.

Policy makers and international aid agencies became increasingly aware of the shrinking income share accruing to labor as the pool of unemployed and informally employed increased. Concerns about low-paid jobs in an increasingly large pool of informally employed workers who remained socially unprotected triggered widespread discontent and political unrest as trade liberalization policies took hold.

According to various studies, however, empirical evidence of the casual impact of trade openness on informality suggests small effects.[4] A recent study on Brazil, for example, found that trade liberalization only accounts for roughly 1 percent of the increase in informality over the 1983–2002 period.[5]

A substantial number of studies, on the other hand, have suggested that it is not trade liberalization but excessive labor protection policies that are at the root of the problem, because such policies involve a delicate trade-off between social protection inclusion for some workers—some but not all unionized—at the expense the vast majority engaged in informal sector activities.

Moreover, Perry et al. (2007) suggest that labor protection policies—a byproduct of democratization—such as minimum wage, severance payments, and excessive labor taxes are themselves causing the pool of informally employed laborers to increase steadily.

Any standard economics textbook contains a section on welfare economics, which explains the well-known tension between equity and efficiency. What happened in Latin America in the 1990s is a perfect example. Specifically, the Latin American workforce—which was formally employed under ISI—lacked the necessary skills to compete with its international counterparts when compared to, for example, the Asian labor force. Moreover, formal sector employees were generally politicized—especially under populist regimes (see chapter 6). This led to exceedingly powerful labor union structures, particularly in SOEs.

More generally, the formally employed public and private sector labor forces under protectionist ISI policies were highly inefficient. At the same time, social security had become extremely fragmented; access was controlled by powerful interest groups and unions, particularly those in SOEs, and especially in the energy sectors. Hence, although loss of efficiency could have been justified on the grounds of equity, our conjecture is that in practice it was not.

Because there were more benefits at stake than just mere above-market-clearing wages, the relationship between the Latin American governments and unions became increasingly strained, with military regimes often attempting to reduce labor unions' strength. The Washington Consensus reforms coincided with democratization. As a result, although the demand for skilled labor increased with the adoption of new technologies, labor rights for all (skilled and unskilled) workers in the 1990s and 2000s were restored de jure and deepened in a vast majority of Latin American countries.

At the same time, empirical evidence from cross-country studies in emerging markets (including Argentina, Brazil, Chile, Colombia, Mexico, and Peru) for the 1996–2009 period shows that labor productivity lags behind real wages, suggesting that labor protection of formal sector employees discouraged firms in this sector from hiring more labor, leading to an expanding informal sector, which in turn lends support to Perry et al.'s (2007) qualitative findings.[6] It is important to note that when labor productivity lags behind wages, countries lose competitiveness.

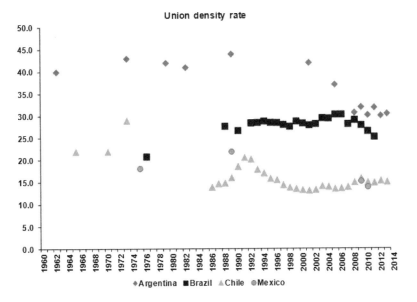

Figure 11.1
Union density rates in Argentina, Brazil, Chile, and Mexico, 1960–2013.
Source: Authors' own construction from Amsterdam Institute for Advanced Labor Studies database (www.uva-aias.net).

But why were real wages so high? In the transition from military regimes to democracy—as we noted in chapter 6—some countries engaged in populist policies via, for example, wage indexation. On the other hand, labor unions lost power. This is particularly true in the manufacturing sector, in which average unionization rates declined by approximately 33 percentage points between 1980 and 2000.[7] Figure 11.1 shows the trend in union density rates in Argentina, Brazil, Chile, and Mexico.

Against this background a dual labor market of formally employed labor in the urban areas emerged. A heavily protected (high wage) labor working in the public sector, which was and still remains heavily unionized on the one hand, and a private (high wage) sector with a pool of high-skilled laborers who were *not* unionized on the other.

It is important to note that the decline in average unionization rates is not a distinguishing feature of Latin America. In fact, deunionization in the private sector is a worldwide trend, as figure 11.2 shows for seven OECD countries. The OECD average of unionized labor—inclusive of highly unionized Nordic countries—shows meager rates of approximately 16 percent of the total labor force.

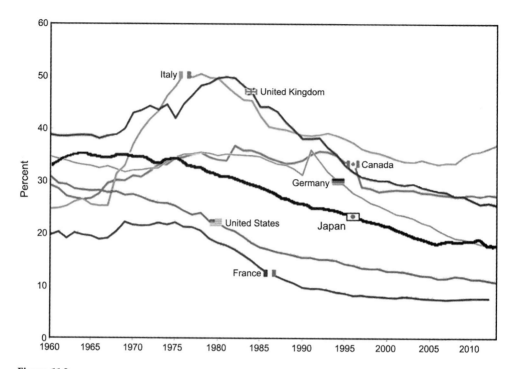

Figure 11.2
Unionization rates in OECD countries, 1960–2013.
Source: OECD 2015.

Unlike in OECD countries, where deunionization is often attributed to deindustrialization, Latin America's declining rates are a by-product of privatization and trade liberalization, which exposed a vast amount of unskilled and skilled labor to international competition. Differences across regions are stark, however, which reflects each country's specificities. Despite a lack of available data, some quantitative figures are revealing. For example, when comparing two of the region's major economies—Argentina in the southern cone and Mexico in the north—we find that although union membership in Argentina declined throughout the entire reform period, Mexico experienced a considerably more pronounced downturn—particularly in the nonagricultural sector, of course.

This difference between two of Latin America's most unionized countries is often attributed to the rapid development of the explosive *maquila* sector in Mexico, reviewed in chapter 10. In this sector, links between union leaders and workers are weak. Union presence and ties with workers are stronger in Argentina, most likely because of historical reasons—specifically, the Argentinean union-managed health care scheme *Obras Sociales*, which dates back to the 1970s. Peronist-style policy responses are a contributing factor.

Latin America is not labor abundant when compared to Asia, and moving away from ISI policies involved harsh competition to attract FDI in labor-intensive manufacturing industries. This, in turn, kept Latin America's real wages down, leading to a de facto flexible labor market. Nonetheless, political economy considerations during the democratization wave led to labor protection laws, such as minimum wages and wage indexation. Consequently, real wage increases were systematically higher than productivity gains in several countries. We will return to this topic in section 11.3.

Relatively high wages in turn discouraged labor absorption by formal private sector employers, which further fueled informal sector activity. According to Thorp (1996), informal sector employment in the 1970s was approximately 13 percent. In contrast, recent statistics from the ILO suggest an increasing trend in informality, surpassing the 50 percent mark over the 2010–2013 period. In short, roughly more than half of the labor force in contemporary Latin America is either self-employed or employed by informal microenterprises.[8]

The rise in informal sector activity and deunionization thus reflects the shift from ISI to export-oriented policies and privatization. ISI facilitated union formation and incorporated unionized labor in political processes.

Subsequent trade liberalization in the 1980s and 1990s led to a decline in unionized public and, most importantly, private sector employment. At the same time, private employment opportunities expanded in the 1980s and 1990s.[9] Private sector workers, particularly in services, are much more difficult to unionize because labor turnover is high. Unskilled workers in the growing informal sector, on the other hand, do not have traditional worker-employer relations and therefore preclude unionization.

The preceding analysis suggests that reconciling efficiency gains from privatization and trade liberalization with equity requires massive investments in education and training for the vast majority of Latin America's labor force.

11.2 Labor Market Deregulation and Deunionization

The theoretical debate on the effects of deregulation on employment is inconclusive. On the one hand, it is often argued that widespread labor reforms in the 1990s have had a negative impact on employment. The most widely documented proxy for deregulation is arguably the decrease in firing costs. It has been suggested that when firing costs decline, firm-level employment is likely to decrease, because higher hiring rates do not compensate for higher firing rates. Yet recent research indicates that a reduction in firing costs leads to an increase in employment.[10]

On the other hand, when we move from firm-specific to macrolevel analysis, the insider-outsider theory predicts that lowering job security provisions boils down to lowering insiders' bargaining power and thus wages, because employers face lower turnover costs, which will in turn increase employment rates.[11] Caballero and Hammour (1997) reach a similar conclusion: In the long run, lower firing costs increase employment as firms shift to more labor-abundant technologies.

Ultimately, however, the effects of deregulation on employment remain an empirical question that deserves further scrutiny. The most comprehensive empirical analysis on Latin America thus far is a study by Nobel Prize laureate James Heckman and his coauthor, Carmen Pagés-Serra (2000), which was sponsored by the Inter-American Development Bank. This study dispels the idea of labor market deregulation in Latin America. In particular, the authors construct a Job Security Index (JSI). The average for Latin America in 1999 is considerably higher than that found in industrialized countries, with most Latin American countries presenting labor markets that are just as inflexible as those in Southern European countries such as Spain and Portugal. Figure 11.3 shows the high levels of job security (proxied by expected dismissal costs upon hiring, expressed in monthly wages) compared to industrialized countries and the large degree of variation across Latin American countries during the reform period in the 1990s. As the figure shows, in Latin America's largest economy, Brazil, the JSI increased in 1999 relative to 1990. It did not change in Mexico and Argentina. Heckman and Pagés-Serra's index did decrease considerably in Colombia, Peru, Venezuela, and Nicaragua, however.

Somewhat surprisingly, the graph also shows that in Chile, which is traditionally viewed as a relatively flexible labor law country, job security not only increased by the end of the twentieth century, but is also higher than in countries such as Mexico and Argentina. Heckman and Pagés-Serra (2000, 114) explain this rather puzzling finding as follows: "While Mexico and Argentina have stronger unions and therefore higher wage rigidities, Chile has higher individual job security provisions." Indeed, it appears that this often misleading perception of the Chilean labor market dates back to the mid-1970s, when firing costs decreased drastically—from approximately four times the average monthly wage under the Allende regime to roughly one month's wages. According to Edwards (2004b), firing costs rose considerably in the aftermath of Chile's labor market reform in 1981 and further increased in 1991, when Chile returned to democracy.

The Chilean example is important, particularly during the 1990s, because most of the Latin American countries during this period transitioned from military

Labor Markets, Informality, and Labor Protection Systems 285

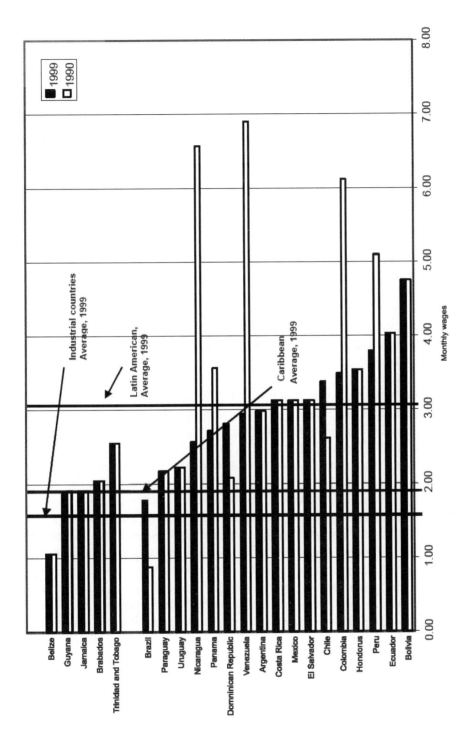

Figure 11.3
Job Security Index in Latin America, 1990–1999.
Source: Heckman and Pagés-Serra 2000.

regimes to democracies, which might in turn explain why most of the region's governments have resisted labor flexibility.

The question then is not what the costs of labor market deregulation in Latin America are. Rather, the focus should be on the costs of continued regulation (or *excessive labor protection*, as Perry et al. 2007 names it). Heckman and Pagés-Serra (2000) convincingly argue that these costs are high in terms of employment and efficiency, with the young bearing a disproportionate share of labor market rigidities in the region. Specifically, Heckman and Pagés-Serra view highly regulated markets in Latin America as one of the main sources of increased income inequalities for three main reasons: first, inflexible labor markets decrease employment prospects for the young, for females, and for a vast majority of unskilled laborers; second, it exacerbates segregation between workers with secure jobs and workers with few prospects of finding a job; and third, it increases the pool of informally employed labor.

Anner (2008) revisits this question from a qualitative standpoint. He looks at unionization and labor laws during "the second round" of labor market laws, extending well into the twenty-first century. His main point is that the reforms in the 1990s were mostly labor friendly because they coincided with democratization wave in the entire Latin American region. However, such laws were never enforced in the vast majority of cases, because trade liberalization imposed, as argued earlier, de facto labor market flexibility.

In our view, the strong downward pressure on wages triggered by trade liberalization discouraged labor from unionizing. Table 11.1 shows that by the turn of the millennium, unionization rates in a majority of Latin American countries in our sample decreased. (As argued in the previous section, deunionization rates in Latin America are in line with the worldwide trends.) What the table reveals is that in many Latin American countries, labor laws were considered to be "union friendly." In these countries, however, unionization rates decreased by more than two digits. Deunionization in Brazil and El Salvador was not as pronounced.

In the case of Brazil, Anner (2008) argues that the relatively small decrease in unionization rates was due to internal political economy considerations granting a great deal of direct de jure empowerment to the unions since 1988; in the case of El Salvador, the cause was external pressures from the United States and the ILO in 1994. In both instances, unionization was promoted via various venues, most notably via constitutional amendments preventing government interference and via enacting simplified unionization procedures. Nonetheless, unionization rates decreased as unions became increasingly decentralized. Overall, unions in Brazil and El Salvador lost power because of poor law enforcement mechanisms and low rates of industrialization.

Table 11.1
Unionization rates in Argentina and Mexico, 1980–2000

Wage earners	AR 1990	AR 2001	MX 1984	MX 1992	MX 1999	MX 2000
Nonagricultural	49	42	30	--	18–21	20
	65	63				
Manufacturing	70	66	30	--	--	20
22		15	50	44		

In sum, although labor market deregulation appears to be a myth, deunionization is a reality—even in countries in which unions have traditionally been strong, such as in Argentina and Mexico, as table 11.2 illustrates. Early assessments of the effects of labor market inflexibility suggest that it has had a negative impact on employment and social indicators: higher unemployment for women and youths, more segregation between the employed and unemployed, and a higher pool of informal sector employment.

Recent reports on public and private sector salaries suggest that they have continued in an upward trend, as shown in table 11.3. Deunionization, on the other hand, reflects the loss of bargaining power from trade liberalization. Specifically, Latin America is a labor-scarce region compared to Asia; exposing unskilled labor to international competition therefore leads to lower real wages.

On a bright note, recent empirical work by, for example, Cornia (2013) and Lustig, Lopez-Calva, and Ortiz-Juarez (2013) suggests that the increase in real wages is not due to excessive regulation. Instead, the authors argue that the factors that might have driven wages upward in the last decade include a larger pool of skilled workers as a result of educational investments in the 1990s and 2000s; an increase in the demand for unskilled workers due to the adoption of competitive exchange rates favoring the unskilled, labor-intensive tradable sector; a decline in the supply of unskilled labor due to higher educational attainment; a fall in birth rates; and an increase in the rate of emigration.

Higher real wages might in turn explain a fall in the skill premium, which has contributed to the decline in income inequalities in the last decade. This decline and, more generally, the overall improvement in the employment situation in Latin America are largely attributed to high and sustained rates of economic growth during the commodity boom, a topic to which we turn next.

11.3 A Labor Market Turning Point

According to the most recent estimates by the ILO (2013), the turning point in Latin America's labor market came in 2004. As of that year, the unemployment

Table 11.2
Labor laws and unionization rates in Latin America, 1990s–2000s

	Main direction of reforms	Percent of workforce unionized	Change in unionization Rate (%)
Argentina	Union-averse (1990s)	28.7 (1995); 25.6 (1999)	-10.80
Bolivia	Union-friendly (1995)	20.9 (1990/1995); 16.4 (1996/2000)	-46.93
Brazil	Union-friendly (1988)	24.88 (1990); 11.3 (1998)	-5.22
Chile	Union-friendly (1990)	13.6 (1990); 11.3 (1998)	16.91
Colombia	Union-friendly (1990)	11.2 (1985); 7.0 (1995)	-37.50
Costa Rica	Union-friendly (1990)	21.4 (1993); 13.8 (2003)	-35.46
Dominican Republic	Union-friendly (1992)	17.3 (1995); 10 (2006)	-42.20
Ecuador	Union-averse (1991)	14.3 (1986/1990); 13.5 (1991/1995)	-5.59
El Salvador	Union-friendly (1994)	5.58 (1994); 4.80 (1999)	-13.78
Guatemala	Mixed (1992, 1995)	2.92 (1990); 1.55 (2004)	-46.91
Honduras	No changes	30.2 (1990); 14 (2003)	-53.64
Mexico	No changes	35.3 (1986/1990); 22.4 (1991/1995)	-36.29
Nicaragua	Mixed (1990, 1996)	32 (1986/1990); 23.4 (1990/1995)	-26.88
Panama	Union-friendly (1995)	17 (1986/1990); 14.2 (1990/1995)	-16.71
Paraguay	Union-friendly (1993)	7.7 (1992); 2.8 (2002)	-63.64
Peru	Union-averse (1991)	30.0 (1991); 10.0 (1998)	-66.67
Venezuela	Union-friendly (1990)	25.9 (1988); 14.9 (1995)	-42.47

rate began to show a sharp decline, and occupational rates increased steadily. Labor force participation also started to show an upward trend.

The ILO 2013 estimates are shown in figure 11.4. The interpretation of this turning point by ILO researchers is that it was not until 2004 that the benefits of the Washington Consensus reforms started to bear fruit. In particular, the ILO report on Latin America in 2013 contends that the region had "turned the page" in the sense that it was not until 2004 that Latin America was able to take advantage of improved terms of trade, higher commodity prices, and high rates of industrialization and economic expansion in China.

Table 11.3
Average monthly wages in selected Latin American countries, 2000–2013

	2000	2005	2010	2011	2012	2013
Brazil	100	93	110	113	117	120
Chile	100	108	121	125	129	133
Colombia	100	105	112	112	114	117
Costa Rica	100	97	111	118	120	122
Ecuador	100	145	165	171	175	179
El Salvador	100	88	82	78	79	79
Honduras	100	95	105	113	107	106
Mexico	100	115	110	107	107	106
Nicaragua	100	118	110	107	105	105
Panama	100	96	105	105	109	118
Paraguay	100	84	91	92	93	95
Peru	100	95	115	119	125	126
Uruguay	100	82	103	106	111	115
Venezuela	100	105	115	120	127	119

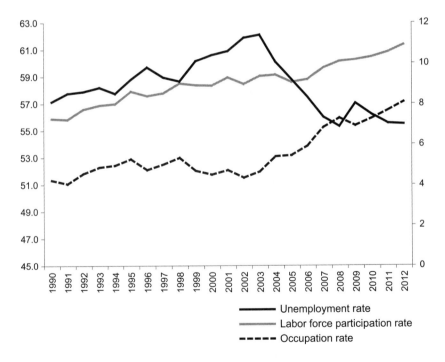

Figure 11.4
Latin America and the Caribbean: Labor force participation, occupation, and unemployment rate, 1990–2012.
Source: ILO 2013.

Rates of economic growth steadily increased for five consecutive years (2004–2008), and Latin America had not witnessed such high and sustained growth over the two preceding decades. Moreover, the region weathered the 2008 subprime crisis relatively well. The ILO (2013) acknowledges that its predictions in 2008 largely overstated the negative effect that the crisis might have had on employment. Unemployment increased by only 0.9 percentage points, but recovery started shortly after, with unemployment falling again from over 7 percent to approximately 6.7 percent. This figure is much lower than the double-digit rates observed at the turn of the millennium.

As table 11.4 shows, the fall in urban unemployment was largest in Argentina, Brazil, Ecuador, Panama, Paraguay, Uruguay, and Venezuela. These countries went from double- to single-digit unemployment rates. Mexico, Latin America's second-largest economy, on the other hand, did not experience a sharp decrease in unemployment. Unemployment might have actually increased there.

We should note, however, that Mexico is the only country in Latin America that has managed to diversify its exports. Under NAFTA, which started in 1994, Mexico moved away from being a primary commodity exporter and therefore benefited the least from the "Chinese miracle," which translated into an extraordinary hike in demand for primary commodities produced in Central America and the southern cone. Contemporary Latin American economies in Central America and the southern cone had not witnessed such high demand for primary commodities since the nineteenth century's belle époque, a period we analyzed in great detail chapter 3.

With regard to labor protective laws in Latin America's nascent democracies, figure 11.5 shows that the average minimum wage increased for the entire region, with the upward trend becoming more pronounced after 2004. Increased average monthly wages and labor productivity, however, differed across countries. As figure 11.6 shows for a selective number of countries for which data is available, average monthly wages from 2004 to 2011 grew in Brazil, Chile, Costa Rica, and Uruguay. In these countries, employment increased as well.

At the other end of the spectrum, we find countries in which monthly average wages increased slightly (e.g., Honduras and Mexico) or remained stagnant (e.g., El Salvador and Nicaragua). Comparatively, the latter countries did not experience an impressive hike in employment figures.

Along the 45-degree upward line, the figure also shows that monthly average wage growth was higher than productivity expansion in some countries—most notably Brazil, Chile, and Costa Rica—which is detrimental to competitiveness, whereas in others, such as Colombia and Panama, average monthly wages were systematically lower than productivity, which is beneficial for competitiveness.

Table 11.4
Unemployment rates in Latin American countries, 2003–2013

País	2004	2005	2006	2007	2008	2009	2010	2011	2012	2013	2013 Quarterly average to 3rd quarter	2014 Trimestre
Latin America												
Argentina	13.6	11.6	10.2	8.5	7.9	6.5	7.7	7.2	7.2	7.3	7.4	...
Bolivia	6.2	8.2	8.0	7.7	6.7	7.9	6.5	...	...	...	...	4.9
Brazil	11.5	9.8	10.0	9.3	7.9	8.1	6.7	6.0	5.5	5.4	5.6	4.9
Chile	10.0	9.2	7.8	7.1	7.8	9.7	8.2	7.1	6.4	5.9	6.0	6.5
Colombia	15.3	13.9	12.9	11.4	11.5	13.0	12.4	11.5	11.2	10.6	11.1	10.3
Costa Rica	6.7	6.9	6.0	4.8	4.8	8.5	8.5	10.1	10.0	9.2	9.6	9.6
Cuba	1.9	1.9	1.9	1.8	1.6	1.7	2.5	3.2	3.5	3.3	...	...
Ecuador	9.7	8.5	8.1	7.3	6.9	8.5	7.6	6.0	4.9	4.7	4.7	5.3
El Salvador	6.5	7.3	5.7	5.8	5.5	7.1	6.8	6.6	6.2	5.6	...	...
Guatemala	4.4	...	...	...	...	...	4.8	3.1	4.0	3.8	3.9	4.2
Honduras	8.0	6.9	5.2	4.1	3.9	4.9	6.4	6.8	5.6	6.0	...	...
Mexico	5.3	4.7	4.6	4.8	4.9	6.6	6.4	5.9	5.8	5.7	5.9	6.0
Nicaragua	8.6	7.0	7.0	6.9	8.0	10.5	10.1	...	7.6	...	...	...
Panama	14.1	12.1	10.4	7.8	6.5	7.9	7.7	5.4	4.8	4.7	5.1	5.0
Paraguay	10.0	7.6	8.9	7.2	7.4	8.2	7.2	7.1	8.1	8.1	8.0	8.5

Table 11.4 (continued)

País	2004	2005	2006	2007	2008	2009	2010	2011	2012	2013	2013 Quarterly average to 3rd quarter Trimestre	2014 Quarterly average to 3rd quarter Trimestre
Peru	9.4	9.6	8.5	8.5	8.4	8.4	7.9	7.7	6.8	6.0	6.0	6.1
Dominican Republic	6.1	6.4	5.5	5.1	4.7	5.3	5.0	5.8	6.5	7.0	7.0	6.8
Uruguay	13.1	12.2	11.3	9.8	8.3	8.2	7.5	6.6	6.7	6.7	6.9	6.9
Venezuela	15.3	12.3	10.0	8.4	7.3	7.9	8.7	8.3	8.1	7.8	7.9	7.3
The Caribbean												
Bahamas	10.2	10.2	7.6	7.9	8.7	14.2	...	15.9	14.7	15.8	16.2	14.3
Barbados	9.6	9.1	8.7	7.4	8.1	10.0	10.8	11.2	11.6	11.6	...	...
Belize	11.6	11.0	9.4	8.5	8.2	13.1	12.5	...	15.3	13.2	12.1	11.1
Jamaica	11.7	11.3	10.3	9.8	10.6	11.4	12.4	12.6	13.8	15.2	15.4	13.6
Trinidad and Tobago	8.3	8.0	6.2	5.5	4.6	5.3	5.9	5.1	5.0	3.7	...	...
Latin America and the Caribbean	10.3	9.0	8.6	7.9	7.3	8.1	7.3	6.7	6.4	6.2	6.5	6.2

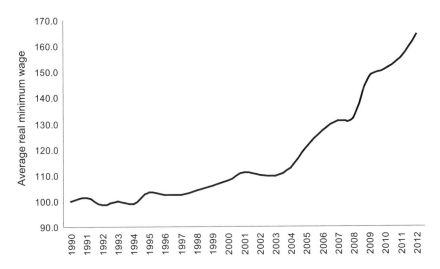

Figure 11.5
Average minimum wage in Latin America, 1990–2012 (1990 = 100).
Source: ILO 2013.

It is important to note that average inflation for the region was in the single digits for the period in question. The consistently high nominal wage in figure 11.5 therefore marks a steep increasing trend in the *real* minimum wage. The upward trend became more pronounced as of the 2004 turning point. Figure 11.6 shows that the increase in wages differs across countries, which might reflect differences in minimum wage legislations. Diverse labor institutions are not confined to minimum wages. Unfortunately, lack of disaggregated data across countries prevents us from making meaningful comparisons and does not allow for labor market conjectures.

Nonetheless, as figure 11.7 shows, average pension coverage for the region became higher for a broad category of workers. For all workers, total coverage increased by around 12 percentage points in 2011 compared to 2000; for total wage workers, 13 percent;[12] for public sector workers, 12 percent; for private sector workers in SMEs, 15 percent; for workers in large firms, 12 percent; for employers, 12 percent; for independent/auxiliary family workers, 8 percent; and for domestic service workers, coverage increased by approximately 11 percent. Against such an encouraging backdrop favoring labor income shares in the twenty-first century, labor protection has been tainted on equity grounds. Specifically, labor protection has been biased in favor of male and elder workers. Indeed, when one looks at women and youth unemployment, twenty-first-century Latin America shows an appalling trend. Figure 11.8 shows that after the turning point in 2004, the trend

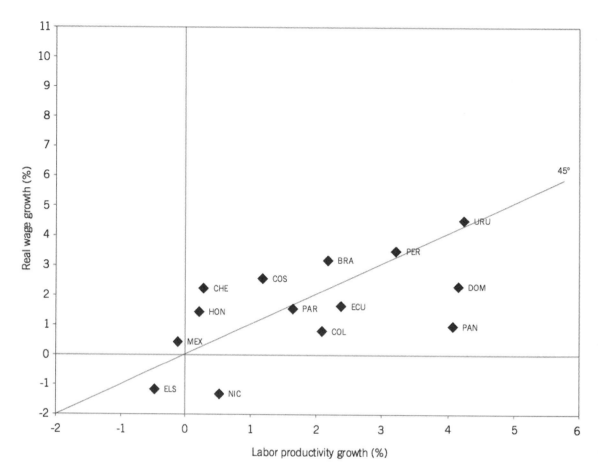

Figure 11.6
Growth in wages and labor productivity in selected Latin American countries, 2004–2011.
Source: ILO 2012–2013.

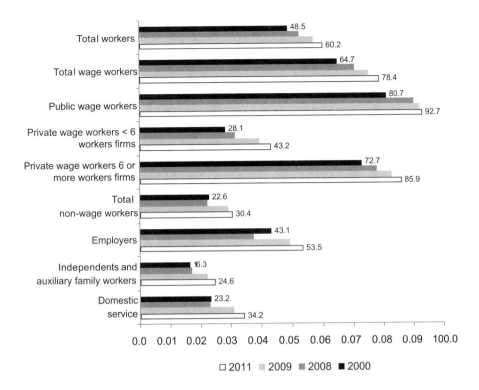

Figure 11.7
Average pension coverage, 2000, 2008, 2009, and 2011.
Source: ILO 2012–2013.

Figure 11.8
Women to men unemployment ratios, 1990–2012.
Source: ILO 2013.

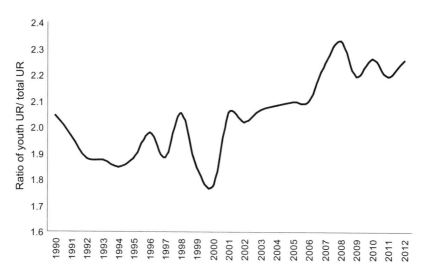

Figure 11.9
Youth to total unemployment, 1990–2012.
Source: ILO 2013.

in the women to men unemployment ratio has increased. In 2012, the ratio reverted to that observed in 1993. Youth unemployment also increased. As figure 11.9 shows, the ratio of youth unemployment to total unemployment increased from approximately 1.8 to 2.3.

11.4 The Informal Sector and Job Quality

According to the OECD (2009), *informal employment* refers primarily to employment in enterprises that lack registration and social security coverage for their employees. It also refers to self-employment and precarious employment in formal enterprises. A distinctive feature of this type of employment is the lack of social coverage and other related benefits. Put simply, informal employment is highly precarious and vulnerable.

There are two main reasons that policy makers should be deeply concerned with regard to informal sector employment. First, the quality of informal sector jobs is lower relative to that in the formal sector, which is partly reflected in wage differentials between skilled and unskilled laborers. This differential—often attributed to skilled-biased technical progress—contributes to chronic income inequalities, one of the main tenets of this book.

Second, there is the problem of underemployment—that is, involuntary part-time jobs. A vast number of Latin Americans work part time and would like to

Table 11.5
Percentage of underemployed workers in selected Latin American countries, 2004–2011

	2008	2009	2010	2011	2012
Argentina	9.5	11.1	9.8	9.1	9.3
Brazil	3.1	3.1	2.7	2.3	2.0
Chile	9.0	10.8	11.5	11.6	11.2
Colombia	9.1	9.5	12.0	11.1	11.7
Costa Rica	10.5	13.5	11.2	13.4	13.8
Ecuador	10.6	11.8	11.5	9.4	7.9
Mexico	6.1	8.9	7.6	7.1	7.0
Panama	2.1	2.1	1.8	1.5	2.4
Paraguay	…	…	7.3	6.3	5.4
Peru	15.6	15.4	14.5	12.4	12.2
Uruguay	10.8	9.1	8.6	7.2	7.1

work more hours to increase their incomes and pull themselves out of poverty. Evidence shows that informally employed labor generally works fewer hours per day than the average formally employed worker. The estimates are staggering: table 11.5 shows that among relatively large Latin American countries such as Argentina, Chile, Colombia, and Peru, the percentage of urban underemployed—mostly women—is between 9 and 12 percentage points.

The underemployed generally lack social protection, which in turn exacerbates poverty and the inequality gap between men and women. In our view, because women are generally the main brokers of health and education within the household, their low income and benefit status compared to their male counterparts is at the root of intergenerational poverty. More generally, social benefits for the average Latin American household derive from social security contributions. Social security coverage is far from being universal. The average for the region, as figure 11.10 shows, is only 30 percent. In other words, roughly 30 percent of those individuals who are formally employed enjoy the benefits of social security contributions! Regional differences are high, however. Argentina, Chile, and Uruguay, for example, show higher than average social security contributions. At the other end of the spectrum, countries such as Colombia, Paraguay, and Peru exhibit lower than average contributions.

Well aware of this problem, some Latin American governments (e.g., Brazil, Chile, Mexico, and Uruguay) in recent years have introduced subsidized pension systems for underemployed and self-employed individuals. In addition, recent research shows that some type of "informal welfare system" for the informally

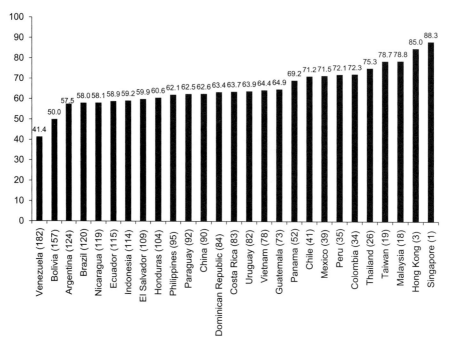

Figure 11.10
Social security contributions as a percentage of employment, 2009–2012.
Source: ILO 2014a.

employed exists in most Latin American regions. In particular, Latin American governments often turn a blind eye to informal sector activity—for example, by not taxing informal employment when government authorities have the constitutional mandate to do so (e.g., not taxing informal street vendors, stands, or stores). Although this might mitigate the perils of income inequalities and help politicians to win congressional elections, such redistributive transfers contribute to the perpetuation of informality.[13]

The region has also witnessed programs aimed at universal coverage. In particular, the "dignity rent" in Bolivia, the "rural pensions" in Brazil, and the "solidarity pensions" in Chile are often cited as examples of social inclusion programs within the framework of antipoverty campaign schemes reviewed in chapter 5.

Besides social concerns, there is another reason that a growing informal sector—currently estimated to account for over 50 percent of the labor force—and poor job quality rank high on Latin American governments' political agendas. Businesses in the informal sector do not pay taxes—partly because of political economy considerations, as argued earlier—and thus further exacerbate the region's fiscal constraints, particularly during recent years, when the slowdown in China and the precipitous fall in commodity prices have adversely affected growth rates in nearly all Latin American countries. As growth rates decrease, so do tax revenues, which in turn prevents governments from providing free access to health and education to a vast majority of poor individuals who remain trapped in poverty. In many instances and regions, lack of access to human capital accumulation also fuels social unrest.

Moreover, although income inequalities, poverty, and social unrest rank high in contemporary Latin American governments' agendas, lowering the size of the informal sector is also important for efficiency. Labor productivity gains are reflected in higher growth and increased real wages only in some cases. As the domestic market grows, the economies of Latin America should be less exposed to business cycles elsewhere—be that China, the United States, or, to a lesser extent, Europe. Domestic labor markets can potentially become stronger via complementary trade integration efforts, such as the Pacific Alliance, MERCOSUR, and the Central American Common Market (CACM), among others, an issue we already discussed in chapter 10.

However, and according to the IDB (2005), the main focus of policy makers wishing to attain the dual objectives of reducing income inequalities and increasing labor productivity in twenty-first-century Latin America should be on the creation of a more business-friendly environment to foster private sector expansion on the one hand and the creation of an institutional framework for good-quality jobs to emerge under the umbrella of effective and enforceable labor protection laws on the other.

With regard to creating a more business-friendly environment, estimates reported by the World Bank (2014a) classify Latin America as one of the least business-friendly regions in the world. For example, Brazil, Latin America's largest economy, is classified as being less business friendly than Zambia, Ecuador, and Jordan. As illustrated in figure 11.11, although cross-country differences within Latin America and the Caribbean are huge, the average for the region is around 40 points below the mark in terms of ease of doing business. The index comprises different components, such as contract enforcement difficulties, regulation, bribes, crime, access to credit, and reliable infrastructure, among others.[14] The figure shows the highest business-friendly environments in countries such as Chile, Colombia, Mexico, and Peru and the lowest in countries such as Argentina, Bolivia, and Venezuela.

With regard to institutional frameworks, protective laws for workers, and enforceability, one of the main obstacles for regulators is the exceedingly large prevalence of microenterprises. These account for approximately 90 percent of all private firms; many are purposely informal in order to avoid taxation.

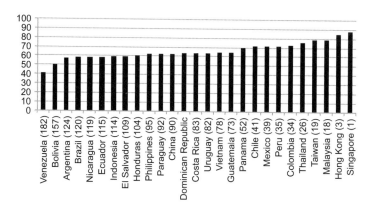

Figure 11.11
The *ease of doing business* rank in Latin America and the Caribbean compared to East Asia, and the distance from the 2014 leader's frontier (rankings in parentheses).
Source: World Bank 2014a.

Approximately 8 percent are SMEs, and the remaining 2 percent are large firms. Against this backdrop, regulatory authorities find it extremely difficult to enforce labor protection laws.

The entrepreneurial structure of the Latin American economies, with only a few private sector firms competing internationally and millions of small microenterprises producing for the internal market, also has an impact on productivity. Microenterprises in the growing urban sector have limited access to technology and credit. Their large numbers imply that average labor productivity is below its potential when compared to a situation in which firms enjoy the benefits of scale economies. However, microenterprises and large firms face the same business-unfriendly environment. Under prevailing bureaucracy, corruption, and excessive regulation, private sector microenterprises deliberately do not grow in order to escape government interference. It pays to remain small and informal from the perspective of an individual firm. However, the social costs in terms of lost tax revenues that could improve social policies, infrastructure, and productivity are huge. Individual firms do not internalize job training costs either.

The IDB (2005) suggests that informality and consequential low labor productivity is linked to high labor mobility across microenterprises, mismatches between workers' expertise and labor demand, lack of skills, and lack of enforceability and low core worker standards. The IDB's report spells out some policy recommendations that include public provision of job-finding services, training and skill acquisition, and better job market institutions.

Some countries, most notably Costa Rica, have already started to devote considerable amounts of government expenditure to on-the-job training. Other countries, such as Argentina, Chile, and Uruguay, have made efforts to include informal sector employees in social security schemes. In Argentina, for example, a 1994 constitutional amendment known as the Integrated System of Retirement and Pensions was enacted in order to mandate extending social security and pension coverage to large number of self-employed individuals over eighteen years of age. Chile introduced a voluntary pension scheme reform in 1981 targeting the self-employed. A mandatory but gradual inclusion of the self-employed in pension and social security schemes was debated in Chile's Congress in 2006. Uruguay reformed its social security and pension scheme system in 1996 in order to include individual owner businesses compulsorily. However, estimates reveal that coverage is limited. Only about 35 percent of self-employed workers are estimated to be covered in Argentina and Uruguay. The figure for Chile is around 27 percent.[15]

On a bright note, however, rapid and sustained employment and output growth rates since the 2004 turning point have triggered a decrease in the informal employment trend. As shown in figure 11.12, employment in informal sector enterprises and nonagricultural self-employment have both decreased.

According to the ILO (2013), those workers who have remained in the informal sector can be broken into three main categories: workers of small enterprises, domestic workers, and own-account or self-employed workers. Typically, informal sector employment comprises a vast majority of the uneducated labor force—which in Latin America is defined as workers who have completed primary school

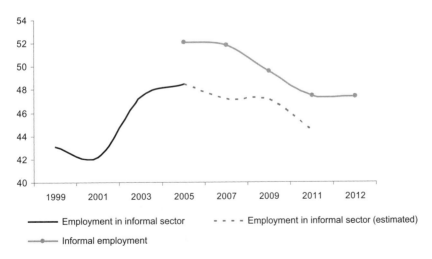

Figure 11.12
Employment in the informal sector and nonagricultural self-employment, 1999–2012.
Source: ILO 2012–2013.

education only—and these workers are generally part of the poorest quintiles of the population.

Needless to say, informal sector employment is inaccurately measured—among other reasons, because of the high labor mobility across microenterprises. Nonetheless, estimates reveal an increasing proportion of the population joining the pool of workers who are formally employed. The estimates are consistent with the view that income inequalities in twenty-first-century Latin America have decreased, as we argued in chapter 5. Such encouraging trends are unlikely to be maintained, however, because recent slowdown in China has adversely affected growth in the region and in other emerging market economies.

11.5 Age Structure and Women in the Labor Force

In an important contribution to our understanding of the Latin American labor markets, Duryea and Székely (1998) emphasize the supply of labor in the region. Specifically, the authors suggest that the demographic transition hypothesis has played an important role. This hypothesis states that as countries become wealthier, fertility and mortality rates fall, leading to a relatively old working population compared to that in less developed countries.

With the exception of Haiti and Nicaragua, most Latin American countries are considered middle-income economies, according to standard World Bank classification—and many statisticians and demographers have noted that Latin America is aging. Since the mid-1960s, population growth has declined, which in turn has two major implications. First, the growth rate of the working-age population has started to fall, and second, the share of the relatively old age group has been increasing.

Nonetheless, because the Latin American region is very diverse, some regions are at early stages of the demographic transition, such as Guatemala, Honduras, and Paraguay. In these countries, the age structure of the population is relatively young compared to that in more developed and more heavily populated countries, such as Argentina, Brazil, Colombia, Mexico, and Peru.[16]

Overall, Duryea and Székely contend that both employment and unemployment have fallen because the rate of growth of the population entering the labor force has started to decrease, from around 3 percent in the 1980s to 2.5 percent in the 1990s. As shown in figure 11.13, and consistent with the predictions of the demographic transition hypothesis, the proportion of working age individuals entering the labor force is expected to decline over the next thirty years.

However, a counter-effect is at work due to an increasing trend of labor force participation by women, as shown in figure 11.14. In the 1970s, women's labor force participation was approximately 22 percent. By the mid-1990s, this rate

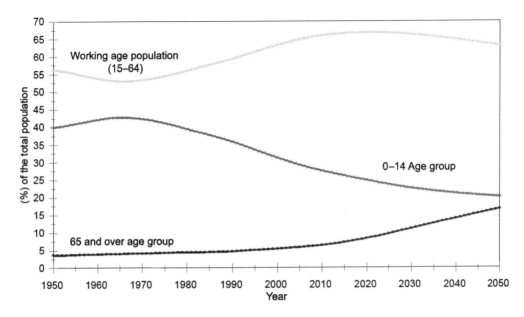

Figure 11.13
Working-age, young-age, and old-age trends, 1950–2050.
Source: Duryea and Székely 1998.

increased to around 37 percent, and again to nearly 55 percent around 2012 (IZA World of Labor 2014).

The higher rate of women in the labor force is in turn explained by several factors, the first of which is the aging population. As women age, their participation in the labor force increases; they have more time to work outside the household, because their children have reached young adulthood. Second, women are more educated, and thus fertility declines as the opportunity cost of having children increases, because wages increase with higher educational attainment. However, wage inequality between men and women persists as men continue to attain higher levels of education. Indeed, as argued previously, not only do women in Latin America earn less than men, but the quality of the jobs they hold in the informal sector also is comparatively low in terms of social protection. Hence, closing the gender gap is another important challenge for employment policy in most of Latin America.

11.6 Concluding Remarks

The Washington Consensus reforms, particularly in the realm of privatization and trade liberalization, triggered a higher pool of informal sector employment as

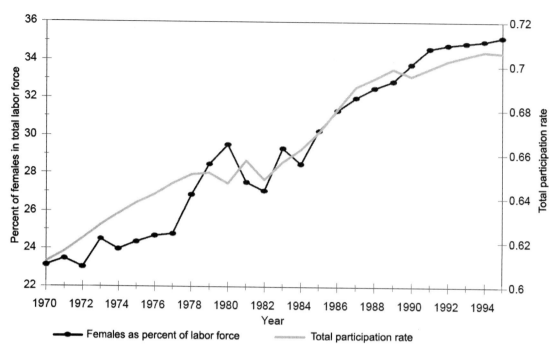

Figure 11.14
Women's labor force participation, 1970–1994.
Source: Duryea and Székely 1998.

newly privatized firms and foreign investors' demand for skilled labor increased, thereby creating a high wage premium that favored a minority of skilled laborers and leaving the majority of unskilled workers behind. The main concern about informally employed labor is that it is socially unprotected.

The reforms coincided with the democratization wave. In an effort to protect labor, real wage increases (inclusive of minimum wage legislation and social protection laws with regard to hiring and firing costs) have been kept above rises in labor productivity in a handful of countries. Moreover, the demographic transition in Latin America has increased labor force participation by youth and women. The results by the turn of the twenty-first century included a higher pool of informal and underemployed workers who were de jure but not de facto socially protected and an increase in low-quality job creation. Women and the young have been particularly affected.

The overall effect on real wages in the 1990s seems to have been negative, which reduced the power of labor as proxied by unionization rates. Nonetheless, the governments in the region's nascent democracies have enacted labor protection laws and promoted unionization—to no avail. Unionization rates in Latin America have fallen, in line with similar declining trends in OECD countries.

Some stylized facts reveal that high and sustained growth rates as of 2004 have increased employment and minimum wages in the formal sector in parallel with expanded social security coverage. The hope is that the trend will continue, leading to higher-quality jobs and expanded social protection as investments in education and skill acquisition take off at a more rapid pace and as antipoverty programs continue to take hold. Outlooks are bleak, however, as Chinese growth has decelerated and commodity prices have fallen in recent years. Most countries' employment figures are likely to be adversely affected—particularly in the southern cone.

The Latin American labor market is still highly regulated and segmented. The formally employed represent a minority of skilled labor employed by, at most, 10 percent of private sector firms that are medium and large and are exposed to international competition. The vast majority of microenterprises along with the self-employed constitute the bulk of unskilled laborers who have not attained higher levels of education and training and whose wages are consequently lower than those of employees in the formal sector.

Allowing the private sector to expand via a set of policies geared toward making the environment more business friendly and promoting expansion of microenterprises should provide high-powered incentives for labor to acquire skills in an enhanced and more dynamic labor market.

Specifically, microenterprises should be incentivized to grow, join the ranks of the formal sector, and contribute to economic growth via increased demand for high productivity jobs and expanded government revenues for financing infrastructure, particularly in the domains of health and education—the two main components of human capital and consequent labor productivity, which seems to be lagging behind the pace of wage acceleration in most countries.

Labor productivity enhancements can also be attained via training. Currently, however, investments in infrastructure for accelerating the pace of human capital accumulation via on-the-job training are relatively slow compared to the growing demand by an increasingly large middle class. The region therefore seems to be stuck in a "bad" equilibrium in which the potentially high demand for skill acquisition is hindered because gaining skills is not within reach for the vast majority of Latin Americans.

More research is needed to fully understand the labor market dynamics in middle- income economies in general and in Latin American countries in particular, where the main engine of growth is the export sector for primary commodities.

Regarding the aging age structure of the population and increased labor force participation by women, early research suggests that increased underemployment due to higher labor force participation by women is dampened by a lower rate of overall participation (mostly from men). As the age structure of the Latin American population increases, the hope is that both the elderly leaving the labor force and the young entering the labor force will be socially protected. Updated empirical research using twenty-first-century data should shed light on this trade-off.

Summary
- Under ISI, a considerable amount of the labor force was employed in inefficient SOEs at higher than market-clearing wages.
- Rural to urban migration flows led to a labor pool of self-employed and informal employment in microenterprises.
- The Washington Consensus reforms, particularly in the realms of privatization and trade liberalization, exacerbated an already segmented labor market with a minority of high-skilled labor employed in the nascent and competitive private sector and a vast majority of unskilled labor employed in microenterprises and self-employment activities.
- Efforts by nascent democracies to protect labor power failed to preserve labor rights because regulation discouraged formal sector employment and led to an increasing pool of informal sector employees.
- Formal employment has nonetheless been protected via regulation, labor laws to incentivize unionization, and social security coverage.
- What triggered higher rates of formal employment, however, were high and sustained rates of growth as of 2004, which marked a labor market turning point.
- Obstacles to further enhancement of formal sector absorption include an unfriendly private business environment, including problems with crime and corruption, and lack of incentives to join the formal sector due to labor laws lacking enforceability and microenterprises attempting to escape taxation to the detriment of government revenues.
- Fiscal constraints have in turn created a vicious circle in which meager investments in training and education discourage unskilled labor from acquiring skills, because private skill acquisition is unaffordable.
- Concerns from the growing middle class have triggered political unrest in some regions.
- The supply of labor has increased mostly because of the increased participation of women in the labor force.
- The skilled versus unskilled wage gap has decreased in the last decade, but more research is needed to elucidate remaining gender wage gaps and income inequalities after the 2004 turning point.

Review Questions
1. What triggered the increasing segmentation of the labor market in the 1990s and beyond?
2. What prevents the private sector from expanding and increasing demand for formal labor employment?
3. To what extent did excessive regulation affect employment in the 1990s compared to the 1980s?
4. What explains the sharp decline in unionization rates?
5. Why is 2004 considered a turning point for labor and formal sector protection?
6. To what extent is the age structure of the population, and the participation of women in the labor force, affecting employment?
7. Can high and sustained economic growth by itself close the gender and skilled versus unskilled wage gaps?
8. Why are most governments in Latin America underinvesting in skill acquisition via schooling and training?

Further Reading
For a comprehensive report on the important changes in labor markets in the commodity booms of the 2000s, see ECLAC and ILO 2013. Informal labor markets in Latin America are explained clearly in Biles 2009. For a comprehensive study on the aging structure of the Latin American labor force, see Cotlear 2011.

12 Growth and Development in Latin America

This closing chapter, though self-contained, covers a wide range of issues of growth and development in Latin America, some of which have been dealt with extensively in chapters 1 through 11. Unsurprisingly, addressing these issues turned out to be a challenging task, because growth and development are indeed multidimensional. Moreover, Latin America has a huge number of pockets of poverty scattered along the entire continent, its income inequalities are high, and it is exceedingly heterogeneous [diverse] in many respects. Nonetheless, there are some common characteristics that are valid for the entire region.

With the exception of Chile, which started in the mid-1970s, Latin America moved away from ISI policies starting in the mid-1980s, when the region's largest economies—notably Mexico—embarked on a broad set of structural transformations better known as the Washington Consensus reforms. With the benefit of hindsight and contrary to what highly regarded economists thought in the early 2000s, Latin American countries benefited from such multilateral, aid agency–sponsored reforms.[1] Growth rates began to gallop by the turn of the twenty-first century. Somewhat paradoxically, Mexico was an exception. Most central and southern cone nations experienced high and sustained growth rates—unseen since the region's nineteenth-century belle époque.

It was probably too little too late; again with the benefit of hindsight, we should note that Asian countries' performance exceeded that of Latin America's stellar performers. However, Latin America can catch up, if better policies for growth with equity are implemented in the region's young democracies. In particular, throughout this chapter we will focus on what is replicable and what is not for improving growth prospects and mitigating the pervasive effects of chronic poverty and income inequalities. Although we recognize that the region's excessive reliance on commodity exports can be a major obstacle, in this chapter we suggest potential solutions in the domain of trade openness, education, and institutions.

Section 12.1 opens this chapter by reviewing the well-known question that compares diverse trajectories in Asia and Latin America. In this section, we highlight savings rates, which are comparatively low in Latin America, although savings are not the main cause of the observed diverging trends, savings rates seem to play an important role. In section 12.2, we pin down structural issues from a Latin American perspective. Then, in section 12.3, we spell out what we think is most important for sustaining inclusive growth in the region—namely, a set of domestic policies in key areas. In section 12.5, we highlight the importance of technological imitation and adaptation—which are the venues many Latin American economists think can be taken to attain much-needed productivity gains. Finally, we summarize the chapter and present concluding remarks in section 12.6.

12.1 Development in Latin America: A Tale of Frustrated Expectations

When we compare per capita income in Latin America and Asia over the last half century, we see that an extraordinary reversal of fortunes has taken place. For example, in 1960, average per capita income in Latin America was US$4,500, whereas income per head in South Korea was US$1,944. Fifty years later, Latin America's average per capita income had tripled, but that of South Korea had increased seventeenfold. Not even Chile, Latin America's best performer—where per capita income quadrupled—can compare to South Korea. A similar story can be told for the entire fifty-year comparison between most countries in Latin America and those in Asia.

Let us take a closer look at what happened in Latin America. Per capita income at PPP 2013 dollars in the region increased from US$4,500 in 1960 to US$12,667 in 2013. Simply stated, it took half a century for per capita income in Latin America to triple.

A recurrent idea in our book is that a great deal of diversity has been observed in the region. Indeed, differences across countries are stark, as shown in figure 12.1. At one end of the spectrum, we find Chile—where per capita income has been rising steadily since the mid-1970s. At the other end, we find countries like Venezuela, where per capita income in the 1960s was more than double that of Chile, but then it stagnated and declined. Partly as a consequence of being an early reformer and partly due to huge differences in the quality of economic management and institutions, average income in Chile in 2013 was roughly 50 percent higher than that in Venezuela.

Growth and Development in Latin America

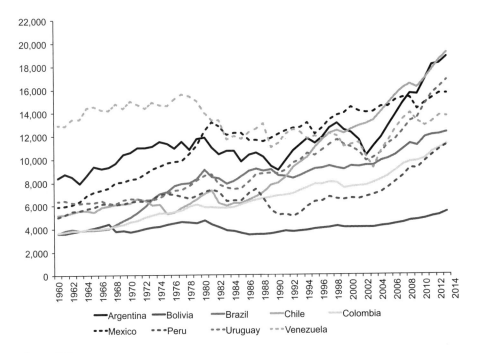

Figure 12.1
Per capita GDP at PPP (constant 2013 US dollars) in selected countries in Latin America, 1960–2013.
Source: Authors' own construction from World Bank (www.worldbank.org) and IMF (www.imf.org) databases.

We now bring Asian countries into the picture. As shown in figure 12.2, two Asian countries—namely, Singapore and Hong Kong—started off at roughly the same per capita income level as Chile and Peru. That is, per capita income at PPP (constant 2013 US dollars) in all four countries was roughly US$4,500 in 1960. In 2013, per capita income in Singapore had reached US$64,586, whereas per capita income in Hong Kong stretched out to US$52,722. Income per capita in Singapore was therefore 18 percent higher than that in Hong Kong. Income per capita in Chile (US$22.543 in 2013) is 95 percent higher than that in Peru (US$11.587 in 2013). What these trends suggest is that although within-region income inequality has increased, the cross-Pacific income gap has become considerably wider.

Key to our understanding of such extraordinary per capita income divergence is the unprecedented growth rates found in some Asian countries. Growth rates of income per capita in Latin America during the 1961–2013 period averaged an annual rate of 3.9 percent. In contrast, per capita income during the same period in three Asian Tigers—South Korea, Singapore, and Hong Kong—grew at roughly 7 percent on average. It is true that other regions have had a slightly worse

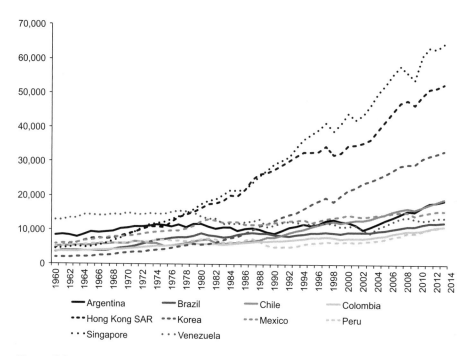

Figure 12.2
Per capita GDP at PPP (constant 2013 US dollars) in selected countries in Latin America and East Asia, 1960–2013.
Source: Authors' own construction from World Bank (www.worldbank.org) and IMF (www.imf.org) databases.

performance than that of Latin America. During the 1961–2013 period, for example, sub-Saharan Africa grew at an annual rate of 3.5 percent, which is slightly lower than that of Latin America. The truth is, however, that both Latin America and sub-Saharan Africa bear an eerie resemblance to one another in many dimensions, not just in their comparatively low rates of growth relative to those in some Asian regions, but also in the realm of income inequalities.

Overall, with the exceptions of Mexico in the sixties, Brazil in the seventies, Chile between 1986 and 1997 and again between 2010 and 2013, and Panama, Peru, and Uruguay in recent years, Latin American economies have usually shown a lackluster performance over the last half a century when compared to Asian best performers. If we were to bring China into our comparative performance analysis, Latin America's growth record over the past fifty years would look considerably worse.

In the remainder of this final chapter, we will discuss theoretical and empirical arguments selectively in order to shed light on such diverse growth performance from a Latin American perspective.

12.2 Growth and Development: A Quest for Answers

It is nearly impossible to point to a single indicator that could explain the divergent trends between Asia and Latin America, if only because policy differences must be considered. It is often argued that Asian governments during the last fifty miraculous years were export led as opposed to inward looking and that Asian governments' interference in myriad industrial sectors, exchange rate regimes, and a range of social policies triggered high and sustained growth with equity. In this section we focus on just two indicators: the savings rate and the initial level of per capita income. Note that our choices shed light on existing theoretical and empirical contributions that we consider particularly relevant to Latin America.

12.2.1 Savings

The Solow 1956 framework has become the traditional starting point to assess per capita income differentials across regions. Solow's neoclassical theory stresses that transitional growth results from physical capital accumulation, albeit with diminishing returns for the stock of per capita capital. Once countries have reached a *steady state* in which the investment rate equals the rate of depreciation plus the population growth rate, output growth is constant unless countries' productivity increases. Productivity, in turn, results from technical progress, which is exogenous in the standard neoclassical framework.

Let us focus first on Solow's concept of transitional growth from a Latin American standpoint. The theory predicts that at low per capita income levels, high savings rates can deliver high transitional growth rates of per capita income.

Cross-country studies on savings and growth abound, and these studies suggest a positive and significant relationship.[2] The importance of the savings rate for explaining differences in growth performance across regions is of utmost relevance to our understanding of the sharp contrast between the poor growth performance of Latin America relative to Asia. As shown in figure 12.3, high-growth Asian economies present significantly higher savings rates. This suggests that relative to Latin America, high savings rates in Asia have led to higher transitional growth and enhanced per capita income.

However, the neoclassical framework does not explain why Asians save more than Latin Americans, because savings rates are exogenous in the Solow model. In the search for savings rate differentials, a simple shortcut is to note that they result from a combination of institutions and culture.[3] Although this might be true, we take the empirically founded view that savings rates can be raised via macroeconomic policies.[4]

Nearly all policy makers in Latin America moved away from ISI policies over the last two decades of the twentieth century and embraced a broad set of

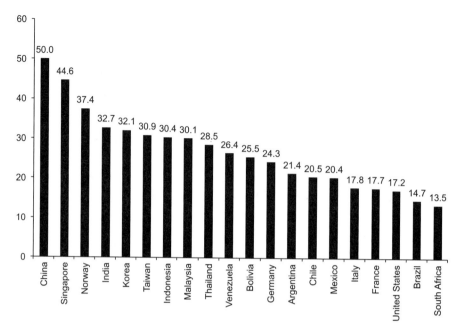

Figure 12.3
Gross national savings in selected countries for 2013 as % of GDP.
Source: Authors' own construction from IMF database (www.imf.org).

market-friendly policies instead. It took nearly a quarter of a century for Latin America to reap the benefits of the new development strategy. Undoubtedly, the legacy of ISI weighed heavily on Latin American citizens, if only because it was difficult for the average Latin American household to think positively about savings under high inflation. Hence, while Asia was growing in a considerably more stable macroeconomic environment over the entire 1960–1990 period, savings and investment in Latin America lagged behind. However, getting the macroeconomic framework "right" in order to experience high and sustained growth rates for more than a decade now does not necessarily mean that savings rates will miraculously increase.

We argued in the previous chapter that not only have social security and pension reforms fallen behind expectations for formally employed individuals and employers, but also that a vast segment of the active workforce, particularly the self-employed and informally employed, is excluded from social security and pension benefits. As a starting point, we therefore suggest the implementation of fully funded social security systems in order to boost savings, without losing sight of Latin America's own specificities; institutions and cultural legacies, which are considerably different from those encountered in Asia.

Policy makers should be exceedingly cautious with regard to where—in Asia or elsewhere—lessons for reform regarding savings can be drawn from, however. Back in figure 12.3, for example, China is at the top of the list. In both China and Latin America, the population is aging. Social security and pension reform cannot wait, but China is certainly not the place from which lessons for these reforms can potentially be drawn. Several empirical studies have shown that it is the absence, not the implementation, of social security and adequate health systems in an environment in which the population is rapidly aging that forces Chinese households to maintain high savings rates.[5]

Moreover, major frictions and capital market imperfections in the Chinese financial markets are also leading to high savings rates. Exceedingly low standards with regard to property rights protection, including a lack of loan contract enforceability and inadequate control of corruption, prevent average Chinese households from accessing credit.[6] Most firms, particularly small and self-owned ones, are also credit constrained and are therefore forced to save in order to finance their investment projects.[7]

Neoclassical theory does not seem to offer much in our quest for the empirical relationship between savings and growth, if only because, as mentioned earlier, savings are exogenous in Solow's contribution. Can endogenous growth theory help? It can, particularly with regard to foreign savings in the form of (long-term) foreign investment and its consequential technology diffusion in the host countries.

During the second half of the 1980s, a huge body of literature on endogenous growth emerged. Romer's (1986, 1991) groundbreaking contributions started the ball rolling. From a Latin American perspective, sweeping reforms on trade and financial liberalization made sense with regard to what the endogenous growth insights might offer.

Recall from chapter 10 that trade and financial liberalization involved the lifting of restrictions on FDI that were enacted during the ISI period—roughly between 1960 and 1985. Technology diffusion was facilitated via trade and financial liberalization in the 1990s. In a nutshell, the prediction from an endogenous growth standpoint is that less developed Latin American economies could more easily catch up with the average per capita income in industrialized countries via foreign investment inflows and the total factor productivity enhancements that come with it.

For this to happen, however, foreign investors must be reassured. The entire Latin America was perceived as a high-risk region, and one way of delivering the reassurance foreign investors were asking for in exchange for their investments might have been to offer domestic entrepreneurs' own savings. These savings can be viewed as a tangible and credible commitment to the costly adoption of superior technologies necessary for foreign investors' returns to be attractive and more secure. Another way was to enact institutional/legal reforms that reduced uncertainty.[8]

Hence, offering a stable macroeconomic environment was a necessary but not a sufficient condition to encourage foreign investors to step in. The insight comes from basic principal agent microeconomic principles: By offering their own savings, local entrepreneurs were assuring foreign investors that high levels of local effort would be put in into their investment projects.[9]

This might imply intraregional income inequality and divergence, however. The poorest Latin American countries were twice cursed in the 1990s: first because they were poor and therefore could not easily implement needed (costly) reforms, and second because entrepreneurial local investors did not have enough savings (or self-owned capital) to reassure risk-averse foreign investors that local effort would be made in technology adoption in order for investment returns to be high.

This explanation sheds light on the current per capita income gap of three to one between Chile and Guatemala, for example (at PPP, 2014 constant dollars). We also know from previous chapters that Chile, an early reformer, is the only country in Latin America that grew steadily from 1985 until 1997—that is, throughout most of the region's reform period. This leads to our next question: Does initial per capita income level matter?

12.2.2 Initial Per Capita Income Level

One key prediction of the Solow paradigm is *conditional convergence*. Simply stated, economies starting farther below their steady state per capita income level experience relatively faster transitional growth when compared to those that start off at a higher level, conditional on all other variables (e.g., savings rates, production functions, rate of technological progress, depreciation, population growth rates, among others) being equal. Because poor economies grow faster because of diminishing returns to per capita capital, the per capita income gap between poor and rich economies will tend to disappear in the long run. This prediction should hold true empirically, after controlling for myriad variables other than initial income.

Solow's convergence prediction has been tested in cross-country studies quite extensively. Most of these studies focus on European countries, and most lend support to the convergence prediction.[10]

Some authors, however, claim that the convergence empirical investigations miss key aspects. For example, Quah (1996c) argues that two mechanisms of growth should be distinguished: (1) pushing forward a country's technological and resource frontier and (2) catching up with richer economies.

In general, traditional empirical analyses using cross-country regressions do not address questions about how countries interact and what those interactions deliver over time, including countries' terms of trade, persistent disadvantages, and poverty.

The literature on convergence has evolved, however, from cross-country to time series analysis.[11] The latter line of empirical investigations has shed light on the notion of *club convergence*—that is, the finding that convergence applies to groups (clubs) of countries rather than being a global phenomenon. An extension of this approach suggests that low-income countries might catch up as long as shocks affecting one country relative to the rest of the countries in the region are temporary. From this literature, evidence of club convergence has been found using time series analysis for a sample of twenty-nine countries between 1900 and 2001.[12] These studies suggest that club convergence is stronger for OECD and European countries and weaker for Latin American nations.

Some studies on club convergence for Latin American economies alone exist.[13] The empirical work carried out thus far suggests some convergence among countries belonging to free trade agreement (FTA) groups like the Latin American Integration Association (LAIA), the Central American Common Market (CACM), and other trade blocs studied in chapter 10. To a lesser extent, club convergence because of geographical proximity seems relevant. Specifically, there appears to be some evidence on club convergence among central countries (Colombia, Costa Rica, Ecuador, El Salvador, Guatemala, Honduras, Mexico, Nicaragua, and Venezuela) and among southern nations (Argentina, Bolivia, Brazil, Chile, Paraguay, Peru, and Uruguay).

By and large, however, there is stronger evidence for club convergence resulting from regional trade integration than for club convergence purely from geographical proximity. For example, a recent study finds convergence across the Americas.[14] Geographically distant countries such as Chile, Costa Rica, and Trinidad and Tobago seem to be converging with per capita income levels in the United States. This trio of countries, two Latin American and one Caribbean, have signed bilateral trade and/or foreign investment agreements with the United States, which might have facilitated North-South technology diffusion.

12.3 Structural Factors

It is widely recognized that structural factors are important for growth and development. For example, population size might matter. All Latin American countries are small in the world stage, with the exceptions of Brazil and possibly Mexico. Geography might be relevant too. As we noted in chapter 1, a vast portion of Latin America's land is close to the equator, which raises several questions: Is tropical weather important? What about other potential geographical suspects, such as proximity to seaports? Many regions in Latin America are far away from world markets, and two countries (Bolivia and Paraguay) are landlocked, lacking any sea access within their territories. Yet another question relates to whether Latin America can be labeled as a resource curse region. All Latin American countries—with the recent exception of Mexico—are highly dependent on natural resources. This section analyzes these three potential sources of underdevelopment—country size, geography, and natural resource abundance—in depth.

12.3.1 Country Size

Many authors have attempted to link *population size* (henceforth *country size*) and economic prosperity.[15] This is important for policy, because it can guide development strategies. For example, it has been argued that relative to the rest of the region, Brazil and Mexico—Latin America's largest economies—had higher than average growth rates under the ISI strategy.[16]

Some stylized facts worldwide are intriguing, however. Heavily populated countries are not necessarily the richest. Among the five most populated countries in the world (China, India, United States, Indonesia, and Brazil), only the United States is considered a high per capita income country. This pattern is similar when considering the ten most populated countries.

At the other end of the spectrum, the two richest countries in the world in terms of per capita GDP at PPP in 2013 are Qatar (US$98,814) and Luxembourg (US$78,670), with roughly two million and half a million inhabitants, respectively. It thus seems that population size is unimportant in that it is possible to be both small and prosperous.

Nonetheless, some studies have argued in favor of size as a contributing factor to economic development. With some exceptions, scale economies are at the root of this argument.[17] In larger economies, the argument goes, the scope for taking advantage of large-scale production for the domestic market is wider. Scale in the provision of public goods is also important. Per capita costs for public security and regulation of the financial system, for example, are considerably lower for larger countries, because these kinds of goods and services have an important fixed-cost component. Some studies carried out using microdata estimate productivity across firms and industries and prove the existence of important scale effects. The evidence is weaker for aggregated data, however.[18]

Rose (2006) used a panel data estimation to examine whether country size, proxied by total population, is linked to some economic or social phenomena, including per capita income. The study concludes that the only robust correlation is that smaller countries are more open to international trade. In contrast, real per capita income, human development measures (inclusive of health and education), institutions, financial depth, and social heterogeneity indices appear not to be associated with size.[19]

Larger economies are in a better position to insure themselves against economic shocks, however; if shocks to a country's different regions are uncorrelated, the economy as a whole is able to diversify risk. Simply stated, when a specific region is in crisis, transfers from other regions can help. This is not the case in small economies, which are more vulnerable to cyclical fluctuations and have limited scope for transfers across regions.

The literature with regard to the effect of trade and country size on economic development (as proxied by income per capita) is extensive, but only a few contributions analyze both effects simultaneously. Alesina and Spolaore (1997) and Alesina, Spolaore, and Wacziarg (2005) studied the relationship between country size and growth. The authors developed a model in which growth is larger when country size and degree of openness are larger. This model suggests that the country size effect becomes lower as the degree of openness increases, which provides an important lesson for small and medium-sized Latin American countries: Incentives are set so as to promote economic growth through trade liberalization at multilateral, unilateral, and regional levels. The evidence shows that this effect is large and statistically significant. (Refer back to chapter 10.)

Alesina, Spolaore, and Wacziarg (2005) suggested two important insights from a Latin American standpoint. First, in an increasingly globalized world in which trade barriers are being dismantled, size advantages are less important. Because it is difficult (and costly) to reconcile heterogeneity in larger and more diverse countries, their framework predicts an increase in the number of countries and a reduction in the average size of countries. Second, the spread of democratic regimes and the downfall of dictatorships has the same effect, because dictators are less sensitive to heterogeneous preferences.

Some stylized facts lend support to the previously mentioned findings, particularly with regard to the substantial increase in the number of countries, especially since 1990. In the last fifty years, the number of independent countries has risen from seventy-six in 1946 to 195 in 2014. A good fraction potentially can be explained by the dismemberment of the USSR and former Yugoslavia. The economic argument is that secession costs have declined, so it is natural to expect more countries to break apart.

Latin America, however, has not experienced dismemberment since the end of World War II. In fact, the number of countries today is the same as half a century ago. On the other hand, stylized facts suggest that the relatively small-sized countries in the region are not at a disadvantage with regard to growth and development prospects in an increasingly globalized twenty-first-century world economy.

12.3.2 Geography

Geography is a largely exogenous determinant of competitiveness and growth. This variable includes weather, exposure to natural disasters, landlockedness, distance to the equator, and ease of access to main world trade centers.

Tropical zones, for example, have lower agricultural productivity and face a variety of diseases, many of which are not fully controlled yet. One of the most severe diseases is malaria, particularly among children. Apart from potential changes in fertility, the direct economic costs of malaria in terms of per capita income can be high. According to Sachs and Warner (1997), countries with tropical climates have lower annual per capita GDP growth by some 0.8 percentage points. In Latin America, malaria is still prevalent in twenty-one countries, but the region represents only 0.1 percent of deaths worldwide, according to WHO's World Malaria Report 2013.

However, geography matters in regions such as Central America and the Caribbean, which are more likely to be hit by natural disasters such as earthquakes, tsunamis, and hurricanes, all of which generate important one-off output losses that might take decades to recoup. Unfortunately, insurance against aggregate shocks is a pending task, for developing countries in general and for Latin America in particular.[20]

Seaport access also correlates with output growth via trade. For example, Sachs and Warner (1997) find that being landlocked implies a lower annual real per capita GDP growth of around 0.6 percentage points. Gallup, Sachs, and Mellinger (1999) show that landlocked countries grow 1 percent less on average than those with access to the sea. Indeed, it appears that the main reason lies in the transport costs faced by these countries, which make international trade more difficult and costly. Remember that we underscored the importance of landlocked regions within countries in Latin America in chapter 2. Within-country income inequality might be explained by these factors, but better infrastructure should lower those costs and thereby ensure that the benefits from trade deliver comparably high growth rates within regions and countries.

On a bright note, a broader view shows that transport and communication costs have declined dramatically, as figure 12.4 shows. New technologies have made these costs progressively lower over time. Yet evidence suggests that developing nations are still at a disadvantage. Transport costs, particularly from the hinterlands to seashores, are still very high. The implication for policy is that nascent democracies in Latin America must invest more in infrastructure. China has been playing an important role in recent years, particularly with regard to foreign investment in routes and railroads in Brazil, Venezuela, and along the Pacific coastline.

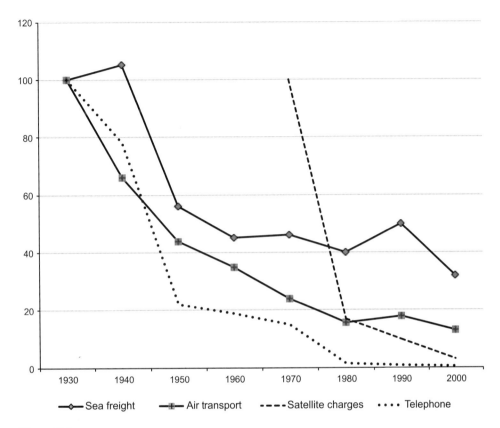

Figure 12.4
Transport and communications costs, 1930–2000 (1930 = 100).
Source: Busse 2003.

12.3.3 Natural Resource Abundance

Latin America is richly endowed with natural resources. As shown in figure 12.5, most countries in the region are highly dependent on primary commodity exports. Yet the relationship between resource abundance and economic growth is controversial. Lack of resources is not a serious impediment to economic development, as the experience of Asian countries shows. On the contrary, natural resource abundance could have a positive impact on economic development, as it seems to be the case in the United States, Australia, New Zealand, and Norway, among others. Although this might hold true historically, many empirical studies using more recent data have found a negative relationship between natural resource abundance and growth. For example, Sachs and Warner (2001) deliver empirical evidence in support of such negative correlation. Two prime examples of major

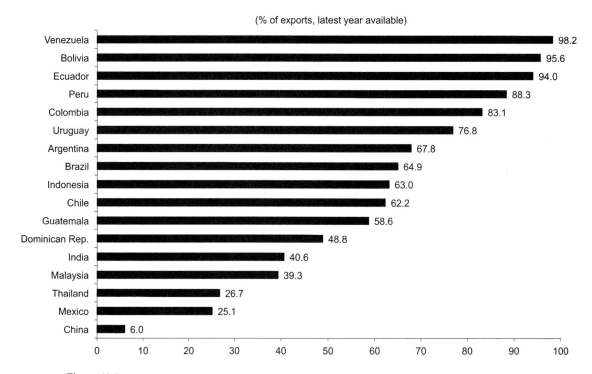

Figure 12.5
Degree of exposure to primary commodities.
Source: Authors' own construction from World Trade Organization (www.wto.org) and Central Bank of Chile (www.bcentral.cl) databases.

development difficulties can be found in the oil-rich countries of Nigeria in Africa and Venezuela in Latin America.

Five arguments attempt to explain the pervasiveness of the concept of "resource curse" economies. First, natural resource abundance tends to cause currency appreciations, which inhibit development of the manufacturing sector. This is the well-known *Dutch disease* phenomenon.[21] Second, natural resource abundance encourages rent-seeking behavior. Specifically, natural resource endowments seem to be positive and statistically significant predictors of high incidence of corruption.[22] Third, natural resource sectors are exposed to large price volatility in international commodity markets. In the absence of risk-spreading mechanisms, commodity price instability can lead to higher and more prolonged business cycle fluctuations.[23] Fourth, natural resources may produce exchange rate volatility, particularly with regard to steep appreciations followed by depreciations, which may cause political and social unrest when accompanied by stagnation and/or a decline in real wages. Finally, it has been argued that natural resources might lower the demand for capital, which reduces economic growth[24].

Real exchange rate volatility in developing countries is estimated to be three times higher than that in developed countries.[25] One reason for this is the greater diversification of exports among the latter countries. Hence, if natural resource endowments are conducive to export-led growth with diversification in domestic production and consequent channeling of export revenues into other sectors and industry, then natural resource endowments may have a positive impact on economic development, as proxied by per capita income growth.

Yet there are very few examples of countries that have fully developed solely on the basis of natural resources but none in Latin America, though Chile—with almost two-thirds of its exports based on natural resources—is the country with the highest per capita income in the region. However, Chile developed strong fiscal institutions to deal with the effects of commodity price volatility, including a structural fiscal rule and a sovereign wealth fund, as we explained in chapter 7.[26]

12.4 Economic Policies and Institutions

As any textbook on the subject suggests, economic development is a multifaceted effort.[27] Thus, while the structural factors underscored in the previous section might play a role, economic and social policies are key. This section analyzes the roles of trade openness, education, fiscal policy, financial development, research and development (R&D), and innovation from a Latin American vantage point.

12.4.1 Trade Openness

Openness contributes to growth through several channels. As we have long known from the Ricardian model of trade (reviewed in chapter 10), we should expect a more efficient allocation of resources as a country specializes in the production and export of goods and services in which the country enjoys comparative advantage. Openness also widens the scope for countries to access new technologies, and, more generally, it allows for less developed countries to more easily benefit from positive R&D spillovers. Moreover, with the advent of external competition, trade openness forces domestic producers to become more efficient, which implies larger productivity gains when compared to countries in which protectionist policies prevail.

A vast body of literature discusses the empirical relationship between trade and economic growth. Openness is measured in terms of the average tariff rate, tariff dispersion, and nontariff trade barriers, as well as in exports and trade volume (as percentages of GDP). A strong positive relationship between growth and openness remains robust and statistically significant.[28]

Are open economies more prone to sudden capital inflow fluctuations?[29] This is a relevant question for the Latin American case, because the entire region is known to have experienced lending booms followed by sudden capital inflow downturns.[30] The trade-offs involved are well-understood. On the one hand, trade and financial openness increase the probability of a country suffering a sudden stop as it increases its exposure to external shocks. On the other hand, openness also makes a country increasingly able to adjust to cutoffs of international capital inflows, because it has a more efficient trade sector and can therefore more easily draw from foreign currency reserves in order to cope with externally generated crises.

The general consensus is that less open economies are more prone to suffering from sudden stops in capital inflows. The effect of trade openness on the probability of a sudden stop is estimated to be statistically significant and large and one of the few significant predictors of sudden stops, the other being current account deficits. As we noted in chapter 4, only the twentieth-century crises that originated in industrialized countries—when Latin America was less open to trade—had a significant impact on growth, particularly during the 1930s and 1980s. This is not the case for twenty-first-century—considerably more open—Latin America.

The potential causal effect of trade openness on growth has also been empirically tested for a larger sample of countries. The general view from existing studies is that, relative to high-income economies, the effect of openness on growth is larger for low-income countries. It has also been suggested that the extent to which openness can spur growth depends on the existence of complementary reforms, including flexible labor markets, public infrastructure provision, and the ease of opening and closing new enterprises.

Timing also seems to matter. Relative to before the 1950s, countries that liberalized trade during the 1950–1998 period seemed to have grown faster. In Latin America, Chile is often cited as an early trade liberalizer, which can in turn explain why Chile, relative to other Latin American regions, was the only country that grew quickly during the 1985–1997 period.[31]

Perhaps more importantly for policy, it appears that the potential positive effects of trade openness on growth are larger in relatively low-income countries.[32] Recent studies also suggest that complementary reforms in support of trade openness are important.[33] Timing is also relevant here. When we compare countries in which the prevalence of trade openness was at the center stage of trade policy from 1950 to 1998 to those in which it was not, the increase in annual growth rate in the former was 2 percentage points. In contrast, the increase in the latter was 1.5 percentage points.[34] Half a percentage point can indeed make a huge difference

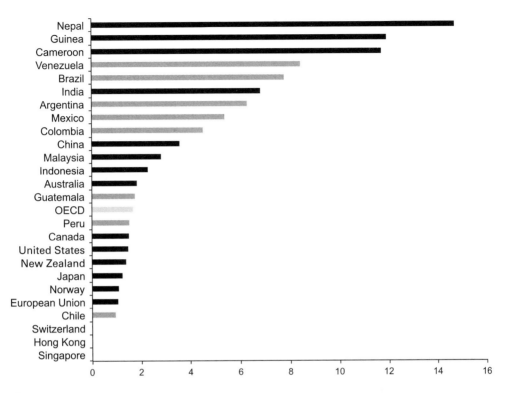

Figure 12.6
Import tariff rate applied, weighted mean, all products (2012 or latest year available, %).
Source: Authors' own construction from World Bank database (www.worldbank.org).

in the long run, which might in turn shed further light on the growth differentials between Asia and Latin America over the past fifty years.

Trade openness in Latin America has increased significantly over the last two decades (see chapter 10), yet it is still well below OECD levels. Figure 12.6 shows that the mean tariff rate in almost all countries in Latin America, except for Chile and Peru, is above the OECD average. If trade openness is measured as total trade as a share of GDP (shown in figure 12.7), then Central American countries, Paraguay, Bolivia, Chile, and Mexico are the most open economies in Latin America. Brazil and Argentina are the least open, regardless of whether openness is proxied by trade shares or by average import tariffs.

Although the degree of trade liberalization might explain some stylized facts and high growth spells in Latin America, there are other complementary policies to consider that took place in parallel with trade liberalization during the two last decades of the twentieth century.

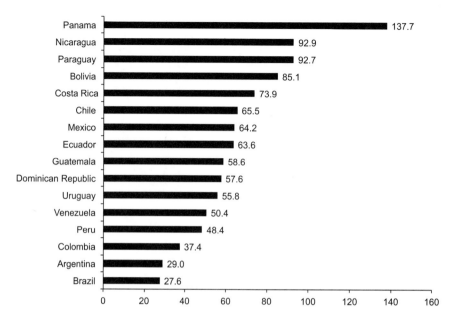

Figure 12.7
Sum of exports and imports of goods and services measured as % of GDP.
Source: Authors' own construction from World Bank database (www.worldbank.org).

12.4.2 Terms of Trade

The price of a country's exports relative to its imports—the *terms of trade*—is an important determinant of economic growth, especially among primary commodity exporters. Although this is intuitive, intuition alone is not enough. The terms of trade and growth relationship has been analyzed empirically in dozens of studies. For example, Barro and Sala-i-Martin (1995) included changes in the terms of trade in their growth regressions. The authors suggest that terms of trade have a positive and significant impact on growth. Easterly et al. (1993) studied the importance of shocks for explaining the lack of persistence of growth across countries and concluded that episodes of high growth are often interrupted by several kinds of shocks, particularly terms of trade shocks. More recently, Bravo-Ortega and De Gregorio (2006) presented further evidence of the positive and robust statistical relationship between terms of trade and economic growth.

Recall that Latin America as a region is highly dependent on commodity exports. Although the evolution in the terms of trade during the twenty-first century does not support the pessimistic Prebisch-Singer view—as we explained in chapter 3—terms of trade volatility in Latin America is significantly larger (on average) than in more advanced economies. The stylized facts in figure 12.8 lend support to this view.

Growth and Development in Latin America

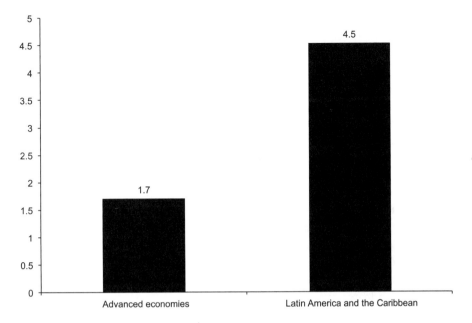

Figure 12.8
Standard deviation of annual % change of terms of trade of goods and services over the period 1983–2013.
Source: Authors' own elaboration based on IMF database (www.imf.org).

Several Latin American countries have adopted policies aimed at decreasing the potential negative effects of terms of trade volatility on their economies, especially via fiscal policy, as we discussed at length in chapter 7. These policies include forward-looking fiscal rules and the implementation of sovereign wealth funds, which can help cushion a country's economy from terms of trade fluctuations.

12.4.3 Education

There is both theoretical and (some) empirical support for a positive relationship between the level of human capital (focusing just on education) and economic growth. Early analyses such as Lucas 1988 account for the role of human capital on growth from a theoretical standpoint. From then on, the role of education in economic growth has been subject to many empirical investigations. Different measures of human capital have been used, and relevant questions arise as to whether it is the quality or the quantity of education that matters and through which mechanisms can human capital affect growth.

Barro and Lee (2013), for example, built an educational database in a sample of countries that allows us to assess the role, if any, of education on economic growth, along with other variables of interest, such as export competitiveness, fertility, income inequality, democracy, institutions, and political freedom. The authors suggest that improved levels of education—as proxied by educational attainment—exert a positive influence on economic growth, competitiveness, democracy, institutions, and income inequality.

Although educational attainment may seem important, other studies have made further inquiries into whether an increased number of years of education is accompanied by educational quality enhancements.[35] Not surprisingly, these studies do show that the quality of education—as proxied by students' performance in international exams—is important for economic growth. It has also been reported that the positive effects of both quality and quantity of education on growth are greater in open economies.

Evidence linking investments in education and economic growth is not as robust as it might seem, however. In a study using US data, Aghion, Boustan et al. (2009) point to several problems when trying to establish the link explicitly. On the one hand, there is a reverse causality issue that has not been dealt with appropriately; richer and faster-growing countries find it easier to increase their educational spending, and hence growth might prompt education increases and not the other way around.

On the other hand, lack of data has compelled numerous researchers to use proxies such as number of years in school—or average school attainment. However, schooling is not the same as education, as Pritchett (2013) has stressed. Moreover, there is a tendency for researchers to neglect omitted variables, which are useful for explaining in detail how education contributes to growth. Is the innovation link more important, because it favors investment in higher education? Or is it better to focus on primary and secondary education? Sapir et al. (2003) present some evidence on the former, whereas Krueger and Lindahl (2011) and Keller (2006) present some evidence on the latter.

In Aghion, Boustan et al. 2009, we also find an assessment of the relative importance of educational spending in a multistate endogenous growth model with two types of education: A "high-brow" education fostering technological innovation and a "low-brow" education increasing the ability to imitate technologies. Educational investment, unlike in previous studies, is measured by spending in dollars per person. The study results support the view that some investments in education have a positive effect on growth. Investment in secondary or tertiary education, for example, appears to be important for high-income countries or countries that are close to the technological frontier. This result could be interpreted as an incentive for less developed regions' residents to acquire more education, because highly educated individuals can potentially migrate to more developed regions and get higher rewards from education. However, we do not believe that migration flows from Latin America to countries close to the technological frontier can be explained this way. If anything, it might explain relatively large migration flows from countries like India to the United States, for example.

Nonetheless, assuming that education indeed has an important role in economic growth, one question follows naturally from a Latin American perspective: Do educational differences have a role to play when attempting to explain differences among per capita income across countries—say, between the Latin American region and the rest of the world? This question was addressed straightforwardly by Castelló and Doménech (2002), who analyzed the impact of human capital inequality on economic growth.

Castelló and Domenech constructed indicators of human capital inequality for a large sample of countries between 1960 and 1990. According to their estimates, the average human capital Gini coefficient for Latin America is 0.447—lower than South Asia (0.846), Middle East and North Africa (0.775), and sub-Saharan Africa (0.774) and slightly lower than East Asia and Pacific (0.484), but greater than OECD and high-income countries (0.251) and Eastern Europe (0.182). The authors then estimated the impact of human capital inequality on economic growth and found a negative relationship. This effect is probably linked to a negative correlation between initial human capital inequality and physical capital accumulation.

Latin American countries have a serious problem with regard to education. Although many countries have emphasized educational policies aiming at greater coverage, educational quality in these countries is far below the standards observed in other economies. This difference is apparent not only when we compare Latin American economies with more developed countries, but also when we compare against other emerging market economies. Table 12.1 shows that Latin American countries' performance on international tests is at the bottom of the table—that is, the worst performers in comparison with other countries.

This result is partly due to low levels of public spending in education. When we examine the effort countries put into improving their educational standards, Latin American countries show relatively little effort (both for quantity and quality). There is a great deal of dispersion within the region, however. Looking at public spending on education, the Latin American and Caribbean average is well below the eurozone level as a share of GDP (see figure 12.9).

But again, large public spending in education does not necessarily correlate with high-quality education, as figure 12.10 suggests. All of Latin America appears as a low-quality region—the bottom of the class—with regard to education. This might be explained not only by low public educational spending, but also by persistent income inequalities and culture.

Consequently, raising the quality of education is a huge challenge for the region. According to Pritchett (2013), the dominant approach to improving school

Table 12.1
PISA scores per test for selected countries, 2012

Country	Mathematics	Reading	Science
Shanghai/China	613	570	580
Singapore	573	542	551
Korea	554	536	538
Japan	536	538	547
Switzerland	531	509	515
Estonia	521	516	541
Finland	519	524	545
Canada	518	523	525
Germany	514	508	524
France	495	505	499
United States	481	498	497
Turkey	448	475	463
Chile	423	441	445
Mexico	413	424	415
Uruguay	409	411	416
Brazil	391	410	405
Argentina	388	396	406
Tunisia	388	404	398
Colombia	376	403	399
Indonesia	375	396	382
Peru	368	384	373

Source: PISA 2012 results, OECD (www.oecd.org/pisa/keyfindings/pisa-2012-results.htm).

quality in developing countries has been to expand known inputs, leading to higher costs per student, but with little impact on learning outcomes.

Randomized control evaluations show that organizational and systemic changes that alter the scope of action, incentives, and accountability of public servants in education are, by and large, more cost-effective for producing higher learning than increasing inputs.[36] In the case of Latin America, the only randomized evaluation on education to date suggests that antipoverty campaigns such as the *Progresa/Oportunidades/Prospera* program in Mexico do have some impact on secondary education.[37]

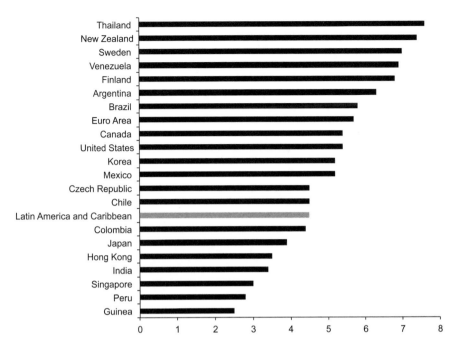

Figure 12.9
Public spending on education, selected countries, 2013 or latest year available (% of GDP).
Source: Authors' own construction from World Bank database (www.worldbank.org).

12.4.4 Fiscal Policy

Fiscal policy is another factor that plays a key role in growth and development. After Barro's 1997 work, several studies documented a negative relationship between government consumption as a share of GDP and economic growth. This result is attributed to government consumption, as proxied by outlays that do not enhance productivity.[38]

Barro's empirical result is an "average effect" for a large sample of countries. As such, it hides different degrees of efficiency in the use of state resources. Figure 12.11 shows, for example, that some countries in Latin America such as Chile have solid performance, whereas others, such as Argentina and Venezuela, do not. Overall, there is a strong perception of waste with regard to government spending in the region as a whole.

On the revenue side, Latin America has higher average tax rates compared to other emerging market regions—although, once more, there is considerable within-region heterogeneity, as shown in figure 12.12. Although countries such as Chile, Honduras, Guatemala, and Peru had a relatively low total tax rate in, for example, the year 2012, Argentina, Colombia, and Brazil in that same year were

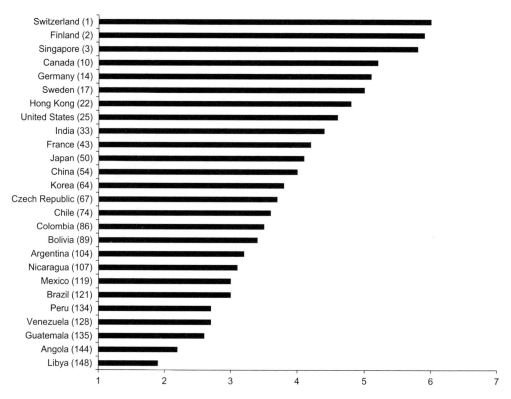

Figure 12.10
Quality of educational system, rankings among 148 countries, 2012–2013 weighted average. (How well does the educational system in your country meet the needs of a competitive economy? 1 = not well at all; 7 = extremely well.)
Source: World Economic Forum 2013.

at the opposite end of the spectrum. This heterogeneity should be factored in when attempting to explain differences in economic growth performance between Latin America and other regions.

In particular, a vast majority of empirical studies suggest that higher corporate taxes reduce economic growth. Table 12.2 provides a list of such studies and their results. Note from the table that all studies after 2000 show a significant negative effect. Indeed, in an increasingly globalized world, it is hard to retain relatively high corporate taxation without considering capital mobility—that is, the fact that companies can move their investments offshore. This limits the extent to which Latin American countries can finance much-needed investments in human capital (health and education) from corporate tax revenues.

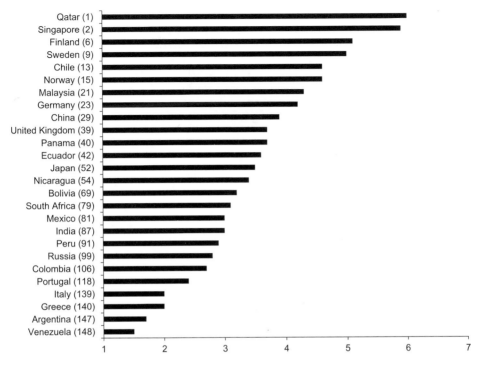

Figure 12.11
Efficiency of public spending, rankings among 148 countries, 2012–2013 weighted average. (In your country, how efficiently does the government spend public revenue? 1 = extremely inefficient; 7 = extremely efficient at providing goods and services.)
Source: World Economic Forum 2013.

12.4.5 Financial Development

Financial development has been extensively analyzed as a relevant factor for growth, because it allows for better risk management and more efficient allocation of capital. It also facilitates human and physical capital accumulation. However, financial crises cause huge losses in terms of output and employment. Since the pioneering work of King and Levine (1993), a positive and significant relationship between financial development and per capita output growth has been established. Subsequent work has assessed the influence of financial development on economic growth. Loayza and Rancière (2006), for example, found a positive relationship between financial intermediation and output growth in the long run, which could coexist with a negative relationship in the short run for financially fragile countries.

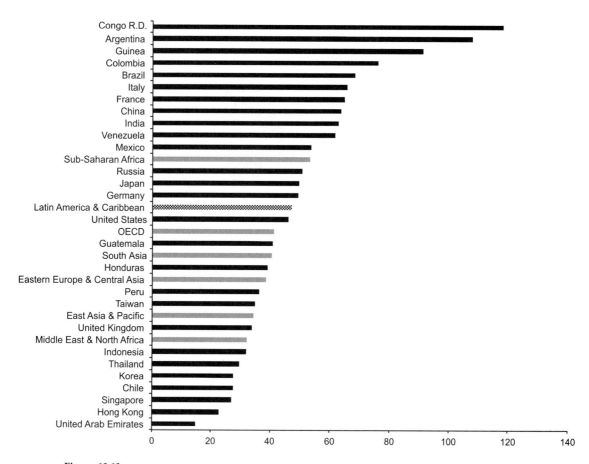

Figure 12.12
Total tax rate, 2012 (corporate tax + labor taxes and contributions + other taxes as % of profits).
Source: World Economic Forum 2013.

The important issue of reverse causality should be brought to light, however: Does financial development cause growth, or is it the other way around? Calderón and Liu (2003) identify causal effects and concluded that financial liberalization promotes growth in all kinds of countries, but that the effect is felt more strongly in developing countries. The channels through which this effect operates include overall productivity, faster capital accumulation, and technological change.

According to Lora (2012), financial liberalization has been one of the areas in which the most significant progress in structural reforms in Latin America has been made since the mid-1980s. The author provides an index ranging between 0

Table 12.2
Empirical research on the effects of corporate taxes on economic growth in different countries and regions

Reference	Effect
Mertens and Ravn 2013	Negative
Hayo and Uhl 2013	Negative
Ferede and Dahlby 2012	Negative
Perotti 2012	Negative
Gemmell, Kneller, and Sanz 2011	Negative
Arnold et al. 2011	Negative
Barro and Redlick 2011	Negative
Widmalm 2011	Negative
Conefrey and Fitz 2011	Negative
Cerda and Larraín 2010	Negative
Romer and Romer 2010	Negative
Alesina and Ardagna 2010	Negative
IMF 2010	Negative
Favero and Giavazzi 2010	Negative
Reed 2008	Negative
Arnold 2008	Negative
Cerda and Larraín 2005	Negative
Lee and Gordon 2005	Negative
Holcombe and Lacombe 2004	Negative
Tomljanovich 2004	Negative
Blanchard and Perotti 2002	Negative
Folster and Henrekson 2001	Negative
Bleaney, Gemmell, and Kneller 2001	Negative
Carroll et al. 2001	Negative
Chernick 1997	Negative
Mendoza, Milesi-Ferretti, and Asea 1997	None
Miller and Russek 1997	Negative
Engen and Skinner 1996	Negative
Easterly and Rebelo 1993	None
Helms 1985	Negative
Katz, Mahler, and Franz 1983	None

Source: Authors' conclusions based on peer-reviewed articles.

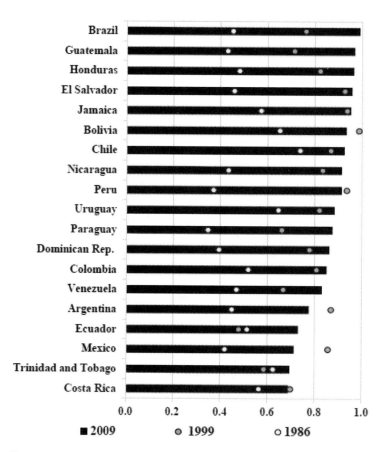

Figure 12.13
Index of financial reform, 1986, 1999, and 2009.
Source: Lora 2012.

and 1, where 1 shows that the reform potential was fully exploited. As shown in figure 12.13, there have been significant increases in that index in most Latin American countries since 1986.

12.4.6 Inflation

Latin America has a well-known record of high inflation, and indeed, inflation appears to be yet another variable affecting growth. Barro (1997), for example, concluded that inflation has a negative effect on growth, but only as far as it crosses over a threshold of 15 percent. Burdekin et al. (2004) lowered the threshold; their analysis shows the potential negative impact to be low for developing countries (3 percent) compared to developed nations (8 percent).[39] One of the main channels through which inflation may affect growth is market frictions.

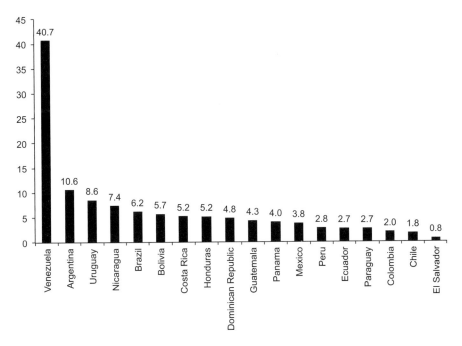

Figure 12.14
Inflation, 2013 (average consumer prices, annual % change).
Source: Authors' own construction from IMF database (www.imf.org).

Despite the fact that Latin America has been typically classified as a high-inflation region, including five cases of hyperinflation, significant improvements have been observed over the past two decades. Specifically, there has been a generalized and significant decline in inflation for the entire region (see chapter 8). This in turn has led to a more stable macroeconomic environment. As shown in figure 12.14, only Argentina and Venezuela had double-digit inflation rates in 2013.

Central bank independence is key, as we noted in chapter 8. Indeed, high inflation in Argentina and Venezuela can be partially attributed to their lack of central bank independence.

12.4.7 Institutions

The quality of institutions—as noted in Acemoglu, Johnson, and Robinson's (2001) seminal contribution, is a crucial factor for explaining differences in economic performance.[40] Dollar and Kraay (2003) studied the importance of the rule of law and political rights for a large sample of countries and concluded that the rule of law has a more significant effect on growth than political rights. However, good democratic political systems allow for voting populations to control administrative procedures, which reduces corruption and has a strong effect on competitiveness and growth (Adserà, Boix, and Payne 2003).

Follow-up empirical work has been rich and somewhat conclusive. Rodrik, Subramanian, and Trebbi (2004) estimated the contribution of institutional quality, geography, and trade on income levels around the world. The authors concluded that institutions have a much greater impact than geography or trade.

Acemoglu, Johnson, and Robinson (2005) also showed that institutions play a crucial role in explaining economic development. They used two natural experiments (Korea's division in 1945 and colonization processes carried out by European countries) in which similar regions received different institutional endowments as evidence of their hypothesis. Institutions appear to condition the economic behavior of individuals and enterprises, and through this channel, institutions prove to be relevant for economic development.

Corruption is relevant for economic growth and development in its own right, for it generates a series of distortions ranging from uncertainty by private sector investors to tax evasion. Empirical evidence has shown a negative and significant correlation between corruption and growth, as in Dreher and Herzfeld 2005 and Gyimah-Brempong and Muñoz de Camacho 2006. In the latter study, the authors estimate that a 10 percent decrease in corruption (measured on the Transparency International (TI) corruption index) increases the income growth rate by 2.6 percent annually in Latin American countries, whereas this magnitude is 1.7 percent in Asian and OECD countries and 2.8 percent in African countries. From a distributional standpoint, the authors estimate that a decline of one standard deviation in corruption reduces the Gini coefficient by 0.33 points in Latin America (the greatest magnitude in the world), by 0.05 in OECD countries, 0.14 in Asia, and 0.25 in Africa.

Overall, and from a Latin American perspective, the evidence is quite conclusive with regard to the positive influence of institutional quality on economic growth when corruption is explicitly introduced into the picture. Thus, efforts made to raise institutional quality levels to worldwide benchmarks like those of Finland, Denmark, Singapore, and Switzerland are a logical step toward economic prosperity. As shown in table 12.3, Chile has similar levels of institutional quality compared to the OECD average, but most other Latin American countries do not.

Political institutions, or the "rules of the game," arguably have an impact in public policy and development as well. Spiller and Tommasi (2003), for example, noted that public policies can be classified according to three dimensions: quality, stability, and coherence. *Quality* captures the social costs associated with the implementation of policy objectives, *stability* refers to the continuity of these policies over time, and *coherence* relates to how consistent and coordinated these

Table 12.3
Dimensions of governance, 2012 (percentile rank, 0–100)

	Voice and accountability	Rule of law	Political stability	Government effectiveness	Regulatory quality	Control of corruption
Argentina	56.9	29.4	48.3	45.5	19.1	38.8
Brazil	60.7	45.8	47.9	50.2	54.6	56.5
Chile	80.1	88.2	59.2	86.6	93.3	93.8
Colombia	45.5	43.6	8.1	62.9	63.6	41.6
Mexico	55	36	24.2	63.2	67	42.6
Peru	57.1	32.7	19.9	48.8	67.9	52.9
Venezuela	22.3	3.3	17.5	12.9	4.8	6.7
Latin America	60.6	51.2	55.3	57.9	55.8	57
OECD	87	87.1	75.4	87.3	87.1	84.9

Source: Authors' own construction from World Bank, Worldwide Governance Indicators 2012 (info.worldbank.org/governance/wgi/index.aspx).

policies are. The authors argued that Argentina's public policies could be considered low quality, unstable, and incoherent. However, we think that both the concept of "political institutions" and the little empirical evidence thus far call for further research to assert the role that the type of institutions mentioned here might have on Latin America as a whole.

12.5 Productivity and Innovation

The main reason behind disappointing rates of economic expansion in Latin American countries is total factor productivity (TFP) growth, which has been negative on average since the 1980s, as shown in figure 12.15. One essential ingredient of productivity is innovation. As Schumpeter pointed out many decades ago, innovation is a crucial element in the development process, and it is tightly linked to R&D investments. The literature is clear in highlighting that more than half of the differences in the level and growth of GDP per capita are explained by differences in TFP and that technological change is the main source of growth in the long run. Yet R&D investments from a Latin American perspective are to be understood as investments in imitation and adaptation of new technologies produced in high-income countries.

Indeed, investment in R&D is a crucial variable to increase TFP, as Romer (1990) and many others have demonstrated.[41] R&D investments can potentially generate important positive externalities, which spread the benefits of R&D activities to the

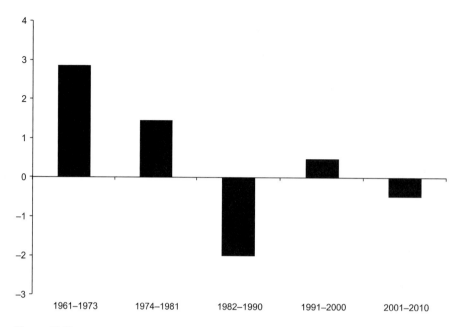

Figure 12.15
Total factor productivity, average annual % change, 1961–2010.
Source: Authors' calculations: data for 1961–1990 from ECLAC database (www.eclac.org); data for 1991–2010 from the Conference Board Total Economy database (www.conference-board.org/data/economydatabase).

rest of the economy. In a similar vein, Jones and Williams (1998) concluded that new knowledge production increases both capital and labor productivity.

From an empirical standpoint, Griffith, Redding, and Van Reenen (2004) showed that investments in R&D are key when trying to explain convergence in growth rates of TFP among OECD countries. The authors reported that the effect of an increase on 1 percent in R&D increases TFP growth between 0.4 percent and 0.9 percent, which translates into an increase in GDP growth of the same magnitude.

Latin American countries show a poor record in R&D investments, even when compared to other emerging economies. For example, figure 12.16 shows the values of R&D expenditure as percentage points of GDP. It is clear from the data that these economies are always below faster-growing countries, and in some cases, such as in Colombia and Bolivia, at levels comparable to those in sub-Saharan countries.

We noted previously that R&D more broadly relates to imitation and adaptation. Thus, even if Latin American countries are not leaders in generating

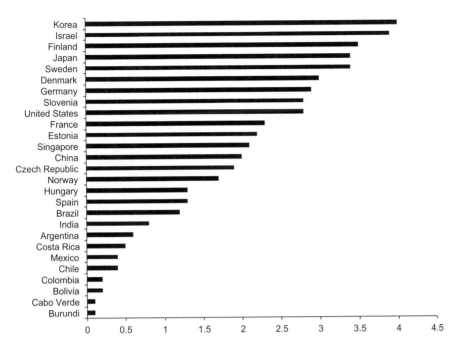

Figure 12.16
Research and development expenditures (% of GDP), latest year available.
Source: Authors' own construction from World Bank, World Development Indicators database (www.worldbank.org).

innovation, they can benefit if and when they are able to absorb available technologies and thus stimulate economic growth.[42] As shown in figure 12.17, countries such as Chile, Costa Rica, and Guatemala have a good record of adapting the latest state-of-the art technologies, whereas others—such as Argentina, Nicaragua, and Venezuela—do not.

The endogenous growth literature distinguishes between major and minor innovations. Undoubtedly, one of the major areas of innovation in the twentieth century has been in information and communication technology (ICT). The extent to which Latin America has benefited from the ICT revolution is difficult to assess empirically. Nonetheless, some stylized facts suggest that ICT penetration is heterogeneous. There are countries such as Argentina and Brazil—two major economies in the region—in which ICT penetration is excellent and comparable to that in Asian countries, whereas others lag far behind, as table 12.4 shows. However, we cannot link ICT and growth from stylized facts alone. To our knowledge, empirical studies on this topic do not exist yet. Overall, what we are reporting here is that Latin America lags behind developed countries in ICT.

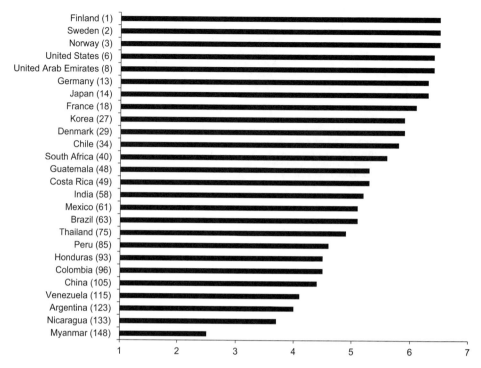

Figure 12.17
Availability of latest technologies, rankings among 148 countries, 2012–2013 weighted average. (In your country, to what extent are the latest technologies available? 1 = not available at all; 7 = widely available.)
Source: World Economic Forum 2013.

However, one conjecture is that ICT penetration might be high in huge urban centers such as Rio de Janeiro and Mexico City, where the IT sector can more easily take advantage of scale economies, and quite low in rural and semirural areas. Another conjecture is that industrial development in some sectors has benefited more from the IT revolution. FDI in those sectors might be important to shed light on the stylized facts, which are hiding important sector dynamics, including information about the (lagging behind) rural sectors and income inequalities.

12.6 Concluding Remarks

This closing chapter has woven together the main ideas about growth and economic development from a Latin American perspective. In our view, growth and development go hand in hand, and for Latin Americans, the words *inclusive growth* do not reflect purely semantic differences within regions and across regions.

Table 12.4
ICT indicators in Latin America and other regions, 2012 or latest year available

	Telephone		Personal computers and Internet				
	Active fixed telephone lines per 100 people	Mobile telephone subscriptions (postpaid and prepaid) per 100 people	% of individuals using the Internet	Fixed broadband Internet subscriptions per 100 people	Mobile broadband Internet subscriptions per 100 people	International Internet bandwidth (kb/s) per Internet user	% of households with a personal computer
Latin America							
Argentina	24.3	151.9	55.8	10.9	20.9	22.0	56.0
Brazil	22.3	125.0	49.8	9.2	33.7	25.1	49.9
Chile	18.8	138.2	61.4	12.4	28.2	40.6	53.7
Colombia	13.2	102.9	49.0	8.2	5.0	12.2	38.4
Mexico	17.4	83.4	38.4	10.5	9.8	16.3	32.2
Peru	11.5	98.0	38.2	4.7	2.9	13.2	29.9
Venezuela	25.6	101.9	44.0	6.7	4.8	10.9	20.2
Asia							
China	20.6	80.8	42.3	12.7	16.9	4.2	40.9
Hong Kong	60.6	229.2	72.8	31.2	83.2	1239.8	80.3
India	2.5	69.9	12.6	1.2	5.0	5.2	10.9
Korea	61.9	109.4	84.1	37.2	105.1	26.0	82.3
Malaysia	15.7	141.3	65.8	8.4	13.4	16.4	66.9

Table 12.4 (continued)

	Telephone		Personal computers and Internet					
	Active fixed telephone lines per 100 people	Mobile telephone subscriptions (postpaid and prepaid) per 100 people	% of individuals using the Internet	Fixed broadband Internet subscriptions per 100 people	Mobile broadband Internet subscriptions per 100 people	International Internet bandwidth (kb/s) per Internet user	% of households with a personal computer
Singapore	37.8	152.1	74.2	25.4	126.1	391.1	87.7
Thailand	9.1	127.3	26.5	8.2	0.1	25.0	26.9
G-7							
Canada	51.9	80.1	86.8	32.5	42.1	101.0	86.6
France	61.9	97.4	83.0	37.5	51.8	84.6	81.0
Germany	61.8	111.6	84.0	33.7	40.8	75.5	87.0
Italy	35.5	159.8	58.0	22.1	52.2	76.2	67.0
Japan	50.8	110.9	79.1	27.7	115.1	33	80.0
United Kingdom	52.6	135.3	87.0	34.0	72.1	188.9	87.0
United States	44.0	95.4	81.0	28.3	88.2	62.3	79.3

Source: World Economic Forum 2013.

To start, we addressed the issue of low savings rates, which require major reforms in existing social security systems. These social security systems not only are inappropriate and poorly funded, but also exclude a vast majority of self-employed and informally employed individuals. With an aging Latin American population, we believe this to be a major challenge for policy makers in the region for two main reasons. First, creating a virtuous circle between savings and growth is key, because Latin Americans cannot rely only on foreign capital, which is constantly fluctuating. Second, and perhaps more importantly, exclusion of the vast majority from social security not only exacerbates income inequalities, at the root of social and political unrest, but also hinders growth and development.

We next addressed structural factors. Again from a Latin American standpoint, we highlighted the potential importance of adverse geography, scarcity of heavily populated countries, and the potentially large number of natural resource–dependent countries. We believe that although these structural factors represent a major challenge for economic growth and development in the region, they do not present insurmountable issues. Adverse geography creates within-region inequalities between the coastline and hinterland regions, for example, but can be mitigated via investments in infrastructure. Country size is unimportant, mostly because the twenty-first century has witnessed a seemingly unstoppable trend of globalization via multilateral, regional, and bilateral trade integration. Finally, while recognizing that most countries might be natural resource dependent, recent trade policies with regard to export diversification are taking hold. We have already experienced the adverse effects of cyclical and volatile output and employment fluctuations, and we view the recent slowdown in growth trends in China as a wake-up call prompting the diversion of export revenues away from commodities into manufacturing, industrial products, and tradable services, which can be competitive under the umbrella of regional trade integration. Overall, widening and deepening trade integration policies are key and within reach.

More important than structural impediments, however, are domestic policies, particularly with regard to trade openness, education, fiscal policy, inflation, financial development, institutions, and political economy. Even if Latin America as a whole has not yet reached OECD numbers, the region has made significant improvements in several areas since the lost decade of the 1980s. Considerable policy improvements have been made in the 1990s to opening trade in nearly all economies in the region, reducing inflation, improving fiscal institutions, and deepening financial liberalization.

More challenging for policy makers are much-needed investments in human capital, particularly in the domain of education. The issue is more difficult when one considers that it is not simply a matter of increasing spending in education but also, and perhaps more importantly, a question of how to enhance educational quality and make high-quality education—particularly secondary and tertiary education—accessible to the vast majority. Even the most benevolent governments in the region's young democracies face difficulties in financing high educational standards.

Important trade-offs are involved. Latin American countries cannot increase significantly corporate and personal income taxation without suffering the consequences of a slowdown in domestic investment, FDI, and capital outflows. On the other hand, other sources of revenue such as VAT might be less difficult to implement, though at the expense of exacerbating income inequalities. This trade-off has increased with the advent of a slowdown in economic growth in recent years and an enlarged and more vocal middle class. If and how Latin American governments will mitigate this trade-off remain open questions. Most likely, just as in other trade-offs confronted before, there will not be a single policy response, because Latin American economies are highly heterogeneous.

Perhaps one area in which institutional strengthening remains a major challenge is corruption. The mere definition of *corruption* is unclear, yet average Latin Americans associate corruption with government interventions, particularly in the exploitation of natural resources and construction. Allowing for open and transparent bidding processes and private sector involvement in key sectors might mitigate the pervasive effects of corruption on economic growth and development. Similarly, construction activities and public services can involve third parties—not just the public sector, but also the private sector, and, more importantly, the public more broadly. Fighting corruption is a more difficult task when private sector interest groups are still lobbying for protection from foreign competition and investors. Antitrust laws and de facto postprivatization regulation waves are still in their infancy. The scope for improvement is important, though context-specific.

Last but not least, and despite the fact that we have covered the ground regarding factor productivity enhancements, in this last chapter we emphasized technology diffusion and adaptation. In our view, R&D in Latin America relates more to adoption of technologies invented in more affluent countries. FDI policies geared toward increasing the intensity of the magnet drawing foreign investors into Latin America should help the region become a natural destination as a technology hub. However, private sector savings might be needed, as we emphasized from the start, if only because foreign investors can more easily be reassured that the necessary effort in technology adoption will be undertaken when local investors' own capital or savings are at stake.

Growth and Development in Latin America

Despite much progress made over nearly the last three decades, Latin America is still at some distance from development. Addressing the remaining challenges—especially in the realms of education and productivity—is key for improving the welfare of some six hundred million Latin American citizens.

Summary
- When comparing Asia with Latin America, growth and development in several Asian countries has outpaced that of Latin America.
- Low savings rates in Latin America might be at the heart of Latin America's poor growth record.
- Domestic savings can potentially play a dual role with regard to inclusive growth. Enhanced commitment from domestic investors can attract more long-term foreign investments, and promoting social security pension reform for Latin America's aging population is important.
- The gap between stellar and less-than-stellar growth performers within Latin America seems to be narrowing with the advent of regional trade integration and openness.
- In an increasingly globalized world, country size does not seem to account for the divergent growth performance across Latin American economies.
- Adverse geography remains a challenge in that much infrastructure is still needed to link the coasts with the hinterlands and thereby increase growth via trade and decrease within-region inequalities.
- Most Latin American economies remain prone to large and sudden terms of trade fluctuations, which might hinder growth and development. Adequate policy responses such as the creation of sovereign wealth funds can considerably mitigate the adverse effects of terms of trade fluctuations.
- Although inflation might hinder growth, most of the region—with the exceptions of Argentina and Venezuela—has managed to lower inflation rates to single digits.
- Financing growth via investments in infrastructure and human capital remains a challenge; Latin American countries have a limited scope for increasing income and corporate taxation, because the entire region remains reliant on foreign savings.
- Most Latin American economies—with the notable exception of Mexico—might be labeled as resource curse economies, and yet channeling natural resource revenues toward industrial sectors can mitigate the adverse effects of the resource curse.

- Corruption remains an important impediment to growth and development in most Latin American regions, and including the private sector in natural resource exploitation might mitigate the problem.
- Further strengthening institutional reform can have an important and positive impact on lowering corruption and private sector regulation in order to enhance efficiency and growth in both the public and private sectors.
- R&D is understood as imitation and adaptation of the latest state-of-the-art technologies invented outside the Latin American region. R&D has important and positive spillovers, which the region will continue to take advantage of via further attraction of long-term capital investments.
- Much-needed investments in high-quality education, particularly secondary and tertiary education, remain a challenge in all Latin American countries, threatening social unrest from the growing middle class, which demands greater access. Governments' lack of ability to provide it is hindering productivity growth.

Review Questions
1. Why is domestic savings promotion important for growth and development in Latin America?
2. In what way can domestic savings generate inclusive growth?
3. Which Latin American countries are more prone to experiencing considerable cyclical fluctuations and why?
4. What are the main impediments for promoting growth and within-region income inequalities via trade openness?
5. Are country size and initial per capita income level the main determinants of growth and development in Latin America? Briefly explain your answer.
6. Briefly comment on the merits of the following statement: "Further institutional strengthening seems to be key for fostering growth and reducing income inequalities in Latin America."
7. Is Latin America a resource curse region?
8. How is R&D understood in developing regions in general and in Latin America in particular?
9. Is there a link between trade and financial openness and productivity enhancements via R&D investments?
10. Briefly comment on the merits of the following statement: "Latin American countries cannot finance investments in secondary and tertiary education via income and corporate taxation."

Further Reading
For a clear and reader-friendly exposition of the Asian miracles in contrast with Latin America's lackluster growth record from a resource curse perspective with emphasis on Brazil, Latin America's largest economy, see Auty 1994. Recent divergent growth trends between North and South American countries as slowdown in China takes hold are discussed in a section titled "Latin America and the Caribbean" in the book *Global Economic Prospects* (World Bank 2015). Aedo and Walker (2012) provide an insightful analysis of the role of educational attainment and quality of education in economic growth in Latin America and the main obstacles of the same.

Notes

1 Geography and the Colonial Legacy

1. Tordesillas is now in the province of Valladolid, Spain. According to the treaty, the dividing line was drawn halfway off the western coast of Africa, some 2,000 kilometers to the west of the Cape Verde islands. The lands to the east would belong to Portugal and the lands to the west to Spain. The treaty was never enforced, however. The Spaniards turned a blind eye to Portuguese settlement in Brazil, for example (Crow 1992). Nevertheless, the *Treaty of Tordesillas* has been cited by Chile in the mid-twentieth century to defend the existence of an Antarctic region extending along a meridian to the South Pole. The treaty was also revived by Argentina in the early 1980s as part of its claim to the Malvinas/Falkland Islands.

2. We herein refer to South America as the entire territory located south of the border between Mexico and the United States including Central America and southern cone countries.

3. For the year 2013, per capita GDP in Latin America was US$9.737, and in the United States it was US$53.101 (IMF 2015). More recent estimates deliver a similar picture: despite growth rates exceeding 4 percent since the 2008 financial meltdown, Latin America's per capita income today is one-sixth that of the United States, relative to one-quarter fifty years ago (Lora and Pagés 2011).

4. See, notably, Sachs and Warner 1997; Bloom et al. 1998; Landes 1998; Sachs 2003; Nordhaus 2006; and Dell, Jones, and Olken 2009, 2012. For a well-cited summary, see Sachs, Mellinger, and Gallup 2001 and Sachs and Malaney 2002.

5. See, notably, Kremer and Zwane 2005.

6. See, notably, López-Casasnovas, Rivera, and Currais 2005; Banerjee-Duflo 2011; and Deaton 2013.

7. This idea was first suggested in the work by Boserup (1965) on agricultural productivity. In the context of endogenous growth models, Kremer (1993) argues that high population density is beneficial for per capita income as the probability of growth-enhancing innovations increases with the population level, because there are more potential talents to advance the frontier of technological change.

8. See, in particular, columns 3 and 4. Dividing column 4 by column 3 delivers population density—as proxied by inhabitants per square mile—which is approximately 29.75 for sub-Saharan Africa and 36.6 for Latin America.

9. See, notably, Thirtle, Lin, and Piese 2003.

10. According to the IMF *World Economic Outlook* (2015), Bolivia is among the five lowest per capita income Latin American countries, alongside Haiti, Nicaragua, Honduras, and Guatemala.

11. See, notably, Glaeser and Shleifer 2002.

12. La Porta, Lopez-de-Silanes, and Shleifer 1999 and La Porta et al. 1997, 1999.

13. See, notably, Larraín and Tavares 2004.

14. See, for example, DeShazo 2007.

15. See World Economic Forum 2012.

16. See Rajan and Zingales 2003.

17. See Musacchio 2009.

18. See Nunn 2012 for a clear exposition.

19. See World Bank Indicators 2014b. Nonetheless, Chile and Uruguay are still considered emerging market economies according to the IMF latest classification.

20. This is the study by Musacchio (2009) referred to in note 17.

21. See Engerman and Sokoloff 2000.

22. See Jaramillo and Sancak 2007 for a detailed analysis.

23. See, notably, Barro and Sala-I-Martin 1995; Quah 1996a; and Johnson 2000.

24. Although the *encomienda* system was formally abolished in 1720, its feudal features persisted nationally and/or locally. In Mexico, for example, it was not until the 1920 Mexican revolution that *encomienda* came to an end constitutionally. This gave rise to the *ejido* system, under which natives were given rights over large plots of land cultivated in a cooperative style, and individual ownership was limited to approximately one hundred hectares of land. In some regions, such as in the southern state of Chiapas, such constitutional changes were not fully implemented, giving rise to the Zapatista uprising in 1994. See O'Neil and Akland 2006 and Castellanos 2007.

25. The *mayorazgo* institution was a Spanish transplant in Latin America. The system allowed Latin America's landed aristocracy to maintain property, such as land, indentured labor, and/or slaves. This property was passed on to the original owners' offspring, generally via the eldest son. The system perpetuated land and indentured labor/slave ownership concentration in only a few hands. Arranged marriages among key family members exacerbated the underlying income inequality problem embedded in the system. A similar institution existed in Portugal under the name of *morgado*, later adopted by Brazil.

26. The *pampas* are the fertile Argentine lowlands, covering more than 700,000 km^2. The pampas include mostly the provinces of Buenos Aires, La Pampa, Santa Fe, Entre Rios, and Cordoba. The climate in the pampas is mild, with precipitation of about 600 mm more or less evenly distributed through the year, making the soil highly propitious to agriculture.

27. This line of reasoning was later formalized by Murphy, Shleifer, and Vishny (1989).

28. This is the interpretation of most Latin American scholars of Acemoglu, Johnson, and Robinson's 2001 institutional approach, discussed further ahead. More recently, however, Frankema (2008) argues that the legacy of income and educational inequalities dating back to the colonial period is not enough to fully understand the persistence of inequality since the 1870s and beyond.

Notes 353

29. Instrumental variables (or IVs) are used to estimate causal relationships in order to obtain consistent estimations when the explanatory variables on the right-hand side are correlated with the error term. For more on IVs, see, for example, Green 2008.

30. See Burkholder 1990; and Carmack, Gasco, and Gossen 2007. Buckholder and Johnson 2003 emphasize the importance of many more *Audiencias*, such as the ones in Bogota, Buenos Aires, Caracas, Charcas, Cusco, Guadalajara, Guatemala, Lima, Mexico, Panama, Quito, and Santo Domingo. These were partially controlled by the viceroyalties, and potential judicial disputes between *Audiencias* and viceroyalties were ultimately resolved by the Council of Indies in Seville, Spain.

31. In practice, as we mentioned in the introduction, much of the land that was supposed to go to Portugal under the Treaty of Tordesillas ended up in the hands of the Spaniards. According to most historians, the main reason was that, relative to Spain, Portugal had less resources—including labor—to colonize the entire eastern hemisphere (see Crow 1992). The rights of Spanish settlers ultimately prevailed, notably in Argentina and Uruguay.

32. We owe this important insight to Maitreesh Ghatak. See https://growthecon.wordpress.com/2014/11/18/the-skeptics-guide-to-institutions-part-1/.

33. The *epidemiological transition* refers to a wave of international health improvements that became available worldwide in the 1940s, sharply reducing the prevalence of disease and thereby increasing life expectancy.

34. See Coatsworth 1998.

35. An alternative view is that it is human capital that shapes institutional quality. See, notably, Glaeser et al. 2004.

36. Dell's econometric analysis differs from that of Acemoglu, Johnson, and Robinson 2001. Specifically, from a methodological standpoint, Dell does not use IVs in order to establish causality. She uses regression discontinuity analysis (RDA) instead. For a practical guide to RDA, see Imbens and Lemieux 2008.

37. One main reason that *mita*-stricken populations were and continue to be worse off is that indentured laborers in the *haciendas* were exposed to better infrastructure for trade and adoption of technological improvements in agriculture, because large estate landlords had privileged access to the ruling elite of Spanish descent.

38. See, notably, Mauro 1995 and Alesina, Baqir, and Easterly 1999.

39. See, notably, Okediji 2008.

40. The reasons Protestantism did not take hold in Latin America are that the entire region remained highly attached to the Catholic Iberian powers even after independence in the early nineteenth century and that European industrialization stepped aside from Spain and Portugal.

41. See Putnam 1993; Landes 1998; Stultz and Williamson 2003; La Porta, Lopez-de-Silanes, and Shleifer 1999; and La Porta et al. 1997, 1999.

42. The BRIC countries are Brazil, Russia, India, and China.

2 Export-Led Growth and the Origins of Protectionism

1. To measure historical income inequalities is a heroic undertaking. Nevertheless, Bértola and Williamson (2006) forcefully argue that income inequalities did indeed increase in postcolonial Latin America. In particular, income inequalities increased further because the governments in the new

republics protected the interest of elites (landowners and later small manufacturers) via high tariffs, which were needed to fill the government coffers to finance wars and political upheavals first and then to maintain peace as a vocal class of urbanites opposed direct taxation. See, in particular, Coatsworth and Williamson 2002.

2. Dom Pedro was crowned the prince of Portugal, but left for Brazil when he was nine years old in 1807. However, he led the fight for independence of Brazil from Portugal from 1821 to 1822.

3. Great Colombia was part of the viceroyalty of New Granada during the colonial period. From 1819 to 1831, Great Columbia included Colombia, Venezuela, Ecuador, and Panama.

4. The term *Dutch disease* is coined after the discovery of North Sea natural gas, which triggered a sharp inflow of foreign currency, leading to currency appreciation in the Netherlands. This ultimately had a negative impact on other Dutch export products, triggering a deindustrialization trend due to currency appreciation (because manufactures could be imported cheaply from other countries).

5. These reforms, originally known as Washington Consensus reforms, involve a list of structural transformation changes that were prescribed for developing countries starting in the 1980s, as stated in Williamson 1990. The reforms encompass a reduction in government deficit, liberalization and deregulation of international trade and cross-border investments, and, more generally, a change of development strategy from ISI to pursue export-led growth.

6. See Bulmer-Thomas 2003.

7. Trade between Iberian colonies and the United States as well as transatlantic trade was largely restricted, but it nevertheless took place, particularly via British, Dutch, and French traders in what Bulmer-Thomas (2003) describes as *contraband trade*.

8. The Bourbon and Pombaline reforms were introduced by Spain and Portugal, respectively with the principal objective of accelerating the pace of economic development in both regions. To this end, both countries sought to take advantage of the export potential of their Latin American colonies. See Fisher 1985 (Bourbon reforms) and Lockhart and Schwartz 1983 (Pombaline reforms).

9. Mercosur comprises five countries: Argentina, Brazil, Paraguay, Uruguay, and Venezuela. CAN is a custom union between Bolivia, Colombia, Ecuador, and Peru. The CARICOM free-trade block includes Antigua and Barbuda, the Bahamas, Barbados, Belize, Dominica, Grenada, Guyana, Haiti, Jamaica, Montserrat, St Lucia, St Kitts and Newis, St Vincent and the Grenadines, Suriname, and Trinidad and Tobago. The MCCA leads trade integration among four central American countries, namely, Guatemala, El Salvador, Honduras, and Nicaragua (or the C4).

10. Mercantilists viewed the accumulation of bullion (gold and silver) as a venue to accumulate foreign reserves that the Sovereign could control. With gold and silver, which were widely accepted, governments could increase their power and exercise greater control within and outside regional borders.

11. See also Prados de la Escosura 2009.

12. See Williamson 2010a, 2010b for a clear exposition and graphic representation of Latin America's terms of trade relative to the rest of the world.

13. *Trade diversion* occurs when a country imports commodities from trade partners as opposed to importing the same commodities from the most efficient countries in terms of cost of production. See Krugman, Obstfeld, and Melitz 2012.

14. See Russell 2010.

Notes

15. See Dobado González, Gómez Galvarriato, and Williamson 2008 for a splendid review of Mexico's deindustrialization during the nineteenth century.

16. According to Bulmer-Thomas (2003), the amount of railway track per one thousand people circa 1912 in Bolivia, Ecuador, Paraguay, and Peru was approximately one-tenth that of Australia, New Zealand, and Canada.

17. See, in particular, Glaeser et al. 2004, which suggests that institutional quality and democratization is shaped by human capital, which was high in Argentina, Chile, and Uruguay relative to the rest of Latin America.

18. See Cardoso and Helwege 1992.

19. See Della Paolera and Taylor 2003.

20. See Lewis 1990.

21. See Prados de la Escosura 2009. His estimates are based on Newland 1998 and Newland and Paulson 1998.

22. The authoritarian regime of Juan Manuel de Rosas in Argentina from 1835 to 1852 remains controversial, especially after the downfall of military regimes in the early 1980s. For an update on human rights violations in Argentina during recent military regimes, see Engstrom 2013.

23. José Batlle y Ordoñez ruled Uruguay intermittently from 1899 to 1915. He is often praised for having put an end to the Uruguayan Civil War.

24. See, in particular, Bulmer-Thomas 2003.

25. See Culver and Reinhart 1989.

26. See Prados de la Escosura 2005a.

27. In contrast, Prados de la Escosura (2009) suggests that income inequalities worsened in Mexico and Brazil throughout most of the nineteenth century.

28. See Williamson 2010a, 2010b.

29. See Bulmer-Thomas 2003.

30. The negative impact of inequality on per capita growth rates is well-documented. See, for example, Alesina and Rodrick 1994; Perotti 1992, 1993, 1996; Persson and Tabellini 1994; and Larraín and Vergara 1998.

31. In comparison, the share of primary commodities as a percentage of total exports in developing Asian economies was 26 percent in 2010. See http://unctad.org/en/pages/InformationNoteDetails.aspx?OriginalVersionID=38.

32. The Stolper-Samuelson theorem states that if the relative price of a particular good increases, then the real wage or rate of return of the factor used intensively in the production of that good also increases, whereas the real wage or rate of return of the other factor(s) of production in other commodities decreases.

3 Import Substitution Industrialization

1. These policies aimed at removing the embedded commodity export bias dating back to the colonial period, which was later exacerbated during the region's belle époque (circa 1870–1914).

2. According to ECLAC 1976.

3. Chile was especially hard-hit due to the collapse of nitrate prices; recall from chapter 2 that nitrate was Chile's main export product at the time.

4. This 1930s protectionist policy was named for Republican Senator Reed Smoot and House of Representatives Republican Willis C. Hawley. The Smoot-Hawley Tariff Act enacted unprecedentedly high tariffs on nearly twenty thousand commodities, mostly agricultural (see Taussig 1931).

5. Unemployment rates reached 25 percent of the labor force (United States Bureau of the Census 1975).

6. The Abnormal Importation Act enacted provisional tariffs of up to 100 percent ad valorem (see Rossiter 2002).

7. See Sachs 1990.

8. See Eichengreen and Portes 1989 and Armendáriz 1992.

9. See, for example, Choudhri and Kochin 1980; Eichengreen and Sachs 1985; Eichengreen 1992; Temin 1993; and Bernanke 1995.

10. See Campa 1990 for details on key measures affecting exchange rates in Latin American countries after 1929.

11. *Exchange rate pass-through*, as defined by Goldberg and Knetter (1997), is the percentage change in local currency import prices resulting from a one percent change in the exchange rate between the importing and the exporting countries. If it is low, as in the case of the aftermath of the Great Depression, then inflation is low.

12. See Thorp 1992, 1998.

13. See Prebisch 1950 and Singer 1950.

14. For a more detailed explanation of how this mechanism works, see Cuddington, Ludema, and Jayasuriya 2007.

15. See Melitz 2005 for a comprehensive review and explanation of conditions for infant argument protection policies to effectively promote industrial development.

16. See Love 2005.

17. This terminology dates back to Hirschman 1958. *Backward linkages* refers to the emergence of industries, which creates demand for inputs; *forward linkages* relate to the growth of raw materials and inputs of production that support industrial development. For follow-up arguments on agglomeration, see Krugman and Venables 1995.

18. See Bulmer-Thomas 2003.

19. *Rent seeking* occurs when resources are used to capture government benefits rather than put to a productive use.

20. The term *X-inefficiency* was originally coined in Harvey Leibenstein's 1966 article in reference to inefficient production by monopolies that were fenced off from competition.

21. The Agreement of Cartagena (1969) of the Andean Pact established that all companies owned by foreign capital should convert to majority domestic ownership within ten years.

22. The savings gap idea dates back to the Harrod-Domar model, named for the articles by Harrod (1939) and Domar (1946). Harrod and Domar contend that the growth rate, g, depends on an

exogenous capital output ratio, k, and a savings rate, s, where k is a proxy for productivity. The well-known Harrod-Domar equation is $g = s/k$. Now, for a target growth rate g^* to be reached when $s < s^*$, where s^* is the needed savings rate to attain g^*, the savings or financial gap is $s^* - s$. This gap can be filled by foreign aid, below-market interest rates (soft loans) from international aid agencies, or both. For an extensive review on the savings gap and criticisms, see Easterly 1997.

23. By *obvious*, we mean those products in industries that did not require "sophisticated" inputs or processes of production and that already existed in craft production. These include textiles, shoes, and other manufactures.

24. Historical data for this period is sketchy. Nevertheless, existing datasets have been put together in a rather coherent way (see, for example, Franko 2007).

25. This term refers to the 1945–1975 period of post–World War II economic prosperity in France, during which per capita output grew at a rate of 4 percent per year from 1950 until the first oil shock in 1973 (see Piketty 2014).

26. See Alexander 1990.

27. See, notably, Murphy, Shleifer, and Vishny 1989.

28. See Mexico's National Statistics, INEGI, and Banco de Mexico, available in www.banxico.org.mx and www.inegi.org.mx.

29. See Santaella 1998.

30. For a detailed discussion of market critics of ISI, see Baer 1972.

31. *Effective protection* attempts to measure the real amount of protection afforded to a particular product or industry by considering the entire tariff structure. In general, in the case in which there is only one input i into the production of a good j, the rate of effective protection for the good $j(g_j)$ is given by the following equation:

$$g_j = \frac{(t_j - a_{ij} t_i)}{1 - a_{ij}}$$

where t_j is the nominal tariff rate on the product j, a_{ij} is the share of the cost of the imported input i in the price of j in the absence of tariffs, and t_i is the nominal tariff on the imported input j. For example, suppose that fifty dollars of imported metallic intermediate goods are required for the production of one refrigerator. Assume also that under free trade the price of the refrigerator is one hundred dollars (then, a_{ij} is 0.5). If the tariff rate on refrigerators is 90 percent, but the tariff rate on intermediate goods is only 30 percent, then the rate of effective protection of the refrigerator is 150 percent (much greater than the nominal rate of 90 percent).

32. *Market failures* in this case involve oligopolistic markets leading to economic inefficiency, whereas *government failures* in this context relate to governments failing to correct economic inefficiencies.

33. See, for example, Furtado 1966.

34. See Piketty 2014.

35. Under a crawling peg system, the central bank allows the domestic currency to adjust according to a prespecified table or equation normally based on macroeconomic variables, such as domestic and international inflation. In principle, a crawling peg system may prevent overvalued exchange rates, sharp and destabilizing domestic currency devaluations, and currency crises.

36. According to Guimaraes 2010, other factors also affected the success of the ISI strategy, such as the failure of the political system to act as an effective channel of conflict negotiation and as a mechanism to insulate the political elite and increase political support for the strategy.

37. *Free on board* (FOB) generally represents the price an exporter obtains for its goods at the local port before shipping costs.

38. Under a *drawback system*, a country pays rebates on tariffs and other import duties on intermediate inputs of production, which are used by exporting industries in their production processes.

39. See, for example, Cardenas, Ocampo, and Thorp 2000.

40. See Dollar 1992; Harrison 1996; Sachs and Warner 1995; Edwards 1998; Chang, Kaltani, and Loayza 2009; and Rassekh 2007, among others.

41. See Labán and Larraín 1995.

4 Debt Crises and the Lost Decade

1. See Mundlak, Cavallo, and Domenech 1992.

2. See Marichal 1989.

3. Note that the current section borrows from Armendáriz 1991 and Armendáriz 1993.

4. *Consols* are long-term (perpetual) loans issued by the United Kingdom since the eighteenth century; they are also known as consolidated annuities.

5. Note that the current section borrows from Armendáriz 1989.

6. Chile had been in default since 1931. According to Chilean law 5580, which was approved in 1935, no more than 50 percent of the government's income from nitrate, iodine, and copper was going to be allocated to interest payments for outstanding debt. The remaining 50 percent was earmarked for purchasing all Chilean debt at market prices.

7. The Colombian government offered its creditors half the sum of the interest on its debt, which had been in default since 1933, and the other half was to be repaid in Colombian currency via *Certificados de la República*—that is, domestic currency–denominated debt.

8. Unlike Chile and Colombia, which defaulted during the Great Depression, Mexico had been in default since 1914 because of the 1910 Mexican Revolution. The offer on this defaulted debt in 1942 involved not only an 80 percent debt reduction, but also a fixed and reduced interest rate of 4.5 percent on the remaining debt.

9. Parts of the current section are based on Larraín and Sachs 1993.

10. The Brady Plan, named after US Treasury Secretary Nicholas Brady, was launched in 1988.

11. See Larraín and Velasco 1990; Armendáriz 1993; and Armendáriz and Ferreira 1999.

12. The use of exchange rates as "nominal anchors" in price stabilization was widespread in Latin America and many Eastern European countries after the fall of the Berlin Wall in 1989. See, for example, Edwards 1993.

13. See Aspe 1993.

14. Whether the crisis was prompted by contagion of the Asian crisis in 1997 remains an open question; see Evangelist and Sathe 2006.

15. See Hausmann and Velasco 2002.

16. Esquivel and Larraín (2000) formally analyze the problem of contagion in currency crises.

17. See Diamond and Rajan 2009.

18. IMF 2015.

19. See Larraín 2008.

5 Poverty and Income Inequality

1. See ECLAC 2013.

2. Lindert and Williamson (2003) and Williamson (2010) argue that in the early nineteenth century, Latin America was less unequal when compared to Western Europe and the United States. In particular, Lindert and Williamson forcefully argue that, just as in any land-abundant backward countries, contemporary Latin America's income inequalities relative to those in industrialized economies started to widen by the end of the nineteenth century, that is, during Latin America's belle époque (1870–1914), not before.

3. See Asian Development Bank 2010.

4. *SEDESOL* stands for *Secretaría de Desarrollo Social*, which is the Ministry of Social Development. It gathers data and finances antipoverty programs via the much-heralded *Progresa/Oportunidades/Prospera* program, and, more recently, via FOSIDES (Fondo Sectorial para la Investigación y el Desarrollo Social).

5. The Gini coefficient is a standard measure of inequalities, which estimates the values of a frequency distribution. The coefficient ranges between zero (perfect equality) and one (perfect inequality). We provide a more detailed explanation in section 5.7.

6. See D'Agostino and Dardanoni 2006 and Ferreira et al. 2012 for more on social mobility measurements and indices.

7. ECLAC (2004, 12), for example, defined poverty as a "situational syndrome in which the associated factors include under-consumption, malnutrition, precarious living conditions, an unstable position in the productive apparatus, feelings of discouragement and anomaly, little participation in the mechanisms of social integration and perhaps adherence to a particular scale of values which differs to some extent from that of the rest of society".

8. In the literature on public economics, the median voter's preferences represent those of the majority, the vote of which leads to an efficient outcome in the political process. See Mas-Colell, Whinston, and Green 1995.

9. See Armendáriz and Morduch 2010.

10. There are other methods for measuring poverty. Notably, poverty can be classified according to objective-subjective and absolute-relative metrics. These classifications are beyond the scope of this chapter, however. See Ray 1998 and Larraín 2008 for extensive discussions on the advantages and drawbacks of different approaches to measure poverty.

11. Hernando de Soto is best known for his work on property rights. Without extended and well-defined property rights over land and housing, de Soto and his followers will proclaim, the standards of living of the poor cannot be raised. See de Soto 1989.

12. See, for example, Besley, Burchardi, and Ghathak 2012 on Sri Lanka.

13. SEDESOL estimates that as many as seven million Mexicans in 2012 were exceedingly poor according to the UBN method. This method combined with the CBN method delivers an astonishing figure of approximately fifty-three million poor in the same year.

14. Many regions, both rural and urban, live on tourism, a sector of growing importance that is also highly volatile due to shocks ranging from natural climate change catastrophes related to El Niño to unexpected upsurges of drug-related armed conflict. Yet according to ECLAC 2011, income derived from tourism accounts for as much as 30 percent of total income in some Latin American regions, particularly in the Caribbean and coastal regions.

15. See Ferreira et al. 2012.

16. See Sen 1976; Preston 1995; Ravallion 1998; Ray 1998; and Deaton 2003.

17. See, for example, Feres 1997.

18. See, for example, Weil 2013.

19. See, notably, Lustig and McCleod 1997; Attanasio and Székely 2001; Wodon et al. 2001; De Ferranti et al. 2003; and Pribble, Huber, and Stephens 2007.

20. Manacorda and colleagues use data for the urban areas of Argentina, Brazil, Chile, Colombia, and Mexico from the 1980s and the 1990s.

21. See, for example, Attanasio, Meghir, and Santiago 2012, which uses data from Mexico.

22. According to the International Labor Organization (ILO), in 2013, up to 17 percent of children who work—instead of going to school—are located in Latin America. Baland and Robinson (2000) demonstrate that child labor is inefficient, because withdrawing children from the labor supply increases low-skilled labor wages, which in turn is good for household heads and future generations; low-income parents earn higher wages, and children increase their future income profile by attending school.

23. Moreover, parallel to ensuring enhanced access to secondary education, policy makers must increase efforts to sustain quality. The quality of primary school education has decreased considerably in most poor and emerging market economies (see, for example, Pritchett 2013). Low quality and limited access in turn have detrimental effects on productivity and growth potential.

24. See Perry et al. 2007 for a full discussion of informality in Latin America.

25. See Wodon et al. 2001.

26. Conditional cash transfers are part of antipoverty programs. Typically, women household heads receive monetary and nonmonetary rewards for sending their children to school and/or taking young children to health centers for vaccinations and preventive health care. A detailed discussion of Latin America's conditional cash transfer programs is offered in section 5.8.

27. See Armendáriz and Morduch 2010.

28. See also Wodon et al. 2001.

29. See Armendáriz and Roell 1994 for a well-documented account of the Zapatista movement.

30. See Piketty 2014. As of the time of writing, the three Latin American countries where the share of income of the top 1 percent is shown for the twenty-first century are Argentina, Colombia, and Uruguay. These three countries combined are relatively small compared to either Mexico or Brazil. It is nevertheless important to point out that, although further behind population-wise, Colombia and

Argentina are among the top five most important economies in the region and that in these two economies, Piketty's dataset suggests that income inequalities have increased. Colombia, the Latin American country for which historical data is most abundant—dating back to 1920—is the only country in that period that surpasses the United States in terms of growing income inequalities, historically and over the past two decades. Further scrutiny into existing data and inclusion of more Latin American countries in Piketty's dataset should help us shed light on recent trends.

31. According to Lustig, Lopez-Calva, and Ortiz-Juarez (2013), the skill premium is affected by demand and supply for workers with different skills and by institutional factors such as the minimum wage. Their results indicate that in Brazil, supply-side, demand-side, and institutional factors played an important role in the fall in the skill premium, but in Mexico institutional factors were unimportant, and this fact was primarily driven by an expansion in the supply of skilled workers.

32. The program has been adopted by other Latin American countries, most notably by Brazil. It has been embraced by a dozen other regions, including New York. A recent World Bank publication identifies 123 conditional cash transfer programs in Africa. See García and Moore 2012.

33. The idea is often credited to two IDB economists—namely, Santiago Lévy and José Gómez de León. See http://www.iadb.org/idbamerica/index.cfm?thisid=3049.

34. See Mullainathan and Shafir 2013.

35. FOSIDES is a branch of SEDESOL.

36. See Harkness 2010.

37. See, notably, Angelucci, Karlan, and Zinman 2014 on Banco Compartamos in Mexico, and, more generally, Armendáriz and Morduch 2010 for an overview of the main microfinance programs in Mexico and other Latin American countries.

38. In 2004, depending on income and family size, cash transfers under BBF ranged between fifteen reals and ninety-five reals.

39. See Scorzafave, Guilherme, and Carvalho de Lima 2010.

6 The Political Economy of Latin American Development

1. With regard to the conceptual link between income inequalities prior to the 1920s and recent manifestations of populism in Latin America, see Prados de la Escosura 2005b; Bértola and Williamson 2006; and Bértola et al. 2008.

2. See Dornbusch and Edwards 1989, 1991.

3. As we will see further ahead, populist upsurges are often linked to natural resource abundance. For the case of Latin America, see, in particular, Kaufman 2007 and Weyland 2009

4. This definition is based on contributions by Joel Horowitz on populism in Argentina, Michael Conniff on Brazil, Paul W. Drake on Chile, Jorge Basurto on Mexico, Steve Stein on Peru, Steve Ellner on Venezuela, Ximena Sosa on Ecuador, and William Francis Robinson on Panama. All in Conniff 2012.

5. See IMF 2013b.

6. See Cavallo, Domenech, and Mundlak 1989.

7. See Horowitz 2012.

8. See Basurto 2012.

9. In a recent visit to Mexico, Ángel Gurría, head of the OECD (a Paris-based think tank), attempted to calm down reform opponents and their followers by declaring that "no one ever declared that the reforms on economic growth and unemployment will take immediate effect" (see El Economista 2014).

10. See Ellner 2012.

11. According to Jorge Basurto, Luis Echeverría is one of the greatest left-wing leaders Mexico has ever had. Under his administration, from 1970 to 1976, nearly 70 percent of Mexico's industry was nationalized. See Basurto 2012.

12. See IMF 2015.

13. According to Conniff (2012), unlike populist predecessor Getúlio Vargas in the 1950s and neopopulist leader Fernando Collor de Mello in the early 1990s, Lula is a democratic socialist (leftist intellectual).

14. The term *stagflation* was coined by British Chancellor of the Exchequer Ian Macleod in 1970, in reference to a situation in which both inflation and unemployment rates increase significantly as economic growth slows down.

15. See Flores 1997 and Larraín and Meller 1990.

16. See table 2 in Dornbusch and Edwards's 1989 article, which is based on Kuczynsky's 1977 estimation and the Peruvian Central Bank and Ministry of Finance approximations.

17. An interesting insider's account of populist policies under the García administration can be found in Carbonetto et al. 1997

18. See table 4 in Dornbusch and Edwards's 1990 article for a full account of key indicators built by the authors using World Bank data combined with data from the Peruvian Ministry of Finance and National Institute of Planning.

19. See Olivera 1967 and Tanzi 1969, 1977.

20. See Sachs 1990.

21. See Blanchard and Kiyotaki 1987.

22. See Bárcena, Prado, and Hopenhayn 2010 for more on subjective perceptions of income by Latin Americans in the 1990s and objective measures of inflation. In the case of Brazil, the correlation coefficient is 0.45.

23. See Aspe 1993 for a comprehensive account of Mexico's heterodox policies, known as *El Pacto Social*.

24. *Orthodox policies* aim to control excess demand via expenditure reduction/budget deficit cuts and expenditure-switching policies—that is, convincing consumers not to demand foreign products via avoiding overvalued exchange rates—in order to reach a disinflation spiral. In contrast, *heterodox policies* attempt to avoid expenditure-reduction costs via imposing controls on prices, wages, and the exchange rate.

25. See also UNDP 2013 for a more detailed analysis of the emergence of the middle class, media, and democracy. Compared to Birdsall 2012, the UNDP report is more cautious, and it portrays the middle class as vulnerable. A slowdown in growth might disrupt the relatively stable social and political environment in the region.

26. See Levy 2008 and Torche and López-Calva 2013.

27. See Barozet and Fierro 2012.

28. See, in particular, Birdsall, de la Torre, and Menezes 2001 and also Stiglitz 2002 and Easterly 2007.

29. The percentage of households living in poverty declined by half, extreme poverty was reduced by 72 percent, income inequality as proxied by the Gini coefficient decreased from 48 to 40, health as proxied by child mortality declined from 21 to 14 deaths per thousand live births, and educational enrollment in primary, secondary and tertiary education increased from 92 to 100 percent. See Weisbrot et al. 2009 for a more detailed assessment.

30. Specifically, the currency board survived the Mexican Tequila crisis in 1994, the Asian crisis in 1997, and the Brazilian and Russian crises in 1998 and 1999.

31. The term *mestizo* in Latin America is used in connection with combined European and indigenous descent. Neighboring Peru also sees a divide between *mestizo*/European descent and the vast majority of indigenous populations. Unlike in Bolivia, however, the leftist Shining Path movement was perceived as a violent guerrilla movement that neglected the rights of Peru's indigenous populations.

32. The Mexican Tequila crisis, which erupted in 1994, was a financial crisis largely perceived as a by-product of overvalued exchange rates under Mexico's stabilization policies. Arguably, there were other domestic factors—in particular, the indigenous upheaval in the southern state of Chiapas and the assassination of PRI candidate Luis Donaldo Colosio. We analyze the 1994 Mexican Tequila crisis in greater detail in chapter 7.

33. See Jácome 2004.

34. According to the World Economic Forum 2010, corruption remains the most important problem of doing business in Ecuador.

35. For a well-known criticism of globalization and market-friendly reforms, see Stiglitz 2002.

36. See World Bank 2001. For an account of privatization in Central America, see Larraín and López-Calva 2001.

37. See, for example, McKenzie and Mookherjee 2003 for an excellent review of the literature.

38. See Bortolotti and Perotti 2007.

39. See, for example, Chong and López-de-Silanes 2003.

40. See, for example, Di Tella and Dubra 2010.

41. See Kornai, Maskin, and Roland 2003.

42. See The Economist 2006 and Financial Times 2012.

7 Fiscal Policy for Development

1. Part of the current section is based on Larraín and Selowsky 1991.

2. See Bértola and Ocampo 2012.

3. See Eichengreen, Hausmann and Panizza 2002; see also chapter 4 in this book for an overview.

4. See, for example, Díaz-Alejandro 1984.

5. The principal-agent problem arises when an economic actor (the principal) depends on the behavior of another actor (the agent), for which the principal does not have perfect information. The problem occurs because sometimes the agent can be motivated to act in his own best interests rather than those of the principal. In the concrete case discussed here, the principal is the owner (shareholders); the

agent is the manager of the public enterprise or institution. An illustration of the principal-agent theory is provided by Gertner, Scharfstein, and Stein 1994.

6. For clear exposition on soft budget constraints, see Maskin 1996 and Qian and Xu 1998. A more comprehensive review of private versus public ownership can be found in Vickers and Yarrow 1988.

7. See Larraín and Sachs 1993, chapter 22.

8. See IMF Data (www.imf.org/en/Data).

9. See Dornbusch and Simonsen 1987.

10. See the database from Reinhart and Rogoff 2009.

11. See chapter 4 for a description of the Baker and Brady plans.

12. See Williamson 1990.

13. For a full discussion, see Birdsall, de la Torre, and Valencia 2011; Rodrik 2006; and Williamson 1990.

14. To some observers, the reforms were progrowth; see, notably, Burnside and Dollar 2000 and Dollar and Kraay 2001. To others, development assistance to implement the Washington Consensus reforms was misleading and did not favor growth (Easterly 2007).

15. *Tagging* links transfers to characteristics that are strongly correlated with income in order to lower the fiscal cost of achieving a given amount of redistribution.

16. See Fiszbein and Schady 2009.

17. A detailed analysis of Chile's fiscal rule can be found in Larraín et al. 2011.

8 The Fight against Inflation

1. According to Reinhart and Rogoff (2011), an *inflation crisis* is an episode in which inflation exceeds 20 percent. *Hyperinflation* is reached when inflation exceeds 50 percent per month, according to the classic work of Cagan (1956). ECLAC (2004) estimates that inflation was 60.9 percent in 1975 and 1,188.5 percent in 1990.

2. The current section borrows extensively from Larraín and Sachs 2013.

3. In essence, the twin deficit hypothesis explains why the budget deficit goes up and down in tandem with the trade deficit. Otherwise stated, an economy is likely to have a twin deficit when it is borrowing from foreigners in exchange of foreign-made goods or imports.

4. See, for example, Gavin, Hausmann, and Leiderman 1996 and Edwards 2000.

5. Simply stated, countercyclical fiscal policies to avoid inflation consist of fiscal contraction when capital inflows are higher than their historical average.

6. *Seigniorage*, from the French word *seigneur*, relates to resources that a sovereign (the government in this case) generates via printing money, typically to finance its own expenditures.

7. According to Eichengreen and Hausmann (1999), *original sin* is the inability of some economies to borrow abroad in their own currency and to borrow long term in local currency domestically.

8. Structuralists would view things differently. Structuralists believe that inflation is to be blamed on institutional rigidities in agriculture and trade, among other sectors. See, for example, Seers 1962. The dispute between monetarists and structuralists is explained in the next section.

9. The standard view of inflation is that it is a monetary phenomenon; that is, $MV = PY$, where M is money supply, V is velocity, P is the price level, and Y is output. Assuming V and Y are stable, changes in the money supply are mainly reflected in a change in prices. When governments can finance their deficits with domestic debt, the need to resort to seigniorage is reduced, and therefore inflation is lowered.

10. Simply stated, *inertial inflation* relates to the influence that past and current inflation have on future inflation expectations and future price and contract adjustments accordingly. Hence, inflation keeps on rising despite the fact that monetary and fiscal indicators may be stable. In most Latin American economies, inflation has been hard to tame, because the past record of inflation triggered an automatic and self-fulfilling price-indexation mechanism.

11. The Olivera-Tanzi effect was coined for the seminal articles by Julio Olivera (1967) and Vito Tanzi (1969).

12. See, for example, Mankiw 2007 and Larraín and Sachs 2013.

13. *Shoe leather costs* relate to the idea that economic agents are unwilling to hold money that is losing value and therefore make regular trips to the bank, where money is at least earning interest. *Menu costs* describe real costs associated with changing prices frequently as a result of inflation (such as costs on restaurant menus and in vending machines). Both shoe leather and menu costs are a waste of resources that could be put to more productive use.

14. There are three main reasons that wages might be sticky downward: first, due to minimum wage policies and labor unions; second, because firms wish to avoid turnover costs; and third, because workers' productivity may depend on the wages firms pay—that is, the efficiency wage. See, for example, Shapiro and Stiglitz 1984.

15. Alesina et al. (1999) created an index for budget institutions or constraints on the deficit by the executive. Unsurprisingly, the index turned out to be high for Mexico, Ecuador, and Chile when compared to that of Brazil, Peru, and Venezuela.

16. See Carstens and Jácome 2005.

17. Among them, Alesina and Summers 1993; Carstens and Jácome 2005; and Carlstrom and Fuerst 2009.

18. At the time of writing, the current president of Brazil, Dilma Russeff, is under intense pressure to grant central bank independence.

19. See Santiso 2004.

20. Under a currency board, monetary authorities are committed to maintaining a completely fixed exchange rate between a domestic and a foreign currency. In the case of Argentina, the currency board dictated a one-to-one exchange rate regime—that is, one Argentinean peso is equal to one US dollar.

21. According to Fischer, Sahay, and Végh (2002), the Mexican, Argentinean, and Brazilian experiences demonstrate that inflation lacks inertia once it reaches high levels; that is, price increases no longer adjust in response to current price indices.

22. See Larraín 2000 and Fostel and Kaminsky 2008.

23. Capital inflow volatility in Latin America is well-documented. See, for example, Gavin and Hausmann 1996; Griffith-Jones 2000; and Larraín 2000.

24. Specifically, the exchange rate pass through is the elasticity of local-currency import prices with respect to local currency price of foreign currency, of import prices resulting from a one percent change in the exchange rate between the importing and exporting countries. Clearly, a change in import prices

has an effect on retail and consumer prices domestically. When the exchange rate pass through is low, there is a less transmission of inflation resulting from local currency depreciations.

25. Because import prices change when the exchange rate depreciates, domestic retail prices increase. This pass-through from the exchange rate to inflation can be high or low, depending on the elasticity of import prices with respect to the local currency price of foreign currency.

26. See Reinhart and Rogoff 2011.

9 Pegging, Sliding, and Floating

1. See IMF 2006 for classification of de facto exchange rate regimes.

2. See Jameson 2003.

3. See Swiston 2011.

4. For an explanation of PPP theory, see Larraín and Sachs 2013, chapter 18.

5. *Sterilization* occurs when countries' central banks attempt to keep the money supply unchanged. In the Latin American context, sterilization took the form of maintaining the value of the currency in order to avoid balance of payments crises.

6. See Frenkel and Rapetti 2010.

7. See chapter 4 for a detailed explanation of this pact.

8. Larraín and Tavares (2003) show than whereas Europe is characterized by a high degree of regional integration, Central and South America (in spite of suggestions for currency integration) display low levels of regional integration.

9. Larraín 2005 provides formal empirical evidence for a large group of countries, concluding that both GDP growth and its volatility behave better under floating exchange rates.

10. See Bernanke and James 1991 and Eichengreen and Temin 1997.

11. See Armendáriz and Reynoso 2013.

12. See, in particular, Hausmann et al. 1999.

13. See, for example, Frankel, Parsley, and Wei 2012.

14. This point has been stressed by Larraín and Velasco (2001, 2002) and by Calvo and Mishkin (2003).

15. This was noted by several policymakers in the region. See, for example, Larraín 2010, 2013.

16. See, in particular, Frenkel and Rapetti 2010.

17. See Gourinchas et al. 2001.

10 Trade and Financial Liberalization

1. *Shadow prices* are those that consider market distortions, which are not part of market prices. For example, when a country borrows, a considerable amount of the loan might be either consumed or invested in nontradable and import-competing goods as opposed to being invested in exportable goods. Such types of incentive-based distortions under ISI were reflected in prices for exportable goods that were too high—higher than world prices—making Latin America's exportable goods uncompetitive. It was this wedge between shadow and world market prices for exportable goods that the region

Notes

aimed to narrow via trade liberalization—that is, by exposing tradable goods to foreign competition (see Brecher and Díaz Alejandro 1977).

2. For an in-depth explanation of the mutually beneficial gains from trade in the Ricardian and Heckscher-Ohlin models, see Krugman, Obstfeld, and Melitz 2012.

3. It was later recognized that trade alone would not trigger growth unless accompanied by institutional reforms. See, for example, Rodrik 2001.

4. Negotiating debt restructuring under the Brady Plan was undeniably very helpful too. In most countries, without debt restructuring it is unlikely that market-oriented reforms, particularly in the realm of trade liberalization, would have brought economic prosperity in the twenty-first century. See Armendáriz and Armendáriz 1999 for the case of Mexico.

5. These estimates are the authors' own, based on the ten-country sample shown in figure 10.1. Earlier estimates based on a larger sample deliver similar numbers. For example, Lora 2001 suggests a fall in tariffs of approximately 38 percentage points during the 1985–1999 period.

6. See, for example, Krueger 1978; Bhagwati 1988; Choksi, Michaely, and Papageorgiou 1991; Edwards 1993; and Agosin 1999.

7. See World Bank 2002.

8. See Edwards 1993.

9. See, for example, Fernández and Rodrik 1991 and Fernández 1997.

10. See Krugman, Obstfeld, and Melitz 2012.

11. See, for example, McCulloch 2002.

12. See Ethier 1998.

13. See European Commission 2015.

14. See Ozden and Parodi 2004.

15. See Echavarría 1998.

16. See Cañas et al. 2011 for an in-depth analysis of the *maquila* export sector.

17. See Tornell, Westermann, and Martinez 2004.

18. See, for example, Pastor 2001.

19. According to Santiso 2013, financial liberalization enabled emerging countries to augment the quantity of multinational companies. Specifically, the Latin American multinationals, or *multilatinas*, have been important in moving financial and industrial wealth from developed to emerging countries and in developing innovation in those countries.

20. For an analysis of capital flows in and out of Latin America during this period, see Larraín 2000. For the factors behind currency crises in emerging markets see Esquivel and Larraín 2000a.

21. This tax is named after Nobel Laureate James Tobin, who suggested a small tax on foreign exchange transactions in order to discourage speculation in the foreign exchange market; see Tobin 1978. For a concise and comprehensive explanation of the Chilean and Colombian experiences with Tobin taxes in the 1990s, see Pradumna 1998 and Larraín 2000.

22. See Ostry et al. 2010.

23. See Rojas-Suarez 2010.

24. See Hernández-Coss 2005.

25. See Passel, Cohn, and Gonzalez-Barrera 2012 and Passel et al. 2014.

26. A detailed analysis of the Chilean experience with capital inflows is provided in Larraín and Labán 2000.

11 Labor Markets, Informality, and Labor Protection Systems

1. Alternatively, above-market-clearing wages can be viewed through the lens of the Lindbeck and Snower (1988) insider-outsider theory. According to this theory, insiders enjoyed high wages because labor turnover costs enable insiders to take advantage of their privileged position vis-à-vis outsiders. Employers do not have an incentive to hire outsiders at such high wages, and thus aggregate labor supply exceeds labor demand, creating unemployment.

2. Urbanization rates in Latin America are estimated to have grown at an average of approximately 3.5 percent per annum from 1950 to 2000. At the same time, the rural population either did not grow at all or declined. The Latin American population living in urban areas swelled from approximately sixty-five million in 1950 to 380 million in 2000, when urban residents accounted for over three-quarters of the Latin American population (Brea 2003).

3. See Stallings and Peres 2000 and Cook 2004.

4. See, for example, Goldberg and Pavcnik 2003 on Colombia and Brazil, and Attanasio, Goldberg, and Pavcnik 2003 on Colombia.

5. See Bosch, Goñi-Pacchioni, and Maloney 2012.

6. See Klein 2012.

7. See, for example, Anner 2008.

8. See ILO 2005.

9. See, notably, Collier and Collier 1991; Drake 1996; and Portes and Hoffman 2003.

10. See, for example, the early literature on the subject: Bertola 1990, Bentolila and Bertola 1990, and Bentolila and Saint Paul 1994. More recent econometric estimates suggest that increased labor flexibility in Latin America can lead to approximately a 2 percent increase in employment (see Kaplan 2009).

11. See, in particular, Lindbeck and Snower 1988 for a comprehensive analysis of insider-outsider theory.

12. *Total wage workers* are formally employed workers whose employers make social security contributions.

13. For a detailed analysis of such traditional welfare systems, see Holland 2014.

14. For a full explanation of the weights of different components and disaggregated indicators, see World Bank 2014a.

15. See Bertranou 2007.

16. According to Clark and Summers 1982, just 60 percent of all teenagers who are out of school are employed, so there is a high youth unemployment rate.

Notes

12 Growth and Development in Latin America

1. See, notably, Easterly 2007.

2. See, notably, Barro 1991.

3. See, for example, Nunn 2012.

4. See, in particular, Dayal-Gulati and Thimann 1997.

5. See Kraay 2000 and Chamon and Prasad 2010.

6. See Allen, Qian, and Qian 2005.

7. See Song, Storesletten, and Zilibotti 2011. The Chinese edition of Armendáriz and Morduch (2012) had to be modified, because the mere meaning of *microfinance* is different in China than it is in Western countries. If and when a project falls into the microfinance category for Chinese standards, the project must involve a minimum fixed cost of approximately US$750,000.

8. For example, Labán and Larraín (1997) showed that liberalizing capital outflow controls induces more capital inflows.

9. See, in particular, Aghion, Comin et al. 2009 for a complete theoretical explanation. A similar argument with regard to diffusion of expertise in long-term projects involving financial institutions can be found in Armendáriz 1999.

10. See, notably, Barro 1991; Mankiw, Romer, and Weil 1992; and Quah 1996b.

11. See, notably, Friedman 1992.

12. See Dawson and Sen 2007.

13. See, notably, Holmes 2005.

14. See Ayala, Cunado, and Alberiko Gil-Alana 2013.

15. See, notably, Alesina 2003.

16. See, for example, Alexander 1990.

17. Kremer (1993) argued that the high size of the population triggers high rates of technology diffusion and economic prosperity.

18. Neither time series studies (Jones 1995) nor cross-country section studies (Backus, Kehoe, and Kehoe 1992; Rose 2006) have found any conclusive evidence of the existence of scale effects at the aggregate level.

19. Coefficients for these variables are not significant or close to nonsignificant. These results are robust in different methodologies, including OLS, fixed-effect panel data, and an instrumental variables (IV) framework.

20. Barahona et al. (2001) provided an analysis of how to reduce the vulnerability to natural disasters in the context of Hurricane Mitch in Central America.

21. The term *Dutch disease* first appeared in the literature in the late 1950s in connection with the decline of the manufacturing sector after natural gas discovery and exploitation in the Netherlands.

22. See Ades and Di Tella 1999 and Acemoglu, Robinson, and Verdier 2004.

23. This line of thought is closely related to the Prebisch-Singer writings on the 1930s (see chapter 3).

24. See Gylfason 2002.

25. See Hausmann, Panizza, and Rigobon 2006.

26. A detailed analysis of Chile's fiscal rule can be found in Larraín et al. 2011.

27. See, notably, Ray 1998.

28. See, for example, Chang, Kaltani, and Loayza 2009; Ari and Zeren 2013; Bulut et al. 2013; and Trejos and Barboza 2014.

29. This question is addressed in Cavallo and Frankel 2008.

30. Gourinchas et al. (2001), for example, estimate that relative to the rest of the world, Latin America is considerably more vulnerable to lending booms and volatility in capital inflows and outflows.

31. See Edwards 1993.

32. See Rassekh 2007.

33. See Chang, Kaltani, and Loayza 2009.

34. See Wacziarg and Welch 2008.

35. See Jamison, Jamison, and Hanushek 2007.

36. See, notably, Kremer and Holla 2009.

37. See Attanasio, Meghir, and Santiago 2012.

38. Note, however, that Barro excluded education and national defense from his econometric equations.

39. Gillman, Harris, and Mátyás 2004, which includes data for OECD and ASEAN countries between 1961 and 1997, supports this view.

40. In their work, the quality of institutions is proxied by expropriation risk.

41. See Aghion and Howitt 1997 for a comprehensive review.

42. See Helpman 1993.

References

Acemoglu, Daron, and Simon Johnson. 2007. "Disease and Development: The Effect of Life Expectancy on Economic Growth." *Journal of Political Economy* 115 (6): 925–985.

Acemoglu, Daron, Simon Johnson, and James Robinson. 2001. "The Colonial Origins of Comparative Development: An Empirical Investigation." *American Economic Review* 91 (5): 1369–1401.

Acemoglu, Daron, Simon Johnson, and James Robinson. 2002. "Reversal of Fortune: Geography and Institutions in the Making of the Modern World Income Distribution." *Quarterly Journal of Economics* 117 (4): 1231–1294.

Acemoglu, Daron, Simon Johnson, and James Robinson. 2005. "Institutions as the Fundamental Cause of Long-Run Growth." In *Handbook of Economic Growth*, edited by Philippe Aghion and Steven Durlauf, 385–472. Amsterdam: North-Holland/Elsevier.

Acemoglu, Daron, James Robinson, and Thierry Verdier. 2004. "Kleptocracy and Divide-and-Rule: A Theory of Personal Rule." *Journal of the European Economic Association* 2 (2–3): 162–192.

Acemoglu, Daron, and James Robinson. 2013. *Why Nations Fail: The Origins of Power, Prosperity and Poverty*. New York: Crown.

Adelman, Irma, and Sherman Robinson. 1989. "Income Distribution and Development." In *Handbook of Development Economics*, vol. 2, edited by Hollis Chenery and T. N. Srinivasan, 949–1003. Amsterdam: North-Holland/Elsevier.

Ades, Alberto, and Rafael Di Tella. 1999. "Rents, Competition and Corruption." *American Economic Review* 89 (4): 982–993.

Adserà, Alicia, Carles Boix, and Mark Payne. 2003. "Are You Being Served? Political Accountability and the Quality of Government." *Journal of Law Economics and Organization* 19 (2): 445–490.

Aedo, Christian, and Ian Walker. 2012. *Skills for the 21st Century in Latin America and the Caribbean*. Washington, DC: World Bank.

Aghion, Philippe, and Peter Howitt. 1997. *Endogenous Growth Theory*. Cambridge, MA: MIT Press.

Aghion, Philippe, Alberto Alesina, and Francesco Trebbi. 2007. "Democracy, Technology and Growth." In *Institutions and Economic Performance* edited by Elhanan Helpman, 511–543. Cambridge, MA: Harvard University Press.

Aghion, Philippe, Leah Boustan, Caroline Hoxby, and Jerome Vandenbussche. 2009. "The Causal Impact of Education on Economic Growth: Evidence from U.S.," *Brookings Paper on Economic Activity*, edited by David Romer and Justin Wolfers, https://www.brookings.edu/wp-content/uploads/2016/07/2009_spring_bpea_aghion_etal.pdf.

Aghion, Phillippe, Diego Comin, Peter Howitt, and Isabel Tecu. 2009. "When Does Domestic Saving Matter for Economic Growth?" NBER Working Paper 12275, Cambridge, MA.

Agosin, Manuel. 1999. "Trade and Growth in Chile." *CEPAL Review*, no. 68: 79–100.

Ahluwalia, Montek S., Nicholas G. Carter, and Hollis B. Chenery. 1979. "Growth and Poverty in Developing Countries." *Journal of Development Economics* 6:255–341.

Alesina, Alberto. 2003. "The Size of Countries: Does it Matter?" *Journal of the European Economic Association* (2–3): 301–316.

Alesina, Alberto, and Silvia Ardagna. 2010. "Large Changes in Fiscal Policy: Taxes versus Spending." *Tax Policy and the Economy* 24: 35-68. .

Alesina, Alberto, Reza Baqir, and William Easterly. 1999. "Public Goods and Ethnic Divisions." *Quarterly Journal of Economics* 114:1243–1284.

Alesina, Alberto, Ricardo Hausmann, Rudolf Hommes, and Ernesto Stein. 1999. "Budget Institutions and Fiscal Performance in Latin America." *Journal of Development Economics* 59:253–273.

Alesina, Alberto, and Roberto Perotti. 1996. "Income Distribution, Political Instability, and Investment." *European Economic Review* 40 (6): 1203–1228.

Alesina, Alberto, and Dani Rodrick. 1994. "Distributive Politics and Economic Growth." *Quarterly Journal of Economics* 109 (2): 465–490.

Alesina, Alberto, and Enrico Spolaore. 1997. "On the Number and Size of Nations." *Quarterly Journal of Economics* 112 (4): 1027–1056.

Alesina, Alberto, Enrico Spolaore, and Romain Wacziarg. 2005. "Trade, Growth and the Size of Countries." In *Handbook of Economic Growth*, edited by Phillippe Aghion and Steven N. Durlauf, 1499–1542. Amsterdam: North-Holland/Elsevier.

Alesina, Alberto, and Lawrence H. Summers. 1993. "Central Bank Independence and Macroeconomic Performance: Some Comparative Evidence." *Journal of Money, Credit and Banking* 25 (2): 151–162.

Alexander, Robert. 1990. "Import Substitution in Latin America in Retrospect." In *Progress Toward Development in Latin America: from Prebisch to technological autonomy*, edited by James Dietz and Dilmus James, 15–28. Boulder: Lynne Rienner Publishers.

Allen, Franklin, Jun Qian, and Meijun Qian. 2005. "Law, Finance, and Economic Growth in China." *Journal of Financial Economics* 77 (1): 57–116.

Allendorf, Henrike, Jorge Coronado, Juan O'Farrell, and Jorge Trefogli. 2011. "Breaking the Mould: How Latin America Is Coping with Volatile Capital Flows." Bretton Woods Project and Latindadd. http://www.brettonwoodsproject.org/wp-content/uploads/2013/10/breakingthemould.pdf.

References

Altimir, Oscar. 1979. "La Dimensión de la Pobreza en América Latina." *Cuadernos de la CEPAL*, no. 27: 1–99.

Angelucci, Manuela, Dean Karlan, and Jonathan Zinman. 2014. "Microcredit Impacts: Evidence from a Randomized Microcredit Program Placement Experiment by Compartamos Banco." NBER Working Paper 19827, Cambridge, MA.

Anner, Mark. 2008. "Meeting the Challenges of Industrial Restructuring: Labor Reform and Enforcement in Latin America." *Latin American Politics and Society* 50 (2): 33–65.

Ari, Ayse, and Fatma Zeren. 2013. "Trade Openness and Economic Growth: A Panel Causality Test." *International Journal of Business and Social Science* 4 (9): 317–324.

Arias, Omar, Nora Lustig, and Jamele Rigolini. 2002. "Poverty Reduction and Economic Growth: the Two-Way Causality" *Inter-American Development Bank, Technical Papers Series*, February. http://www.iadb.org/sds/doc/GrowthIneqDualCaus.pdf.

Armendáriz, Beatriz. 1989. "Acuerdos de deuda extranjera con varios acreedores." 1989. *Cuadernos Económicos del I.C.E.*, no. 43.

Armendáriz, Beatriz. 1991. "Foreign Debt Negotiations: An Historical and Theoretical Analysis." PhD diss., Massachusetts Institute of Technology.

Armendáriz, Beatriz. 1992. "On the Pricing of LDC Debt: An Analysis Based on Historical Evidence from Latin America." OECD Development Centre Working Papers 52, Paris.

Armendáriz, Beatriz. 1993. "Analytical Issues on LDC Debt: A Survey." *The World Economy* 16 (4): 467–482.

Armendáriz, Beatriz. 1999. "Development Banking." *Journal of Development Economics* 58:83–100.

Armendáriz, Beatriz, and Patricia Armendáriz. 1999. "Debt Relief, High Growth and Stabilization in Mexico." *Journal of Development Economics* 48:135–149.

Armendáriz, Beatriz, and Francisco Ferreira. 1995. "The World Bank and the Analysis of the International Debt Crisis." In *The New Institutional Economics and Third World Development*, edited by John Harris, Janet Hunter, and Colin Lewis, 215–233. New York: Routledge.

Armendáriz, Beatriz, and Jonathan Morduch. 2010. *The Economics of Microfinance*. Cambridge, MA: MIT Press.

Armendáriz, Beatriz, and Jonathan Morduch. 2012. *The Economics of Microfinance*. Chinese edition. Beijing: Renmin University Press.

Armendáriz, Beatriz, and Alejandro Reynoso. 2013. "On the Design of a Temporary Exit of Insolvent Countries from the Eurozone." Typescript, University College London and Harvard University.

Armendáriz, Beatriz, and Sophie Roell. 1994. "Economic Strategies for Peace in Chiapas." Working paper no. 238. In *State of Violence: The Limits to National Sovereignty in Mexico*. London: Institute of Latin American Studies (ILAS).

Arnold, Jens. 2008. "Do Tax Structures Affect Aggregate Economic Growth? Empirical Evidence from a Panel of OECD Countries." OECD Economics Department Working Papers 643, Paris.

Arnold, Jens, Bert Brys, Christopher Heady, Asa Johansson, Cyrille Schwellnus, and Laura Vartia. 2011. "Tax Policy for Economic Recovery and Growth." *Economic Journal* 121:59–80.

Asian Development Bank. 2010. Annual Report. http://www.adb.org/documents/adb-annual-report-2010.

Aspe, Pedro. 1993. *Economic Transformation the Mexican Way*. Cambridge, MA: MIT Press.

Attanasio, Orazio, Pinelopi K. Goldberg, and Nina Pavcnik. 2003. "Trade Reforms and Wage Inequality in Colombia." NBER Working Paper 9830, Cambridge, MA.

Attanasio, Orazio, Costas Meghir, and Ana Santiago. 2012. "Education Choices in Mexico: Using a Structural Model and a Randomized Experiment to Evaluate PROGRESA." *Review of Economic Studies* 79 (1): 37–66.

Attanasio, Orazio, and Miguel Székely. 1999. "An Asset-Based Approach to the Analysis of Poverty in Latin America". IDB Working Paper No. 109. http://ssrn.com/abstract=1814653 or http://dx.doi.org/10.2139/ssrn.1814653.

Attanasio, Orazio, and Miguel Székely. 2001. "Going beyond Income: Redefining Poverty in Latin America." In *Portrait of the Poor: An Assets-Based Approach*, edited by Orazio Attanasio and Miguel Székely, 1–43. Baltimore: Johns Hopkins University Press.

Auty, Richard M. 1994. "Industrial Policy Reform in Six Large Newly Industrializing Countries: The Resource Curse Thesis." *World Development* 22 (1): 11–26.

Ayala, Astrid, Juncal Cunado, and Luis Alberiko Gil-Alana. 2013. "Real Convergence: Empirical Evidence for Latin America." *Applied Economics* 45 (22): 3220–3229.

Backus, David, Patrick Kehoe, and Timothy Kehoe. 1992. "In Search of Scale Effect in Trade and Growth." *Journal of Economic Theory* 58:377–409.

Baer, Werner. 1972. "Import Substitution and Industrialization in Latin America: Experience and Interpretations." *Latin American Research Review* 7 (1): 95–111.

Baland, Jean-Marie, and James Robinson. 2000. "Is Child Labor Inefficient?" *Journal of Political Economy* 108:663–679.

Balisacan, Arsenio M., Ujjayant Chakravorty, and Majah-Leah V. Ravago. 2015. *Sustainable Economic Development: Resources, Environment, and Institutions*. Amsterdam: Academic Press/Elsevier B.V.

Banerjee, Abhijit V., and Esther Duflo. 2011. *Poor Economics: A Radical Rethinking of the Way to Fight Global Poverty*. New York: Public Affairs.

Banerjee, Abhijit, and Andrew Newman. 1994. "Poverty, Incentives, and Development." *American Economic Review* 84 (2): 211–215.

Bank for International Settlements. 2008. "Financial Liberalization and Emerging Market Capital Flows." BIS Paper No. 44. Basel, Switzerland: Bank for International Settlements.

Barahona, Juan Carlos, Eduardo Doryan, Felipe Larraín, and Jeffrey Sachs. 2001. "Reducing the Vulnerability to Natural Disasters: Hurricane Mitch and Central America." In *Structural Reform*, vol. 2 of *Economic Development in Central America*, edited by Felipe Larraín, 269–307. Cambridge, MA: Harvard Studies in International Development, Harvard University Press.

Bárcena, Alicia, Antonio Prado, and Martín Hopenhayn. 2010. "Time for Equality: Closing the Gaps, Opening Trails." Santiago, Chile: Economic Commision for Latin America and the Caribbean.

Barozet, Emmanuelle, and Jaime Fierro. 2011. "Clase Media en Chile, 1990–2011: Algunas Implicancias Sociales y Políticas." Konrad Adenauer-Stiftung, Serie de Estudios no. 4, 82 p.

Barro, Robert. 1991. "Economic Growth in a Cross Section of Countries." *Quarterly Journal of Economics* 106 (2): 407–443.

Barro, Robert. 1997. *The Determinants of Economic Growth: A Cross-Country Empirical Study*. Cambridge, MA: MIT Press.

Barro, Robert. 2000. "Inequality and Growth in a Panel of Countries." *Journal of Economic Growth* 5 (1): 5–32.

Barro, Robert, and Jong-Wha Lee. 2013. "A New Data Set of Educational Attainment in the World, 1950–2010." *Journal of Development Economics* 104:184–198.

Barro, Robert, and Charles J. Redlick. 2011. "Macroeconomic Effects of Government Purchases and Taxes." *Quarterly Journal of Economics* 126:51–102.

Barro, Robert, and Xavier Sala-i-Martin. 1995. *Economic Growth*. New York: McGraw Hill.

Basurto, Jorge. 2012. "Populism in Mexico: From Cárdenas to López Obrador." In *Populism in Latin America*, 2nd ed., edited by Michael Conniff, 86–109. Tuscaloosa: University of Alabama Press.

Bentolila, Samuel, and Giuseppe Bertola. 1990. "Firing Costs and Labour Demand: How Bad Is Eurosclerosis?" *Review of Economic Studies* 57 (3): 381–402.

Bentolila, Samuel, and Gilles Saint Paul. 1994. "A Model of Labor Demand with Linear Adjustment Costs." *Labour Economics* 1 (3–4): 303–326.

Berganza, Juan Carlos. 2012. "Fiscal Rules in Latin America: A Survey." Banco de España, documentos ocasionales, no. 1208.

Berins Collier, Ruth, and David Collier. 1991. *Shaping the Political Arena: Critical Junctures, the Labor Movement, and Regime Dynamics in Latin America*. Princeton, NJ: Princeton University Press.

Bernanke, Ben. 1995. "The Macroeconomics of the Great Depression: A Comparative Approach." *Journal of Money, Credit and Banking* 27 (1): 1–28.

Bernanke, Ben, and Harold James. 1991. "The Gold Standard, Deflation, and Financial Crisis in the Great Depression: An International Comparison." NBER Working Paper 3488, Cambridge, MA.

Berrios, Ruben, Andrae Marak, and Scott Morgenstern. 2010. "Explaining Hydrocarbon Nationalization in Latin America: Economics and Political Ideology." *Review of International Political Economy* 18 (5): 1–25.

Bertola, Giuseppe. 1990. "Job Security, Employment and Wages." *European Economic Review* 34 (4): 851–886.

Bértola, Luis, Cecilia Castelnovo, Javier Rodríguez, and Henry Willebald. 2008. "Income Distribution in the Latin American Southern Cone during the First Globalization Boom and Beyond." *International Journal of Comparative Sociology* 50 (5–6): 452–485.

Bértola, Luis, and José Antonio Ocampo. 2012. *The Economic Development of Latin America since Independence*. Oxford: Oxford University Press.

Bértola, Luis, and José Antonio Ocampo. 2013. *Economic Development of Latin America since Independence*. Oxford: Oxford University Press.

Bértola, Luis, and Jeffrey Williamson. 2006. "Globalization in Latin America before 1940." In *The Cambridge Economic History of Latin America*, vol. 2, edited by Victor Bulmer-Thomas, John Coatsworth, and Roberto Cortés Conde, 11–56. New York: Cambridge University Press.

Bertranou, Fabio. 2007. *Informal Economy, Independent Workers and Social Security Coverage in Argentina, Chile and Uruguay*. Santiago, Chile: International Labor Office.

Besley, Timothy J., Konrad B. Burchardi, and Maitreesh Ghatak. 2012. "Incentives and the De Soto Effect." *Quarterly Journal of Economics* 127:237–282.

Bhagwati, Jagdish. 1988. *Protectionism*. Cambridge, MA: MIT Press.

Bianchi, Andrés, Robert Devlin, and Joseph Ramos. 1987. "The Adjustment Process in Latin America, 1981–1986." Paper presented at "World Bank—IMF Symposium on Growth Oriented Adjustment Programs," Washington, DC, February 25–27.

Biles, James. 2009. "Informal Work in Latin America: Competing Perspectives and Recent Debates." *Geography Compass* 3 (1): 214–236.

Birdsall, Nancy. 2012. "A Note on the Middle Class in Latin America." Center for Global Development Working Paper 303, Washington, DC.

Birdsall, Nancy, Augusto de la Torre, and Rachel Menezes. 2001. "Washington Contentious: Economic Policies and Social Equity in Latin America." Washington, DC: Carnegie Endowment for International Peace.

Birdsall, Nancy, Augusto de la Torre, and Felipe Valencia. 2011. "The Washington Consensus: Assessing a Damaged Brand." In *The Oxford Handbook of Latin American Economics*, edited by José Antonio Ocampo and Jaime Ros, 79–106. Oxford: Oxford University Press.

Blanchard, Olivier, and Nobuhiro Kiyotaki. 1987. "Monopolistic Competition and the Effects of Aggregate Demand." *American Economic Review* 77 (4): 647–666.

Blanchard, Olivier, and Roberto Perotti. 2002. "An Empirical Characterization of the Dynamic Effects of Changes in Government Spending and Taxes on Output." *Quarterly Journal of Economics* 107:1329–1368.

Bleaney, Michael, Norman Gemmell, and Richard Kneller. 2001. "Testing the Endogenous Growth Model: Public Expenditure, Taxation, and Growth over the Long Run." *Canadian Journal of Economics* 34 (1): 36–57.

Bloom, David, Jeffrey Sachs, Paul Collier, and Christopher Udry. 1998. "Geography, Demography, and Economic Growth in Africa." *Brookings Papers on Economic Activity* 1998 (2): 207–295.

Bortolotti, Bernardo, and Enrico Perotti. 2007. "From Government to Regulatory Governance: Privatization and the Residual Role of the State." *World Bank Research Observer* 22 (1): 53–66.

Bosch, Mariano, Edwin Goñi-Pacchioni, and William Maloney. 2012. "Trade Liberalization, Labor Reforms and Formal–Informal Employment Dynamics." *Labour Economics* 19 (5): 653–667.

Boserup, Ester. 1965. *The Conditions of Agricultural Growth: The Economics of Agrarian Change under Population Pressure*. London: George Allen Unwin.

Bourguignon, Francois. 2003. "The Growth Elasticity of Poverty Reduction: Explaining Heterogeneity across Countries and Time Periods." In *Inequality and Growth: Theory and Policy Implications*, edited by Theo S. Eicher and Stephen J. Turnovsky, 3–26. Cambridge, MA: MIT Press.

Braga, Carlos. 2010. "Import Substitution Industrialization in Latin America: Experience and Lessons for the Future." In *Economic Development in Latin America*, edited by Hadi Esfahani, Giovanni Facchini, and Geoffrey Hewings, 34–42. Basingstoke, Hampshire, UK: Palgrave Macmillan.

Braun, Juan, Matías Braun, Ignacio Briones, and José Díaz. 2000. "Economía Chilena 1810–1995, Estadísticas Históricas." Working Paper 187, Pontificia Universidad Católica de Chile, January.

Bravo-Ortega, Claudio, and José De Gregorio. 2006. "The Relative Richness of the Poor? Natural Resources, Human Capital and Economic Growth." In *Neither Curse nor Destiny: Natural Resources and Development*, edited by Daniel Lederman and William F. Maloney, 71–99. Stanford University Press, Palo Alto.

Brea, Jorge. 2003. "Population Dynamics in Latin America." *Population Bulletin* 58 (1): 1–36.

Brecher, Richard, and Carlos Díaz Alejandro. 1977. "Tariffs, Foreign Capital and Immiserizing Growth." *Journal of International Economics* 7 (4): 317–322.

Buckholder, Mark, and Lyman Johnson. 2003. *Colonial Latin America*. 5th ed. Oxford: Oxford University Press.

Bulmer-Thomas, Victor. 2003. *The Economic History of Latin America since Independence*. 2nd ed. Cambridge, UK: Cambridge University Press.

Bulut, Sahin, Metín Dam, Ismet Gocer, and Mehmet Mercan. 2013. "The Effect of Openness on Economic Growth for BRIC-T Countries: Panel Data Analysis." *Eurasian Journal of Business and Economics* 6:1–14.

Burdekin, Richard C. K., Arthur T. Denzau, Manfred W. Keil, Thitithep Sitthiyot, and Thomas D. Willett. 2004. "When Does Inflation Hurt Economic Growth? Different Nonlinearities for Different Economies." *Journal of Macroeconomics* 26:519–532.

Burkholder, Mark. 1990. *Colonial Latin America*. Oxford, UK: Oxford University Press.

Burnside, Craig, and David Dollar. 2000. "Aid, Policies, and Growth." *American Economic Review* 90 (4): 847–868.

Busse, Matthias. 2003. "Tariffs, Transport Costs, and the WTO Doha Round: The Case of Developing Countries." *Journal of International Law and Trade Policy* 4 (1): 15–31.

Caballero, Ricardo, and Mohamad Hammour. 1998. "Jobless Growth: Appropriability, Factor Substitution and Unemployment." Carnegie-Rochester Conference Series on Public Policy, vol. 48, 51–94, June.

Cagan, Phillip. 1956. "The Monetary Dynamics of Hyperinflation." In *Studies in the Quantity Theory of Money*, edited by Milton Friedman, 25–117. Chicago: University of Chicago Press.

Calderón, César, and Eduardo Levy Yeyati. 2009. "Zooming In: From Aggregate Volatility to Income Distribution." World Bank Policy Research Working Paper 4895. Washington, DC: World Bank.

Calderón, César, and Lin Liu. 2003. "The Direction of Causality between Financial Development and Economic Growth." *Journal of Development Economics* 72:321–334.

Calvo, Guillermo A., and Frederic S. Mishkin. 2003. "The Mirage of Exchange Rate Regimes for Emerging Market Countries." *Journal of Economic Perspectives* 17 (4): 99–118.

Campa, José Manuel. 1990. "Exchange Rates and Economic Recovery in the 1930s: An Extension to Latin America." *Journal of Economic History* 50:677–682.

Cañas, Jesús, Roberto A. Coronado, Robert W. Gilmer, and Eduardo Saucedo. 2011. "The Impact of the Maquiladora Industry on U.S. Border Cities." Research Department Working Paper 1107, Federal Reserve of Dallas.

Carbonetto Daniel, M. Inés C. de Cabellos, Oscar Dancourt, César Ferrari, Daniel Martinez, Jaime Mezzera, Gustavo Saberbein, Javier Tantaleán, and Pierre Vigier. 1997. *El Perú Heterodoxo. Un Modelo Económico*. Lima, Perú: Instituto Nacional de Planificación.

Cardenas, Enrique, Jose Antonio Ocampo, and Rosemary Thorp. 2000. *An Economic History of Twentieth Century Latin America*. Vol. 3, Industrialization and the State in Latin America: The Post War Years. New York: Palgrave Press and St. Martins.

Cardoso, Eliana. "Inflation and Poverty." 1992. NBER Working Paper 4006, Cambridge, MA.

Cardoso, Eliana, and Ann Helwege. 1992. *Latin America's Economy: Diversity Trends and Conflicts*. Cambridge, MA: MIT Press.

Cardoso, Fernando Henrique, and Henrique Brignoli. 1979. *Historia Económica de América Latina*. Vol. 2, *Economía de la Exportación y Desarrollo Capitalista*. Barcelona, España: Editorial Crítica.

Cardoso, Fernando Henrique, and Enzo Faletto. 1969. *Dependencia y Desarrollo en América Latina: Ensayo de interpretación sociológica*. México D.F., Mexico: Siglo XXI.

Carlstrom, Charles, and Timothy Fuerst. 2009. "Central Bank Independence and Inflation: A Note." *Economic Inquiry* 47 (1): 182–186.

Carmack, Robert, Janine Gasco, and Gary Gossen. 2007. *The Legacy of Mesoamerica: History and Culture of a Native American Civilization*. 2nd ed. Upper Saddle River, NJ: Pearson Education, Inc.

Carroll, Robert, Douglas Holtz-Eakin, Mark Rider, and Harvey Rosen. 2001. "Personal Income Taxes and the Growth of Small Firms." *Tax Policy and the Economy* 15:121–147.

Carstens, Agustín, and Luis Jácome. 2005a. "The 1990s Institutional Reform of Monetary Policy in Latin America." Working Papers 343, Central Bank of Chile.

Carstens, Agustín, and Luis Jácome. 2005b. "Latin American Central Bank Reform: Problems and Challenges." Working Paper WP/05/114. Washington, DC: International Monetary Fund.

Castellanos, Laura. 2007. *México Armado: 1943–1981*. México D.F., México: Editorial Era.

Castelló, Amparo, and Rafael Doménech. 2002. "Human Capital Inequality and Economic Growth: Some New Evidence." *Economic Journal* 112 (478): 187–200.

Cavallo, Eduardo, and Jeffrey Frankel. 2008. "Does Openness to Trade Make Countries More Vulnerable to Sudden Stops, or Less? Using Gravity to Establish Causality." *Journal of International Money and Finance* 27 (8): 1430–1452.

Cavallo, Domingo, Roberto Domenech, and Yair Mundlak. 1989. *La Argentina que pudo ser: Los costos de la represión económica*. Buenos Aires: Ediciones Manantial.

Celasun, Oya, Francesco Grigoli, Keiko Honjo, Javier Kapsoli, Alexander Klemm, Bogdan Lissovolik, Jan Luksic, Marialuz Moreno Badia, Joana Pereira, Marcos Poplawski-Ribeiro, Baoping Shang, and Yulia Ustyugova. 2015. *Fiscal Policy in Latin America: Lessons and Legacies of the Global Financial Crisis*. Washington, DC: International Monetary Fund.

Cerda, Rodrigo, and Felipe Larraín. 2005. "Inversión Privada e Impuestos Corporativos: Evidencia para Chile." *Cuadernos de Economía* 42 (126): 257–281.

Cerda, Rodrigo, and Felipe Larraín. 2010. Corporate Taxes and the Demand for Labor and Capital in Developing Countries. *Small Business Economics* 34 (2): 187–201.

Chamon, Marcos, and Eswar Prasad. 2010. "Why Are Saving Rates of Urban Households in China Rising?" *American Economic Journal. Macroeconomics* 2 (1): 93–130.

Chang, Roberto, Linda Kaltani, and Norman Loayza. 2009. "Openness Can Be Good for Growth: The Role of Policy Complementarities." *Journal of Development Economics* 90:33–49.

Chenery, Hollis, Sherman Robinson, and Moshe Syrquin. 1986. *Industrialization and Growth: A Comparative Study*. New York: Published for the World Bank by Cambridge University Press.

Chernick, Howard. 1997. "Tax Progressivity and State Economic Performance." *Economic Development Quarterly* 11 (3): 249–267.

Choksi, Ameane M., Michael Michaely, and Demetris Papageorgiou. 1991. *Liberalizing Foreign Trade: The Experience of Argentina, Chile, and Uruguay*. Vol. 1. Cambridge, MA: Basil Blackwell.

Chong, Alberto, and Florencio López-de-Silanes. 2003. "The Truth about Privatization in Latin America." IDB Working Paper #R-486, Washington, DC.

Choudhri, Ehsan, and Levis Kochin. 1980. "The Exchange Rate and the International Transmission of Business Cycle Disturbances: Some Evidence from the Great Depression." *Journal of Money, Credit and Banking* 12 (4): 565–574.

Clark, Kim B., and Lawrence H. Summers. 1979. "Labor Market Dynamics and Unemployment: A Reconsideration." *Brookings Papers on Economic Activity* 1979 (1): 13–72.

Clark, Kim B., and Lawrence H. Summers. 1982. "The Dynamics of Youth Unemployment." In *The Youth Labor Market Problem: Its Nature, Causes, and Consequences*, edited by Richard B. Freeman and David A. Wise, 199–234. Chicago: University of Chicago Press.

Coatsworth, John. 1998. "Economic and Institutional Trajectories in Nineteenth-Century Latin America." In *Latin America and the World Economy since 1800*, edited by John Coatsworth and Alan Taylor, 23–54. Cambridge, MA: Harvard University Press.

Coatsworth, John, and Jeffrey Williamson. 2002. "The Roots of Latin American Protectionism: Looking before the Great Depression." NBER Working Paper 8999, Cambridge, MA.

Collier, Paul. 2010a. *The Plundered Planet: Why We Must—and How We Can—Manage Nature for Global Prosperity*. Oxford: Oxford University Press.

Collier, Paul. 2010b. "The Political Economy of Natural Resources." *Social Research* 77 (4): 1105–1132.

Conefrey, Thomas, and John Fitz. 2011. "The Macro-Economic Impact of Changing the Rate of Corporation Tax." *Economic Modelling* 28 (3): 991–999.

The Conference Board. 2015. "The Conference Board: Productivity Brief 2015." New York.

Conniff, Michael. 2012. *Populism in Latin America*. 2nd ed. Tuscaloosa: University of Alabama Press.

Connolly, M. P., and J. Gunther. 1999. "Mercosur: Implications for Growth in Member Countries." *Current Issues in Economics and Finance* 5 (7): 1–6.

Cook, María Lorena. 2004. "Unions, Markets, and Democracy in Latin America." In *The Future of Labor Unions: Organized labor in the 21st Century*, edited by Julius Getman and F. Ray Marshall, 237–254. Austin: Ray Marshall Center for the Study of Human Resources, Lyndon B. Johnson School for Public Affairs, University of Texas.

Corbo, Vittorio. 1991. "National Economic Policies in Latin America." In *National Economic Policies*, edited by Dominick Salvatore, 205–230. Westport, CT: Greenwood Press.

Corbo, Vittorio. 1992. *Development Strategies and Policies in Latin America: A Historical Perspective*. San Francisco: International Center for Economic Growth.

Cornia, Giovanni. 2010. "Income Distribution under Latin America's Center-Left Regimes." *Journal of Human Development and Capabilities* 11 (1): 85–114.

Cornia, Giovanni. 2013. "Inequality Trends and Determinants: Latin America over 1990–2010." In *Falling Inequality in Latin America: Policy Changes and Lessons*, edited by Giovanni Cornia, 23–48. Oxford: Oxford University Press.

Cotlear, Daniel. 2011. *Population Is Aging: Is Latin America Ready?* Washington, DC: World Bank.

Crow, John. 1992. *The Epic of Latin America*. San Francisco: University of California Press.

Cuddington, John, Rodney Ludema, and Shamila Jayasuriya. 2007. "Prebisch-Singer Redux." In *Natural Resources: Neither Curse nor Destiny*, edited by Daniel Lederman and William Maloney, 103–140. Stanford, CA: Stanford University Press.

Culver, William, and Cornel J. Reinhart. 1989. "Capitalist Dreams: Chile's Response to Nineteenth-Century World Copper Competition." *Comparative Studies in Society and History* 31 (4): 722–744.

Curtin, Phillip. 1989. *Death by Migration: Europe's Encounter with the Tropical World in the Nineteenth Century*. New York: Cambridge University Press.

D'Agostino, Marcello, and Valentino Dardanoni. 2006. "The Measurement of Mobility: A Class of Distance Indices." The London School of Economics Working Paper no. 1104.

Dawson, John, and Amit Sen. 2007. "New Evidence on the Convergence of International Income from a Group of 29 Countries." *Empirical Economics* 33:199–230.

Dayal-Gulati, Anuradha, and Christian Thimann. 1997. "Saving in Southeast Asia and Latin America Compared: Searching for Policy Lessons." In *Macroeconomic Issues Facing ASEAN Countries*, edited by J. Hicklin, D. Robinson and A. Singh, 130–149. Washington, DC: International Monetary Fund.

Deaton, Angus. 2003. "Health, Inequality and Economic Development." *Journal of Economic Literature* 41 (1): 113–158.

Deaton, Angus. 2013. *The Great Escape: Health, Wealth, and the Origins of Inequality*. Princeton, NJ: Princeton University Press.

de Ferranti, David, Daniel Lederman, Guillermo Perry, and Rodrigo Suescún. 2003. "Trade for Development in Latin America and the Caribbean." World Bank Policy Research Paper. Washington, DC: World Bank. http://documents.worldbank.org/curated/en/378611468016145623/Trade-for-development-in-Latin-America-and-the-Caribbean.

de Ferranti, David, Guillermo E. Perry, Francisco Ferreira, and Michael Walton. 2004. *Inequality in Latin America: Breaking with History?* Washington, DC: World Bank.

De Gregorio, José. 2010. "The Role of Central Banks after the Financial Crisis." Economic Policy Papers of the Central Bank of Chile, no. 36.

De Janvry, Alain, and Elisabeth Sadoulet. 2000. "Growth, Poverty and Inequality in Latin America: A Causal Analysis, 1970–94." *Review of Income and Wealth* 46 (3): 267–.

Delamonica, Enrique, Alberto Minujin, and Jan Vandemoortele. 2002. "Economic Growth, Poverty and Children." *Environment and Urbanization* 14 (2): 23–43.

Dell, Melissa. 2010. "The Persistence Effects of Peru's Mining Mita." *Econometrica* 78:1863–1903.

Dell, Melissa. 2014. "Trafficking Networks and the Mexican Drug War." Typescript, Harvard University.

Dell, Melissa, Benjamin Jones, and Benjamin Olken. 2009. "Temperature and Income: Reconciling New Cross-Sectional and Panel Estimates." *American Economic Review* 99:198–204.

Dell, Melissa, Benjamin Jones, and Benjamin Olken. 2012. "Temperature Shocks and Economic Growth: Evidence from the Last Half Century." *American Economic Journal: Macroeconomics* 4 (3): 66–95.

Della Paolera, Gerardo, and Alan M. Taylor. 2003. *A New Economic History of Argentina*. Cambridge, UK: Cambridge University Press.

de Paula, Luiz Fernando, Fernando Ferrari-Filho, and Aline M. Gomes. 2014. "Capital Flows, International Imbalances and Economic Policies in Latin America." Typescript, University of the Rio de Janeiro State University.

DeShazo, Peter. 2007. "Anticorruption Efforts in Latin America: Lessons Learned." Policy Papers on the Americas, vol. 18, study 3, 21 p.

de Soto, Hernando. 1989. *The Other Path: The Economic Answer to Terrorism*. New York: Basic Books.

Di Tella, Rafael, and Juan Dubra. 2010. "Peronist Beliefs and Interventionist Policies." NBER Working Paper 16621, Cambridge, MA.

Diamond, Douglas W., and Raghuram Rajan. 2009. "The Credit Crisis: Conjectures about Causes and Remedies." *American Economic Review* 99 (2): 606–610.

Díaz-Alejandro, Carlos. 1984. "Latin American Debt: I Do Not Think We Are in Kansas Anymore." *Brookings Papers on Economic Activity* 1984 (2): 335–403.

Dobado González, Rafael, Aurora Gómez Galvarriato, and Jeffrey Williamson. 2008. "Mexican Exceptionalism: Globalization and De-Industrialization, 1750–1877." *Journal of Economic History* 68 (3): 758–811.

Dollar, David. 1992. "Outward-Oriented Developing Economies Really Do Grow More Rapidly: Evidence from 95 LDCs, 1976–1985." *Economic Development and Cultural Change* 40 (3): 523–544.

Dollar, David, and Aart Kraay. 2001. "Growth is Good for the Poor." World Bank Policy Research Working Paper 2587. Washington, DC: World Bank.

Dollar, David, and Aart Kraay. 2003. "Institutions, Trade and Growth: Revisiting the Evidence." *Journal of Monetary Economics* 50 (1): 133–162.

Dollar, David, and Aart Kraay. 2004. "Trade, Growth and Poverty." *Economic Journal* 114 (493): F22–F49.

Domar, Evsey. 1946. "Capital Expansion, Rate of Growth, and Employment." *Econometrica* 14:137–147.

Domínguez, Jorge I. 2006. *Cuba hoy: Analizando su pasado, imaginando su futuro*. Madrid: Editorial Colibrí.

Dornbusch, Rudiger, and Sebastian Edwards. 1989. "Macroeconomic Populism in Latin America." NBER Working Paper 2986, Cambridge, MA.

Dornbusch, Rudiger, and Sebastian Edwards. 1990. "Macroeconomic Populism." *Journal of Development Economics* 32:247–277.

Dornbusch, Rudiger, and Sebastian Edwards. 1991. *The Macroeconomics of Populism in Latin America*. Chicago: University of Chicago Press.

Dornbusch, Rudiger, and Mario Henrique Simonsen. 1987. "Inflation Stabilization with Incomes Policy Support." NBER Working Paper 2153, Cambridge, MA.

Drake, Paul. 1996. *Labor Movements and Dictatorships: The Southern Cone in Comparative Perspective*. Baltimore: Johns Hopkins University Press.

Drake, Paul W. 2012. "Chile's Populism Reconsidered, 1920s–1990s." In *Populism in Latin America*, 2nd ed., edited by Michael L. Conniff, 71–85. Tuscaloosa: Alabama University Press.

Dreher, Axel, and Thomas Herzfeld. 2005. "The Economic Cost of Corruption: A Survey and New Evidence." http://ssrn.com/abstract=734184 or http://dx.doi.org/10.2139/ssrn.734184.

Duflo, Esther. 2002. "The Medium Run Effects of Educational Expansion: Evidence from a Large School Construction Program in Indonesia." NBER Working Paper 8710, Cambridge, MA.

Duryea, Suzanne, and Miguel Székely. 1998. "Labor Markets in Latin America: A Supply-Side Story." IDB Working Paper 310.

Easterly, William. 1997. "The Ghost of Financing Gap: How the Harrod-Domar Growth Model Still Haunts Development Economics." World Bank Policy Research Working Paper 1807. Washington, DC: World Bank.

Easterly, William. 2007. "Was Development Assistance a Mistake?" *American Economic Review* 97 (2): 328–332.

Easterly, William, Norman Loayza, and Peter Montiel. 1997. "Has Latin America's post-reform growth been disappointing?" *Journal of International Economics* 43 (3): 287–311.

Easterly, William, and Sergio Rebelo. 1993. "Fiscal Policy and Economic Growth: An Empirical Investigation." *Journal of Monetary Economics* 32:417–458.

Easterly, William, Michael Kremer, Lant Pritchett, and Lawrence Summers. 1993. "Good Policy or Good Luck? Country Growth Performance and Temporary Shocks." *Journal of Monetary Economics* 32:459–483.

Echavarría, Juan José. 1997. "Trade Flows in the Andean Countries: Unilateral Liberalization or Regional Preferences." In *Trade: Towards Open Regionalism*, edited by Shahid Javed Burki, Guillermo E. Perry, and Sara Calvo, 79–102. Washington, DC: World Bank.

Echavarría, Juan José, and Cristina Gamboa. 2000. "Colombia and Venezuela after the Uruguay Round: Trade Policy Reform and Institutional Adjustments." Latin American Trade Network Working Paper 11.

ECLAC. 1976. *America Latina: Relación de precios del intercambio*. Santiago, Chile: Economic Commission for Latin America.

ECLAC. 1999. *International Capital Flows to Latin America: Their Implications for International and National Policies*. Santiago, Chile: Economic Commission for Latin America and the Caribbean.

ECLAC. 2002. *Social Panorama of Latin America 2001–2002*. Santiago, Chile: Economic Commission for Latin America and the Caribbean.

ECLAC. 2003. *Análisis de Resultados del Programa Puente*. Santiago, Chile: Social Development Division.

ECLAC. 2004. *Understanding Poverty from a Gender Perspective.*. Santiago, Chile: Women and Development Unit.

ECLAC. 2007. *Progreso técnico y cambio estructural en América Latina*. Santiago, Chile: Economic Commission for Latin America and the Caribbean.

ECLAC. 2008. *Social Panorama of Latin America 2008*. Santiago, Chile: Economic Commission for Latin America and the Caribbean.

ECLAC. 2011. *Social Panorama 2011*. Santiago, Chile: Economic Commission for Latin America and the Caribbean.

ECLAC. 2012. *Eslabones de la desigualdad, Heterogeneidad estructural, empleo y protección social*. Santiago, Chile: Economic Commission for Latin America and the Caribbean.

ECLAC. 2013. *Social Panorama of Latin America 2013*. Santiago, Chile: Economic Commission for Latin America and the Caribbean.

ECLAC. 2015. *Balance Preliminar de las Economías de America Latina y el Caribe*. Santiago, Chile: Economic Commission for Latin America and the Caribbean.

ECLAC and ILO. 2013. "The Employment Situation in Latin America and the Caribbean: Advances and Challenges in Measuring Decent Work." ECLAC-ILO Bulletin no. 8.

The Economist. 2006. "The Return of Populism." *The Economist*, April 12. http://www.economist.com/node/6802448.

Edwards, Sebastian. 1993. "Openess, Trade Liberalization, and Growth in Developing Countries." *Journal of Economic Literature* 31 (3): 1358–1393.

Edwards, Sebastian. 1995. *Crisis and Reform in Latin America: From Despair to Hope*. Oxford: Oxford University Press.

Edwards, Sebastian. 1998. "Openness, Productivity and Growth: What Do We Really Know?" *Economic Journal* 108 (447): 383–398.

Edwards, Sebastian. 2000. "Exchange Rate Regimes, Capital Controls, and Crisis Prevention." Working Paper for the NBER Conference on Financial Crises in Emerging Market Economies, University of California, Los Angeles.

Edwards, Sebastian, ed. 2004a. *Capital Controls and Capital Flows in Emerging Economies: Policies, Practices and Consequences*. Chicago: University of Chicago Press.

Edwards, Sebastian. 2004b. "Labor Reform and Employment in Latin America." In *Law and Employment: Lessons from Latin America and the Caribbean*, edited by James Heckman and Carmen Pagés, 349–363. Chicago: University of Chicago Press.

Edwards, Sebastian. 2009. "Forty Years of Latin America's Economic Development: From the Alliance for Progress to the Washington Consensus." NBER Working Paper 15190, Cambridge, MA.

Edwards, Sebastian, Gerardo Esquivel, and Graciela Márquez. 2007. *The Decline of Latin American Economies: Growth, Institutions, and Crises*. Chicago: University of Chicago Press.

Eichengreen, Barry. 1992. *Golden Fetters: The Gold Standard and the Great Depression, 1919–1939*. Oxford: Oxford University Press.

Eichengreen, Barry, and Ricardo Hausmann. 1999. "Exchange Rates and Financial Fragility." Paper presented at symposium "New Challenges for Monetary Policy," Jackson Hole, WY, August 27–29.

Eichengreen, Barry, Ricardo Hausmann, and Hugo Panizza. 2002. "Original Sin: The Pain, the Mystery, and the Road to Redemption." Paper presented at conference "Currency and Maturity Matchmaking: Redeeming Debt from Original Sin," Inter-American Development Bank, Washington, DC, November 21–22.

Eichengreen, Barry, and Douglas Irwin. 2010. "The Slide to Protectionism in the Great Depression: Who Succumbed and Why?" *Journal of Economic History* 70 (4): 871–897.

Eichengreen, Barry, and Richard Portes. 1989a. "Dealing with Debt: The 1930s and the 1980s." In *Dealing with the Debt Crisis*, edited by Ishrat Hussain and Ishac Diwan, 69–88. Washington, DC: World Bank.

Eichengreen, Barry, and Richard Portes. 1989b. "Resolving Debt Crises: An Historical Perspective." In *Latin American Debt: Perspectives and Solutions*, edited by Sebastian Edwards and Felipe Larraín, 68–96. Oxford: Blackwell.

Eichengreen, Barry, and Jeffrey Sachs. 1985. "Exchange Rates and Economic Recovery in the 1930s." *Journal of Economic History* 45 (4): 925–946.

Eichengreen, Barry, and Peter Temin. 1997. "The Gold Standard and the Great Depression." NBER Working Paper 6060, Cambridge, MA.

El Economista. 2014. "Reformas fiscales deben reducir la inequidad: FMI." *El Economista*, March 24. http://eleconomista.com.mx/economia-global/2014/03/14/reformas-fiscales-deben-reducir-inequidad-fmi.

Ellner, Steve. 2012. "The Heyday of Radical Populism in Venezuela and Its Reappearance." In *Populism in Latin America*, 2nd ed., edited by Michael Conniff, 132–158. Tuscaloosa: University of Alabama Press.

Engen, Eric, and Jonathan Skinner. 1996. "Taxation and Economic Growth." NBER Working Paper 5826, Cambridge, MA.

Engerman, Stanley, and Kenneth Sokoloff. 2000. "History Lessons: Institutions, Factor Endowments, and Paths of Development in the New World." *Journal of Economic Perspectives* 14 (3): 217–232.

Engstrom, Par. 2013. "Addressing the Past, Avoiding the Present, Ignoring the Future? Ongoing Human Rights Trials in Argentina." Typescript, UCL Institute of the Americas, London.

Esquivel, Gerardo, and Felipe Larraín. 2000a. "Determinantes de las Crisis Cambiarias." *El Trimestre Economico* 67 (266): 191–237.

Esquivel, Gerardo, and Felipe Larrain. 2000b. "Latin America Confronting the Asian Crisis." In *Private Capital Flows in the Age of Globalization: The Aftermath of the Asian Crisis*, edited by U. Dadush, D. Das Gupta and M. Uzan, 81–104. Northhampton: Elgar Publisher.

Ethier, Wilfred. 1998. "The New Regionalism." *Economic Journal* 108 (449): 1149–1161.

European Commission. 2015. "Trade Policy Countries and Regions: Argentina." http://ec.europa.eu/trade/policy/countries-and-regions/countries/argentina/.

Evangelist, Mike, and Valerie Sathe. 2006. "Brazil's 1998–1999 Currency Crisis." Typescript, University of Michigan.

Fajnzylber, Pablo, and J. Humberto López. 2008. *Remittances and Development: Lessons from Latin America*. Washington, DC: World Bank.

Favero, Carlo, and Francesco Giavazzi. 2010. "Reconciling VAR-Based and Narrative Measures of the Tax Multiplier." CEPR Discussion Papers 7769.

Feinberg, Richard E. 2013. "Latin American–Asian Trade Flows: No Turning Back." Paper presented at "Reaching across the Pacific: Latin America and Asia in the New Century," Woodrow Wilson International Center for Scholars, Washington, DC, June 20.

Ferede, Ergete, and Bev Dahlby. 2012. "The Impact of Tax Cuts on Economic Growth: Evidence from the Canadian Provinces." *National Tax Journal* 63:563–594.

Feres, Juan Carlos. 1997. "Notas sobre la Medición de la Pobreza según el Método del Ingreso." *CEPAL Review*, no. 61: 145–163.

Fernández, Raquel. 1997. "Returns to Regionalism: An Evaluation of Nontraditional Gains from Regional Trade Agreements." World Bank Policy Research Working Paper 1816. Washington, DC: World Bank.

Fernández, Raquel, and Dani Rodrik. 1991. "Resistance to Reform: Status Quo Bias in the Presence of Individual-Specific Uncertainty." *American Economic Review* 81 (5): 1146–1155.

Ferreira, Francisco H. G., Anna Fruttero, Philippe Leite, and Leonardo Luccetti. 2011. "Raising Food Prices and Household Welfare: Evidence from Brazil 2008." World Bank Policy Research Working Paper 5652, May. Washington, DC: World Bank.

Ferreira, Francisco, Julian Messina, Jamele Rigolini, Luis-Felipe López-Calva, María Ana Lugo, and Renos Vakis. 2012. *Economic Mobility and the Rise of the Latin American Middle Class*. Washington, DC: World Bank.

Financial Times. 2012. "Bolivia Seizes Spanish Energy Group." *Financial Times*, May 1. http://www.ft.com/cms/s/0/8b563a14-93b3-11e1-8c6f-00144feab49a.html#axzz4G7Bbmp1b.

Fischer, Stanley, Ratna Sahay, and Carlos A. Végh. 2002. "Modern Hyper- and High Inflations." *Journal of Economic Literature* 40 (3): 837–880.

Fisher, John Robert. 1985. *Commercial Relations between Spain and Spanish America in the Era of Free Trade, 1778–1796*. Liverpool: University of Liverpool.

Fiszbein, Ariel, and Norbert Schady. 2009. *Conditional Cash Transfers: Reducing Present and Future Poverty*. Washington, DC: World Bank.

Flores, William. 1997. "New Citizens vs. Citizenry: Undocumented Immigrants and Latino Cultural Citizenship." In *Latino Cultural Citizenship: Claiming Identity, Space and Rights*, edited by William Vincent Flores and Rina Benmayor, 255–277. Boston: Beacon Press.

Folster, Stefan, and Magnus Henrekson. 2001. "Growth Effects of Government Expenditure and Taxation in Rich Countries." *European Economic Review* 45:1501–1520.

Foreign Bondholders Protective Council. 1936. Annual report. http://sul-derivatives.stanford.edu/derivative?CSNID=00014820&mediaType=application/pdf.

Fostel, Ana, and Graciela Kaminsky. 2008. "Latin America's Access to International Capital Markets: Good Behavior or Global Liquidity?" In *Current Account and External Financing*, vol. 12, edited by Kevin Cowan, Sebastián Edwards, and Rodrigo O. Valdés, 117–158. Santiago: Central Bank of Chile.

Frankel, Jeffrey A., David Parsley, and Shang-Jin Wei. 2012. "Slow Pass-Through around the World: A New Import for Developing Countries?" *Open Economies Review* 23 (2): 213–251.

Frankema, Ewout. 2008. "Wage Inequality in Twentieth Century Latin America: A Comparative Perspective." Typescript, University of Groningen, The Netherlands.

Franko, Patrice. 2007. *The Puzzle of Latin American Economic Development*. 3rd ed. Lanham, MD: Rowman and Littlefield Publishers.

Frenkel, Roberto, and Martín Rapetti. 2010. "A Concise History of Exchange Rate Regimes in Latin America." Economics Department Working Paper Series 2010-01, University of Massachusetts Amherst.

Friedman, Milton. 1963. *Inflation: Causes and Consequences*. New York: Asia Publishing House.

Friedman, Milton. 1992. "Do Old Fallacies Ever Die?" *Journal of Economic Literature* 30 (4): 2129–2132.

Furceri, Davide, Stéphanie Guichard, and Elena Rusticelli. 2012. "Episodes of Large Capital Inflows, Banking and Currency Crises, and Sudden Stops." *International Finance* 15 (1): 1–35.

Furtado, Celso. 1966. "U.S. Hegemony and the Future of Latin America." *World Today* 22 (9): 375–385.

Furtado, Celso. 1967. "La concentración del poder económico en los Estados Unidos y sus proyecciones en América latina." *Estudios Internacionales* 1 (3–4): 323–336.

Gallego, Francisco, and Norman Loayza. 2002. "The Golden Period for Growth in Chile: Explanations and Forecasts." In *Economic Growth: Sources, Trends, and Cycles*, edited by Norman Loayza and Raimundo Soto, 417–463. Santiago: Central Bank of Chile.

Gallup, John Luke, Jeffrey D. Sachs, and Andrew D. Mellinger. 1999. "Geography and Economic Development." *International Regional Science Review* 22 (2): 179–232.

Galván, Javier A. 2004. "The Bittersweet Chapter in the 19th Century Cuba, 1817–1886." *Revista de Humanidades: Tecnológico de Monterrey*, no. 16: 211–231. Mexico: Instituto Tecnológico de Estudios Superiores de Monterrey.

García, Marito, and Charity M. T. Moore. 2012. *The Cash Dividend: The Rise of Cash Transfers in Sub-Saharan Africa*. Washington, DC: World Bank.

Gasparini, Leonardo, Guillermo Cruces, and Leopoldo Tornarolli. 2009. "Recent Trends in Income Inequality in Latin America." ECINEQ Working Paper 132, Society for the Study of Economic Inequality.

Gavin, Michael, and Ricardo Hausmann. 1996. *Macroeconomic Volatility and Economic Development*. Paris: OECD Development Centre Publication.

Gavin, Michael, Ricardo Hausmann, and Leonardo Leiderman. 1996. "Macroeconomics of Capital Flows in Latin America: Experience and Policy Issues." In *Volatile Capital Flows: Taming Their Impact on Latin America*, edited by Ricardo Hausmann and Liliana Rojas-Suárez, 2–59. Washington, DC: IDB/Johns Hopkins University.

Gemmell, Norman, Richard Kneller, and Ismael Sanz. 2011. "The Timing and Persistence of Fiscal Policy Impacts on Growth: Evidence from OECD Countries." *Economic Journal* 21:33–58.

Gertler, Paul J., and Simone Boyce. 2001."An Experiment in Incentive-Based Welfare: The Impact of PROGRESA on Health in Mexico." University of California, Berkeley.

Gertner, Robert, David Scharfstein, and Jeremy Stein. 1994. "Internal versus External Capital Markets." *Quarterly Journal of Economics* 109 (4): 1211–1230.

Ghosh, Amit. 2013. "Exchange Rate Pass-Through, Macro Fundamentals and Regime Choice in Latin America." *Journal of Macroeconomics* 35:163–171.

Gillman, Max, Mark Harris, and Laszlo Mátyás. 2004. "Inflation and Growth: Explaining a Negative Effect." *Empirical Economics* 29:149–167.

Glaeser, Edward, and Andrei Shleifer. 2002. "Legal Origins." *Quarterly Journal of Economics* 117:1193–1230.

Glaeser, Edward, Rafael La Porta, Florencio Lopez-de-Silanes, and Andrei Shleifer. 2004. "Do Institutions Cause Growth?" *Journal of Economic Growth* 9 (3): 271–303.

Goldberg, Pinelopi, and Michael Knetter. 1997. "Goods Prices and Exchange Rates: What Have We Learned?" *Journal of Economic Literature* 35:1243–1292.

Goldberg, Pinelopi K., and Nina Pavcnik. 2003. "The Response of the Informal Sector to Trade Liberalization." *Journal of Development Economics* 72 (2): 463–496.

Gómez, Juan Carlos, and Juan Pablo Jiménez. 2012. "Tax Structure and Tax Evasion in Latin America." United Nations, Economic Commission for Latin America and the Caribbean, No. 5350.

Goñi, Edwin, J. Humberto López, and Luis Servén. 2011. "Fiscal Redistribution and Income Inequality in Latin America." *World Development* 39 (9): 1558–1569.

Goudie, Andrew, and Paul Ladd. 1999. "Economic Growth, Poverty and Inequality." *Journal of International Development* 11:177–195.

Gourinchas, Pierre Olivier, Rodrigo Valdés, Oscar Landerretche, Ernesto Talvi, and Adhijit V. Banerjee. 2001. "Lending Booms: Latin America and the World." *Economía* 1 (2): 47–99.

Green, Duncan, and Sue Branford. 2013. *Faces of Latin America*. 4th ed. New York: Monthly Review Press.

Green, William H. 2008. *Econometric Analysis*. 6th ed. Upper Saddle River, NJ: Prentice-Hall.

Griffith-Jones, Stephany and José Antonio Ocampo. 1999. "International Capital Flows to Latin America: Their Implications for International and National Policies," no. 31385, Economic Comission for Latin America and the Caribbean. http://repositorio.cepal.org/bitstream/handle/11362/7536/1/S2000560_en.pdf.

Griffith, Rachel, Stephen Redding, and John Van Reenen. 2004. "Mapping the Two Faces of R&D: Productivity Growth in a Panel of OECD Industries." *Review of Economics and Statistics* 86:883–895.

Grilli, Enzo, and Maw Cheng Yang. 1988. "Primary Commodity Prices, Manufactured Goods Prices, and the Terms of Trade of Developing Countries: What the Long Run Shows." *World Bank Economic Review* 2 (1): 1–47.

Guimaraes, Alexandre. 2010. "State Capacity and Economic Development: The Advances and Limits of Import Substitution in Brazil." *Luso-Brazilian Review* 47 (2): 49–73.

Gupta, Indrani, and Arup Mitra. 2004. "Economic Growth, Health and Poverty: An Exploratory Study for India." *Development Policy Review* 22:193–206.

Gutierrez, Hector. 1986. "La Mortalite des Eveques Latino-Americains aux XVIIe et XVIIIe Siecles." *Annales de Demographie Historique* 1986 (1), 29–39.

Gutiérrez, Mario, and Julio E. Revilla. 2010. "Building Countercyclical Fiscal Policies in Latin America: The International Experience." World Bank Policy Research Working Paper 5251. Washington, DC: World Bank.

Gyimah-Brempong, Kwabena, and Samaria Muñoz de Camacho. 2006. "Corruption, Growth and Income Distribution: Are There Regional Differences?" *Economics of Governance* 7:245–269.

Gylfason, Thorvaldur. 2002. "Natural Resources and Economic Growth: What Is the Connection?" In *Fostering Sustainable Growth in Ukraine*, edited by Stephan Cramon-Taubadel and Iryna Akimova, 48–66. Heidelberg: Physica-Verlag.

Harberger, Arnold. 1970. "Economic Policy Problems in Latin America: A Review." *Journal of Political Economy* 78 (4): 1007–1016.

Harkness, Susan. 2010. "The Contribution of Women's Employment and Earnings to Household Income Inequality: A Cross-Country Analysis." Luxembourg Income Study Working Paper Series, Working Paper 531.

Harris, John R., and Michael P. Todaro. 1970. "Migration, Unemployment, and Development: A Two-Sector Analysis." *American Economic Review* 60 (1): 126–142.

Harrison, Ann. 1996. "Openness and Growth: A Time-Series, Cross-Country Analysis for Developing Countries." *Journal of Development Economics* 48:419–447.

Harrod, Roy. 1939. "An Essay in Dynamic Theory." *Economic Journal* 49:14–33.

Hausmann, Ricardo, Michael Gavin, Carmen Pagés-Serra, and Ernesto H. Stein. 1999. "Financial Turmoil and Choice of Exchange Rate Regime." Working paper no. 400, Intera-American Development Bank.

Hausmann, Ricardo, Ugo Panizza, and Roberto Rigobon. 2006. "The Long-Run Volatility Puzzle of the Real Exchange Rate." *Journal of International Money and Finance* 25:93–134.

Hausmann, Ricardo, and Andrés Velasco. 2002. "Hard Money's Soft Underbelly: Understanding the Argentine Crisis." *Brookings Trade Forum* 2002 (1): 59–104.

Hayo, Berndt, and Matthias Uhl. 2013. "The Macroeconomic Effects of Legislated Tax Changes in Germany." *Oxford Economic Papers* 66:397–418.

Heckman, James, and Carmen Pagés-Serra. 2000. "The Cost of Job Security Regulation: Evidence from Latin American Labor Markets." *Economía* 1 (1): 109–154.

Helms, Jay. 1985. "The Effect of State and Local Taxes on Economic Growth: A Time Series–Cross Section Approach." *Review of Economics and Statistics* 67 (4): 574–582.

Helpman, Elhanan. 1993. "Innovation, Imitation and Intellectual Property Rights." *Econometrica* 61 (6): 1247–1280.

Heltberg, Rasmus. 2002. "The Growth Elasticity of Poverty." Helsinki: United Nations University, World Institute for Development Economics Research.

Hernández-Coss, Raúl. 2005. "The U.S.–Mexico Remittance Corridor: Lessons on Shifting from Informal to Formal Transfer Systems." World Bank Working Paper 47. Washington, DC: World Bank.

Hirschman, Albert. 1958. *The Strategy of Economic Development*. New Haven, CT: Yale University Press.

Holcombe, Randall, and Donald Lacombe. 2004. "The Effect of State Income Taxation on Per Capita Income Growth." *Public Finance Review* 32:292–312.

Holland, Alisha. 2014. "Forbearance as Redistribution: Enforcement Politics in Urban Latin America." PhD diss., Harvard University.

Holmes, Mark. 2005. "New Evidence on Long-Run Output Convergence among Latin American Countries." *Journal of Applied Econometrics* 8 (2): 299–319.

Horowitz, Joel. 2012. "Populism and Its Legacies in Argentina." In *Populism in Latin America*, 2nd ed., edited by Michael L. Conniff, 23–47. Tuscaloosa: University of Alabama Press.

IDB. 1996. *Economic and Social Progress in Latin America*. Washington, DC: IBD.

IDB. 2004. *Good Jobs Wanted: Labor Markets in Latin America*. Washington, DC: IDB.

IDB. 2005. *Summit of the Americas: The IDB and Job Creation in the Americas*. Mar del Plata, Argentina: Inter-American Development Bank.

ILO. 2005. *2005 Labor Overview: Latin America and the Caribbean*. Lima: ILO/Regional Office for Latin America and the Caribbean.

ILO. 2011. *2011 Labour Overview: Latin America and the Caribbean*. Lima: ILO/Regional Office for Latin America and the Caribbean.

ILO. 2012–2013. *Global Wage Report: Wages and Equitable Growth*. Geneva: ILO.

ILO. 2013. *2013 Labour Overview: Latin America and the Caribbean*. Lima: ILO/Regional Office for Latin America and the Caribbean.

ILO. 2014a. *La Estrategia de Desarrollo de los Sistemas de Seguridad Social de la OIT. El Papel de los Pisos de Protección Social en América Latina y el Caribe*. Lima: OIT, Oficina Regional para América Latina y el Caribe.

ILO. 2014b. *Social Panorama*. Geneva: ILO.

Imbens, Guido, and Thomas Lemieux. 2008. "Regression Discontinuity Designs: A Guide to Practice." *Journal of Econometrics* 142 (2): 615–635.

IMF. 1985. *Annual Report on Exchange Arrangements and Exchange Restrictions*. Washington, DC: IMF.

IMF. 1995. *Policies for Growth: The Latin American Experience*. Edited by André Lara Resende and Joaquín Muns. Washington, DC: International Monetary Fund.

IMF. 1997. *World Economic Outlook 1997 : Interim Assessment, Crisis in Asia: Regional and Global Implications*. Washington, DC: International Monetary Fund.

IMF. 2000. *Annual Report on Exchange Arrangements and Exchange Restrictions*. Washington, DC: IMF.

IMF. 2002. IMF Survey, Vol. 31, No. 20. Washington, DC: International Monetary Fund. http://www.elibrary.imf.org/abstract/IMF023/14874-9781451926729/14874-9781451926729/14874-9781451926729.xml?rskey=SiKBu0&result=5&redirect=true.

IMF. 2004. "Macroeconomic and Structural Policies in Fund Supported Programs—Review of Experience." Washington, DC: International Monetary Fund. https://www.imf.org/external/np/pdr/2004/eng/macro.htm.

IMF. 2006. "De Facto Classification of Exchange Rate Regimes and Monetary Policy Framework." July 31. https://www.imf.org/external/np/mfd/er/2006/eng/0706.htm.

IMF. 2008. *De Facto Classification of Exchange Rate Regimes and Monetary Frameworks*. Washington, DC: International Monetary Fund.

IMF. 2009. *World Economic Outlook: Crisis and Recovery*. Washington, DC: IMF.

IMF. 2010. "Will It Hurt? Macroeconomic Effects of Fiscal Consolidation." In *World Economic Outlook: Recovery, Risk, and Rebalancing*, 93–124. Washington, DC: IMF.

IMF. 2013a. *Government Financial Statistics Yearbook, 2012*. Washington, DC: IMF.

IMF. 2013b. *World Economic and Financial Surveys, Regional Economic Outlook, Western Hemisphere, Latin America and the Caribbean*. Washington, DC: IMF.

IMF. 2013c. "Fiscal Rules Dataset, 1985–2013." www.imf.org/external/FiscalRules/map/map.htm.

IMF. 2014a. *Annual Report on Exchange Arrangements and Exchange Restrictions 2014*. Washington, DC: IMF.

IMF. 2014b. "Fiscal Policy and Income Inequality." IMF Policy Paper, Washington, DC.

IMF. 2015. *World Economic Outlook: Adjusting to Lower Commodity Prices*. Washington, DC: IMF.

IZA World of Labor. 2014. *Female Labor Force Participation in Developing Countries*. Bonn: IZA World of Labor.

Jácome, Luis Ignacio. 2004. "The Late 1990s Financial Crisis in Ecuador: Institutional Weaknesses, Fiscal Rigidities, and Financial Dollarization at Work." IMF Working Paper 04/12, Washington, DC.

Jalles, Joao Tovar. 2011. "Growth, Poverty, and Inequality: Evidence from Post- Communist Economies." *Journal of Poverty* 15:277–308.

Jameson, Kenneth. 2003. "Dollarization in Latin America: Wave of the Future or Flight to the Past?" *Journal of Economic Issues* 37 (3): 643–663.

Jaramillo, Laura, and Cemile Sancak. 2007. "Growth in the Dominican Republic and Haiti: Why Has the Grass Been Greener on One Side of Hispaniola." IMF Working Paper WP/07/63, Washington, DC.

Jamison, Eliot, Dean Jamison, and Eric Hanushek. 2007. "The Effects of Education Quality on Income Growth and Mortality Decline." *Economics of Education Review* 26 (6): 771–788.

Jensen, Robert. 2010. "The Perceived Returns to Education and Demand for Schooling." *Quarterly Journal of Economics* 125 (2): 515–548.

Jiménez, Juan Pablo, and Osvaldo Kacef. 2011. "Volatilidad macroeconómica, espacio fiscal y gobernanza." In *La política fiscal para el afianzamiento de las democracias en América Latina: Reflexiones a partir de una serie de estudios de caso*, edited by Alicia Bárcena and Osvaldo Kacef, 53–69. Santiago: CEPAL.

Jiménez, Juan Pablo, and Isabel López. 2012. "¿Disminución de la desigualdad en América Latina? El rol de la política fiscal." Working Paper 33, Research Network on Interdependent Inequalities in America Latina.

Johnson, Paul. 2000. "A Nonparametric Analysis of Income Convergence across the US States." *Economics Letters* 69:219–223.

Jones, Charles. 1995. "Time Series Tests of Endogenous Growth Models." *Quarterly Journal of Economics* 110 (2): 495–525.

Jones, Charles, and John Williams. 1998. "Measuring the Social Rate of Return to R&D." *Quarterly Journal of Economics* 113 (4): 1119–1135.

Kakwani, Nanak, and Medhi Krongkaew. 2000. "Economic Growth, Poverty and Income Inequality in the Asia-Pacific Region." *Journal of the Asia Pacific Economy* 5 (1–2): 9–13.

Kaplan, David. 2009. "Job Creation and Labor Reform in Latin America." *Journal of Comparative Economics* 37 (1): 91–105.

Katz, Claudio, Vincent Mahler, and Michael Franz. 1983. "The Impact of Taxes on Growth and Distribution in Developed Capitalist Countries: A Cross-National Study." *American Political Science Review* 77 (4): 871–886.

Kaufman, Robert. 2007. "Political Economy and the New Left." In *The New Left and Democratic Governments in Latin America*, edited by Cynthia J. Arnson and José Raúl Perales, 24–30. Washington, DC: Woodrow Wilson International Center for Scholars.

Keller, Katarina. 2006. "Investment in Primary, Secondary, and Higher Education and the Effects on Economic Growth." *Contemporary Economic Policy* 24: 18–24.

King, Robert G., and Ross Levine. 1993. "Financial Intermediation and Economic Development." In *Financial Intermediation in the Construction of Europe*, edited by Colin Mayer and Xavier Vives, 156–189. London: Centre for Economic Policy Research.

Klein, Nir. 2012. "Real Wage, Labor Productivity, and Employment Trends in South Africa: A Closer Look." IMF Working Paper WP/12/92, Washington, DC.

Klemm, Alexander. 2014. "Fiscal Policy in Latin America over the Cycle." IMF Working Paper 14/59, Washington, DC.

Kornai, János, Eric Maskin, and Gérard Roland. 2003. "Understanding the Soft Budget Constraint." *Journal of Economic Literature* 41 (4): 1095–1136.

Kose, M. Ayhan, Guy M. Meredith, and Christoper M. Towe. 2004. "How Has NAFTA Affected the Mexican Economy? Review and Evidence." Working Paper WP/04/59, Washington, DC: IMF.

Kraay, Aart. 2000. "Household Saving in China." *World Bank Economic Review* 14 (3): 545–570.

Kremer, Michael. 1993. "Population Growth and Technological Change: One Million B.C. to 1990." *Quarterly Journal of Economics* 108 (3): 681–716.

Kremer, Michael, and Alaka Holla. 2009. "Improving Education in the Developing World: What Have We Learned from Randomized Evaluations?" *Annual Review of Economics* 1:513–542.

Kremer, Michael, and Alix Peterson Zwane. 2005. "Encouraging Private Sector Research for Tropical Agriculture." *World Development* 33 (1): 87–105.

Kristensen, Nicolai, and Wendy Cunningham. 2006. "Do Minimum Wages in Latin America and the Caribbean Matter: Evidence from 19 Countries." World Bank Policy Research Paper 3870. Washington, DC: World Bank.

Krueger, Alan, and Mikael Lindahl. 2011. "Education for Growth: Why and for Whom?" *Journal of Economic Literature* 39:1101–1136.

Krueger, Anne. 1978. *Liberalization Attempts and Consequences: Foreign Trade Regime and Economic Development*. Cambridge, MA: Ballinger Publishing Company.

Krugman, Paul, Maurice Obstfeld, and Marc Melitz. 2012. *International Economics: Theory and Policy*. 9th ed. Boston: Addison-Wesley/Pearson.

Krugman, Paul, and Anthony Venables. 1995. "Globalization and the Inequality of Nations." *Quarterly Journal of Economics* 110 (4): 857–880.

Kurtz, Marcus. 2004. "The Dilemmas of Democracy in the Open Economy: Lessons from Latin America." *World Politics* 56 (2): 262–302.

Kuznets, Simon. 1955. "Economic Growth and Income Inequality." *American Economic Review* 45:1–28.

Labán, Raúl, and Felipe Larraín. 1995. "Continuity, Change, and the Political Economy of Transition in Chile." In *Reform, Recovery, and Growth: Latin America and the Middle East*, edited by Rudiger Dornbusch and Sebastian Edwards, 115–149. Chicago: University of Chicago Press.

Labán, Raúl, and Felipe Larraín. 1997. "Can a Liberalization of Capital Outflows Increase Net Capital Inflows?" *Journal of International Money and Finance* 16:415–431.

Laeven, Luc, and Fabián Valencia. 2013. "Systemic Banking Crises Database." *IMF Economic Review* 61 (2): 225–270.

Laffont, Jean-Jacques, and Jean Tirole. 1993. *A Theory of Incentives in Procurement and Regulation*. Cambridge, MA: MIT Press.

Landes, David. 1998. *The Wealth and Poverty of Nations: Why Some Are So Rich and Some So Poor*. New York: Norton.

La Porta, Rafael, Florencio Lopez-de-Silanes, and Andrei Shleifer. 1999. "Corporate Ownership around the World." *Journal of Finance* 54 (2): 471–517.

La Porta, Rafael, Florencio Lopez-de-Silanes, Andrei Shleifer, and Robert Vishny. 1997. "Legal Determinants of External Finance." *Journal of Finance* 52:1131–1150.

La Porta, Rafael, Florencio Lopez-de-Silanes, Andrei Shleifer, and Robert Vishny. 1999. "The Quality of Government." *Journal of Law Economics and Organization* 15 (1): 222–279.

Larraín, Felipe. 2000. *Capital Flows, Capital Controls and Currency Crises: Latin America in the 1990s*. Ann Arbor: University of Michigan Press.

Larraín, Felipe. 2003. "Lights and Shadows of Latin American Competitiveness." In *The Global Competitiveness Report 2002–2003*, edited by Peter K. Cornelius, 198–223. Oxford: Oxford University Press.

Larraín, Felipe. 2005. "Flotar o dolarizar: ¿Qué nos dice la evidencia?" *El Trimestre Economico* 71 (285): 5–28.

Larraín, Felipe. 2008. "Cuatro Millones de Pobres en Chile: Actualizando la Línea de Pobreza." *Estudios Públicos* 109: 102–148.

Larraín, Felipe. 2010. "Both China and the US at Fault in Currency War." *Financial Times*, October 18.

Larraín, Felipe. 2013. "Remember the Effect of QE on the Emerging Economies." *Financial Times*, February 5.

Larraín, Felipe, Rosanna Costa, Rodrigo Cerda, Mauricio Villena, and Andrés Tomaselli. 2011. "Una política fiscal de balance estructural de segunda generación para Chile" (A second-generation fiscal policy of structural balance for Chile). Studies in Public Finance. Santiago, Chile: Budget Office, Ministry of Finance.

Larraín, Felipe, and Raúl Labán. 2000. "Private Capital Flows to Chile in the 1990s: Causes, Effects and Policy Reactions." In *Capital Flows, Capital Controls and Currency Crises: Latin America in the 1990s*, edited by Felipe Larraín, 223–230. Ann Arbor: University of Michigan Press.

Larraín, Felipe, and Luis F. López-Calva. 2001. "Privatization: Fostering Economic Growth through Private Sector Development." In *Structural Reform*, edited by Felipe Larraín. Vol. 2 of *Economic Development in Central America*, edited by Felipe Larraín, 66–106. Cambridge, MA: Harvard University Press.

Larraín, Felipe, and Patricio Meller. 1990. "La experiencia socialista-populista chilena: La Unidad Popular, 1970–73." *Cuadernos de Economia* , no. 82: 317–355.

Larraín, Felipe, and Francisco Parro. 2008. "Chile Menos Volatil?" *El Trimestre Economico* 75 (299): 563–596.

Larraín, Felipe, and Jeffrey D. Sachs. 1993. *Macroeconomics in the Global Economy*. Upper Saddle River, NJ: Prentice Hall.

Larraín, Felipe, and Jeffrey Sachs. 2013. *Macroeconomía en la Economía Global Tercera Edición*. Santiago, Chile: Pearson.

Larraín, Felipe, and Marcelo Selowsky. 1991. *The Public Sector and the Latin American Crisis*. San Francisco: ICS Press.

Larraín, Felipe and José Tavares. 2003. "Regional Currencies versus Dollarization: Options for Asia and the Americas." *Journal of Policy Reform* 6 (1): 35–49.

Larraín, Felipe, and José Tavares. 2004. "Does Foreign Direct Investment Decrease Corruption?" *Cuadernos de Economia* 41 (123): 217–230.

Larraín, Felipe, and Andrés Velasco. 1990. *Can Swaps Solve the Debt Crisis? Lessons from the Chilean Experience*. Princeton, NJ: International Finance Section, Department of Economics, Princeton University.

Larraín, Felipe, and Andrés Velasco. 2001. *Exchange-Rate Policy in Emerging-Market Economies: The Case for Floating*. Princeton, NJ: International Economics Section, Department of Economics, Princeton University.

Larrain, Felipe, and Andrés Velasco. 2002. "How Should Emerging Economies Float Their Currencies?" *Economics of Transition* 10 (2): 365–392.

Larraín, Felipe, and Rodrigo Vergara. 1998. "Income Distribution, Investment and Growth." In *Social Inequality: Values, Growth and the State*, ed. Andrés Solimano, 120–139. Ann Arbor: University of Michigan Press.

Larrañaga, Osvaldo. 1994. "Pobreza, crecimiento y desigualdad: Chile, 1987–92." *Revista de Análisis Económico* 9:69–92.

League of Nations. 1939. *World Production and Prices 1938/39*. Geneva: League of Nations.

Lederman, Daniel, William F. Maloney, and Luis Servén. 2003. *Lessons from NAFTA from Latin America and the Caribbean (LAC): A Summary of Research Findings*. Washington, DC: World Bank.

Lederman, Daniel, Marcelo Olarreaga, and Guillermo E. Perry, eds. 2009. *China's and India's Challenge to Latin America: Opportunity or Threat?* Washington, DC: World Bank.

Lee, Neil, Paul Sissons, Ceri Hughes, Anne Green, Gaby Atfield, Duncan Adam, and Andrés Rodríguez-Pose. 2014. *Cities, Growth and Poverty: Evidence Review*. York, UK: Joseph Rowntree Foundation.

Lee, Young, and Roger Gordon. 2005. "Tax Structure and Economic Growth." *Journal of Public Economics* 89:1027–1043.

Leibenstein, Harvey. 1966. "Allocative Efficiency vs. 'X-Efficiency.'" *American Economic Review* 56 (3): 392–415.

Levy, Santiago. 2008. *Good Intentions, Bad Outcomes: Social Policy, Informality and Economic Growth in Mexico*. Washington, DC: Brookings Institution Press.

Levy Yeyati, Eduardo. 2006. "Exchange Rate Regimes in the 2000s: A Latin American Perspective." Universidad Torcuato di Tella, Centro de Investigación en Finanzas, Documento de Trabajo 07/2006, Buenos Aires, Argentina.

Lewis, Colin M. 1990. "Las Economías de Exportación: América Latina, c. 1870–1930." Typescript, London School of Economics and Political Sciences.

Lindbeck, Assar, and Dennis J. Snower. 1988. *The Insider-Outsider Theory of Employment and Unemployment*. Cambridge, MA: MIT Press.

Lindert, Peter H., and Jeffrey Williamson. 2003. "Does Globalization Make the World More Unequal?" In *Globalization in Historical Perspective*, edited by Michael Bordo, Allan Taylor, and Jeffrey Williamson, 227–276. Chicago: University of Chicago Press.

Loayza, Norman, and Romain Rancière. 2006. "Financial Development, Financial Fragility and Growth." *Journal of Money, Credit and Banking* 38 (4): 1051–1076.

Lockhart, James, and Stuart Schwartz. 1983. *Early Latin America: A History of Colonial Spanish America and Brazil*. Cambridge, UK: Cambridge University Press.

López-Calva, Luis F., and Nora Lustig. 2010. "Explaining the Decline in Inequality in Latin America: Technological Change, Educational Upgrading, and Democracy." In *Declining Inequality in Latin America: A Decade of Progress?*, edited by Luis F. López-Calva and Nora Lustig, 1–24. New York: United Nations Development Program, and Washington, DC: Brookings Institution Press.

López-Casanovas, Guillem, Berta Rivera, and Luis Currais. 2005. *Health and Economic Growth: Findings and Policy Implications*. Cambridge, MA: MIT Press.

Lora, Eduardo. 2001. "Structural Reforms in Latin America: What Has Been Reformed and How to Measure It." IDB, Research Department, Working Paper 466.

Lora, Eduardo. 2012. "Structural Reforms in Latin America: What Has Been Reformed and How to Measure It (Updated Version)." IDB, Working Paper IDB-WP-346, Washington, DC.

Lora, Eduardo, and Carmen Pagés. 2011. "Face-to-Face with Productivity." *Finance & Development* 48 (1): 16–19.

Lorenz, Max Otto. 1905. "Methods of Measuring the Concentration of Wealth." *Publications of the American Statistical Association* 9 (7): 209–219.

Love, Joseph. 2005. "The Rise and Decline of Economic Structuralism in Latin America: New Dimensions." *Latin American Research Review* 40 (3): 100–125.

Lucas, Robert. 1988. "On the Mechanics of Economic Development." *Journal of Monetary Economics* 22 (1): 3–42.

Lucas, Robert. 2002. *Lectures on Economic Growth*. Cambridge, MA: Harvard University Press.

Lustig, Nora, Omar Arias, and Jamele Rigolini. 2002. *Reducción de la pobreza y crecimiento económico: La doble Causalidad*. Washington, DC: Banco Interamericano de Desarrollo.

Lustig, Nora, Luis F. Lopez-Calva, and Eduardo Ortiz-Juarez. 2011. "The Decline in Inequality in Latin America: How Much, Since When, and Why?" ECINE Society for the Study of Income Inequality, Working Paper Series WP 2011-211.

Lustig, Nora, Luis F. Lopez-Calva, and Eduardo Ortiz-Juarez. 2013. "Declining Inequality in Latin America in the 2000s: The Case of Argentina, Brazil, and Mexico." *World Development* 44:129–141.

Lustig, Nora, and Darryl McLeod. 1997. "Minimum Wages and Poverty in Developing Countries: Some Empirical Evidence." In *Labour Markets in Latin America*, edited by Sebastian Edwards and Nora C. Lustig, 62–103. Washington, DC: Brookings Institution Press.

The Maddison-Project. 2009. The Maddison-Project, 2009 version. http://www.ggdc.net/maddison/maddison-project/home.htm.

Maizels, Alfred. 1992. *Commodities in Crisis: The Commodity Crisis of the 1980s and the Political Economy of International Commodity Policies*. Oxford: Clarendon Press.

Maldonado, René, and María Luisa Hayem. 2014. *Remittances to Latin America and the Caribbean in 2013: Still Below Pre-Crisis Levels*. Washington, DC: IDB.

Manacorda, Marco, Carolina Sánchez-Páramo, and Norbert Schady. 2010. "Changes in Returns to Education in Latin America: The Role of Demand and Supply of Skills." *Industrial & Labor Relations Review* 63:307–326.

Mankiw, Gregory. 2007. *Macroeconomics*. 6th ed. New York: Worth Publishers.

Mankiw, Gregory, David Romer, and David N. Weil. 1992. "A Contribution to the Empirics of Economic Growth." *Quarterly Journal of Economics* 107:407–437.

Marcano, Cristina, and Alberto Barrera. 2005. *Hugo Chávez Sin Uniforme: Una Historia personal*. Caracas: Debate.

Marichal, Carlos. 1989. *A Century of Debt Crises from Independence to the Great Depression*. Princeton, NJ: Princeton University Press.

Marshall, Adriana. 2005. "Labor Regulations and Unionization Trends: Comparative Analysis of Latin American Countries." Working Paper, Cornell University School of Industrial and Labor Relations, International Programs.

Mas-Colell, Andrew, Michael D. Whinston, and Jerry H. Green. 1995. *Microeconomic Theory*. Oxford: Oxford University Press.

Maskin, Eric. 1996. "Theories of the Soft Budget Constraint." *Japan and the World Economy* 8:125–133.

Mauro, Paolo. 1995. "Corruption and Growth." *Quarterly Journal of Economics* 110 (3): 681–712.

McCulloch, Rachel. 2002. "Unilateral and Reciprocal Trade Reform in Latin America." In *Going Alone: The Case for Relaxed Reciprocity in Freeing Trade*, edited by Jagdish Bhaghwati, 395–441. Cambridge, MA: MIT Press.

McKay, Andrew. 1997. "Poverty Reduction through Economic Growth: Some Issues." *Journal of International Development* 9 (4): 665–673.

McKenzie, David, and Dilip Mookherjee. 2003. "Distributive Impact of Privatization in Latin America: An Overview of Evidence from Four Countries." *Economía* 3 (2): 161–233.

Meier, Andre. 2015. "Watching the Tide." *Finance and Development* 52 (3): 17–19.

Melitz, Marc. 2005. "When and How Should Infant Industries Be Protected?" *Journal of International Economics* 66:177–196.

Mendoza, Enrique, Gian Milesi-Ferretti, and Patrick Asea. 1997. "On the Effectiveness of Tax Policy in Altering Long-Run Growth: Harberger's Superneutrality Conjecture." *Journal of Public Economics* 61:99–126.

Mertens, Karel, and Morten Ravn. 2013. "The Dynamic Effects of Personal and Corporate Income Tax Changes in the United States." *American Economic Review* 103:1212–1247.

Miller, Stephen, and Frank Russek. 1997. "Fiscal Structures and Economic Growth: International Evidence." *Economic Inquiry* 35:603–613.

Ministry of Social Development of Chile. 2015. Casen survey 2013. http://www.ministeriodesarrollosocial.gob.cl/resultados-encuesta-casen-2013/.

Minujin, Alberto, Jan Vandemoortele, and Enrique Delamonica. 2002. "Economic Growth, Poverty and Children." *Environment and Urbanization* 4 (2): 23–43.

Mishkin, Frederic, and Klaus Schmidt-Hebbel. 2002. "A Decade of Inflation Target in the World: What Do We Know and What Do We Need to Know." In *Inflation Targeting: Design, Performance, Challenges*, edited by Norman Loayza and Raimundo Soto, 171–219. Santiago: Central Bank of Chile.

Mullainathan, Sendhil, and Eldar Shafir. 2013. *Scarcity: Why Having Too Little Means So Much*. New York: Times Books.

Mundell, Robert. 1961. "The Theory of Optimal Currency Areas." *American Economic Review* 51 (3): 657–665.

Mundlak, Yair, Domingo Cavallo, and Roberto Domenech. 1993. "Agriculture and Growth: The Experience of Argentina, 1913–1984." In *The Bias against Agriculture: Trade and Macroeconomic Policies in Developing Countries*, edited by Romeo Bautista and Alberto Valdes, 159–176. San Francisco: Institute for Contemporary Studies.

Murphy, Kevin, Andrei Shleifer, and Robert Vishny. 1989. "Industrialization and the Big Push." *Journal of Political Economy* 97 (5): 1003–1026.

Musacchio, Aldo. 2009. *Experiments in Financial Democracy: Corporate Governance and Financial Development in Brazil, 1872–1950*. Cambridge, UK: Cambridge University Press.

Nenci, Silvia, and Carlo Pietrobelli. 2008. "Does Tariff Liberalization Promote Trade? Latin American Countries in the Long-Run (1900–2000)." *Global Economy Journal* 8 (4): 1–30.

Newland, Carlos. 1998. "Economic Development and Population Change: Argentina, 1810–1870." In *Latin America and the World Economy since 1800*, edited by John H. Coatsworth and Alan Taylor, 207–222. Cambridge, MA: Harvard University.

Newland, Carlos, and Barry Paulson. 1998. "Purely Animal: Pastoral Production in Early Argentine Economic Growth, 1825–1865." *Explorations in Economic History* 35 (3): 325–345.

Nordhaus, William. 2006. "Geography and Macroeconomics: New Data and Findings." *Proceedings of the National Academy of Sciences of the United States of America* 103:3510–3517.

Nunn, Nathan. 2009. "The Importance of History for Economic Development." *Annual Review of Economics* 1 (1): 65–92.

Nunn, Nathan. 2012. "Culture and the Historical Process." *Economic History of Developing Regions* 27 (1): S108–S126.

O'Neil, Mathieu, and Robert Ackland. 2006. "The Structural Role of Nanotechnology-Opposition in Online Environmental-Activist Networks." Paper presented at the 26th International Sunbelt Social Network Conference, Vancouver, April 24–30.

Ocampo, José A., and Juliana Vallejo. 2012. "Economic Growth, Equity and Human Development in Latin America." *Journal of Human Development and Capabilities* 13 (1): 107–133.

OECD. 2009. *Is Informal Normal? Towards More and Better Jobs in Developing Countries*. Paris: OECD.

OECD. 2012. "Less Income Inequality and More Growth—Are They Compatible? Part 3. Income Redistribution via Taxes and Transfers Across OECD Countries." OECD Economics Department Working Papers 926, Paris.

OECD. 2015. *Better Policies for Better Lives*. Paris: OECD.

Okediji, Tade. 2008. "The Color of Brazil: Law, Ethnic Fragmentation, and Economic Growth." *Chicago-Kent Law Review* 83 (1): 185–199.

Olivera, Julio H. G. 1967. "Money, Prices, and Fiscal Lags: A Note on the Dynamics of Inflation." *Banco Nazionale del Lavoro Quarterly Review* 20 (82): 258–267.

Ortíz, Guillermo. 2014. "The Challenges of Achieving Sustainable Growth in Latin America." Paper presented at "Think Tank 20: Growth, Convergence and Income Distribution, the Road from Brisbane G-20 Summit," November 15–16. http://www.guntramwolff.net/wp-content/uploads/2015/05/TT20-Nov-7-FINAL-Web-v2.pdf.

Ostry, Jonathan D., Atish R. Ghosh, Karl Habermeier, Marcos Chamon, Mahvash S. Qureshi, and Dennis B. S. Reinhardt. 2010. "Capital Inflows: The Role of Controls." IMF Staff Position Note SPN/10/04, February.

Ozden, Caglar, and Francisco J. Parodi. 2004. "Customs Unions Theory and Evidence from Mercosur's Auto Industry." Working Paper 282, Central Bank of Chile, Santiago.

Passel, Jeffrey S., D'Vera Cohn, and Ana Gonzalez-Barrera. 2012. "Net Migration from Mexico Falls to Zero—and Perhaps Less." *Pew Research Center: Hispanic Trends*, April 23. http://www.pewhispanic.org/2012/04/23/net-migration-from-mexico-falls-to-zero-and-perhaps-less/.

Passel, Jeffrey S., D'Vera Cohn, Jens Manuel Krogstad, and Ana Gonzalez-Barrera. 2014. "As Growth Stalls, Unauthorized Migrant Population Becomes More Settled." *Pew Research Center: Hispanic Trends*, September 3. http://www.pewhispanic.org/2014/09/03/as-growth-stalls-unauthorized-immigrant-population-becomes-more-settled/.

Pastor, Robert. 2001. *Toward a North American Community: Lessons from the Old World for the New*. Washington, DC: Washington Institute for International Economics.

Perotti, Roberto. 1992. "Fiscal Policy, Income Distribution, and Growth." Columbia University Working Paper 636.

Perotti, Roberto. 1993. "Political Equilibrium, Income Distribution, and Growth." *Review of Economic Studies* 60 (4): 755–776.

Perotti, Roberto. 1996. "Growth, Income Distribution, and Democracy: What the Data Say." *Journal of Economic Growth* 1 (2): 149–187.

Perotti, Roberto. 2012. "The Effects of Tax Shocks on Output: Not So Large, but Not Small Either." *American Economic Journal: Economic Policy* 4:214–237.

Perry, Guillermo, Omar S. Arias, J. Humberto López, William F. Maloney, and Luis Servén. 2006. *Poverty Reduction and Growth: Virtuous and Vicious Circles*. Washington, DC: World Bank.

Perry, Guillermo, William F. Maloney, Omar S. Arias, Pablo Fajnzylber, Andrew D. Mason, and Jaime Saavedra-Chanduvi. 2007. *Informality: Exit and Exclusion*. Washington, DC: World Bank.

Persson, Torsten, and Guido Tabellini. 1994. "Is Inequality Harmful for Growth?" *American Economic Review* 84 (3): 600–621.

Piketty, Thomas. 2014. *Capital in the Twenty-First Century*. Cambridge, MA: Harvard University Press.

Pill, Huw. 2002. *Mexico: The Tequila Crisis 1994–95*. Cambridge, MA: Harvard Business School Publication.

Portes, Alejandro, and Kelly Hoffman. 2003. "Latin American Class Structures: The Composition and Change during the Neoliberal Era." *Latin American Research Review* 38 (1): 41–82.

Prados de la Escosura, Leandro. 2005a. "Colonial Independence and Economic Backwardness in Latin America." Working Paper 10/05, Departamento de Historia e Instituciones, Universidad Carlos III de Madrid, Spain.

Prados de la Escosura, Leandro. 2005b. "Growth, Inequality, and Poverty in Latin America: Historical Evidence, Controlled Conjectures." Working Papers in Economic History no. 05-41(04), Universidad Carlos III, Instituto Figuerola de Historia y Ciencias Sociales.

Prados de la Escosura, Leandro. 2009. "Lost Decades? Economic Performance in Post-Independence Latin America." *Journal of Latin American Studies* 41:279–307.

Pradumna, Rana. 1998. "Controls on Short-Term Capital Inflows: The Latin American Experience and Lessons for DMCs." EDRC Briefing Notes, no. 2. Economics and Development Resource Center, Asian Development Bank.

Prebisch, Raul. 1950. *The Economic Development of Latin America and Its Principal Problems*. Lake Success, NY: UN Department of Economic Affairs.

Preston, Ian. 1995. "Sampling Distributions of Relative Poverty Statistics." *Journal of the Royal Statistical Society: Series A (General)* 44 (1): 91–99.

Pribble, Jennifer, Evelyne Huber, and John D. Stephens. 2005. "The Politics of Poverty in Latin America." Unpublished paper.

Pritchett, Lant. 1996. "Measuring Outward Orientation in Developing Countries: Can It Be Done?" *Journal of Development Economics* 49 (2): 307–335.

Pritchett, Lant. 2013. *The Rebirth of Education: Schooling Ain't Learning*. Washington, DC: Center for Global Development.

Putnam, Robert. 1993. *Making Democracy Work: Civic Traditions in Modern Italy*. Princeton, NJ: Princeton University Press.

Qian, Yingyi, and Cheng-Gang Xu. 1998. "Innovation and Bureaucracy under Soft and Hard Budget Constraints." *Review of Economic Studies* 65:151–164.

Quah, Danny. 1996a. "Convergence Empirics across Economies with (Some) Capital Mobility." *Journal of Economic Growth* 1 (1): 95–124.

Quah, Danny. 1996b. "Regional Convergence Clusters across Europe." *European Economic Review* 40:951–958.

Quah, Danny. 1996c. "Twin Peaks: Growth and Convergence in Models of Distribution Dynamics." *Economic Journal* 106 (437): 1045–1055.

Rajan, Raghuram, and Luigi Zingales. 2003. "The Emergence of Strong Property Rights: Speculation from History." NBER Working Paper 9478, Cambridge, MA.

Ramírez, Miguel. 2011. "Foreign Direct Investment and Its Determinants in the Chilean Case: Single Break Unit Root and Co-integration Analysis." *Applied Econometrics and International Development* 11 (1): 91–110.

Rassekh, Farhad. 2007. "Is International Trade More Beneficial to Lower Income Economies? An Empirical Inquiry." *Review of Development Economics* 11 (1): 159–169.

Ravallion, Martin. 1995. "Growth and Poverty: Evidence for Developing Countries in the 1980s." *Economics Letters* 48:411–417.

Ravallion, Martin. 1998. "Poverty Lines in Theory and Practice." Living Standards Measurement Study, Working Paper 133. Washington DC: World Bank.

Ray, Debraj. 1998. *Development Economics*. Princeton, NJ: Princeton University Press.

Reed, Robert. 2008. "The Robust Relationship between Taxes and U.S. State Income Growth." *National Tax Journal* 61 (1): 57–80.

Reinhart, Carmen, and Kenneth Rogoff. 2009. *This Time Is Different: Eight Centuries of Financial Folly*. Princeton, NJ: Princeton University Press.

Reinhart, Carmen, and Kenneth Rogoff. 2011. "From Financial Crash to Debt Crisis." *American Economic Review* 101:1676–1706.

Robinson, William Francis. 2012. "Panama for the Panamenians: The Populism of Arnufo Arias Madrid." In *Populism in Latin America*, 2nd ed., edited by Michael Conniff, 184–200. Tuscaloosa: University of Alabama Press.

Rodrik, Dani. 2001. "The Global Governance of Trade as if Development Really Mattered." Typescript, Harvard University. http://www.giszpenc.com/globalciv/rodrik1.pdf.

Rodrik, Dani. 2006. "Goodbye Washington Consensus, Hello Washington Confusion? A Review of the World Bank's Economic Growth in the 1990s: Learning from a Decade of Reform." *Journal of Economic Literature* 44 (4): 973–987.

Rodrik, Dani, Arvind Subramanian, and Francesco Trebbi. 2004. "Institutions Rule: The Primacy of Institutions Over Geography and Integration in Economic Development." *Journal of Economic Growth* 9 (2): 131–165.

Rojas-Suarez, Liliana. 2010. "The International Financial Crisis: Eight Lessons for and from Latin America." Center for Global Development, Working Paper 202.

Rojas-Suarez, Liliana, and Steven I. Weisbrod. 1995. "Resolving the Banking Crises of the 1990s in Latin America." *The Brown Journal of World Affairs* 2 (2): 219–226.

Romer, Paul. 1986. "Increasing Returns and Long-Run Growth." *Journal of Political Economy* 94 (5): 1002–1037.

Romer, Paul. 1990. "Endogenous Technical Change." *Journal of Political Economy* 98:71–102.

Romer, Paul. 1991. "Increasing Returns and New Developments in the Theory of Growth." In *Equilibrium Theory and Applications: Proceedings of the Sixth International Symposium in Economic Theory and Econometrics*, edited by William A. Barnett, Bernard Cornet, Claude D'Aspremont, Jean Gabszewicz, and Andreu Mas-Colell, 83–110. Cambridge, UK: Cambridge University Press.

Romer, Christina, and David Romer. 2010. "The Macroeconomic Effects of Tax Changes: Estimates Based on a New Measure of Fiscal Shocks." *American Economic Review* 100 (3): 763–801.

Rose, Andrew. 2006. "Size Really Doesn't Matter: In Search of a National Scale Effect." *Journal of the Japanese and International Economies* 20 (4): 482–507.

Rossiter, Clinton. 2002. *Constitutional Dictatorship: Crisis Government in the Modern Democracies*. Rev. 2nd ed. Piscataway, NJ: Transaction Publishers.

Russell, Philip L. 2011. "Early Nineteenth Century Mexico, 1821–1855." In *The History of Mexico: From Pre-Conquest to Present*, edited by Philip Russell, 141–194. New York: Routledge.

Sachs, Jeffrey D. 1987. "Trade and Exchange Rate Policies in Growth-Oriented Adjustment Programs." In *Growth-Oriented Adjustment Programs*, edited by Vittorio Corbo, Morris Goldstein, and Mohsin Khan, 291–325. Washington, DC: International Monetary Fund / World Bank.

Sachs, Jeffrey D. 1990. "Social Conflict and Populist Policies in Latin America." In *Labour Relations and Economic Performance*, edited by Renato Brunetta and Carlo Dell'Aringa, 137–169. London: Palgrave Macmillan.

Sachs, Jeffrey D. 2003. "Institutions Don't Rule: Direct Effects of Geography on Per Capita Income." National Bureau of Economic Research, Working Paper 9490.

Sachs, Jeffrey D., and Pia Malaney. 2002. "The Economic and Social Burden of Malaria." *Nature* 415: 680–685.

Sachs, Jeffrey D., Andrew D. Mellinger, and John M. Gallup. 2001. "The Geography of Poverty." *Scientific American* 284 (3): 70–75.

Sachs, Jeffrey D., and Andrew Warner. 1995. "Economic Reform and the Process of Global Integration." *Brookings Papers on Economic Activity* 1995 (1): 1–118.

Sachs, Jeffrey D., and Andrew Warner. 1997. "Fundamental Sources of Long-Run Growth." *American Economic Review* 87 (2): 184–188.

Sachs, Jeffrey D., and Andrew Warner. 2001. "The Curse of Natural Resources." *European Economic Review* 45:827–838.

Santaella, Julio. 1998. "El crecimiento económico de México: Explorando causas de su caída secular." *Gaceta de Economía* 3 (6): 5–46.

Santiso, Carlos. 2004. "Legislatures and Budget Oversight in Latin America: Strengthening Public Finance Accountability in Emerging Economies." *OECD Journal on Budgeting* 4 (2): 47–76.

Santiso, Javier. 2013. *The Decade of the Multilatinas*. Cambridge, UK: Cambridge University Press.

Sapir, André, Phillipe Aghion, Giuseppe Bertola, Martin Hellwig, Jean Pisani-Ferry, Dariusz Rosario, José Viñaks, and Helen Wallace. 2003. *An Agenda for a Growing Europe: The Sapir Report*. Oxford: Oxford University Press.

Schmidt-Hebbel, Klaus. 2011. "Central Banking in Latin America: Changes, Achievements, Challenges." Banco de España Occasional Papers 1102.

Scorzafave, Luis Guilherme, and Érica Marina Carvalho de Lima. 2010. "Inequality Evolution in Brazil and South Africa: The Role of Cash Transfer Programs and Other Income Sources." In *Studies in Applied Welfare Analysis: Papers from the Third ECINEQ Meeting*, edited by John A. Bishop, 107–129. Bingley: Emerald Group Publishing.

Seers, Dudley. 1962. "A Theory of Inflation and Growth in Underdeveloped Economies Based on the Experience of Latin America." *Oxford Economic Papers* 14 (2): 173–195.

Seligson, Michell. 2007. "The Rise of Populism and the Left in Latin America." *Journal of Democracy* 18 (3): 81–95.

Sen, Amartya. 1976. "Poverty: An Ordinal Approach to Measurement." *Econometrica* 44 (2): 219–231.

Shafer, Robert. 1978. *A History of Latin America*. Lexington, MA: D.C. Heath and Co.

Shapiro, Carl, and Joseph E. Stiglitz. 1984. "Equilibrium Unemployment as a Worker Discipline Device." *American Economic Review* 74 (3): 433–444.

Singer, Hans. 1950. "The Distribution of Gains between Investing and Borrowing Countries." *American Economic Review* 40 (2): 473–485.

Singh, Anoop, Agnès Belaisch, Charles Collyns, Paula de Masi, Reva Krieger, Guy Meredith, and Robert Rennhack. 2005. *Stabilization and Reform in Latin America: A Macroeconomic Perspective on the Experience since the Early 1990s*. IMF.

Solow, Robert. 1956. "A Contribution to the Theory of Economic Growth." *Quarterly Journal of Economics* 70 (1): 65–94.

Solow, Robert. 1957. "Technical Change and the Aggregate Production Function." *Review of Economics and Statistics* 39 (3): 312–320.

Song, Zheng, Kjetil Storesletten, and Fabrizio Zilibotti. 2011. "Growing Like China." *American Economic Review* 101 (1): 196–233.

Spiller, P., and M. Tommasi. 2003. "The Institutional Foundations of Public Policy: A Transactions Approach with Application to Argentina." *Journal of Law Economics and Organization* 19 (2): 281–306.

Stallings, Barbara, and Wilson Peres. 2000. *Growth, Employment, and Equity: The Impact of Economic Reforms in Latin America and the Caribbean*. Washington, DC: Brookings Institution Press, United Nations Commission for Latin American and the Caribbean.

Stiglitz, Joseph. 2002. *Globalization and Its Discontents*. New York: Norton.

Stolper, Wolfgang, and Paul Samuelson. 1941. "Protection and Real Wages." *Review of Economic Studies* 9 (1): 58–73.

Stulz, R., and R. Williamson. 2003. "Culture, Openness, and Finance." *Journal of Financial Economics* 70: 313–349.

Swiston, Andrew. 2011. "Official Dollarization as a Monetary Regime: Its Effects on El Salvador." IMF Working Paper 11/129, 1–25. Washington, DC. https://ssrn.com/abstract=1864432.

Tanzi, Vito. 1969. *The Individual Income Tax and Economic Growth*. Baltimore: Johns Hopkins University Press.

Tanzi, Vito. 1977. "Inflation, Lags in Collection, and the Real Value of Taz Revenue." *IMF Staff Papers* 24 (1): 154–167.

Taussig, Frank. 1931. *The Tariff History of the United States*. 8th ed. New York: Putnam and Sons.

Temin, Peter. 1993. "Transmission of the Great Depression." *Journal of Economic Perspectives* 7:87–102.

Thirtle, Colin, Lin Lin, and Jenifer Piese. 2003. "The Impact of Research-Led Agricultural Productivity Growth on Poverty Reduction in Africa, Asia and Latin America." *World Development* 31 (12): 1959–1975.

Thorp, Rosemary. 1992. "A Reappraisal of the Origins of Import-Substituting Industrialisation: 1930–1950." In *The Colonial and Post-Colonial Experience: Five Centuries of Spanish and Portuguese America*, edited by T. Halperín Donghi, Victor Bulmer-Thomas, and Laurence Whitehead, special issue, *Journal of Latin American Studies* 24:181–195. Cambridge, UK: Cambridge University Press.

Thorp, Rosemary. 1996. "Import Substitution: A Good Idea in Principle." In *Latin America and the World Economy: Dependency and Beyond*, edited by Richard J. Salvucci, 140–146. Lexington, MA: Health.

Thorp, Rosemary. 1998. *Progress, Poverty and Exclusion: An Economic History of Latin America in the 20th Century*. Baltimore: Johns Hopkins University Press.

Tobin, James. 1978. "A Proposal for International Monetary Reform." *Eastern Economic Journal* 4 (3–4): 153–159.

Tomljanovich, Marc. 2004. "The Role of State Fiscal Policy in State Economic Growth." *Contemporary Economic Policy* 22:318–330.

Torche, Florencia, and Luis F. López-Calva. 2013. "The Stability and Vulnerability of the Latin American Middle Class." *Oxford Development Studies* 41 (4): 409–435.

Tornell, Aaron, Frank Westermann, and Lorenza Martinez. 2004. "NAFTA and Mexico's Economic Performance." CESifo Working Paper 1155.

Trejos, Sandra, and Gustavo Barboza. 2014. "Dynamic Estimation of the Relationship between Trade Openness and Output Growth in Asia." *Journal of Asian Economics* 36:110–125.

United States Bureau of the Census. 1975. *Historical Statistics of the United States, Colonial Times to 1970*. Washington, DC: U.S. Department of Commerce.

US Census Bureau. 2011. "The Hispanic Population: 2010." Census Brief, May. http://www.census.gov/prod/cen2010/briefs/c2010br-04.pdf.

UNCTAD. 1994. *Directory of Import Regimes*. New York: United Nations.

UNCTAD. 2014. *Trade and Development Report, 2014*. http://unctad.org/en/PublicationsLibrary/tdr2014_en.pdf.

UNDP. 2013. *Human Development Report: The Rise of the South*. New York: United Nations. http://www.undp.org/content/undp/en/home/librarypage/hdr/human-development-report-2013.html.

Ventura-Dias, Vivianne. 2010. *Beyond Trade Barriers: The Gender Implications of Trade Liberalization in Latin America*. Winnipeg: International Institute for Sustainable Development.

Vickers, John, and George K. Yarrow. 1988. *Privatization: An Economic Analysis*. Cambridge, MA: MIT Press.

Wacziarg, Romain, and Karen Horn Welch. 2008. "Trade Liberalization and Growth: New Evidence." *World Bank Economic Review* 22:187–231.

Weber, Max. 1958. *The Protestant Ethic and the Spirit of Capitalism*. Translated by Talcott Parsons. New York: Scribner.

Weil, David. 2013. *Economic Growth*. Upper Saddle River, NJ: Prentice Hall/Pearson.

Weisbrod, Steven, and Liliana Rojas-Suarez. 1995. "Financial Fragilities in Latin America: The 1980s and 1990s." IMF Occasional Papers 132.

Weisbrot, Mark, Rebecca Ray, Jake Johnston, José Antonio Cordero, and Juan Antonio Montecino. 2009. *IMF-Supported Macroeconomic Policies and the World Recession: A Look at Forty-One Borrowing Countries*. Washington, DC: Center for Economic Policy Research.

Weisbrot, Mark, Rebecca Ray, and Luis Sandoval. 2009. *The Chávez Administration at 10 Years: The Economic and Social Indicators*. Washington, DC: The Center for Economic and Policy Research.

Weyland, Kurt. 2009. "The Rise of Latin America's Two Lefts: Insights from Rentier State Theory." *Comparative Politics* 41 (2): 145–164.

WHO. 2013. "World Malaria Report 2013." http://www.who.int/iris/bitstream/10665/97008/1/9789241564694_eng.pdf.

Widmalm, Frida. 2011. "Tax Structure and Growth: Are Some Taxes Better than Others?" *Public Choice* 107 (3–4): 199–219.

Williamson, Jeffrey. 1998. "Growth, Distribution and Demography: Some Lessons from History." *Explorations in Economic History* 35 (3): 241–271.

Williamson, Jeffrey. 2009. "Five Centuries of Latin American Income Inequality." NBER Working Paper 15305, Cambridge, MA.

Williamson, J. G. 2010a. "Latin American Growth-Inequality Trade-Offs: The Impact of Insurgence and Independence." NBER Working Paper 15680, Cambridge, MA.

Williamson, Jeffrey. 2010b. "Five Centuries of Latin American Inequality." *Journal of Iberian and Latin American Economic History* 28 (2): 227–252.

Williamson, Jeffrey. 2015. "Latin American Inequality: Colonial Origins, Commodity Booms, or a Missed 20th Century Great Leveling?" *Journal of Human Development and Capabilities* 16 (3): 1–18.

Williamson, John. 1990. "What Washington Means by Policy Reform." In *Latin American Adjustment: How Much Has Happened?*, edited by John Williamson, 7–20. Washington, DC: Institute for International Economics.

Williamson, John. 2006. "After the Washington Consensus: Latin American Growth and Sustainable Development." Paper presented at the Seminar on Latin American Financing and the Role of Development Banks, Belo Horizonte, Brazil, March 30–31.

WITS. 2015. World Integrated Trade Solution website. http://wits.worldbank.org/.

Wodon, Quentin, Rodrigo Castro-Fernandez, Kihoon Lee, Gladys Lopez-Acevedo, Corinne Siaens, Carlos Sobrado, and Jean-Philippe Tre. 2001. "Poverty in Latin America: Trends (1986–1998) and Determinants." *Cuadernos de Economia* 38 (114): 127–153.

World Bank. 1987. *World Development Report 1987: Barriers to Adjustment and Growth in the World Economy*. New York: Oxford University Press.

World Bank. 1997. *World Development Report 1997: The State in a Changing World*. New York: Oxford University Press.

World Bank. 2001. *World Development Report 2000/2001: Attacking Poverty*. Washington, DC: World Bank.

World Bank. 2002. "Chile's High Growth Economy: Poverty and Income Distribution, 1987–1998." World Bank Country Study. Washington, DC: World Bank.

World Bank. 2008. *Doing Business 2009: Comparing Regulation in 181 Economies*. Washington, DC: World Bank Group.

World Bank. 2013a. *Regulating Foreign Direct Investment in Latin America*. Washington, DC: World Bank.

World Bank. 2013b. "Shifting Gears to Accelerate Shared Prosperity in Latin America and the Caribbean." Latin America and the Caribbean Poverty and Labor Brief. Washington, DC: World Bank. http://www.worldbank.org/content/dam/Worldbank/document/LAC/PLB%20Shared%20 Prosperity%20FINAL.pdf.

World Bank. 2014a. *Doing Business 2015: Going Beyond Efficiency*. Washington, DC: World Bank Group.

World Bank. 2014b. "World Development Indicators." http://databank.worldbank.org/data/reports .aspx?source=world-development-indicators.

World Bank. 2015. *Global Economic Prospects, June 2015: The Global Economy in Transition*. Washington, DC: World Bank.

World Economic Forum. 2010. *The Global Competitiveness Report 2010–2011*. Geneva, Switzerland: World Economic Forum.

World Economic Forum. 2012. *World Economic Forum on Latin America 2012 Report: Regional Transformation in a New Global Context*. Geneva, Switzerland: World Economic Forum.

World Economic Forum. 2013. *The Global Competitiveness Report 2013–2014*. Geneva, Switzerland: World Economic Forum.

WTO. 2011. *World Trade Report 2011, The WTO and Preferential Trade Agreements: From Co-existence to Coherence*. Geneva. https://www.wto.org/english/res_e/booksp_e/anrep_e/world_trade_report11_e .pdf.

WTO. 2015. *The WTO and the Millennium Development Goals*. Geneva: WTO.

Yeats, Alexander. 1998. "Does Mercosur's Trade Performance Raise Concerns about the Effects of Regional Trade Arrangements?" *World Bank Economic Review* 12 (1): 1–28.

Index

Page numbers followed by t refer to tables; page numbers followed by f refer to figures.

Abnormal Importation Act, 62, 356n6
Acción Democratica (Democratic Action) (AD), 149
Acemoglu, Daron, 20–21, 24, 26–27, 33, 36, 337–338, 352n28, 353n36
Adserà, Alicia, 338
Aedo, Christian, 349
Africa
  cash transfer programs and, 361n32
  colonial legacies and, 5–7, 15, 18, 28, 30–31, 351n1
  export-led growth and, 36, 45, 57
  fiscal policy and, 178–179
  growth and development and, 312, 322, 329, 338
  poverty and, 111, 113, 115, 131, 142
African Americans, 36, 111, 131, 142
Age
  labor and, 301–303, 306
  pensions and, 126, 133, 142, 176, 193, 208, 278, 293, 297–298, 301, 314–315, 347
  poverty and, 112, 120, 128–129, 133
Aghion, Phillipe, 328
Agriculture. *See also specific product*
  Brazil and, 16
  climate and, 15–16, 26, 29–31, 122, 320, 352n26, 360n14
  exchange rates and, 239
  export-led growth and, 40, 44, 46, 49, 51, 52t

factor endowments hypothesis and, 4, 15–20, 29, 44
fiscal policy and, 183, 192
geography and, 5, 7
grains and, 15, 17, 39t, 44
growth and development and, 320
import substitution industrialization (ISI) and, 62, 67–74, 80, 84, 278
income inequality and, 29, 279
inflation and, 364n8
innovation and, 44
plantations and, 15–19, 27, 31, 48–51, 54, 56
political economy and, 151, 162
productivity and, 7–8, 351n7
reform and, 73, 151
research and development (R&D) in, 7, 16–17
self-employment and, 301
soil and, 8, 15–17, 29, 31, 60, 352n26
tariffs and, 356
technology and, 5
trade liberalization and, 247, 254–257, 259t
unions and, 282
Alesina, Alberto, 119, 319
Allende, Salvador, 150–152, 284
Allendorf, Henrike, 276
American Civil War, 16, 18, 48–49
Andean Pact, 76, 356n21
Anner, Mark, 286
Argentina
  Andean Pact and, 76, 356n21

Argentina (cont.)
  Catholicism and, 29
  climate of, 16–17
  colonial legacies and, 353n31
  convertibility system collapse and, 99–100, 228
  corruption and, 10t
  currency board and, 365n20
  debt crises and, 87, 96, 99–100, 105–106, 268
  European character of, 18
  exchange rates and, 223–232, 236, 239–240
  export-led growth and, 36–42, 45–49, 53–55
  expropriation risk and, 27
  factor endowments and, 16
  financial liberalization and, 266, 269, 271, 273
  fiscal policy and, 182, 195, 200
  G-20 membership of, 29
  gold standard and, 63
  growth and development and, 317, 325, 331, 337–341, 347
  human capital and, 355n17
  human rights and, 355n22
  import substitution industrialization (ISI) and, 63–65, 72–76, 79, 83–84
  income inequality and, 134
  inflation and, 206, 210–213, 216–221, 365n20
  Kirchners and, 149, 162–163, 169
  labor and, 280–284, 287–290, 297–302
  legal origins hypothesis and, 14
  Macri and, 163, 169, 219
  manufacturing and, 19
  military and, 355n22
  mortality rates and, 21, 23t, 24
  National Electricity Regulatory Authority and, 166
  per capita GDP and, 11
  Peróns and, 149, 154
  political economy and, 148–149, 154, 160–170
  populism and, 148–149, 161–163, 361n4
  poverty and, 118, 130, 360n30
  regulatory capture and, 166
  relative size of, 360n30
  Rosas and, 47, 355n22
  Rúa and, 162
  San Martin and, 36
  small indigenous population of, 17–18
  trade liberalization and, 249, 253–255, 262, 264
  Treaty of Asunción and, 253
  Treaty of Tordesillas and, 351n1, 353n31
  wars of, 42t
  Yrigoyen and, 149
Armendáriz, Beatriz, 356n8, 358nn3,5,11, 359n9, 360nn27, 29, 361n37, 366n11, 367n4, 369nn7,9

Asian Tigers, 59, 71–72, 79–80, 311
Association of South East Asian Nations (ASEAN), 253, 365, 370n39
Attansio, Orazio, 124, 139
Audiencias, 21–24, 353n30
Australia, 264
Autarky, 19, 66, 82
Authoritarian regimes, 118, 153–154, 156, 355n22

Backward linkages, 356n17
Baer, Werner, 74, 85
Bahamas, 23, 354n9
Banco Mercantil del Norte (Banorte), 98
Bands, 226–228
Banerjee, Abhijit V., 119
Bank for International Settlements (BIS), 271
Bankruptcy, 210–211
Barbados, 354n9
Bargaining power, 90, 257, 284, 287
Barrera, Alberto, 171
Barro, Robert, 326–327, 331, 336, 370n38
Battle y Ordóñez, 47
Beef, 16, 193t
Belize, 3, 11t, 354n9
Benefício de Prestação Continuada (BPC), 112, 140
Berganza, Juan Carlos, 202
Berlin Wall, 155
Betancourt, Rómulo, 149
Bianchi, Andrés, 81
Birdsall, Nancy, 157, 362n25
Blancos (Whites, political faction), 47
Boix, Carles, 338
Bolívar, Simón, 36
Bolivia
  Andean Pact and, 76, 356n21
  CAN and, 354n9
  corruption and, 10t
  export-led growth and, 41, 47, 51, 355n16
  extractive institutions and, 27
  fiscal policy and, 181–182, 192
  growth and development and, 317–318, 325, 340
  human capital and, 27
  import substitution industrialization (ISI) and, 63, 76
  inflation and, 206
  labor and, 298–300
  large indigenous population of, 16–17
  Morales and, 163–165, 167
  mortality rates and, 23t

Index 407

official languages and, 28
per capita GDP and, 11t, 27
political economy and, 148, 160, 163–164, 167–169, 171, 363n31
populism and, 148, 163–164, 256
poverty and, 134
railways and, 355n16
revolution and, 160–161, 256
trade liberalization and, 249, 253, 256
wars of, 42t, 47
Bolsa Família (BF), 140
Bondholders Protective Council Corporation, 89–90, 95
Bonds, 63, 76, 84, 88–91, 95–96, 105, 162, 205, 237
Bourbon reforms, 38, 41, 354n8
Boustan, Leah, 328
Boyce, Simone, 138
Brady Plan, 94, 201, 367n4
Braga, Carlos, 85
Bravo-Ortega, Claudio, 326
Brazil
  Afro-Latin population of, 37
  agricultural research and, 7, 16–17
  Bolsa Família (BF) and, 140
  boom/bust cycles of, 49
  Catholicism and, 29
  colonial legacies and, 3, 16, 352n25
  corruption and, 10
  crawling peg and, 76–77
  debt crises and, 89, 93, 98–100, 105, 268
  Dom Pedro and, 35, 354n2
  exchange rates and, 223, 226–230, 234–236, 239–240
  expenditure rule of, 196t
  export-led growth and, 35, 37–38, 42–43, 45, 48–50, 54–56
  extractive institutions and, 27
  financial liberalization and, 134, 136–137, 140–141, 266–268, 271, 273
  fiscal policy and, 195, 196t, 200
  G-20 membership of, 29
  globalization and, 16
  growth and development and, 14, 312, 317–318, 320, 325, 330–331, 341, 349
  import substitution industrialization (ISI) and, 49, 60–63, 65, 71–78, 83–85
  income inequality and, 140, 355n27
  independence from Portugal, 48
  indigenous population of, 20, 131
  inflation and, 206, 210, 212–214, 217, 220–222, 365nn15,21
  labor and, 20, 279–281, 284, 286–290, 297–302

large economy of, 20, 31, 360n30
legal origins hypothesis and, 14
Lula da Silva and, 150, 162
mortality rates and, 23t
natural resources of, 48–49
per capita GDP of, 11t, 27, 49–50
plantations and, 16, 19
political economy and, 150, 154, 162–163
populism and, 150
poverty and, 112–113, 131, 361n31
railways and, 49
reform and, 76
Russeff and, 365n18
slavery and, 48
Spanish Crown and, 21
trade liberalization and, 142–144, 247–249, 253–257, 264, 266
Treaty of Asunción and, 253
Treaty of Tordesillas and, 351n1
wars of, 42t
Brazil, Russia, India, and China (BRIC), 29
Brazilian miracle, 60, 73, 76, 84, 226
British pound, 63–64
Brunei, 264
Bulmer-Thomas, Victor, 44–45, 354n7, 355n16
Bulnes, Manuel, 47
Burdekin, Richard C. K., 336

Caballero, Ricardo, 284
Cacao, 38, 39t
Calderón, César, 189, 334
Canada
  debt crises and, 87, 96
  expropriation risk and, 27
  factor endowments and, 15–20
  financial liberalization and, 273–275
  growth and development and, 15–18, 26–29
  North American Free Trade Agreement (NAFTA) and, 20, 51, 54, 96–97, 249, 257–263, 273–275, 290
  per capita GDP and, 27
  railways and, 355n16
  trade liberalization and, 249, 257–264, 273–275
Capital inflows
  debt crises and, 94–97
  exchange rates and, 225, 227, 230, 232, 235–237, 239–240
  financial liberalization and, 266–269, 271–275
  growth and development and, 324
  import substitution industrialization (ISI) and, 61, 70, 76
  inflation and, 204–208, 217–221, 364n5, 365n23

408 Index

Capital outflows
  debt crises and, 100
  financial liberalization and, 271, 369n8
  growth and development and, 346, 369n8
  inflation and, 207, 219
  political economy and, 153
Cárdenas, Lázaro, 149, 166
Cardoso, Eliana, 222
Carstens, Agustin, 222
Cash transfers
  conditional, 7, 112, 130, 136–138, 140–141, 144, 187–188, 360n26, 361n32
  fiscal policy and, 185–188, 201
  income inequality and, 136–138
  poverty and, 112, 130, 133, 136–138, 141, 144, 361n38
  unconditional, 138, 140
  World Bank and, 361n32
Castelló, Amparo, 329
Castro, Raúl, 57
Catholicism, 28–30, 353n40
Cattle, 17, 27, 39t, 47, 193t
Celasun, Oya, 202
Cenepa War, 164
Central American Common Market (CACM), 299, 317
Central American Free Trade Agreement (CAFTA), 257–263, 273–275
Chávez, Hugo, 149–150, 160–161, 168–169, 256
Chenery, Hollis, 53
Chile, 9
  Advisory Fiscal Council and, 194
  Allende and, 150–152, 284
  Andean Pact and, 76, 356n21
  Bulnes and, 47
  Catholicism and, 29
  climate of, 16–17
  contract enforcement and, 14
  copper and, 47, 78, 194, 231
  corruption and, 10
  debt crises and, 90–91, 93, 96, 358nn6,8
  Economic and Social Stabilization Fund (ESSF) and, 193
  economic collapse of, 152
  European character of, 18
  exchange rates and, 226–229, 231–236, 239–240
  export-led growth and, 19, 36–37, 40, 45, 47–49, 51–55, 78–79, 81, 83–84
  expropriation risk and, 27
  factor endowments and, 16
  financial liberalization and, 268, 271–275
  fiscal policy and, 177, 181–182, 192, 195, 196t, 200–201
  Fiscal Responsibility Law and, 193
  golden age of, 81
  growth and development and, 309–317, 322–325, 331, 338, 341
  human capital and, 355n17
  import substitution industrialization (ISI) and, 60–62, 65, 72–74, 76, 78
  income inequality and, 112, 114, 116–117, 133, 140–141
  inflation and, 78, 206, 210–213, 216–217, 219, 221, 365n15
  Ingreso Ético Familiar (IEF) and, 112, 140–141, 158
  labor and, 280–281, 284, 290, 297–301
  loans and, 228
  military and, 79, 81, 152, 249, 284–285
  Ministry of Finance and, 194
  Montt and, 47
  mortality rates and, 23t, 24
  nitrate prices and, 356n3
  O'Higgins and, 36
  Pacific Alliance and, 246, 264–265, 273–274, 299
  Pension Reserve Fund (PRF) and, 193
  per capita GDP and, 11t
  political economy and, 150–152, 157–158, 169
  populism and, 150
  poverty and, 112, 114, 116–117, 133, 144
  public sector and growth and, 177
  recession of, 152
  small indigenous population of, 17–18
  Spanish Crown and, 21
  stagflation of, 152
  structural balance rules and, 192–194, 195
  take-it-or-leave-it offers and, 90–91
  Tobin taxes and, 367n21
  trade liberalization and, 247–252, 264–266, 367n21
  Treaty of Tordesillas and, 351n1
  wars of, 42t, 47
Chilean miracle, 252
China, 20
  debt crises and, 88, 101, 103–104, 106
  exchange rates and, 225–226, 238–239
  export-led growth and, 37, 41, 52, 55–56
  financial liberalization and, 271–275
  growth and development and, 312, 315, 318, 320, 322, 345, 349
  import substitution industrialization (ISI) and, 81
  increased trade with, 7

Index 409

industrialization and, 7, 19, 37, 41, 52, 56
inflation and, 221
labor and, 288, 299, 302
loans and, 104, 165
political economy and, 165, 170
savings and, 101
slowdown in, 81–82, 88, 104, 144, 170–171, 221, 238–239, 274, 299, 302, 349
tensions with United States and, 265
trade liberalization and, 246, 255–256, 263–265
Chinese miracle, 290
Cholera, 5
Civil law, 4, 9–14, 29, 32
Climate
 agriculture and, 15–16, 26, 29–31, 122, 320, 352n26, 360n14
 investment, 9, 29
 soil and, 15
 urbanization and, 5
Climate change, 360n14
Club convergence, 317
Coatsworth, John, 26, 36, 40, 353–354n1
Coherence, 338–339
Collier, Paul, 57, 158
Colombia
 agricultural research and, 7
 Andean Pact and, 76, 356n21
 CAN and, 354n9
 corruption and, 10t
 crawling peg and, 17
 debt crises and, 90–96, 358nn7,8
 exchange rates and, 224, 226, 229–236, 239–240
 export-led growth and, 19, 36, 51
 financial liberalization and, 268, 271, 273–274
 fiscal policy and, 180–182, 195, 197t, 200
 Great Colombia and, 36, 354n3
 growth and development and, 317, 331, 340
 import substitution industrialization (ISI) and, 60, 75–78, 83
 inflation and, 206, 213, 216–217, 219–221
 labor and, 280, 284, 290, 297–302
 lack of default from, 93
 mortality rates and, 11t, 23t, 24
 Pacific Alliance and, 246, 264–265, 273–274, 299
 per capita GDP and, 11t, 24
 political economy and, 154, 159, 169
 poverty and, 133–134, 360n30
 ProExpo and, 77
 public sector contraction and, 180–181
 reform and, 77–78
 relative size of, 360n30

revolution and, 159
structural balance rules and, 195
take-it-or-leave-it offers and, 90–91
Tobin taxes and, 367n21
trade liberalization and, 247, 256–257, 264
wars of, 42t
Colonial legacies
 Africa and, 5–7, 15, 18, 28, 30–31, 351n1
 Argentina and, 353n31
 Audiencias and, 21–24, 353n30
 Brazil and, 3, 16, 352n25
 corruption and, 9–11, 29
 Cuba and, 16, 19
 Dominican Republic and, 16
 elitism and, 15–20, 27, 31–32, 353n37
 ethnolinguistic fragmentation and, 28–29, 31–32
 geography and, 20, 24, 26, 29, 31–32
 gross domestic product (GDP) and, 10–11, 16–17, 20–27, 351n3
 Guatemala and, 353n30
 Haiti and, 16, 23
 income inequality and, 3–4, 15, 17–19, 31–32, 352n25
 indentured labor and, 15, 17, 19, 30, 36, 45, 48, 56, 352n25, 353n37
 independence and, 23, 26–27, 32, 353n40
 institutional legacy and, 4, 20–27, 32
 International Monetary Fund (IMF) and, 352nn10,19
 Mexico and, 15–20, 27, 29–31, 352n24, 353n30
 military and, 14
 Panama and, 353n30
 political stability and, 28
 Portugal and, 3–4, 18, 21, 23, 26–28
 property rights and, 9, 11, 14, 27–29, 31–32
 research and development (R&D) and, 15
 slavery and, 15–20, 27, 32, 352n25
 Spain and, 4, 17–18, 21, 27
 viceroyalties and, 21–24, 30, 353n30, 354n3
Colorados (Reds, political faction), 47
Colosio, Luis Donaldo, 228
Commodity lottery, 44–45
Commodity prices
 debt crises and, 103–104
 exchange rates and, 230–234, 238–240
 export-led growth and, 36, 41
 financial liberalization and, 271, 273
 fiscal policy and, 178, 191–192, 199t
 growth and development and, 322–323
 import substitution industrialization (ISI) and, 81

Commodity prices (cont.)
　inflation and, 203–206, 216, 219–222
　labor and, 288, 299, 305
　natural resources and, 321–323
　political economy and, 170
　Stolper-Samuelson theorem and, 55, 355n32
　trade liberalization and, 260
Common law, 4, 9, 11–14, 29, 31–32
Communications, 166, 258, 320–321, 341
Communidad Andina de las Naciones (Andean Community of Nations) (CAN), 38, 256–257, 354n9
Communidad del Caribe (Caribbean Community and Common Market) (CARICOM), 38, 354n9
Conditional convergence, 316
Conniff, Micahel, 148
Consols, 88, 358n4
Convertibility system collapse, 99–100, 228
Copper, 47, 78, 151, 193–195, 196t, 231, 266, 358n6
Cornia, Giovanni, 114, 287
Correa, Rafael, 164–165
Corruption
　Argentina and, 10t
　Brazil and, 10
　Chile and, 10
　Colombia and, 10t
　colonial legacies and, 9–11, 29
　Costa Rica and, 10
　defining, 346
　Ecuador and, 10t, 363n34
　El Salvador and, 10t
　fiscal policy and, 200
　foreign direct investment (FDI) and, 10
　growth and development and, 315, 322, 338, 339t, 346, 348
　Guatemala and, 10t
　Haiti and, 10
　labor and, 300, 306
　natural resources and, 322
　Panama and, 10t
　Paraguay and, 10t
　political economy and, 148, 154, 159, 164–165, 167
　poverty and, 116
　Transparency International (TI) and, 338
　Uruguay and, 10
　Venezuela and, 10t
Costa Rica
　corruption and, 10
　debt crises and, 89

　fiscal policy and, 195, 197t
　growth and development and, 317
　labor and, 290, 300
　mortality rates and, 23t
　per capita GDP and, 11t
　political economy and, 156
　poverty and, 114, 117, 126
　trade liberalization and, 260
Cost of basic needs (CBN), 120–122, 128, 142–143, 360n13
Cotlear, Daniel, 307
Cotton, 16, 38, 39t, 43, 193t
Country size, 318–319
Crawling bands, 227–228
Crawling pegs, 76–78, 84, 98, 207, 226–229, 239, 357n35
Credit markets, 116
Creditors, 14, 62, 89–91, 96, 105, 180–181, 358n7
Creoles, 35–36
Cruces, Guillermo, 187
Cuba
　Afro-Latin population of, 37
　agriculture and, 17
　colonial legacies and, 16, 19
　export-led growth and, 37, 40, 45, 48–50, 54, 56–57
　growth and development and, 14
　indigenous population of, 20
　labor and, 20, 50
　legal origins hypothesis and, 14
　per capita GDP of, 49–50
　plantations and, 16
　political economy and, 161
　slavery and, 48
　sugar and, 50
　trade liberalization and, 247
　wars of, 42t
Currency boards
　exchange rates and, 223, 225–226, 228, 235t, 239–240
　fiscal policy and, 161–162, 363n30
　inflation and, 216–217, 365n20
Currency unions, 231
Cyclically adjusted balance rule, 192–193

Debt crises, xiv–xv
　1930s, 89–91
　1980s, 91–96
　1990s, 96–101
　Argentina and, 87, 96, 99–100, 105–106, 268
　Brady Plan and, 94, 201, 367n4
　Brazil and, 89, 93, 98–100, 105, 268

Index 411

Canada and, 87, 96
capital inflows and, 94–97
capital outflows and, 100
Chile and, 90–91, 93, 96, 358nn6,8
China and, 88, 101, 103–104, 106
Colombia and, 90–96, 358n7
commodity prices and, 103–104
Costa Rica and, 89
creditors and, 14, 62, 89–91, 96, 105, 180–181, 358n7
default and, 41, 60, 62–63, 76, 80, 83–84, 87–90, 93, 105, 358nn6–8
depreciation and, 98–100
exchange rates and, 96–100, 358n12
foreign currency and, 87, 93, 96–98, 100, 105
foreign direct investment (FDI) and, 96, 98, 106
globalization and, 88, 96, 100
Great Depression and, 87–91, 96, 100, 105
gross domestic product (GDP) and, 93, 95, 99–104
import substitution industrialization (ISI) and, 60, 94
income inequality and, 102, 105
independence and, 88
industrialization and, 87–88, 91–93, 101–102, 104–105
infrastructure and, 89, 91
interest rates and, 88–89, 92–94, 98, 101, 105, 358n8
International Monetary Fund (IMF) and, 95, 98
loans and, 87–91, 104, 358n4
lower export revenues and, 93
macroeconomics and, 87–88, 92
Mexico and, 88, 90–100, 105, 358n8
middle class and, 105
natural resources and, 104
North American Free Trade Agreement (NAFTA) and, 96–97
oil and, 91–93, 105
overvaluations and, 97–98, 100, 105
Peru and, 93t, 95t
political stability and, 89, 100
privatization and, 96–98, 105
productivity and, 102–104
protectionism and, 87, 94
prudential regulation and, 96–97
public sector and, 104, 180–183
recession and, 88, 92–94, 101, 104–105
reform and, 93, 95–96, 98–99, 104–106
renegotiation of, 63, 89–90, 105, 162

Russia and, 99
stabilization and, 96, 98, 105, 358n12
state-owned enterprises (SOEs) and, 96, 104
take-it-or-leave-it offers and, 90–91, 105
taxes and, 104
technology and, 96
tequila crisis and, 99, 164, 223, 228, 236, 240, 260, 267–268, 363nn30,32
terms of trade and, 103
trade liberalization and, 96, 105
twenty-first century, 101–104
unemployment and, 100
United States and, 88–89, 92, 96, 101, 104–106
Venezuela and, 93, 104
World Bank and, 91, 95
World War I era and, 89
World War II era and, 90–91
Debt rescheduling, 95
Decentralization, 38, 142, 148
Default
 cyclical, 87
 debt crises and, 41, 60, 62–63, 76, 80, 83–84, 87–90, 93, 105, 358nn6–8
 debt rescheduling and, 95
 exchange rates and, 225, 228, 235
 export-led growth and, 41
 fiscal policy and, 176, 180, 201
 Great Depression and, 87–91, 96, 100, 105
 import substitution industrialization (ISI) and, 60, 62–63, 76, 80, 83–84
 political economy and, 165
 sovereign, 41, 62, 76, 83, 87–88, 105, 176, 180, 225
De Gregorio, José, 326
Deindustrialization, 36, 51, 254n4, 255n15, 282
Dell, Melissa, 27, 261, 353n36
Democracy, 9, 28, 81, 118, 156, 158, 281, 284, 328, 362n25
Dengue, 5
Denmark, 358
Depreciation
 debt crises and, 98–100
 exchange rates and, 226–228, 233, 240
 financial liberalization and, 269
 fiscal policy and, 182, 201
 growth and development and, 313, 316, 322
 import substitution industrialization (ISI) and, 63–64
 inflation and, 213, 216, 219, 221, 366n25
 political economy and, 162
Deregulation, 96, 184, 252, 277, 283–287, 354n5
Deunionization, 281–287

Devaluation
　debt crises and, 98
　exchange rates and, 225, 227, 229, 238
　import substitution industrialization (ISI) and, 63–65, 357n35
　inflation and, 207–208
　political economy and, 152–153, 162
Devlin, Robert, 81
Dictatorships, 47, 73, 81, 152, 249, 319
Disease, 5, 8, 26, 29, 320, 353n33
Disinflation, 219, 362n24
Distrito Federal (Federal District) (DF), 73
Doha Round, 247, 252, 273
Dollar, David, 337–338
Dollarization, 153, 164, 216, 221, 223–225, 229, 268–269
Doménech, Rafael, 329
Domínguez, Jorge I., 57
Dominican Republic
　colonial legacies and, 16
　corruption and, 10t
　mortality rates and, 23t
　per capita GDP and, 11t, 16
　poverty and, 124
　trade liberalization and, 260
Dom Pedro, 35, 354n2
Dornbusch, Rudiger, 147, 150–151, 154, 171
Drake, Paul W., 150
Drawback system, 41, 78, 358n10
Dreher, Axel, 338
Drugs, 158, 260–261, 273, 275, 360n14
Duflo, Esther, 123
Duryea, Suzanne, 302
Dutch disease, 36–37, 42, 55, 322, 354n4, 369n21

Easterly, William, 107, 326
Economic and Social Stabilization Fund (ESSF), 193
Economic Commission for Latin America and the Caribbean (ECLAC)
　import substitution industrialization (ISI) and, 66, 81
　inflation and, 209, 364n1
　labor and, 278, 307
　political economy and, 151
　poverty and, 113, 118, 359n7, 360n14
　trade and, 246–247
Ecuador
　Andean Pact and, 76, 356n21
　CAN and, 354n9
　Central Bank of, 164
　Correa and, 164–165
　corruption and, 10t, 363n34
　exchange rates and, 224–225, 229
　export-led growth and, 51, 52t, 53f, 354nn3,9, 355n16
　fiscal policy and, 192, 195, 197t
　Great Colombia and, 354n3
　growth and development and, 317
　import substitution industrialization (ISI) and, 76
　indigenous population of, 131
　inflation and, 210–211, 213, 216, 221, 365n15
　labor and, 290, 299
　mortality rates and, 24
　oil and, 225
　per capita GDP and, 11t, 24
　political economy and, 148, 160, 164–165, 167–169, 363n34
　populism and, 148, 164–165
　poverty and, 114f, 116f, 127t–128t, 131
　railways and, 355n16
　structural balance rules and, 195
　trade liberalization and, 249, 256, 270
　wars of, 42t, 164
Education
　fiscal policy and, 183, 201
　growth and development and, 310, 318, 323–331, 345–349
　high-brow vs. low-brow, 328–329
　import substitution industrialization (ISI) and, 59, 84
　income inequality and, 134, 139–140, 352n28
　investments in, 8, 59
　labor and, 283, 287, 297, 299–306
　political economy and, 158
　poverty and, 111–112, 116–126, 129–130, 360n23, 363n29
　as premium, 124
　quality of, 360n23
　slavery and, 27
Edwards, Sebastian, 33, 66, 80, 147, 150–151, 154, 171, 266, 284
Effective protection, 74, 357n31
Egypt, 177
Eichengreen, Barry, 64, 107
Electricity, 47, 73, 120, 163, 166, 170, 198t
Elitism
　colonial legacies and, 15–20, 27, 31–32, 353n37
　encomienda system and, 16–20, 27, 31–32, 48, 352n24
　export-led growth and, 36, 48, 54–55
　political economy and, 149, 163, 167

Index

El Salvador
  corruption and, 10t
  exchange rates and, 224–225, 229
  financial liberalization and, 269
  fiscal policy and, 195
  growth and development and, 317
  inflation and, 216, 221
  labor and, 286–290
  MCCA and, 354n9
  mortality rates and, 23t
  per capita GDP of, 11t
  poverty and, 143
  trade liberalization and, 260
  wars of, 42t
Emergency social funds (ESFs), 134, 143
Emerging Markets Bond Index Plus (EMBI+), 237–238
Encomienda system, 16–20, 27, 31–32, 48, 352n24
Endogenous growth theory, 315, 328, 341, 351n7
Engerman, Stanley, 15–19
Equator, 4–5, 29, 317, 320
Escosura, Prados de la, 57
Esquivel, Gerardo, 33, 236
Ethnicity, 112, 131, 142
Ethnolinguistic fragmentation, 28–29, 31–32
European Union (EU)
  fiscal policy and, 186
  liberalization and, 273–275
  political economy and, 167, 169
  trade and, 253, 255–256, 263–264, 275
Eurozone, 229, 323, 329
Exchange rates, xv
  agriculture and, 239
  Argentina and, 223–232, 236, 239–240
  bands and, 226–228
  Brazil and, 223, 226–230, 234–236, 239–240
  capital inflows and, 225, 227, 230, 232, 235–237, 239–240
  characterization of different regimes for, 224–226
  Chile and, 226–229, 231–236, 239–240
  China and, 225–226, 238–239
  Colombia and, 224, 226, 229–236, 239–240
  commodity prices and, 230–234, 238–240
  convertibility system collapse and, 99–100, 228
  crises avoidance and, 235–238
  currency boards and, 223, 225–226, 228, 235t, 239–240
  currency unions and, 231
  debt crises and, 96–100, 358n12
  default and, 225, 228, 235
  depreciation and, 226–228, 233, 240
  devaluations and, 63–65, 98, 152–153, 162, 207–208, 225, 227, 229, 238, 357n35
  disinflation and, 219, 362n24
  dollarization and, 153, 164, 216, 221, 223–225, 229, 268–269
  Ecuador and, 224–225, 229
  El Salvador and, 224–225, 229
  financial liberalization and, 266, 269, 271–275
  fiscal policy and, 182
  fixed, 62–63, 84, 96, 98–100, 161–162, 213, 216–217, 223–232, 236–240, 365n20
  floating and, 78, 217, 221, 223–224, 226–236, 239–241, 366n9
  foreign currency and, 224–228
  foreign direct investment (FDI) and, 225
  globalization and, 230, 235, 239–240
  gold standard and, 62–64, 84, 232
  gross domestic product (GDP) and, 224–225, 228, 236t, 237f, 366n9
  growth and development and, 313, 322
  Guatemala and, 234
  import substitution industrialization (ISI) and, 60–65, 68–70, 76–80, 82–84, 354n5, 356n11, 357n35
  independence and, 224, 233
  indigenous populations and, 228
  inflation and, 204–207, 209, 213–222, 266n25, 365nn20,24
  informality and, 233
  interest rates and, 225, 229
  International Monetary Fund (IMF) and, 224, 234, 238–239
  labor and, 287
  loans and, 228
  macroeconomics and, 224–225
  Mexico and, 223, 226–229, 232–236, 239–240
  NAFTA and, 97
  natural resources and, 230, 322–323
  nominal anchors and, 226
  oil and, 225, 227, 229, 231, 239
  overvaluations and, 227–228 (*see also* Overvaluations)
  Panama and, 224–225, 229
  pass-through and, 64, 219–220, 233, 240, 356n11, 365n24, 366n25
  pegs and, 63–64, 76–78, 84, 97–99, 207, 217, 219, 223, 225–230, 234t–235t, 239, 357n35
  Peru and, 229, 231–232, 234, 235t–236t, 239–240
  political economy and, 151–152, 162, 362n24, 363n32
  political stability and, 228
  poverty and, 130–131

Exchange rates (cont.)
  recession and, 232, 236, 239
  reform and, 228, 235
  Russia and, 223, 228, 230, 236
  savings and, 153
  sliding, 217, 228
  sovereign debt and, 227, 235
  stabilization and, 225–227, 238
  tablitas system and, 227
  trade liberalization and, 245, 252–254, 275
  undervaluation and, 97, 268
  unemployment and, 224
  United States and, 224–226, 231–234
  Venezuela and, 232, 236, 239
Export bias, 35, 49, 52, 59, 69, 76, 78, 84, 247, 355n1
Export-led growth
  Africa and, 36, 45, 57
  agriculture and, 40, 44, 46, 49, 51, 52t
  Argentina and, 36–42, 45–49, 53–55
  belle époque of, 37, 40–41, 44, 48, 53–56
  Bolivia and, 41, 47, 51, 355n16
  Brazil and, 35, 37–38, 42–43, 45, 48–50, 54–56
  Chile and, 19, 36–37, 40, 45, 47–49, 51–55, 78–79, 81, 83–84
  China and, 37, 41, 52, 55–56
  Colombia and, 19, 24, 36, 51
  commodity lottery and, 44–45
  commodity prices and, 36, 41
  creoles and, 35–36
  Cuba and, 37, 40, 45, 48–50, 54, 56–57
  cyclically adjusted balance rule and, 192–193
  default and, 41
  divergent trends in, 45–48
  Dutch disease and, 36–37, 42, 55, 322, 354n4, 369n21
  Ecuador and, 51, 52t, 53f, 354nn3,9, 355n16
  elitism and, 36, 48, 54–55
  foreign direct investment (FDI) and, 46, 49, 266–267, 270–271, 273–274
  geography and, 47
  globalization and, 37, 51, 55
  gross domestic product (GDP) and, 40t, 43, 47, 49–50, 54
  human capital and, 45
  income inequality and, 35–37, 42, 46–49, 54–57, 353–354n1, 355n27
  independence and, 35–43, 48–49, 53, 55, 57, 354n2
  India and, 55
  indigenous populations and, 56
  industrialization and, 35–44, 51–56
  infrastructure and, 37, 41–43, 46–47, 49, 54, 56
  intendencia system and, 38
  loans and, 41
  manufacturing and, 35–37, 41, 45, 51, 53–55, 354n4
  Mexico and, 19, 35–36, 41–45, 48, 51–55
  natural resources and, 37, 44–46, 48, 57
  nineteenth-century vs. modern, 51–52
  North American Free Trade Agreement (NAFTA) and, 51, 54
  Peru and, 19, 36, 39t, 40t, 41, 42t, 45, 47–48, 51, 52t–53t, 354n9, 355n16
  political stability and, 43, 46–47
  Portugal and, 35–38, 41, 48
  productivity and, 45, 48, 51, 55
  protectionism and, 36, 43, 51, 54–55
  reform and, 37–38, 41, 354nn5,8
  regional diversity and, 43–45
  slavery and, 36, 45, 48–50, 56
  Spain and, 37–38, 41, 45–47, 50
  tariffs and, 36, 41, 54
  taxes and, 36, 41, 54, 353–354n1
  terms of trade and, 36, 41–42, 55
  trade agreements and, 37, 41, 51, 55
  trade blocs and, 354n9
  trade liberalization and, 51
  transportation and, 43–44, 46
  United States and, 36–44, 47–55, 354n7
  urbanization and, 353–354n1
  Uruguay and, 37, 45–47, 49, 54–55, 226–227, 234, 239
  War of the Pacific and, 41, 42t, 47
  World War I era and, 36–37, 43, 45, 53
  World War II era and, 42

Factor endowments hypothesis, 4, 15–20, 29, 44
Falkland Islands, 3, 42t, 351n1
Ferreira, Francisco, 116, 140, 145
Fertility, human, 18, 302–303, 320, 328
Fertility, soil, 8
Financial liberalization
  Argentina and, 266, 269, 271, 273
  banking crises and, 268–272
  Brazil and, 134, 136–137, 140–141, 266–268, 271, 273
  Canada and, 273–275
  capital inflows and, 266–269, 271–275
  capital outflows and, 271, 369n8
  Chile and, 268, 271–275
  China and, 271–275
  Colombia and, 268, 271, 273–274
  commodity prices and, 271, 273

defining, 245
depreciation and, 269
El Salvador and, 269
European Union (EU) and, 273–275
exchange rates and, 266, 269, 271–275
foreign currency and, 269
foreign direct investment (FDI) and, 266–275
gross domestic product (GDP) and, 271, 274
growth and development and, 333–336
industrialization and, 267, 273–274
interest rates and, 268, 271, 274
International Monetary Fund (IMF) and, 266–269
liability dollarization and, 268–269
loans and, 266–269, 366n1
macroeconomics and, 266, 268
manufacturing and, 273
Mexico and, 266–275
North American Free Trade Agreement (NAFTA) and, 273
oil and, 266, 270
overvaluations and, 266, 271, 274–275
Peru and, 271, 273–275
political stability and, 273
privatization and, 268, 272
purchasing power parity (PPP) and, 227
recession and, 269
reform and, 266, 272
Russia and, 267
savings and, 268
stabilization and, 266, 272–273
supervision and, 268–272
tariffs and, 273–274
taxes and, 268
technology and, 266, 273–274
terms of trade and, 271
trade liberalization and, 266, 271–272
United States and, 267, 270–275
Uruguay and, 273, 290, 297, 301
Venezuela and, 271
worker remittances and, 269–271
Finland, 358
Firing costs, 132, 283–284, 304
Fiscal discipline, 164, 175–176, 183, 195, 200, 215, 232
Fiscal policy, xv
  Advisory Fiscal Council and, 194
  Africa and, 178–179
  agriculture and, 183, 192
  Argentina and, 182, 195, 200
  Bolivia and, 181–182, 192
  Brady Plan and, 94, 201, 367n4
  Brazil and, 195, 196t, 200
  cash transfers and, 185–188, 201
  Chile and, 177, 181–182, 192, 195, 196t, 200–201
  Colombia and, 180–182, 195, 197t, 200
  commodity prices and, 178, 191–192, 199t
  corruption and, 200
  Costa Rica and, 195, 197t
  countercyclical, 175, 195, 196t, 200–202
  creditors and, 180–181
  currency boards and, 161–162, 363n30
  cyclically adjusted balance rule and, 192–193
  default and, 176, 180, 201
  depreciation and, 182, 201
  deregulation and, 96, 184, 252, 277, 283–287, 354n5
  economic contraction and, 189, 191
  Ecuador and, 192, 195, 197t
  education and, 183, 201
  El Salvador and, 195
  European Union (EU) and, 186
  exchange rates and, 182, 224–228
  expansionary, 175–179, 189, 195, 197t
  foreign currency and, 178
  foreign direct investment (FDI) and, 178
  globalization and, 191
  Great Depression and, 14, 176
  gross domestic product (GDP) and, 176, 177t, 181–183, 185f, 186, 187f, 191f, 192, 194–195, 196t–199t
  growth and development and, 175–202, 331–332
  health issues and, 183, 201
  human capital and, 188, 201
  import substitution industrialization (ISI) and, 176
  income inequality and, 179, 189, 191
  independence and, 184
  industrialization and, 176
  inflation and, 175–176, 178, 181–183, 200–201
  infrastructure and, 183, 199t
  institutional changes in, 191–195
  interest rates and, 178, 180–181
  International Monetary Fund (IMF) and, 183, 187–188, 202
  loans and, 176, 178
  macroeconomics and, 178–180, 183, 187, 189, 191, 195, 201
  Mexico and, 180, 182, 192, 195, 198t
  middle class and, 176
  military and, 199t
  natural resources and, 178, 197t

Fiscal policy (cont.)
  oil and, 176–179, 192–195, 197t–198t
  Organisation for Economic Co-operation and Development (OECD) and, 186–187
  orthodox, 157, 204, 208–212, 217, 220–222, 362n24
  Panama and, 198t
  pensions and, 176, 193
  Peru and, 177t, 182, 183t, 186t, 188t, 189f, 193t, 195, 199t, 200
  populism and, 176, 179, 191
  principal-agent problem and, 363n5
  private sector and, 178–179, 182, 184, 299
  privatization and, 184, 201
  protectionism and, 175–176
  public expenditure and, 177–178, 182–185
  public sector and, 176–182, 184, 195, 198t–199t, 200
  recession and, 177, 182, 192
  redistributive effects of, 184–191
  reform and, 175–176, 183–184, 191, 198t, 200–201, 364n14
  role of state and, 183–184
  savings and, 198t, 315
  social security and, 198t
  sovereign debt and, 200–201
  stabilization and, 182, 193, 197t–198t, 201
  state intervention and, 175
  state-owned enterprises (SOEs) and, 175–177, 182, 184
  structural balance rules and, 192–195
  structuralists and, 151, 208–209, 364n8
  tariffs and, 175–176
  taxes and, 176–179, 182, 184–189, 192, 195, 200–201
  terms of trade and, 179, 182
  unemployment and, 189
  United States and, 177–178
  Uruguay and, 182, 195
  Venezuela and, 182, 195
  Washington Consensus and, 159, 183–185, 277, 280, 288, 303, 306, 309, 354n5, 364n14
  World Bank and, 176, 183, 188
Fiscal Responsibility Law, 193
Floating. *See also* Pegs
  consensus for, 229–235
  debt crises and, 99, 99z
  dollarization and, 223
  exchange rates and, 78, 217, 221, 223–236, 239–241, 366n9
  import substitution industrialization (ISI) and, 78
  independent, 226, 229, 230t, 239
  inflation and, 181
  interest rates and, 93
  managed, 226, 230t, 239
  trends in, 223–224
Fondo Sectorial para la Investigatión y el Desarrollo Social (Sector Fund for Research and Social Development) (FOSIDES), 139, 359n4
Forceful contraction, 182, 204–205, 210, 221
Foreign currency
  debt crises and, 87, 93, 96–98, 100, 105
  Dutch disease and, 36–37, 42, 55, 322, 354n4, 369n21
  financial liberalization and, 266, 269
  fiscal policy and, 178
  growth and development and, 324
  import substitution industrialization (ISI) and, 62–63, 77, 84
  inflation and, 205, 209
Foreign direct investment (FDI)
  corruption and, 10
  debt crises and, 96, 98, 106
  exchange rates and, 225
  export-led growth and, 46, 49, 266–267, 270–271, 273–274
  financial liberalization and, 266–275
  fiscal policy and, 178
  globalization and, 31
  gross domestic product (GDP) and, 10
  growth and development and, 315–316, 342, 346
  import substitution industrialization (ISI) and, 70, 76, 80, 83, 315
  inflation and, 214, 218
  labor and, 283
  lifting restrictions on, 315–316
  political economy and, 149, 167
  savings and, 76, 80, 83
  technology transfer and, 31
  trade liberalization and, 245, 255, 260
  transportation and, 46, 49
Formal sector, 126, 132–133, 140, 277–280, 296, 305–306
Forward linkages, 356n17
France, 4, 9, 40, 42t, 45, 357n25
Free on board (FOB), 6t, 77, 358n37
Free trade agreement (FTA), 317
Free Trade Area of the Americas (FTAA), 162
Frenkel, Roberto, 241
Friedman, Milton, 208

Index

Fuerzas Armadas Revolucionarias de Colombia (Revolutionary Armed Forces of Colombia) (FARC), 159
Fujimori, Alberto, 153–154
Furceri, Davide, 237
Furtado, Celso, 151, 209

Gallup, John Luke, 320
Galván, Javier A., 50
García, Alan, 151–153
Gas, 47, 73, 140, 163, 166–170, 193t, 354n4, 369n21
Gasparani, Leonardo, 187
Gender
  labor and, 303, 306
  poverty and, 112, 129–130, 142–143
General Agreement on Trade and Tariffs (GATT), 247
Geography
  agriculture and, 5, 7
  climate and, 15–16, 26, 29–31, 122, 320, 352n26, 360n14
  colonial legacies and, 20, 24, 26, 29, 31–32
  equator and, 4–5, 29, 317, 320
  export-led growth and, 47
  gross domestic product (GDP) and, 8
  growth and development and, 5–9, 317–318, 320, 338, 345, 347
  hypothesis of, 4–9
  institutional legacy and, 20, 24, 26, 29, 31–32
  landlocked countries and, 5–7, 29, 43, 318, 320
  Mexico and, 351n2
  pampas and, 17, 352n26
  poverty and, 122
  transportation and, 7
  Treaty of Tordesillas and, 3, 21, 351n1, 353n31
Germany, 14
Gertler, Paul J., 135–136
Ghosh, Amit, 233
Gini coefficient
  economic contraction and, 189–190
  income inequality and, 115–116, 135–139, 142–143, 165, 186, 189, 329, 338, 359n5, 363n29
  poverty and, 115–116
  quintile indices and, 116
Glaeser, Edward, 33
Global Economic Prospects (World Bank), 349
Globalization
  Brazil and, 16
  debt crises and, 88, 96, 100
  exchange rates and, 230, 235, 239–240

  export-led growth and, 37, 51, 55
  fiscal policy and, 191
  foreign direct investment (FDI) and, 31
  growth and development and, 319, 332, 345, 347
  import substitution industrialization (ISI) and, 69, 83
  inflation and, 217
  political economy and, 154, 160, 165, 167
  trade liberalization and, 7, 253, 262
Gold, 38, 39t, 62–64, 84, 193t, 232, 354n10
Goñi, Ewin, 186
Grain, 15, 17, 39t, 44
Great Colombia, 36, 354n3
Great Depression, xiv
  debt crises and, 87–91, 96, 100, 105
  fiscal policy and, 14, 176
  growth and development and, 356, 358
  import substitution industrialization (ISI) and, 60–64, 66, 82, 82–85
  legal origin concept and, 11–12
Great Venezuela Plan, 149
Greece, 229, 232
Griffith, Rachel, 340
Gross domestic product (GDP)
  civil law countries and, 11
  colonial legacies and, 10–11, 16–17, 20–27, 351n3
  debt crises and, 93, 95, 99–104
  exchange rates and, 224–225, 228, 236t, 237f, 366n9
  export-led growth and, 40t, 43, 47, 49–50, 54
  financial liberalization and, 271, 274
  fiscal policy and, 176, 177t, 181–183, 185f, 186, 187f, 191f, 192, 194–195, 196t–199t
  foreign direct investment (FDI) and, 10
  geography and, 8
  growth and development and, 311f–312f, 314f, 318, 320, 324–325, 329, 331, 339–340, 341f
  import substitution industrialization (ISI) and, 68, 70t, 71–73, 76–78, 84
  income inequality and, 136
  inflation and, 206, 207t, 210f–211f, 221
  Latin America vs. U.S., 4, 40t
  political economy and, 150–152, 155f, 160, 165
  purchasing power parity (PPP) and, 11t, 21
  trade and, 245, 264
Growth and development, xiv, xvi
  Africa and, 312, 322, 329, 338
  agriculture and, 320
  Argentina and, 317, 325, 331, 337–341, 347
  Bolivia and, 317–318, 325, 340

Growth and development (cont.)
  Brazil and, 14, 312, 317–318, 320, 325, 330, 331, 341, 349
  Canada and, 15–18, 26–29
  capital inflows and, 324
  capital outflows and, 346, 369n8
  Chile and, 309–317, 322–325, 331, 338, 341
  China and, 312, 315, 318, 320, 322, 345, 349
  club convergence and, 317
  coherence and, 338–339
  Colombia and, 317, 331, 340
  commodity prices and, 322–323
  comparison to Asian countries, 310–312
  conditional convergence and, 316
  corruption and, 315, 322, 338, 339t, 346, 348
  Costa Rica and, 317
  country size and, 318–319
  Cuba and, 14
  depreciation and, 313, 316, 322
  Ecuador and, 317
  education and, 310, 318, 323–331, 345–349
  El Salvador and, 317
  endogenous growth theory and, 315, 328, 341, 351n7
  exchange rates and, 313, 322
  financial liberalization and, 333–336
  fiscal policy and, 175–202, 331–332
  foreign currency and, 324
  foreign direct investment (FDI) and, 315–316, 342, 346
  frustrated expectations and, 310–312
  geography and, 5–9, 317–318, 320, 338, 345, 347
  globalization and, 319, 332, 345, 347
  Great Depression and, 356, 358
  gross domestic product (GDP) and, 311f–312f, 314f, 318, 320, 324–325, 329, 331, 339–340, 341f
  Guatemala and, 316–317, 331, 341
  health issues and, 315, 318, 332
  heterogeneity and, 28, 32, 159, 247, 249, 309, 319, 331–332, 341, 346
  Honduras and, 317, 331
  human capital and, 327, 329, 332, 345, 347
  import substitution industrialization (ISI) and, 309, 313–315, 318
  inclusive growth and, 342, 347
  income inequality and, 309–312, 316, 320, 328–329, 342, 345–346
  independence and, 337
  India and, 318, 329
  inflation and, 336–337
  information and communication technology (ICT) and, 341–342
  infrastructure and, 320, 324, 345, 347
  innovation and, 339–342
  institutions and, 337–339
  lack of, xiii
  loans and, 315
  macroeconomics and, 313–316, 337
  manufacturing and, 322, 345
  Mexico and, 309, 312, 317–318, 325, 330, 342, 347
  multidimensional nature of, 309
  natural resources and, 316, 318, 321–323, 345–348
  Nicaragua and, 317, 341
  oil and, 322
  Organisation for Economic Co-operation and Development (OECD) and, 317, 325, 329, 338–340, 345
  Panama and, 312
  Paraguay and, 317–318, 325
  pensions and, 314–315, 347
  per capita income and, 5, 8–11, 18, 27–32, 40, 43, 45, 47, 60, 72, 102, 149, 186, 191, 310–320, 323, 329, 351nn3,7, 352n10
  Peru and, 311–312, 317, 325, 331
  political stability and, 339t
  private sector and, 338, 346, 348
  privatization and, 346
  productivity and, 232, 310, 313, 315, 318, 320, 331, 334, 339–342, 346–348
  property rights and, 315
  protectionism and, 323
  public sector and, 176–179, 346
  purchasing power parity (PPP) and, 310–311, 316, 318
  quality and, 338
  reform and, 309–310, 314–316, 324, 334, 336, 345, 347–348
  research and development (R&D) and, 323, 340, 346, 348
  savings and, 310, 313–316, 345–347
  social security and, 314–315, 345, 347
  stabilization and, 155–157
  stagnation and, 40, 49, 55, 71, 102, 104, 182, 251, 270, 279, 290, 310, 323
  structural factors and, 317–323
  tariffs and, 323–325
  taxes and, 331–332, 338, 346–348
  technology and, 315–317, 341, 346, 369n17
  terms of trade and, 36, 41–42, 55, 61, 103, 179, 182, 217, 271, 288, 317, 326–327, 347, 354n12

total factor productivity (TFP) and, 339–340
trade blocs and, 317
trade liberalization and, 319, 324–325
trade openness and, 54, 82, 252–254, 274–275, 279, 310, 323–325, 345
transportation and, 320
United States and, 28–30, 317–318, 321, 329
Uruguay and, 312, 317
Venezuela and, 310, 317, 320–321, 331, 337, 341, 347
Washington Consensus and, 309
World Bank and, 349
Guano, 45
Guatemala
  colonial legacies and, 353n30
  corruption and, 10t
  exchange rates and, 234
  growth and development and, 316–317, 331, 341
  income inequality and, 136
  indigenous population of, 16–17, 131
  inflation and, 217
  labor and, 302
  MCCA and, 354n9
  mortality rates and, 23t
  per capita GDP and, 11t
  poverty and, 131
  trade liberalization and, 249, 260
  wars of, 42t
Guerrillas, 158, 363n31
Guichard, Stephanie, 237
Gutiérrez, Mario, 202
Guyana, 23, 354n9
Gyimah-Brempong, Kwabena, 338

Haciendas, 27, 30, 353n37
Haiti
  colonial legacies and, 16, 23
  corruption and, 10
  income inequality and, 29
  independence of, 23
  labor and, 302
  per capita GDP and, 11t, 16, 24
  poverty and, 29, 114, 124
Hammour, Mohamad, 284
Harberger, Arnold, 85
Harris-Todaro model, 71, 278–279
Harrod-Domar model, 356n22
Health issues
  children and, 27, 360n26, 363n29
  disease and, 5, 8, 26, 29, 320, 353n33
  fiscal policy and, 183, 201

growth and development and, 315, 318, 332
hospitals and, 73
import substitution industrialization (ISI) and, 59, 84
income inequality and, 134, 138–141, 143–144
infrastructure investments and, 8
labor and, 283, 297, 299, 305
life expectancy and, 353n33
mortality rates and, 20–27, 30, 302, 363n29
Obras Sociales and, 283
poverty and, 7, 116–121, 131–133
slavery and, 27
technology and, 5
Heckman, James, 284, 286
Hecksher-Ohlin theorem, 246, 275, 367n2
Helwege, Ann, 222
Herzfeld, Thomas, 338
Heterodox policies
  inflation and, 204, 208–212, 221–222
  stabilization and, 152–153, 157, 204, 208–212, 221–222, 362nn23,24
Heterogeneity, 28, 32, 159, 247, 249, 309, 319, 331–332, 341, 346
Hidalgo, Miguel, 36
Honduras
  growth and development and, 317, 331
  income inequality and, 136
  labor and, 290, 302
  MCCA and, 354n9
  per capita GDP and, 11t
  poverty and, 114–115, 134
  trade liberalization and, 249, 260
Hong Kong, 14, 59, 311
Hospitals, 73
Huber, Evelyne, 126
Human capital
  education and, 327–330 (*see also* Education)
  export-led growth and, 45
  fiscal policy and, 188, 201
  growth and development and, 327, 329, 332, 345, 347
  health issues and, 27 (*see also* Health issues)
  immigrants and, 14, 18
  import substitution industrialization (ISI) and, 59
  income inequality and, 128, 139–140
  institutional quality and, 353n35, 355n17
  labor and, 299, 305
  poverty and, 128, 142
Human rights, 131, 154, 355n22
Hyperinflation, 153, 159, 181–182, 203, 206, 208, 219, 232, 337, 364n1

Immigration, 14, 45–46, 48–49
Import barriers, 64, 79
Imported inflation, 219–220
Import prices, 41, 69, 356n11, 365n24, 366n25
Import substitution industrialization (ISI), xiv
  adjustments to strategy of, 75–79
  agriculture and, 62, 67–74, 80, 84, 278
  Argentina and, 63–65, 72–76, 79, 83–84
  backward linkages and, 356n17
  Bolivia and, 63, 76
  Brazil and, 49, 60–63, 65, 71–78, 83–85
  capital inflows and, 61, 70, 76
  Chile and, 60–62, 65, 72–74, 76, 78
  China and, 81
  Colombia and, 60, 75–78, 83
  commodity prices and, 81
  country size and, 318
  criticism of, 74–75
  debt crises and, 60, 94
  default and, 60, 62–63, 76, 80, 83–84
  depreciation and, 63–64
  Economic Commission for Latin American and the Caribbean (ECLAC) and, 66, 81
  Ecuador and, 76
  education and, 59, 84
  exchange rates and, 60–65, 68–70, 76–80, 82–84, 354n5, 356n11, 357n35
  factor endowments and, 15
  fall of stellar performers and, 72–74
  fiscal policy and, 176
  floating and, 78
  foreign currency and, 62–63, 77, 84
  foreign direct investment (FDI) and, 70, 76, 80, 83, 315
  forward linkages and, 356n17
  globalization and, 69, 83
  Great Depression and, 60–64, 66, 82–85
  gross domestic product (GDP) and, 68, 70t, 71–73, 76–78, 84
  growth and development and, 309, 313–315, 318
  Harris-Todaro model and, 71
  health issues and, 59, 84
  historical perspective on, 60–66
  human capital and, 59
  income inequality and, 73, 75, 82–83
  infant industry argument and, 67
  inflation and, 60, 206
  informal sector and, 71, 80
  infrastructure and, 68, 73, 77, 80, 83
  interest rates and, 61, 70, 356n22
  International Monetary Fund (IMF) and, 80–81
  labor and, 278–280, 283, 306
  LAFTA and, 75–76
  legacies of, 83, 314
  loans and, 62, 81, 356n22
  macroeconomics and, 60, 65, 80, 357n35
  manufacturing and, 60, 65–70, 73–74, 76–80, 82, 84, 357n23
  Mexico and, 60–61, 71–74, 78, 83–84
  new consensus for, 79–82
  oil and, 59, 77–78
  overvaluations and, 69–70, 76–77, 80, 84
  Paraguay and, 63
  performance indicators for, 71–79
  Peru and, 61, 76
  policies of, 66–71
  privatization and, 60, 81
  productivity and, 67, 69, 71, 73, 81–82
  protectionism and, 59–76, 80–85, 280, 356n4
  public sector and, 61
  recession and, 61–62, 64
  reform and, 73, 76–79, 81, 83–84
  research and development (R&D) and, 67
  savings and, 313–314
  self-sufficiency and, 66, 82
  shadow prices and, 366n1
  sovereign debt and, 60, 62–63, 76
  stabilization and, 60, 76–81
  state intervention and, 60, 66, 68, 75, 79, 84
  state-owned enterprises (SOEs) and, 60, 83, 85
  structuralists and, 151
  tariffs and, 61–62, 68, 76–78
  taxes and, 76–80
  terms of trade and, 61
  trade liberalization and, 60, 65, 79–81, 85, 246–247, 275, 278
  unemployment and, 62, 64, 67, 71, 84
  United States and, 59, 61–62, 64, 66, 79, 84
  Uruguay and, 63, 72–75, 79, 84
  Venezuela and, 63, 76, 83
  World Bank and, 80
  World War I era and, 59, 61–62, 85
  World War II era and, 61, 65–66, 79, 82, 84–85
  X-inefficiency and, 69, 84, 356n20
Income inequality, xv
  agriculture and, 29, 279
  Argentina and, 134
  Brazil and, 140, 355n27
  Chile and, 112, 114, 116–117, 133, 140–141
  colonial legacies and, 3–4, 15, 17–19, 31–32, 352n25
  conditional cash transfers and, 136–138

Index

conditional convergence and, 316
debt crises and, 102, 105
diversity and, 113–117
education and, 134, 139–140, 352n28
elitism and, 15–20 (*see also* Elitism)
export-led growth and, 35–37, 42, 46–49, 54–57, 353–354n1, 355n27
fiscal policy and, 179, 189, 191
FOSIDES and, 139, 359n4
Gini coefficient and, 115–116, 135–139, 142–143, 165, 186, 189, 329, 338, 359n5, 363n29
gross domestic product (GDP) and, 136
growth and development and, 309–312, 316, 320, 328–329, 342, 345–346
Guatemala and, 136
Haiti and, 29
health issues and, 134, 138–141, 143–144
Honduras and, 136
human capital and, 128, 139–140
income quintiles and, 135–136
indigenous populations and, 17
inflation and, 204
informal sector and, 278
infrastructure and, 134
interest rates and, 139
labor and, 278–279, 286–287, 296–299, 302, 306
language and, 4
loans and, 139
manufacturing and, 30
measurement of, 134–141
Mexico and, 134, 136–139, 355n27
middle class and, 134–135, 137, 139
minimum wage and, 126, 132, 278, 280, 283, 290, 293, 304–305, 361n31, 365n14
Nicaragua and, 29, 136
per capita income and, 5, 8–11, 18, 27–32, 40, 43, 45, 47, 60, 72, 102, 149, 186, 191, 310–311, 313, 315–320, 323, 329, 351nn3,7, 352n10
Peru and, 134, 137
political economy and, 147–148, 154, 160, 165, 168–170, 361n1, 363n29
populism and, 361n1
poverty and, 112, 114–116, 134–141, 359n2, 360n30
productivity and, 134, 139
public sector and, 134
recent trends in, 113–117, 134–141
tariffs and, 353–354n1
United States and, 360n30
Washington Consensus and, 159, 183–185, 277, 280, 288, 303, 306, 309, 354n5, 364n14
World Bank and, 134, 136

Indentured labor, 15, 17, 19, 30, 36, 45, 48, 56, 352n25, 353n37
Independence
 backwardness and, 26–27
 colonial legacies and, 23, 26–27, 32, 353n40
 debt crises and, 88
 economic consequences of, 38–43
 exchange rates and, 224, 233
 export-led growth and, 35–43, 48–49, 53, 55, 57, 354n2
 fiscal policy and, 184
 growth and development and, 337
 Haiti and, 23
 inflation and, 212–213, 219, 365n18
 performance after, 32, 35
 poverty and, 118
India, 55, 265, 318, 329
Indigenous populations
 Argentina and, 17–18
 Bolivia and, 16
 Brazil and, 20, 131
 Chile and, 17–18
 Cuba and, 20
 Ecuador and, 131
 ethnolinguistic fragmentation and, 28
 exchange rates and, 228
 export-led growth and, 56
 Guatemala and, 16–17, 131
 income inequality and, 17
 mestizos and, 131, 147, 363nn31,32
 Mexico and, 16–17, 131
 Peru and, 16–17, 131
 political economy and, 147, 163–164
 poverty and, 111, 131
 property rights and, 27
 slavery and, 15
 Uruguay and, 17–18
Indigo, 38, 39t
Industrialization, 5
 China and, 7, 19, 37, 41, 52, 56
 debt crises and, 87–88, 91–93, 101–102, 104–105
 deindustrialization and, 36, 51, 254n4, 255n15, 282
 delayed, 30, 32
 Dutch disease and, 36–37, 42, 55, 322, 354n4, 369n21
 Europe and, 19, 353n40
 export-led growth and, 35–44, 51–56
 financial liberalization and, 267, 273–274
 fiscal policy and, 176
 growth and development and, 315, 323
 infant industry argument and, 67

Industrialization (cont.)
  innovation and, 7, 43, 260, 323, 328, 339, 341, 351n7, 367n19
  ISI and, 15 (*see also* Import substitution industrialization [ISI])
  labor and, 282, 284, 286, 288
  manufacturing and, 19 (*see also* Manufacturing)
  political economy and, 149
  poverty and, 132
  R&D and, 7, 15, 67, 167, 323, 339–340, 346, 348
  standard of living and, 16, 43, 78, 93, 102, 104, 118, 170, 359n11
  supply-side considerations and, 20
  trade liberalization and, 262, 264–265
  United States and, 18
  urbanization and, 26
Inertial inflation, 207, 209, 221, 365n10
Infant industry argument, 67
Inflation, xv
  agriculture and, 364n8
  Argentina and, 206, 210–213, 216–221, 365n20
  bankruptcy and, 210–211
  Bolivia and, 206
  Brazil and, 206, 210, 212–214, 217, 220–222, 365n21
  capital inflows and, 204–208, 217–221, 364n5, 365n23
  capital outflows and, 207, 219
  central bank autonomy and, 212–214
  Chile and, 78, 206, 210–213, 216–217, 219, 221
  China and, 221
  Colombia and, 206, 213, 216–217, 219–221
  commodity prices and, 203–206, 216, 219–222
  costs of, 208
  currency boards and, 216–217, 365n20
  defining, 20–23
  depreciation and, 213, 216, 219, 221, 366n25
  disinflation and, 219, 362n24
  Economic Commission for Latin American and the Caribbean (ECLAC) and, 209, 364n1
  Ecuador and, 210–211, 213, 216, 221, 365n15
  El Salvador and, 216, 221
  exchange rates and, 204–207, 209, 213–222, 266n25, 365nn20,24
  fiscal policy and, 175–176, 178, 181–183, 200–201, 205, 209
  fiscal prudence and, 215
  forceful contraction and, 182, 204–205, 210, 221
  foreign direct investment (FDI) and, 214, 218
  globalization and, 217
  gross domestic product (GDP) and, 206, 207t, 210f–211f, 221
  growth and development and, 336–337
  Guatemala and, 217
  heterodox policies and, 204, 208–212, 221–222
  hyperinflation and, 153, 159, 181–182, 203, 206, 208, 219, 232, 337, 364n1
  imported, 219–220
  import substitution industrialization (ISI) and, 60, 206
  income inequality and, 204
  independence and, 212–213, 219, 365n18
  inertial, 207, 209, 221, 365n10
  institutions and, 215–216
  interest rates and, 212, 214
  International Monetary Fund (IMF) and, 209, 216, 218, 222
  loans and, 208, 217
  macroeconomics and, 203–204, 208, 218
  main roots of, 204–208
  Mexico and, 78, 206, 210–213, 216–217, 219–221, 365n15
  oil and, 205–206
  Olivera-Tanzi effect and, 153, 182, 207, 365n11
  orthodox policies and, 157, 204, 208–212, 217, 220–222, 362n24
  overvaluations and, 206, 214, 217, 219–220
  Panama and, 216, 221
  pensions and, 208
  Peru and, 207t, 210, 213, 216, 219, 221, 365n15
  populism and, 130, 155–157, 219
  poverty and, 130–131
  private sector and, 97
  productivity and, 365n14
  public sector and, 206
  reform and, 210, 213–220, 222
  Russia and, 211, 220
  savings and, 204, 208
  shoe leather costs and, 208, 365n13
  sovereign debt and, 206, 215
  stabilization and, 155–157, 204, 206, 208–212, 216–217, 219–222
  stagflation and, 141, 150–152, 159, 219, 362n14
  standard view of, 365n9
  structuralists and, 208–209, 364n8
  targeting and, 60, 78, 83, 168, 212–213, 217–221, 226, 229, 233–239
  taxes and, 204, 206–208, 215, 220
  terms of trade and, 217
  twin deficit hypothesis and, 204, 364n3
  unemployment and, 209, 362n14
  United States and, 206, 219

Index 423

Uruguay and, 211–212, 216–217
Venezuela and, 204, 210–213, 219–221
Informality
  exchange rates and, 233
  increasing trend in, 283
  job quality and, 277, 296–302
  mobility and, 300
  poverty and, 124–126
  redistributive transfers and, 298
  trade openness and, 279
  unemployment and, 124–126
  wage indexation and, 233
Informal sector
  deunionization and, 283, 287
  import substitution industrialization (ISI) and, 71, 80
  income inequality and, 278
  job quality and, 296–303
  poverty and, 126–132, 277
  private sector and, 283
  reform and, 277
  self-employed and, 111, 121, 128, 132–133, 279, 283, 296–297, 301, 305–306, 314, 345
  trade liberalization and, 280, 303–304
Information and communication technology (ICT), 341–342
Infrastructure
  debt crises and, 89, 91
  electricity and, 47, 73, 120, 163, 166, 170, 198t
  export-led growth and, 37, 41–43, 46–47, 49, 54, 56
  fiscal policy and, 183, 199t
  gas and, 47, 73, 140, 163, 166–170, 193t, 354n4, 369n21
  growth and development and, 320, 324, 345, 347
  import substitution industrialization (ISI) and, 68, 73, 77, 80, 83
  income inequality and, 134
  investment in, 7–8, 20, 31
  labor and, 299–300, 305, 353n37
  loans for, 41
  oil and, 59 (*see also* Oil)
  political economy and, 163–169
  transportation and, 20
  water and, 73, 131, 163
Ingreso Ética Familiar (IEF), 112, 140–141, 158
Innovation, 260, 351n7, 367n19
  chemicals and, 43
  electricity and, 43
  growth and development and, 328, 339–342
  iron making and, 43

  petroleum refining and, 43
  productivity and, 339–342
  R&D and, 7, 15, 67, 167, 323, 339–340, 346, 348
  steam power and, 43
  textiles and, 43
Insider-outsider theory, 278, 284, 368n1
Institutional legacy, 4, 20–27, 32
Institutional quality, 9, 14, 24, 26–27, 30–31, 338, 353n35, 355n17
Instrumental variables (IVs), 20, 353n29, 369n19
Intendencia system, 38
Inter-American Development Bank (IDB), 126, 176, 299–300, 361n33
Interest rates
  debt crises and, 88–89, 92–94, 98, 101, 105, 358n8
  exchange rates and, 225, 229
  financial liberalization and, 268, 271, 274
  fiscal policy and, 178, 180–181
  import substitution industrialization (ISI) and, 61, 70, 356n22
  income inequality and, 139
  inflation and, 212, 214
  political economy and, 152
International Labour Organization (ILO), 125, 278, 283, 286–290, 301, 307, 360n22
International Monetary Fund (IMF)
  colonial legacies and, 352nn10,19
  debt crises and, 95, 98
  exchange rates and, 224, 234, 238–239
  financial liberalization and, 266–269
  fiscal policy and, 183, 187–188, 202
  import substitution industrialization (ISI) and, 80–81
  inflation and, 209, 216, 218, 222
  political economy and, 150, 152, 163–164
  role of, 80–81
  World Economic Outlook and, 238, 352n10
Israel, 177
Italy, 18, 45

Jácome, Luis, 222
Jamaica, 23, 156, 354n9
Japan, 43–44, 264–265, 273
Jensen, Robert, 124
Job quality, 260, 277–278, 296–305
Job security, 124, 284
Job Security Index (JSI), 284
Johnson, Simon, 20–21, 24, 26–27, 33, 36, 337–338, 353nn28,36
Jones, Charles, 340
Juárez, Benito, 163

Keller, Katarina, 328
King, Robert G., 333
Kirchner, Cristina Fernández de, 149, 162
Kirchner, Néstor, 149, 162
Klemm, Alexander, 195
Kraay, Aart, 337–338
Krueger, Alan, 328

Labor, xvi
  age and, 301–303, 306
  agriculture and, 15–19 (*see also* Agriculture)
  Argentina and, 280–284, 287–290, 297–302
  Bolivia and, 298–300
  Brazil and, 20, 279–281, 284, 286–290, 297–302
  Chile and, 280–281, 284, 290, 297–301
  China and, 288, 299, 302
  Colombia and, 280, 284, 290, 297–302
  commodity prices and, 288, 299, 305
  corruption and, 300, 306
  Costa Rica and, 290, 300
  Cuba and, 20, 50
  debt crises and, 87–107
  deregulation and, 277, 283–287
  deunionization and, 281–287
  Economic Commission for Latin American and the Caribbean (ECLAC) and, 278, 307
  Ecuador and, 290, 299
  education and, 283, 287, 297, 299–306
  El Salvador and, 286–290
  emergency job creation and, 133–134
  encomienda system and, 16–20, 27, 31–32, 48, 352n24
  excessive protection of, 286
  exchange rates and, 223–241, 287
  factor endowments hypothesis and, 4, 15–20, 29, 44
  firing costs and, 132, 283–284, 304
  foreign direct investment (FDI) and, 283
  formal sector and, 126, 132–133, 140, 277–280, 296, 305–306
  gender and, 303, 306
  Guatemala and, 302
  Haiti and, 302
  Harris-Todaro model and, 278–279
  health issues and, 283, 297, 299, 305
  Honduras and, 290, 302
  human capital and, 299, 305
  human rights and, 131, 154, 355n22
  immigrants and, 14, 45–46, 48–49
  import substitution industrialization (ISI) and, 59–85, 278–280, 283, 306

  income inequality and, 278–279, 286–287, 296–299, 302, 306
  indentured, 15, 17, 19, 30, 36, 45, 48, 56, 352n25, 353n37
  informality and, 124–126, 127t, 233, 277, 279, 283, 296–302
  infrastructure and, 299–300, 305, 353n37
  innovation and, 7, 43, 260, 323, 328, 339, 341, 351n7, 367n19
  insider-outsider theory and, 278, 284, 368n1
  International Labour Organization (ILO) and, 125, 278, 283, 286–290, 301, 307, 360n22
  job quality and, 260, 277–278, 296–305
  job security and, 124, 284
  labor and, 277–307
  manufacturing and, 281, 283
  market turning point and, 287–296
  mayorazgo institution and, 17, 48, 352n25
  Mexico and, 280–284, 287–290, 297–302
  military and, 280–281, 284–285
  minimum wage and, 126, 132, 278, 280, 283, 290, 293, 304–305, 361n31, 365n14
  mita (forced), 17, 20, 27, 30, 32, 48, 353n37
  mobility and, 300
  mortality rates and, 20–27, 30, 302, 363n29
  Nicaragua and, 284, 290, 302
  North American Free Trade Agreement (NAFTA) and, 290
  Organisation for Economic Co-operation and Development (OECD) and, 281–282, 296, 305
  Panama and, 290
  Paraguay and, 290, 297, 302
  payroll taxes and, 133
  pensions and, 126, 133, 142, 176, 193, 208, 278, 293, 297–298, 301, 314–315, 347
  per capita income and, 5, 8–11, 18, 27–32, 40, 43, 45, 47, 60, 72, 102, 149, 186, 191, 310–311, 313, 315–320, 323, 329, 351nn3,7, 352n10
  Peru and, 280, 284, 288t–289t, 292t, 297–302
  PETI and, 140
  plantations and, 15–19, 27, 31, 48–51, 54, 56
  populism and, 280–281
  Portugal and, 284, 352n25
  poverty and xxx, 35–57, 111–134
  private sector and, 96 (*see also* Private sector)
  privatization and, 277, 282–283, 303–304, 306
  productivity and, 280, 283, 290, 299–300, 304–305
  protectionism and, 280
  public sector and, 61 (*see also* Public sector)
  real wages and, 130, 151–153, 170, 280–281, 283, 287, 299, 304, 323, 355n32

Index 425

reform and, 277–288, 301, 303–304, 306
scarcity of, 4, 16–17
self-employed and, 111, 121, 128, 132–133, 279, 283, 296–297, 301, 305–306, 314, 345
shortages in, 15, 45, 48, 50–51
social security and, 280, 296–297, 301, 305–306, 368n12
Spain and, 284
state-owned enterprises (SOEs) and, 280, 306
taxes and, 133, 279–280, 298–300, 306
technology and, 300
terms of trade and, 288
total wage workers and, 293, 368n12
trade liberalization and, 278–283, 286–287, 303, 306
type of employment and, 128
unemployment and, 62, 64, 67, 71 (see also Unemployment)
unions and, 73, 76, 80, 83, 97, 148, 151, 167, 257, 277–287, 288t, 304–306, 365n14
United States and, 286, 299, 356n5
unskilled, 47, 126, 132, 134, 137, 279–280, 282–283, 286–287, 296, 304–306
urbanization and, 278, 368n2
Venezuela and, 284, 290, 299
worker remittances and, 269–271
World Bank and, 299, 302
Laffont, Jean-Jacques, 166
Larraín, Felipe, 150–151, 195, 233, 236, 359n10, 366nn8,9
Latin America. *See also specific country*
backwardness of, 3
belle époque of, 37, 40–41, 44, 48, 53–56, 83, 89, 107, 235, 265, 290, 309, 355n1
debt crises and, 87–107
demographics of, xiii
ECLAC and, 66, 81, 113, 118, 151, 209, 246–247, 278, 307, 360n14
ethnolinguistic fragmentation and, 28–29, 31–32
exchange rates and, 223–241
export-led growth and, 35–57
financial liberalization and, 266–276
fiscal policy and, 175–202
foreign control over, 3–4
frustrated expectations of, 310–312
growth and development and, 309–349
import substitution industrialization (ISI) and, 59–85
income inequality and, 134–141 (see also Income inequality)
inflation and, 203–222

labor and, 277–307 (see also Labor)
political economy and, 147–171
poverty and, 111–134
trade liberalization and, 245–266
Latin American Free Trade Association (LAFTA), 75–76
Latin American Integration Association (LAIA), 317
Latin America's Economy: Diversity Trends and Conflicts (Cardoso and Helwege), 222
Lederman, Daniel, 241
Lee, Jong-Wha, 327
Legal issues
civil law and, 4, 9–14, 29, 32
colonial legacies and, 9–14
common law and, 4, 9, 11–14, 29, 31–32
transparency and, 9, 19t, 166, 197t, 200, 213, 215–216, 338
Less developed countries (LDCs), 67, 74–75
Levine, Ross, 333
Levy Yeyati, Eduardo, 189, 241
Liability dollarization, 268–269
Life expectancy, 353n33
Lindahl, Mikael, 328
Lindbeck, Assar, 368n1
Liu, Lin, 334
Loans
belle époque, 89
bonds and, 63, 76, 84, 88–91, 95–96, 105, 162, 205, 237
Brady Plan and, 94, 201, 367n4
Bretton Woods and, 81
central bank and, 151
Chile and, 228
China and, 104, 165
commercial bank, 217, 269
concessional, 176
consols, 88, 356n22
creditors and, 14, 62, 89–91, 96, 105, 180–181, 358n7
debt crises and, 87–91, 104, 358n4
debt rescheduling and, 95
default and, 87 (see also Default)
dollar-denominated, 269
enforceability and, 315
exchange rates and, 228
export-led growth and, 41
extended, 176, 178
external, 178
financial liberalization and, 266–269, 366n1
fiscal policy and, 176, 178
foreign currency, 178

Loans (cont.)
  growth and development and, 315
  import substitution industrialization (ISI) and, 62, 81, 356n22
  income inequality and, 139
  inflation and, 208, 217
  infrastructure financing and, 41
  interest rates and, 139 (*see also* Interest rates)
  long-term, 91, 356n22
  microfinance and, 119, 130, 139, 361n37, 369n7
  microloans and, 139
  Monroe Doctrine and, 88
  perpetual, 356n22
  political economy and, 150–151, 165
  poor-quality, 268
  prudential regulation and, 96–97
  renegotiation of, 63, 89–90, 105, 162
  risk premium and, 88
  shadow prices and, 245, 366n1
  short-term, 266
  soft, 356n22
  Venezuela and, 150
Loayza, Norman, 333
López, J. Humberto, 186
Lopez-Calva, Luis F., 139–140, 187, 287, 361n31
Lora, Eduardo, 334, 336
Lorenz curve, 135–136
Lucas, Robert, 43, 327
Lula da Silva, Luis Ignácio, 150, 162
Lustig, Nora, 139–140, 187, 287, 361n31
Luxembourg, 318

Macri, Mauricio, 163, 169, 219
Macroeconomics
  debt crises and, 87–88, 92
  exchange rates and, 224–225
  financial liberalization and, 266, 268
  fiscal policy and, 178–180, 183, 187, 189, 191, 195, 201
  growth and development and, 313–316, 337
  import substitution industrialization (ISI) and, 60, 65, 80, 357n35
  inflation and, 203–204, 208, 218
  political economy and, 147–148, 150–159, 167–171
  populism and, 143, 147, 150–159, 169–170
  poverty and, 143
  protectionism and, 60
  trade liberalization and, 260
Maduro, Nicolás, 150, 161
Maquila assembly plants, 258, 260, 282
Malaria, 5, 320

Malaysia, 264
Malvinas, 3, 351n1
Manufacturing
  domestic demand and, 19–20
  Dutch disease and, 36–37, 42, 55, 322, 354n4, 369n21
  export-led growth and, 35–37, 41, 45, 51, 53–55, 60, 65–70, 73–74, 76–80, 82, 84, 354n4
  financial liberalization and, 273
  growth and development and, 322, 345
  import substitution industrialization (ISI) and, 60, 65–70, 357n23
  income inequality and, 30
  infrastructure investments and, 20
  labor and, 281, 283
  maquila assembly plants and, 258, 260, 282
  political economy and, 151
  research and development (R&D) and, 7
  slavery and, 19
  trade liberalization and, 245–246, 258–260, 263, 265
Maquila assembly plants, 258, 260, 282
Marcano, Cristina, 171
Márquez, Graciela, 33
Mayorazgo institution, 17, 48, 352n25
Meghir, Costas, 139
Meller, Patricio, 150–151
Mellinger, Andrew D., 320
Mercado Común Centroamericano (Central American Customs Union) (MCCA), 38
Mercado Común del Sur (Southern Common Market) (MERCOSUR), 249, 253–257, 263–264, 273–274, 299, 354n9
Mercury, 38, 39t
Mestizos, 131, 147, 363nn31,32
Mexican Conditional Cash Transfer Program (MCCTP), 138–139
Mexico, xv
  Aztecs and, 3
  Cárdenas and, 73, 149, 166
  Catholicism and, 29
  Chiapas, 228
  colonial legacies and, 15–20, 27, 29–31, 352n24, 353n30
  Colosio and, 228
  corruption and, 10t
  debt crises and, 88, 90–100, 105, 358n8
  Echeverria and, 78
  exchange rates and, 223, 226–229, 232–236, 239–240
  export-led growth and, 19, 35–36, 41–45, 48, 51–55

expropriation risk and, 27
factor endowments and, 15
financial liberalization and, 266–275
fiscal policy and, 180, 182, 192, 195, 198t
G-20 membership of, 29
geographical advantage of, 19–20, 351n2
growth and development and, 309, 312,
  317–318, 325, 330, 342, 347
Hidalgo and, 36
import substitution industrialization (ISI) and,
  60–61, 71–74, 78, 83–84
income inequality and, 134, 136–139, 355n27
indentured labor and, 15, 17
indigenous population of, 16–17, 131
inflation and, 78, 206, 210–213, 216–217,
  219–221, 365n15
labor and, 280–284, 287–290, 297–302
large economy of, 31, 360n30
maquila assembly plants and, 258, 260, 282
mortality rates and, 23t
North American Free Trade Agreement
  (NAFTA) and, 20, 51, 54, 96–97, 249, 257–263,
  273–275, 290
Pacific Alliance and, 246, 264–265, 273–274, 299
Peña Nieto and, 138, 166
per capita GDP and, 11t
political economy and, 148–149, 157–158, 163,
  166, 169, 362nn9,11 363n32
populism and, 149–150
poverty and, 112–113, 124, 128, 131–133,
  142–144, 350n30, 361n31
production modes in, 20
Progresa/Oportunidades/Prospera program and, 7,
  112, 138–139, 142, 158, 330, 359n4
public sector contraction and, 180
regulatory capture and, 166
revolution and, 73, 118, 352n24, 358n8
rise of, 72–74
Solidarity Pact and, 228
stabilization policies and, 363n32
take-it-or-leave-it offers and, 90–91
tequila crisis and, 99, 164, 223, 228, 236, 240,
  260, 267–268, 363nn30,32
trade and, 245–249, 257–261, 264–265
wars of, 42t
Washington Consensus and, 309
Microfinance, 119, 130, 139, 361n37, 369n7
Middle class
  blue-collar, 83
  buying power of, 7
  debt crises and, 105
  factor endowments and, 15

fiscal policy and, 176
growth of, 15, 60, 105, 111–112, 135, 137,
  143–145, 157–158, 305–306, 346, 348, 362n25
income inequality and, 134–135, 137, 139
market influence of, 7, 15
measurement of, 122, 134–135
political economy and, 148–149, 154, 157–159,
  164–165, 169
populism and, 157–158
postprotectionism and, 60
power of, 15, 83, 105, 116–117, 119, 135, 142,
  346
productivity and, 111
rise of, 157–158
social services and, 116
social stability and, 157–158
unrest and, 157–158
World Bank studies and, 14, 29
Military, 156
  Argentina and, 355n22
  Chile and, 79, 81, 152, 249, 284–285
  colonial legacies and, 14
  fiscal policy and, 199t
  industrialization and, 65
  labor and, 280–281, 284–285
  poverty and, 118
  United States and, 160
  Uruguay and, 79
  Venezuela and, 149
Minimum wage, 126, 132, 278, 280, 283, 290, 293,
  304–305, 361n31, 365n14
Mining, 7, 44, 51, 52t, 60, 69–70, 163
Mita (forced labor), 17, 20, 27, 30, 32, 48, 353n37
Monroe Doctrine, 88
Montt, Manuel, 47
Morales, Evo, 163–165, 167
Mortality rates, 20–27, 30, 302, 363n29
Movimiento al Socialismo (Movement to
  Socialism) (MAS), 163
Multinationals, 75, 159, 367n19
Muñoz de Camacho, Samaria, 338

Napoleon, 9, 35
Natural resources. *See also specific resource*
  abundance of, 158–159, 321–323
  commodity prices and, 321–323
  corruption and, 322
  debt crises and, 104
  demand for capital and, 323
  Dutch disease and, 36–37, 42, 55, 322, 354n4,
    369n21
  exchange rates and, 230

Natural resources (cont.)
  exploitation of, 32, 37, 104, 348
  export-led growth and, 37, 44–46, 48, 57
  fiscal policy and, 178, 197t
  growth and development and, 316, 318, 321–323, 345–348
  political economy and, 154, 158–159, 167
  populism and, 361n3
  rent-seeking and, 322
  trade liberalization and, 254–255
Nenci, Silvia, 276
New Granada, 21, 24, 354n3
Newman, Andrew, 119
New-Marxism, 75
New Zealand, 264, 321, 355n16
Nicaragua
  extractive institutions and, 27
  growth and development and, 317, 341
  income inequality and, 29, 136
  labor and, 284, 290, 302
  MCCA and, 354n9
  mortality rates and, 24
  per capita GDP and, 11t, 27
  poverty and, 29, 114, 124, 126, 134
  trade liberalization and, 260
Nigeria, 160, 322
Nitrate, 47, 356n3, 358n6
Nominal anchors, 226
Nongovernmental organizations (NGOs), 131
North American Free Trade Agreement (NAFTA)
  CAFTA and, 257–263, 273–275
  debt crises and, 96–97
  expansion of, 20
  export-led growth and, 51, 54
  financial liberalization and, 273
  labor and, 290
  maquila assembly plants and, 258, 260, 282
  MERCOSUR and, 253, 273
  trade and, 20, 51, 54, 96–97, 249, 257–263, 273–275, 290
Norway, 59, 321

Obama, Barack, 57
Obras Sociales (health care scheme), 21139
Ocampo, José Antonio, 71, 114
O'Higgins, Bernardo, 36
Oil
  debt crises and, 91–93, 105
  Ecuador and, 225
  exchange rates and, 225, 227, 229, 231, 239
  financial liberalization and, 266, 270
  fiscal policy and, 176–179, 192–195, 197t–198t
  growth and development and, 322
  import substitution industrialization (ISI) and, 59, 77–78
  inflation and, 205–206
  Operation Desert Storm and, 160
  petrodollars and, 92, 105, 178, 205, 235
  political economy and, 148–150, 159–162, 164–168
  shocks and, 77–78, 91, 105, 179, 195, 227, 239, 357n25
Olarreaga, Marcelo, 241
Olivera-Tanzi effect, 153, 182, 207, 365n11
Operation Desert Storm, 160
Organisation for Economic Co-operation and Development (OECD)
  fiscal policy and, 186–187
  growth and development and, 317, 325, 329, 338–340, 345
  labor and, 281–282, 296, 305
  political economy and, 362n9
Organization of the Petroleum Exporting Countries (OPEC), 177
Orthodox policies, 157, 204, 208–212, 217, 220–222, 362n24
Ortiz-Juarez, Eduardo, 139–140, 187, 287, 361n31
Overvaluations
  capital inflows and, 227
  crawling pegs and, 357n35
  debt crises and, 97–98, 100, 105
  depression and, 228
  disinflation and, 219, 362n24
  financial liberalization and, 266, 271, 274–275
  import substitution industrialization (ISI) and, 69–70, 76–77, 80, 84
  inflation and, 206, 214, 217, 219–220
  political economy and, 152, 161
  poverty and, 131
  stabilization policies and, 363n32
  trade liberalization and, 252–253
  undervaluations and, 97, 268

Pacific Alliance, 246, 264–265, 273–274, 299
Pagés-Serra, Carmen, 284, 286
Pampas, 17, 352n26
Panama
  colonial legacies and, 353n30
  corruption and, 10t
  exchange rates and, 224–225, 229
  fiscal policy and, 198t
  Great Colombia and, 354n3
  growth and development and, 312

Index

inflation and, 216, 221
labor and, 290
mortality rates and, 11t, 23t, 24
per capita GDP and, 11t
Panama Canal, 198t, 224
Paraguay
  corruption and, 10f
  growth and development and, 317–318, 325
  import substitution industrialization (ISI) and, 63
  labor and, 290, 297, 302
  mortality rates and, 23t
  official languages and, 28
  per capita GDP and, 11t
  railways and, 355n16
  trade liberalization and, 253
  Treaty of Asunción and, 253
  wars of, 42t
Partido Acción Nacional (National Action Party) (PAN), 138, 158, 261
Partido Revolucionario Institucional (Institutional Revolutionary Party) (PRI), 98, 138, 149–150, 158, 228, 363n32
Pass-through, 64, 219–220, 233, 240, 356n11, 365n24, 366n25
Payne, Mark, 338
Payroll taxes, 133
Pegs
  bands and, 226, 226–228
  conventional, 235t
  crawling, 76–78, 84, 98, 207, 226–229, 239, 357n35
  dollarization and, 153, 164, 216, 221, 223–225, 229, 268–269
  exchange rates and, 63–64, 76–78, 84, 97–99, 207, 217, 219, 223, 225–230, 234t–235t, 239, 357n35
  hard, 223, 239
  nominal anchors and, 226
Peña Nieto, Enrique, 138, 166
Pension Reserve Fund (PRF), 193
Pensions
  fiscal policy and, 176, 193
  growth and development and, 314–315, 347
  inflation and, 208
  labor and, 126, 133, 142, 176, 193, 208, 278, 293, 297–298, 301, 314–315, 347
  national systems for, 126
  poverty and, 126, 133, 142
  private sector and, 293
  public sector and, 293
  reform and, 176, 314–315, 347

Pérez, Carlos Andrés, 149, 160
Perón, Evita, 149, 154
Perón, Juan, 149, 154
Perotti, Roberto, 119
Perry, Guillermo E., 119, 124, 241, 280, 286
Peru
  Andean Pact and, 76, 356n21
  CAN and, 354n9
  corruption and, 10t
  debt crises and, 93t, 95t
  exchange rates and, 229, 231–232, 234, 235t–236t, 239–240, 247–249, 257, 259t, 264–266
  export-led growth and, 19, 36, 39t, 40t, 41, 42t, 45, 47–48, 51, 52t–53t, 354n9, 355n16
  factor endowments and, 15
  financial liberalization and, 271, 273–275
  fiscal policy and, 177t, 182, 183t, 186t, 188t, 189f, 193t, 195, 199t, 200
  Fumimori and, 153–154
  García and, 151–153
  growth and development and, 311–312, 317, 325, 331
  guano and, 45
  human capital and, 27
  import substitution industrialization (ISI) and, 61, 76
  Incas and, 3
  income inequality and, 134, 137
  indentured labor and, 15, 17
  indigenous population of, 16–17, 131
  inflation and, 207t, 210, 213, 216, 219, 221, 365n15
  labor and, 280, 284, 288t–289t, 292t, 297–302
  mineral wealth of, 15
  mortality rates and, 23t
  Pacific Alliance and, 246, 264–265, 273–274, 299
  per capita GDP and, 11t
  political economy and, 151–153, 156t, 157f, 164, 166, 168t, 169, 363n31
  poverty and, 114t, 120, 127t–128t, 130t, 131, 133–134
  production modes in, 20
  railways and, 355n16
  San Martin and, 36
  Shining Path and, 153–154, 363n31
  Spanish Crown and, 21
  structural balance rules and, 195
  trade liberalization and, 247–249, 257, 259t, 264
  wars of, 42t, 47
Petrobras (Petróleo Brasileiro S.A.), 150
Petrodollars, 92, 105, 178, 205, 235
Petróleos de Venezuela S.A. (PDVSA), 149–150

Petróleos Mexicanos (PEMEX), 198t
Petroleum, 43, 160
Pietrobelli, Carlo, 276
Plantations, 15–19, 27, 31, 48–51, 54, 56
Political economy, xv
  agriculture and, 151, 162
  Argentina and, 148–149, 154, 160–170
  Bolivia and, 148, 160, 163–164, 167–169, 171, 363n31
  Brazil and, 150, 154, 162–163
  capital outflows and, 153
  Chile and, 150–152, 157–158, 169
  China and, 165, 170
  Colombia and, 154, 159, 169
  commodity prices and, 170
  corruption and, 148, 154, 159, 164–165, 167
  Costa Rica and, 156
  Cuba and, 161
  default and, 165
  depreciation and, 162
  Economic Commission for Latin American and the Caribbean (ECLAC) and, 151
  Ecuador and, 148, 160, 164–165, 167–169, 363n34
  education and, 158
  elitism and, 149, 163, 167
  European Union (EU) and, 167, 169
  exchange rates and, 151–152, 162, 362n24, 363n32
  fall of macroeconomic populism and, 154–159
  foreign direct investment (FDI) and, 149, 167
  globalization and, 154, 160, 165, 167
  gross domestic product (GDP) and, 150–152, 155f, 160, 165
  heterodox policies and, 152–153, 157, 204, 208–212, 221–222, 362nn23,24
  income inequality and, 147–148, 154, 160, 165, 168–170, 361n1, 363n29
  indigenous populations and, 147, 163–164
  industrialization and, 149
  infrastructure and, 163–169
  interest rates and, 152
  International Monetary Fund (IMF) and, 150, 152, 163–164
  loans and, 150–151, 165
  macroeconomics and, 147–148, 150–159, 167–171
  manufacturing and, 151
  Mexico and, 148–149, 157–158, 163, 166, 169, 362nn9,11, 363n32
  middle class and, 148–149, 154, 157–159, 164–165, 169
  natural resources and, 154, 158–159, 167
  oil and, 148–150, 159–162, 164–168
  Olivera-Tanzi effect and, 153, 182, 207, 365n11
  Organisation for Economic Co-operation and Development (OECD) and, 362n9
  orthodox policies and, 157, 204, 208–212, 217, 220–222, 362n24
  overvaluations and, 152, 161
  Peru and, 151–153, 156t, 157f, 164, 166, 168t, 169, 363n31
  political stability and, 158, 164, 170
  populism and, 147–155, 159–165, 167–171, 362nn13,17
  privatization and, 148, 154, 159, 165–169
  productivity and, 148, 152, 155, 166
  protectionism and, 162, 167
  public sector and, 148, 151, 167
  recession and, 152, 154, 161
  reform and, 147–152, 154–161, 164–166, 170, 362n9, 363n35
  regulatory capture and, 148, 165–171
  research and development (R&D) and, 167
  social security and, 151
  stabilization and, 152, 154–157, 159, 161, 164, 168, 170, 363n32
  state intervention and, 147, 149, 161–163
  state-owned enterprises (SOEs) and, 148, 151–152, 165–167, 169
  structuralist policies and, 151
  taxes and, 152–153, 162–163, 170
  technology and, 162
  trade liberalization and, 154, 159, 162, 248
  transportation and, 160
  unemployment and, 151, 153
  United States and, 160, 162, 164
  urbanization and, 155, 163
  Venezuela and, 148–150, 160–171
  World Bank and, 158, 165–166, 362n18
Political Risk Services, 27
Political stability
  colonial legacies and, 28
  debt crises and, 89, 100
  exchange rates and, 228
  export-led growth and, 43, 46–47
  financial liberalization and, 273
  growth and development and, 339t
  political economy and, 158, 164, 170
  poverty and, 119
  trade liberalization and, 256
Pombaline reforms, 38, 41, 354n8
Populism
  Argentina and, 148–149, 161–163, 361n4

Index   431

autocrats and, 19
Bolivia and, 148, 163–164, 256
Brazil and, 150
Chile and, 150
defining, 147–148
downfall of, 154–159
Ecuador and, 148, 164–165
fiscal policy and, 176, 179, 191
historical perspective on, 148–150
income inequality and, 361n1
indigenous language and, 28
inflation and, 130, 155–157, 219
labor and, 280–281
macroeconomic, 143, 147, 150–159, 169–170
Mexico and, 149–150
middle class and, 157–158
natural resources and, 158–159, 361n3
policy impacts of, 28
political economy and, 147–155, 159–165, 167–171, 362nn13,17
poverty and, 116, 118–119, 130, 143, 361n4
rebirth of, 159–165
reform and, 148, 154–159
regulatory capture and, 165, 167
stabilization and, 155–157
trade liberalization and, 256
unsustainability of, 119
Venezuela and, 148–150, 160–161
Portugal
  Catholicism and, 353n40
  colonial legacies of, 3–4, 18, 21, 23, 26–28
  Dom Pedro and, 35, 354n2
  export-led growth and, 35–38, 41, 48
  labor and, 284, 352n25
  reforms by, 354n8
  Treaty of Tordesillas and, 351n1, 353n31
Poultry, 16
Poverty, xv
  Africa and, 111, 113, 115, 131, 142
  age and, 112, 120, 128–129, 133
  antipoverty campaigns and, 7, 18, 83, 105, 112, 119–120, 130, 138, 140–145, 158, 298, 305, 330, 359n4, 360n26
  Argentina and, 118, 130, 360n30
  Bolivia and, 134
  Brazil and, 112–113, 131, 361n31
  cash transfers and, 112, 130, 133, 136–138, 141, 144
  Chile and, 112, 114, 116–117, 133, 144
  Colombia and, 133–134, 360n30
  consequences of, 117–119
  corruption and, 116
  Costa Rica and, 114, 117, 126
  cost of basic needs (CBN) approach and, 120–122, 128, 142–143, 360n13
  credit markets and, 116
  defining, 117–119, 359n7
  direct/indirect approach to, 119–120
  diversity and, 113–117
  Dominican Republic and, 124
  Economic Commission for Latin American and the Caribbean (ECLAC) and, 113, 118, 359n7, 360n14
  Ecuador and, 114f, 116f, 127t–128t, 131
  education and, 111–112, 116–119, 121, 123–124, 126, 129–130, 143–144, 360n23, 363n29
  El Salvador and, 143
  emergency job creation and, 133–134
  eradication policies and, 111–112, 115–119, 130, 165
  ethnicity and, 131
  exchange rates and, 130–131
  firing costs and, 132
  fundamental causes of, 122, 131
  gender and, 112, 129–130, 142–143
  geography and, 122
  Gini coefficient and, 115–116
  Guatemala and, 131
  Haiti and, 29, 114, 124
  health issues and, 7, 116–121, 131–133
  Honduras and, 114–115, 134
  human capital and, 128, 142
  income inequality and, 112, 114–116, 134–141, 359n2, 360n30
  independence and, 118
  indigenous populations and, 111, 131
  industrialization and, 132
  inflation and, 130–131
  informality and, 124–126, 127t
  informal sector and, 126–132, 277
  job security and, 124, 284
  labor markets and, 131–133
  macroeconomics and, 143
  main determinants of, 122–131
  measurement of, 119–122, 359n10
  metrics for, 116–117
  Mexico and, 112–113, 124, 128, 131–133, 142–144, 350n30, 361n31
  military regimes and, 118
  minimum wage and, 126, 132, 278, 280, 283, 290, 293, 304–305, 361n31, 365n14
  Nicaragua and, 29, 114, 124, 126, 134
  overvaluations and, 131
  payroll taxes and, 133

Poverty (cont.)
pensions and, 126, 133, 142
Peru and, 114t, 120, 127t–128t, 130t, 131, 133–134
political stability and, 119
populism and, 116, 118–119, 130, 143, 361n4
productivity and, 111–112, 119, 122, 128, 133, 360n23
Progresa/Oportunidades/Prospera program and, 7, 112, 138–139, 142, 158, 330, 359n4
protectionism and, 125–126
proximate causes of, 122–123
racial discrimination and, 131
recent trends in, 113–117
reform and, 111, 114, 119, 133, 141–142
SEDESOL and, 113, 359n4, 360n13
social security and, 126, 133, 142
taxes and, 126, 133
technology and, 122
transportation and, 121
type of employment and, 128
unemployment and, 124–134, 142–143
unsatisfied basic needs (UBN) approach and, 120–121, 142–143, 360n13
urbanization and, 123, 131
Uruguay and, 133, 360n30
Venezuela and, 130
vulnerability and, 117
World Bank and, 113–114, 118, 122, 131–132, 145
Prebisch, Raul, 66–69, 81, 151, 246–247, 326
Pribble, Jennifer, 126
Price indexes, 155, 207, 209, 365n10
Principal-agent problem, 363n5
Pritchett, Lant, 252, 328–330, 360n23
Private sector
deregulation and, 96
excess employment and, 277
expropriation fears and, 76
fiscal policy and, 178–179, 182, 184, 299
growth and development and, 338, 346, 348
high wage, 281
inflation and, 97
informal sector and, 283
international competition and, 300, 305–306
microenterprises and, 300
pensions and, 293
productivity and, 152
protectionism and, 83, 280
regulatory capture and, 148, 165–167
salary trends in, 287
unions and, 83, 97, 151, 281–282

Privatization
debt crises and, 96–98, 105
financial liberalization and, 268, 272
fiscal policy and, 184, 201
growth and development and, 346
import substitution industrialization (ISI) and, 60, 81
labor and, 277, 282–283, 303–304, 306
political economy and, 148, 154, 159, 165–169
trade liberalization and, 245, 252
Productivity
agriculture and, 7–8, 351n7
capital output ratio and, 356n20
debt crises and, 102–104
export-led growth and, 45, 48, 51, 55
growth and development and, 232, 310, 313, 315, 318, 320, 331, 334, 339–342, 346–348
import substitution industrialization (ISI) and, 67, 69, 71, 73, 81–82
income inequality and, 134, 139
inflation and, 365n14
innovation and, 7, 43–44, 260, 323, 328, 339–342, 351n7, 367n19
labor and, 280, 283, 290, 299–300, 304–305
lower level of in tropics, 29, 55
maquila assembly plants and, 258, 260, 282
political economy and, 148, 152, 155, 166
poverty and, 111–112, 119, 122, 128, 133, 360n23
private sector and, 152
savings and, 81
trade liberalization and, 246, 256
ProExpo, 77
Programa de Erradicação do Trabalho Infantil (Program to Eradicate Child Labor) (PETI), 140
Progresa/Oportunidades/Prospera program, 7, 112, 138–139, 142, 158, 330, 359n4
Property rights
colonial legacies and, 9, 11, 14, 27–29, 31–32
de Soto and, 359n11
growth and development and, 315
indigenous populations and, 27
reform and, 9
Protectionism, 16
debt crises and, 87, 94
effective protection and, 74, 357n31
export-led growth and, 36, 43, 51, 54–55
fiscal policy and, 175–176
growth and development and, 323
import substitution industrialization (ISI) and, 59–76, 80–85, 280, 356n4

Index   433

labor and, 280
macroeconomics and, 60
origins of, 36, 43, 51, 54–55
political economy and, 162, 167
poverty and, 125–126
Prebisch-Singer paradigm and, 66–67, 81, 151, 246–247, 326
private sector and, 83, 280
tariffs and, 62 (*see also* Tariffs)
trade liberalization and, 246–247, 249, 262
Protestantism, 28, 353n40
Prudential regulation, 96–97
Public expenditure, 177–178, 182–185
Public sector
  debt crises and, 104
  fiscal policy and, 176–182, 184, 195, 198t–199t, 200
  forceful contraction of, 180–182
  growth and development and, 346
  high wage, 281
  import substitution industrialization (ISI) and, 61
  income inequality and, 134
  inflation and, 206
  pensions and, 293
  political economy and, 148, 151, 167
  reform and, 277
Puerto Rico, 45
Purchasing power parity (PPP)
  exchange rates and, 227
  GDP and, 11t, 21
  growth and development and, 310–311, 316, 318
  Pension Reserve Fund (PRF) and, 193

Qatar, 318
Quah, Danny, 316
Quechua, 28, 163–164

Racial discrimination, 131, 142
Railways, 41, 43, 49, 83, 89, 91, 163, 355n16
Ramírez, Miguel, 271
Ramos, Joseph, 81
Rancière, Romain, 333
Ravallion, Martin, 145
Real wages, 130, 151–153, 170, 280–281, 283, 287, 299, 304, 323, 355n32
Recession
  debt crises and, 88, 92–94, 101, 104–105
  exchange rates and, 232, 236, 239
  financial liberalization and, 269
  fiscal policy and, 177, 182, 192

import substitution industrialization (ISI) and, 61–62, 64
political economy and, 152, 154, 161
Redding, Stephen, 340
Reform
  agrarian, 73, 151
  antipoverty campaigns and, 7, 18, 83, 105, 112, 119–120, 130, 138, 140–145, 158, 298, 305, 330, 359n4, 360n26
  Bourbon, 38, 41, 354n8
  Brazil and, 76–77
  Colombia and, 77–78
  debt crises and, 93, 95–96, 98–99, 104–106
  decentralization, 38, 142, 148
  economic, 76–81, 83, 99, 156t, 170, 235, 253, 277
  exchange rates and, 228, 235
  export-led growth and, 37–38, 41, 354nn5,8
  fall of macroeconomic populism and, 154–159
  financial liberalization and, 266, 272
  fiscal policy and, 175–176, 183–184, 191, 198t, 200–201, 364n14
  growth and development and, 309–310, 314–316, 324, 334, 336, 345, 347–348
  import substitution industrialization (ISI) and, 73, 76–79, 81, 83–84
  inflation and, 210, 213–220, 222
  informal sector and, 277
  institutional, 175–176, 316, 348, 367n3
  labor and, 277–288, 301, 303–304, 306
  land, 18
  market-oriented, 37, 81, 95–96, 98, 104–105, 148, 154, 157, 159, 161, 164, 200, 245, 266, 272, 278, 284, 367n4
  pensions and, 176, 314–315, 347
  political economy and, 147–161, 164–166, 170, 362n9, 363n35
  Pombaline, 38, 41, 354n8
  populism and, 148, 154–159
  poverty and, 111, 114, 119, 133, 141–142
  property rights and, 9
  public sector and, 277
  social security and, 142
  structural, 9, 93, 96, 106, 111, 114, 119, 147–148, 154, 156, 160, 165, 183–184, 191, 218, 220, 222, 334
  tax, 176, 184, 215
  trade liberalization and, 245, 248–256, 367nn3,4
  unemployment and, 362n9
  Washington Consensus and, 159, 183–185, 277, 280, 288, 303, 306, 309, 354n5, 364n14
Regression discontinuity analysis (RDA), 353n36

Regulatory capture, 148, 165–171
Reinhart, Carmen, 87, 364n1
Religion, 28–32, 353n40
Rent-seeking, 69, 322
Research and development (R&D), 7, 15, 67, 167, 323, 339–340, 346, 348
　agriculture and, 7, 16–17
　colonial legacies and, 15
　growth and development and, 323, 340, 346, 348
　import substitution industrialization (ISI) and, 67
　political economy and, 167
　region-specific, 7
Revilla, Julio E., 202
Revolution
　Bolivia and, 160–161, 256
　Colombia and, 159
　Mexico and, 73, 118, 352n24, 358n8
　poverty and, 112, 120, 128–129, 133
　Venezuela and, 161
Risk premium, 88
Robinson, James, 20–21, 24, 26–27, 33, 36, 337–338, 353nn28,36, 360n22
Robinson, Sherman, 53
Rodrik, Dani, 338
Rogoff, Kenneth, 87, 364n1
Romer, David, 315, 339
Römer, Enrique Salas, 161
Rosas, Juan Manuel de, 47, 355n22
Rose, Andrew, 318
Rosenstein-Rodan, Paul, 19
Rúa, Fernando de la, 162
Russeff, Dilma, 365n18
Russia, 319
　debt crises and, 99
　exchange rates and, 223, 228, 230, 236
　financial liberalization and, 267
　inflation and, 211, 220
　trade liberalization and, 256
Rusticelli, Elena, 237

Sachs, Jeffrey, 7, 64, 154, 320–321
Salai-i-Martin, Xavier, 326
San Martín, José de, 36
Sapir, André, 328
Savings
　China and, 101
　domestic, 70, 80, 103, 347
　exchange rates and, 153
　financial liberalization and, 268
　fiscal policy and, 198t, 315

　foreign direct investment (FDI) and, 76, 80, 83
　gap in, 70, 76, 356n22
　García project and, 153
　growth and development and, 310, 313–316, 345–347
　import substitution industrialization (ISI) and, 313–314
　inflation and, 204, 208
　populism and, 167
　productivity and, 81
　Solow framework and, 313, 315–316
Schmidt-Hebbel, Klaus, 213
Schumpeter, Joseph, 339
Secretaría de Desarrollo Social (Ministry of Social Development) (SEDESOL), 113, 359n4, 360n13
Self-employed, 111, 121, 128, 132–133, 279, 283, 296–297, 301, 305–306, 314, 345
Seligson, Michell, 171
Sen, Amartya, 145
Servén, Luis, 186
Shadow prices, 245, 366n1
Shining Path (El Sendero Luminosa) movement, 153–154, 363n31
Shoe leather costs, 208, 365n13
Silver, 38, 39t, 44, 47, 193t, 354n10
Singapore, 59, 264–265, 311, 338
Singer, Hans, 66–67, 81, 151, 246–247, 326
Slavery
　colonial legacies and, 15–20, 27, 32, 352n25
　education and, 27
　export-led growth and, 36, 45, 48–50, 56
　health issues and, 27
　indentured labor and, 15, 17, 19, 30, 36, 45, 48, 56, 352n25, 353n37
　indigenous populations and, 15
　mayorazgo institution and, 17, 48, 352n25
　mita (forced labor) and, 17, 20, 27, 30, 32, 48, 353n37
Sliding, 217, 228
Small and medium enterprises (SMEs), 126, 293, 300
Smoot-Hawley Tariff Act, 61–62, 356n4
Snower, Dennis J., 368n1
Social security
　fiscal policy and, 198t
　growth and development and, 314–315, 345, 347
　labor and, 280, 296–297, 301, 305–306, 368n12
　payroll taxes and, 133
　political economy and, 151
　poverty and, 126, 133, 142

reform and, 142
total wage workers and, 293, 368n12
Soil, 8, 15–17, 29, 31, 60, 352n26
Sokoloff, Kenneth, 15–19
Solidarity Pact, 228
Solow, Robert, 313, 315–316, 339
South Korea, 53, 59, 73, 310–311
Sovereign debt
  crises in, 89 (*see also* Debt crises)
  default and, 41, 62, 76, 83, 87–88, 105, 176, 180, 225
  exchange rates and, 227, 235
  fiscal policy and, 200–201
  import substitution industrialization (ISI) and, 60, 62–63, 76
  inflation and, 206, 215
Soybeans, 7, 16, 162, 193t, 231, 255, 266
Spain
  Audiencias and, 21–24, 353n30
  Catholicism and, 353n40
  colonial legacies and, 4, 17–18, 21, 27
  Council of Indies and, 353n30
  export-led growth and, 37–38, 41, 45–47, 50
  labor and, 284
  mayorazgo institution and, 17, 48, 352n25
  reforms and, 354n8
  Spanish Crown and, 17, 21
  trade liberalization and, 270
  Treaty of Tordesillas and, 351n1, 353n31
  viceroyalties of, 21–24, 30, 353n30, 354n3
  wars of, 42t
Spiller, P., 338
Spillover, 45, 167, 323, 348
Spolaore, Enrico, 319
Stabilization
  debt crises and, 96, 98, 105, 358n12
  exchange rates and, 225–227, 238
  financial liberalization and, 266, 272–273
  fiscal policy and, 182, 193, 197t–198t, 201
  growth and development and, 155–157
  heterodox policies and, 152–153, 157, 204, 208–212, 221–222, 362nn23,24
  import substitution industrialization (ISI) and, 60, 76–81
  inflation and, 155–157, 204, 206, 208–212, 216–217, 219–222
  orthodox policies and, 204, 208–212, 217, 220–222
  political economy and, 152, 154–157, 159, 161, 164, 168, 170, 363n32
  populism and, 155–157
  trade liberalization and, 246, 252–253

Stagflation, 141, 150–152, 159, 219, 362n14
Stagnation, 40, 49, 55, 71, 102, 104, 182, 251, 270, 279, 290, 310, 323
Standard of living, 16, 43, 78, 93, 102, 104, 118, 170, 359n11
State intervention
  fiscal policy and, 175
  import substitution industrialization (ISI) and, 60, 66, 68, 75, 79, 84
  political economy and, 147, 149, 161–163
State-owned enterprises (SOEs)
  debt crises and, 96, 104
  fiscal policy and, 175–177, 182, 184
  import substitution industrialization (ISI) and, 60, 83, 85
  labor and, 280, 306
  political economy and, 148, 151–152, 165–167, 169
Stephens, John D., 126
Stolper-Samuelson theorem, 55, 355n32
Structural balance rule, 192–195
Structuralists, 151, 208–209, 364n8
Subramanian, Arvind, 338
Sugar, 15–16, 19, 38–40, 44, 49–50, 193t
Switzerland, 206, 338
Syria, 177
Syrquin, Moshe, 53
Székely, Miguel, 124, 302

Tablitas system, 227
Tagging, 188, 364n15
Taiwan, 59
Tariffs
  Abnormal Importation Act and, 62, 356n6
  drawback system and, 41, 78, 358nn10,38
  effective protection and, 74, 357n31
  export-led growth and, 36, 41, 54
  financial liberalization and, 273–274
  fiscal policy and, 175–176
  growth and development and, 323–325
  import substitution industrialization (ISI) and, 61–62, 68, 76–78
  income inequality and, 353–354n1
  recession and, 62
  Smoot-Hawley Tariff Act and, 61–62, 356n4
  trade liberalization and, 245–249, 252–254, 257, 274
Taxes
  debt crises and, 104
  export-led growth and, 36, 41, 54, 353–354n1
  financial liberalization and, 268

Taxes (cont.)
    fiscal policy and, 176–179, 182, 184–189, 192, 195, 200–201
    growth and development and, 331–332, 338, 346–348
    import substitution industrialization (ISI) and, 76–80
    inflation and, 204, 206–208, 215, 220
    labor and, 133, 279–280, 298–300, 306
    Olivera-Tanzi effect and, 153, 182, 207, 365n11
    payroll, 133
    political economy and, 152–153, 162–163, 170
    poverty and, 126, 133
    reform and, 176, 184, 215
    Tobin, 268, 367n21
    value-added (VAT), 54, 74, 186, 188t, 215, 346
Technology
    agriculture and, 5
    debt crises and, 96
    financial liberalization and, 266, 273–274
    foreign direct investment (FDI) and, 31
    growth and development and, 315–317, 341, 346, 369n17
    health issues and, 5
    import substitution industrialization (ISI) and, 73, 75, 82–83
    information and communication technology (ICT) and, 341–342
    innovation and, 7, 43, 260, 323, 328, 339, 341, 351n7, 367n19
    labor and, 300
    political economy and, 162
    poverty and, 122
    R&D and, 7, 15, 67, 167, 323, 339–340, 346, 348
    spillover and, 45, 167, 323, 348
    trade liberalization and, 245, 256
    transfer of, 8, 31, 96
Tequila crisis, 99, 164, 223, 228, 236, 240, 260, 267–268, 363nn30,32
Terms of trade
    debt crises and, 103
    export-led growth and, 36, 41–42, 55
    financial liberalization and, 271
    fiscal policy and, 179, 182
    growth and development and, 36, 41–42, 55, 61, 103, 179, 182, 217, 271, 288, 317, 326–327, 347, 354n12
    import substitution industrialization (ISI) and, 61
    inflation and, 217
    labor and, 288
Textiles, 35, 39t, 42–43, 45, 53, 247, 257n23

Thailand, 267
Tirole, Jean, 166
Tobacco, 39t
Tobin tax, 268, 367n21
Tommasi, M., 338
Tornarolli, Leopoldo, 187
Total factor productivity (TFP), 339–340
Total wage workers, 293, 368n12
Trade
    CAFTA and, 257–263, 273–275
    debt crises and, 96
    ECLAC and, 246–247
    European Union (EU) and, 253, 255–256, 263–264, 275
    export-led growth and, 37, 41, 51, 55
    foreign direct investment (FDI) and, 275
    free trade agreement (FTA) groups and, 317
    gross domestic product (GDP) and, 245, 264
    LAFTA and, 75–76
    MERCOSUR and, 249, 253–257, 263–264, 273–274, 299
    NAFTA and, 20, 51, 54, 96–97, 249, 253, 257–263, 273–277, 290
    Pacific Alliance and, 246, 264–265, 273–274, 299
    trade blocs and, 252–263
    Trans-Pacific Trade Partnership (TPP) and, 264
    World Trade Organization (WTO) and, 37, 55, 247, 252, 261–262, 273
Trade balance, 70, 97t, 182
Trade blocs
    export-led growth and, 354n9
    growth and development and, 317
    liberalization and, 249, 252–263, 273–275
    trade agreements and, 252–263
Trade diversion, 41, 253, 256, 273–274, 354n13
Trade liberalization, xv–xvi, 19, 276
    agriculture and, 247, 254–257, 259t
    Argentina and, 249, 253–255, 262, 264
    bilateral agreements and, 252–263
    blocs and, 249, 252–263, 273–275
    Bolivia and, 249, 253, 256
    Brady Plan and, 367n4
    Brazil and, 142–144, 247–249, 253–257, 264, 266
    Canada and, 249, 257–264, 273–275
    Chile and, 247–252, 264–266, 367n21
    China and, 246, 255–256, 263–265
    Colombia and, 247, 256–257, 264
    commodity prices and, 260
    Costa Rica and, 260
    Cuba and, 247
    debt crises and, 96, 105
    Doha Round and, 247, 252, 273

Dominican Republic and, 260
Ecuador and, 249, 256, 270
El Salvador and, 260
exchange rates and, 245, 252–254, 275
export-led growth and, 51
financial liberalization and, 266, 271–272
foreign direct investment (FDI) and, 245, 255, 260
globalization and, 7, 253, 262
growth and development and, 319, 324–325
Guatemala and, 249, 260
Hecksher-Ohlin theorem and, 246, 275
Honduras and, 249, 260
import substitution industrialization (ISI) and, 60, 65, 79–81, 85, 246–247, 275, 278
India and, 265
industrialization and, 262, 264–265
informal sector and, 279–280, 303–304
labor and, 278–283, 286–287, 303, 306
macroeconomics and, 260
manufacturing and, 245–246, 258–260, 263, 265
maquila assembly plants and, 258, 260, 282
most favored nation principle and, 252
natural resources and, 254–255
Nicaragua and, 260
overvaluations and, 252–253
Paraguay and, 253
Peru and, 247–249, 257, 259t, 264
political economy and, 154, 159, 162, 248
political stability and, 256
populism and, 256
Prebisch-Singer hypothesis and, 246
privatization and, 245, 252
productivity and, 246, 256
protectionism and, 246–247, 249, 262
reform and, 245, 248–256, 367nn3,4
Russia and, 256
shadow prices and, 245, 366n1
Spain and, 270
stabilization and, 246, 252–253
tariffs and, 245–249, 252–254, 257, 274
technology and, 245, 256
trade creation/diversion and, 252–253
transportation and, 256, 260–261
Treaty of Asunción and, 253
unilateral wave of, 246–252
United States and, 249, 257–258, 260, 264–265
Uruguay and, 247, 252–253, 273
Venezuela and, 253, 256–257, 262, 266
World Bank and, 249, 260
Trade openness, 54, 82, 252–254, 274–275, 279, 310, 323–325, 345

Trans-Pacific Trade Partnership (TPP), 264
Transparency, 9, 19t, 166, 197t, 200, 213, 215–216, 338
Transparency International (TI), 338
Transportation
costs of, 7, 29, 46, 320
export-led growth and, 43–44, 46
foreign direct investment (FDI) and, 46, 49
geography and, 7
growth and development and, 320
infrastructure and, 20
innovation and, 43–44
political economy and, 160
poverty and, 121
railways and, 41, 43, 49, 83, 89, 91, 163, 355n16
sea trade and, 5, 29, 43
trade liberalization and, 256, 260–261
Treaty of Asunción, 253
Treaty of Tordesillas, 3, 21, 351n1, 353n31
Trebbi, Francesco, 338
Twin deficit hypothesis, 204, 364n3

Undervaluation, 97, 268
Unemployment
age and, 128–129, 287, 293, 296, 368n16
benefits for, 278
debt crises and, 100
decrease of, 290, 302
exchange rates and, 224
fiscal policy and, 189
gender and, 287, 293, 296
import substitution industrialization (ISI) and, 62, 64, 67, 71, 84
increase of, 290, 356n5
inflation and, 209, 362n14
informality and, 124–126, 127t
partial, 279
participation rates and, 277
political economy and, 151, 153
poverty and, 124–134, 142–143
reform and, 362n9
severance payments and, 278
supply-demand and, 368n1
Unidad Popular coalition, 152
Unions
custom, 38, 76, 253, 354n9
deunionization and, 281–287
labor and, 73, 76, 80, 83, 97, 148, 151, 167, 257, 277–287, 288t, 304–306, 365n14
private sector and, 83, 97, 151, 281–282
trade, 257
United Kingdom, 3, 28, 62, 80, 105, 232, 358n4

United Nations Conference on Trade and
  Development (UNCTAD), 249
United Nations Development Program (UNDP),
  362n25
United States
  American Civil War and, 16, 18, 48–49
  common law and, 32
  debt crises and, 88–89, 92, 96, 101, 104–106
  dollarization and, 153, 164, 216, 221, 223–225,
    229, 268–269
  entrepreneurship and, 28
  exchange rates and, 224–226, 231–234
  export-led growth and, 36–44, 47–55, 354n7
  expropriation risk and, 27
  factor endowments and, 15–16
  financial liberalization and, 267, 270–275
  fiscal policy and, 177–178
  growth and development and, 28–30, 317–318,
    321, 329
  import substitution industrialization (ISI) and,
    59, 61–62, 64, 66, 79, 84
  income inequality and, 360n30
  industrialization and, 18
  inflation and, 206, 219
  labor and, 286, 299, 356n5
  military and, 160
  Monroe Doctrine and, 88
  Operation Desert Storm and, 160
  Panama Canal and, 198t, 224
  per capita GDP and, 4, 351n3
  political economy and, 160, 162, 164
  Protestants and, 28
  recovering economy of, 270–271
  riches of, 26
  Smoot-Hawley Tariff Act and, 61–62, 356n4
  tensions with China and, 265
  trade liberalization and, 249, 257–258, 260,
    264–265
  urbanization of, 18
  wars of, 42t
Unsatisfied basic needs (UBN), 120–121,
  142–143, 360n13
Urbanization
  climate and, 5
  export-led growth and, 353–354n1
  labor and, 278, 368n2
  political economy and, 155, 163
  population density and, 26
  poverty and, 123, 131
  United States and, 18
Uruguay
  climate of, 16–17
  contract enforcement and, 14
  corruption and, 10
  European character of, 18
  exchange rates and, 226–227, 234, 239
  export-led growth and, 37, 45–47, 49, 54–55
  factor endowments and, 16
  financial liberalization and, 273, 290, 297, 301
  fiscal policy and, 182, 195
  gold standard and, 63
  growth and development and, 312, 317
  human capital and, 355n17
  import substitution industrialization (ISI) and,
    63, 72–75, 79, 84
  inflation and, 211–212, 216–217
  military and, 79
  mortality rates and, 21, 23t, 24
  per capita GDP and, 11t
  poverty and, 133, 360n30
  relative size of, 360n30
  small indigenous population of, 17–18
  trade liberalization and, 247, 252–253
  Treaty of Tordesillas and, 353n31
  wars of, 42t
  WTO negotiations and, 247, 252, 273
Uruguay Round, 247, 252, 273
US Census Bureau, 260
US Department of State, 89
US Federal Reserve System, 224

Vallejo, Juliana, 114
Value-added tax (VAT), 54, 74, 186, 188t, 215,
  346
Van Reenen, John, 340
Venezuela
  Andean Pact and, 76, 356n21
  Betancourt and, 149
  Bolívar and, 36, 160–161, 256
  Chávez and, 149–150, 160–161, 168–169, 256
  corruption and, 10t
  debt crises and, 93, 104
  exchange rates and, 232, 236, 239
  export-led growth and, 36, 51
  financial liberalization and, 271
  fiscal policy and, 182, 195
  Great Colombia and, 354n3
  Great Venezuela Plan and, 149
  growth and development and, 310, 317,
    320–321, 331, 337, 341, 347
  import substitution industrialization (ISI) and,
    63, 76, 83
  inflation and, 204, 210–213, 219–221, 365n15
  labor and, 284, 290, 299

Index 439

loans and, 150
Maduro and, 150, 161
military and, 149
mortality rates and, 11t, 23t, 24
per capita GDP and, 11t, 24
Pérez and, 149, 160
political economy and, 148–150, 160–171
populism and, 148–150, 160–161
poverty and, 130
revolution and, 161
structural balance rules and, 195
trade liberalization and, 253, 256–257, 262, 266
Venezuela and, 36, 51
Viceroyalties, 21–24, 30, 353n30, 354n3

Wacziarg, Romain, 319
Walker, Ian, 349
Warner, Andrew, 320–321
War of the Pacific, 41, 42t, 47
Washington Consensus, 159, 183–185, 277, 280, 288, 303, 306, 309, 354n5, 364n14
Water, 5, 73, 131, 163
Wheat, 15, 38, 39t, 44–45, 47, 193t, 255
Williams, John, 340
Williamson, Jeffrey, 36, 40, 55, 159, 354nn1,5, 359n2
Wodon, Quentin, 124, 126, 128–129
Worker remittances, 269–271
World Bank
 cash transfer and, 361n32
 corruption and, 10t
 debt crises and, 91, 95, 362n18
 fiscal policy and, 176, 183, 188
 growth and development and, 349
 import substitution industrialization (ISI) and, 80
 income inequality and, 134, 136
 labor and, 299, 302
 middle class and, 14, 29
 political economy and, 158, 165–166
 poverty and, 113–114, 118, 122, 131–132, 145
 trade liberalization and, 249, 260
World Economic Outlook (IMF), 238, 352n10
World Health Organization (WHO), 320
World Trade Organization (WTO), 37, 55, 247, 252, 261–262, 273
World War I era, xiv, 32
 debt crises and, 89
 export-led growth and, 36–37, 43, 45, 53
 import substitution industrialization (ISI) and, 59, 61–62, 85

World War II era
 debt crises and, 90–91
 export-led growth and, 42
 growth and development and, 319, 357
 import substitution industrialization (ISI) and, 61, 65–66, 79, 82, 84–85

X-inefficiency, 69, 84, 356n20

Yacimientos Petrolíficos Fiscales (Fiscal Oilfields) (YPF), 162
Yellow fever, 5
Yom Kippur War, 177
Yrigoyen, Hipólito, 149
Yugoslavia, 319